BUSINESS COMMUNICATION

>> PROCESS AND PRODUCT

SECOND
BRIEF
CANADIAN
EDITION

MARY ELLEN GUFFEY
Professor of Business Emerita
Los Angeles Pierce College

KATHLEEN RHODES
Durham College

PATRICIA ROGIN
Durham College

THOMSON
NELSON™

Australia Canada Mexico Singapore Spain United Kingdom United States

Business Communication: Process and Product, Second Brief Canadian Edition

by Mary Ellen Guffey, Kathleen Rhodes, and Patricia Rogin

Associate Vice President, Editorial Director
Evelyn Veitch

Publisher:
Joanna Cotton

Marketing Manager:
Sandra Green

Developmental Editor:
Linda Sparks

Permissions Coordinator:
Terri Rothman

Senior Production Editor:
Natalia Denesiuk

Copy Editor and Proofreader:
Wayne Herrington

Indexer:
Christopher Blackburn

Senior Production Coordinator:
Hedy Sellers

Design Director:
Ken Phipps

Interior Design:
Liz Harasymczuk

Cover Design:
Liz Harasymczuk

Cover Image:
Linda Bleck/Stock Illustration Source

Compositor:
Carol Magee

Printer:
Quebecor World

Printed and bound in the United States
2 3 4 5 10 09 08 07

For more information contact Nelson, 1120 Birchmount Road, Toronto, Ontario, M1K 5G4. Or you can visit our Internet site at http://www.nelson.com

ISBN-13: 978-0-17-640710-0
ISBN-10: 0-17-640710-3

Library and Archives Canada Cataloguing in Publication

Guffey, Mary Ellen

Business communication : process and product / Mary Ellen Guffey, Kathleen Rhodes, Patricia Rogin. — 2nd brief Canadian ed.

Includes bibliographical references and index.
ISBN 0-17-640710-3

1. Business communication—Textbooks. 2. Business writing—Textbooks.
I. Rhodes, Kathleen, 1951–
II. Rogin, Patricia, 1958– III. Title.

HF5718.3.G82 2006 651.7
C2005-907515-5

Brief Contents

Detailed Contents

Preface

At the request of instructors who liked *Business Communication: Process and Product* but found that it contained more material than they could cover in their courses, we introduced the first Brief Canadian Edition in 2003. Based on instructor feedback, much of the nice-to-know information, such as the case studies and career track profiles, was removed to the Instructor's Web site. In addition, the number of end-of-chapter activities was reduced. The content of the information was not compromised in any way, but was condensed to focus on key elements.

Business Communication: Process and Product, Second Brief Canadian Edition, remains true to Mary Ellen Guffey's 3-×-3 writing process. This systematic approach provides students with a practical plan for solving communication problems and creating successful communication products. The nine-stage approach of analyzing-anticipating-adapting, researching-organizing-approaching, and revising-proofreading-evaluating makes the process understandable.

New to the Second Brief Canadian Edition

We have responded to changes in the workplace by expanding and updating coverage in the areas of communication and technology, listening and speaking, and currency and clarity of information. Some key changes include

- revised discussion of collaboration technology that includes timely coverage of conferencing (audio, video, desktop, and media) as well as Internet relay chat, webcasting, and other meeting tools;
- expanded discussion of e-mail coverage. Chapter 8 now applies the 3-×-3 writing process to e-mails and memos;
- integrated discussions of mobile communication tools, such as instant messaging and wireless networking;
- reinforced focus on effective workplace communication by adding new strategies and tips for listening to colleagues and teammates;
- renamed headings in Unit 2 that further reinforce the 3-×-3 writing process;
- new and updated end-of-chapter exercises; and
- updated references to current news and research.

Appreciation for Support

We are very pleased to present the Second Brief Canadian Edition of *Business Communication: Process and Product.* As always, we owe a huge debt of gratitude to Dr. Mary Ellen Guffey, who continues to produce timely, market-driven texts and ancillaries that form the basis of our work.

In addition, we continue to appreciate the support from the team at Thomson Nelson. This edition saw many new faces added to the team, including Mike Thompson and Linda Sparks. We look forward to developing the same wonderful working relationship with them as we have had in the past with Chris Carson, Rebecca Rea, and Natalia Denesiuk.

We particularly appreciate those instructors and students who continue to choose *Business Communication: Process and Product*, especially those who provide both formal and informal feedback. Those who had a specific impact on the content of this edition include Denise Blay, Fanshawe College; Steffie Hawrylak-Young, Nova Scotia Community College; Marion Hohener, Seneca College; Gerald Horne, Kwantlen University College; and Linda Large, Canadore College.

The support of colleagues and friends at Durham College and other institutions continues to play an important part in our work. We thank you all.

Finally, as always, we thank our families for their unswerving support.

Kathleen Rhodes
Patricia Rogin

Support Package

A rich variety of instructional resources supplement and support *Business Communication: Process and Product*, Second Brief Canadian Edition. These materials give you excellent working tools to create a dynamic, exciting, and effective course.

For the Instructor:

Instructor's Manual/Test Bank (0-17-610354-6)
This comprehensive Instructor's Resource Manual contains both the **Instructor's Manual** and the **Printed Test Bank**.

The ***Instructor's Manual*** includes chapter synopses, teaching ideas, lecture enrichment material, classroom management techniques, answers for chapter review questions, suggested discussion guides for critical thinking questions, and solution guides for case study questions and applications.

Each chapter of the ***Printed Test Bank*** contains between 60 and 150 test questions. A special feature of this edition is the inclusion of feedback for the response to each question. Every chapter opens with a correlation table that identifies questions by chapter learning objective and by content: factual, conceptual, or application. Page references to the text ensure quick reference.

Instructor's Resource CD-ROM (0-17-610363-5)
Using key course resources is now easier than ever! The Instructor's CD-ROM combines popular text supplement material in one easy-to-use format. You'll have complete access to the Instructor's Manual (chapter outlines, bonus lecture material, before-and-after documents, and solutions to select chapter activities). Includes:

Microsoft® PowerPoint® Presentation Slides
This comprehensive lecture system offers summaries, explanations, and illustrations of key chapter concepts, plus lecture enrichment material not included in the text. With Microsoft® PowerPoint® software, instructors can easily customize any slide to support their lectures.

Computerized Test Bank

All items from the printed test bank are available through this automated testing program using the ExamView testing program. Create exams by selecting provided questions, modifying existing questions, and adding questions. It is provided free to adopters of this text.

Instructor's Manual/Test Bank

You'll have complete access to the Instructor's Manual (chapter outlines, bonus lecture material, before-and-after documents, and solutions to select chapter activities) and word-processing files for the test bank.

Book-Specific Web Site **http://www.guffeybrief2e.nelson.com**

The book-specific Web site contains a link to Instructor's Resources providing access to downloadable versions of the Instructor's Manual and Microsoft® PowerPoint® slides. The book-specific site also contains links to professional organizations, media resources, online writing labs, and much more! Contact your local sales representative for a password to the Instructor Resources portion of the site.

For the Student:

Student Web Site **http://www.guffeybrief2e.nelson.com**

This powerful site features chapter-by-chapter quizzes and Web links, career and job search information, Web media resources, online writing labs, and much more!

Unit 1
Communication Foundations

Chapter 1

Communicating at Work

LEARNING OBJECTIVES

1. *Identify changes in the workplace and the importance of communication skills.*

2. *Describe the process of communication.*

3. *Discuss barriers to interpersonal communication and the means of overcoming those barriers.*

4. *Analyze the functions and procedures of communication in organizations.*

5. *Assess the flow of communication in organizations including barriers and methods for overcoming those barriers.*

6. *List the goals of ethical business communication and describe important tools for doing the right thing.*

ENSURING THAT YOU SUCCEED IN THE NEW WORKPLACE

1

Employees at many organizations are experiencing change and upheaval. In fact, the entire work world you are about to enter is changing dramatically. The kind of work you'll do, the tools you'll use, the form of management, the environment where you'll work, the people with whom you'll interact—all are undergoing a profound transformation. Many of the changes in this dynamic workplace revolve around processing and communicating information. As a result, the most successful players in this new world of work will be those with highly developed communication skills.

Succeeding in today's world of work demands that you read, listen, speak, and write effectively.

The abilities to read, listen, speak, and write effectively, of course, are not inborn. Thriving in the dynamic and demanding work world depends on many factors, some of which you cannot control. But one factor that you do control is how well you communicate. The goals of this book and this course are to teach you basic business communication skills, such as how to write a memo or letter and how to make a presentation. You will also learn additional powerful communication skills that will equip you with the skills most needed in today's dynamic workplace. The book provides you with not only the process but also the products of effective communication. That's why many students decide that this is one book they will keep.

To become an effective communicator, you need practice—with meaningful feedback. You need someone such as your instructor to tell you how to modify your responses so that you can improve.

Yes, the workplace is undergoing profound changes. As a businessperson and especially as a business communicator, you will undoubtedly be affected by many transformations. Some of the most significant changes include global competition, flattened management hierarchies, and team-based projects. Other changes reflect our constantly evolving information technology, new work environments, a diverse work force, and the emergence of a knowledge-based economy. The following brief look at this new world of work reveals how directly your success in it will be tied to possessing excellent communication skills.

Heightened Global Competition

Communication is more complicated with people who have different religions, customs, and lifestyles.

Small, medium, and large companies increasingly find themselves competing in global rather than local markets. Improved systems of telecommunication, advanced forms of transportation, and saturated local markets—all of these developments have encouraged companies to move beyond familiar territories to emerging markets around the world.

Doing business in far-flung countries means dealing with people who are very different from you. They have different religions, engage in different customs, live different lifestyles, and rely on different approaches in business. Now add the complications of multiple time zones, vast distances between offices, and different languages. No wonder global communicators can blunder.[1]

Successful communication in these new markets requires developing new skills and attitudes such as cultural knowledge and sensitivity, flexibility, patience, and tolerance. Because these are skills and attitudes that most of us need to polish, you will receive special communication training to help you deal with intercultural business transactions.

Flattened Management Hierarchies

In response to intense global competition and other pressures, businesses have for years been cutting costs and flattening their management hierarchies. This flattening means that fewer layers of managers separate decision makers from line workers. In traditional companies, information flows through many levels of managers. In flat organizations, however, where the lines of communication are shorter, decision makers can react more quickly to market changes.

Flatter organizations demand that every employee be a skilled communicator.

Progressive organizations are in the midst of changing from "command and control" to "coordination and cultivation" management styles. This means that work is organized to let people use their own talents more wisely.[2] But today's flatter organizations also bring greater communication challenges. In the past, authoritarian and hierarchical management structures did not require that every employee be a skilled communicator. Managers simply passed along messages to the next level. Today, however, front-line employees as well as managers participate in decision making. Their input and commitment are necessary for their organizations to be successful in global markets. What's more, everyone has become a writer and a communicator.[3] Nearly all employees have computers and write their own messages. Administrative assistants no longer "clean up" their bosses' writing.

Expanded Team-Based Management

Along with flatter chains of command, companies are also turning to the concept of team-based operations. Nearly 80 percent of employees in all industries have adopted some form of quality circles or self-directed teams.

However, when companies form cross-functional teams, individuals must work together and share information. What's tough is that these individuals often don't share the same background, knowledge, or training. Some companies must hire communication coaches to help existing teams get along. They work to develop interpersonal, negotiation, and collaboration techniques. But companies would prefer to hire new workers who already possess these skills. That's why so many advertisements for new employees say "must possess good communication skills."

Innovative Communication Technologies

E-mail, voice mail, fax, videoconferencing, and the Web are revolutionizing the way we exchange information.

Because technology has completely revolutionized the way we communicate, recruiters are also looking for people with good computer skills. We now exchange information and stay in touch through e-mail, instant messaging, text messaging, fax, voice mail, two-way pagers, cell phones, powerful laptop computers, wireless networking, and satellite communications.[4] Through teleconferencing and videoconferencing, we can conduct meetings with associates around the world. Interactive software enables dozens or even hundreds of users to collaborate on projects. We now make tremendous use of the Internet and the Web for collecting information, serving customers, and selling products and services.

Just as companies are scrambling to use the Web most effectively, individual businesspeople are eagerly embracing the new technologies and revamping the way they communicate. E-mail is now the most popular communication channel; it's even replacing face-to-face talk.[5] To use these new resources most effectively, you, as a skilled business communicator, must develop a tool kit of new communication skills. For example, you will want to know how to design documents for screen appeal, how to select the best medium for a message, and how to use online search tools efficiently.

New Work Environments

As a result of global competition, restructuring, and the Internet, we are also seeing dramatic changes in work environments. Thanks to advances in communication and mobile technologies, experts estimate that there are over 1.5 million teleworkers in Canada.[6] They have flexible working arrangements so that they can work at home at least part of the time. At first telecommuting was rare, but now working at home or in remote locations is widely embraced thanks to broadband high-speed connections.[7] Tools such as instant and text messaging, file sharing, and wireless networking make it easy for employees to collaborate.[8]

Global competition, restructuring, and mobile technologies are encouraging flexible working arrangements such as telecommuting.

Tight quarters, intense cost-cutting measures, demands for increased productivity, and round-the-clock workdays—all are creating stress for today's workers. Combined with new responsibilities of team problem solving, business communicators can expect to need interpersonal skills that deal with heightened levels of emotion. Especially important are listening to and empathizing with fellow employees. Equally significant is respecting others' periodic need for uninterrupted, focused work time.[9] And employees in remote locations face added communication challenges since staying connected with the office often requires exchanging more messages than if they were face to face with their colleagues.[10]

Increasingly Diverse Work Force

Changes in today's work environments include more than innovative technology, team management, and different work routines. You can also expect to see hordes of new faces. No longer, say the experts, will the workplace be overwhelmingly male- or Anglo-oriented. In the last two decades, the number of women working in Canada increased almost 50 percent to more than 7.5 million, while the number of men working rose only 18 percent to 8.5 million.[11] Canada is truly a global nation with its heterogeneous diversity, and by 2017, it is projected that the Canadian immigration population will hit 22 percent, with one in five Canadians representing a visible minority.[12] In addition to increasing numbers of minorities, the work force will see a big jump in older workers. In 2001, people in the 37 to 55 age group made up 47 percent of the labour force. In 2011, more than half of this group will be 55 or older.[13] As the baby boomers begin to retire, the "Y Generation"—those born between 1978 and 1988 who comprise approximately 19 percent of Canada's work force according to Statistics Canada—will begin to fill the void.[14] As a result of these and other demographic trends, you can count on interacting with many coworkers who differ from you in race, ethnicity, gender, age, and many other ways.

Communicating with workers who differ in race, ethnicity, gender, and age requires new attitudes and skills.

Communicating in this diverse work environment requires new attitudes and skills. Acquiring these new employment skills is certainly worth the effort because of the benefits diversity brings to consumers, work teams, and business organizations. A diverse staff is better able to read trends and respond to the increasingly diverse customer base in local and world markets. In the workplace, diversity also makes good business sense. Teams made up of different people with different experiences are more likely to create the different products that consumers demand. Customers also want to deal with companies that respect their values. Learning to cooperate and communicate successfully with diverse coworkers should be a major priority for all businesspeople.

Thriving in the Age of Knowledge

Knowledge workers deal with symbols, such as words, figures, and data.

We're now witnessing the emergence of a new economy based on information and knowledge. Physical labour, raw materials, and capital are no longer the key ingredients in the creation of wealth. Knowledge workers engage in mind work. They deal with symbols: words, figures, and data.

What does all this mean for you? As a future knowledge worker, you can expect to be generating, processing, and exchanging information. Whether you work in the new economy of e-commerce or the old economy of *brick and mortar* companies, three out of four jobs will involve some form of mind work. Jobs that require thinking, brain power, and decision-making skills are likely to remain plentiful. To be successful in these jobs, you must be able to think critically, make decisions, and communicate those decisions.

Learning to Think Critically. Management and employees alike will be making decisions in such areas as product development, quality control, and customer satisfaction. You will be asked to think critically. This means having opinions that are backed by reasons and evidence. When your boss or team leader says, "What do you think we ought to do?" you want to be able to supply good ideas. The accompanying Career Coach box provides a five-point critical thinking plan to help you solve problems and make decisions. But having a plan is not enough. You also need chances to try the plan out and get feedback from colleagues and your boss (your instructor, for the time being). At the end of each chapter, you'll find activities and problems that will help you develop and apply your critical thinking skills.

CAREER COACH

Sharpening Your Skills for Critical Thinking, Problem Solving, and Decision Making

Gone are the days when management expected workers to do only as told. As a knowledge worker, you'll be expected to think critically. You'll be solving problems and making decisions. Much of this book is devoted to helping you learn how to solve problems and communicate those decisions to management, coworkers, clients, the government, and the public.

Faced with a problem or an issue, most of us do a lot of worrying before separating the issues or making a decision. All that worrying can become directed thinking by channelling it into the following procedure.

1. **Identify and Clarify the Problem.** Your first task is to recognize that a problem exists. Some problems are big and unmistakable, such as failure of an air-freight delivery service to get packages to customers on time. Other problems may be continuing annoyances, such as regularly running out of toner for an office copy machine. The first step in reaching a solution is pinpointing the problem area.
2. **Gather Information.** Learn more about the problem situation. Look for possible causes and solutions. This step may mean checking files, calling suppliers, or brainstorming with fellow workers. For example, the air-freight delivery service would investigate the tracking systems of the commercial airlines carrying its packages to determine what went wrong.
3. **Evaluate the Evidence.** Where did the information come from? Does it represent various points of view? What biases could be expected from each source? How accurate is the information gathered? Is it fact or opinion? For example, it is a fact that packages are missing; it is an opinion that they are merely lost and will turn up eventually.
4. **Consider Alternatives and Implications.** Draw conclusions from the gathered evidence and pose solutions. Then weigh the advantages and disadvantages of each alternative. What are the costs, benefits, and consequences? What are the obstacles, and how can they be handled? Most important, what solution best serves your goals and those of your organization? Here's where your creativity is especially important.
5. **Choose and Implement the Best Alternative.** Select an alternative and put it into action. Then, follow through on your decision by monitoring the results of implementing your plan. The freight company decided to give its unhappy customers free delivery service to make up for the lost packages and downtime. Be sure to continue monitoring and adjusting the solution to ensure its effectiveness over time.

Taking Charge of Your Career. In the new world of work, you can look forward to being in constant training to acquire new skills that will help you keep up with improved technologies and procedures. You can also expect to be exercising greater control over your career. Many workers today will not find nine-to-five jobs, lifetime security, predictable promotions, and even conventional workplaces, as you have learned earlier. Don't presume that companies will provide you with a clearly defined career path or planned developmental experiences. And don't wait for someone to "empower" you. You have to empower yourself.[15] To thrive in the new work world, you must be flexible and continually willing to learn new skills that supplement the strong foundation of basic skills you acquire in college or university.

Constantly changing technologies and work procedures mean continual training for employees.

Learning to Communicate. Probably the most important foundation skill for knowledge workers in the new environment is the ability to communicate. This means being able to listen and to express your ideas effectively in writing and in speech. As you advance in your career, communication skills become even more important. The number one requirement for promotion to management is the ability to communicate.

EXAMINING THE PROCESS OF COMMUNICATION

2

Since communication is a central factor in the emerging knowledge economy and a major consideration for anyone entering today's work force, we need to look more closely at the total process of communication. Just what is communication? For our purposes, communication is the *transmission of information and meaning from one individual or group to another.* The crucial element in this definition is *meaning.* Communication has as its central objective the transmission of meaning. The process of communication is successful only when the receiver understands an idea as the sender intended it. Both parties must agree not only on the information transmitted but also on the meaning of that information. This entire book is devoted to one objective: teaching you the skills of communication so that you can transmit meaning along with information. How does an idea travel from one person to another? Despite what you may have seen in futuristic science fiction movies, we can't just glance at another person and transfer meaning directly from mind to mind. We engage in a sensitive process of communication that generally involves five steps, discussed here and depicted in Figure 1.1.

The communication process has five steps: idea formation, message encoding, message transmission, message decoding, and feedback.

Sender Has Idea

The process of communication begins when the person with whom the message originates—the *sender*—has an idea. The form of the idea will be influenced by complex factors surrounding the sender: mood, frame of reference, background, culture, and physical makeup, as well as the context of the situation and many other factors. The way you greet people on campus or on the job, for example, depends a lot on how you feel, whom you are addressing, and what your culture has trained you to say.

The form of the idea, whether a simple greeting or a complex idea, is shaped by assumptions based on the sender's experiences. A manager sending an e-mail announcement to employees assumes they will be receptive, while direct mail advertisers assume that receivers will give only a quick glance to their message. The ability to accurately predict how a message will affect its receiver and skill in adapting that message to its receiver are key factors in successful communication.

Predicting the effect of a message and adapting the message to a receiver are key factors in successful communication.

FIGURE 1.1 The Communication Process

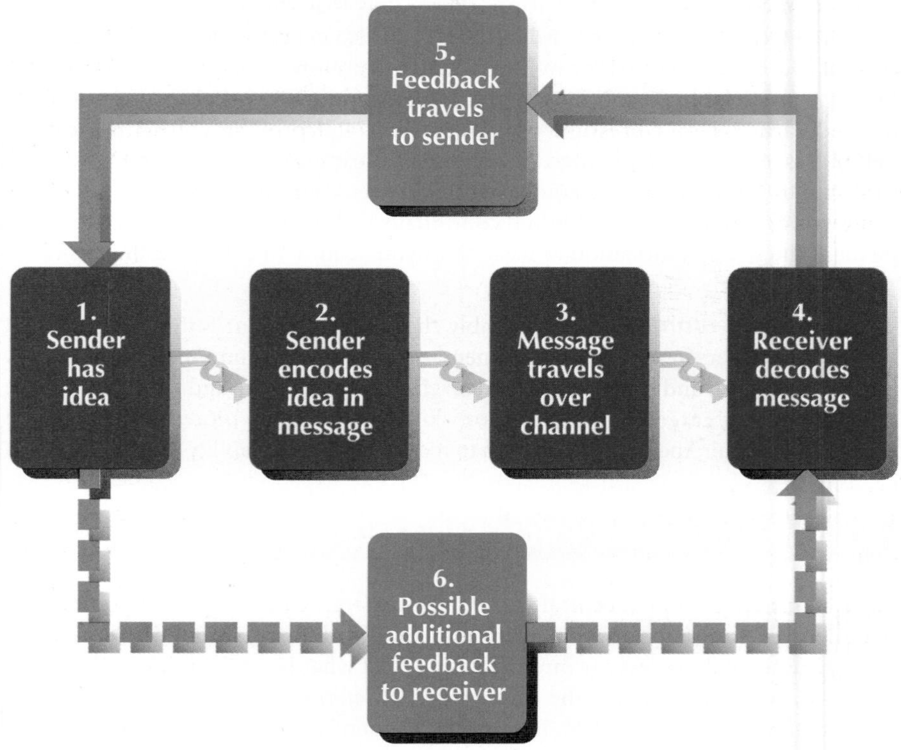

Sender Encodes Idea in Message

The next step in the communication process involves *encoding.* This means converting the idea into words or gestures that will convey meaning. A major problem in communicating any message verbally is that words have different meanings for different people. When misunderstandings result from missed meanings, it's called *bypassing.* Recognizing how easy it is to be misunderstood, skilled communicators choose familiar words with concrete meanings on which both senders and receivers agree. In selecting proper symbols, senders must be alert to the receiver's communication skills, attitudes, background, experiences, and culture: How will the selected words affect the receiver? Because the sender initiates a communication transaction, he or she has primary responsibility for its success or failure. Choosing appropriate words or symbols is the first step.

Message Travels Over Channel

The medium over which the message is physically transmitted is the *channel.* Messages may be delivered by computer, telephone, cell phone, letter, memorandum, report, announcement, picture, spoken word, fax, pager, Web page, or through some other channel. Because communication channels deliver both verbal and nonverbal messages, senders must choose the channel and shape the message carefully. A company may use its annual report, for example, as a channel to deliver many messages to shareholders. The verbal message lies in the report's financial and organizational news. Nonverbal messages, though, are conveyed by the report's appearance (showy versus bland), layout (ample white space versus tightly packed columns of print), and tone (conversational versus formal).

Anything that interrupts the transmission of a message in the communication process is called *noise.* Channel noise ranges from static that disrupts a telephone conversation to typographical and spelling errors in a letter or e-mail message. Such errors damage the credibility of the sender. Channel noise might even include the annoyance a receiver feels when the sender chooses an improper medium for sending a message, such as announcing a loan rejection via postcard or firing an employee by e-mail.

Channels are the media—computer, telephone, letter, fax, and so on—that transmit messages.

Receiver Decodes Message

The individual for whom the message is intended is the *receiver.* Translating the message from its symbol form into meaning involves *decoding.* Only when the receiver understands the meaning intended by the sender—that is, successfully decodes the message—does communication take place. Such success, however, is difficult to achieve because no two people share the same life experiences and because many barriers can disrupt the process.

Decoding can be disrupted internally by the receiver's lack of attention to or bias against the sender. It can be disrupted externally by loud sounds or illegible words. Decoding can also be sidetracked by semantic obstacles, such as misunderstood words or emotional reactions to certain terms. A memo that refers to all the women in an office as "girls," for example, may disturb its receivers so much that they fail to comprehend the total message.

Feedback Travels to Sender

The verbal and nonverbal responses of the receiver create *feedback,* a vital part of the communication process. Feedback helps the sender know that the message was received and understood. Although the receiver may respond with additional feedback to the sender, we'll concentrate here on the initial message flowing to the receiver and the resulting feedback.

Asking questions encourages feedback that clarifies communication.

Senders can encourage feedback by asking questions such as, *Am I making myself clear?* and *Is there anything you don't understand?* Senders can further improve feedback by timing the delivery appropriately and by providing only as much information as the receiver can handle. Receivers can improve the process by paraphrasing the sender's message with comments, such as, *Let me try to explain that in my own words.* The best feedback is descriptive rather than evaluative. An evaluative response is judgmental and doesn't tell the sender whether the receiver actually understood the message.

OVERCOMING INTERPERSONAL COMMUNICATION BARRIERS

3

The communication process is successful only when the receiver understands the message as intended by the sender. It sounds quite simple. Yet, it's not. How many times have you thought that you delivered a clear message, only to learn later that your intentions were totally misunderstood? Most messages that we send reach their destination, but many are only partially understood.

Obstacles That Create Misunderstanding

You can improve your chances of communicating successfully by learning to recognize barriers that are known to disrupt the process. The most significant barriers for individuals are bypassing, frames of reference, lack of language skill, and distractions.

Barriers to successful communication include bypassing, differing frames of reference, lack of language or listening skills, emotional interference, and physical distractions.

Bypassing. One of the biggest barriers to clear communication involves words. Each of us attaches a little bundle of meanings to every word, and these meanings are not always similar. *Bypassing* happens when people miss each other with their meanings.[16] Bypassing can lead to major miscommunication because people assume that meanings are contained in words. Actually, meanings are in people. For communication to be successful, the receiver and sender must attach the same symbolic meanings to their words.

Miscommunication often results when the sender's frame of reference differs markedly from the receiver's.

Differing Frames of Reference. Another barrier to clear communication is your *frame of reference.* Everything you see and feel in the world is translated through your individual frame of reference. Your unique frame is formed by a combination of your experiences, education, culture, expectations, personality, and many other elements. As a result, you bring your own biases and expectations to any communication situation. Because your frame of reference is totally different from everyone else's, you will never see things exactly as others do. Wise business communicators strive to prevent communication failure by being alert to both their own frames of reference and those of others.

Successful communication requires good oral and written language skills.

Lack of Language Skill. No matter how extraordinary the idea, it won't be understood or fully appreciated unless the communicators involved have good language skills. Each individual needs an adequate vocabulary, a command of basic punctuation and grammar, and skill in written and oral expression. Moreover, poor listening skills can prevent us from hearing oral messages clearly and thus responding properly.

Distractions. Other barriers include emotional interference and physical distractions. Shaping an intelligent message is difficult when you're feeling joy, fear, resentment, hostility, sadness, or some other strong emotion. To reduce the influence of emotions on communication, both senders and receivers should focus on the content of the message and try to remain objective. Physical distractions such as faulty acoustics, noisy surroundings, or a poor cell phone connection can disrupt oral communication. Similarly, sloppy appearance, poor printing, careless formatting, and typographical or spelling errors can disrupt written messages.

Overcoming the Obstacles

To overcome obstacles, communicators must anticipate problems in encoding, transmitting, and decoding.

Careful communicators can conquer barriers in a number of ways. Half the battle in communicating successfully is recognizing that the entire process is sensitive and susceptible to breakdown. Like a defensive driver anticipating problems on the road, a good communicator anticipates problems in encoding, transmitting, and decoding a message. Effective communicators also focus on the receiver's environment and frame of reference. They ask themselves questions such as, *How is that individual likely to react to my message?* or *Does the receiver know as much about the subject as I do?*

Misunderstandings are less likely if you arrange your ideas logically and use words precisely. But communicating is more than expressing yourself well. A large part of successful communication is listening.

Overcoming interpersonal barriers often involves questioning your preconceptions. Successful communicators continually examine their personal assumptions, biases, and prejudices. The more you pay attention to subtleties and know "where you're coming from" when you encode and decode messages, the better you'll communicate.

Finally, effective communicators create an environment for useful feedback. In oral communication this means asking questions such as, *Do you understand?* and *What questions do you have?* as well as encouraging listeners to repeat instructions or paraphrase ideas. As a listener it means providing feedback that describes rather than evaluates. And in written communication it means asking questions and providing access: *Do you have my telephone number in case you have questions?* or *Here's my e-mail address so that you can give me your response immediately.*

Good communicators ask questions to stimulate feedback.

COMMUNICATING IN ORGANIZATIONS

Until now, you've probably been thinking about the communication you do personally. But business communicators must also be concerned with the bigger picture, and that involves sharing information in organizations. Creating and exchanging knowledge are critical to fostering innovation, the key challenge in today's knowledge economy. On the job you'll be exchanging information by communicating internally and externally.

Internal and External Functions

Internal communication includes sharing ideas and messages with superiors, coworkers, and subordinates. When those messages must be written, you'll probably choose e-mail or a printed memorandum. When you are communicating externally with customers, suppliers, government, and the public, you will generally send letters on company stationery.

Internal communication often consists of e-mail, memos, and voice messages; external communication generally consists of letters.

Some of the functions of internal communication are to issue and clarify procedures and policies, inform management of progress, develop new products and services, persuade employees or management to make changes or improvements, coordinate activities, and evaluate and reward employees. External functions are to answer inquiries about products or services, persuade customers to buy products or services, clarify supplier specifications, issue credit, collect bills, respond to government agencies, and promote a positive image of the organization.

In all of these tasks employees and managers use a number of communication skills: reading, listening, speaking, and writing. You probably realize that you need to improve these skills to the proficiency level required for success in today's knowledge society. This book and this course will provide you with practical advice on how to do just that.

Organizational communication has three basic functions: to inform, to persuade, and/or to promote goodwill.

Now look back over the preceding discussion of internal and external functions of communication in organizations. Although there appear to be a large number of diverse business communication functions, they can be summarized in three simple categories, as Figure 1.2 shows: (1) to inform, (2) to persuade, and/or (3) to promote goodwill.

New Emphasis on Interactive, Mobile, and Instant Communication

The flattening of organizations coupled with the development of sophisticated information technology has greatly changed the way we communicate internally and

FIGURE 1.2 Functions of Business Communication

Canadian icon Marshall McLuhan coined the phrase "the medium is the message." McLuhan observed the impact of technology on shaping our culture and saw the telephone as a liberating device. Amazing wireless and mobile technologies are changing where, when, and how we communicate and work.

externally. We're seeing a major shift away from one-sided and rather slow forms of communication, such as memos and letters, to more interactive, fast-results communication. Speeding up the flow of communication are technologies such as e-mail, instant messaging (IM), text messaging, voice mail, cell phones, and wireless fidelity (Wi-Fi) networks. Wi-Fi lets mobile workers connect to the Internet at ultra-fast speeds without cables. Using IM, workers can communicate simultaneously with clients, colleagues, and friends. Many workers also rely on text messaging on their cell phones, laptops, or handheld devices. In addition to dependence on IM, many businesspeople rely on their cell phones.

Cell phones have proliferated so rapidly that their careless use has become an annoyance in many public places. See the accompanying Career Coach box for tips on using this technological privilege courteously and responsibly.

Other forms of interactive communication include intranets (company versions of the Internet), Web sites, video transmission, and videoconferencing. You'll be learning more about these forms of communication in subsequent chapters. Despite the range of interactive technologies, communicators are still working with two basic forms of communication: oral and written. Each has advantages and disadvantages.

Oral communication minimizes miscommunication but provides no written record.

Oral Communication. Nearly everyone agrees that the best way to exchange information is orally in face-to-face conversations or meetings. Oral communication has many advantages. For one thing, it minimizes misunderstandings because communicators can immediately ask questions to clarify uncertainties. For another, it enables communicators to see each other's facial expressions and hear voice inflections, further improving the process. Oral communication is also an efficient way to develop consensus when many people must be consulted. Finally, most of us enjoy face-to-face interpersonal communication because it's easy, feels warm and natural, and promotes friendships.

CAREER COACH

Practising Courteous and Responsible Cell Phone Use

Business communicators find cell phones to be enormously convenient and real time-savers. But rude users have generated a backlash of sorts. Most of us have experienced thoughtless and offensive cell phone behaviour. Although the cell phone industry vigorously opposes restrictive legislation, many major manufacturers admonish users to be courteous. Here are specific suggestions for using cell phones safely and responsibly:

- **Be courteous to those around you.** Don't force those near you to hear your business. Think first of those in close proximity instead of those on the other end of the phone. Apologize and make amends gracefully for occasional cell phone blunders.
- **Observe wireless-free quiet areas.** Don't allow your cell phone to ring in theatres, restaurants, museums, classrooms, important meetings, and similar places. Use the cell phone's silent/vibrating ring option. A majority of travellers prefer that cell phone conversations not be held on most forms of public transportation.
- **Speak in low, conversational tones.** Microphones on cell phones are quite sensitive, thus making it unnecessary to talk loudly. Avoid "cell yell."
- **Take only urgent calls.** Make full use of your cell phone's caller ID feature to screen incoming calls. Let voice mail take those calls that are not pressing.
- **Drive now, talk later.** Pull over if you must make a call. Talking while driving increases the chance of accidents fourfold, about the same as driving while intoxicated.

The main disadvantages of oral communication are that it produces no written record, sometimes wastes time, and may be inconvenient. When individuals meet face to face or speak on the telephone, someone's work has to be interrupted. And how many of us are able to limit a conversation to just business? Nevertheless, oral communication has many advantages. The forms and advantages of both oral and written communication are summarized in Figure 1.3.

FIGURE 1.3 Forms of Organizational Communication

Oral Communication	Written Communication
Form	**Form**
Phone call	Announcement
Conversation	Memo, e-mail, fax
Interview	Letter
Meeting	Report, proposal
Conference	Newsletter
Advantages	**Advantages**
Immediate feedback	Permanent record
Nonverbal cues	Convenience
Warm feeling	Economy
Forceful impact	Careful message
Multiple input	Easy distribution

Written communication provides a permanent record but lacks immediate feedback.

Written Communication. Written communication is impersonal in the sense that two communicators cannot see or hear each other and cannot provide immediate feedback. Most forms of business communication—including e-mail, announcements, memos, faxes, letters, newsletters, reports, proposals, and manuals—fall into this category.

Written messages demand good writing skills, which can be developed through training.

Organizations rely on written communication for many reasons. It provides a permanent record, a necessity in these times of increasing litigation and extensive government regulation. Writing out an idea instead of delivering it orally enables communicators to develop an organized, well-considered message. Written documents are also convenient. They can be composed and read when the schedules of both communicators permit, and they can be reviewed if necessary.

Written messages have drawbacks, of course. They require careful preparation and sensitivity to audience and anticipated effects. Words spoken in conversation may soon be forgotten, but words committed to hard or soft copy become a public record—and sometimes an embarrassing or dangerous one.

Another drawback to written messages is that they are more difficult to prepare. They demand good writing skills, and such skills are not inborn. But writing proficiency can be learned. Because as much as 90 percent of all business transactions may involve written messages and because writing skills are so important to your business success, you will be receiving special instruction in becoming a good writer and a good communicator.

Avoiding Information Overload and Productivity Meltdown

Although communication tools like e-mail and voice mail were expected to make workers more productive, the truth is that many employees are feeling stressed and unable to function.

Although technology provides a myriad of communication channel choices, the sheer volume of messages is overwhelming many employees. The average North American worker receives 54 e-mails per day, and this number seems to have stabilized. However, the number of nonessential messages has increased by 41 percent. According to Christina Cavanagh, a professor at the Richard Ivey School of Business, the cost of e-mail overload is approximately 12 percent of yearly corporate payrolls.[17] Additionally, meaning may also be lost since reading on a computer screen has been shown to yield just 75 percent of the comprehension of reading on paper.[18]

Information overload and resulting productivity meltdown are becoming serious problems for workers and their employers. While some software programs can now automatically sort messages into limited categories, one expert says that "human brainpower"—not new technology—is the key to managing e-mail overload.[19] Suggestions for controlling the e-mail monster are shown in the accompanying Tech Talk box.

5 IMPROVING THE FLOW OF INFORMATION IN ORGANIZATIONS

Information within organizations flows through formal and informal communication channels. A free exchange of information helps organizations respond rapidly to changing markets, increase efficiency and productivity, build employee morale, serve the public, and take full advantage of the ideas of today's knowledge workers. Barriers, however, can obstruct the flow of communication.

TECH TALK

Tips for Managing Your E-Mail

In an amazingly short time, e-mail has become one of the most powerful and useful communication channels in the workplace. But it has also produced information overload for many workers. The following techniques can help you control the e-mail monster:

- Send only business messages that you would have sent in a memo format. If a quick phone call or a short in-person chat could solve the problem immediately, avoid sending an e-mail.
- Check your e-mail in-box only at specific times each day, say at 9 a.m. and again at 4 p.m.
- Print important memos to read during free time away from your desk.
- Deal with a message only once. Answer it, delegate it to someone else, or move it to a project-specific folder for later action.
- Avoid using the copy function and sending unnecessary replies.
- Pick up your incoming messages online, but answer them offline. Take time to think about your responses. Compose them on your word processor and upload them to your mail program, thus saving valuable network connection time.
- Practise e-mail triage. This means focusing on the most urgent messages first. Read the subject lines; then delete unwanted messages (spam) and those that require no response.
- Use an alternate address when registering for anything on the Web. Avoid giving out your primary e-mail address.
- Subscribe only to mailing lists in which you are really interested.[20]

Formal Channels

Formal communication channels follow an organization's chain of command.

Formal channels of communication generally follow an organization's hierarchy of command. Information about policies and procedures originates with executives and flows down through managers to supervisors and finally to lower-level employees. Many organizations have formulated official communication policies that encourage regular open communication, suggest means for achieving it, and spell out responsibilities. Official information among workers typically flows through formal channels in three directions: downward, upward, and horizontally.

Job plans, policies, instructions, feedback, and procedures flow downward from managers to employees.

Downward Flow. Information flowing downward generally moves from decision makers, including the CEO and managers, through the chain of command to workers. This information includes job plans, policies, and procedures. Managers also provide feedback about employee performance and instill a sense of mission in achieving the organization's goals.

One obstacle that can impede the downward flow of information is distortion resulting from long lines of communication. If, for example, the CEO wanted to change an accounting procedure, she or he would probably not send a memo directly to the staff or cost accountants who would implement the change. Instead, the CEO would relay the idea through proper formal channels—from the vice president for finance, to the accounting manager, to the senior accountant, and so on—until the message reached the affected employees. Obviously, the longer the lines of communication, the greater the chance that a message will be distorted.

To improve communication and to compete more effectively, many of today's companies have "reengineered" themselves into smaller operating units and work teams. Rather than being bogged down with long communication chains, management speaks directly to team leaders, thus speeding up the entire process.[21] Management is also improving the downward flow of information through newsletters, announcements, meetings, videos, and company intranets. Instead of hoarding information at the top, today's managers recognize how essential it is to let workers know how well the company is doing and what new projects are planned.

Feedback from employees forms the upward flow of communication in most organizations.

Upward Flow. Information flowing upward provides feedback from nonmanagement employees to management. Subordinate employees describe progress in completing tasks, report roadblocks encountered, and suggest methods for improving efficiency. Channels for upward communication include phone messages, e-mail, memos, reports, departmental meetings, and suggestion systems. Ideally, the heaviest flow of information should be upward, with information being fed steadily to decision makers.

A number of obstacles, however, can interrupt the upward flow of communication. Employees who distrust their employers are less likely to communicate openly. Employees cease trusting managers if they feel they are being tricked, manipulated, criticized, or treated unfairly. Unfortunately, some employees today no longer have a strong trusting attitude toward employers. Downsizing, cost-cutting measures, the tremendous influx of temporary workers, discrimination and harassment suits, substantial compensation packages for chief executives, and many other factors have eroded the feelings of trust and pride that employees once felt toward their employers and their jobs. Other obstacles include fear of reprisal for honest communication, lack of adequate communication skills, and differing frames of reference. Imperfect communication results when individuals are not using words or symbols with similar meanings, when they cannot express their ideas clearly, or when they come from different backgrounds.

To improve the upward flow of communication, some companies are (1) hiring communication coaches to train employees, (2) asking employees to report customer complaints, (3) encouraging regular meetings with staff, (4) providing a trusting, nonthreatening environment in which employees can comfortably share their observations and ideas with management, and (5) offering incentive programs that encourage employees to collect and share valuable feedback. Companies are also building trust by setting up hotlines for anonymous feedback to management and by installing *ombudsman* programs. An *ombudsman* is a mediator who hears employee complaints, investigates, and seeks to resolve problems fairly.

Workers coordinate tasks, share information, solve problems, and resolve conflicts through horizontal communication.

Horizontal Flow. Lateral channels transmit information horizontally among workers at the same level. These channels enable individuals to coordinate tasks, share information, solve problems, and resolve conflicts. Horizontal communication takes place through personal contact, telephone, e-mail, memos, voice mail, and meetings. Most traditional organizations have few established regular channels for the horizontal exchange of information. Restructured companies with flattened hierarchies and team-based management, however, have discovered that when employees combine their knowledge with that of other employees, they can do their jobs better. Much of the information in these organizations is travelling horizontally among team members.[22]

Obstacles to the horizontal flow of communication, as well as to upward and downward flow, include poor communication skills, prejudice, ego involvement, and turf wars. Some employees avoid sharing information if doing so might endanger their status or chances for promotion within the organization. Competition within units and an uneven reward system may also prevent workers from freely sharing information.

To improve horizontal communication, companies are (1) training employees in teamwork and communication techniques, (2) establishing reward systems based on team achievement rather than individual achievement, and (3) encouraging full participation in team functions. However, employees must also realize that they are personally responsible for making themselves heard, for really understanding what other people say, and for getting the information they need. Developing those business communication skills is exactly what this book and this course will do for you.

To improve horizontal communication, companies are training and rewarding employees.

Informal Channels

Not all information within an organization travels through formal channels. Often, it travels in informal channels called the *grapevine.* These channels are usually based on social relationships in which individuals talk about work when they are having lunch, meeting at the water cooler, working out, golfing, or car-pooling to work. Alert managers find the grapevine an excellent source of information about employee morale and problems. They have also used the grapevine as a "break it to them gently" device, planting "rumours," for example, of future layoffs or other changes.

Informal organizational communication transmits unofficial news through the grapevine.

Researchers studying communication flow within organizations know that the grapevine can be a major source of information. Is this bad? Well, yes and no. The grapevine can be a fairly accurate and speedy source of organization information. However, grapevine information is often incomplete because it travels in headlines. When employees obtain most of their company news from the grapevine, it's a pretty sure bet that management is not releasing sufficient information through formal channels.

The truth is that most employees want to know what's going on. In fact, one study found that regardless of how much information organization members reported receiving, they wanted more.[23] Many companies today have moved away from a rigid authoritarian management structure in which only managers were privy to vital information, such as product success and profit figures. Employees who know the latest buzz feel like important members of the team.[24] Through formal lines of communication, smart companies are keeping employees informed. Thus, the grapevine is reduced to carrying gossip about who's dating whom and what restaurant is trendy for lunch.

Employees prefer to receive vital company information through formal channels.

FACING INCREASING ETHICAL CHALLENGES

The work world is indeed changing. One of the most remarkable changes involves ethics in the workplace. According to Eugene Ellen, executive director of the Social Investment Organization in Canada, the issue of business ethics is becoming more mainstream. "It has become good hard business practice to establish corporate liability in various areas, including ethics and environment."[25]

Many businesses have recognized that ethical practices make good business sense. Ethical companies endure less litigation, less resentment, and less government regulation.[26] As a result, companies are adding ethics officers, hotlines, workshops, training programs, and codes of conduct. If you go to work for a large company, chances are good that you'll be asked to comply with its code of conduct.

Ethical awareness grows as companies recognize that ethical practices make good business sense.

Achieving Ethical Behaviour

Despite this trend, however, the business world continues to be plagued by unethical behaviour and a poor public image. With downsized staffs and fewer resources, employees feel pressure to increase productivity—by whatever means. Knowingly or

The business world suffers from a poor public image resulting from unethical behaviour by some organizations.

not, managers under pressure to make profit quotas may send the message to workers that it's acceptable to lie, cheat, or steal to achieve company goals.[27] Couple these pressures with a breakdown in the traditional attitudes of trust and loyalty toward employers, and it's easy to see why ethical lapses are causing concern in the workplace.

Five Common Ethical Traps

In making ethical decisions, business communicators commonly face five traps that can make arriving at the right decision more difficult.[28]

Recognizing five ethical traps can help communicators avoid them.

The False Necessity Trap. People act from the belief that they're doing what they must do. They convince themselves that they have no other choice, when in fact it's generally a matter of convenience or comfort. When people fall into the false necessity trap, they overestimate the cost of doing the right thing and underestimate the cost of failing to do so.[29]

The Doctrine-of-Relative-Filth Trap. Unethical actions sometimes look good when compared with the worse behaviour of others.

The Rationalization Trap. In falling into the rationalization trap, people try to explain away unethical actions by justifying them with excuses.

The Self-Deception Trap. People may persuade themselves that a lie is not really a lie. Self-deception is justifying our beliefs to ourselves by convincing ourselves to accept as true what is false or invalid.

The Ends-Justify-the-Means Trap. Taking unethical actions to accomplish a desirable goal is a common trap.

Goals of Ethical Business Communication

Business communicators can minimize the danger of falling into ethical traps by setting specific ethical goals. Although the following goals hardly comprise a formal code of conduct, they will help business writers maintain a high ethical standard.

Goals of ethical communicators include telling the truth, labelling opinions, being objective, communicating clearly, and giving credit.

Telling the Truth. Ethical business communicators do not intentionally make statements that are untrue or deceptive. We become aware of dishonesty in business when violators break laws, notably in advertising, packaging, and marketing.

Half-truths, exaggerations, and deceptions constitute unethical communication. But conflicting loyalties in the workplace sometimes blur the line between right and wrong.

***Facts* are verifiable; *opinions* are beliefs held with conviction.**

Labelling Opinions. Sensitive communicators know the difference between facts and opinions. Facts are verifiable and often are quantifiable; opinions are beliefs held with confidence but without substantiation. Stating opinions as if they were facts is unethical.

Being Objective. Ethical business communicators recognize their own biases and strive to keep them from distorting a message. Honest reporting means presenting the whole picture and relating all facts fairly.

Communicating Clearly. Ethical business communicators feel an obligation to write clearly so that receivers understand easily and quickly. Many organizations, such as banks and insurance companies, have even created "Plain English" guidelines to ensure that policies, warranties, and contracts are in language comprehensible to average readers. Plain English means short sentences, simple words, and clear organization. Communicators who intentionally obscure the meaning with long sentences and difficult words are being unethical. A thin line, however, separates unethical communication from ethical communication. Some might argue that writers and speakers who deliver wordy, imprecise messages requiring additional correspondence or inquiry to clarify the meaning are acting unethically. However, the problem may be one of experience and skill rather than ethics. Such messages waste the time and resources of both senders and receivers. However, they are not unethical unless the intent is to deceive.

"Plain English" guidelines require simple, understandable language in policies, contracts, warranties, and other documents.

Giving Credit. As you probably know, using the written ideas of others without credit is called *plagiarism*. Ethical communicators give credit for ideas by (1) referring to originators' names within the text; (2) using quotation marks; and (3) documenting sources with endnotes, footnotes, or internal references. In school or on the job, stealing ideas or words from others is unethical.

Tools for Doing the Right Thing

In composing messages or engaging in other activities on the job, business communicators can't help being torn by conflicting loyalties. Acting ethically means doing the right thing given the circumstances. Each set of circumstances requires analyzing issues, evaluating choices, and acting responsibly.

Resolving ethical issues is never easy, but the task can be made less difficult if you know how to identify key issues. The following questions may be helpful.

- **Is the action you are considering legal?** No matter who asks you to do it or how important you feel the result will be, avoid anything that is prohibited by law.
- **How would you see the problem if you were on the opposite side?** Looking at all sides of an issue helps you gain perspective. By weighing both sides of the issue, you can arrive at a more equitable solution.
- **What are alternative solutions?** Consider all dimensions of other options. Would the alternative be more ethical? Under the circumstances, is the alternative feasible? Can an alternative solution be implemented with a minimum of disruption and with a high degree of probable success?
- **Can you discuss the problem with someone whose advice you trust?** Talking about your dilemma with a coworker or with a colleague in your field might give you helpful insights and lead to possible alternatives.
- **How would you feel if your family, friends, employer, or coworkers learned of your action?** If the thought of revealing your action publicly disturbs you, your choice is probably not a wise one. Losing the faith of your friends or the confidence of your customers is not worth whatever short-term gains might be realized.

Business communicators can help resolve ethical issues through self-examination.

Discussing an ethical problem with a coworker or colleague might lead to helpful alternatives.

Perhaps the best advice in ethical matters is contained in the Golden Rule: Do unto others as you would have others do unto you. The ultimate solution to all ethics problems is treating others fairly and doing what is right to achieve what is good. In succeeding chapters you will find additional discussions of ethical questions as they relate to relevant topics.

STRENGTHENING YOUR COMMUNICATION SKILLS

You've just taken a brief look at the changing workplace, the process of communication, the flow of communication in organizations, and ethical challenges facing business communicators today. Each topic provided you not only with the latest information about an issue but also with tips and suggestions that will help you function successfully in the changing workplace. After all, it's not enough to know the problems; you also need to know some of the solutions. Our goal is to help you recognize the problems and also to equip you with techniques for overcoming the obstacles that others have faced.

Remember, communication skills are not inherent; they must be learned. Remember, too, to take advantage of the unique opportunity you now have. You have an expert who is willing to work with you to help improve your writing, speaking, and other communication skills. Many organizations pay thousands of dollars to communication coaches and trainers to teach employees the very skills that you are learning in this course. Your coach is your instructor. Get your money's worth! Pick his or her brains. With this book as your guide and your instructor as your coach, you will find that this course, as we mentioned earlier, could very well be the most important in your entire postsecondary curriculum.

SUMMARY OF LEARNING OBJECTIVES

1 **Identify changes in the workplace and the importance of communication skills.** The workplace has undergone profound changes, such as the emergence of heightened global competition, flattened management hierarchies, expanded team-based management, innovative communication technologies, new work environments, and an increasingly diverse work force. In this dynamic workplace you can expect to be a knowledge worker; that is, you will deal with words, figures, and data. The most important foundation skill for knowledge workers is the ability to communicate. You can improve your skills by studying the principles, processes, and products of communication provided in this book and in this course.

2 **Describe the process of communication.** The sender encodes (selects) words or symbols to express an idea. The message is sent verbally over a channel (such as a letter, e-mail message, or telephone call) or is expressed nonverbally, perhaps with gestures or body language. "Noise"—such as loud sounds, misspelled words, or other distractions—may interfere with the transmission. The receiver decodes (interprets) the message and attempts to make sense of it. The receiver responds with feedback, informing the sender of the effectiveness of the message. The objective of communication is the transmission of meaning so that a receiver understands a message as intended by the sender.

3 **Discuss barriers to interpersonal communication and the means of overcoming those barriers.** *Bypassing* causes miscommunication because people have different meanings for the words they use. One's *frame of reference* creates a filter through which all ideas are screened, sometimes causing distortion and lack of objectivity. *Weak language skills* as well as *poor listening skills* impair communication efforts. *Emotional interference*—joy, fear, anger, and so forth—hampers the sending

and receiving of messages. *Physical distractions*—noisy surroundings, faulty acoustics, and so forth—can disrupt oral communication. You can reduce or overcome many interpersonal communication barriers if you (a) realize that the communication process is imperfect, (b) adapt your message to the receiver, (c) improve your language and listening skills, (d) question your preconceptions, and (e) plan for feedback.

4 **Analyze the functions and procedures of communication in organizations.** Internal functions of communication include issuing and clarifying procedures and policies, informing management of progress, persuading others to make changes or improvements, and interacting with employees. External functions of communication include answering inquiries about products or services, persuading customers to buy products or services, clarifying supplier specifications, and so forth. Oral, face-to-face communication is most effective, but written communication is often more expedient. The volume of messages today is overwhelming many employees, who must institute techniques to control information overload and productivity meltdown.

5 **Assess the flow of communication in organizations including barriers and methods for overcoming those barriers.** Formal channels of communication follow an organization's hierarchy of command. Information flows downward from management to workers. Long lines of communication tend to distort information. Many organizations are improving the downward flow of communication through newsletters, announcements, meetings, videos, and company intranets. Information flows upward from employees to management, thus providing vital feedback for decision makers. Obstacles include mistrust, fear of reprisal for honest communication, lack of adequate communication skills, and differing frames of reference. To improve upward flow, companies are improving relations with staff, offering incentive programs that encourage employees to share valuable feedback, and investing in communication training programs. Horizontal communication is among workers at the same level. Obstacles include poor communication skills, prejudice, ego involvement, competition, and turf wars. Techniques for overcoming the obstacles include (a) training employees in communication and teamwork techniques, (b) establishing reward systems, and (c) encouraging full participation in team functions. Informal channels of communication, such as the grapevine, deliver unofficial news—both personal and organizational—among friends and coworkers.

6 **List the goals of ethical business communication and describe important tools for doing the right thing.** Ethical business communicators strive to (a) tell the truth, (b) label opinions so that they are not confused with facts, (c) be objective and avoid distorting a message, (d) write clearly and avoid obscure language, and (e) give credit when using the ideas of others. When you face a difficult decision, the following questions serve as valuable tools in guiding you to do the right thing: (a) Is the action you are considering legal? (b) How would you see the problem if you were on the opposite side? (c) What are alternative solutions? (d) Can you discuss the problem with someone whose advice you trust? (e) How would you feel if your family, friends, employer, or coworkers learned of your action?

CHAPTER REVIEW

1. How are business communicators affected by the emergence of global competition, flattened management hierarchies, and expanded team-based management? (Obj. 1)
2. How are business communicators affected by the emergence of innovative communication technologies, new work environments, and an increasingly diverse work force? (Obj. 1)
3. What are knowledge workers? Why are they hired? (Obj. 1)
4. Define *communication* and explain its most critical factor. (Obj. 2)
5. Describe the five steps in the process of communication. (Obj. 2)
6. List four barriers to interpersonal communication. Be prepared to discuss each. (Obj. 3)
7. Name five specific ways in which you can personally reduce barriers in your communication. (Obj. 3)
8. What are the three main functions of organizational communication? (Obj. 4)
9. What are the advantages of oral, face-to-face communication? (Obj. 4)
10. What are the advantages of written communication? (Obj. 4)
11. How do formal and informal channels of communication differ within organizations? (Obj. 5)
12. Describe three directions in which communication flows within organizations and what barriers can obstruct each. (Obj. 5)
13. How can barriers to the free flow of information in organizations be reduced? (Obj. 5)
14. Discuss five thinking traps that block ethical behaviour. (Obj. 6)
15. When faced with a difficult ethical decision, what questions should you ask yourself? (Obj. 6)

INFOTRAC® COLLEGE EDITION

Building Knowledge and Research Skills

Today's digital workplace requires you to find and evaluate information on the Internet. As a student purchasing a new copy of *Business Communication: Process and Product,* Second Brief Canadian Edition, you have an extraordinary opportunity to develop these research skills. For four months, you have special access to InfoTrac College Edition, a comprehensive Web-based collection of over 10 million full-text articles from nearly 5000 scholarly and popular periodicals. You can access this online database 24 hours a day, 7 days a week from any computer with Internet access. Since InfoTrac College Edition's articles are updated daily, you can access the most current information. At the time of publication, InfoTrac links were up-to-date. You will find research activities and questions in this text that will help you build knowledge and develop research skills using InfoTrac. Watch for the InfoTrac icon.

How to Use InfoTrac College Edition

1. Visit the InfoTrac site at <http://infotrac.thomsonlearning.com>. Click on *Register New Account.*
2. Enter the passcode on the card packaged with your textbook.
3. Create your own user name.
4. Fill out the registration form completely to activate your account. Enter your newly created user name (step 3). Create your own password. Make up a question to which only you know the answer; then provide the answer. Provide your contact information. Your account is now registered. (If you forget your password, InfoTrac uses the security question to verify access and will e-mail your password back to you.)

Search Methods

Subject Search: Select *Subject Guide* on the menu bar. Enter the subject, and click *Search.*

a. After a list of articles appears, select an article by clicking on its title. If your search words do not match the Subject Guide database, a list of similar and related subjects will appear.
b. Select the subject that most closely matches your topic. A list containing bibliographic information for each article appears.
c. To view an article, click on the citation.
d. To print the article, click *Print* on the menu bar.
e. To return to the citation list, click *Citations* on the menu bar.
f. To start a new search, click *Search* on the menu bar.

Keyword Search: Click *Keyword Search* on the menu bar. This search matches keywords in the articles.

a. Click on the entry box, and type your search term. Click *Search.*

The search will return with a list of articles containing the keyword(s). Results are listed from most recent to oldest publication date.

b. To print an article, return to the citation list, or start a new search, refer to the above.

Advanced Search: Click *Advanced Search* on the menu bar. This allows you to select from the index to narrow your search.

a. Select an index. Each article is indexed by variables such as author, title, publication name, and where and when it was published.
b. Type your search criteria into the entry box. Click *Search.*

CRITICAL THINKING

1. Why should students and professionals strive to improve their communication skills, and why is it difficult or impossible to do so on your own? (Obj. 1)
2. Recall a time when you experienced a problem as a result of poor communication. What were the causes of and possible remedies for the problem? (Objs. 2 and 3)
3. How would you respond to this complaint? Some companies say that the more information provided to employees, the more employees want. (Objs. 4 and 5)
4. As a channel of communication, what are the advantages and disadvantages of e-mail? (Objs. 4 and 5)
5. How are the rules of ethical behaviour that govern businesses different from those that govern your personal behaviour? (Obj. 6)

ACTIVITIES

1.1 Communication Self-Assessment (Objs. 2 and 3)

You know more about yourself than anyone else. That makes you the best person to assess your present communication skills. Take an honest look at your current skills and rank them using the chart below. How well you communicate will be an important factor in your future career—particularly if you are promoted into management, as many postsecondary graduates are. For each skill, circle the number from 1 (indicating low ability) to 5 (indicating high ability) that best reflects your perception of yourself.

Now analyze your scores. Where are you strongest? Weakest? How do you think outsiders would rate you on these skills and traits? Are you satisfied with your present skills? The first step to improvement is recognition of a need. Put check marks next to the five traits you feel you should begin working on immediately.

		Low				High
Writing Skills						
1.	Possess basic spelling, grammar, and punctuation skills	1	2	3	4	5
2.	Am familiar with proper memo, letter, and report formats for business documents	1	2	3	4	5
3.	Can analyze a writing problem and quickly outline a plan for solving the problem	1	2	3	4	5
4.	Am able to organize data coherently and logically	1	2	3	4	5
5.	Can evaluate a document to determine its probable success	1	2	3	4	5
Reading Skills						
1.	Am familiar with specialized vocabulary in my field as well as general vocabulary	1	2	3	4	5
2.	Can concentrate despite distractions	1	2	3	4	5
3.	Am willing to look up definitions whenever necessary	1	2	3	4	5
4.	Am able to move from recreational to serious reading	1	2	3	4	5
5.	Can read and comprehend postsecondary material	1	2	3	4	5
Speaking Skills						
1.	Feel at ease in speaking with friends	1	2	3	4	5
2.	Feel at ease in speaking before a group of people	1	2	3	4	5
3.	Can adapt my presentation to the audience	1	2	3	4	5
4.	Am confident in pronouncing and using words correctly	1	2	3	4	5
5.	Sense that I have credibility when I make a presentation	1	2	3	4	5
Listening Skills						
1.	Spend at least half the time listening during conversations	1	2	3	4	5
2.	Am able to concentrate on a speaker's words despite distractions	1	2	3	4	5
3.	Can summarize a speaker's ideas and anticipate what's coming during pauses	1	2	3	4	5
4.	Provide feedback, such as nodding, paraphrasing, and asking questions	1	2	3	4	5
5.	Listen with the expectation of gaining new ideas and information	1	2	3	4	5

1.2 Getting to Know You (Objs. 1 and 2)

E-MAIL

Your instructor wants to know more about you, your motivation for taking this course, your career goals, and your writing skills.

Your Task. Send an e-mail or write a memo of introduction to your instructor. See Chapter 8 for tips on preparing an e-mail message. In your message include the following:

- **a.** Your reasons for taking this class
- **b.** Your career goals (both temporary and long term)
- **c.** A brief description of your employment, if any, and your favourite activities
- **d.** An assessment and discussion of your current communication skills, including your strengths and weaknesses
- **e.** A brief discussion of your familiarity with e-mail and other communication technologies

1.3 Information Overload: Dangerous to Employees? (Obj. 4)

CRITICAL THINKING TEAM INFOTRAC

Psychologist David Lewis coined the phrase "Information Fatigue Syndrome." He warns that businesses may face litigation and financial liability for failing to protect employees from the health consequences of exposure to excessive amounts of information. (Proceed to "Your Task.")

Your Task. To learn more about information overload, use InfoTrac to find Marsha White and Steve M. Dorman's article, "Confronting Information Overload," *Journal of School Health*, April 2000, Article No. A61995006. After reading the article, organize into teams to discuss these questions:

- **a.** What evidence did you find in the article to support the contention that North Americans are overwhelmed with information?
- **b.** How could employers avoid the possibility of being sued for allowing employees to suffer from information overload?
- **c.** What strategies are suggested for living with information overload? Can you add other strategies?

1.4 Small-Group Presentation: Getting to Know Each Other (Objs. 1 and 2)

LISTENING SPEAKING TEAM

Many business organizations today use teams to accomplish their goals. To help you develop listening, speaking, and teamwork skills, your instructor may assign team projects. One of the first jobs in any team is selecting members.

Your Task. Your instructor will divide your class into small groups or teams. At your instructor's direction, either (a) interview another group member and introduce that person to the group or (b) introduce yourself to the group. Think of this as an informal interview for a team assignment or for a job. You'll want to make notes from which to speak. Your introduction should include information such as the following:

- **a.** Where did you grow up?
- **b.** In what work and extracurricular activities have you engaged?
- **c.** What are your interests and talents? What are you good at doing?
- **d.** What have you achieved?
- **e.** How familiar are you with various computer technologies?
- **f.** What are your professional and personal goals?
- **g.** Where do you expect to be five years from now?

To develop listening skills, team members should practise good listening techniques (see Chapter 2) and take notes. They should be prepared to discuss three important facts as well as remember details about each speaker.

1.5 Communication Skills: What Do Employers Really Want? (Obj. 1)

TEAM WEB

What do employers request when they list job openings in your field?

Your Task. To learn what employers request in classified ads, check out the listings at an online job board. Visit a job board such as Monster.ca or Workopolis. Use your favourite search engine to locate their sites. Follow the instructions to search job categories and locations. Study the jobs listed. Find five or more job listings in your field. If possible, print the results of your search. If you cannot print, make notes on what you find. Study the skills requested. How often do the ads mention communication, teamwork, and computer skills? What tasks do the ads mention? Discuss your findings with your team members. Prepare a list of the most frequently requested skills. Your instructor may ask you to submit your findings and/or report to the class. If you are not satisfied with the job selection at this site, choose another job board.

1.6 Communication Process: Analyzing the Process (Obj. 2)

Review the communication process and its barriers as described in the text. Now imagine that you are the boss in an organization where you've worked and you wish to announce a new policy aimed at improving customer service. Examine the entire communication process from sender to feedback. How will the message be encoded? What assumptions must you make about your audience? How should you announce the new policy? How can you encourage feedback? What noise may interfere with transmission? What barriers should you expect? How can you overcome them? Your instructor may ask you to write a memo describing your responses to these questions.

1.7 Workplace Writing: Separating Myths From Facts (Obj. 1)

Today's knowledge workers are doing more writing on the job than ever before. Flattened management hierarchies, heightened global competition, expanded team-based management, and heavy reliance on e-mail have all contributed to more written messages.
Your Task. In teams discuss the following statements. Are they myths or facts?

a. Because I'm in a technical field, I'll work with numbers, not words.
b. Administrative assistants will clean up my writing problems.
c. Technical writers do most of the real writing on the job.
d. Computers can fix any of my writing mistakes.
e. I can use form letters for most messages.

1.8 Document for Analysis: Barriers to Communication (Objs. 3, 4, and 5)

The following memo is from an exasperated manager to his staff.
Your Task. Comment on the memo's effectiveness, tone, and potential barriers to communication. Your instructor may ask you to revise the memo improving its tone, grammar, and organization.

DATE: Current

TO: All Employees

FROM: Harold Robinson, Operations Manager

SUBJECT: Cleanup!

You were all suppose to clean up your work areas last Friday, but that didn't happen. A few people cleaned their desks, but no one pitched in to clean the common areas, and you all seen what a mess they were in!

So we're going to try again. As you know, we don't hardly have a big enough custodial budget anymore. Everyone must clean up himself. This Friday I want to see action in the copy machine area, things like emptying waste baskets and you should organize paper and toner supplies. The lunch room is a disaster area. You must do something about the counters, the refrigerator, the sinks, and the coffee machine. And any food left in the refrigerator on Friday afternoon should be throwed out because it stinks by Monday. Finally, the office supply shelves should be straightened.

If you can't do a better job this Friday, I will have to assign individuals to a specific cleaning schedule. Which I don't want to do, but you may force me to.

1.9 Communicating in Organizations: Managing Your E-Mail (Obj. 4)

Eric S. has been working at HotStuff Software for six months. He loved e-mail when he first joined HotStuff, but now it's overwhelming him. Every day he receives between 200 and 300 messages, some important and some junk. To keep caught up, Eric checks his e-mail every hour—sometimes more often if he's expecting a response. He joined five mailing lists because they sounded interesting and helpful. But when a topic really excites the subscribers, Eric's e-mail box is jammed with 50 or 60 postings at once. Reading all his messages prevents him from getting his real work done. If he ignores his e-mail, though, he may miss something important. What really frustrates him is what to do with messages that he must retain until he gathers the necessary information to respond.
Your Task. What suggestions can you make to lessen Eric's e-mail overload?

1.10 Ethics: Does White-Collar Crime Pay? (Obj. 6)

INFOTRAC

You've been asked to participate in a panel discussing white-collar crime. Some people argue that executives seldom serve prison time for white-collar crime. You think that high-profile people have actually been sentenced to prison.
Your Task. Using InfoTrac, look for ammunition for your position. Try to find at least five examples of individuals who have been sentenced for corporate wrongdoing. What did they do, and what penalty did they receive? Be sure to document your sources, including author, title, publication, date, and page. If you wish to expand your topic, examine companies that have paid fines, suffered bad press, or been forced into bankruptcy for corporate malfeasance. Remember that InfoTrac requires good search terms to return good results. Try "white collar crime" and "corporate scandals," along with other search terms. Discuss your findings in class or in a memo to your instructor. Can you draw any conclusions from your findings?

C.L.U.E. REVIEW 1

Each chapter includes an exercise based on Appendix A, "Competent Language Usage Essentials (C.L.U.E.)." This appendix is a business communicator's condensed guide to language usage, covering 54 of the most used, and abused, language elements. The following ten sentences are packed with errors based on concepts from the appendix. If you are rusty on these language essentials, spend some time studying the guidelines and examples in Appendix A. Then, test your skills with the chapter C.L.U.E. exercises. You will find the corrections for these exercises at the end of the text. On a separate sheet, edit the following sentences to correct faults in grammar, punctuation, numbers, spelling, and word use.

1. In todays average buziness office employes spend approximately 60% of there time processing documents.
2. My friend and me was serprised to learn that more information has been produced in the last thirty years then in the previous five thousand years.
3. A typical Manager by the way reads 1 000 000 words every week. Which is equal to reading one and a half full length novels everyday.
4. If you are defining *communication* a principle element are the transmission of information and meaning.
5. When Ms Diaz had 3 messages to send she chose e-mail because it was definitly the most fastest comunication channel.
6. 5 factors that make up your unique frame of reference are the following, Experience, Education, Culture, Expectations and Personality.
7. Just between you and I whom do you think will be reccomended for the award.
8. To many workers balancing family and work demands are more important then earning big salarys.
9. Matt felt that he done good on the exam but he wants to do even better when its given again next Fall.
10. The grapevine may be a excelent source of employe information however it should not replace formal lines of communication.

Chapter 2

Communicating in Small Groups and Teams

LEARNING OBJECTIVES

1. *Discuss why groups and teams are formed and how they are different.*

2. *Describe team development, team and group roles, dealing with conflict, and methods for reaching group decisions.*

3. *Identify the characteristics of successful teams.*

4. *List techniques for organizing team-based written and oral presentations.*

5. *Discuss how to plan and participate in productive meetings.*

6. *Describe collaboration technologies used to facilitate meetings, manage projects, and make decisions.*

PREPARING TO WORK WITH GROUPS AND TEAMS

1

Like employees at many organizations, you will probably find yourself working with small groups or in a team-oriented environment. You may already be part of one or more groups or teams. That's good, because experience on a team has become one of the top requests among recruiters looking over job candidates. To participate most effectively on a team, however, you need to learn about groups and teams. In this chapter you'll study why groups and teams are formed, how they differ, how they develop, typical roles members play, and how to deal with dysfunctional behaviour. In addition, you'll study how to collaborate in team-based written and oral presentations and how to plan and participate in productive meetings.

Why Form Groups and Teams?

Organizations are forming teams for better decisions, faster response, increased productivity, greater "buy-in," less resistance to change, improved morale, and reduced risks.

As organizations in the past decade were downsized, restructured, and reengineered, one reality became increasingly clear: Companies were expected to compete globally, meet higher standards, and increase profits—but often with fewer people and fewer resources.[1] Striving to meet these seemingly impossible goals, organizations began developing groups and teams for the following specific reasons:[2]

- **Better decisions.** Decisions are generally more accurate and effective because group and team members contribute different expertise and perspectives.
- **Faster response.** When action is necessary to respond to competition or to solve a problem, small groups and teams can act rapidly.
- **Increased productivity.** Because they are often closer to the action and to the customer, team members can see opportunities for improving efficiencies.
- **Greater "buy-in."** Decisions derived jointly are usually better received because members are committed to the solution and are more willing to support it.
- **Less resistance to change.** People who have input into making decisions are less hostile, aggressive, and resistant to change.
- **Improved employee morale.** Personal satisfaction and job morale increase when teams are successful.
- **Reduced risks.** Responsibility for a decision is diffused, thus carrying less risk for any individual.

Some companies rejected teams because they slowed decisions, shielded workers from responsibility, and reduced productivity.

Teams can be very effective in solving problems; however, they are not a panacea for all workplace problems. Some critics complain that they are the latest in a succession of management fads. Others charge that they are a screen behind which management intensifies its control over labour.[3] Some major organizations have retreated from teams, finding that they slowed decision making, shielded workers from responsibility, and created morale and productivity problems.[4] Yet, in most models of future organizations, teams, not individuals, function as the primary performance unit.[5]

Some organizations are even creating *virtual teams*, which are connected by the Internet, intranets, and electronic media. To learn more about communicating in these digital groups, see the accompanying Tech Talk box.

TECH TALK

Techniques for Staying Connected in Virtual Teams

When Roger Richards goes to work at WishBone Software in Waterloo, Ontario, he connects with a team of customer support people in Maryland, the United Kingdom, and Japan. He has never met these people and probably never will. Richards is one of many workers and managers who belong to *virtual* teams. These are teams with members in remote locations who communicate electronically. With videoconferences, e-mail, the Internet, and sophisticated groupware, it's possible for teams to complete projects no matter where they are geographically based. You'll learn more about groupware and videoconferencing shortly.

Richards and others working on virtual teams must overcome many obstacles not faced by intact groups. Because team members may be separated by geography, time zones, and cultures, they must work especially hard to develop understanding, commitment, and trust. Virtual team managers offer the following recommendations to help members work together.

- **Select team members carefully.** Choose team members who are self-starters, good communicators, flexible, trusting, and experts in areas needed by the team.
- **Invest in beginnings.** Team processes are expedited by spending time initially in reaching consensus about goals, tasks, and procedures. If possible, meet face to face to work out procedures and to bond.
- **Redefine "we."** Team members should be present in one another's thoughts even when not in their physical presence. Encourage behaviour that reflects unity, such as including one another in decisions and sharing information. Consider having a team photograph taken and made into something used frequently, such as a mouse pad or computer wallpaper.
- **Get the maximum benefit from technology.** Make use of speaker phones, groupware, the Internet, and videoconferencing. But be sure that members are well trained in their use.
- **Concentrate on building credibility and trust.** Team members should pay close attention to the way that others perceive them. Consistency of actions, fulfilling promises, considering other members' schedules, and responding promptly to e-mail and voice messages help to build credibility and trust.
- **Put communication on the agenda.** Members should discuss how and when it is appropriate to communicate with one another. They should establish clear expectations about response times.
- **Avoid misinterpreting messages.** Because it's so easy to misunderstand e-mail messages, one virtual manager advises team members to always doubt their first instinct about another team member if the response is negative. Always take time to question your reactions.

Comparing Groups and Teams

Although teams and groups are similar, they are not identical. A *group* is a collection of three or more individuals who perceive themselves as a group but who may work independently to achieve organizational goals. A *team* is a group of individuals who interact over time to achieve a purpose. Members recognize a need for each other's expertise, talents, and commitment to achieve their goals.

A group may work independently, but a team must interact.

Much of the emphasis today is on *self-directed teams.* They are different from single-leader work groups in a number of dimensions, as shown in Figure 2.1. Self-directed teams are most useful to solve problems that require people with different skills to work together. Single-leader work groups are most useful in solving problems quickly when the leader already knows how to proceed.

Self-directed teams are best to solve problems requiring people with different skills.

FIGURE 2.1 Comparing Self-Directed Teams and Single-Leader Work Groups

DIMENSION	SELF-DIRECTED TEAM	SINGLE-LEADER WORK GROUP
Best business use	Most useful to solve problems that require people with various skill sets working together	Most useful to solve problems in which time is of the essence and the leader already knows how to proceed
Leadership	Shifts to member best suited to lead tasks at hand	Formally assigned to one person, usually the senior member
Goals and agenda	Set by group, based on dialogue about purpose	Set by leader, often in consultation with sponsoring executive
Conflict	Recognized as constructive	Avoided by members
Work style	Determined by members	Determined by leader
Success	Defined by members' aspirations	Defined by leader's aspirations
Speed and efficiency	Low until group learns to function as a team; afterward, as fast as a single-leader group	Higher at first because members need no time to develop commitment or to learn to work as a team
End products	Best produced by collective group working together	Best produced by individuals working on their own
Accountability	Set by team who hold one another mutually accountable	Set by leader who holds individuals accountable for their output

Ideally, the most successful self-directed teams will have many of the following characteristics:

- Clearly stated goals
- Autonomy
- Decision-making authority
- Frequent communication
- Ongoing training

UNDERSTANDING TEAM DEVELOPMENT AND ROLES

Small groups and teams may be formed to complete single tasks or to function as permanent ongoing bodies. Regardless of their purpose, successful teams normally go through predictable phases as they develop. Team members also perform in a number of functional and dysfunctional roles. You'll also study the role of conflict and how to apply a six-step plan for resolving conflict.

Four Phases of Team Development

Successful teams generally go through four phases: forming, storming, norming, and performing.

When groups are formed, they generally evolve through four phases, as identified by psychologist B. A. Tuckman. These phases include *forming*, *storming*, *norming*, and *performing*.[6] Some groups get lucky and move quickly from forming to performing. But most struggle through disruptive, although ultimately constructive, team-building stages.

Forming. During the first stage individuals get to know one another. They often are overly polite and feel a bit awkward. As they search for similarities and attempt to bond, they begin to develop trust in each other. Members will discuss fundamental topics such as why the team is necessary, who "owns" the team, whether membership is mandatory, how large it should be, and what talents members can contribute. A leader functions primarily as a traffic director. Groups and teams should resist the efforts of some members to sprint through the first stages and vault to the performing stage. Moving slowly through the stages is necessary in building a cohesive, productive unit.

Storming. During the second phase, members define their roles and responsibilities, decide how to reach their goals, and iron out the rules governing how they interact. Unfortunately, this stage often produces conflict, resulting in *storming.* A good leader, however, should step in to set limits, control the chaos, and offer suggestions. The leader will be most successful if she or he acts like a coach rather than a cop. Teams composed of dissimilar personality types may take longer to progress through the storming phase. Tempers may flare, sleep may be lost, leaders may be deposed. But most often the storm passes, and a cohesive group emerges.

Norming. Once the sun returns to the sky, teams and groups enter the *norming* stage. Tension subsides, roles clarify, and information begins to flow among members. The group periodically checks its agenda to remind itself of its progress toward its goals. People are careful not to shake the hard-won camaraderie and formation of a single-minded purpose. Formal leadership is unnecessary since everyone takes on leadership functions. Important data is shared with the entire group, and mutual interdependence becomes typical. The group or team begins to move smoothly in one direction. Members make sure that procedures are in place to resolve future conflicts.

In the norming stage, tensions subside, roles clarify, and information flows among team members.

Performing. In Tuckman's team growth model, some groups never reach the final stage of *performing.* Problems that may cause them to fail are shown in Figure 2.2. For those that survive the first three phases, however, the final stage is gratifying. Group members have established a pace and a shared language. They develop loyalty and a willingness to resolve all problems. A "can-do" mentality pervades as they progress toward their goal. Fights are clean, and members continue working together without grudges. Best of all, information flows freely, deadlines are met, and production exceeds expectations.

Typical Team and Group Roles

Team members play different roles when they work together in groups. These roles can be grouped into three categories. *Task roles* are those that help the group meet its goals. *Relationship roles* facilitate the smooth functioning of the group. *Dysfunctional roles* are those that hinder a group from moving forward to achieve its purpose.[7]

Group Task Roles. Group members who are committed to achieving the group's purpose contribute to the group in a number of positive roles. You can be a better group member if you assume one or more of the following task roles.

Members who assume positive task roles help a team achieve its purpose.

- **Initiator.** Defines problems, sets rules, contributes ideas.
- **Information seeker/information giver.** Asks for or supplies relevant information.
- **Opinion giver/opinion seeker.** Asks for and offers personal opinions, attitudes, and beliefs.
- **Direction giver.** Tells how to perform task at hand.

FIGURE 2.2 Why Teams Fail: Typical Problems, Symptoms, and Solutions

PROBLEM	SYMPTOM	SOLUTION
Confused goals	People don't know what they're supposed to do	Clarify team purpose and expected outcomes
Mismatched needs	People with private agendas working at cross-purposes	Get hidden agendas on table by asking what people personally want from team
Unresolved roles	Team members are uncertain what their jobs are	Inform team members what is expected of them
Senseless procedures	Team is at the mercy of an ineffective employee handbook	Throw away the book and develop procedures that make sense
Bad leadership	Leader is tentative, inconsistent, or foolish	Leader must learn to serve the team and keep its vision alive or give up role
Antiteam culture	Organization is not committed to the idea of teams	Team for the right reasons or don't team at all; never force people onto a team
Poor feedback	Performance is not being measured; team members are groping in the dark	Create system of free flow of useful information to and from all team members

- **Summarizer.** Reviews significant points, synthesizing points of agreement and group's progress toward goal.
- **Diagnoser.** Analyzes task and discussion. Tells what is needed to reach goal.
- **Energizer.** Exhorts members to stay on task, offers encouraging remarks.
- **Gatekeeper.** Controls participants, drawing in nontalkers and cutting off monopolizers.
- **Reality tester.** Compares group's ideas with feasibility of real-world implementation.

Members who carry out relationship roles help teams achieve harmony and strong bonds.

Group Relationship Roles. In addition to contributing to task functions, effective members of groups perform relationship functions. When you assume these roles, you are helping to build harmony and strong relationships among group members.

- **Participation encourager.** Seeks to involve silent members.
- **Harmonizer/tension reliever.** Resolves differences, relaxes atmosphere, reduces tension—sometimes with the use of humour or informality.
- **Evaluator of emotional climate.** Reflects the feelings of the group.
- **Praise giver.** Encourages warm, supportive climate by praising and agreeing with others.
- **Empathic listener.** Shows interest by listening actively without interrupting or evaluating.

Dysfunctional Group Roles. When group members perform the following roles, they disrupt the group and slow progress toward its goal. As you study the following list, think about groups you know and individuals who may have played these self-serving roles.

- **Blocker.** Constantly puts down the ideas and suggestions of others.

- **Attacker.** Insults, criticizes, and aggresses against others.
- **Recognition-seeker.** Wastes group's time with unnecessary and irrelevant recounting of personal achievements and successes.
- **Joker.** Distracts group with excessive joke-telling, inappropriate comments, and disruptive antics.
- **Withdrawer.** Participates very little or not at all. Refuses to be drawn out or to offer opinions.

Members who play dysfunctional roles disrupt the group's progress toward its goal.

Resolving Workplace Conflicts

Conflict is a normal part of every workplace and every team. Although the word alone is enough to make your heart go into overdrive, conflict is not always negative. When managed properly, conflict can improve decision making, clarify values, increase group cohesiveness, stimulate creativity, decrease tensions, and undermine dissatisfaction. Unresolved conflict, however, can destroy productivity and seriously undermine morale. You will be better prepared to resolve workplace conflict if you know the five most common response patterns as well as study a six-step procedure for dealing with conflict.

Common Conflict Response Patterns. Recall a time when you were very upset with a workplace colleague, boss, or teammate. How did you respond? Experts who have studied conflict say that most of us deal with conflict in one of the following predictable patterns:[8]

- **Avoidance/withdrawal.** Instead of trying to resolve the conflict, one person or the other simply withdraws. Avoidance of conflict generally results in a "lose–lose" situation because the problem festers and no attempt is made to understand the issues causing the conflict. On the other hand, avoidance may be the best response when the issue is trivial, when potential losses from an open conflict outweigh potential gains, or when insufficient time is available to work through the issue adequately.

Although avoidance does not solve conflicts, it may be the best response to some situations such as when the issue is trivial.

- **Accommodation/smoothing.** When one person gives in quickly, the conflict is smoothed over and surface harmony results. This accommodation/smoothing strategy may be the best method when the issue is minor, when damage to the relationship would harm both parties, and when tempers are too hot for productive discussion.
- **Compromise.** When both people give up something of lesser importance to gain something more important, a compromise results. This may be the best approach when both parties stand to gain, when a predetermined "ideal" solution is not required, and when time is short.
- **Competition/forcing.** In some contests, one person comes out on top, leaving the other with a sense of failure. This method forces the end of the conflict, but it may result in hurt feelings and potential future problems from the loser. This competition/forcing strategy is appropriate when a decision or action must be immediate. It also works when the parties recognize the power relationship between themselves.
- **Collaboration/problem solving.** If both parties are willing to collaborate to reach consensus, the problem may be solved. This approach works when the involved people have common goals, but they disagree over how to reach them. Conflict may arise from misunderstanding or a communication breakdown. Collaboration works best when all parties are trained in problem-solving techniques.

Resolving conflict through the collaboration/problem-solving method is best, but this technique requires training and commitment.

Six-Step Procedure for Dealing With Conflict. Probably the best pattern for resolving conflicts entails collaboration and problem-solving procedures. But this method requires a certain amount of training. Fortunately, experts in the field of negotiation have developed a six-step pattern that you can try the next time you need to resolve a conflict.[9]

Following an effective six-step procedure can help you resolve conflicts through collaboration and cooperation.

1. **Listen.** To be sure you understand the problem, listen carefully. If the other person doesn't seem to be listening to you, you need to set the example and be the first to listen.
2. **Understand the other point of view.** Once you listen, it's much easier to understand the other's position. Show your understanding by asking questions and paraphrasing. This will also verify what you think the other person means.
3. **Show a concern for the relationship.** By focusing on the problem, not the person, you can build, maintain, and even improve relationships. Show an understanding of the other person's situation and needs. Show an overall willingness to come to an agreement.
4. **Look for common ground.** Identify your interests and help the other side identify its interests. Learn what you have in common, and look for a solution to which both sides can agree.
5. **Invent new problem-solving options.** Spend time identifying the interests of both sides. Then brainstorm to invent new ways to solve the problem. Be open to new options.
6. **Reach an agreement based on what's fair.** Seek to determine a standard of fairness that is acceptable to both sides. Then weigh the possible solutions, and choose the best option.

Avoiding Groupthink

Groupthink means that team members agree without examining alternatives or considering contingency plans.

Conflict is normal in team interactions, and successful teams are able to resolve conflict using methods you've just learned. But some teams avoid conflict. They smooth things over and, in doing so, may fall victim to *groupthink*. This is a term coined by theorist Irving Janis to describe faulty decision-making processes by team members who are overly eager to agree with one another. Several conditions can lead to groupthink: team members with similar backgrounds, a lack of methodical procedures, a demand for a quick decision, and a strong leader who favours a specific decision. Symptoms of groupthink include pressures placed on a member who argues against the group's shared beliefs, self-censorship of thoughts that deviate from the group consensus, collective efforts to rationalize, and an unquestioned belief in the group's inherent morality. Teams suffering from groupthink fail to examine alternatives, are biased in collecting and evaluating information, and ignore the risks of the preferred choice. They may also forget to work out a contingency plan in case the preferred choice fails.[10]

Effective teams avoid groupthink by striving for team diversity—in age, gender, backgrounds, experience, and training. They encourage open discussion, search for relevant information, evaluate many alternatives, consider how a decision will be implemented, and plan for contingencies in case the decision doesn't work out.

Reaching Group Decisions

The manner in which teams reach decisions greatly affects the morale and commitment of a team, as well as the implementation of any team decision. In North American culture the majority usually rules, but other methods, five of which are discussed here, may be more effective. As you study these methods, think about which methods would be best for routine decisions and which methods would be best for dealing with emergencies.

- **Majority.** Group members vote and a majority wins. This method results in a quick decision but may leave an alienated minority uncommitted to implementation.
- **Consensus.** Discussion continues until all team members air their opinions and, ultimately, agree. This method is time-consuming, but it produces creative, high-quality discussion and generally elicits commitment by all members to implement the decision.
- **Minority.** Typically, a subcommittee investigates and makes a recommendation for action. This method is useful when the full group cannot get together to make a decision or when time is short.
- **Averaging.** Members haggle, bargain, cajole, and negotiate to reach a middle position, which often requires compromise. With this method, the opinions of the least knowledgeable members may cancel the opinions of the most knowledgeable.
- **Authority rule with discussion.** The leader, boss, or manager listens to team members' ideas, but the final decision is his or hers. This method encourages lively discussion and results in participatory decision making. However, team members must have good communication skills. This method also requires a leader who is willing to make decisions.

Although time-consuming, consensus decisions generally produce the most team commitment.

CHARACTERISTICS OF SUCCESSFUL TEAMS

3

The use of teams has been called the "solution" to many ills in the current workplace.[11] Someone even observed that as an acronym, TEAM means "Together, Everyone Achieves More."[12] Yet, many teams do not work well together. In fact, some teams can actually increase frustration, lower productivity, and create employee dissatisfaction. Experts who have studied team workings and decisions have discovered that effective teams share some or all of the following characteristics.

Small Size, Diverse Makeup. For most functions the best teams range from 2 to 25 members, although 4 or 5 is optimum for many projects. Larger groups have trouble interacting constructively, much less agreeing on actions.[13] For the most creative decisions, teams generally have male and female members who differ in age, social background, training, and experience. Members should bring complementary skills to a team. Diverse teams can produce innovative solutions with broader applications than homogeneous teams can.

Small, diverse teams often produce more creative solutions with broader applications than homogeneous teams.

Agreement on Purpose. An effective team begins with a common purpose. Working from a general purpose to specific goals typically requires a huge investment of time and effort. Meaningful discussions, however, motivate team members to "buy into" the project.

Agreement on Procedures. The best teams develop procedures to guide them. They set up intermediate goals with deadlines. They assign roles and tasks, requiring all members to contribute equivalent amounts of real work. They decide how they will reach decisions using one of the strategies discussed earlier. Procedures are continually evaluated to ensure movement toward attainment of the team's goals.

Ability to Confront Conflict. Poorly functioning teams avoid conflict, preferring sulking, gossip, or backstabbing. A better plan is to acknowledge conflict and address the root of the problem openly. Although it may feel emotionally risky, direct confrontation saves time and enhances team commitment in the long run. To be constructive, however, confrontation must be task-oriented, not person-oriented. An open airing of differences, in which all team members have a chance to speak their minds, should focus on strengths and weaknesses of the different positions and ideas—not on personalities. After hearing all sides, team members must negotiate a fair settlement, no matter how long it takes. The best decisions are based on consensus: all members agree.

Good teams exchange information freely and collaborate rather than compete.

Use of Good Communication Techniques. The best teams exchange information and contribute ideas freely in an informal environment. Team members speak clearly and concisely, avoiding generalities. They encourage feedback. Listeners become actively involved, read body language, and ask clarifying questions before responding. Tactful, constructive disagreement is encouraged. Although a team's task is taken seriously, successful teams are able to inject humour into their interactions.

Ability to Collaborate Rather Than Compete. Effective team members are genuinely interested in achieving team goals instead of receiving individual recognition. They contribute ideas and feedback unselfishly. They monitor team progress, including what's going right, what's going wrong, and what to do about it. They celebrate individual and team accomplishments.

Ethical teams should represent the organization's view and respect its privileged information.

Acceptance of Ethical Responsibilities. Teams as a whole have ethical responsibilities to their members, to their larger organizations, and to society. Members have a number of specific responsibilities to each other. As a whole, groups have a responsibility to represent the organization's view and respect its privileged information. They should not discuss with outsiders any sensitive issues without permission. In addition, groups have a broader obligation to avoid advocating actions that would endanger members of society at large.

Shared Leadership. Effective teams often have no formal leader. Instead, leadership rotates to those with the appropriate expertise as the team evolves and moves from one phase to another. Many teams operate under a democratic approach. This approach can achieve buy-in to team decisions, boost morale, and create fewer hurt feelings and less resentment. But in times of crisis, a strong team member may need to step up as leader.

Demonstration of Good Workplace Manners. Rudeness and bad manners have become alarmingly common in the North American workplace. Successful team members treat each other and colleagues politely and respectfully. This may involve a few more *pleases* and *thank yous,* as well as showing consideration for others. Good team members are aware of noise levels when colleagues are trying to concentrate. They offer support to colleagues with heavy workloads, and they respect others' boundaries and need for privacy.

CHECKLIST FOR DEVELOPING TEAM EFFECTIVENESS

 **Establish small teams.** Teams with fewer members are thought to function more efficiently and more effectively than larger teams.

- **Encourage diversity.** Innovative teams typically include members who differ in age, gender, and background. Team members should possess technical expertise, problem-solving skills, and interpersonal skills.
- **Determine purpose, procedures, and roles.** Members must understand the task at hand and what is expected of them. Teams function best when operating procedures are ironed out early on and each member has a specific role.
- **Acknowledge and manage conflict.** Conflict is productive when it motivates a team to search for new ideas, increase participation, delay premature decisions, or discuss disagreements. Keep conflict centred on issues rather than on people.
- **Cultivate good communication skills.** Effective team members are willing and able to articulate ideas clearly and concisely, recognize nonverbal cues, and listen actively.
- **Advance an environment of open communication.** Teams are most productive when members trust each other and feel free to discuss all viewpoints openly in an informal atmosphere.
- **Encourage collaboration and discourage competition.** Sharing information in a cooperative effort to achieve the team purpose must be more important than competing with other members for individual achievement.
- **Share leadership.** Members with the most expertise should lead at various times during the project's evolution.
- **Create a sense of fairness in making decisions.** Effective teams resolve issues without forcing members into a win–lose situation.
- **Lighten up.** The most successful teams take their task seriously, but they are also able to laugh at themselves and interject humour to enliven team proceedings.
- **Continually assess performance.** Teams should establish checkpoints along the way to determine whether they are meeting their objectives and adjust procedures if progress is unsatisfactory.

ORGANIZING TEAM-BASED WRITTEN AND ORAL PRESENTATIONS

4

Companies form teams for many reasons. The goal of some teams is an oral presentation to pitch a new product or to win a high-stakes contract. The goal of other teams is to investigate a problem and submit recommendations to decision makers in a report. The end product of any team is often a written report or an oral presentation.

Guidelines for Team Writing and Oral Presentations

Whether your team's project produces written reports or oral presentations, you generally have considerable control over how the project is organized and completed. If you've been part of any team efforts before, you also know that such projects can be very frustrating—particularly when some team members don't carry

Team projects proceed more smoothly when members agree on ground rules.

their weight or when members cannot resolve conflict. On the other hand, team projects can be harmonious and productive when members establish ground rules and follow guidelines related to preparing, planning, collecting information for, organizing, rehearsing, and evaluating team projects.

Preparing to Work Together. Before you begin talking about a specific project, it's best to discuss some of the following issues in regard to how your group will function.

- Name a meeting leader to plan and conduct meetings, a recorder to keep a record of group decisions, and an evaluator to determine whether the group is on target and meeting its goals.
- Decide whether your team will be governed by consensus (everyone must agree), by majority rule, or by some other method.
- Compare schedules of team members in order to set up the best meeting times. Plan to meet often. Make team meetings a top priority. Avoid other responsibilities that might cause disruption during these meetings.
- Discuss the value of conflict. By bringing conflict into the open and encouraging confrontation, your team can prevent personal resentment and group dysfunction. Confrontation can actually create better final products by promoting new ideas and avoiding groupthink. Conflict is most beneficial when team members are allowed to air their views fully.
- Discuss how you will deal with team members who are not pulling their share of the load.

Teams must decide whether they will be governed by consensus, by majority rule, or by some other method.

Planning the Document or Presentation. Once you've established ground rules, you're ready to discuss the final document or presentation. Be sure to keep a record of the following decisions your team makes.

- Establish the specific purpose for the document or presentation. Identify the main issues involved.
- Decide on the final format. For a report, determine what parts it will include, such as an executive summary, figures, and an appendix. For a presentation, decide on its parts, length, and graphics.
- Discuss the audience(s) for the product and what questions it would want answered in your report or oral presentation. If your report is persuasive, consider what appeals might achieve its purpose.
- Develop a work plan. Assign jobs. Set deadlines. If time is short, work backward from the due date. For oral presentations build in time for content and creative development as well as for a series of rehearsals.
- For oral presentations give each team member a written assignment that details his or her responsibilities for researching content, producing visuals, developing handout materials, building transitions between segments, and showing up for rehearsals.
- For written reports decide how the final document will be composed: individuals working separately on assigned portions, one person writing the first draft, the entire group writing the complete document together, or some other method.

In planning a team document or presentation, develop a work plan, assign jobs, and set deadlines.

Collecting Information. The following suggestions help teams generate and gather accurate information. Unless facts are accurate, the most beautiful report or the best high-powered presentation will fail.

- Brainstorm for ideas; consider cluster diagramming.
- Assign topics. Decide who will be responsible for gathering what information.
- Establish deadlines for collecting information.
- Discuss ways to ensure the accuracy of the information collected.

Unless facts are accurate, reports and presentations will fail.

Organizing, Writing, and Revising. As the project progresses, your team may wish to modify some of its earlier decisions.

- Review the proposed organization of your final document or presentation and adjust it if necessary.
- Compose the first draft of a written report or presentation. If separate team members are writing segments, they should use the same word processing and/or presentation graphics program to facilitate combining files.
- Meet to discuss and revise the draft(s) or rehearse the presentation.
- If individuals are working on separate parts of a written report, appoint one person (probably the best writer) to coordinate all the parts, striving for consistent style and format. Work for a uniform look and feel to the final product.
- For oral presentations be sure each member builds a bridge to the next presenter's topic and launches it smoothly. Strive for logical connections between segments.

For team reports assign one person to coordinate all the parts and make the style consistent.

Editing, Rehearsing, and Evaluating. Before the presentation is made or the final document is submitted, complete the following steps.

- For a written report give one person responsibility for finding and correcting grammatical and mechanical errors.
- For a written report meet as a group to evaluate the final document. Does it fulfill its purpose and meet the needs of the audience? Successful group documents emerge from thoughtful preparation, clear definition of contributors' roles, commitment to a group-approved plan, and willingness to take responsibility for the final product.
- For oral presentations assign one person the task of merging the various files, running a spell checker, and examining the entire presentation for consistency of design, format, and vocabulary.
- Schedule at least five rehearsals, say the experts.[14] Consider videotaping one of the rehearsals so that each presenter can critique his or her own performance.
- Schedule a dress rehearsal with an audience at least two days before the actual presentation. Practise fielding questions.

Schedule at least five rehearsals for a team presentation.

More information about writing business reports and making individual presentations appears in subsequent chapters of this book.

PLANNING AND PARTICIPATING IN PRODUCTIVE MEETINGS

5

As businesses become more team-oriented and management becomes more participatory, people are attending more meetings than ever. It is estimated that senior managers spend three quarters of their workdays in meetings,[15] yet meetings are almost universally disliked. In spite of employee reluctance and despite terrific advances in communication and team technology, face-to-face meetings are not going to disappear. Our task as business communicators is to learn how to make them efficient, satisfying, and productive.

Because you can expect to attend many meetings, learn to make them efficient, satisfying, and productive.

Meetings consist of three or more individuals who gather to pool information, solicit feedback, clarify policy, seek consensus, and solve problems. But meetings have another important purpose. They represent opportunities. Because they are a prime tool for developing staff, they are career-critical. At meetings judgments are formed and careers are made. Therefore, instead of treating them as thieves of your valuable time, try to see them as golden opportunities to demonstrate your leadership, communication, and problem-solving skills. So that you can make the most of these opportunities, here are techniques for planning and conducting successful meetings.

Deciding Whether a Meeting Is Necessary

Call meetings only when necessary, and invite only key people.

No meeting should be called unless the topic is important, can't wait, and requires an exchange of ideas. If the flow of information is strictly one way and no immediate feedback will result, then don't schedule a meeting. For example, if people are merely being advised or informed, send an e-mail, memo, or letter. Leave a telephone or voice mail message, but don't call a costly meeting. Remember, the real expense of a meeting is the lost productivity of all the people attending. To decide whether the purpose of the meeting is valid, it's a good idea to consult the key people who will be attending. Ask them what outcomes are desired and how to achieve those goals. This consultation also sets a collaborative tone and encourages full participation.

Selecting Participants

Problem-solving meetings should involve five or fewer people.

The number of meeting participants is determined by the purpose of the meeting, as shown in Figure 2.3. If the meeting purpose is motivational, such as an awards ceremony, then the number of participants is unlimited. But to make decisions, according to studies at 3M Corporation, the best number is five or fewer participants.[16] Ideally, those attending should be people who will make the decision and people with information necessary to make the decision. Also attending should be people who will be responsible for implementing the decision and representatives of groups who will benefit from the decision.

Distributing Advance Information

Pass out a meeting agenda showing topics to be discussed and other information.

At least two days in advance of a meeting, distribute an agenda of topics to be discussed. Also include any reports or materials that participants should read in advance. For continuing groups, you might also include a copy of the minutes of the previous meeting. To keep meetings productive, limit the number of agenda items. Remember, the narrower the focus, the greater the chances for success. A good agenda, as illustrated in Figure 2.4, covers the following information:

- Date and place of meeting
- Start time and end time

FIGURE 2.3 Meeting Purpose and Number of Participants

PURPOSE	IDEAL SIZE
Intensive problem solving	5 or fewer
Problem identification	10 or fewer
Information reviews and presentations	30 or fewer
Motivational	Unlimited

FIGURE 2.4 Typical Meeting Agenda

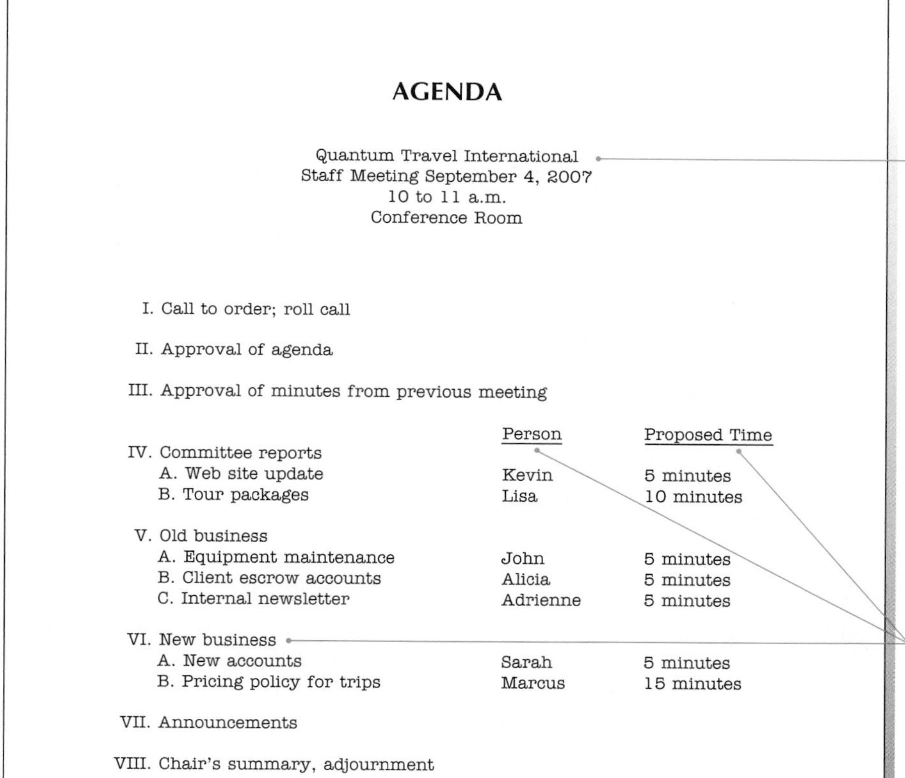

AGENDA

Quantum Travel International
Staff Meeting September 4, 2007
10 to 11 a.m.
Conference Room

I. Call to order; roll call

II. Approval of agenda

III. Approval of minutes from previous meeting

	Person	Proposed Time
IV. Committee reports		
A. Web site update	Kevin	5 minutes
B. Tour packages	Lisa	10 minutes
V. Old business		
A. Equipment maintenance	John	5 minutes
B. Client escrow accounts	Alicia	5 minutes
C. Internal newsletter	Adrienne	5 minutes
VI. New business		
A. New accounts	Sarah	5 minutes
B. Pricing policy for trips	Marcus	15 minutes

VII. Announcements

VIII. Chair's summary, adjournment

Heading identifies all important details including time allocation.
Items, responsibilities, and time lines provide clarity and ensure the meeting proceeds smoothly.

- Brief description of each topic, in order of priority, including the names of individuals who are responsible for performing some action
- Proposed allotment of time for each topic
- Any premeeting preparation expected of participants

Getting the Meeting Started

Start meetings on time and open with a brief introduction.

To avoid wasting time and irritating attendees, always start meetings on time—even if some participants are missing. Waiting for latecomers causes resentment and sets a bad precedent. For the same reasons, don't give a quick recap to anyone who arrives late. At the appointed time, open the meeting with a three- to five-minute introduction that includes the following:

- Goal and length of the meeting
- Background of topics or problems
- Possible solutions and constraints
- Tentative agenda
- Ground rules to be followed

A typical set of ground rules might include arriving on time, communicating openly, being supportive, listening carefully, participating fully, confronting conflict frankly, and following the agenda. More formal groups follow parliamentary procedures based on *Robert's Rules of Order.* After establishing basic ground rules, the leader should ask if participants agree thus far. The next step is to assign one attendee to take minutes and one to act as a recorder. The recorder stands at a flipchart or whiteboard and lists the main ideas being discussed and agreements reached.

Moving the Meeting Along

Keep the meeting moving by avoiding issues that sidetrack the group.

After the preliminaries, the leader should say as little as possible. Remember that the purpose of a meeting is to exchange views, not to hear one person, even the leader, do all the talking. This technique also encourages quieter participants to speak up.

To avoid allowing digressions to sidetrack the group, try generating a "Parking Lot" list. This is a list of important but divergent issues that should be discussed at a later time. Another way to handle digressions is to say, "Folks, we are getting off track here. Forgive me for pressing on, but I need to bring us back to the central issue of . . . ."[17] It's important to adhere to the agenda and the time schedule. Equally important, when the group seems to have reached a consensus, is to summarize the group's position and check to see whether everyone agrees.

Recording Information

Ensure minutes of the meeting are transcribed for consistency of information and distribution to all stakeholders. Minutes must be objective and action-oriented. Verbatim minutes are long and tedious, and may include personal and irrelevant "chatter." To capture discussion, a point-by-point summary is effective. Action-oriented minutes permit one to chair the meeting and take notes at the same time.[18]

Managing Conflict in Meetings

As you learned earlier, conflict is natural and even desirable, but it can cause awkwardness and uneasiness. In meetings, conflict typically develops when people feel unheard or misunderstood. If two people are in conflict, the best approach is to encourage each to make a complete case while group members give their full attention. Let each one question the other. Then, the leader should summarize what was said, and the group should offer comments. The group may modify a recommendation or suggest alternatives before reaching consensus on a direction to follow.

When a conflict develops between two members, allow each to make a complete case before the group.

Managing Dysfunctional Group Members

When individuals are performing in any of the dysfunctional roles described earlier (such as blocker, attacker, joker, and withdrawer), they should be handled with care and tact. The following specific techniques can help a leader or gatekeeper control some group members and draw others out.[19]

To control dysfunctional behaviour, team leaders should establish rules and seat problem team members strategically.

- Lay down the rules in an opening statement
- Seat potentially dysfunctional members strategically
- Avoid direct eye contact
- Assign dysfunctional members specific tasks
- Ask members to speak in a specific order
- Interrupt monopolizers
- Encourage nontalkers
- Give praise and encouragement

Ending With a Plan

End the meeting at the agreed time. The leader should summarize what has been decided, who is going to do what, and by what time. It may be necessary to ask people to volunteer to take responsibility for completing action items agreed to in the meeting. No one should leave the meeting without a full understanding of what was accomplished. One effective technique that encourages full participation is "once around the table." Everyone is asked to summarize briefly his or her interpretation of what was decided and what happens next. Of course, this closure technique works best with smaller groups. The leader should conclude by asking the group to set a time for the next meeting. He or she should also assure the group that a report will follow and thank participants for attending.

End the meeting with a summary of accomplishments.

Following Up Actively

Minutes should be distributed within a couple of days after the meeting. It is up to the leader to see that what was decided at the meeting is accomplished. The leader may need to call people to remind them of their assignments and also to volunteer to help them if necessary.

Follow up by reminding participants of their assigned tasks.

Meetings are a necessary evil for today's team-oriented workplace. The following checklist can help you use them effectively and perhaps accelerate your career.

CHECKLIST FOR PLANNING AND PARTICIPATING IN PRODUCTIVE MEETINGS

Before the Meeting

- ✓ **Consider alternatives.** Unless a topic is important and pressing, avoid calling a meeting. Perhaps an e-mail message, telephone call, or announcement would serve the purpose as well.

- ✓ **Invite the right people.** To make decisions, invite those people who have information and authority to make the decision and implement it.

- ✓ **Distribute an agenda.** Prepare and distribute an agenda that includes the date and place of meeting, the starting and ending times, a brief description of each topic, the names of people responsible for any action, and a proposed time allotment for each topic.

During the Meeting

- ✓ **Start on time and introduce the agenda.** Discuss the goal and length of the meeting, provide background of topics for discussion, suggest possible solutions and constraints, propose a tentative agenda, and clarify the ground rules for the meeting.

- ✓ **Appoint a secretary and a recorder.** Ask one attendee to make a record of the proceedings, and ask another person to record discussion topics on a flipchart or whiteboard.

- ✓ **Encourage balanced participation.** Strive to be sure that all participants' views are heard and that no one monopolizes the discussion. Avoid digressions by steering the group back to the topics on the agenda.

- ✓ **Confront conflict frankly.** Encourage people who disagree to explain their positions completely. Then, restate each position and ask for group comments. The group may modify a recommendation or suggest alternatives before agreeing on a plan of action.

- ✓ **Summarize along the way.** When the group seems to reach a consensus, summarize and see whether everyone agrees.

Ending the Meeting and Following Up

- ✓ **Review meeting decisions.** At the end of the meeting, summarize what has been decided, discuss action items, and establish a schedule for completion.

- ✓ **Distribute minutes of meeting.** A few days after the meeting, arrange to have the recorder or scribe distribute the minutes.

- ✓ **Remind people of action items.** Follow up by calling people to see if they are completing the actions recommended at the meeting.

USING COLLABORATION TECHNOLOGY TO FACILITATE MEETINGS, MANAGE PROJECTS, AND MAKE DECISIONS

Collaboration technology (sometimes called *groupware*) refers to software designed to facilitate group activities. The term relates to a number of constantly evolving technologies that help groups exchange information, collaborate in team projects, and make decisions. New technologies are continually appearing, resulting in significant cost savings, greater efficiency, and more intuitive equipment.

6

Collaboration technology (sometimes called groupware) facilitates group activities and can help companies, team members, and customers exchange information efficiently using the Web.

Collaboration tools that you may use on the job include teleconferencing, Web conferencing, screen sharing, chat servers, instant messaging, folder sharing, intranets, message boards, and e-mail, to name a few. These tools are increasingly important when members of organizations must work together to solve problems, develop products, forecast future performance, and complete other team projects. The tools are equally useful whether team members are just down the hall, across the country, or around the world.

Let's say, for example, that a motorcycle manufacturing team is working to solve a gear-making problem. The team's goal is to reduce gear noise, which is perceived as poor quality, and to give customers more exhaust noise. The project manager is in Montreal; two engineers are in Winnipeg; and the production staff is in Toronto. Rather than travel to meet face to face, they gather in a private online room using a Web-based conferencing tool. They work with an online whiteboard using different coloured markers until they reach agreement on the gear design. Then the manager assigns action items, and the meeting is over. And no one had to travel farther than the PC on his or her desk!

Although Bernd Pischetsrieder speaks at a Volkswagen press conference in Wolfsburg, Germany, his presentation can be broadcast to dealerships around the world by means of webcasting.

First-generation collaboration tools involved expensive, cumbersome, and complex software systems. Many required local area networks with well-trained technical staffs to keep them functioning. The latest tools, however, enable companies, team members, and customers to exchange information more efficiently, often using the Web. Today's collaboration tools are most often employed to help teams with three important functions: project management, meeting facilitation, and decision support.

Project Management

Completing a project successfully generally requires unrestricted sharing of information. Project management software can allow remote team members, suppliers, partners, and others with an interest in the project's successful completion to view

Project management software helps distant team members, suppliers, partners, and others clarify project goals, set deadlines, and anticipate obstacles.

the project and modify their own tasks via the Web. For example, users can input time sheet information, submit status reports, and delegate tasks. Some programs provide guides that help managers identify project phases, clarify goals, establish deadlines, and anticipate obstacles. Executives can even create a portfolio view to determine the status of all projects under way as well as search more deeply for detailed descriptions of key events. Team members can work together more easily by using software features such as shared calendaring, scheduling, and shared folders.

Meeting Facilitation

The most commonly used meeting tool is teleconferencing, which connects speakers by telephones.

Everyone agrees that the best meetings are face to face. But when distance or other factors prevent face-to-face gatherings, numerous collaboration tools enable far-flung colleagues to meet. One of the simplest tools is *teleconferencing* (sometimes called *audioconferencing*). It involves one or two people who confer with others by telephone. Phone "bridges" may be engaged to allow a limitless number of people to share the same call. Teleconferences may involve several people in a room with an enhanced speakerphone that enables people at both ends to speak and be heard simultaneously. Thanks to cellular service, you can even participate in a conference call from an airplane or your home. Although teleconferencing is not as glitzy as other collaboration tools, it is really the "bread and butter" of the entire teleconferencing industry.[20] More people use it than any other of the collaboration meeting tools.

Videoconferencing enables real-time collaboration by combining video, audio, and networking technologies.

If team members need to see each other, they use *videoconferencing*. This collaboration tool combines video, audio, and communications networking technologies for real-time interaction. Generally, participants meet in special conference rooms equipped with cameras and television screens for transmitting images and documents. Because participants do not have to journey to distant meetings, organizations can reduce travel expenses, travel time, and employee fatigue. But first-generation videoconferencing equipment was expensive, and only large organizations could afford it.

More recently companies have turned to *desktop videoconferencing*. It combines personal computing with audio, video, and networking technologies to provide real-time interaction from desktop computers.

Media conferencing combines PC functionality with media features that emulate face-to-face meetings.

The latest technologies use a *media conferencing* approach. Relying heavily on the Web, it facilitates meetings by incorporating PC functionality with media features that emulate "real-life" meetings. The media conferencing approach enables participants to present PowerPoint slides or share spreadsheets, just as they might do in a face-to-face meeting. They can even demonstrate products and make changes in real time during a meeting without having to interrupt the flow of the presentation. Companies are now able to turn instant messenger sessions into interactive WebEx meetings.

Microsoft features Live Meeting™, which requires only a phone, a PC, and an Internet connection. The service allows groups of two to thousands to share applications, mark up documents, illustrate ideas, and create flowcharts—all in real time without the cost and hassle of business travel.

Internet relay chat allows people to exchange comments in a chat room at a prearranged time.

Team members who merely want to chat find *Internet relay chat* (IRC) a simple alternative to other forms of conferencing. The cyber equivalent of CB radio, IRC gives ordinary folks the ability to chat in real time. Team members prearrange a time and enter a chat room where everyone can "hear" what everyone else is saying. It's more efficient than individual e-mails with copies to other participants.

Webcasting involves the delivery of one-way live audio and video programs to large groups via the Internet. Webcasts are rapidly replacing conference calls and press meetings as a cheaper, more convenient way to reach a large number of people when limited interactivity is necessary. For example, let's say an organization wants all dealers to see the launching of a flashy sales promotion. The company could webcast the launching with live audio and video, thus enabling dealers to experience the hype without leaving their desks.

Webcasting involves sending audio and video programs to large groups over the Internet.

Driven by a number of factors, from the grassroots adoption of instant messaging to frustration with e-mail's limitations, richer kinds of technology-enabled meeting and collaboration tools will continue to evolve. The most sophisticated companies want to embed *presence awareness*. This is the ability to detect the online status of others so that employees can find available experts, project team members, and managers without even looking away from their screens.

Decision Support

Another group of software products helps teams and organizations analyze information and make decisions based on solid data. Sometimes called *business intelligence software* or, more fashionably, *digital dashboards*, these tools bring together data from internal and external sources. Equipped with a "digital dashboard," team members and managers can check actual performance and make adjustments. A company, for instance, can study sales figures on a regional, product, or customer basis. What products should it produce, and how many of them will sell and in what parts of the country? Using sophisticated business intelligence tools, companies can find answers to sales trends even in the middle of a promotion. They can also play "what if" scenarios to test plans before implementing them.

Business intelligence software, including digital dashboards, helps people analyze information and make rapid decisions.

As decision support tools continue to evolve, they become more useful in gathering, analyzing, and manipulating data to assist in planning and decision making. Today's tools are more scalable, which means that they can run on multiprocessor servers. This makes it possible to gather more data and crunch more information in shorter periods of time. Team members are able to develop their own queries and report on information relevant to their jobs. Most of the time, they receive answers in near real time. Connected to live data sources, such as sales transactions, digital dashboards enable team members to create reports with information that can help forecast or explain shifts in business performance. Every business welcomes tools that help it analyze performance and make decisions regarding the future.

Connected to live sources, digital dashboards help teams explain and forecast future performance.

STRENGTHENING YOUR TEAMWORK SKILLS NOW

At one time or another in your current or future job and certainly in your postsecondary career, you will be working on a team, so you need to start developing teamwork skills now. You can't just turn them on when you want them. They need to be studied, modelled, nurtured, and practised. You've just taken a look at the inner workings of teams, including the four phases of team development, the role of conflict, the characteristics of successful teams, functional and dysfunctional team roles, and participating in productive meetings. In this book, in this course, and throughout your academic career, you will have opportunities to work with teams. Begin to analyze their dynamics. Who has the power and why? Who are the most successful team members and why? What would make a team function more effectively? How can you improve your teamwork skills?

Developing effective teamwork skills requires study, modelling, nurturing, and practice.

Remember, job recruiters consider team skills among the most important requirements for many of today's jobs. You can become the number one candidate for your dream job by developing team skills and acquiring experience now.

SUMMARY OF LEARNING OBJECTIVES

1 **Discuss why groups and teams are formed and how they are different.** Many organizations have found that groups and teams are more effective than individuals because groups make better decisions, respond faster, increase productivity, achieve greater buy-in, reduce resistance to change, improve employee morale, and result in reduced risk for individuals. A *group* is a collection of three or more individuals who perceive themselves as a group but who may complete their tasks independently. A *team* is a group that interacts over time to achieve a purpose. Businesses are increasingly turning to *self-directed teams*, which are characterized by clearly stated goals, autonomy, decision-making authority, frequent communication, and ongoing training.

2 **Describe team development, team and group roles, dealing with conflict, and methods for reaching group decisions.** Teams typically go through four stages of development: *forming, storming, norming,* and *performing*. Team members may play functional or dysfunctional roles. Common conflict response patterns include avoidance/withdrawal, accommodation/smoothing, compromise, competition/forcing, and collaboration/problem solving. To resolve conflict, team members should listen, understand the other's point of view, look for common ground, invent new problem-solving options, and reach an agreement based on what is fair. Open discussion of conflict prevents *groupthink*, a condition that leads to faulty decisions. Methods for reaching group decisions include majority, consensus, minority, averaging, and authority rule with discussion.

3 **Identify the characteristics of successful teams.** The most effective teams are usually small and diverse; that is, they are made up of people representing different ages, genders, and backgrounds. Successful teams agree on their purpose and procedures. They are able to channel conflict into constructive discussion and reach consensus. They accept their ethical responsibilities, encourage open communication, listen actively, provide feedback, and have fun. Members are able to collaborate rather than compete, and leadership is often a shared responsibility depending on the situation and expertise required. Successful team members are polite and courteous.

4 **List techniques for organizing team-based written and oral presentations.** In preparing to work together, teams should limit their size, name a meeting leader, and decide whether they wish to make decisions by consensus, majority rule, or some other method. They should work out their schedules, discuss the value of conflict, and decide how to deal with team members who do not do their share. They should decide on the purpose, form, and procedures for preparing the final document or presentation. They must brainstorm for ideas, assign topics, establish deadlines, and discuss how to ensure information accuracy. In composing the first draft of a report or presentation, they should use the same software and meet to discuss drafts and rehearsals. For written reports one person should probably compose the final draft, and the group should evaluate it. For group presentations they need to work for consistency of design, format, and vocabulary. At least five rehearsals, one of which should be videotaped, will enhance the final presentation.

5 **Discuss how to plan and participate in productive meetings.** Call a meeting only when urgent two-way communication is necessary. Limit participants to those directly involved. Distribute an agenda in advance, start the meeting on time, and keep the discussion on track. Confront conflict openly by letting each person present her or his views fully before having the group decide which direction to take. Summarize what was said and end the meeting on time. Follow up by distributing minutes of the meeting and verifying that action items are being accomplished.

6 **Describe collaboration technologies used to facilitate meetings, manage projects, and make decisions.** Today's collaboration tools help team members exchange information, work together in team projects, and make decisions. To facilitate meetings, teams may take part in *teleconferencing* using telephones or *videoconferencing,* which combines video, audio, and networking technologies. *Desktop videoconferencing* provides real-time interaction from personal computers. *Media conferencing* incorporates features that emulate face-to-face meetings such as PowerPoint and spreadsheets. *Internet relay chat* enables individuals to exchange ideas in an Internet chat room. *Webcasting* involves the delivery of one-way audio and video programs to large groups via the Internet. Project management software enables remote team members, suppliers, partners, and others to work together in clarifying goals, establishing deadlines, and completing other project tasks. Decision support software, sometimes called *business intelligence software* or *digital dashboards,* helps teams and organizations analyze information and make decisions based on solid data.

CHAPTER REVIEW

1. List seven reasons that explain why organizations are forming groups and teams. (Obj. 1)
2. To be most successful, self-directed teams need to have what characteristics? (Obj. 1)
3. What are the four phases of team development? Is it best to move through the stages quickly? Why or why not? (Obj. 2)
4. Name five team roles that relate to tasks and five roles that relate to developing relationships. Which roles do you think are most important and why? (Obj. 2)
5. Name five dysfunctional team roles. (Obj. 2)
6. What is *groupthink*? (Obj. 2)
7. Why can diverse teams be more effective than homogeneous teams? (Obj. 3)
8. Why are team decisions based on consensus generally better than decisions reached by majority rule? (Obj. 3)
9. What is the best way to set team deadlines when time is short to complete a project? (Obj. 4)
10. In completing a team-written report, should all team members work together to write the report? Why or why not? (Obj. 4)
11. When groups or teams meet, what are seven ground rules with which they should begin? (Obj. 5)
12. Name five techniques for handling dysfunctional group members. (Obj. 5)
13. Name three important functions served by collaboration technology. Describe six tools available to facilitate team or group meetings. (Obj. 6)

CRITICAL THINKING

1. Compare the advantages and disadvantages of using teams in today's workplace. (Objs. 1, 2, and 3)
2. What kinds of conflict could erupt during the "storming" phase of team development? Should conflict be avoided? (Obj. 2)
3. What are the advantages and disadvantages of diverse teams? (Obj. 3)
4. Compare the advantages and disadvantages of face-to-face meetings with virtual meetings using teleconferencing and videoconferencing. (Obj. 5)

ACTIVITIES

2.1 Advantages of Teams: Convincing Your Boss (Obj. 1)

Your boss or organization leader comes to you and asks you to take on a big job. Use your imagination to select a task such as developing a Web site or organizing a fund-raising campaign. You are flattered that your boss respects you and thinks you capable of completing the task, but you think that a team could do a better job than an individual.

Your Task. What arguments would you use to convince your boss that a team could work better than an individual?

2.2 Responding to Workplace Conflicts (Obj. 2)

TEAM

Experts say that we generally respond to conflict in one of the following patterns: avoidance/withdrawal, accommodation/smoothing, compromise, competition/forcing, or collaboration/problem solving.

Your Task. For each of the following conflict situations, name an appropriate response pattern(s) and be prepared to explain your choice.

a. A company policy manual is posted and updated at an internal Web page. Employees must sign that they have read and understand the manual. A conflict arises when one manager insists that employees should sign electronically. Another manager thinks that a paper form should be signed by employees so that better records may be kept. What conflict response pattern is most appropriate?
b. A manager and his assistant plan to attend a conference together at a resort location. Six weeks before the conference, the company announces a cutback and limits conference support to only one person. The assistant, who has developed a presentation specifically for the conference, feels that he should be the one to attend. Travel arrangements must be made immediately. What conflict response pattern will most likely result?
c. Customer service rep Jackie comes to work one morning and finds Alexa sitting at Workstation 2. Although the customer service reps have no special workstation assigned to them, Jackie has the longest seniority and has always assumed that Workstation 2 was hers. Other workstations were available, but the supervisor told Alexa to use Workstation 2 that

morning because she didn't know that Jackie would be coming in. When Jackie arrives and sees her workstation occupied, she becomes angry and demands that Alexa vacate "her" station. What conflict response pattern might be most appropriate for Alexa and the supervisor?

2.3 Reaching Group Decision: Which Method? (Objs. 1 and 2)

TEAM

In small groups decide which decision strategy is best for the following situations:

a. Union employees numbering 600 or more must decide to strike or remain on the job.
b. The owner of your company is meeting with all managers to decide which departments will be allowed to move into a new facility.
c. Members of a homeowners' association must decide which members will become directors.
d. The human resources department of a large company must work with employees to develop a new benefits package within its budget.
e. A large association of realtors must decide how to organize a member Web site. Only a few members have technical expertise.

2.4 Group Roles: Observing a Group in Action (Objs. 1, 2, 3, and 5)

Watching a school board, city council, campus organization, or other public meeting in which problems and solutions are discussed can be useful in understanding group actions and roles.
Your Task. Attend the meeting of an organized group. Analyze the roles played by participants. What roles related to completing the task at hand? What roles related to developing group relationships? Did any participants play dysfunctional roles? How was conflict resolved?

2.5 Group Roles: Revealing Comments (Obj. 2)

In teams or in class discussion, analyze the following statements in relation to the group roles presented in this chapter. What group role does each statement represent? Is it a positive or negative contribution to the team?

a. "I don't think the two of you are as far apart as you think. Kevin, are you saying . . . . And Jeff, you seem to be saying . . . . Is that what you mean?"
b. "Hey, did you all hear the one about the . . . ."
c. "What a great idea! Stacy, you're really on to something. We need more input like this."
d. "I know it's a little off the subject, but you're going to love this. Wait till I tell you about what happened to me today."
e. "Rachel, you've been awfully quiet. What do you think about this?"

2.6 Workplace Etiquette: Avoiding Shooting Yourself in the Foot (Obj. 2)

INFOTRAC

When the economy slows down, business interactions seem to become more formal, according to two etiquette experts. Dining manners, greeting etiquette, and body language awareness become more important in tough times. You can learn how to avoid "shooting yourself in the foot" by reading an interview about how to gain a competitive edge.
Your Task. Using InfoTrac, search for "Manners Matter" by Andy Cohen (Article No. A108838323) and answer the following questions.

a. According to the two etiquette experts, how have business interactions changed in the last few years?
b. When is profanity appropriate?
c. In what ways are people misusing e-mail and cell phones?

2.7 Team Presentations: Oh, No, Not Me! (Obj. 4)

WEB

You have just been named to a class team that must research a topic, produce a report, and make a class presentation. Alternatively, assume that you have been asked to head a team that is to produce an organizational five-year plan for your company. You know this assignment will end with a written report and a presentation to management and stockholders. Your first reaction is dismay. But you decide that if you must take on this task, you want to make sure you know what you are doing.
Your Task. Using your favourite search tool such as <**www.google.ca**>, see what you can find that might be helpful in preparing a team report or oral presentation. Use search terms such as "team writing" or "team presentation." Surrounding your term with quotation marks ensures that it will be searched as a unit. Ignore commercial sites trying to sell you services or software. Focus on finding practical

advice. In a class discussion or in a memo to your instructor, name at least five good tips that were not discussed in this chapter. Identify and evaluate the Web sites where you find the best information.

2.8 Meetings: Planning a Gathering (Obj. 5)

Assume that the next meeting of your student association will discuss preparations for a careers day in the spring. The group will hear reports from committees working on speakers, business recruiters, publicity, reservation of campus space, setup of booths, and any other matters you can think of.

Your Task. As president of your SA, prepare an agenda for the meeting. Compose your introductory remarks to open the meeting. Your instructor may ask you to submit these two documents or use them in staging an actual meeting in class.

2.9 Videoconferencing: Using the Web for Research (Obj. 5)

WEB

Your boss wants to learn more about workplace videoconferencing, but she is busy and a Web novice. She asks you to find three or four sites that will help her learn more about terminology, resources, and services.

Your Task. Use a search engine such as <**www.google.ca**> to locate helpful sites. Consider sites with videoconferencing glossaries, FAQs (frequently asked questions), and guides. Submit a list of the three best sites that you find. Provide a short description of each site and why you think it will be helpful.

C.L.U.E. REVIEW 2

On a separate sheet edit the following sentences to correct faults in grammar, punctuation, spelling, numbers, proofreading, and word use.

1. Companys are forming teams for at least 3 good reasons; better decisions, more faster response times and increase productivity.
2. Although they do not hold face to face meetings virtual teams exchange information and make desisions electronically.
3. Successful self directed teams are autonomous, that is they can hire fire and discipline there own member.
4. We all ready have a number of teams, however our CEO and several Vice Presidents are advicing us to add more.
5. At last months Staff meeting the Manager and him encouraged a warm supportive climate with praise and helpful comments.
6. When conflict erupted at our teams febuary meeting we made a conscience effort to confront the underlying issues.
7. The best method for reaching group decisions involve consensus but this method is very time-consuming.
8. The Team Leader and myself think however that all speakers have a right to a fair hearing.
9. 75 people are expected to attend the Training Session on May 15th consequently her and I must find a more larger room.
10. Lawyers in our legal services department distributed a agenda for participants attending there January 3rd meeting.

Chapter 3

Workplace Listening and Nonverbal Communication

LEARNING OBJECTIVES

1. *Explain the importance of listening in the workplace and describe three types of workplace listening.*

2. *Discuss the listening process and its barriers.*

3. *Enumerate ten techniques for improving workplace listening.*

4. *Define nonverbal communication and explain its functions.*

5. *Describe the forms of nonverbal communication and how they can be used positively in your career.*

6. *List specific techniques for improving nonverbal communication skills in the workplace.*

LISTENING IN THE WORKPLACE

1

Today's employers are becoming increasingly aware that listening is a critical employee and management skill. In addition, listening to customers takes on increasing importance as our economy becomes ever more service-oriented.

But, you may be thinking, everyone knows how to listen. Most of us believe that listening is an automatic response to noise. We do it without thinking. Perhaps that explains why so many of us are poor listeners. You can develop good listening habits by learning more about the process and by studying specific techniques. In this chapter we'll explore the importance of listening, the kinds of listening required in the workplace, the listening process, listening barriers, and how to become a better listener. Although many of the tips will be effective in your personal life, our discussion centres primarily on workplace and employment needs.

Workers are doing more communicating than ever before, largely because of the Internet, team environments, global competition, and an increasing emphasis on customer service. A vital ingredient in every successful workplace is high-quality communication. And three quarters of high-quality communication involves listening.[1]

Listening skills are critical for career success, organization effectiveness, and worker satisfaction.

Listening skills are important for career success, organization effectiveness, and worker satisfaction. Numerous studies report that good listeners make good managers and that good listeners advance more rapidly in their organizations.[2]

Listening is especially important in the workplace because we spend so much time doing it. Most workers spend 30 to 45 percent of their communication time listening,[3] while executives spend 60 to 70 percent of their communication time listening.[4]

Poor Listening Habits

Most of us listen at only 25 percent efficiency.

Although executives and workers devote the bulk of their communication time to listening, research suggests that they're not very good at it. In fact, most of us are poor listeners. Some estimates indicate that only half of the oral messages heard in a day are completely understood.[5] Experts say that we listen at only 25 percent efficiency. In other words, we ignore, forget, distort, or misunderstand 75 percent of everything we hear.

We are inefficient listeners due to lack of training, competing sounds, slowness of speech, and daydreaming.

Poor listening habits may result from several factors. Lack of training is one significant reason. Few schools give as much emphasis to listening as they do to the development of reading, speaking, and writing skills. In addition, our listening skills may be less than perfect because of the large number of competing sounds and stimuli in our lives that interfere with concentration. Finally, we are inefficient listeners because we are able to process speech much faster than others can speak. While most speakers talk at about 125 to 250 words per minute, listeners can think at 1000 to 3000 words per minute.[6] The resulting lag time fosters daydreaming, which clearly reduces listening efficiency.

Types of Workplace Listening

In an employment environment, you can expect to be involved in many types of listening. These include listening to superiors, listening to colleagues and teammates, and listening to customers. As an entry-level employee, you will be most concerned with listening to superiors. But as you advance in your career and enter the ranks of management, you will need skills for listening to colleagues and teammates. Finally, the entire organization must listen to customers to compete in today's service-oriented economy.

Listening to Superiors. On the job one of your most important tasks will be listening to instructions, assignments, and explanations about how to do your work. You will be listening to learn and to comprehend. To focus totally on the speaker, be sure you are not distracted by noisy surroundings or other tasks. Don't take phone calls, and don't try to complete another job while listening with one ear. Show your interest by leaning forward and striving for good eye contact.

Listening to superiors involves hearing instructions, assignments, and explanations of work procedures.

Above all, take notes. Don't rely on your memory. Details are easy to forget. Taking selective notes also conveys to the speaker your seriousness about hearing accurately and completely. Don't interrupt. When the speaker finishes, paraphrase the instructions in your own words. Ask pertinent questions in a nonthreatening manner. And don't be afraid to ask "dumb" questions, if it means you won't have to do a job twice. Avoid criticizing or arguing when you are listening to a superior. Your goals should be to hear accurately and to convey an image of competence.

Listen carefully, take selective notes, and don't interrupt.

Listening to Colleagues and Teammates. Much of your listening will result from interactions with fellow workers and teammates. In these exchanges two kinds of listening are important. *Critical listening* enables you to judge and evaluate what you are hearing. You will be listening to decide whether the speaker's message is fact, fiction, or opinion. You will also be listening to decide whether an argument is based on logic or emotion. Critical listening requires an effort on your part. You must remain objective, particularly when you disagree with what you are hearing. Control your tendency to prejudge. Let the speaker have a chance to complete the message before you evaluate it. *Discriminative listening* is necessary when you must understand and remember. It means you must identify main ideas, understand a logical argument, and recognize the purpose of the message.

Listening to colleagues and teammates involves critical listening and discriminative listening.

Three listening strategies will be especially useful to you in team and group interactions: *dampening, redirecting*, and *reflecting*.[7] *Dampening* involves listening with minimal response and maximum acceptance. It is particularly necessary when group members are in conflict. If one team member is unhappy about something, it is often best to let that person vent without interrupting. Dampening is also appropriate in situations requiring politeness. You listen courteously, for example, when team members are introducing themselves or when a valued employee describes a stressful encounter with a customer. *Redirecting* involves asking questions, restating the message, and getting the speaker back on track. For example, "I believe, Jeff, that our goal is to find a way to reduce travel expenses. Although your comments on airport delays are interesting, do you have specific suggestions for cutting back travel expenses?"

Dampening means listening with minimal response and maximum acceptance; redirecting involves restating the message; and reflecting clarifies content and feeling.

Reflecting is useful to clarify both content and feeling. By reflecting emotions, you are better able to interpret a message in the proper context. Reflecting is a helpful tool in managing conflict. A wise strategy, for instance, is to repeat the speaker's message and acknowledge the feeling that goes with it. Paraphrase what has been said and check with the speaker to make sure you understand. For example, "I understand, Holly, that you were upset and inconvenienced because we changed the meeting date without consulting you. Is that correct?"

Although dampening, redirecting, and reflecting are listening techniques that work well in group interactions, they are equally effective in listening to customers.

Organizations that listen to customers improve sales and profitability.

Listening to Customers. As the North American economy becomes increasingly service-oriented, the new management mantra has become "customers rule." Yet, despite 50 years of talk about customer service, the concept of "customer-centric" business is still in its infancy.[8] Many organizations are just learning that listening to customers results in increased sales and profitability as well as improved customer acquisition and retention. As one salesperson says, "Price is almost always the number one factor for the buyer. But once you develop a relationship, even if your price is a little high, the customers will want to find a reason to stay with you."[9] The simple truth is that consumers just feel better about companies that value their opinions. Listening is an acknowledgment of caring and is a potent retention tool. Customers want to be cared about, thus fulfilling a powerful human need.

How can organizations improve their customer listening techniques? Since employees are the eyes and ears of the organization, smart companies begin by hiring employees who genuinely care about customers. Listening organizations also train their employees to listen actively and to ask gentle, probing questions to ensure clear understanding.

THE LISTENING PROCESS AND ITS BARRIERS

2

Listening takes place in four stages, including perception, interpretation, evaluation, and action, as illustrated in Figure 3.1. Barriers, however, can obstruct the listening process. These barriers may be mental or physical.

The four stages of listening are perception, interpretation, evaluation, and action.

Perception. The listening process begins when you hear sounds and concentrate on them. The conscious act of listening begins when you focus on the sounds around you and select those you choose to hear. You tune in when you (1) sense that the message is important, (2) are interested in the topic, or (3) are in the mood to listen. Perception is reduced by impaired hearing, noisy surroundings, inattention, and pseudolistening. *Pseudolistening* occurs when listeners "fake" it. They look as if they are listening, but their minds are wandering far off.

Interpretation. Once you have focused your attention on a sound or message, you begin to interpret, or decode, it. As described in Chapter 1, interpretation of a message is coloured by your cultural, educational, and social frames of reference. The meanings you attach to the speaker's words are filtered through your expectations and total life experiences. Thus, your interpretation of the speaker's meaning may be quite different from what the speaker intended because your frame of reference is different.

Evaluation involves separating fact from opinion and judging messages objectively.

Evaluation. After interpreting the meaning of a message, you analyze its merit and draw conclusions. To do this, you attempt to separate fact from opinion. Good listeners try to be objective, and they avoid prejudging the message. Thus, to evaluate a message accurately and objectively, you should (1) consider all the information, (2) be aware of your own biases, and (3) avoid jumping to hasty conclusions.

Action involves storing a message in memory, reacting, or supplying feedback.

Action. Responding to a message may involve storing the message in memory for future use, reacting with a physical response (a frown, a smile, a laugh), or supplying feedback to the speaker. Listener feedback is essential because it helps clarify the message so that it can be decoded accurately. Feedback also helps the speaker to find out whether the message is getting through clearly. In one-to-one conversation, of course, no clear distinction exists between the roles of listener and speaker—you give or receive feedback as your role alternates.

Enhancing Retention. Unfortunately, most of us will be able to recall only 50 percent of information we heard a day earlier and only 20 percent after two days.[10] How can we improve our retention?

FIGURE 3.1 The Listening Process and Its Barriers

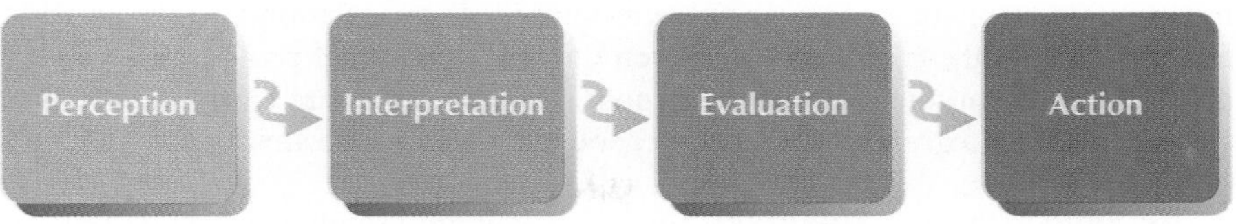

COMMON LISTENING BARRIERS

Mental Barriers	Physical and Other Barriers
Inattention	Hearing impairment
Prejudgment	Noisy surroundings
Frame of reference	Speaker's appearance
Closed-mindedness	Speaker's mannerisms
Pseudolistening	Lag time

Memory training specialists say that effective remembering involves three factors: (1) deciding to remember, (2) structuring the incoming information to form relationships, and (3) reviewing. In the first step you determine what information is worth remembering. Once you have established a positive mindset, you look for a means of organizing the incoming information to form relationships. Chain links such as acronyms or rhymes can help you associate the unfamiliar with something familiar.

Retention can be improved by deciding to remember, structuring incoming information to form relationships, and reviewing.

One of the most reliable ways to improve retention is to take notes of the important ideas to be remembered. Rewriting within ten minutes of completing listening improves your notes and takes advantage of peak recall time, which immediately follows listening.

To further improve retention, take notes and rewrite them immediately after listening.

The final step in improving retention is reviewing your notes, repeating your acronym, or saying your rhyme to move the targeted information into long-term memory. Frequent reviews help strengthen your memory connections.

IMPROVING WORKPLACE LISTENING

Listening on the job is more difficult than listening in classes where professors present well-organized lectures and repeat important points. Workplace listening is more challenging because information is often exchanged casually. It may be disorganized, unclear, and cluttered with extraneous facts. Moreover, your coworkers are usually friends. Because they are familiar with one another, they may not be as polite and respectful as they are with strangers. Friends tend to interrupt, jump to conclusions, and take each other for granted.

Workplace listening is challenging because information may be disorganized, unclear, and cluttered with extraneous facts.

Ten Keys to Building Powerful Listening Skills

Despite the complexities and challenges of workplace listening, good listeners on the job must remember that their goal is to listen carefully and to *understand* what is being said so that they can do their work well. The following recommendations can help you improve your workplace listening effectiveness.

You listen better when you control distractions, become actively involved, separate facts from opinions, and identify important facts.

Listening on the job involves controlling external and internal distractions, becoming actively involved, identifying important facts, and taking notes. When listening to your boss, ask clarifying questions, but wait for the right moment.

1. Control External and Internal Distractions. Move to an area where you can hear without conflicting noises or conversations. Block out surrounding physical distractions. Internally, try to focus totally on the speaker. If other projects are on your mind, put them on the back burner temporarily. When you are emotionally upset, whether angry or extremely happy, it's a good idea to postpone any serious listening.

2. Become Actively Involved. Show that you are listening closely by leaning forward and maintaining eye contact with the speaker. Don't fidget or try to complete another task at the same time you are listening. Listen to more than the spoken words. How are they said? What implied meaning, reasoning, and feelings do you hear behind the spoken words? Does the speaker's body language (eye contact, posture, movements) support or contradict the main message?

3. Separate Facts From Opinions. Facts are truths known to exist; opinions are statements of personal judgments or preferences. Some opinions are easy to recognize because speakers preface them with statements such as *I think, It seems to me,* and *As far as I'm concerned.*[11] Often, however, listeners must evaluate assertions to decide their validity. Good listeners consider whether speakers are credible and speaking within their areas of competence. They don't automatically accept assertions as facts.

4. Identify Important Facts. Speakers on the job often intersperse critical information with casual conversation. Unrelated topics pop up—ball scores, a customer's weird request, a computer glitch, the boss's extravagant new SUV. Your task is to select what's important and register it mentally. What step is next in your project? Who does what? What is your role?

5. Don't Interrupt. While someone else has the floor, don't interrupt with a quick reply or opinion. And don't show nonverbal disagreement such as negative head shaking, rolling eyes, sarcastic snorting, or audible sighs. Good listeners let speakers have their say. Interruptions are not only impolite, but they also prevent you from hearing the speaker's complete thought. Listeners who interrupt with their opinions sidetrack discussions and cause hard feelings.

You listen better when you refrain from interrupting, ask clarifying questions, paraphrase, capitalize on lag time, take notes, and observe gender differences.

6. Ask Clarifying Questions. Good listeners wait for the proper moment and then ask questions that do not attack the speaker. Instead of saying, "But I don't understand how you can say that," a good listener seeks clarification with questions such as, "Please help me understand by explaining more about . . . ." Because questions can put you in the driver's seat, think about them in advance. Use open questions (those without set answers) to draw out feelings, motivations, ideas, and suggestions. Use closed fact-finding questions to identify key factors in a discussion.[12] And, by the way, don't ask a question unless you are ready to be quiet and listen to the answer.

7. Paraphrase to Increase Understanding. To make sure you understand a speaker, rephrase and summarize a message in your own words. Be objective and nonjudgmental. Remember, your goal is to understand what the speaker has said—not to show how mindless the speaker's words sound when parroted. Remember, too, that other workplace listeners will also benefit from a clear summary of what was said.

8. Capitalize on Lag Time. While you are waiting for a speaker's next idea, use the time to review what the speaker is saying. Separate the central idea, key points, and details. Sometimes you may have to supply the organization. You can also use lag time to silently rephrase and summarize the speaker's message in your own words. Most important, keep your mind focused on the speaker and her or his ideas—not on all the other work waiting for you.

9. Take Notes to Ensure Retention. Don't trust your memory. If you have a hallway conversation with a colleague and don't have a pencil handy, make a mental note of the important items. Then write them down as soon as possible. Even with seemingly easily remembered facts or instructions, jot them down to ease your mind and also to be sure you understand them correctly. Two weeks later you'll be glad that you did. Be sure you have a good place to store notes of various projects, such as file folders, notebooks, or computer files.

10. Be Aware of Gender Differences. Men tend to listen for facts, whereas women tend to perceive listening as an opportunity to connect with the other person on a personal level.[13] Men tend to use interrupting behaviour to control conversations, while women generally interrupt to communicate assent, to elaborate on an idea of another group member, or to participate in the topic of conversation.[14] Women listeners tend to be attentive, provide steady eye contact, remain stationary, and nod their heads.[15] Male listeners are less attentive, provide sporadic eye contact, and move around. Being aware of these tendencies will make you a more sensitive and knowledgeable listener.

CHECKLIST FOR IMPROVING LISTENING

- ✓ **Stop talking.** Accept the role of listener by concentrating on the speaker's words, not on what your response will be.
- ✓ **Work hard at listening.** Become actively involved; expect to learn something.
- ✓ **Block out competing thoughts.** Concentrate on the message. Don't allow yourself to daydream during lag time.
- ✓ **Control the listening environment.** Move to a quiet area where you won't be interrupted by telephone calls or visitors. Check to be certain that listeners can hear speakers.
- ✓ **Maintain an open mind.** Know your biases and try to correct for them. Be tolerant of less-abled and different-looking speakers. Provide verbal and nonverbal feedback. Encourage the speaker with comments such as "Yes," "I see," "OK," and "Uh huh," and ask polite questions. Look alert by leaning forward.
- ✓ **Paraphrase the speaker's ideas.** Silently repeat the message in your own words, sort out the main points, and identify supporting details. In conversation sum up the main points to confirm what was said.
- ✓ **Listen between the lines.** Observe nonverbal cues and interpret the feelings of the speaker: What is really being said?
- ✓ **Distinguish between facts and opinions.** Know the difference between factual statements and opinions stated as assertions.
- ✓ **Capitalize on lag time.** Use spare moments to organize, review, anticipate, challenge, and weigh the evidence.

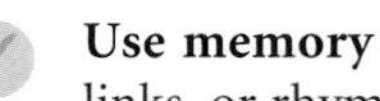

Use memory devices. If the information is important, develop acronyms, links, or rhymes to help you remember.

Take selective notes. If you are hearing instructions or important data, record the major points; then, revise your notes immediately or verify them with the speaker.

COMMUNICATING THROUGH NONVERBAL MESSAGES

Nonverbal communication includes all unwritten and unspoken messages, both intentional and unintentional.

Understanding messages often involves more than merely listening to spoken words. Nonverbal cues also carry powerful meanings. Nonverbal communication includes all unwritten and unspoken messages, both intentional and unintentional. Eye contact, facial expression, body movements, space, time, distance, appearance—all of these nonverbal cues influence the way a message is interpreted, or decoded, by the receiver. Many of the nonverbal messages that we send are used intentionally to accompany spoken words. But people can also communicate nonverbally even when they don't intend to. And not all messages accompany words.

Because nonverbal communication can be an important tool for you to use and control in the workplace, you need to learn more about its functions and forms.

Functions of Nonverbal Communication

Nonverbal cues function in five ways: to complement and illustrate, to reinforce and accentuate, to replace and substitute, to control and regulate, and to contradict.

Nonverbal communication functions in at least five ways to help convey meaning. As you become more aware of the following functions of nonverbal communication, you will be better able to use these silent codes to your advantage in the workplace.

- **To complement and illustrate.** Nonverbal messages can amplify, modify, or provide details for a verbal message.
- **To reinforce and accentuate.** Skilled speakers raise their voices to convey important ideas, but they whisper to suggest secrecy. A grimace forecasts painful news, while a big smile intensifies good news.
- **To replace and substitute.** Many gestures substitute for words: nodding your head for "yes," giving a "V" for victory. In fact, a complex set of gestures totally replaces spoken words in sign language.
- **To control and regulate.** Nonverbal messages are important regulators in conversation. Shifts in eye contact, slight head movements, changes in posture, raising of eyebrows, nodding of the head, and voice inflection—all of these cues tell speakers when to continue, to repeat, to elaborate, to hurry up, or to finish.
- **To contradict.** To be sarcastic, a speaker might hold his nose while stating that your new perfume is wonderful. In the workplace, individuals may send contradictory messages with words or actions.

Because nonverbal messages may speak louder than words, make sure that your nonverbal cues reinforce your spoken words.

In the workplace people may not be aware that they are sending contradictory messages. Researchers have found that when verbal and nonverbal messages contradict each other, listeners tend to believe and act on the nonverbal message.

Effective communicators must make sure that all their nonverbal messages reinforce their spoken words and their professional goals. To make sure that you're on the right track to nonverbal communication competency, let's look more carefully at the specific forms of nonverbal communication.

Forms of Nonverbal Communication

Instead of conveying meaning with words, nonverbal messages carry their meaning in a number of different forms ranging from facial expressions to body language and even clothes. Each of us sends and receives thousands of nonverbal messages daily in our business and personal lives. Although the following discussion covers all forms of nonverbal communication, we will be especially concerned with workplace applications. As you learn about the messages sent by eye contact, facial expressions, posture, and gestures, as well as the use of time, space, territory, and appearance—think about how you can use these nonverbal cues positively in your career.

5

The eyes are thought to be the most accurate predictor of a speaker's true feelings.

Eye Contact. Communicators consider the eyes to be the most accurate predictor of a speaker's true feelings and attitudes. Most of us cannot look another person straight in the eyes and lie. As a result, we tend to believe people who look directly at us. We have less confidence in and actually distrust those who cannot maintain eye contact. Sustained eye contact suggests trust and admiration; brief eye contact signifies fear or stress. Prolonged eye contact, however, can be intrusive and intimidating.

Good eye contact enables the message sender to determine whether a receiver is paying attention, showing respect, responding favourably, or feeling distress. From the receiver's perspective, good eye contact reveals the speaker's sincerity, confidence, and truthfulness. Since eye contact is a learned skill, however, you must be respectful of people who do not maintain it. You must also remember that nonverbal cues, including eye contact, have different meanings in various cultures.

Facial Expression. The expression on a communicator's face can be almost as revealing of emotion as the eyes. Researchers estimate that the human face can display over 250 000 different expressions.[16] Although a few people can control these expressions and maintain a "poker face" when they want to hide their feelings, most of us display our emotions openly. Raising or lowering the eyebrows, squinting the eyes, swallowing nervously, clenching the jaw, smiling broadly—these voluntary and involuntary facial expressions supplement or entirely replace verbal messages.

Erect posture sends a message of confidence, competence, diligence, and strength.

Posture and Gestures. An individual's general posture can convey anything from high status and self-confidence to shyness and submissiveness. Leaning toward a speaker suggests attraction and interest; pulling away or shrinking back denotes fear, distrust, anxiety, or disgust. Similarly, gestures can communicate entire thoughts via simple movements. But remember that these nonverbal cues may have vastly different meanings in different cultures.

In the workplace a simple way to leave a good impression is to make sure your upper body is aligned with the person to whom you're talking. Erect posture sends a message of confidence, competence, diligence, and strength. Gestures are also important, if used effectively.

Being on time sends a positive nonverbal message in North American workplaces.

Time. How we structure and use time tells observers about our personality and attitudes. For example, when someone gives a visitor a prolonged interview, she signals her respect for, interest in, and approval of the visitor or the topic to be discussed. By sharing her valuable time, she sends a clear nonverbal message. Likewise, when an individual twice arrives late for a meeting, it could mean that the meeting has low priority to him, that he is a self-centred person, or that he has little self-discipline. These are assumptions that typical North Americans might make. In other cultures and regions, though, punctuality is viewed differently.

In the workplace you can send positive nonverbal messages by being on time for meetings and appointments, staying on task during meetings, and giving ample time to appropriate projects and individuals.

The way an office is arranged can send nonverbal messages about the openness of its occupant.

Space. How we arrange things in the space around us tells something about ourselves and our objectives. Whether the space is a dorm room, an office, or a department, people reveal themselves in the design and grouping of furniture within that space. Generally, the more formal the arrangement, the more formal and closed the communication environment.

Territory. Each of us has certain areas that we feel are our own territory, whether it's a specific spot or just the space around us. We all maintain zones of privacy in which we feel comfortable. Figure 3.2 categorizes the four zones of social interaction among North Americans, as formulated by anthropologist Edward T. Hall.

Your appearance and the appearance of your documents convey nonverbal messages.

Appearance of Business Documents. The way a letter, memo, or report looks can have either a positive or a negative effect on the receiver. Envelopes through their postage, stationery, and printing can suggest routine, important, or junk mail. Letters and reports can look neat, professional, well organized, and attractive—or just the opposite. Among the worse offenders are e-mail messages.

Although they seem like conversation, e-mails are business documents that create a permanent record and often a bad impression. Sending an e-mail message full of errors conveys a damaging nonverbal message. The receiver immediately doubts the credibility of the sender. How much faith can you put in someone who can't spell, capitalize, or punctuate and won't make the effort to communicate clearly?

In succeeding chapters you'll learn how to create documents that send positive nonverbal messages through their appearance, format, organization, readability, and correctness.

Appearance of People. The way you look—your clothing, grooming, and posture—sends an instant nonverbal message about you. Based on what they see, viewers make quick judgments about your status, credibility, personality, and potential. Business communicators who look the part are more likely to be successful in working with superiors, colleagues, and customers.

Invest in appropriate, professional-looking clothing and accessories; quality is more important than quantity. Avoid flashy garments, clunky jewellery, garish

FIGURE 3.2 Four Space Zones for Social Interaction

Intimate Zone (30 TO 45 CM)

Personal Zone (45 CM TO 1 M)

Social Zone (1 TO 3.65 M)

Public Zone (3.65 M OR MORE)

makeup, and overpowering colognes. Pay attention to good grooming, including a neat hairstyle, body cleanliness, polished shoes, and clean nails. Project confidence in your posture, both standing and sitting.

Although the current trend is toward one or more days per week of casual dress at work, casual clothes change the image you project and also may affect your work style. A recent survey found that 70 percent of employees feel that workplace attire affects an employee's state of mind, behaviour, and productivity. The survey also reported that 69 percent of employees would prefer a more professional dress code, and they would be willing to give up casual attire if it would help their career progression.[17]

In the preceding discussion of nonverbal communication, you have learned that each of us gives and responds to thousands of nonverbal messages daily in our personal and work lives. You can harness the power of silent messages by reviewing Figure 3.3 and by studying the tips in the following checklist.

CHECKLIST OF TECHNIQUES FOR IMPROVING NONVERBAL COMMUNICATION SKILLS IN THE WORKPLACE

- ✓ **Establish and maintain eye contact.** Remember that in North America appropriate eye contact signals interest, attentiveness, strength, and credibility.
- ✓ **Use posture to show interest.** Encourage communication interaction by leaning forward, sitting or standing erect, and looking alert.
- ✓ **Reduce or eliminate physical barriers.** Move out from behind a desk or lectern; shorten lines of communication; arrange meeting chairs in a circle.
- ✓ **Improve your decoding skills.** Watch facial expressions and body language to understand the complete verbal and nonverbal message being communicated.

FIGURE 3.3 Sending Positive Nonverbal Signals in the Workplace

Eye contact	Maintain direct but not prolonged eye contact.
Facial expression	Express warmth with frequent smiles.
Posture	Convey self-confidence with erect stance.
Gestures	Suggest accessibility with open-palm gestures.
Time	Be on time, use time judiciously.
Space	Maintain neat, functional work area.
Territory	Use closeness to show warmth and to reduce status differences.
Business documents	Produce careful, neat, professional, well-organized messages.
Appearance	Be well groomed, neat, and appropriately dressed.

- **Probe for more information.** When you perceive nonverbal cues that contradict verbal meanings, politely seek additional clues (*I'm not sure I understand, Please tell me more about . . . ,* or *Do you mean that . . .*).
- **Avoid assigning nonverbal meanings out of context.** Make nonverbal assessments only when you understand a situation or a culture.
- **Associate with people from diverse cultures.** Learn about other cultures to widen your knowledge and tolerance of intercultural nonverbal messages.
- **Appreciate the power of appearance.** Keep in mind that the appearance of your business documents, your business space, and yourself send immediate positive or negative messages to receivers.
- **Observe yourself on videotape.** Ensure that your verbal and nonverbal messages are in sync by taping and evaluating yourself making a presentation.
- **Enlist friends and family.** Ask them to monitor your conscious and unconscious body movements and gestures to help you become a more effective communicator.

SUMMARY OF LEARNING OBJECTIVES

1 **Explain the importance of listening in the workplace and describe three types of workplace listening.** A large part of the communication process involves listening. Good listeners advance more rapidly in their careers, and listening skills are increasingly important in our economy's emphasis on customer service. Workplace listening involves listening to superiors, to colleagues and teammates, and to customers. When listening to superiors, take selective notes, don't interrupt, ask pertinent questions, and paraphrase what you hear. When listening to fellow workers, avoid being judgmental, confirm the message being sent, and affirm the relationship. When listening to customers, employees should defer judgment, pay attention to content rather than form, listen completely, control emotions, give affirming statements, and invite additional comments.

2 **Discuss the listening process and its barriers.** The listening process involves (a) perception of sounds, (b) interpretation of those sounds, (c) evaluation of meaning, and (d) action, which might involve a physical response or storage of the message in memory for future use. Mental barriers to listening include inattention, prejudgments, differing frames of reference, closed-mindedness, and pseudolistening. Physical and other barriers include hearing impairment, noisy surroundings, speaker's appearance, speaker's mannerisms, and lag time. Retention can be improved by developing a positive mindset, structuring the incoming information to form relationships, and reviewing.

3 **Enumerate ten techniques for improving workplace listening.** Listeners can improve their skills by controlling external and internal distractions, becoming actively involved, separating facts from opinions, identifying important facts, refraining from interrupting, asking clarifying questions, paraphrasing, taking advantage of lag time, taking notes to ensure retention, and being aware of gender differences.

4 Define nonverbal communication and explain its functions. Nonverbal communication includes all unwritten and unspoken messages, both intentional and unintentional. Its primary functions are to complement and illustrate, to reinforce and accentuate, to replace and substitute, to control and regulate, and to contradict. When verbal and nonverbal messages contradict each other, listeners tend to believe the nonverbal message.

5 Describe the forms of nonverbal communication and how they can be used positively in your career. Nonverbal communication takes many forms including eye contact, facial expressions, posture and gestures, as well as the use of time, space, and territory. Appearance of business documents and of people also sends silent messages. Eye contact should be direct but not prolonged; facial expression should express warmth with frequent smiles. Posture should convey self-confidence, and gestures should suggest accessibility. Being on time and maintaining neat, functional work areas send positive nonverbal messages. Use closeness to show warmth and to reduce status differences. Strive for neat, professional, well-organized business messages, and be well groomed, neat, and appropriately dressed.

6 List specific techniques for improving nonverbal communication skills in the workplace. To improve your nonverbal skills, establish and maintain eye contact, use posture to show interest, reduce or eliminate physical barriers, improve your decoding skills, probe for more information, avoid assigning nonverbal meanings out of context, associate with people from diverse cultures, appreciate the power of appearance, observe yourself on videotape, and enlist friends and family to monitor your conscious and unconscious body movements and gestures.

CHAPTER REVIEW

1. According to experts, we ignore, forget, distort, or misunderstand 75 percent of everything we hear. Why are we such poor listeners? (Obj. 1)
2. How can workers improve their listening when superiors are giving instructions, assignments, and explanations? (Obj. 1)
3. How can companies and managers do a better job of listening to employees? (Obj. 1)
4. How can employees do a better job of listening to customers? (Obj. 1)
5. Describe the four elements in the listening process. (Obj. 2).
6. How can listeners improve retention? (Obj. 2)
7. What are ten techniques for improving workplace listening? Be prepared to explain each. (Obj. 3)
8. Define *nonverbal communication.* (Obj. 4)
9. List five functions of nonverbal communication. Give an original example of each. (Obj. 4)
10. When verbal and nonverbal messages disagree, which message does the receiver consider more truthful? Give an example. (Obj. 4)
11. North Americans are said to be a little "standoffish." What does this mean? (Obj. 5)
12. How can posture send nonverbal messages? (Obj. 5)
13. How can the use of space send nonverbal messages? (Obj. 5)
14. What nonverbal messages are sent by organizations with casual dress codes? (Obj. 5)
15. List ten techniques for improving nonverbal communication skills in the workplace. (Obj. 6)

CRITICAL THINKING

1. Why do executives and managers spend more time listening than do workers? (Obj. 1)
2. North Americans are said to have the world's worst listening skills.[18] Why do you think this reputation has been earned? (Objs. 1–3)
3. Why is it acceptable behaviour for two 127-kg professional football players to slap each other on the rear end during a game but inappropriate during a business meeting? What principle of nonverbal communication can you extract from this example? (Obj. 4)
4. What arguments could you give for or against the idea that body language is a science with principles that can be interpreted accurately by specialists? (Obj. 4)

ACTIVITIES

3.1 Bad Listening Habits (Objs. 1–3)

Focusing on your own listening can reveal a number of bad habits.

Your Task. Concentrate for three days on your listening habits in class and on the job. What bad habits do you detect? Be prepared to discuss five bad habits and specific ways you could improve your listening skills. Your instructor may ask you to report your analysis in a memo.

3.2 Listening in the Workplace (Objs. 1 and 5)

TEAM

Do the listening skills and behaviours of individuals differ depending on their careers?

Your Task. Your instructor will divide you into teams and give each team a role to discuss, such as business executive, teacher, physician, police officer, lawyer, accountant, administrative assistant, mentor, or team leader. Create a list of verbal and nonverbal cues that a member of this profession would display to indicate that he or she is listening. Would the cues and behaviour change if the person were trying to listen discriminatively versus critically? How?

3.3 Evaluating Trained and Untrained Listeners (Objs. 1–3)

Play the part of a training consultant hired to help improve customer service at a high-volume travel agency. During one training session, you hear the following comments from current customer service representatives.

Your Task. Based on what you learned in this chapter, would you characterize the speaker as a trained or an untrained listener, and what advice would you give to improve the speaker's listening skills?

a. "You know what I can't stand? Those customers who call to complain but distort and exaggerate what happened. I nail them on every point that I know can't be true."
b. "It's pretty hard to take seriously a customer whose accent and grammar are so bad that you know she could never afford the trip to Hawaii that she's asking about."
c. "My biggest gripe are those people who want to complain about something that went wrong—but they can't stick to the facts. They insist on telling you every little detail."
d. "When I have a customer who wants to tell a long story, I cut her off and get the conversation under control with my questions."
e. "I think the best way to handle unhappy customers is silence. I try not to encourage them."

3.4 Distinguishing Facts From Opinions (Obj. 3)

TEAM

Good listeners make an effort to distinguish facts from opinions. Facts can be checked and verified through objective evidence. Opinions express beliefs, feelings, or judgments that cannot be proven.
Your Task. In teams, discuss the following statements. Decide whether they are facts or opinions. Be prepared to justify your choices.

- **a.** Most workers spend 30 to 40 percent of their communication time listening, whereas executives spend 60 to 70 percent of their communication time listening.
- **b.** Because they have been promoted, managers have better listening skills than subordinates do.
- **c.** Feedback helps a receiver know whether the message got through clearly.
- **d.** Women are good listeners.
- **e.** Most people who learn how to listen more accurately are amazed when they find out what they have been missing.

3.5 Document Appearance (Objs. 5 and 6)

How does the appearance of a document send a nonverbal message?
Your Task. Select a business letter and envelope that you have received at home or work. Analyze the appearance and nonverbal message the letter and envelope send. Consider the amount of postage, method of delivery, correctness of address, kind of stationery, typeface(s), format, and neatness. What assumptions did you make when you saw the envelope? How about the letter itself?

3.6 Body Language (Objs. 5 and 6)

What attitudes do the following body movements suggest to you? Do these movements always mean the same thing? What part does context play in your interpretations?

- **a.** Whistling, wringing hands
- **b.** Bowed posture, twiddling thumbs
- **c.** Steepled hands, sprawling position
- **d.** Rubbing hand through hair
- **e.** Open hands, unbuttoned coat
- **f.** Wringing hands, tugging ears

3.7 Nonverbal Communication: How to Be More Influential (Obj. 6)

Assume you've just been hired into a prestigious job and you want to make a good impression. You also want very much to become influential in the organization.
Your Task. When you attend meetings, what nonverbal behaviours and signals can you send that will make a good impression as well as improve your influence? In interacting with colleagues, what nonverbal behaviour will make you more impressive and influential?

3.8 Verbal vs. Nonverbal Signals (Objs. 4–6)

To show the power of nonverbal cues, the president of a large East Coast consulting company uses the following demonstration with new employees. Raising his right hand, he touches his pointer finger to his thumb to form a circle. Then he asks new employees in the session to do likewise. When everyone has a finger-thumb circle formed, the president tells them to touch that circle to their *chin*. But as he says this, he touches his own finger-thumb circle to his *cheek*. What happens? You guessed it! About 80 percent of the group follow what they see the president do rather than following what they hear.[19]
Your Task. Try this same demonstration with several of your friends, family members, or work colleagues. Which is more effective—verbal or nonverbal signals? What conclusion could you draw from this demonstration? Do you think that nonverbal signals are always more meaningful than verbal ones? What other factors in the communication process might determine whether verbal or nonverbal signals were more important?

3.9 Defining "Business Casual" (Objs. 5 and 6)

WEB TEAM

Although many business organizations are adopting business casual dress, most people cannot define the term. Your boss asks your internship team to use the Web to find out exactly what "business casual" means.
Your Task. Using a good search engine, such as <**www.google.ca**>, search the Web for "business casual dress code." A few Web sites actually try to define the term and give examples of appropriate clothing. Visit several sites and decide whether they are reliable enough to use as sources of accurate information. Print several relevant pages. Get together with your team and compare notes. Then write a memo to your boss explaining what men and women should and shouldn't wear on business casual days.

C.L.U.E. REVIEW 3

On a separate sheet edit the following sentences to correct faults in grammar, punctuation, numbers, spelling, proofreading, and word use.

1. Although listening is a principle activity of employees experts say that many listen at only twenty-five percent effecency.

2. When listening too instructions be sure to take notes and review them immedeately.

3. In a poll of over nine thousand employees only 1/3 felt that their companys' sought their opinions and suggestion.

4. Well trained customer service represenatives ask gentle probing questions to insure clear understanding.

5. The appearance and mannerisms of a speaker effects a listeners evaluation of a message.

6. Remembering important points involve 3 factors, (1) Deciding to remember, (2) Forming relationships, and (c) Reviewing.

7. A list of suggestions for paraphrasing a speakers ideas are found in an article titled Best Listening Habits which appeared in Fortune.

8. Skilled speakers raise there voices to convey important ideas, however they whisper to infer secrecy.

9. One successful Manager says that he can tell from peoples eyes whether they are focused receptive or distant.

10. On March 5th the President of the Company announced a casual dress policy consequently I must buy a hole new wardrobe.

Chapter 4

Communicating Across Cultures

LEARNING OBJECTIVES

1. *Discuss three significant trends related to the increasing importance of intercultural communication.*

2. *Define culture. Describe five significant characteristics of culture, and compare and contrast five key dimensions of culture.*

3. *Explain the effects of ethnocentrism, tolerance, and patience in achieving intercultural proficiency.*

4. *Illustrate how to improve nonverbal and oral communication in intercultural environments.*

5. *Illustrate how to improve written messages in intercultural environments.*

6. *Explain the challenge of capitalizing on work force diversity, including its dividends and its divisiveness. List tips for improving harmony and communication among diverse workplace audiences.*

THE INCREASING IMPORTANCE OF INTERCULTURAL COMMUNICATION

1

The "global village" predicted many years ago is increasingly becoming a reality. National and even local businesses push products across borders and seek customers in diverse foreign markets. Especially in North America, this movement toward a global economy has swelled to a torrent. To better compete, many organizations form multinational alliances. But many expanding companies stumble when they are forced to confront obstacles never before encountered.

Learning more about how culture affects behaviour helps you reduce friction and misunderstandings.

Significant obstacles involve misunderstandings and contrary views resulting from intercultural differences. You may face such intercultural differences in your current or future jobs. Your employers, fellow workers, or clients could very well be from other countries. You may travel abroad for your employer or on your own. Learning more about the powerful effect that culture has on behaviour will help you reduce friction and misunderstanding in your dealings with people from other cultures. Before examining strategies for helping you surmount intercultural obstacles, let's take a closer look at three significant trends: (1) the globalization of markets, (2) technological advancements, and (3) an intercultural work force.

Globalization of Markets

National boundaries mean less as businesses expand through mergers, alliances, and acquisitions.

Doing business beyond our borders is now commonplace. Procter & Gamble is selling disposable diapers in Asia; Rubbermaid would like to see its plastic products in all European kitchens; and McDonald's and Starbucks have establishments throughout the world. Not only are market borders blurring, but acquisitions, mergers, and alliances are obscuring the nationality of many companies.

North American companies in global markets must adapt to other cultures.

To be successful in this interdependent global village, North American companies are increasingly finding it necessary to adapt to other cultures. To sell ketchup in Japan, H. J. Heinz had to overcome a cultural resistance to sweet flavours. Thus, it offered Japanese homemakers cooking lessons instructing them how to use the sugary red sauce on omelettes, sausages, and pasta.[1] Domino's Pizza also catered to the Japanese by adding squid to its pizza toppings.[2]

Favourable trade agreements and the growth of the middle class fuel the expansion of global markets.

What has caused this rush toward globalization of markets and blurring of national identities? One significant factor is the passage of favourable trade agreements. The General Agreement on Tariffs and Trade (GATT) promotes open trade globally, while the North American Free Trade Agreement (NAFTA) expands free trade among Canada, the United States, and Mexico. NAFTA created the largest and richest free-trade region on earth.[3] The opening of Eastern Europe and the shift away from communism in Russia have also fuelled the progress toward expanding world markets. And China's admission to the World Trade Organization opens its skyrocketing economy to world markets.[4]

Equally important to expanding global markets is the explosive growth of the middle class. Parts of the world formerly considered underdeveloped now boast robust middle classes. And these consumers crave everything from cola to cellular phones. But probably the most important factor in the rise of the global market is the development of new transportation and information technologies.

Technological Advancements

Amazing new transportation and information technologies are major contributors to the development of our global interconnectivity. Equally significant in creating the global village are incredible advancements in communication technologies. The

Internet now permits instantaneous oral and written communication across time zones and continents.

Moreover, the growth of electronic commerce (e-commerce) has made every marketer with a Web site a global company. Companies depend on the Web to sell products, provide technical support, offer customer service, investigate the competition, and link directly to suppliers. Many multinational companies are now establishing country-specific Web sites, as discussed in the Tech Talk box on page 72.

Internal Web networks called *intranets* streamline business processes and improve access to critical company information. Through intranets employees have access to information that formerly had to be printed, such as a company phone book, training manuals, job postings, employee newsletters, sales figures, price lists, and even confidential reports, which can be password-protected. The Internet and the Web have changed the way we do business and the way we communicate. These advancements in communication and transportation have made markets more accessible and the world of business more efficient and more globally interdependent.

Intercultural Work Force

As world commerce mingles more and more, another trend gives intercultural communication increasing importance: people are on the move. Lured by the prospects of peace, prosperity, education, or a fresh start, persons from many cultures are moving to countries promising to fulfill their dreams. For generations the two most popular destinations have been Canada and the United States.

Canada has always welcomed immigrants, and immigration is expected to increase. By 2017 Statistics Canada reports that people born in a different country will make up more than one fifth of Canadian residents. The new population will be more diverse than ever. In the past, immigrants arrived from Europe, but the new influx of workers will be made up almost entirely of Chinese, Indian, black, Arab, and other West Asian groups.[5]

This influx of immigrants has reshaped Canadian society. Author Michael Ignatieff noted that Canadians "have always had an advantage, in that they live in a country held together by shared values rather than shared roots. And the very notion of a mosaic society, as opposed to a melting pot, tells new Canadians that they can think of citizenship in a less exclusionary way."[6] Individuals are invited to join the nation and still retain their cultural identifies, complete with traditions, languages, and customs. Although Canada's two official languages are English and French, unofficially it is a land of many languages. Instead of being the exception, cultural diversity is increasingly the norm. As we seek to accommodate multiethnic neighbourhoods, multinational companies, and a multicultural work force, we can expect some changes to happen smoothly. Other changes may involve conflict and resentment, especially for people losing their positions of power and privilege. Learning how to manage intercultural conflict is an important part of the education of any business communicator.

Canadian society is often referred to as a cultural mosaic.

UNDERSTANDING CULTURE

Every country or region within a country has a unique common heritage, joint experience, or shared learning. This shared background produces the culture of a region, country, or society. For our purposes, *culture* may be defined as the complex system of values, traits, morals, and customs shared by a society. Culture teaches people how to behave, and it conditions their reactions.

TECH TALK

Being Interculturally Correct on the Web

Early Web sites were almost always in English and meant for North Americans. But as online access grows around the world, multinational companies are revamping their sites. Sony now hosts Web sites in six regions of the world. In Europe it sponsors sites in 42 countries with native language content. The National Football League launched a Chinese version of its usual NFL.com fare but with the text translated into Mandarin Chinese. And the National Basketball Association now has nine versions of NBA.com aimed at foreign markets. As Internet use grows abroad, people in other countries are increasingly asserting their right to be spoken to in their own language. What should companies do when they decide to go global on the Web?

- **Learn the local lingo.** Other countries have developed their own Web jargon and iconography. *Home page* is "page d'accueil" (welcome page) in French and "pagina inicial" (initial page) in Spanish. Experts warn against simply translating English words page by page. Hiring a proficient translator is a better idea.[7]
- **Check icons.** North American Web surfers easily recognize the mailbox, but in Europe a more universal icon would be an envelope. Test images with local residents.
- **Relax restrictions on consistency.** Allow flexibility to meet local tastes. For example, McDonald's main site greets visitors with the golden arches and a Ronald McDonald–red background. The Japanese site, though, complements the McDonald's red and gold with pinks and browns, which are more pleasing in their culture.
- **Keep the message simple.** Whether in English or the local language, use simple, easily translated words. Avoid slang, jargon, acronyms, or ambiguous expressions.
- **Customize Web content.** Avoid conflict with local customs and attitudes. For example, the Web page of a car manufacturer showed a hiker standing next to a car. But in Mexico, hikers are poor people who can't afford cars, so it wasn't acceptable to show someone who wanted to be a hiker.[8] Tailor Web marketing content to local holidays and events.
- **Develop the site together.** The best foreign Web sites for multinational companies are developed when domestic and foreign webmasters work together. Start early and build rapport, recommends Judy Newby, McDonald's webmaster.[9]

Anthropologists Edward T. Hall and Mildred Reed Hall suggested that culture is "a system for creating, sending, storing, and processing information." Society programs men and women to act differently. Gender, race, age, religion, and many other factors affect our behaviour and cause us to behave in certain patterns.

People from one culture may have difficulty getting through to those from another culture because individuals do not always behave as expected. People are further differentiated by their environments. For example, work cultures differ remarkably from one organization to another. When people conditioned to work in casual surroundings are placed in work cultures that are more formal and regimented, they may experience culture shock.

The important thing to remember is that culture is a powerful operating force that conditions the way we think and behave. As thinking individuals, we are extraordinarily flexible and are capable of phenomenal change. The purpose of this chapter is to broaden your view of culture and open your mind to flexible attitudes so that you can avoid frustration when cultural adjustment is necessary.

Understanding basic characteristics of culture helps us make adjustments and accommodations.

Characteristics of Culture

Culture is shaped by attitudes learned in childhood and later internalized in adulthood. As we enter this current period of globalization and interculturalism, we should expect to make adjustments and adopt new attitudes. Adjustment and accommodation will be easier if we understand some basic characteristics of culture.

Culture Is Learned. Rules, values, and attitudes of a culture are not inherent. They are learned and passed down from generation to generation. For example, in many Middle Eastern and some Asian cultures, same-sex people may walk hand in hand in the street, but opposite-sex people may not do so. In Arab cultures conversations are often held in close proximity, sometimes nose to nose. But in Western cultures if a person stands too close, one may react as if violated. Cultural rules of behaviour learned from your family and society are conditioned from early childhood.

Cultures Are Inherently Logical. The rules in any culture originated to reinforce that culture's values and beliefs. They act as normative forces. Although current cultural behaviour may sometimes seem silly and illogical, nearly all serious rules and values originate in deep-seated beliefs. Rules about how close to stand are linked to values about sexuality, aggression, modesty, and respect. Acknowledging the inherent logic of a culture is extremely important when learning to accept behaviour that differs from one's own cultural behaviour.

Culture Is the Basis of Self-Identity and Community. Culture is the basis for how we tell the world who we are and what we believe. People build their identities through cultural overlays to their primary culture. North Americans, for example, make choices in education, career, place of employment, and life partner. Each of these choices brings with it a set of rules, manners, ceremonies, beliefs, language, and values. They add to one's total cultural outlook, and they represent major expressions of a person's self-identity.

Culture determines our sense of who we are and our sense of community.

Culture Combines the Visible and Invisible. To outsiders, the way we act—those things that we do in daily life and work—are the most visible parts of our culture. In Japan, for instance, harmony with the environment is important. Thus, when attending a flower show, a woman might dress in pastels rather than primary colours to avoid detracting from the beauty of the flowers.[10] Such practices are outward symbols of deeper values that are invisible but that pervade everything we think and do.

Culture Is Dynamic. Over time, cultures will change. Changes are caused by advancements in technology and communication, as discussed earlier. Change is also caused by events such as migration, natural disasters, and wars. Attitudes, behaviours, and beliefs change in open societies more quickly than in closed societies.

Attitudes, behaviours, and beliefs in a culture change as a result of migration, disasters, and wars.

About Stereotypes, Prototypes, Prejudices, and Generalizations

Most experts recognize that it is impossible to talk about cultures without using mental categories, representations, and generalizations to describe groups. These categories are sometimes considered *stereotypes.* Because the term *stereotype* has a negative meaning, intercultural authors Varner and Beamer suggest that we distinguish between *stereotype* and *prototype.*

Stereotypes are oversimplified behavioural patterns applied uncritically to groups; _prototypes_ describe general characteristics that are dynamic and may change.

A *stereotype* is an oversimplified behavioural pattern applied uncritically to groups. Stereotypes are fixed and rigid. Although they may be exaggerated and overgeneralized beliefs when applied to groups of people, stereotypes are not always entirely false.[11] Often they contain a grain of truth. When a stereotype develops into a rigid attitude and when it's based on erroneous beliefs or preconceptions, then it should be called a *prejudice*.

Varner and Beamer recommend the use of the term *prototype* to describe "mental representations based on general characteristics that are not fixed and rigid, but rather are open to new definitions."[12] Prototypes, then, are dynamic and change with fresh experience. Prototypes based on objective observations usually have a considerable amount of truth in them. That's why they can be helpful in studying culture.

Being able to draw valid generalizations is necessary for learning and education.

Some people object to making any generalizations about cultures whatsoever. Yet, it is wise to remember that whenever we are confronted with something new and unfamiliar, we naturally strive to categorize the data in order to make sense out of it. In categorizing these new data, we are making generalizations. Much of what we teach in university or college courses could be called generalizations. Being able to draw generalizations from masses of data is a sign of intelligence and learning. Unfounded generalizations about people and cultures, of course, can lead to bias and prejudice. But for our purposes, when we discuss cultures, it's important to be able to make generalizations and describe cultural prototypes.

An inukshuk was chosen as the emblem for the 2010 Olympic Winter Games in Vancouver as a uniquely Canadian symbol of friendship, hospitality, strength, teamwork, and the vast Canadian landscape.

Dimensions of Culture

The more you know about culture in general and your own culture in particular, the better able you will be to adapt to an intercultural perspective. The diverse Canadian society is really a group of cultures. Canada also has several regional subcultures. Those living on the west coast of Canada may have a different way of thinking and a different spirit from those on the east coast; Canadians living on the Prairies are distinct from those in Ontario, as are Québécois and Newfoundlanders.[13] When Vancouver announced the emblem for the 2010 Olympic Winter Games, a uniquely Canadian symbol of friendship, hospitality, strength, teamwork, and the vast Canadian landscape was unveiled. The new inukshuk logo speaks to "the humanity of the country, the people, the culture and the values we have" according to organizing committee CEO John Furlong.[14] A typical Canadian has habits and beliefs similar to those of other members of Western, technologically advanced societies. In our limited space in this book, it's impossible to cover fully the infinite facets of culture. But we can outline some key dimensions of culture and look at them from different views.

So that you will better understand your culture and how it contrasts with other cultures, we will describe five key dimensions of culture: context, individualism, formality, communication style, and time orientation.

Low-context cultures (North America, Western Europe) depend less on the environment of a situation to convey meaning than do high-context cultures (Japan, China, and Arab countries).

People in low-context cultures tend to be logical, analytical, and action-oriented.

Context. Context is probably the most important cultural dimension and also the most difficult to define. It's a concept developed by cultural anthropologist Edward T. Hall. In his model, context refers to the stimuli, environment, or ambience surrounding an event. Communicators in low-context cultures (such as those in North America, Scandinavia, and Germany) depend little on the context of a situation to convey their meaning. They assume that listeners know very little and must be told practically everything. In high-context cultures (such as those in Japan, China, and Arab countries), the listener is already "contexted" and does not need to be given much background information.[15] To identify low- and high-context countries, Hall arranged them on a continuum, as shown in Figure 4.1.

Individualism. An attitude of independence and freedom from control characterizes individualism. Members of low-context cultures, particularly North Americans, tend to value individualism. They believe that initiative and self-assertion result in

FIGURE 4.1 Comparing Low- and High-Context Cultures

Low Context	High Context
Tends to prefer direct verbal interaction	Tends to prefer indirect verbal interaction
Tends to understand meaning at one level only	Tends to understand meanings embedded at many sociocultural levels
Is generally less proficient in reading nonverbal cues	Is generally more proficient in reading nonverbal cues
Values individualism	Values group membership
Relies more on logic	Relies more on context and feeling
Employs linear logic	Employs spiral logic
Says *no* directly	Talks around point; avoids saying *no*
Communicates in highly structured (contexted) messages, provides details, stresses literal meanings, gives authority to written information	Communicates in simple, ambiguous, noncontexted messages; understands visual messages readily

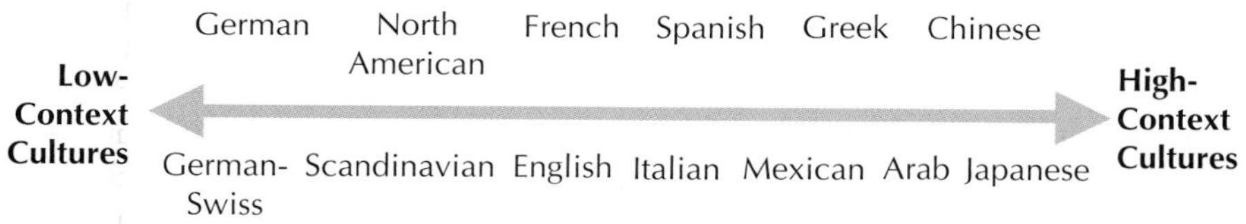

Low-Context Cultures ⟷ **High-Context Cultures**

German-Swiss, German, Scandinavian, North American, English, French, Italian, Spanish, Mexican, Greek, Arab, Chinese, Japanese

personal achievement. They believe in individual action and personal responsibility, and they desire a large degree of freedom in their personal lives.

Members of many low-context cultures value independence and freedom from control.

Members of high-context cultures are more collectivist. They emphasize membership in organizations, groups, and teams; they encourage acceptance of group values, duties, and decisions. They typically resist independence because it fosters competition and confrontation instead of consensus. In group-oriented cultures like many Asian societies, for example, self-assertion and individual decision making are discouraged. Business decisions are often made by all who have competence in the matter under discussion. Similarly, in China managers also focus on the group rather than on the individual, preferring a "consultative" management style over an autocratic style.[16]

Many cultures, of course, are quite complex and cannot be characterized as totally individualistic or group-oriented. For example, Canadians of European descent are generally quite individualistic, while those with Asian backgrounds may be closer to the group-centred dimension.[17]

Formality. People in some cultures place less emphasis on tradition, ceremony, and social rules than do members of other cultures. While Canadians tend to be generally reserved and formal in their business dealings,[18] levels of formality vary across the country. In Quebec, where etiquette and politeness are considered very important, first names and informal greetings are generally not used, and modes of dress are more conservative than in the rest of Canada.[19] In other parts of Canada, business dress may be more casual, and business acquaintances are soon on a first-name

Tradition, ceremony, and social rules are more important in some cultures.

The Quilt of Belonging is a project designed to create a better understanding of Canadians of all origins to recognize our common humanity and promote harmony and passion among our people.

basis. While French Canadians may be more formal in business settings, they may also have a tendency to be less reserved—gesturing more expansively, requiring less personal space, and engaging in more touching—than English Canadians.[20] Directness and a tendency to come right to the point often characterize a lack of formality in business. In many cases, lack of directness is thought to be a waste of time—another valuable commodity in Western culture.

This informality and directness may be confusing abroad. In Mexico, for instance, a typical business meeting begins with handshakes, coffee, and an expansive conversation about the weather, sports, and other light topics.[21] In Japan signing documents and exchanging business cards are important rituals. In Europe first names are never used without invitation. In Arab, South American, and Asian cultures, a feeling of friendship and kinship must be established before business can be transacted.

In Western cultures people are more relaxed about social status and appearance of power.[22] Deference is not generally paid to individuals merely because of their wealth, position, seniority, or age. In many Asian cultures, however, these characteristics are important and must be respected.

Words are used differently by people in low- and high-context cultures.

Communication Style. People in low- and high-context cultures tend to communicate differently with words. To North Americans and Germans, words are very important, especially in contracts and negotiations. People in high-context cultures, on the other hand, place more emphasis on the surrounding context than on the words describing a negotiation. A Greek may see a contract as a formal statement announcing the intention to build a business for the future. The Japanese may treat contracts as statements of intention, and they assume changes will be made as a project develops. Mexicans may treat contracts as artistic exercises of what might be accomplished in an ideal world. They do not necessarily expect contracts to apply consistently in the real world. An Arab may be insulted by merely mentioning a contract; a person's word is more binding.[23]

Westerners value a direct, straightforward communication style.

Westerners tend to take words literally, while Hispanics enjoy plays on words. Arabs and South Americans sometimes speak with extravagant or poetic figures of speech that may be misinterpreted if taken literally. Nigerians prefer a quiet, clear form of expression; and Germans tend to be direct but understated.[24]

In communication style Canadians value straightforwardness, are suspicious of evasiveness, and distrust people who might have a "hidden agenda" or who "play their cards too close to the chest."[25] Canadians and Americans also tend to be uncomfortable with silence and impatient with delays. Some Asian businesspeople have learned that the longer they drag out negotiations, the more concessions impatient North Americans are likely to make.

Western cultures have developed languages that use letters describing the *sounds* of words. But Asian languages are based on pictographical characters representing the *meanings* of words. Asian language characters are much more complex than the Western alphabet; therefore, Asians are said to have a higher competence in the discrimination of visual patterns.

Time Orientation. Punctuality is an important Western value. Most North Americans consider time a precious commodity to be conserved. They correlate time with productivity, efficiency, and money. Keeping people waiting for business appointments wastes time and is also rude. In other cultures time may be perceived as an unlimited and never-ending resource to be enjoyed.

North Americans tend to correlate time with productivity, efficiency, and money.

ACHIEVING INTERCULTURAL PROFICIENCY

3

Being aware of your own culture and how it contrasts with others is an important first step in achieving intercultural proficiency. Another step involves recognizing barriers to intercultural accommodation and striving to overcome them. Some of these barriers occur quite naturally and require conscious effort to surmount. You might be thinking, why bother? Probably the most important reasons for becoming interculturally competent are that your personal life will be more satisfying and your work life will be more productive, gratifying, and effective.

Avoiding Ethnocentrism

The belief in the superiority of one's own race is known as *ethnocentrism*, a natural attitude inherent in all cultures. If you were raised in Canada, many of the dimensions of culture described previously probably seem "right" to you.

Ethnocentrism, the belief in the superiority of one's own race, tends to cause us to judge others by our own values.

Ethnocentrism causes us to judge others by our own values. As Professor Usha George points out, "We all try to interpret the world through our own cultural lens."[26] We expect others to react as we would, and they expect us to behave as they would. Misunderstandings naturally result. Ethnocentric reactions can be reduced through knowledge of other cultures and development of increased intercultural sensitivity.

Bridging the Gap

Developing cultural competence often involves changing attitudes. Remember that culture is learned. Through exposure to other cultures and through training, such as you are receiving in this course, you can learn new attitudes and behaviours that help bridge gaps between cultures.

Because culture is learned, you can learn new attitudes and behaviours through training.

Tolerance. One desirable attitude in achieving intercultural sensitivity is that of *tolerance.* Closed-minded people cannot look beyond their own ethnocentrism. But as global markets expand and as our own society becomes increasingly multiethnic, tolerance becomes especially significant. Some job descriptions now include statements such as "Must be able to interact with ethnically diverse personnel."

To improve tolerance, you'll want to practise *empathy.* This means trying to see the world through another's eyes. It means being less judgmental and more eager to seek common ground. Accepting cultural differences and adapting to them with tolerance and empathy often results in a harmonious compromise.

Empathy, which means trying to see the world through another's eyes, helps you be more tolerant and less judgmental.

Saving Face. In business transactions North Americans often assume that economic factors are the primary motivators of people. It's wise to remember, though, that strong cultural influences are also at work. *Saving face*, for example, is important in many parts of the world. *Face* refers to the image a person holds in his or her social network. People in low-context cultures are less concerned with face.

Saving face may require indirectness to respect the feelings and dignity of others.

Tolerance sometimes involves being patient and silent.

Patience. Being tolerant also involves patience. If a foreigner is struggling to express an idea in English, North Americans must avoid the temptation to finish the sentence and provide the word that they presume is wanted. When we put words into their mouths, our foreign friends often smile and agree out of politeness, but our words may in fact not express their thoughts. Remaining silent is another means of exhibiting tolerance. Instead of filling every lapse in conversation, North Americans, for example, should recognize that in Asian cultures people deliberately use periods of silence for reflection and contemplation.

IMPROVING COMMUNICATION WITH INTERCULTURAL AUDIENCES

Business success may depend on working harmoniously with people from different cultures.

Thus far we've discussed the increasing importance of intercultural sensitivity as a result of globalization of markets, increasing migration, and technological advancements. We've described characteristics and dimensions of cultures, and we've talked about avoiding ethnocentrism. Remember, the key to future business success may very well lie in finding ways to work harmoniously with people from different cultures.

Adapting Messages to Intercultural Audiences

As business communicators, we need to pay special attention to specific areas of communication to enhance the effectiveness of intercultural messages. To minimize the chance of misunderstanding, we'll look more closely at nonverbal communication, oral messages, and written messages.

Understanding nonverbal messages is particularly difficult when cultures differ.

Nonverbal Communication. Verbal skills in another culture can generally be mastered if one studies hard enough. But nonverbal skills are much more difficult to learn. Nonverbal behaviour includes areas such as eye contact, facial expression, posture, gestures, and the use of time, space, and territory. The messages sent by body language and the way we arrange time and space have always been open to interpretation. Deciphering nonverbal communication is difficult for people who are culturally similar, and it is even more troublesome when cultures differ.

In Western cultures, for example, people perceive silence as a negative trait. It suggests rejection, unhappiness, depression, regret, embarrassment, or ignorance. However, the Japanese admire silence and consider it a key to success. Silence is equated with wisdom.

Gestures can create different reactions in multicultural environments.

Although nonverbal behaviour is ambiguous within cultures and even more problematic between cultures, it nevertheless conveys meaning. If you've ever had to talk with someone who does not share your language, you probably learned quickly to use gestures to convey basic messages. Since gestures can create very different reactions in different cultures, one must be careful in using and interpreting them.

As businesspeople increasingly interact with their counterparts from other cultures, they will become more aware of these differences. Some behaviours are easy to warn against, such as touching people from the Middle East with the left hand (because it is considered unclean and is used for personal hygiene). We're also warned not to touch anyone's head (even children) in Thailand, as the head is considered sacred. Numerous lists of cultural do's and don'ts have been compiled. However, learning all the nuances of nonverbal behaviour in other cultures is impossible, and such lists are merely the tip of the cultural iceberg.

Although we can't ever hope to understand fully the nuances of meaning transmitted by nonverbal behaviour in various cultures, we can grow more tolerant, more flexible, and eventually, more competent. An important part of achieving nonverbal competence is becoming more aware of our own nonverbal behaviours and their meanings. Much of our nonverbal behaviour is learned in early childhood from our families and from society, and it is largely unconscious. Once we become more aware of the meaning of our own gestures, posture, eye gaze, and so on, we will become more alert and more sensitive to variations in other cultures. Striving to associate with people from different cultures can further broaden our intercultural competence.

Becoming more aware of your own use of nonverbal cues can make you more sensitive to variations in other cultures.

From a practical standpoint, when interacting with businesspeople in other cultures, it's always wise to follow their lead. If they avoid intense eye contact, don't stare. If no one is putting his or her elbows on a table, don't be the first to do so. Until you are knowledgeable about the meaning of gestures, it's probably a good idea to keep yours to a minimum. Learning the words for *please*, *yes*, and *thank you* is even better than relying on gestures.[27] Achieving intercultural competence in regard to nonverbal behaviour may never be totally attained, but sensitivity, nonjudgmentalism, and tolerance go a long way toward improving interactions.

Oral Messages. Although it's best to speak a foreign language fluently, many of us lack that skill. Fortunately, global business transactions are often conducted in English; however, the level of proficiency may be limited among those for whom it is a second language. English has become the language of technology and the language to know in global business even for traditionally non-English-speaking countries. English is so dominant in business that when Koreans go to China, English is the language they use to conduct business.[28] Travellers abroad make a big mistake in thinking that people who speak English always understand what is being said. Comprehension can be fairly superficial. The following suggestions are helpful for situations in which one or both communicators may be using English as a second language.

- **Learn foreign phrases.** In conversations, even when English is used, foreign nationals appreciate it when you learn greetings and a few phrases in their language. Practise the phrases phonetically so that you will be understood.
- **Use simple English.** Speak in short sentences (under 15 words), and try to stick to the 3000 to 4000 most common English words. For example, use *old* rather than *obsolete* and *rich* rather than *luxurious* or *sumptuous.* Eliminate puns, sports and military references, slang, and jargon (special business terms). Be especially alert to idiomatic expressions that can't be translated, such as *burn the midnight oil* and *under the weather.*

Use simple English and avoid puns, sports references, slang, and jargon when communicating with people for whom English is a second language.

- **Speak slowly and enunciate clearly.** Avoid fast speech, but don't raise your voice. Overpunctuate with pauses and full stops. Always write numbers for all to see.
- **Observe eye messages.** Be alert to a glazed expression or wandering eyes—these tell you the listener is lost.
- **Encourage accurate feedback.** Ask probing questions, and encourage the listener to paraphrase what you say. Don't assume that a *yes*, a nod, or a smile indicates comprehension.
- **Check frequently for comprehension.** Avoid waiting until you finish a long explanation to request feedback. Instead, make one point at a time, pausing to check for comprehension. Don't proceed to B until A has been grasped.
- **Accept blame.** If a misunderstanding results, graciously accept the blame for not making your meaning clear.

- **Listen without interrupting.** Curb your desire to finish sentences or to fill out ideas for the speaker. Keep in mind that North Americans abroad are often accused of listening too little and talking too much.
- **Remember to smile!** Roger Axtell, international behaviour expert, calls the smile the single most understood and most useful form of communication in either personal or business transactions.[29]
- **Follow up in writing.** After conversations or oral negotiations, confirm the results and agreements with follow-up letters. For proposals and contracts, engage a translator to prepare copies in the local language.

5

Written Messages. In sending letters and other documents to businesspeople in other cultures, try to adapt your writing style and tone appropriately. For example, in cultures where formality and tradition are important, be scrupulously polite. Don't even think of sharing the latest joke. Humour translates very poorly and can cause misunderstanding and negative reactions. Familiarize yourself with accepted channels of communication. Are letters, e-mail, and faxes common? Would a direct or indirect organizational pattern be more effective? The following suggestions, coupled with the earlier guidelines, can help you prepare successful written messages for intercultural audiences.

To improve written messages, adopt local formats, use short sentences and short paragraphs, avoid ambiguous expressions, strive for clarity, use correct grammar, cite numbers carefully, and accommodate readers in organization, tone, and style.

- **Adopt local formats.** Learn how documents are formatted and addressed in the intended reader's country. Use local formats and styles.
- **Use short sentences and short paragraphs.** Sentences with fewer than 15 words and paragraphs with fewer than 7 lines are most readable.
- **Avoid ambiguous expressions.** Include relative pronouns (*that, which, who*) for clarity in introducing clauses. Stay away from contractions (especially ones like *Here's the problem*). Avoid idioms (*once in a blue moon*), slang (*my presentation really bombed*), acronyms (*ASAP* for *as soon as possible*), abbreviations (*DBA* for *doing business as*), jargon (*input, bottom line*), and sports references (*play ball, slam dunk, ballpark figure*). Use action-specific verbs (*purchase a printer* rather than *get a printer*).
- **Strive for clarity.** Avoid words that have many meanings (the word *light* has 18 different meanings!). If necessary, clarify words that may be confusing. Replace two-word verbs with clear single words (*return* instead of *bring back*; *delay* instead of *put off*; *maintain* instead of *keep up*).
- **Use correct grammar.** Be careful of misplaced modifiers, dangling participles, and sentence fragments. Use conventional punctuation.
- **Cite numbers carefully.** For international trade it's a good idea to use the metric system. In citing numbers use figures (*15*) instead of spelling them out (*fifteen*). Always convert dollar figures into local currency. Avoid using figures to express the month of the year.
- **Accommodate the reader in organization, tone, and style.** Organize your message to appeal to the reader. If flowery tone, formal salutations, indirectness, references to family and the seasons, or unconditional apologies are expected, strive to accommodate.

Making the effort to communicate with sensitivity across cultures pays big dividends. "Much of the world wants to like us," says businessman and international consultant Kevin Chambers. "When we take the time to learn about others, many will bend over backward to do business with us."[30] The following checklist summarizes suggestions for improving communication with intercultural audiences.

CHECKLIST FOR IMPROVING INTERCULTURAL SENSITIVITY AND COMMUNICATION

- **Study your own culture.** Learn about your customs, biases, and views and how they differ from those in other societies. This knowledge can help you better understand, appreciate, and accept the values and behaviour of other cultures.

- **Learn about other cultures.** Education can help you alter cultural misconceptions, reduce fears, and minimize misunderstandings. Knowledge of other cultures opens your eyes and teaches you to expect differences. Such knowledge also enriches your life.

- **Curb ethnocentrism.** Avoid judging others by your personal views. Get over the view that the other cultures are incorrect, defective, or primitive. Try to develop an open mindset.

- **Avoid judgmentalism.** Strive to accept other behaviour as different, rather than as right or wrong. Try not to be defensive in justifying your culture. Strive for objectivity.

- **Seek common ground.** When cultures clash, look for solutions that respect both cultures. Be flexible in developing compromises.

- **Observe nonverbal cues in your culture.** Become more alert to the meanings of eye contact, facial expression, posture, gestures, and the use of time, space, and territory. How do they differ in other cultures?

- **Use plain English.** Speak and write in short sentences using simple words and standard English. Eliminate puns, slang, jargon, acronyms, abbreviations, and any words that cannot be easily translated.

- **Encourage accurate feedback.** In conversations ask probing questions and listen attentively without interrupting. Don't assume that a yes or a smile indicates assent or comprehension.

- **Adapt to local preferences.** Shape your writing to reflect the reader's document styles, if appropriate. Express currency in local figures. Write out months of the year for clarity.

CAPITALIZING ON WORK FORCE DIVERSITY

At the same time that North American businesspeople are interacting with people from around the world, the domestic work force is becoming more diverse. This diversity has many dimensions—race, ethnicity, age, religion, gender, national origin, physical ability, and countless other qualities. No longer, say the experts, will the workplace be predominantly Anglo-oriented or male. According to Statistics

Canada, by 2017 one in five Canadians will be a visible minority.[31] In addition, the number of the world's older population is seen as the century's defining demographic trend. Predictions indicate the workplace revolution ahead will rival the gender revolution of a quarter century ago when women's educational levels and labour force participation soared.[32] Jeff Taylor, who launched Monster.com over ten years ago, predicts that by 2010 we will see the worst labour shortages in our lifetime as less than half of the number of workers will replace the number of retiring baby boomers.[33]

Dividends of Diversity

Rajesh Subramanian, president of FedEx Canada, notes, "We have a tendency to reject what is different. And at the same time, we need what is different. Because what is different is the only way we can grow. Sameness is suicide in the business world—particularly now as we operate in the global economy."[34] As society and the work force become more diverse, successful interaction and communication among the various identity groups brings distinct challenges and dividends in three areas.

A diverse work force benefits consumers, work teams, and business organizations.

Consumers. A diverse staff is better able to read trends and respond to the increasingly diverse customer base in local and world markets. Diverse consumers now want specialized goods and services tailored to their needs. Teams made up of different people with different experiences are better able to create the different products that these markets require. Consumers also want to deal with companies that respect their values.

Work Teams. As you learned in Chapter 2, employees today work in teams. Team members with different backgrounds may come up with more creative and effective problem-solving techniques than homogeneous teams. Chains of command, narrow job descriptions, and hierarchies are gradually becoming things of the past. Today's teams are composed of knowledgeable, diverse individuals who are concerned with sustainability, competence, and ownership within the project, team, and organization.[35]

Diversity can improve employee relationships and increase productivity.

Business Organizations. Companies that set aside time and resources to cultivate and capitalize on diversity will suffer fewer discrimination lawsuits, fewer union clashes, and less government regulatory action. Most important, though, is the growing realization among organizations that diversity is a critical bottom-line business strategy to improve employee relationships and to increase productivity. Developing a diverse staff that can work together cooperatively is one of the biggest challenges facing business organizations today.

Divisiveness of Diversity

Diversity can cause divisiveness, discontent, and clashes.

Diversity can be a positive force within organizations. But all too often it can also cause divisiveness, discontent, and clashes. Many of the identity groups, the so-called work force "disenfranchised," have legitimate gripes.

The *glass ceiling* is an invisible barrier of attitudes, prejudices, and "old boy networks" that block women from reaching important positions.

Women complain of the *glass ceiling,* that invisible barrier of attitudes, prejudices, and "old boy networks" blocking them from reaching important corporate positions. In 2002 women held only 14 percent of corporate officer positions in Canada according to Catalyst.[36] Some women feel that they are the victims of sexual harassment, unequal wages, sexism, and even their style of communication. On the other hand, men, too, have gender issues. One manager described gender discrimination in his office: "My boss was a woman and was very verbal about the opportunities for women to advance in my company. I have often felt she gave much more attention to the women in the office than the men."[37]

Older employees feel that the deck is stacked in favour of younger employees. Older workers often feel that they are perceived as being more expensive, lacking in fresh skills, less adaptable, and less technology-savvy.[38] Minorities complain that they are discriminated against in hiring, retention, wages, and promotions. Physically challenged individuals feel that their limitations should not hold them back, and they fear that their potential is often prejudged. Individuals with different religions may feel uncomfortable working beside each other.

Tips for Improving Communication Among Diverse Workplace Audiences

Integrating all this diversity into one seamless work force is a formidable task and a vital one. Harnessed effectively, diversity can enhance productivity and propel a company to success well into the twenty-first century. Mismanaged, it can become a tremendous drain on a company's time and resources. How companies deal with diversity will make all the difference in how they compete in an increasingly global environment. And that means that organizations must do more than just pay lip service to these issues. Harmony and acceptance do not happen automatically when people who are dissimilar work together. The following suggestions can help you and your organization find ways to improve communication and interaction.

A diverse work force may reduce productivity unless trained to value differences.

- **Seek training.** Especially if an organization is experiencing problems in managing diversity, awareness-raising sessions may be helpful. Spend time reading and learning about work force diversity and how it can benefit organizations. Look on diversity as an opportunity, not a threat. Intercultural communication, team building, and conflict resolution are skills that can be learned in diversity training programs.
- **Understand the value of differences.** Diversity makes an organization innovative and creative. Sameness fosters an absence of critical thinking called "groupthink," which you learned about in Chapter 2. Diversity in problem-solving groups encourages independent and creative thinking.
- **Don't expect conformity.** Gone are the days when businesses could say, "This is our culture. Conform or leave."[39] Paul Fireman, CEO of Reebok, stresses seeking people who have new and different stories to tell. "And then you have to make real room for them, you have to learn to listen, to listen closely, to their stories. It accomplishes next to nothing to employ those who are different from us if the condition of their employment is that they become the same as us. For it is their differences that enrich us, expand us, provide us the competitive edge."[40]

Don't expect all workers to think or act alike.

- **Learn about your cultural self.** Begin to think of yourself as a product of your culture, and understand that your culture is just one among many. Try to stand outside and look at yourself. Do you see any reflex reactions and automatic thought patterns that are a result of your upbringing? These may be invisible to you until challenged by difference. Remember, your culture was designed to help you succeed and survive in a certain environment. Be sure to keep what works and yet be ready to adapt as environments change.
- **Make fewer assumptions.** Be careful of seemingly insignificant, innocent workplace assumptions. For example, don't assume that everyone wants to observe the holidays with a Christmas party and a decorated tree. Celebrating only Christian holidays in December and January excludes those who honour Hanukkah, Kwanza, and the Chinese New Year. Moreover, in workplace discussions don't assume that everyone is married or wants to be or is even heterosexual, for that matter. For invitations, avoid phrases such as *managers and their*

wives. Spouses or *partners* is more inclusive. Valuing diversity means making fewer assumptions that everyone is like you or wants to be like you.

In times of conflict, look for areas of agreement and build on similarities.

- **Build on similarities.** Look for areas where you and others not like you can agree or at least share opinions. Be prepared to consider issues from many perspectives, all of which may be valid. Accept that there is room for different points of view to coexist peacefully. Although you can always find differences, it's much harder to find similarities. Look for common ground in shared experiences, mutual goals, and similar values. Concentrate on your objective even when you may disagree on how to reach it.[41]
- **Adapt communication style** based on age, gender, culture, technical competence, and special needs of audience.

SUMMARY OF LEARNING OBJECTIVES

1 **Discuss three significant trends related to the increasing importance of intercultural communication.** Three trends are working together to crystallize the growing need for developing intercultural sensitivities and improved communication techniques. First, the globalization of markets means that you can expect to be doing business with people from around the world. Second, technological advancements in transportation and information are making the world smaller and more intertwined. Third, more and more immigrants from other cultures are settling in North America, thus changing the complexion of the work force. Successful interaction requires awareness, tolerance, and accommodation.

2 **Define *culture*. Describe five significant characteristics of culture, and compare and contrast five key dimensions of culture.** *Culture* is the complex system of values, traits, morals, and customs shared by a society. Each of us is shaped by the elements of our culture. Some of the significant characteristics of culture include the following: (1) culture is learned, (2) cultures are inherently logical, (3) culture is the basis of self-identity and community, (4) culture combines the visible and invisible, and (5) culture is dynamic. Members of low-context cultures (such as those in North America, Scandinavia, and Germany) depend on words to express meaning, while people in high-context cultures (such as those in Japan, China, and Arab countries) rely more on context (social setting, a person's history, status, and position) to communicate meaning. Other key dimensions of culture include individualism, degree of formality, communication style, and time orientation.

3 **Explain the effects of ethnocentrism, tolerance, and patience in achieving intercultural proficiency.** *Ethnocentrism* refers to an individual's feeling that the culture you belong to is superior to all others and holds all truths. To function effectively in a global economy, we must acquire knowledge of other cultures and be willing to change attitudes. Developing tolerance often involves practising *empathy*, which means trying to see the world through another's eyes. Saving face and promoting social harmony are important in many parts of the world. Moving beyond narrow ethnocentric views often requires tolerance and patience.

4 **Illustrate how to improve nonverbal and oral communication in intercultural environments.** We can minimize nonverbal miscommunication by recognizing that meanings conveyed by eye contact, posture, and gestures

are largely culture dependent. Nonverbal messages are also sent by the use of time, space, and territory. Becoming aware of your own nonverbal behaviour and what it conveys is the first step in broadening your intercultural competence. In improving oral messages, you can learn foreign phrases, use simple English, speak slowly and enunciate clearly, observe eye messages, encourage accurate feedback, check for comprehension, accept blame, listen without interrupting, smile, and follow up important conversations in writing.

5 **Illustrate how to improve written messages in intercultural environments.** To improve written messages, adopt local formats, use short sentences and short paragraphs, avoid ambiguous expression, strive for clarity, use correct grammar, and cite numbers carefully. Also try to accommodate the reader in organization, tone, and style.

6 **Explain the challenge of capitalizing on work force diversity, including its dividends and its divisiveness. List tips for improving harmony and communication among diverse workplace audiences.** Having a diverse work force can benefit consumers, work teams, and business organizations. However, diversity can also cause divisiveness among various identity groups. To promote harmony and communication, many organizations develop diversity training programs. As an individual, you must understand and accept the value of differences. Don't expect conformity, and create zero tolerance for bias and prejudice. Learn about your cultural self, make fewer assumptions, and seek common ground when disagreements arise.

CHAPTER REVIEW

1. Why is it increasingly important for businesspeople to develop intercultural communication skills? (Obj. 1)
2. In what ways is the Web used to promote e-commerce? (Obj. 1)
3. What is culture and how is culture learned? (Obj. 2)
4. Describe five major dimensions of culture. (Obj. 2)
5. Briefly, contrast high- and low-context cultures. (Obj. 2)
6. What is *ethnocentrism*? (Obj. 3)
7. How is a *stereotype* different from a *prototype*? (Obj. 3)
8. Why is nonverbal communication more difficult to study and learn than verbal communication? (Obj. 4)
9. Name three processes that are effective in achieving competence in dealing with nonverbal messages in other cultures. (Obj. 4)
10. Describe five specific ways in which you can improve oral communication with a foreigner. (Obj. 4)
11. Describe five specific ways in which you can improve written communication with a foreigner. (Obj. 5)
12. Name three groups that benefit from work force diversity and explain why. (Obj. 6)
13. Describe six tips for improving communication among diverse workplace audiences. (Obj. 6)

CRITICAL THINKING

1. Since English is becoming the world's business language, why should Canadians bother to learn about other cultures? (Objs. 1, 2, and 6)
2. If the rules, values, and attitudes of a culture are learned, can they be unlearned? Explain. (Obj. 2)
3. Some economists argue that the statement that "diversity is an economic asset" is an unproved and perhaps unprovable assertion. Should social responsibility or market forces determine whether an organization strives to create a diverse work force? Why? (Obj. 6)

ACTIVITIES

4.1 Cross-Cultural Gap at Resort Hotel in Thailand (Objs. 1–4)

TEAM

The Laguna Beach Resort Hotel in Phuket, Thailand, nestled between a tropical lagoon and the sparkling Andaman Sea, is one of the most beautiful resorts in the world. (You can take a virtual tour by using Google and searching for "Laguna Beach Resort Phuket.") When Brett Peel arrived as the director of the hotel's kitchen, he thought he had landed in paradise. On the job for only six weeks, he began wondering why his Thai staff would answer *yes* even when they didn't understand what he had said. Other foreign managers discovered that junior staff managers rarely spoke up and never expressed an opinion contrary to those of senior executives. And guests with a complaint thought that Thai employees were not taking them seriously because the Thais smiled at even the worst complaints. Thais also did not seem to understand deadlines or urgent requests.[42]

Your Task. In teams decide how you would respond to the following. If you were the director of this hotel, would you implement a training program for employees? If so, would you train only foreign managers, or would you include local Thai employees as well? What topics should a training program include? Would your goal be to introduce Western ways to the Thais? At least 90 percent of the hotel guests are non-Thai.

4.2 Interpreting Intercultural Proverbs (Objs. 2 and 3)

Proverbs, which tell truths with metaphors and simplicity, often reveal fundamental values held by a culture.

Your Task. Discuss the following proverbs and explain how they relate to some of the cultural values you studied in this chapter. What additional proverbs can you cite and what do they mean?

Japanese proverbs

The pheasant would have lived but for its cry.
The nail that sticks up gets pounded down.
To say nothing is a flower.

North American proverbs

The squeaking wheel gets the grease.
A stitch in time saves nine.
A bird in hand is worth two in the bush.
A man's home is his castle.

German proverbs

No one is either rich or poor who has not helped himself to be so.
He who is afraid of doing too much always does too little.

4.3 Negotiating Traps (Objs. 2, 3, 4, and 5)

It's often difficult for businesspeople to reach agreement on the terms of contracts, proposals, and anything that involves bargaining. It's even more difficult when the negotiators are from different cultures.

Your Task. Discuss the causes and implications of the following common mistakes made by North Americans in their negotiations with foreigners.

a. Assuming that a final agreement is set in stone
b. Lacking patience and insisting that matters progress more quickly than the pace preferred by the locals
c. Thinking that an interpreter is always completely accurate
d. Believing that individuals who speak English understand every nuance of your meaning
e. Ignoring or misunderstanding the significance of rank

4.4 *Designing a Cell Phone Manual for Low- and High-Context Cultures* (Obj. 2)

CRITICAL THINKING

Sometime in the early twenty-first century, many are predicting that China will emerge as the world's largest consumer of electronics products.[43] Well aware of this prediction, Siemens AG, a German cellular telephone manufacturer, is preparing to sell its popular German model to the Chinese. To develop the cell phone user manual, the firm conducted focus groups with Chinese and German consumers. The traditional German manual was translated into Chinese, and both German and Chinese focus groups were given nine tasks to perform using the same manual.

The focus groups produced contrasting results. When Chinese users first approach a manual, they want to see basic operations illustrated in colour on single pages with pictures. They reported having "no patience" to learn functions they might not use. They also noted that they learned to use the phone by asking friends, but if they had a problem they would never admit it to a friend. The Germans, on the other hand, wanted a manual that would present a clear but detailed overview of all the phone functions, not just basic operations. They thought that it would be useful in the long run to know all the different functions. The Germans read the words in the manual carefully, sometimes complaining when sentences were illogical or contradictory.

The Chinese preferred the "help" key to the printed manual. One said, "It gives you a very foolish feeling to use the phone at the same time you use the manual. It is ridiculous." The Chinese requested a videotape to show operations, and they also recommended that the size of the characters in the manual correlate with the importance of the information.
Your Task. Based on your knowledge of high- and low-context cultures, how do the reactions of these focus groups reflect cultural expectations? If you were the researcher in this study, would you suggest to Siemens that a totally different user manual be developed for the Chinese market? What design recommendations would you make regarding the Chinese manual?

4.5 *Analyzing a Problem International Letter* (Obj. 5)

North American writers sometimes forget that people in other countries, even if they understand English, are not aware of the meanings of certain words and phrases.
Your Task. Study the following letter[44] to be sent by a North American firm to a potential supplier in another country. Identify specific weaknesses that may cause troubles for intercultural readers.

Dear Hashi:

Because of the on-again/off-again haggling with one of our subcontractors, we have been putting off writing to you. We were royally turned off by their shoddy merchandise, the excuses they made up, and the way they put down some of our customers. Since we have our good name to keep up, we have decided to take the bull by the horns and see if you would be interested in bidding on the contract for spare parts.

By playing ball with us, your products are sure to score big. So please give it your best shot and fire off your price list ASAP. We'll need it by 3/8 if you are to be in the running.

Yours,

4.6 *Diversity Role-Playing: Hey, We're All Clones!* (Obj. 6)

Reebok International, the athletic footwear and apparel company, swelled from a $12-million-a-year company to a $3-billion footwear powerhouse in less than a decade. "When we were growing very, very fast, all we did was bring another friend into work the next day," recalls Sharon Cohen, Reebok vice president. "Everybody hired nine of their friends. Well, it happened that nine white people hired nine of their friends, so guess what? They were white, all about the same age. And then we looked up and said, 'Wait a minute. We don't like the way it looks here.'"[45] Assume you are a manager for a successful, fast-growing company like Reebok. One day you look around and notice that everyone looks alike.
Your Task. Pair off with a classmate to role-play a discussion in which you strive to convince another manager that your organization would be better if it were more diverse. The other manager (your classmate), however, is satisfied with the status quo. Suggest advantages for diversifying the staff. The opposing manager argues for homogeneity.

4.7 *Locating Diversity Training Consultants* (Obj. 6)

WEB **E-MAIL**

Management thought it was doing the right thing in diversifying its staff. But now signs of friction are appearing. Staff meetings are longer, and conflicts have arisen in solving problems. Some of the new people say they aren't taken seriously and that they are expected to blend in and become just like everybody else. A discrimination suit was filed in one department.

Your Task. CEO William Somers asks you, a human resources officer, to present suggestions for overcoming this staff problem. Make a list of several suggestions, based on what you have learned in this chapter. In addition, go to the Web and locate three individuals, teams, or firms who you think might be possibilities for developing a diversity training program for your company. Prepare a memo or an e-mail to Mr. Somers outlining your suggestions and listing your recommendations for possible diversity training consultants. Describe the areas of expertise of each potential consultant.

4.8 Searching International Publications for Business News

WEB

Your company seeks to expand its markets overseas. Your boss asks you to check three newspapers (your choice) every week to keep track of business-related events. She's interested in a variety of subjects and is always intrigued by whatever you uncover.

Your Task. Go to <**www.businessindepth.com**>, where you'll find English editions of international newspapers from many countries. Select three to five articles to summarize in a memo to your boss, Susan Plutsky. Include a short description of each newspaper.

C.L.U.E. REVIEW 4

On a separate sheet edit the following sentences to correct faults in grammar, punctuation, spelling, and word use.

1. Gifts for the children of an arab are welcome however gifts for an arabs wife are not advisible.
2. In latin america knifes are not proper gifts, they signify cutting off a relationship.
3. statistics canada reports that 1/3 of the foreign born population of canada are from: asia, the caribbean, and the middle east.
4. Although international business was all ready common among big companys we now find many smaller companys seeking global markets.
5. On April 15th an article entitled Practicle Cross-Cultural persuasion strategies appeared in The Journal of International Business.
6. 3 executives agreed that there companys overseas project with france was taking twice as long as expected.
7. They reccommend therefor that a committee study the cultural and language issues for a 3 week period, and submit a report of it's findings.
8. The three hundred represenatives were told that the simple act of presenting a bussiness card is something to which canadians give little thought but it is a serious formality in japan.
9. Each of the seventy-five delegates were charged a fee of forty dollars to attend the cultural training session although formally the charge had been only thirty dollars.
10. Both the President and Senior Vice President agrees that all staff members suggestions should be sent to: Human Relations.

Unit 2

Guffey's 3-×-3 Writing Process

CHAPTER 5

Writing Process Phase 1: Analyze, Anticipate, Adapt

CHAPTER 6

Writing Process Phase 2: Research, Organize, Compose

Writing Process Phase 3: Revise, Proofread, Evaluate

Chapter 5

Writing Process Phase 1: Analyze, Anticipate, Adapt

LEARNING OBJECTIVES

1

Identify three basics of business writing, summarize Guffey's 3-×-3 writing process, and explain how a writing process helps a writer.

2

Explain how the writing process may be altered and how it is affected by team projects.

3

Clarify what is involved in analyzing a writing task and selecting a communication channel.

4

Describe anticipating and profiling the audience for a message.

5

Specify six writing techniques that help communicators adapt messages to the task and audience.

6

Explain why communicators must adapt their writing in four high-risk areas.

APPROACHING THE WRITING PROCESS SYSTEMATICALLY

1

Preparing and writing any business message—whether a letter, e-mail, memo, or sales presentation—is easier when the writer or presenter has a systematic plan to follow.

The Basics of Business Writing

Business writing is purposeful, economical, and reader-oriented.

Business writing differs from other writing you may have done. Secondary or post-secondary compositions and term papers may have required you to describe your feelings, display your knowledge, and meet a minimum word count. Business writing, however, has different goals. In preparing business messages and oral presentations, you'll find that your writing needs to be:

- **Purposeful.** You will be writing to solve problems and convey information. You will have a definite purpose to fulfill in each message.
- **Economical.** You will try to present ideas clearly but concisely. Length is not rewarded.
- **Reader-oriented.** You will concentrate on looking at a problem from the reader's perspective instead of seeing it from your own.

Business writers seek to *express* rather than *impress*.

These distinctions actually ease the writer's task. In writing most business documents, you won't be searching your imagination for creative topic ideas. You won't be stretching your ideas to make them appear longer. Conciseness is what counts in business. Furthermore, you won't be trying to dazzle readers with your extensive knowledge, powerful vocabulary, or graceful phrasing. The goal in business writing is to *express* rather than *impress*. You will be striving to get your ideas across naturally, simply, and clearly.

In many ways business writing is easier than academic writing, yet it still requires hard work, especially from beginners. But following a process, studying models, and practising the craft can make nearly anyone a successful business writer and speaker. This book provides all three components: process, products (models), and practice. First, you'll focus on the process of writing business messages.

Guffey's 3-×-3 Writing Process for Business Messages and Oral Presentations

The phases of Guffey's 3-×-3 writing process are prewriting, writing, and revising.

This book divides the writing process into three distinct phases: prewriting, writing, and revising. As shown in Figure 5.1, each phase is further divided into three major activities. Guffey's 3-×-3 process provides you with a systematic plan for developing all your business communications, from simple memos and informational reports to corporate proposals and oral presentations.

Collecting data, organizing it, and composing a first draft make up the second phase of the writing process.

The time spent on each phase varies with the deadline, purpose, and audience for the message. The first phase (prewriting) prepares you to write and involves analyzing, anticipating, and adapting. The second phase (writing) involves researching, organizing, and then composing the message. Equipped with a plan, you're ready to compose the first draft. The third phase of the process (revising) involves revising, proofreading, and evaluating. After writing the first draft, you'll revise the message for clarity, conciseness, tone, and readability. You'll proofread carefully to ensure correct spelling, grammar, punctuation, and format. Finally, you'll evaluate the message to see whether it accomplishes your goal.

FIGURE 5.1 Guffey's 3-×-3 Writing Process

Prewriting 1

Analyze: Decide on your purpose. What do you want the receiver to do or believe? What channel is best?

Anticipate: Profile the audience. What does the receiver already know? Will the receiver's response be neutral, positive, or negative?

Adapt: What techniques can you use to adapt your message to its audience and anticipated reaction?

Writing 2

Research: Gather data to provide facts. Search company files, previous correspondence, and the Internet. What do you need to know to write this message?

Organize: Group similar facts together. Decide how to organize your information. Outline your plan and make notes.

Compose. Prepare a first draft, usually writing quickly.

Revising 3

Revise: Edit your message to be sure it is clear, conversational, concise, and readable.

Proofread: Read carefully to find errors in spelling, grammar, punctuation, names, numbers, and format.

Evaluate: Will this message achieve your purpose? Have you thought enough about the audience to be sure this message is appropriate and appealing?

2

Adapting and Altering the Writing Process

Although our diagram of the writing process shows the three phases equally, the time you spend on each varies.

In the writing process revising takes the most time.

Scheduling the Process. One expert gives these rough estimates for scheduling a project: 25 percent worrying and planning (Phase 1), 25 percent writing (Phase 2), 45 percent revising, and 5 percent proofreading (Phase 3). These are rough guides, yet you can see that good writers spend most of their time revising. Much depends, of course, on your project, its importance, and your familiarity with it. What's critical to remember, though, is that revising is a major component of the writing process.

This process may seem a bit complicated for the daily messages and oral presentations that many businesspeople prepare. Does this same process apply to memos and short letters? And how do collaborators and modern computer technologies affect the process?

Although good writers proceed through each phase of the writing process, some steps may be compressed for short, routine messages. Brief, everyday documents enlist Guffey's 3-×-3 process, but many of the steps are performed quickly, without prolonged deliberation. For example, prewriting may take the form of a few moments of reflection. The writing phase may consist of looking in the files quickly, jotting a few notes in the margin of the original document, and composing at your computer. Revising might consist of reading a printout, double-checking the spelling and grammar, and making a few changes. Longer, more involved documents—such as persuasive memos, sales letters, management reports, proposals, and résumés—require more attention to all parts of the process.

Steps in the writing process may be rearranged, shortened, or repeated.

Recursive Nature of the Process. One other point about Guffey's 3-×-3 writing process needs clarification. It may appear that you perform one step and progress to the next, always following the same order. Most business writing, however, is not that rigid. Although writers perform the tasks described, the steps may be rearranged, abbreviated, or repeated. Some writers revise every sentence and paragraph as they go. Many find that new ideas occur after they've begun to write, causing them to back up, alter the organization, and rethink their plan. You should expect to follow Guffey's 3-×-3 process closely as you begin developing your business communication skills. With experience, though, you'll become like other good writers and presenters who alter, compress, and rearrange the steps as needed.

Working With Teams. As you learned in Chapter 2, many of today's workers will spend some time working with teams to complete projects. Experts say that 40 to 50 percent of the work force will soon be working in some kind of team environment.[1] Because much of a team's work involves writing, you can expect to be putting your writing skills to work as part of a team.

Team-written documents and presentations produce better products.

When is writing collaboration necessary? It is especially important for (1) big tasks, (2) items with short deadlines, and (3) team projects that require the expertise or consensus of many people. Businesspeople sometimes collaborate on short documents, such as memos, letters, information briefs, procedures, and policies. But more often, teams work together on big documents and presentations.

Team-written documents and presentations are standard in most organizations because collaboration has many advantages. Most important, collaboration produces a better product. Many heads are better than one. In addition, team members and organizations benefit from team processes. Working together helps socialize members. They learn more about the organization's values and procedures. They are able to break down functional barriers, and they improve both formal and informal chains of communication. Additionally, they "buy into" a project when they are part of its development. Members of effective teams are eager to implement their recommendations.

Team-written projects are necessary for big tasks, jobs with short deadlines, and projects that require the expertise or consensus of many people. Team members generally work together to brainstorm and make assignments, but they work separately to do the writing.

In preparing big projects, teams may not actually function together for each phase of the writing process. Typically, team members gather at the beginning to brainstorm. They iron out answers to questions about the purpose, audience, content, organization, and design of their document or presentation. They develop procedures for team functioning, as you learned in Chapter 2. Then, they often assign segments of the project to individual members. Thus, teams work together closely in Phase 1 (prewriting) of the writing process. However, members generally work separately in Phase 2 (writing), when they conduct research, organize their findings, and compose a first draft. During Phase 3 (revising) teams may work together to synthesize their drafts and offer suggestions for revision. They might assign one person the task of preparing the final document and another the job of proofreading. The revision and evaluation phase might be repeated several times before the final product is ready for presentation.

One of the most frustrating tasks for teams is writing shared documents. Keeping the different versions straight and recognizing who made what comment can be confusing. Microsoft Word, however, provides a number of wonderful tools that enable team members to track changes and insert comments while editing one team document. The following Tech Talk box presents these tools.

WRITING PROCESS PHASE 1: ANALYZE

Whether you're writing with a team, composing by yourself, or preparing an oral presentation, the product of your efforts can be improved by following the steps described in Guffey's 3-×-3 writing process. Not only are you more likely to get your message across, but you'll feel less anxious and your writing will progress more quickly. The remainder of this chapter concentrates on the prewriting phase of composition: analyzing, anticipating, and adapting.

TECH TALK

Using Technology to Edit and Revise Collaborative Documents

Collaborative writing and editing projects are challenging. Fortunately, Microsoft Word offers many useful tools to help team members edit and share documents electronically. Two simple but useful editing tools are *Highlight* and *Font Colour*. These tools, which are found on the **Formatting** toolbar, enable reviewers to point out errors and explain problematic passages through the use of contrast. However, some projects may require more advanced editing tools such as *Track Changes* and *Insert Comments*.

Track Changes. To suggest specific editing changes to other team members, *Track Changes* is handy. The revised wording is visible on-screen, and deletions show up in call-out balloons that appear in the right-hand margin. Suggested revisions offered by different team members are identified and dated. The original writer may accept or reject these changes. In recent versions of Word, you'll find *Track Changes* on the **Tools** menu.

Insert Comments. Probably the most useful editing tool is *Insert Comments*. This tool allows users to point out problematic passages or errors, ask or answer questions, and share ideas without changing or adding text. When additional people add comments, the comments appear in different colours and are identified by the individual writer's name and a date/time stamp. To use this tool in newer versions of Word, each reviewer must click **Tools, Options,** and fill in the **User Information** section. In older versions of Word, this collaborative tool was called *Annotation*. To facilitate adding, reviewing, editing, or deleting comments, Word now provides a special toolbar. You can activate it by using the **View** pull-down menu (click **Toolbars** and **Reviewing**). On the **Reviewing** toolbar, click **New Comment.** Then type your comment, which can be seen in the web or print layout view (click **View** and **Print Layout** or **Web Layout**).

In analyzing the composition task, you'll first need to identify the purpose of the message and select the best channel or form in which to deliver it.

Identifying Your Purpose

As you begin to compose a message, ask yourself two important questions: (1) Why am I sending this message? and (2) What do I hope to achieve? Your responses will determine how you organize and present your information.

Your message may have primary and secondary purposes. For academic work your primary purpose may be merely to complete the assignment; secondary purposes might be to make yourself look good and to get a good grade. The primary purposes for sending business messages are typically to inform and to persuade. A secondary purpose is to promote goodwill: you and your organization want to look good in the eyes of your audience.

Most business communication has both primary purposes (to inform or persuade) and secondary purposes (to promote goodwill).

Most business messages do nothing more than *inform*. They explain procedures, announce meetings, answer questions, and transmit findings. Some business messages, however, are meant to *persuade*. These messages sell products, convince managers, motivate employees, and win over customers. Informative messages are developed differently than persuasive messages.

Selecting the Best Channel

After identifying the purpose of your message, you need to select the most appropriate communication channel. As you learned in Chapter 1, some information is most efficiently and effectively delivered orally. Other messages should be written, and still others are best delivered electronically. Whether to set up a meeting, send a message by e-mail, or write a report depends on some of the following factors:

- Importance of the message
- Amount and speed of feedback required
- Necessity of a permanent record
- Cost of the channel
- Degree of formality desired

The foregoing factors could help you decide which of the channels shown in Figure 5.2 is most appropriate for delivering a message.

FIGURE 5.2 Choosing Communication Channels

Channel	Best Use
Face-to-face conversation	When you want to be persuasive, deliver bad news, or share a personal message.
Telephone call	When you need to deliver or gather information quickly, when nonverbal cues are unimportant, and when you cannot meet in person.
Voice mail message	When you wish to leave important or routine information that the receiver can respond to when convenient.
Fax	When your message must cross time zones or international boundaries, when a written record is significant, or when speed is important.
E-mail	When you need feedback but not immediately. Lack of security makes it problematic for personal, emotional, or private messages. Effective for communicating with a large, dispersed audience.
Face-to-face group meeting	When group decisions and consensus are important. Inefficient for merely distributing information.
Video or teleconference	When group consensus and interaction are important, but members are geographically dispersed.
Memo	When you want a written record to clearly explain policies, discuss procedures, or collect information within an organization.
Letter	When you need a written record of correspondence with customers, the government, suppliers, or others outside an organization.
Report or proposal	When you are delivering complex data internally or externally.

Choosing the best channel to deliver a message depends on the importance of the message, the feedback required, the need for a permanent record, the cost, and the degree of formality needed.

WRITING PROCESS PHASE 1: ANTICIPATE

Some messages miss the mark. A good writer anticipates the audience for a message: What is the reader like? How will that reader react to the message? Although you can't always know exactly who the reader is, you can imagine some characteristics of the reader. Picturing a typical reader is important in guiding what you write. By profiling your audience and shaping a message to respond to that profile, you are more likely to achieve your communication goals.

Profiling the Audience

By profiling your audience before you write, you can identify the appropriate tone, language, and channel.

Visualizing your audience is a pivotal step in the writing process. The questions in Figure 5.3 will help you profile your audience. How much time you devote to answering these questions depends greatly on your message and its context. No matter how short your message, though, spend some time thinking about the audience so that you can tailor your words to your readers or listeners. "The most often unasked question in business and professional communication," claims a writing expert, "is as simple as it is important: *Have I thought enough about my audience?*"[2]

Responding to the Profile

Anticipating your audience helps you make decisions about shaping the message. You'll discover what kind of language is appropriate, whether you're free to use specialized technical terms, whether you should explain everything, and so on. You'll decide whether your tone should be formal or informal, and you'll select the most desirable channel. Imagining whether the receiver is likely to be neutral, positive, or negative will help you determine how to organize your message.

Another result of profiling your audience will be knowing whether a secondary audience is possible. If so, you'll provide more background information and be more specific in identifying items than would be necessary for the primary audience only.

FIGURE 5.3 Asking the Right Questions to Profile Your Audience

Primary Audience	Secondary Audience
Who is my primary reader or listener?	Who might see or hear this message in addition to the primary audience?
What is my personal and professional relationship with that person?	How do these people differ from the primary audience?
What position does the individual hold in the organization?	
How much does that person know about the subject?	
What do I know about that person's education, beliefs, culture, and attitudes?	
Should I expect a neutral, positive, or negative response to my message?	

Analyzing the task and anticipating the audience assists you in adapting your message so that it will accomplish what you intend.

WRITING PROCESS PHASE 1: ADAPT

After analyzing your purpose and anticipating your audience, you must convey your purpose to that audience. Adaptation is the process of creating a message that suits your audience.

5

One important aspect of adaptation is *tone*. Conveyed largely by the words in a message, tone reflects how a receiver feels upon reading or hearing a message. For example, think how you would react to these statements:

You must return the form by 5 p.m.

Would you please return the form by 5 p.m.

Ways to adapt to the audience include choosing the right words and tone, spotlighting reader benefits, cultivating a "you" attitude, and using sensitive, courteous language.

The wording of the first message establishes an aggressive or negative tone—no one likes being told what to do. The second message is reworded in a friendlier, more positive manner. Poorly chosen words may sound demeaning, condescending, discourteous, pretentious, or demanding.

Skilled communicators create a positive tone in their messages by using a number of adaptive techniques, some of which are unconscious. These include spotlighting receiver benefits; cultivating a "you" attitude; and avoiding gender, racial, age, and disability bias. Additional adaptive techniques include being courteous, using familiar words, and choosing precise words.

Spotlighting Receiver Benefits

Empathic communicators envision the receiver and focus on benefits to that person.

Focusing on the audience is a fundamental guideline for today's business communicators. A communication consultant gives this solid advice to his business clients: "Always stress the benefit to the readers of whatever it is you're trying to get them to do. If you can show them how you're going to save *them* frustration or help them meet their goals, you have the makings of a powerful message."[3]

***Empathy* means trying to understand another's situation, feelings, and motives.**

Adapting your message to the receiver's needs means putting yourself in that person's shoes. It's called *empathy*. Empathic senders think about how a receiver will decode a message. They try to give something to the receiver, solve the receiver's problems, save the receiver's money, or just understand the feelings and position of that person. Which of the following messages are more appealing to the receiver?

Sender-Focused	**Receiver-Focused**
To enable us to update our shareholder records, we ask that the enclosed card be returned.	So that you may promptly receive dividend cheques and information related to your shares, please return the enclosed card.
We offer a CD language course in which we have complete faith.	The sooner you order the CD language program, the sooner the rewards will be yours.

Cultivating the "You" View

Notice how many of the previous receiver-focused messages included the word *you*. In concentrating on receiver benefits, skilled communicators naturally develop the "you" view. They emphasize second-person pronouns (*you, your*) instead of

Effective communicators develop the "you" view in a sincere, not manipulative or critical, tone.

first-person pronouns (*I/we, us, our*). Whether your goal is to inform, persuade, or promote goodwill, the catchiest words you can use are *you* and *your*. Compare the following examples.

"I/We" View	**"You" View**
I have scheduled your vacation to begin May 1.	You may begin your vacation May 1.
"I/We" View	**"You" View**
We have shipped your order by FedEx, and we are sure it will arrive in time for the sales promotion January 15.	Your order will be delivered by FedEx in time for your sales promotion January 15.

Avoid overusing *you* or including it when it suggests blame.

Your goal is to focus on the reader, but second-person pronouns can be overused and misused. Readers appreciate genuine interest; on the other hand, they resent obvious attempts at manipulation. Some sales messages, for example, are guilty of overkill when they include *you* dozens of times in a direct-mail promotion. Furthermore, the word can sometimes create the wrong impression. Consider this statement: *You cannot return merchandise until you receive written approval. You* appears twice, but the reader feels singled out for criticism. In the following version the message is less personal and more positive: *Customers may return merchandise with written approval.* In short, avoid using *you* for general statements that suggest blame and could cause ill will.

In recognizing the value of the "you" attitude, however, writers do not have to sterilize their writing and avoid any first-person pronouns or words that show their feelings. Skilled communicators are able to convey sincerity, warmth, and enthusiasm by the words they choose. Don't be afraid to use phrases such as *I'm happy* or *We're delighted*, if you truly are.

When speaking face to face, communicators show sincerity and warmth with nonverbal cues such as a smile and pleasant voice tone. In letters, memos, and e-mail messages, however, only expressive words and phrases can show these feelings. These phrases suggest hidden messages that say to readers and customers "You are important, I hear you, and I'm honestly trying to please you."

Using Bias-Free Language

In adapting a message to its audience, be sure your language is sensitive and bias-free. Few writers set out to be offensive. Sometimes, though, we all say things that we never thought might be hurtful. The real problem is that we don't think about the words that stereotype groups of people, such as *the boys in the mailroom* or *the girls in the front office.* Be cautious about expressions that might be biased in terms of gender, race, ethnicity, age, and disability.[4]

Avoiding Gender Bias. You can defuse gender time bombs by replacing words that exclude or stereotype women (sometimes called *sexist language*) with neutral, inclusive expressions. The following examples show how sexist terms and phrases can be replaced with neutral ones.

Gender-Biased	Improved
female doctor, woman lawyer, cleaning woman	doctor, lawyer, cleaner
waiter/waitress, authoress, stewardess	server, author, cabin attendant
mankind, man-hour, man-made	humanity, working hours, artificial
office girls	office workers
the doctor . . . he	doctors . . . they
the teacher . . . she	teachers . . . they
executives and their wives	executives and their spouses
foreman, flagman, workman	lead worker, flagger, worker
businessman, salesman	businessperson, sales representative
Each worker had his picture taken.	Each worker had a picture taken. All workers had their pictures taken. Each worker had his or her picture taken.

Generally, you can avoid gender-biased language by leaving out the words *man* or *woman*, by using plural nouns and pronouns, or by changing to a gender-free word (*person* or *representative*). Avoid the "his or her" option whenever possible. It's wordy and conspicuous. With a little effort, you can usually find a construction that is graceful, grammatical, and generic.

Avoiding Racial or Ethnic Bias. You need indicate racial or ethnic identification only if the context demands it.

Racially or Ethnically Biased	Improved
An Indian accountant was hired.	An accountant was hired.
James Lee, a Native Canadian, applied.	James Lee applied.

Avoiding Age Bias. Again, specify age only if it is relevant, and avoid expressions that are demeaning or subjective.

Age-Biased	Improved
The law applied to old people.	The law applied to people over 65.
Sally Kay, 55, was transferred.	Sally Kay was transferred.
a spry old gentleman	a man
a little old lady	a woman

Avoiding Disability Bias. Unless relevant, do not refer to an individual's disability. When necessary, use terms that do not stigmatize disabled individuals.

Disability-Biased	Improved
afflicted with, suffering from, crippled by	has
defect, disease	condition
confined to a wheelchair	uses a wheelchair

The preceding examples give you a quick look at a few problem expressions. The real key to bias-free communication, though, lies in your awareness and commitment. Always be on the lookout to be sure that your messages do not exclude, stereotype, or offend people.

Expressing Yourself Positively

Certain negative words create ill will because they appear to blame or accuse readers. For example, opening a letter to a customer with *You claim that* suggests that you don't believe the customer. Other loaded words that can get you in trouble are *complaint, criticism, defective, failed, mistake,* and *neglected.* Often the writer is unconscious of the effect of these words. To avoid angry reactions, restrict negative words and try to find positive ways to express ideas. You provide more options to the reader when you tell what can be done instead of what can't be done.

Positive language creates goodwill and gives more options to readers.

Negative	Positive
You failed to include your credit card number, so we can't mail your order.	We'll mail your order as soon as we receive your credit card number.
You won't be sorry that	You will be happy that . . . .
The problem cannot be solved without the aid of top management.	With the aid of top management, the problem can be solved.

Being Courteous

Maintaining a courteous tone involves not just guarding against rudeness but also avoiding words that sound demanding or preachy. Expressions like *you should, you must,* and *you have to* cause people to instinctively react with "Oh, yeah?" One remedy is to turn these demands into rhetorical questions that begin with *Will you please* . . . . Giving reasons for a request also softens the tone.

Less Courteous	More Courteous
You must complete this report before Friday.	Will you please complete the report by Friday.
You should organize a car pool in this department.	Organizing a car pool will reduce your transportation costs and help preserve the environment.

Even when you feel justified in displaying anger, remember that losing your temper or being sarcastic will seldom accomplish your goals as a business communicator to inform, to persuade, and to create goodwill. When you are irritated, frustrated, or infuriated, keep cool and try to defuse the situation. Concentrate on the real problem. What must be done to solve it?

Negative expressions can often be rephrased to sound positive.

You May Be Thinking This	Better to Say This
This is the second time I've written. Can't you get anything right?	Please credit my account for $843. My latest statement shows that the error noted in my letter of June 2 has not been corrected.

Am I the only one who can read the operating manual?	Let's review the operating manual together so that you can get your documents to print correctly next time.

Simplifying Your Language

In adapting your message to your audience, whenever possible use short, familiar words that you think readers will recognize. Don't, however, avoid a big word that conveys your idea efficiently and is appropriate for the audience. Your goal is to shun pompous and pretentious language. Instead, use "GO" words. If you mean *begin*, don't say *commence* or *initiate*. If you mean *give*, don't write *render*.[5] By substituting everyday, familiar words for unfamiliar ones, as shown in the following list, you help your audience comprehend your ideas quickly.

Unfamiliar	**Familiar**
commensurate	equal
conceptualization	idea
interrogate	question
materialize	appear
remunerate	pay
terminate	end

At the same time, be selective in your use of jargon. *Jargon* describes technical or specialized terms within a field. These terms enable insiders to communicate complex ideas briefly, but to outsiders they mean nothing. Human resources professionals, for example, know precisely what's meant by *cafeteria plan* (a benefits option program), but most of us would be thinking about lunch. Geologists refer to *plate tectonics*, and physicians discuss *metastatic carcinomas*, but these terms mean little to most of us. Use specialized language only when the audience will understand it. And don't forget to consider secondary audiences: Will those potential readers understand any technical terms used?

Using Precise, Vigorous Words

Using familiar but precise language helps receivers understand.

Strong verbs and concrete nouns give readers more information and keep them interested. Don't overlook the thesaurus (or the thesaurus program on your computer) for expanding your word choices and vocabulary. Whenever possible, use specific words as shown here.

Imprecise, Dull	**More Precise**
a change in profits	a 10 percent plunge in profits
a jump in profits	a 23 percent hike in profits
to think about	to identify, diagnose, analyze to probe, examine, inspect
to say	to promise, confess, understand to allege, assert, assume

By reviewing the tips in the following checklist, you can master the steps of writing preparation. As you review these tips, remember the three basics of prewriting: analyzing, anticipating, and adapting.

CHECKLIST FOR ADAPTING A MESSAGE TO ITS AUDIENCE

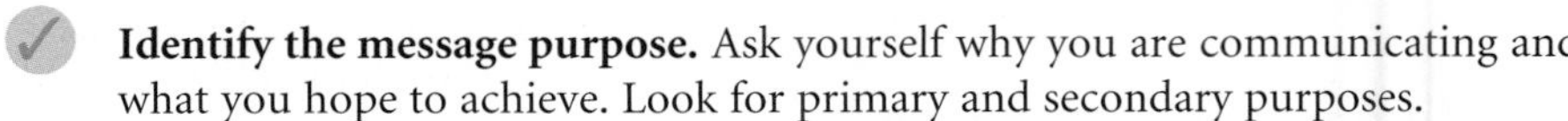

- **Identify the message purpose.** Ask yourself why you are communicating and what you hope to achieve. Look for primary and secondary purposes.

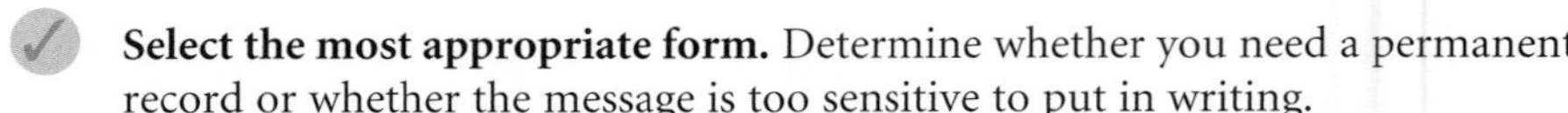

- **Select the most appropriate form.** Determine whether you need a permanent record or whether the message is too sensitive to put in writing.

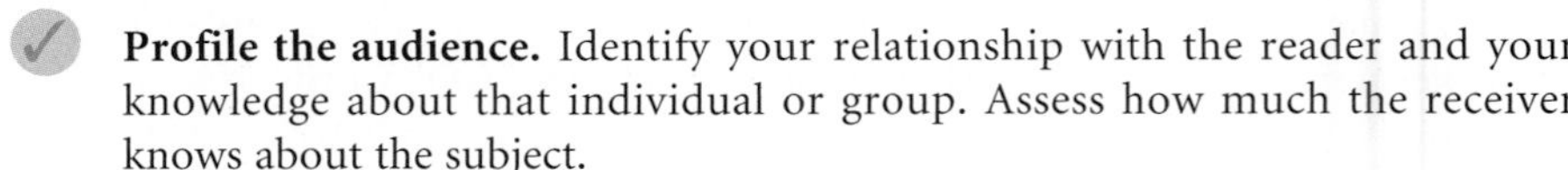

- **Profile the audience.** Identify your relationship with the reader and your knowledge about that individual or group. Assess how much the receiver knows about the subject.
- **Focus on reader benefits.** Phrase your statements from the reader's viewpoint, not the writer's. Concentrate on the "you" view (*Your order will arrive, You can enjoy, Your ideas count*).
- **Avoid gender and racial bias.** Use bias-free words (*businessperson* instead of *businessman*; *working hours* instead of *man-hours*). Omit ethnic identification unless the context demands it.
- **Avoid age and disability bias.** Include age only if relevant. Avoid potentially demeaning expressions (*spry old gentleman*), and use terms that do not stigmatize disabled people (*he is disabled* instead of *he is a cripple* or *he has a handicap*).
- **Express ideas positively rather than negatively.** Instead of *Your order can't be shipped before June 1*, say *Your order can be shipped June 1.*
- **Use short, familiar words.** Use technical terms and big words only if they are appropriate for the audience (*end* not *terminate*, *required* not *mandatory*).
- **Search for precise, vigorous words.** Use a thesaurus if necessary to find strong verbs and concrete nouns (*announces* instead of *says*, *brokerage* instead of *business*).

ADAPTING TO LEGAL RESPONSIBILITIES

6

One of your primary responsibilities in writing for an organization or for yourself is to avoid language that may land you in court. In our current business environment, lawsuits abound, many of which centre on the use and abuse of language. You can protect yourself and avoid litigation by knowing what's legal and by adapting your language accordingly. Be especially careful when communicating in the following four areas: investments, safety, marketing, and human resources. Because these information areas generate the most lawsuits, we will examine them more closely.[6]

Careful communicators should familiarize themselves with information in four information areas: investments, safety, marketing, and human resources.

Investment Information

Writers describing the sale of stocks or financial services must follow specific laws written to protect investors. Any messages—including letters, newsletters, and pamphlets—must be free from misleading information, exaggerations, and half-truths. Experienced financial writers know that careless language and even poor timing may provoke litigation.

Safety Information

Writers describing potentially dangerous products worry not only about protecting people from physical harm but also about being sued. Although there are far fewer product liability cases filed in Canada than in the United States,[7] litigation arising from these cases is an active area of tort law (tort law involves compensating those who have been injured by the wrongdoing of others).[8] Under the law of product liability, a manufacturer is responsible to those injured by a product with a defect caused by either the manufacturing process or the product's design.[9] Manufacturers are obligated to warn consumers of any risks in their products. These warnings must do more than suggest danger; they must also clearly tell people how to use the product safely. In writing warnings, concentrate on major points. Omit anything that is not critical. In the work area describe a potential problem and tell how to solve it. For example, *Lead dust is harmful and gets on your clothes. Change your clothes before leaving work.*

Warnings on dangerous products must be written especially clearly.

Clearly written safety messages use easy-to-understand words, such as *doctor* instead of *physician*, *clean* instead of *sanitary*, and *burn* instead of *incinerate*. Technical terms are defined. For example, *Asbestos is a carcinogen (something that causes cancer).*[10] Effective safety messages also include highlighting techniques, such as using headings and bullets. In coming chapters you'll learn more about these techniques for improving readability.

Marketing Information

Sales and marketing messages are illegal if they falsely advertise prices, performance capability, quality, or other product characteristics. Marketing messages must not deceive the buyer in any way. According to Canada's Competition Bureau, "misleading advertising occurs when representation is made to the public that is materially misleading."[11] If the consumer purchases the product or service based on the advertising, it is material. To determine whether an advertisement is misleading, the courts consider the "general impression" it conveys as well as the literal meaning.[12] Sellers of services must also be cautious about the language they use to describe what they will do. Letters, reports, and proposals that describe services to be performed are interpreted as contracts in court. Therefore, the language must not promise more than intended. Here are some dangerous words (and recommended alternatives) that have created misunderstandings leading to lawsuits.[13]

Sales and marketing messages must not make claims that can't be verified.

Dangerous Word	Court Interpretation	Recommended Alternative
inspect	to examine critically, to investigate and test officially, to scrutinize	to review, to study, to tour the facility
determine	to come to a decision, to decide, to resolve	to evaluate, to assess, to analyze

Human Resources Information

The vast number of lawsuits relating to employment makes this a treacherous area for business communicators. In evaluating employees in the workplace, avoid making unsubstantiated negative comments. It's also unwise to assess traits (*she is unreliable*) because they require subjective judgment. Concentrate instead on specific incidents (*in the last month she missed four work days and was late three times*). Defamation lawsuits have become so common that some companies no longer provide letters of recommendation for former employees. To be safe, give recommendations only when the former employee authorizes the recommendation and when you can say something positive. Stick to job-related information.

The safest employment recommendations contain positive, job-related information.

Statements in employee handbooks also require careful wording, because a court might rule that such statements are "implied contracts." Companies are warned to avoid promissory phrases in writing job advertisements, application forms, and offer letters. Phrases that suggest permanent employment and guaranteed job security can be interpreted as contracts.[14]

In adapting messages to meet today's litigious business environment, be sensitive to the rights of others and to your own rights. The key elements in this adaptation process are awareness of laws, sensitivity to interpretations, and careful use of language.

SUMMARY OF LEARNING OBJECTIVES

1 **Identify three basics of business writing, summarize the three phases of Guffey's 3-×-3 writing process, and explain how a writing process helps a writer.** Business writing differs from academic writing in that it strives to solve business problems, it is economical, and it is reader-oriented. Phase 1 of the writing process (prewriting) involves analyzing the message, anticipating the audience, and considering ways to adapt the message to the audience. Phase 2 (writing) involves researching the topic, organizing the material, and composing the message. Phase 3 (revising) includes proofreading and evaluating the message.

2 **Explain how the writing process may be altered and how it is affected by team projects.** The writing process may be compressed for short messages; steps in the process may be rearranged. Team writing, which is necessary for large projects or when wide expertise is necessary, alters the writing process. Teams often work together in brainstorming and working out their procedures and assignments. Then individual members write their portions of the report or presentation during Phase 2. During Phase 3 (revising) teams may work together to combine their drafts. Collaboration software helps teams working on shared documents.

3 **Clarify what is involved in analyzing a writing task and selecting a communication channel.** Communicators must decide why they are delivering a message and what they hope to achieve. Although many messages only inform, some must also persuade. After identifying the purpose of a message, communicators must choose the most appropriate channel. That choice depends on the importance of the message, the amount and speed of feedback required, the need for a permanent record, the cost of the channel, and the degree of formality desired.

4 **Describe anticipating and profiling the audience for a message.** A good communicator tries to envision the audience for a message. What does the receiver know about the topic? How well does the receiver know the sender? What is known about the receiver's education, beliefs, culture, and attitudes? Will the response to the message be positive, neutral, or negative? Is the secondary audience different from the primary audience?

5 **Specify six writing techniques that help communicators adapt messages to the task and audience.** Skilled communicators strive to (a) spotlight reader benefits; (b) look at a message from the receiver's perspective (the "you" view); (c) use sensitive language that avoids gender, racial, ethnic, and disability

biases; (d) state ideas positively; (e) show courtesy; and (f) use short, familiar, and precise words.

6 **Explain why communicators must adapt their writing in four high-risk areas.** Actions and language in four information areas generate the most lawsuits: investments, safety, marketing, and human resources. In writing about investments, communicators must avoid misleading information, exaggerations, and half-truths. Safety information, including warnings, must tell people clearly how to use a product safely and motivate them to do so. In addition to being honest, marketing information must not promise more than intended. And communicators in the area of human resources must use careful wording (particularly in employment recommendations and employee handbooks) to avoid potential lawsuits.

CHAPTER REVIEW

1. Explain how business writing differs from writing academic essays and term papers. (Obj. 1)
2. Describe the components in each stage of Guffey's 3-×-3 writing process. (Obj. 1)
3. List five factors to consider when selecting a communication channel. (Obj. 3)
4. Why should you "profile" your audience before composing a message? (Obj. 4)
5. What is *empathy*, and how does it apply to business writing? (Obj. 5)
6. Discuss the effects of first- and second-person pronouns. (Obj. 5)
7. What is bias-free language? Give examples. (Obj. 5)
8. What is *jargon*, and when is it appropriate for business writing? (Obj. 5)
9. What's wrong with using words such as *commence, mandate,* and *interrogate*? (Obj. 5)
10. What four information areas generate the most lawsuits? (Obj. 6)
11. How can business communicators protect themselves against litigation? (Obj. 6)

CRITICAL THINKING

1. Business communicators are encouraged to profile or "visualize" the audience for their messages. How is this possible if you don't really know the people who will receive a sales letter or who will hear your business presentation? (Obj. 4)
2. How can Guffey's 3-×-3 writing process help the writer of a business report as well as the writer of an oral presentation? (Obj. 1)
3. If adapting your tone to the receiving audience and developing reader benefits are so important, why do we see so much writing that does not reflect these suggestions? (Objs. 3–5)
4. Discuss the following statement: "The English language is a landmine—it is filled with terms that are easily misinterpreted as derogatory and others that are blatantly insulting. . . . Being fair and objective is not enough; employers must also appear to be so."[15] (Obj. 5)

ACTIVITIES

5.1 Document for Analysis (Obj. 5)

Your Task. Discuss the following memo, which is based on an actual document sent to employees. How can you apply what you learned in this chapter to improving this memo? Revise the memo to make it more courteous, positive, and precise. Focus on developing the "you" view and using familiar language. Remove any gender-biased references.

TO: All Employees Using HP 5000 Computers

It has recently come to my attention that a computer security problem exists within our organization. I understand that the problem is twofold in nature:

a. You have been sharing computer passwords.
b. You are using automatic log-on procedures.

Henceforth, you are prohibited from sharing passwords for security reasons that should be axiomatic. We also must forbid you to use automatic log-on files because they empower anyone to have access to our entire computer system and all company data.

5.2 Selecting Communication Channels (Obj. 3)

Your Task. Using Figure 5.2, suggest the best communication channels for the following messages. Assume that all channels shown are available. Be prepared to explain your choices.

a. You need to know whether Elizabeth in Reprographics can produce a special brochure for your department within two days.
b. A prospective client in Italy wants price quotes for a number of your products—pronto!
c. As assistant to the vice president, you are to investigate the possibility of developing internship programs with several nearby colleges and universities.
d. As manager, you must inform an employee that continued tardiness is jeopardizing her job.
e. As department manager, you need to inform nine staff members of a safety training session scheduled for the following month.

5.3 Analyzing Audiences (Obj. 4)

Your Task. Using the questions in Figure 5.3, write a brief analysis of the audience for each of the following communication tasks.

a. An e-mail memo to your district sales manager describing your visit to a new customer who demands special discounts.
b. A letter of application for a job advertised in your local newspaper. Your qualifications match the job description.
c. An e-mail memo to your boss persuading her to allow you to attend a computer class that will require you to leave work early two days a week for ten weeks.
d. An unsolicited sales letter promoting life insurance to a targeted group of executives.

e. A letter from the municipal water department explaining that the tap water may taste and smell bad; however, it poses no threats to health.

5.4 Reader Benefits and the "You" View (Obj. 5)

Your Task. Revise the following sentences to emphasize the reader's perspective and the "you" view.

a. To help us expand and grow our business, we are proud to announce that videoconferencing is now available at 125 of our branches.
b. To prevent us from possibly losing large sums of money, our bank now requires verification of any large cheque presented for immediate payment.
c. So that we may bring our customer records up-to-date and eliminate the expense of duplicate mailings, we are asking you to complete the enclosed card.
d. We're requesting all employees to complete the enclosed questionnaire so that we may develop a master schedule for summer vacations.
e. I think my background and my education match the description of the manager trainee position you advertised.

5.5 Language Bias (Obj. 5)

Your Task. Revise the following sentences to eliminate gender, racial, age, and disability stereotypes.

a. How many man-hours will the project require?
b. James is afflicted with arthritis, but his crippling rarely interferes with his work.
c. Debbie Sanchez, 24, was hired; Tony Morris, 57, was promoted.
d. All conference participants and their wives are invited to the banquet.
e. Our company encourages the employment of handicapped people.

5.6 Positive Expression (Obj. 5)

Your Task. Revise the following statements to make them more positive.

a. Because of a mistake in its address, your letter did not arrive until January 3.
b. In response to your e-mail complaint, we are investigating our agent's poor behaviour.
c. It is impossible to move forward without community support.
d. Customers are ineligible for the 10 percent discount unless they show their membership cards.
e. You won't be disappointed with the many electronic services we now offer.

5.7 Courteous Expression (Obj. 5)

Your Task. Revise the following messages to show greater courtesy.

a. We will be forced to deactivate your debit card if you don't call this 800 number immediately to activate it.
b. This is the last time I'm writing to try to get you to record my January 6 payment of $500 to my account. Anyone who can read can see from the attached documents that I've tried to explain this to you before.
c. As manager of your department, you will have to get your employees to use the correct forms.
d. To the Staff: Can't anyone around here read instructions? Page 12 of the operating manual for our copy machine very clearly describes how to remove jammed paper. But I'm the only one who ever does it, and I've had it! No more copies will be made until you learn how to remove jammed paper.
e. If you had listened to our agent more carefully, you would know that your policy does not cover accidents outside Canada.

5.8 Familiar Words (Obj. 5)

Your Task. Revise the following sentences to avoid unfamiliar words.

a. The salary we are offering is commensurate with other managers' remuneration.
b. To expedite ratification of this agreement, we urge you to vote in the affirmative.
c. In a dialogue with the manager, I learned that you plan to terminate our agreement.
d. Did the steering problem materialize subsequent to our recall effort?
e. Pursuant to your invitation, we will interrogate our manager.

5.9 Precise Words (Obj. 5)

Your Task. From the choices in parentheses, select the most precise, vigorous words.

a. When replying to e-mail, *(bring in, include, put)* enough of the old message for *(someone, the person, the recipient)* to recognize the original note.
b. For a *(hard, long, complicated)* e-mail message, *(make, create, have)* the note in your word processing program.
c. If an e-mail *(thing, catch, glitch)* interferes while writing, you can easily *(get, have, retrieve)* your message.
d. We plan to *(acknowledge, publicize, applaud)* the work of exemplary employees.
e. Ryan's excellent report has *(a lot of, many, a warehouse of)* relevant facts.

For the following sentences provide more precise alternatives for the italicized words.

f. In her e-mail memo she said that she would (a) *change* overtime hours in order to (b) *fix* the budget.
g. Our new manager (a) *said* that only (b) *the right kind of* applicants should apply.
h. After (a) *reading* the report, I decided it was (b) *bad.*
i. Rebecca said the movie was (a) *different,* but her remarks weren't very (b) *clear* to us.
j. I'm (a) *going* to Moncton tomorrow, and I plan to (b) *find out* the real problem.

5.10 Legal Language (Obj. 6)

Your Task. To avoid possible litigation, revise the italicized words in the following sentences taken from proposals.

a. We will *inspect* the building plans before construction begins.
b. Our goal is to *assure* completion of the project on schedule.
c. We will *determine* the amount of stress for each supporting column.

5.11 Is Instant Messaging a Valid Business Channel Choice? (Obj. 3)

INFOTRAC

Should instant messaging become one of the accepted communication channels for business? Once "dismissed as a toy for teenagers and lonely hearts," instant messaging is making its way into the office.

Your Task. Using InfoTrac, conduct a keyword search for "instant messaging." Find David LaGesse's article "Instant Message Phenom Is, Like, Way Beyond E-mail," *U.S. News & World Report,* 5 March 2001, Article No. A70910699.

a. How many users are estimated to be sending instant messages by 2004?
b. What are the advantages to instant messages for businesspeople?
c. What are the disadvantages?

C.L.U.E. REVIEW 5

On a separate sheet edit the following sentences to correct faults in grammar, punctuation, spelling, and word use.

1. If I was you I would memorize the following three parts of the writing process; prewriting writing and revising.
2. A writers time is usualy spent as follows; twenty-five percent worrying, twenty-five percent writing, forty-five percent revising and five percent proofreading.
3. At least 4 or 5 members of our team will probaly attend the meeting scheduled with our company Vice President at three p.m. on Tuesday March 4th.
4. Were not asking the team to altar it's proposal we are asking team members to check the proposals figures.
5. A writer may use computer software to fight writers block as well as to help him collect information electronically.
6. Will you please fax me a list of all independant pubishers names and addresses?
7. A writer has many communication channels from which to chose, therefore he should choose carefully.
8. Over two hundred fifty years ago one of Canada's founding fathers recognized a fundamental writing principal.
9. If you are trying to persuade someone be sure that your proposal and request is benificial to him.
10. By substituting every day familiar words for unfamilar ones you can make you audience comprehend your ideas more quicker.

Chapter 6

Writing Process Phase 2: Research, Organize, Compose

LEARNING OBJECTIVES

1. *Apply Phase 2 of Guffey's 3-×-3 writing process, which begins with formal and informal methods for researching data and generating ideas.*

2. *Specify how to organize data into lists and alphanumeric or decimal outlines.*

3. *Compare direct and indirect patterns for organizing ideas.*

4. *Discuss composing the first draft of a message, focusing on techniques for creating effective sentences.*

5. *Define a paragraph and describe three classic paragraph plans and techniques for composing meaningful paragraphs.*

WRITING PROCESS PHASE 2: RESEARCH

1 Business communicators face daily challenges that require data collection, idea generation, and concept organization. These activities are part of the second phase of the writing process, which includes researching, organizing, and composing.

No smart businessperson would begin writing a message before collecting all the needed information. We call this collection process *research*, a rather formal-sounding term. For simple documents, though, the procedure can be quite informal. Research is necessary before beginning to write because the information you collect helps shape the message. Discovering significant data after a message is half-completed often means starting over and reorganizing. To avoid frustration and inaccurate messages, collect information that answers a primary question:

Before writing, conduct formal or informal research to collect or generate necessary data.

- *What does the receiver need to know about this topic?*

When the message involves action, search for answers to secondary questions:

- *What is the receiver to do?*
- *How is the receiver to do it?*
- *When must the receiver do it?*
- *What will happen if the receiver doesn't do it?*

Whenever your communication problem requires more information than you have in your head or at your fingertips, you must conduct research. This research may be formal or informal.

Formal Research Methods

Formal research may involve searching electronic databases and libraries or investigating primary sources (interviews, surveys, and experimentation).

Long reports and complex business problems generally require some use of formal research methods. To conduct formal research, you could:

- **Access electronically.** Like other facets of life, the research process has been changed considerably by the computer. Most businesspeople begin any research process by seeing what they can find electronically. Much of the current printed material is now available from the Internet, databases, or CDs that can be accessed by computer. Database providers, such as the InfoTrac service that comes with this textbook, enable you to search millions of magazine, newspaper, and journal articles. The Internet also provides a wealth of information from public records, public and private organizations, and many other sources.
- **Search manually.** You'll find helpful background and supplementary information through manual searching of resources in public and institutional libraries. These traditional sources include periodical indexes for lists of newspaper, magazine, and journal articles, along with the card catalogue for books. Other manual sources are book indexes, encyclopedias, reference books, handbooks, dictionaries, directories, and almanacs.
- **Investigate primary sources.** To develop firsthand, primary information for a project, go directly to the source. For example, you could conduct interviews or surveys, put together questionnaires, or organize focus groups. Formal research includes scientific sampling methods that enable investigators to make accurate judgments and valid predictions.
- **Experiment scientifically.** Another source of primary data is experimentation. Instead of merely asking for the target audience's opinion, scientific researchers present choices with controlled variables.

Informal Research Methods

Most routine tasks—such as composing e-mail messages, memos, letters, informational reports, and oral presentations—require data that you can collect informally. For some projects, though, you rely more on your own ideas instead of—or in addition to—researching existing facts. Here are some techniques for collecting informal data and for generating ideas:

Informal research may involve looking in the files, talking with your boss, interviewing the audience, and conducting an informal survey.

- **Look in the files.** Before asking others for help, see what you can find yourself. For many routine messages you can often find previous documents to help you with content and format.
- **Talk with your boss.** Get information from the individual making the assignment. What does that person know about the topic? What slant should be taken? What other sources would she or he suggest?
- **Interview the target audience.** Consider talking with individuals at whom the message is aimed. They can provide clarifying information that tells you what they want to know and how you should shape your remarks.
- **Conduct an informal survey.** Gather unscientific but helpful information via questionnaires or telephone surveys. In preparing a memo report predicting the success of a proposed fitness centre, for example, circulate a questionnaire asking for employee reactions.

Generating Ideas by Brainstorming

One popular method for generating ideas is brainstorming. We should point out, however, that some critics argue that brainstorming groups "produce fewer and poorer quality ideas than the same number of individuals working alone."[1] Proponents say that if "you've had bad luck with brainstorming, you're just not doing it right."[2] Here are suggestions for productive group brainstorming:

The most productive group brainstorming sessions begin with defining the problem and creating an agenda.

- Define the problem and create an agenda that outlines the topics to be covered.
- Establish time limits, remembering that short sessions are best.
- Set a quota, such as a minimum of 100 ideas. The goal is quantity, not quality.
- Require every participant to contribute ideas, accept the ideas of others, or improve on ideas.
- Encourage wild, "out of the box" thinking. Allow no one to criticize or evaluate ideas.
- Write ideas on flipcharts or on sheets of paper hung around the room.
- Organize and classify the ideas, retaining the best. Consider using cluster diagrams, discussed shortly.

Collecting Information and Generating Ideas on the Job

Assume you work in the corporate offices of Gap Inc., and you have been given the task of developing a student recruiting brochure for all Gap stores. You think this is a great idea because many students don't know about exciting career opportunities and benefits at Old Navy and Gap. You know right away that you want the brochure to be colourful, exciting, concise, youthfully oriented, lightweight (because it has to be carried to campuses), and easily updated. Beyond that, you realize that you need ideas from others on how to develop this recruiting brochure.

To collect data for this project, you decide to use both formal and informal research methods. You study recruiting brochures from other companies and talk with students to ask what information they would like to see in a brochure. You conduct more formal research among recently hired employees and among Gap division presidents and executives to learn what they think a recruiting brochure should include.

More complex projects may require both formal and informal research.

Working with an outside consultant, you prepare a questionnaire, to use in personal interviews with executives and employees. The interviews include some open-ended questions, such as "How did you start with the company?" They also contain more specific questions about the number of employees in their departments, intended career paths, academic requirements, personality traits desired, and so forth.

Next you ask five or six fellow employees and team members to help brainstorm ideas for the brochure. In the session, your team comes up with the cluster diagram shown in Figure 6.1. The ideas range from the cost of the brochure to career development programs and some of your company's appealing locations.

From the jumble of ideas in the initial cluster diagram, you see that you can organize most of the information into three main categories relating to the brochure—Development, Form, and Content. You eliminate, simplify, and consolidate some ideas and add other new ideas. Then you organize the ideas into subclusters shown in Figure 6.2. This set of subclusters could form the basis for an outline. Or you could make another set of subclusters, further outlining the categories.

WRITING PROCESS PHASE 2: ORGANIZE

2

Writers of well-organized messages group similar ideas together so that readers can see relationships and follow arguments.

Well-organized messages group similar items together; ideas follow a sequence that helps the reader understand relationships and accept the writer's views. Unorganized messages proceed freeform, jumping from one thought to another. Such messages fail to emphasize important points. Puzzled readers can't see how the pieces fit together, and they become frustrated and irritated. Many communication experts regard poor organization as the greatest failing of business writers. Two simple techniques can help you organize data: the scratch list and the outline.

Using Lists and Outlines to Organize Ideas

In developing simple messages, some writers make a quick scratch list of the topics they wish to cover. Writers often jot this scratch list in the margin of the letter or memo to which they are responding—and the majority of business messages are written in response to other documents. These writers then compose a message at their computers directly from the scratch list.

Alphanumeric outlines show major and minor ideas; decimal outlines show how ideas relate to one another.

Most writers, though, need to organize their ideas—especially if the project is complex—into a hierarchy, such as an outline. The beauty of preparing an outline is that it gives you a chance to organize your thinking before you get bogged down in word choice and sentence structure.[3] Figure 6.3 shows two outline formats: alphanumeric and decimal. The familiar alphanumeric format uses Roman numerals, letters, and numbers to show major and minor ideas. The decimal format, which takes a little getting used to, has the advantage of showing how every item at every level relates to the whole. Both outlining formats force you to focus on the topic, identify major ideas, and support those ideas with details, illustrations, or evidence. Many

FIGURE 6.1 Creating a Cluster Diagram to Generate Ideas for Old Navy/Gap Recruiting Brochure

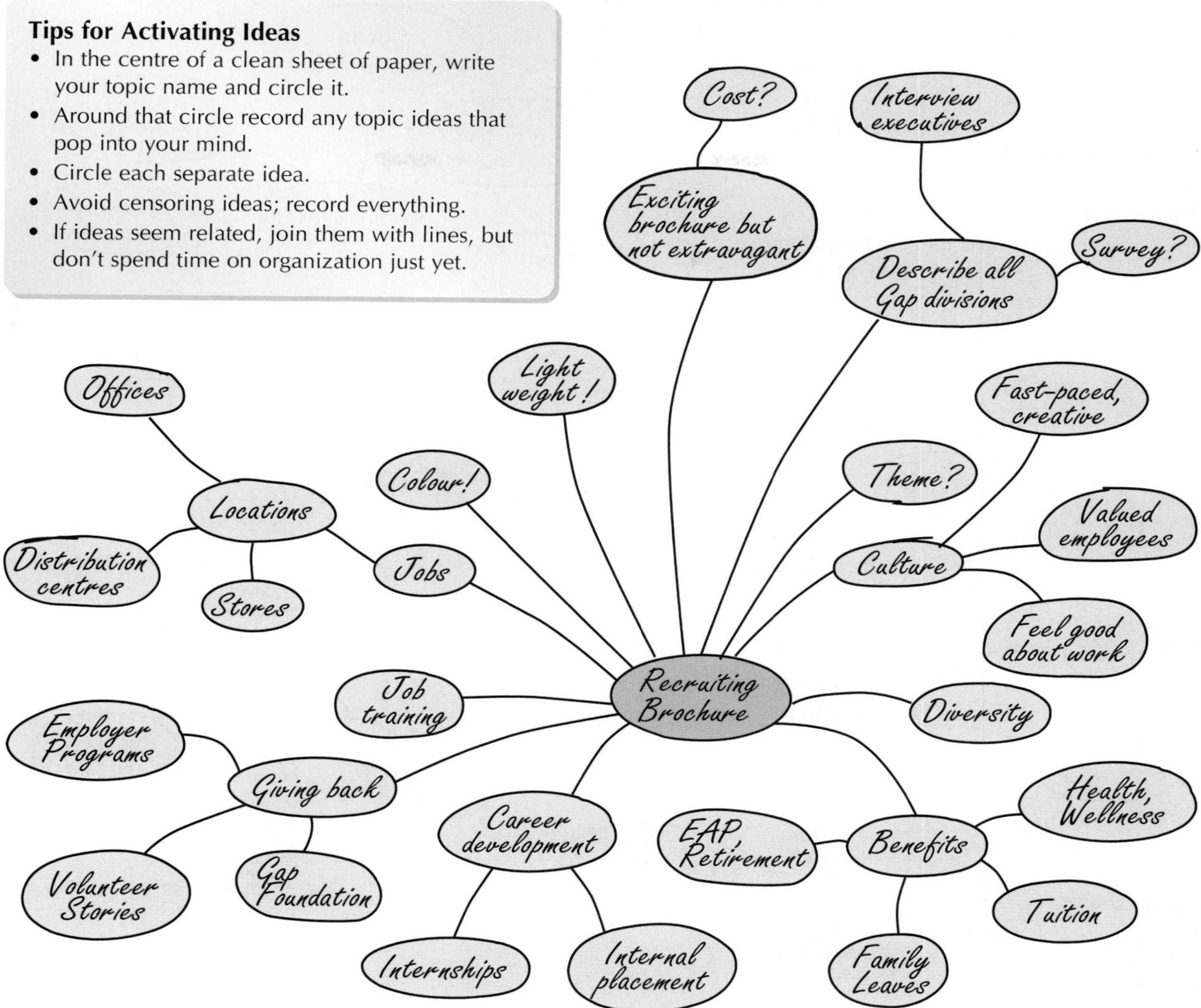

computer outlining programs now on the market make the mechanics of the process a real breeze.

Grouping ideas into categories is the hardest part of outlining.

The hardest part of outlining is grouping ideas into components or categories—ideally three to five in number. By the way, these major categories will become the major headings in your report. If you have more than five components, look for ways to combine smaller segments into broader topics. The following example shows how a portion of the Gap recruiting brochure subcluster (Figure 6.2) can be organized into an alphanumeric outline.[4]

I. Introduction
   A. Brief history of Gap Inc.
      1. Founding
      2. Milestones

FIGURE 6.2 Organizing Ideas From a Cluster Diagram Into Subclusters

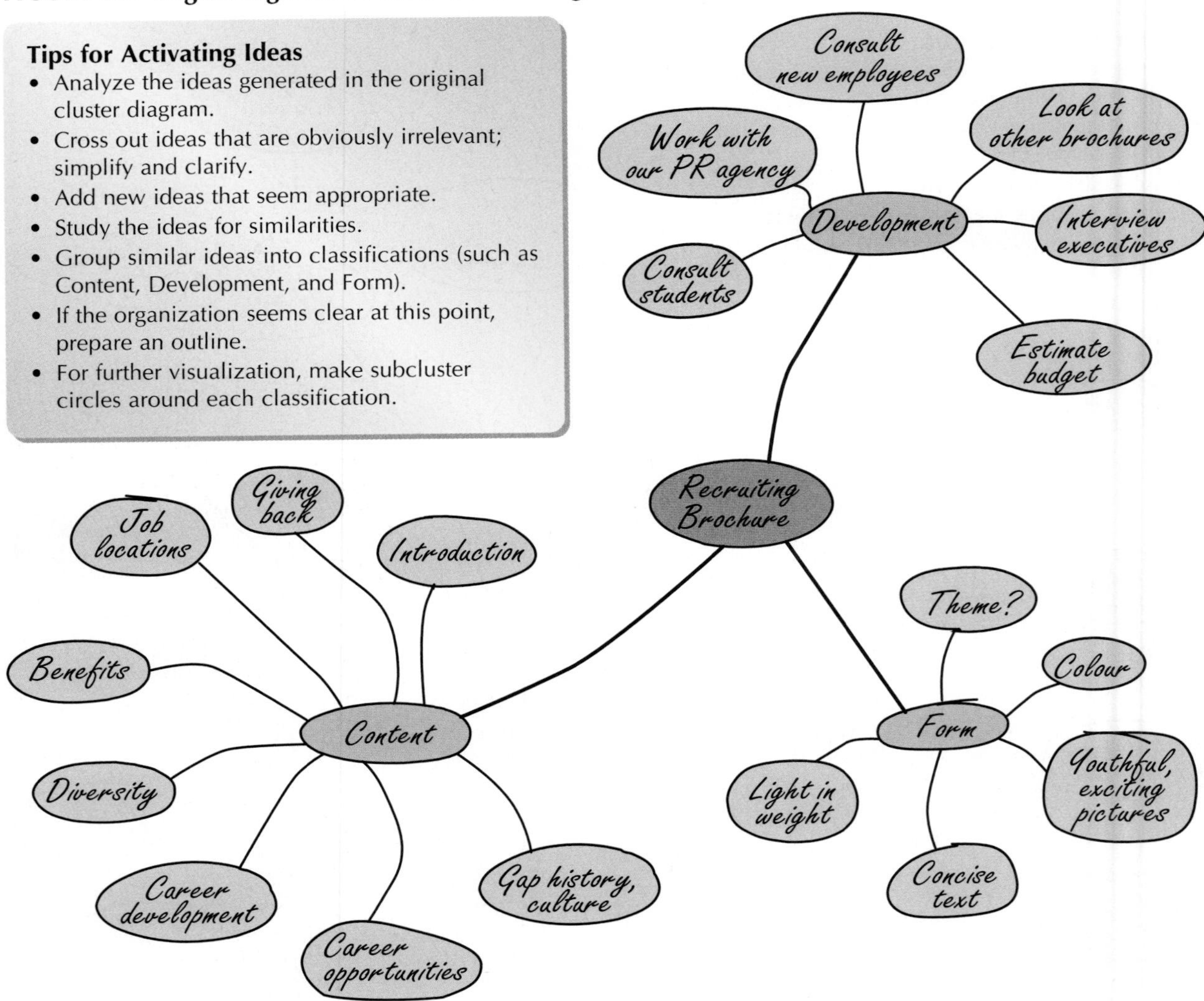
Tips for Activating Ideas
• Analyze the ideas generated in the original cluster diagram.
• Cross out ideas that are obviously irrelevant; simplify and clarify.
• Add new ideas that seem appropriate.
• Study the ideas for similarities.
• Group similar ideas into classifications (such as Content, Development, and Form).
• If the organization seems clear at this point, prepare an outline.
• For further visualization, make subcluster circles around each classification.
Recruiting Brochure
Development
Consult new employees
Look at other brochures
Work with our PR agency
Interview executives
Consult students
Estimate budget
Content
Job locations
Giving back
Introduction
Benefits
Diversity
Career development
Career opportunities
Gap history, culture
Form
Theme?
Colour
Youthful, exciting pictures
Light in weight
Concise text

An alphanumeric outline divides items into major and minor categories.

B. Corporate culture
   1. Fast-paced, creative, feel good about work
   2. Valuing diversity, employees
   3. Social responsibility

II. Careers
   A. Opportunities
      1. Internships
      2. Management trainee programs
   B. Development
      1. Internal promotion
      2. Job training

FIGURE 6.3 Two Outlining Formats

Tips for Making Outlines

- Define the main topic (purpose of message) in the title.
- Divide the main topic into major components or classifications (preferably three to five). If necessary, combine small components into one larger category.
- Break the components into subpoints.
- Don't put a single item under a major component; if you have only one subpoint, integrate it with the main item above it or reorganize.
- Strive to make each component exclusive (no overlapping).
- Use details, illustrations, and evidence to support subpoints.

Format for Alphanumeric Outline

Title: Major Idea, Purpose

I. First major component
   A. First subpoint
      1. Detail, illustration, evidence
      2. Detail, illustration, evidence
   B. Second subpoint
      1.
      2.
II. Second major component
   A. First subpoint
      1.
      2.
   B. Second subpoint
      1.
      2.
III. Third major component
   A.
      1.
      2.
   B.
      1.
      2.

(This method is simple and familiar.)

Format for Decimal Outline

Title: Major Idea, Purpose

1.0. First major component
   1.1. First subpoint
      1.1.1. Detail, illustration, evidence
      1.1.2. Detail, illustration, evidence
   1.2. Second subpoint
      1.2.1.
      1.2.2.
2.0. Second major component
   2.1. First subpoint
      2.1.1.
      2.1.2.
   2.2. Second subpoint
      2.2.1.
      2.2.2.
3.0. Third major component
   3.1.
      3.1.1.
      3.1.2.
   3.2.
      3.2.1.
      3.2.2.

(This method relates every item to the overall outline.)

Notice that each major category is divided into at least two subcategories. These categories are then fleshed out with examples, details, statistics, case histories, and other data. In moving from major point to subpoint, you are progressing from large abstract concepts to small concrete ideas. And each subpoint could be further subdivided with more specific illustrations if you desired. You can determine the appropriate amount of detail by considering what your audience (primary and secondary) already knows about the topic and how much persuading you must do.

Every major category in an outline should have at least two subcategories.

How you group ideas into components depends on your topic and your channel of communication. Business documents do not have rigid page constraints. They usually contain typical components arranged in traditional patterns, as shown in Figure 6.4.

FIGURE 6.4 Typical Major Components in Business Outlines

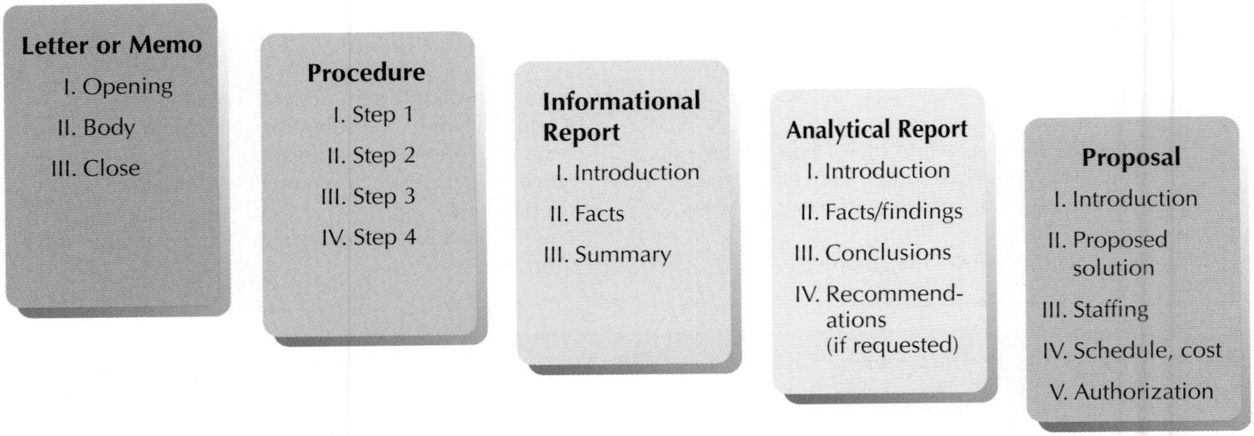

Letter or Memo
I. Opening
II. Body
III. Close

Procedure
I. Step 1
II. Step 2
III. Step 3
IV. Step 4

Informational Report
I. Introduction
II. Facts
III. Summary

Analytical Report
I. Introduction
II. Facts/findings
III. Conclusions
IV. Recommend-ations (if requested)

Proposal
I. Introduction
II. Proposed solution
III. Staffing
IV. Schedule, cost
V. Authorization

Thus far, you've seen how to collect information, generate ideas, and prepare an outline. How you order the information in your outline, though, depends on what pattern or strategy you choose.

Organizing Ideas Into Patterns

3

Two organizational patterns provide plans of action for typical business messages: the direct pattern and the indirect pattern. The primary difference between the two patterns is where the main idea is placed. In the direct pattern the main idea comes first, followed by details, explanation, or evidence. In the indirect pattern the main idea follows the details, explanation, and evidence. The pattern you select is determined by how you expect the audience to react to the message, as shown in Figure 6.5.

Business messages typically follow either the (1) direct pattern, with the main idea first, or (2) the indirect pattern, with the main idea following explanation and evidence.

Direct Pattern for Receptive Audiences. In preparing to write any message, you need to anticipate the audience's reaction to your ideas and frame your message accordingly. When you expect the reader to be pleased, mildly interested, or, at worst, neutral—use the direct pattern. That is, put your main point—the purpose of your message—in the first or second sentence. As quickly as possible, tell why you are writing. Compare the direct and indirect patterns in the following memo openings. Notice how long it takes to get to the main idea in the indirect opening.

Indirect Opening
Our company has been concerned with attracting better-qualified prospective job candidates. For this reason, the Management Council has been gathering information about an internship program for postsecondary students. After considerable investigation, we have voted to begin a pilot program starting next fall.

Direct Opening
The Management Council has voted to begin a postsecondary internship pilot program next fall.

Explanations and details should follow the direct opening. What's important is getting to the main idea quickly. This direct method, also called *frontloading*, has at least three advantages:

FIGURE 6.5 Audience Response Determines Pattern of Organization

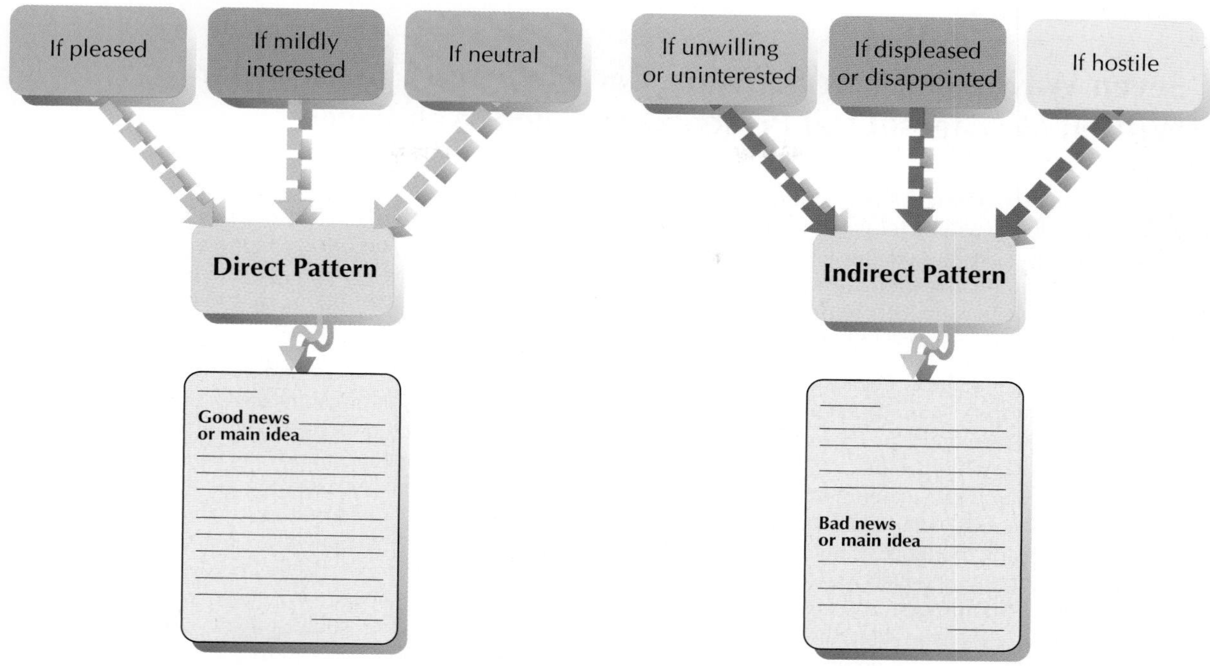

- **Saves the reader's time.** Many of today's businesspeople can devote only a few moments to each message. Messages that take too long to get to the point may lose their readers along the way.
- **Sets a proper frame of mind.** Learning the purpose up front helps the reader put the subsequent details and explanations in perspective. Without a clear opening, the reader may be thinking, "Why am I being told this?"
- **Prevents frustration.** Readers forced to struggle through excessive verbiage before reaching the main idea become frustrated. They resent the writer. Poorly organized messages create a negative impression of the writer.

Frontloading saves the reader's time, establishes the proper frame of mind, and prevents frustration.

This frontloading technique works best with audiences that are likely to be receptive to or at least not disagree with what you have to say. Typical business messages that follow the direct pattern include routine requests and responses, orders and acknowledgments, nonsensitive memos, e-mail messages, informational reports, and informational oral presentations. All these tasks have one element in common: none has a sensitive subject that will upset the reader.

Indirect Pattern for Unreceptive Audiences. When you expect the audience to be uninterested, unwilling, displeased, or perhaps even hostile, the indirect pattern is more appropriate. In this pattern you don't reveal the main idea until after you have offered explanation and evidence. This approach works well with three kinds of messages: (1) bad news, (2) ideas that require persuasion, and (3) sensitive news, especially when being transmitted to superiors. The indirect pattern has these benefits:

The indirect pattern respects the feelings of the audience, facilitates a fair hearing, and minimizes a negative reaction.

- **Respects the feelings of the audience.** Bad news is always painful, but the trauma can be lessened when the receiver is prepared for it.

TECH TALK

Seven Ways Computer Software Can Help You Create Better Written Messages, Oral Presentations, and Web Pages

Although computers and software programs cannot actually do the writing for you, they provide powerful tools that make the composition process easier and the results more professional. Here are seven ways your computer can help you improve your written documents, oral presentations, and even Web pages.

1. **Fighting writer's block.** Because word processors enable ideas to flow almost effortlessly from your brain to a screen, you can expect fewer delays resulting from writer's block. You can compose rapidly, and you can experiment with structure and phrasing, later retaining and polishing your most promising thoughts. Many authors "sprint write," recording unedited ideas quickly, to start the composition process and also to brainstorm for ideas on a project. Then, they tag important ideas and use computer outlining programs to organize those ideas into logical sequences.
2. **Collecting information electronically.** As a knowledge worker in an information economy, you will need to find information quickly. Much of the world's information is now accessible by computer. You can locate the titles of books, as well as many full-text articles from magazines, newspapers, and government publications. Massive amounts of information are available from the Internet, CD-ROMs, and online services. Through specialized information-retrieval services (such as ABI-INFORM, InfoTrac, or Dow Jones News/Retrieval Service), you can have at your fingertips up-to-the-minute legal, scientific, scholarly, and business information. The most amazing source of electronic information is the Web, with its links to sites around the world, some incredibly helpful and others worthless. You'll learn more about these exciting electronic resources in Unit 4.
3. **Outlining and organizing ideas.** Most high-end word processors include some form of "outliner," a feature that enables you to divide a topic into a hierarchical order with main points and subpoints. Your computer keeps track of the levels of ideas automatically so that you can easily add, cut, or rearrange points in the outline. This feature is particularly handy when you're preparing a report or organizing a presentation. Some programs even enable you to transfer your outline directly to slide frames to be used as visual aids in a talk.
4. **Improving correctness and precision.** Nearly all word processing programs today provide features that catch and correct spelling and typographical errors. Poor spellers and weak typists universally bless their spell checkers for repeatedly saving them from humiliation. Most high-end word processing programs today also provide grammar checkers that are markedly improved over earlier versions. They now detect many errors in capitalization, word use (such as *it's, its*), double negatives, verb use, subject–verb agreement, sentence structure, number agreement, number style, and other writing faults. However, most grammar programs don't actually correct the errors they detect. You must know how to do that. Still, grammar checkers can be very helpful. In addition to spelling and grammar programs, thesaurus programs help you choose precise words that say exactly what you intend.
5. **Adding graphics for emphasis.** Your letters, memos, and reports may be improved by the addition of graphs and artwork to clarify and illustrate data. You can import charts, diagrams, and illustrations created in database, spreadsheet, graphics, or draw-and-paint programs. Moreover, ready-made pictures, called clip art, can be used to symbolize or illustrate ideas.
6. **Designing and producing professional-looking documents, presentations, and Web pages.** Most high-end word processing programs today include a large selection of scalable fonts (for different character sizes and styles), italics, boldface, symbols, and styling techniques to aid you in producing consistent formatting and professional-looking results. Moreover, today's presentation software enables you to incorporate

(continued)

showy slide effects, colour, sound, pictures, and even movies into your talks for management or customers. Web document builders also help you design and construct Web pages.

7. **Using collaborative software for team writing.** Assume you are part of a group preparing a lengthy proposal to secure a government contract. You expect to write one segment of the proposal yourself and help revise parts written by others. Special word processing programs with commenting and strikeout features allow you to revise easily and to identify each team member's editing. Some collaborative programs, called groupware, as you learned in Chapter 2, also include decision-support tools to help groups generate, organize, and analyze ideas more efficiently than in traditional meetings.

- **Encourages a fair hearing.** Messages that may upset the reader are more likely to be read when the main idea is delayed. Beginning immediately with a piece of bad news or a persuasive request, for example, may cause the receiver to stop reading or listening.
- **Minimizes a negative reaction.** A reader's overall reaction to a negative message is generally improved if the news is delivered gently.

Typical business messages that could be developed indirectly include letters and memos that refuse requests, deny claims, and disapprove credit. Persuasive requests, sales letters, sensitive messages, and some reports and oral presentations also benefit from the indirect strategy. You'll learn more about how to use the indirect pattern in Chapters 10 and 11.

In summary, business messages may be organized directly, with the main idea first, or indirectly, with the main idea delayed. Although these two patterns cover many communication problems, they should be considered neither universal nor inviolate. Every business transaction is distinct. Some messages are mixed: part good news, part bad; part goodwill, part persuasion. In upcoming chapters you'll practise applying the direct and indirect patterns in typical situations. Then, you'll have the skills and confidence to evaluate communication problems and vary these patterns depending on the goals you wish to achieve.

WRITING PROCESS PHASE 2: COMPOSE

Once you've researched your topic, organized the data, and selected a pattern of organization, you're ready to begin composing. Most writers expect to use their computers for composition, but many are unaware of all the ways a computer can help create better written messages, oral presentations, and Web pages. See the accompanying Tech Talk box to learn how you can take full advantage of your computer.

Even with a computer, some writers have trouble getting started, especially if they haven't completed the preparatory work. Organizing your ideas and working from an outline are very helpful in overcoming writer's block. Composition is also easier if you have a quiet environment in which to concentrate. Businesspeople with messages to compose set aside a given time and allow no calls, visitors, or other interruptions. This is a good technique for students as well.

As you begin composing, keep in mind that you are writing the first draft, not the final copy. Experts suggest that you write quickly (*sprint writing*). Get your thoughts down now and refine them in later versions.[5] As you take up each idea, imagine that you are talking to the reader. Don't let yourself get bogged down. If you can't think of the right word, insert a substitute or type "find perfect word later."[6] Sprint writing works especially well for those composing on a computer because it's simple to make changes at any point of the composition process. If you are hand-writing the first draft, double-space so that you have room for changes.

Creating Effective Sentences

Sentences must have subjects and verbs and must make sense.

As you create your first draft, you'll be working at the sentence level of composition. Although you've used sentences all your life, you may be unaware of how they can be shaped and arranged to express your ideas most effectively. First, let's review some basic sentence elements.

Complete sentences have subjects and verbs and make sense.

SUBJECT (report) VERB (is)
This report is clear and concise.

SUBJECT (employees) VERB (write)
Our employees write many reports.

Clauses have subjects and verbs, but phrases do not.

Clauses and phrases, the key building blocks of sentences, are related groups of words. Clauses have subjects and verbs; phrases do not.

PHRASE (of that organization) PHRASE (to our staff)
The CEO of that organization sent a letter to our staff.

CLAUSE (Because she writes well) CLAUSE (Tracy answers most customer letters)
Because she writes well, Tracy answers most customer letters.

Independent clauses may stand alone; dependent clauses may not.

Clauses may be divided into two groups: independent and dependent. Independent clauses are grammatically complete. Dependent clauses depend for their meaning on independent clauses. In the preceding example, the clause beginning with *Because* is dependent. Dependent clauses are often introduced by words such as *if, when, because,* and *as.*

DEPENDENT CLAUSE (When she writes to customers) INDEPENDENT CLAUSE (Tracy uses simple language)
When she writes to customers, Tracy uses simple language.

By learning to distinguish phrases, independent clauses, and dependent clauses, you'll be able to punctuate sentences correctly and avoid three basic sentence faults: the fragment, the run-on sentence, and the comma splice. In Guides 1–3, Appendix A, we examine these writing problems in greater detail. For now, however, let's look at some ways to make your sentences more readable.

Effective sentences are short and stress important ideas.

Preferring Short Sentences. Because your goal is to communicate clearly, you're better off limiting your sentences to about 20 or fewer words. The American Press Institute reports that reader comprehension drops off markedly as sentences become longer.[7] Thus, in crafting your sentences, think about the relationship between sentence length and comprehension:

Sentence Length	Comprehension Rate
8 words	100%
15 words	90%
19 words	80%
28 words	50%

Sentences of 20 or fewer words have the most impact.

Instead of stringing together clauses with *and, but,* and *however,* break some of those complex sentences into separate segments. Business readers want to grasp ideas immediately. They can do that best when thoughts are separated into short sentences. On the other hand, too many monotonous short sentences will sound "grammar schoolish" and may bore or even annoy the reader. Strive for a balance between longer sentences and shorter ones. Your computer probably can point out long sentences and give you an average sentence length.

Ensure instructions are readable by shortening sentences, emphasizing important ideas with graphic highlighting, and using active-voice verbs.

Emphasizing Important Ideas. You can stress prominent ideas mechanically by underscoring, italicizing, or boldfacing. You'll learn more about these graphic highlighting devices shortly. You can also emphasize important ideas with five stylistic devices.

- **Use vivid words.** Vivid words are emphatic because the reader can picture ideas clearly.
- **Label the main idea.** If an idea is significant, tell the reader.
- **Place the important idea first or last in the sentence.** Ideas have less competition from surrounding words when they appear first or last in a sentence.
- **Place the important idea in a simple sentence or in an independent clause.** Don't dilute the effect of the idea by making it share the spotlight with other words and clauses.
- **Make sure the important idea is the sentence subject.** You'll learn more about active and passive voice shortly, but at this point just focus on making the important idea the subject.

Emphasize an important idea by using vivid words, labelling the main idea, placing the idea first or last in a sentence, and making the idea the sentence subject.

Managing Active and Passive Voice. In sentences with active-voice verbs, the subject is the doer of the action. In passive-voice sentences, the subject is acted upon.

In active-voice sentences the subject is the doer; in passive-voice sentences, the subject is acted upon.

Active verb	Passive verb
Brandon *completed* his tax return before the April 30 deadline. (The subject, *Brandon,* is the doer of the action.)	The tax return *was completed* before the April 30 deadline. (The subject, *tax return,* is acted upon.)

In the first sentence, the active-voice verb emphasizes Brandon. In the second sentence, the passive-voice verb emphasizes the tax return. Active-voice sentences are more direct because they reveal the performer immediately. They're easier to understand and shorter. Most business writing should be in the active voice.

Passive-voice sentences are useful for tact and to direct attention to actions instead of people.

Yet, passive verbs are useful in certain instances. In sentences with passive-voice verbs, the doer of the action may be revealed or left unknown. In business writing, as well as in personal interactions, some situations demand tact and sensitivity. Instead of using a direct approach with active verbs, we may prefer the indirectness that passive verbs allow. Rather than making a blunt announcement with an active verb (*Tyler made a major error in the estimate*), we can soften the sentence with a passive construction (*A major error was made in the estimate*).

Here's a summary of the best uses of active- and passive-voice verbs:

- **Use the active voice for most business writing.** *Our company gives drug tests to all applicants.*

- **Use the passive voice to emphasize an action or the recipient of the action.** *Drug tests are given to all applicants.*
- **Use the passive voice to deemphasize negative news.** *Your monitor cannot be repaired.*
- **Use the passive voice to conceal the doer of an action.** *A major error was made in the estimate.*

How can you tell whether a verb is active or passive? Identify the subject of the sentence and decide whether the subject is doing the acting or whether it is being acted upon. For example, in the sentence *An appointment was made for January 1*, the subject is *appointment.* The subject is being acted upon; therefore, the verb (*was made*) is passive. Another clue in identifying passive-voice verbs is that they generally include a *to be* helping verb, such as *is, are, was, were, being,* or *been.*

Modifiers must be close to the words they describe or limit.

Avoiding Dangling and Misplaced Modifiers. For clarity, modifiers must be close to the words they describe or limit. A dangling modifier describes or limits a word or words that are missing from the sentence. A misplaced modifier occurs when the word or phrase it describes is not close enough to be clear. In both instances, the solution is to position the modifier closer to the word(s) it describes or limits. Introductory verbal phrases are particularly dangerous; be sure to follow them immediately with the words they can logically describe or modify.

Dangling Modifier	**Improved**
Driving on the Cabot Trail, the ocean suddenly came into view. (*Is the ocean driving on the Cabot Trail?*)	As we drove on the Cabot Trail, the ocean suddenly came into view.

Try this trick for detecting and remedying dangling modifiers. Ask the question *who?* or *what?* after any introductory phrase. The words immediately following should tell the reader *who* or *what* is performing the action. Try the "who?" test on the previous dangler and on the following misplaced modifier.

A modifier is misplaced when the word or phrase it describes is not close enough to be clear.

Misplaced Modifier	**Improved**
A wart appeared on my left hand that I want removed. (*Is the left hand to be removed?*)	A wart that I want removed appeared on my left hand.

Drafting Meaningful Paragraphs

5

From composing sentences, we progress to paragraphs. A paragraph is one or more sentences designated as a separate thought group. To avoid muddled paragraphs, writers must recognize basic paragraph elements, conventional sentence patterns, and ways to organize sentences into one of three classic paragraph patterns. They must also be able to polish their paragraphs by linking sentences and using transitional expressions.

Discussing One Topic. Well-constructed paragraphs discuss only one topic. They reveal the primary idea in a main sentence that usually, but not always, appears first. Other ideas, connected logically with transitional expressions (verbal road signs), support or illustrate that idea.

Organizing Sentences Into Paragraphs. Paragraphs are generally composed of three kinds of sentences:[8]

Main sentence: Expresses the primary idea of the paragraph.

Supporting sentence: Illustrates, explains, or strengthens the primary idea.

Limiting sentence: Opposes the primary idea by suggesting a negative or contrasting thought; may precede or follow the main sentence.

These sentences may be arranged in three classic paragraph plans: direct, pivoting, and indirect.

Using the Direct Paragraph Plan to Define, Classify, Illustrate, or Describe. Paragraphs arranged in the direct plan begin with the main sentence, followed by supporting sentences. Most business messages use this paragraph plan because it clarifies the subject immediately. This plan is useful whenever you must define (a new product or procedure), classify (parts of a whole), illustrate (an idea), or describe (a process). Simply start with the main sentence; then strengthen and amplify that idea with supporting ideas, as shown here:

The direct paragraph pattern is appropriate when defining, classifying, illustrating, or describing.

Main Sentence	A social audit is a report on the social performance of a company.
Supporting Sentences	Such an audit may be conducted by the company itself or by outsiders who evaluate the company's efforts to produce safe products, engage in socially responsible activities, and protect the environment. Many companies publish the results of their social audits in their annual reports. Commitment to the environment and social responsibility have been core values for Vancouver City Savings Credit Union (Vancity) since 1993. The company conducts social audits to combine measures of financial return, social responsibility, and environmental performance.[9]

You can alter the direct plan by adding a limiting sentence if necessary. Be sure, though, that you follow with sentences that return to the main idea and support it, as shown here:

Main Sentence	Flexible work scheduling could immediately increase productivity and enhance employee satisfaction in our entire organization.
Limiting Sentence	Such scheduling, however, is impossible for all employees.
Supporting Sentences	Managers would be required to maintain their regular hours. For many other employees, though, flexible scheduling permits extra time to manage family responsibilities. Feeling less stress, employees are able to focus their attention better at work; hence they become more relaxed and more productive.

The pivoting paragraph pattern is appropriate when comparing and contrasting.

Using the Pivoting Paragraph Plan to Compare and Contrast. Paragraphs arranged in the pivoting plan start with a limiting sentence that offers a contrasting or negative idea before delivering the main sentence. Notice in the following example how two limiting sentences about drawbacks to military careers open the paragraph; only then do the main and supporting sentences describing rewards in military service appear. The pivoting plan is especially useful for comparing and contrasting ideas. In using the pivoting plan, be sure you emphasize the turn in direction with an obvious *but* or *however.*

Limiting Sentences	Military careers are certainly not for everyone. Many are in remote countries where harsh climates, health hazards, security risks, and other discomforts exist.
Main Sentence	However, careers in the military offer special rewards for the special people who qualify.
Supporting Sentences	Military employees enjoy the pride and satisfaction of representing their country abroad. They enjoy frequent travel, enriching cultural and social experiences in living abroad, and action-oriented work.

The indirect paragraph pattern is appropriate when delivering bad news.

Using the Indirect Paragraph Plan to Explain and Persuade. Paragraphs arranged in the indirect plan start with the supporting sentences and conclude with the main sentence. This useful plan enables you to build a rationale, a foundation of reasons, before hitting the audience with a big idea—possibly one that is bad news. It enables you to explain your reasons and then in the final sentence draw a conclusion from them. In the following example the vice president of a large accounting firm begins by describing the trend toward casual dress and concludes with a recommendation that his firm change its dress code. This indirect plan works well for describing causes followed by an effect.

Supporting Sentences	According to a recent poll, more than half of all white-collar workers are now dressing casually at work. Many high-tech engineers and professional specialists have given up suits and ties, favouring khakis and sweaters instead. In our own business our consultants say they stand out like "sore thumbs" because they are attired in traditional buttoned-down styles, while the businesspeople they visit are usually wearing comfortable, casual clothing.
Main Sentence	Therefore, I recommend that we establish an optional "business casual" policy allowing consultants to dress casually, if they wish, as they perform their duties both in and out of the office.

You'll learn more techniques for implementing direct and indirect writing strategies when you prepare letters, memos, e-mail messages, reports, and oral presentations in subsequent chapters.

Coherent paragraphs link ideas by sustaining the main idea, using pronouns, dovetailing sentences, and using transitional expressions.

Linking Ideas to Build Coherence. Paragraphs are coherent when ideas are linked, that is, when one idea leads logically to the next. Well-written paragraphs take the reader through a number of steps. When the author skips from Step 1 to Step 3 and forgets Step 2, the reader is lost. You can use several techniques to keep the reader in step with your ideas.

Sustaining the Key Idea. This involves simply repeating a key expression or using a similar one. For example:

> Our philosophy holds that every customer is really a guest. All new employees to our theme parks are trained to treat *guests* as *VIPs*. These *VIPs* are never told what they can or cannot do.

Notice how the repetition of *guest* and *VIP* connects ideas.

Using Pronouns. Familiar pronouns, such as *we, they, he, she,* and *it,* help build continuity, as do demonstrative pronouns, such as *this, that, these,* and *those.* These words confirm that something under discussion is still being discussed. For example:

Using pronouns strategically helps build coherence and continuity.

> All new park employees receive a two-week orientation. They learn that every staffer has a vital role in preparing for the show. This training includes how to maintain enthusiasm.

Be careful with *this, that, these,* and *those,* however. These words usually need a noun with them to make their meaning absolutely clear. In the last example notice how confusing *this* becomes if the word *training* is omitted.

Dovetailing Sentences. Sentences are "dovetailed" when an idea at the end of one connects with an idea at the beginning of the next. For example:

Dovetailing sentences means connecting ending and beginning ideas.

> New hosts and hostesses learn about the theme park and its *facilities*. These facilities include telephones, food services, bathrooms, and attractions, as well as the location of *offices*. Knowledge of administrative offices and internal workings of the company, such as who's who in administration, ensures that staffers will be able to *serve guests* fully. *Serving guests,* of course, is our number one priority.

Dovetailing of sentences is especially helpful with dense, difficult topics. This technique, however, should not be overused.

Showing Connections With Transitional Expressions. Transitional expressions are another excellent device for achieving paragraph coherence. These words, some of which are shown in Figure 6.6, act as verbal road signs to readers and listeners. Transitional expressions enable the receiver to anticipate what's coming, to reduce uncertainty, and to speed up comprehension. They signal that a train of thought is moving forward, being developed, possibly detouring, or ending. Transitions are especially helpful in persuasive writing.

Transitional expressions help readers anticipate what's coming, reduce uncertainty, and speed comprehension.

As Figure 6.6 shows, transitions can add or strengthen a thought, show time or order, clarify ideas, show cause and effect, contradict thoughts, and contrast ideas. Thus, you must be careful to select the best transition for your purpose. Look back at the examples of direct, pivoted, and indirect paragraphs to see how transitional expressions and other devices build paragraph coherence. Remember that coherence in communication rarely happens spontaneously; it requires effort and skill.

Composing Short Paragraphs for Readability. Although no rule regulates the length of paragraphs, business writers recognize the value of short paragraphs. Paragraphs with eight or fewer lines look inviting and readable, whereas long, solid chunks of print appear formidable. If a topic can't be covered in eight or fewer printed lines (not sentences), consider breaking it up into smaller segments.

Paragraphs with eight or fewer lines are inviting and readable.

The following checklist summarizes the key points of writing a first draft.

FIGURE 6.6 Transitional Expressions to Build Coherence

TO ADD OR STRENGTHEN	TO SHOW TIME OR ORDER	TO CLARIFY	TO SHOW CAUSE AND EFFECT	TO CONTRADICT	TO CONTRAST
additionally	after	for example	accordingly	actually	as opposed to
again	before	for instance	as a result	but	at the same time
also	earlier	I mean	consequently	however	by contrast
besides	finally	in other words	for this reason	in fact	conversely
likewise	first	that is	so	instead	on the contrary
moreover	meanwhile	this means	therefore	rather	on the other hand
further	next	thus	thus	still	
furthermore	now	to put it another way	under the circumstances	though	
	previously			yet	

CHECKLIST FOR COMPOSING SENTENCES AND PARAGRAPHS

For Effective Sentences

- ✓ **Use short sentences.** Keep in mind that sentences with 20 or fewer words are easier to read. Use longer sentences occasionally, but rely primarily on short sentences.
- ✓ **Emphasize important ideas.** Place main ideas at the beginning of short sentences for emphasis.
- ✓ **Apply active and passive verbs carefully.** Use active verbs (*She sent the e-mail* instead of *The e-mail was sent by her*) most frequently; they immediately identify the doer. Use passive verbs to be tactful, to emphasize an action, or to conceal the performer.
- ✓ **Eliminate misplaced modifiers.** Be sure that introductory verbal phrases are followed by the words that can logically be modified. To check the placement of modifiers, ask *who?* or *what?* after such phrases.

For Meaningful Paragraphs

- ✓ **Develop one idea.** Use main, supporting, and limiting sentences to develop a single idea within each paragraph.
- ✓ **Use the direct plan.** Start most paragraphs with the main sentence followed by supporting sentences. This direct plan is useful in defining, classifying, illustrating, and describing.
- ✓ **Use the pivoting plan.** To compare and contrast ideas, start with a limiting sentence; then, present the main sentence followed by supporting sentences.
- ✓ **Use the indirect plan.** To explain reasons or causes first, start with supporting sentences. Build to the conclusion with the main sentence at the end of the paragraph.

- ✓ **Build coherence by linking sentences.** Hold ideas together by repeating key words, using pronouns, and dovetailing sentences (beginning one sentence with an idea from the end of the previous sentence).

- ✓ **Provide road signs with transitional expressions.** Use verbal signals to help the audience know where the idea is going. Words like *moreover, accordingly, as a result,* and *thus* function as idea pointers.

- ✓ **Limit paragraph length.** Remember that paragraphs with eight or fewer printed lines look inviting. Consider breaking up longer paragraphs if necessary.

SUMMARY OF LEARNING OBJECTIVES

1 **Apply Phase 2 of Guffey's 3-×-3 writing process, which begins with formal and informal methods for researching data and generating ideas.** The second phase of the writing process includes researching, organizing, and writing. Researching means collecting information using formal or informal techniques. Formal research for long reports and complex problems may involve searching library data manually or electronically, as well as conducting interviews, surveys, focus groups, and experiments. Informal research for routine tasks may include looking in company files, talking with your boss, interviewing the target audience, conducting informal surveys, brainstorming for ideas, and cluster diagramming.

2 **Specify how to organize data into lists and alphanumeric or decimal outlines.** One method for organizing data in simple messages is to list the main topics to be discussed. Organizing more complex messages usually requires an outline. To prepare an outline, divide the main topic into three to five major components. Break the components into subpoints consisting of details, illustrations, and evidence. For an alphanumeric outline arrange items using Roman numerals (I, II), capital letters (A, B), and numbers (1, 2). For a decimal outline show the ordering of ideas with decimals (1.0., 1.1., 1.1.1.).

3 **Compare direct and indirect patterns for organizing ideas.** The direct pattern places the main idea first. This pattern is useful when audiences will be pleased, mildly interested, or neutral. It saves the reader's time, sets the proper frame of mind, and prevents reader frustration. The indirect pattern places the main idea after explanations. This pattern is useful for audiences that will be unwilling, displeased, or hostile. It respects the feelings of the audience, encourages a fair hearing, and minimizes negative reactions.

4 **Discuss composing the first draft of a message, focusing on techniques for creating effective sentences.** Compose the first draft of a message in a quiet environment where you won't be interrupted. Compose quickly, preferably at a computer. Plan to revise. As you compose, remember that sentences are most effective when they are short (under 20 words). A main idea may be emphasized by making it the sentence subject, placing it first, and removing competing ideas. Effective sentences use active verbs, although passive verbs may be necessary for tact or deemphasis. Effective sentences avoid dangling and misplaced modifiers.

5 **Define a paragraph and describe three classic paragraph plans and techniques for composing meaningful paragraphs.** A paragraph consists of one or more sentences designated as a separate thought group. Typical paragraphs follow one of three plans. Direct paragraphs (main sentence followed by supporting sentences) are useful to define, classify, illustrate, and describe. Pivoting paragraphs (limiting sentence followed by main sentence and supporting sentences) are useful to compare and contrast. Indirect paragraphs (supporting sentences followed by main sentence) build a rationale and foundation of ideas before presenting the main idea. Paragraphs may be improved through the use of coherence techniques and transitional expressions.

CHAPTER REVIEW

1. What are the three main activities involved in the second phase of Guffey's 3-×-3 writing process? (Obj. 1)
2. Name seven specific techniques for a productive group "brainstorming" session. (Obj. 1)
3. What is a cluster diagram, and when might it be useful? (Obj. 1)
4. Describe an alphanumeric outline. (Obj. 2)
5. What is the relationship between the major categories in an outline and those in a report written from the outline? (Obj. 2)
6. Distinguish between the direct and indirect patterns of organization for typical business messages. (Obj. 3)
7. Why should most messages be "frontloaded"? (Obj. 3)
8. List some business messages that should be frontloaded and some that should not be frontloaded. (Obj. 3)
9. Why should writers plan for revision? How can they do it? (Obj. 4)
10. Name three ways to emphasize important ideas in sentences. (Obj. 4)
11. Distinguish between active-voice sentences and passive-voice sentences. Give examples. (Obj. 4)
12. Give an original example of a dangling or misplaced modifier. Why are introductory verbal phrases dangerous? (Obj. 4)
13. Describe three kinds of sentences used to develop ideas in paragraphs. (Obj. 5)
14. Describe three paragraph plans. Identify the uses for each. (Obj. 5)
15. What is coherence, and how is it achieved? (Obj. 5)

CRITICAL THINKING

1. Why is cluster diagramming considered an intuitive process while outlining is considered an analytical process? (Obj. 1)
2. Why is audience analysis so important in choosing the direct or indirect pattern of organization for a business message? (Obj. 3)
3. In what ways do you imagine that writing on the job differs from the writing you do in your academic studies? Consider process as well as product. (Obj. 1)
4. Why are short sentences and short paragraphs appropriate for business communication? (Objs. 4 and 5)

ACTIVITIES

6.1 Document for Analysis (Objs. 3, 4, and 5)

The following interoffice memo is hard to read. It suffers from numerous writing faults discussed in this chapter.
Your Task. First, read the memo to see whether you can understand what the writer requests from all Western Division employees. Then, discuss why this memo is so hard to read. How long are the sentences? How many passive-voice constructions can you locate? How effective is the paragraphing? Can you spot four dangling or misplaced modifiers? (Superscript numbers in the following sentences are provided to help you identify problem sentences.)

TO: All Western Division Employees

[1]Personal computers and all the software to support these computers are appearing on many desks of Western Division employees. [2]After giving the matter considerable attention, it has been determined by the Systems Development Department (SDD) that more control should be exerted in coordinating the purchase of hardware and software to improve compatibility throughout the division so that a library of resources may be developed. [3]Therefore, a plan has been developed by SDD that should be followed in making all future equipment selections and purchases. [4]To make the best possible choice, SDD should be contacted as you begin your search because questions about personal computers, word processing programs, hardware, and software can be answered by our knowledgeable staff, who can also provide you with invaluable assistance in making the best choice for your needs at the best possible cost.

[5]After your computer and its software arrive, all your future software purchases should be channelled through SDD. [6]To actually make your initial purchase, a written proposal and a purchase request form must be presented to SDD for approval. [7]A need for the purchase must be established; benefits that you expect to derive resulting from its purchase must be analyzed and presented, and an itemized statement of all costs must be submitted. [8]By following these new procedures, coordinated purchasing benefits will be realized by all employees. [9]I may be reached at X466 if you have any questions.

6.2 Collaborative Brainstorming (Obj. 1)

TEAM SPEAKING

Brainstorming can be a productive method for generating problem-solving ideas. You can improve your brainstorming skills through practice.

Your Task. In teams of four or five, analyze a problem on your campus such as the following: unavailable classes, unrealistic degree requirements, lack of student intern programs, poor parking facilities, inadequate registration process, lack of diversity among students on campus, and so forth. Use brainstorming techniques to generate ideas that clarify the problem and explore its solutions. Each team member should prepare a cluster diagram to record the ideas generated. Either individually or as a team, organize the ideas into an outline with three to five main points and numerous subpoints. Assume that your ideas will become part of a letter to be sent to an appropriate campus official or to your campus newspaper discussing the problem and your solution. Remember, however, your role as a student. Be polite, positive, and constructive—not negative, hostile, or aggressive.

6.3 Outlining (Obj. 2)

Web designers at Gap Inc. are complaining about their assignment to develop Web pages describing Gap's employment benefits. Although Gap Inc. offers one of the most comprehensive benefits packages around, the jumble of information has the Web designers totally confused.

The benefits programs include health and wellness benefits covering medical, dental, and vision care. To promote peace of mind among employees and their eligible dependants, Gap offers life insurance, disability insurance, accidental death and dismemberment insurance, and protection against business travel accidents. Another health benefit is a special health care flexible spending account.

Gap Inc. also offers a service that allows employees to speak with a registered nurse 24 hours a day, seven days a week. It's called NurseLine. To prepare for the future, Gap offers a pension plan plus a separate employee stock purchase option. As a "helping hand" to employees, it provides an Employee Assistance Program (EAP) called Life Resources. This is a confidential service that provides counselling resources to help employees and their families cope with personal problems. Gap also offers home loans, moving and relocation assistance, and travel assistance. One special benefit aimed at career development is the tuition reimbursement plan. Gap also encourages employees to develop their careers through its internal placement program.

Your Task. As part of the human resources staff at Gap Inc., you've been asked to make sense of the preceding information so that your Web designers can build it into a coherent presentation. Arrange the benefits information into a simple outline with about five major headings and a title.

6.4 Sentence Elements (Obj. 4)

Your Task. In the following sentences underscore and identify dependent clauses (DC), independent clauses (IC), and phrases (P). Circle subjects and verbs in clauses.

a. We hire talented undergraduates in our intern program.

b. If you qualify, you should send an application to us.

c. In the summer, interns appreciate a program if it offers a learning experience.

6.5 Sentence Length (Obj. 4)

Your Task. Break the following sentences into shorter sentences. Use appropriate transitional expressions.

a. If firms have a substantial investment in original research or development of new products, they should consider protecting those products with patents, although all patents eventually expire and what were once trade secrets can become common knowledge in the industry.

b. As soon as consumers recognize a name associated with a product or service, that name is entitled to legal protection as a trademark; in fact, consumers may even create a trademark where none existed or create a second trademark by using a nickname as a source indicator, such as the name "Coke," which was legally protected even before it had ever been used by the company.

c. Although no magic formula exists for picking a good trademark name, firms should avoid picking the first name that pops into someone's head; moreover, they should be aware that unique and arbitrary marks are best, while descriptive terms such as "car" or "TV repair" are useless, and surnames and geographic names are weak because they lack distinction and exclusivity.

6.6 Active and Passive Voice (Obj. 4)

Your Task. In the following sentences convert passive-voice verbs to active-voice verbs. Add subjects if necessary. Be prepared to discuss which sentence version is more effective.

a. Programs were created by our board so that employees could become volunteers.

b. Employees are encouraged to take up to five hours a month of paid time to volunteer.

c. Café-style restaurants are provided for employees in our corporate buildings.

d. When it was realized that transportation was a problem, interoffice shuttles were established.

e. Our company was named in *Fortune* magazine's "100 Best Places to Work."

Now convert active-voice verbs to passive-voice verbs, and be prepared to discuss which sentence version is more effective.

f. We cannot authorize repair of your DVD because you have allowed the warranty period to expire.

g. I cannot give you a cash refund for merchandise that you purchased 90 or more days ago.
h. ValleyView Golf Course does not accept players who are not members.
i. You must submit your résumé and cover letter by e-mail.
j. Jennifer added the two columns instead of subtracting them, thus producing the incorrect total.

6.7 Dangling and Misplaced Modifiers (Obj. 4)

Your Task. Remedy any dangling or misplaced modifiers in the following sentences. Add subjects as needed, but retain the introductory phrases. Mark "C" if correct.

a. Ignoring the warning prompt on the screen, the computer was turned off resulting in the loss of data.
b. Using a number of creative search terms, the Web site was finally found.
c. By working as a summer intern, your chance of permanent employment is greatly improved.
d. Acting as team leader, the meeting was organized and led by Matt.
e. To prevent head injuries, wear a helmet when cycling.

6.8 Transitional Expressions (Obj. 5)

Your Task. Add transitional expressions to the following sentences to improve the flow of ideas (coherence).

a. We recognize that giving your time to important causes is just as important as giving your money. We've created several programs that make it easy and rewarding for our employees to get involved.
b. Our computerized file includes all customer data. It provides space for name, address, and other vital information. It has an area for comments, a feature that comes in handy and helps us keep our records up-to-date.
c. No one likes to turn out poor products. We began highlighting recurring problems. Employees make a special effort to be more careful in doing their work right the first time. It doesn't have to be returned to them for corrections.
d. In-depth employment interviews may be structured or unstructured. Structured interviews have little flexibility. All candidates are asked the same questions in the same order. Unstructured interviews allow a free-flowing conversation. Topics are prepared for discussion by the interviewer.
e. Fringe benefits consist of life, health, and dental insurance. Some fringe benefits might include paid vacations and sick pay. Other fringe benefits include holidays, funeral leave, and emergency leave. Paid lunch, rest periods, tuition reimbursement, and child care are also sometimes provided.

6.9 Paragraph Organization (Obj. 5)

Your Task. The following poorly written paragraphs follow the indirect plan. Locate the main sentence in each paragraph. Then revise each paragraph so that it is organized directly. Improve coherence by using the techniques described in this chapter.

a. Many of our customers limp through their business despite problems with their disk drives, printers, and peripherals. We cannot service their disk drives, printers, and peripherals. These customers are unable to go without this equipment long enough for the repair. We've learned that there are two times when we can get to that equipment. We can do our repairs in the middle of the night or on Sunday. All of our staff of technicians now works every Sunday. Please authorize additional budget for my department to hire technicians for night and weekend service hours.
b. Air express is one of the ways SturdyBilt power mowers and chain saws may be delivered. Air express promises two-day delivery but at a considerable cost. The cheapest method is for retailers to pick up shipments themselves at our nearest distribution centre. We have distribution centres in Regina, Winnipeg, and Thunder Bay. Another option involves having our trucks deliver the shipment from our distribution centre to the retailer's door for an additional fee. These are the options SturdyBilt provides for the retailers purchasing our products.

C.L.U.E. REVIEW 6

Edit the following sentences to correct faults in grammar, punctuation, spelling, and word use.

1. Whether you are writting a short memo or a thirty page report you should expect to conduct formal, or informal research.
2. Our company Vice President came to the President and I asking for help with 2 complex but seperate desktop publishing problems.
3. Because neither of us are particularly creative we decided to organize a brainstorming session.
4. To develop a better sense of design we collected desireable samples from: books, magazines, brochures and newsletters.
5. We noticed that, poorly-designed projects often was filled with cluttered layouts, incompatible typefaces, and to many typefaces.
6. Our brain storming session included the following individuals; Troy, Rhonda, Amanda and Matt.

7. We encouraged participants to think visually but most was reluctant to draw pictures.

8. One of our principle goals were to create one hundred ideas in thirty minutes however we were prepared to meet up to 1 hour.

9. Because we know that ideas continue to incubate we encouraged every one to continue too submit ideas, after the session ended.

10. Robyn Clarkes article titled A Better way to brainstorm which appeared in the magazine Black Enterprise proved to be very helpful.

Chapter 7

Writing Process Phase 3: Revise, Proofread, Evaluate

LEARNING OBJECTIVES

1. *Apply Phase 3 of Guffey's 3-×-3 writing process, which begins with techniques to make a message clear, conversational, and concise.*

2. *Describe revision tactics that make a document vigorous and direct.*

3. *Discuss revision strategies that improve readability.*

4. *List problem areas that good proofreaders examine carefully.*

5. *Compare the proofreading of routine and complex documents.*

6. *Evaluate a message to judge its success.*

WRITING PROCESS PHASE 3: REVISE

1 The final phase of Guffey's 3-×-3 writing process focuses on revising, proofreading, and evaluating. Revising means improving the content and sentence structure of your message. Proofreading involves correcting its grammar, spelling, punctuation, format, and mechanics. Evaluating is the process of analyzing whether your message achieved its purpose. Many businesspeople realize that their ideas are worth little unless they can be communicated effectively to coworkers and to management. In the communication process the techniques of revision can often mean the difference between the acceptance or rejection of ideas.

While the composition process differs for individuals and situations, this final phase should occupy a significant share of the total time you spend on a message. As you learned earlier, some experts recommend devoting about half of the total composition time to revising and proofreading.[1]

Because few writers can produce a satisfactory copy on the first attempt, revision is an important step in the writing process.

Rarely is the first or even second version of a message satisfactory. The revision stage is your chance to make sure your message says what you mean. Many professional writers compose the first draft quickly without worrying about language, precision, or correctness. Then they revise and polish extensively. Other writers, however, prefer to revise as they go—particularly for shorter business documents.

Important messages—such as those you send to management or to customers or turn in to instructors for grades—deserve careful revision and proofreading. When you finish a first draft, plan for a cooling-off period. Put the document aside and return to it after a break, preferably after 24 hours or longer.[2]

Whether you revise immediately or after a break, you'll want to examine your message critically. You should be especially concerned with ways to improve its clarity, conciseness, vigour, and readability.

Keeping It Clear

The goal of business writing is to express rather than impress.

One of the first revision tasks is assessing the clarity of your message. A clear message is one that is immediately understood. To achieve clarity, resist the urge to show off or be fancy. Remember that your goal is not to impress an instructor. Instead, the goal of business writing is to *express*, not *impress*. This involves two simple rules: (1) keep it simple and (2) keep it conversational.

Why do some communicators fail to craft simple, direct messages? For several reasons:

- Untrained executives and professionals worry that plain messages don't sound important.
- Subordinates fear that plain talk won't impress the boss.
- Unskilled writers create foggy messages because they have not learned how to communicate clearly.
- Unethical writers intentionally obscure a message to hide the truth.

To achieve clarity, remember to KISS: Keep It Short and Simple!

Whatever the cause, you can eliminate the fog by applying the familiar KISS formula: Keep It Short and Simple! One way to achieve clear writing is to use active-voice sentences that avoid foggy, indirect, and pompous language.

Foggy
To be sure of obtaining optimal results, it is essential that you give your employees the implements that are necessary for completion of the job.

Clear
To get the best results, give employees the tools they need to do the job.

Keeping It Conversational

Clarity is further enhanced by language that sounds like conversation. This doesn't mean that your letters and memos should be chatty or familiar. Rather, you should strive to sound professional, yet not artificial or formal. This means avoiding legal terminology, technical words, and third-person constructions (*the undersigned, the writer*). Business messages should sound warm, friendly, and conversational—not stuffy and formal.[3] To sound friendly, include occasional contractions (*can't, doesn't*) and first-person pronouns (*I/we*). This warmth is appropriate in all but the most formal business reports. You can determine whether your writing is conversational by trying the kitchen test. If it wouldn't sound natural in your kitchen, it probably needs revision. Note how the following formal sentence was revised to pass the kitchen test.

To achieve a conversational tone, sound professional but not stilted.

Formal
Our organization would like to inform you that your account is being credited in the aforementioned sum.

Conversational
We're crediting your account for $78.

Keeping It Concise

In revising, make certain that a message makes its point in the fewest possible words. In explaining a five-page letter to a friend, former British Prime Minister Winston Churchill once said, "I would have written a short letter, but I didn't have the time."[4]

Main points are easier to understand in concise messages.

Messages without flabby phrases and redundancies are easier to comprehend and more emphatic because main points stand out. Efficient messages also save the reader valuable time.

But concise writing is not easy. To turn out slim sentences and lean messages, you do not have to be brusque, rude, or simple-minded. Instead, you must take time in the revision stage to "trim the fat." And before you can do that, you must learn to recognize it. Locating and excising wordiness involves (1) removing opening fillers, (2) deleting long lead-ins, (3) eliminating redundancies, (4) reducing compound prepositions, and (5) purging empty words.

Short messages require more effort than long, flabby ones.

Removing Opening Fillers. Openers like *there is* and *it is* fill in sentences but generally add no meaning. These fillers reveal writers spinning their wheels until deciding where the sentence is going. Train yourself to question these constructions. About 75 percent of sentence-opening fillers can be eliminated, almost always resulting in more emphatic and more efficient sentences.

Wordy
There are three vice presidents who report directly to the president.

Concise
Three vice presidents report directly to the president.

Long lead-ins delay getting to the "meat" of the sentence.

Deleting Long Lead-Ins. Delete unnecessary introductory words. The meat of the sentence often follows the words *that* and *because.* In addition, many long lead-ins say what is obvious.

Wordy	**Concise**
This is to inform you that you can redeem travel awards at our Web site.	You can redeem travel awards at our Web site.

Redundancies convey the same meaning more than once.

Eliminating Redundancies. Expressions that repeat meaning or include unnecessary words are redundant. To say *unexpected surprise* is like saying "surprise surprise" because *unexpected* carries the same meaning as *surprise.* Excessive adjectives, adverbs, and phrases often create redundancies and wordiness. The following list represents a tiny segment of the large number of redundancies appearing in business writing today.

What word in each expression creates the redundancy?

Redundancies to Avoid

advance warning	exactly identical	perfectly clear
alter or change	few in number	personal opinion
assemble together	free and clear	potential opportunity
basic fundamentals	grateful thanks	positively certain
collect together	great majority	proposed plan
consensus of opinion	integral part	serious interest
contributing factor	last and final	refer back
dollar amount	midway between	true facts
each and every	new changes	visible to the eye
end result	past history	unexpected surprise

Wordy prepositional phrases can be shortened to single words.

Reducing Compound Prepositions. Single words can often replace wordy prepositional phrases. In the following examples notice how the shorter forms say the same thing but more efficiently.

Wordy Compound Preposition	**Shorter Form**
as to whether	whether
at a later date	later
at this point in time	now
at such time, at which time	when
by means of, in accordance with	by
despite the fact that	although
due to the fact that, inasmuch as, in view of the fact that	because
for the amount of	for
in advance of, prior to	before
subsequent to	after
the manner in which	how
until such time as	until

Purging Empty Words. Familiar phrases roll off the tongue easily, but many contain expendable parts. Be alert to these empty words and phrases: *case, degree, the*

Although stockbrokers understand the meaning of their finger gestures in buying and selling stocks, investors were often confused by the language appearing in investment literature. Plain language guidelines offer suggestions to avoid redundancies, long sentences, wordy phrases, passive voice, and abstract words. These techniques are helpful to all business communicators.

fact that, factor, instance, nature, and *quality.* Notice how much better the following sentences sound when we remove all the empty words:

> Except for ~~the instance of~~ Mazda, Japanese imports sagged.
>
> She chose a career in a field that was analytical ~~in nature~~. (Or, *She chose a career in an analytical field.*)
>
> Student writing in that class is excellent ~~in quality~~.

Good writers avoid saying what is obvious.

Also avoid saying the obvious. In the following examples notice how many unnecessary words we can omit through revision:

> ~~When it arrived,~~ I cashed your cheque immediately. (*Announcing the cheque's arrival is unnecessary. That fact is assumed in its cashing.*)
>
> ~~This is to inform you that~~ the meeting will start at 2 p.m. (*Avoid unnecessary lead-in.*)

Finally, look carefully at clauses beginning with *that, which,* and *who.* They can often be shortened without loss of clarity. Search for phrases, such as *it appears that.* Such phrases can be reduced to a single adjective or adverb, such as *apparently.*

> Changing the name of a ^successful^ company ~~that is successful~~ is always risky.
>
> All employees ~~who are among those~~ completing the course will be reimbursed.

REVISING FOR VIGOUR AND DIRECTNESS

2

Much business writing has been criticized as lifeless, cautious, and "really, really boring."[5] This boredom results not so much from content as from wordiness and dull, trite expressions. You've already studied ways to improve clarity and conciseness. You can also reduce wordiness and improve vigour by (1) kicking the noun habit and (2) dumping trite business phrases.

Kicking the Noun Habit

Some writers become addicted to nouns, needlessly transforming verbs into nouns (*we make a recommendation of* instead of *we recommend*). This bad habit increases sentence length, drains verb strength, slows the reader, and muddies the thought. Notice how efficient, clean, and forceful the verbs below sound compared with their noun phrase counterparts.

Much business writing is plagued by wordiness and triteness.

Wordy Noun Phrase	Verb
conduct a discussion of	discuss
create a reduction in	reduce
engage in the preparation of	prepare
give consideration to	consider
make an assumption of	assume
make a discovery of	discover
perform an analysis of	analyze
reach a conclusion about	conclude
take action on	act

Dumping Trite Business Phrases

To sound "businesslike," many writers repeat the same stale expressions that other writers have used over the years. Your writing will sound fresher and more vigorous if you eliminate these phrases or find more original ways to convey the idea.

Avoid trite expressions that are overused in business writing.

Trite Phrase	Improved Version
as per your request	as you request
pursuant to your request	at your request
enclosed please find	enclosed is
every effort will be made	we'll try
in accordance with your wishes	as you wish
in receipt of	have received
please do not hesitate to	please
thank you in advance	thank you
under separate cover	separately
with reference to	about

REVISING FOR READABILITY

3

To help receivers anticipate and comprehend ideas quickly, a number of graphic highlighting techniques are helpful. You can use (1) parallelism, which involves balanced writing, (2) lists and bullets, which facilitate quick comprehension, (3) highlighting, which makes important points more visible, and (4) other highlighting techniques to improve readability.

Developing Parallelism for Balance

As you revise, be certain that you express similar ideas in balanced or parallel construction. For example, the phrase *clearly, concisely, and correctly* is parallel because all the words end in *-ly*. To express the list as *clearly, concisely, and with correctness* is jarring because the last item is not what the receiver expects. Instead of an adverb, the series ends with a noun. To achieve parallelism, match nouns with nouns, verbs with verbs, phrases with phrases, and clauses with clauses. Avoid mixing active-voice verbs with passive-voice verbs.

Parallelism means matching nouns with nouns, verbs with verbs, phrases with phrases, and so on.

Not Parallel	**Improved**
Good managers analyze a problem, collect data, and alternatives are evaluated.	Good managers analyze a problem, collect data, and evaluate alternatives. *(Series matches verb forms.)*

Be alert to a list or series of items; the use of *and* or *or* should signal you to check for balanced construction. When elements cannot be balanced fluently, consider revising to subordinate or separate the items.

Not Parallel	**Improved**
Foreign service employees must be able to communicate rapidly, concisely, and be flexible in handling diverse responsibilities.	Foreign service employees must be able to communicate rapidly and concisely; they must also be flexible in handling diverse responsibilities.

Using Numbered and Bulleted Lists for Quick Comprehension

One of the best ways to ensure rapid comprehension of ideas is through the use of numbered or bulleted lists. Ideas formerly buried within sentences or paragraphs stand out when listed. Readers not only understand your message more rapidly and easily but also consider you efficient and well organized. Lists provide high "skim value." This means that readers use lists to read quickly and grasp main ideas. By breaking up complex information into smaller chunks, lists improve readability, comprehension, and retention. They also force the writer to organize ideas and write efficiently. Use numbered lists for items that represent a sequence or reflect a numbering system. Use bulleted lists to highlight items that don't necessarily show a chronology.

Graphic devices such as lists, bullets, headings, and white space spotlight important ideas.

In listing items vertically, capitalize the word at the beginning of each line. Add end punctuation only if the statements are complete sentences, and be sure to use parallel construction. Notice in the numbered list that each item begins with a verb. In the bulleted list each item follows an adjective/noun sequence.

Lists offset from the text and introduced with bullets or numbers have a strong visual impact.

Bulleted List

Chez Hélène attracts upscale customers by featuring the following:

- Quality fashions
- Personalized service
- Generous return policy

Numbered List

Chez Hélène advises recruiters to follow these steps in hiring applicants:

1. Examine application
2. Interview applicant
3. Check references

Adding Headings for Visual Impact

Headings are an important tool for highlighting information and improving readability. They encourage the writer to organize carefully so that similar material is grouped together. And they help the reader separate major ideas from details. Moreover, headings enable a busy reader to skim familiar or less important information. They also provide a quick preview or review. Although headings appear more often in reports, they are equally helpful in complex letters and memos. Here, they are used with bullets to summarize categories:

Category Headings
Chez Hélène focuses on the following areas in the employment process:

- **Attracting applicants.** We advertise for qualified applicants, and we also encourage current employees to recommend good people.
- **Interviewing applicants.** Our specialized interviews include simulated customer encounters as well as scrutiny by supervisors.
- **Checking references.** We investigate every applicant thoroughly, including conversations with former employers and all listed references.

Improving Readability With Other Graphic Techniques

Headings help writers to organize information and enable readers to absorb important ideas.

Vertical lists and headings are favourite tools for improving readability, but other graphic techniques can also focus attention. To highlight individual words, use CAPITAL letters, <u>underlining</u>, **bold** type, or *italics.* Be careful with these techniques, though, because readers may feel they are being shouted at.

One final technique to enhance comprehension is blank space. Space is especially important in e-mail messages when formatting techniques don't always work. Grouped ideas under a capitalized heading with blank space preceding the heading can greatly improve readability.

The following chapters supply additional ideas for grouping and spotlighting data. Although highlighting techniques can improve comprehension, they can also clutter a message if overdone. Many of these techniques also require more space, so use them judiciously.

Measuring Readability

Formulas can measure how easy, or difficult, a message is to read. Two well-known formulas are Robert Gunning's Fog Index and the Flesch-Kincaid Index. Both measure word and sentence length to determine readability. The longer a sentence, the more difficult it is to read. If you are using a current version of Microsoft Word, the software will calculate a readability score for any passages you highlight.* Word shows a "reading ease" score as well as the Flesch-Kincaid grade level score. A score of 10, for example, means that the passage can be easily read by a person with 10 years of schooling.

*On the **Tools** menu, click **Options,** and then click the **Spelling & Grammar** tab. Select the **Check grammar with spelling** check box. Select the **Show readability statistics** check box, and then click **OK.** When Microsoft Word finishes checking spelling and grammar, it displays information about the reading level of the highlighted passage.

Your goal should be to keep your writing between the levels of 8 and 12. Magazines and newspapers that strive for wide readership keep their readability between these grade levels.

Readability formulas, however, don't always tell the full story. Although they provide a rough estimate, those based solely on word and sentence counts fail to measure meaningfulness. Even short words (such as *skew, onus,* and *wane*) can cause trouble if readers don't recognize them. More important than length are a word's familiarity and meaningfulness to the reader. In Chapter 5 you learned to adapt your writing to the audience by selecting familiar words. Other techniques that can improve readability include well-organized paragraphs, transitions to connect ideas, headings, and lists.

Readability formulas based on word and sentence length do not always measure meaningfulness.

The task of revision, summarized in the following checklist, is hard work. It demands objectivity and a willingness to cut, cut, cut. Although painful, the process is gratifying. It's a great feeling when you realize your finished message is clear, concise, and readable.

CHECKLIST FOR REVISING MESSAGES

- ✓ **Keep the message simple.** Express ideas directly. Don't show off or use fancy language.
- ✓ **Be conversational.** Include occasional contractions (*hasn't, don't*) and first-person pronouns (*I/we*). Use natural-sounding language.
- ✓ **Avoid opening fillers.** Omit sentence fillers such as *there is* and *it is* to produce more direct expression.
- ✓ **Shun redundancies.** Eliminate words that repeat meanings, such as *mutual cooperation.* Watch for repetitious adjectives, adverbs, and phrases.
- ✓ **Tighten your writing.** Check phrases that include *case, degree, the fact that, factor,* and other words and phrases that unnecessarily increase wordiness. Avoid saying the obvious.
- ✓ **Don't convert verbs to nouns.** Keep your writing vigorous by avoiding the noun habit (*analyze,* not *make an analysis of*).
- ✓ **Avoid trite phrases.** Keep your writing fresh, direct, and contemporary by skipping such expressions as *enclosed please find* and *pursuant to your request.*
- ✓ **Strive for parallelism.** Help receivers anticipate and comprehend your message by using balanced writing (*planning, drafting, and constructing,* not *planning, drafting, and construction*).
- ✓ **Highlight important ideas.** Use graphic techniques such as letters, numerals, bullets, headings, capital letters, underlining, boldface, and italics to spotlight ideas and organization.
- ✓ **Consider readability.** Strive to keep the reading level of a message between Grades 8 and 12. Remember that short, familiar words and short sentences help readers comprehend.

WRITING PROCESS PHASE 3: PROOFREAD

Once you have the message in its final form, it's time to proofread it. Don't proofread earlier because you may waste time checking items that eventually are changed or omitted.

What to Watch for in Proofreading

Proofreading before a document is completed is generally a waste of time.

Careful proofreaders check for problems in these areas:

- **Spelling.** Now's the time to consult the dictionary. Is *recommend* spelled with one *c* or two? Do you mean *affect* or *effect*? Use your computer spell checker, but don't rely on it totally. See the following Tech Talk box to learn more about the benefits and hazards of computer spell checkers.
- **Grammar.** Locate sentence subjects. Do their verbs agree with them? Do pronouns agree with their antecedents? Review the C.L.U.E. principles in Appendix A if necessary. Use your computer's grammar checker, but be suspicious. See the following Tech Talk box.
- **Punctuation.** Make sure that introductory clauses are followed by commas. In compound sentences put commas before coordinating conjunctions (*and, or, but, nor*). Double-check your use of semicolons and colons.
- **Names and numbers.** Compare all names and numbers with their sources because inaccuracies are not immediately visible. Especially verify the spelling of the names of individuals receiving the message. Most of us immediately dislike someone who misspells our name.
- **Format.** Be sure that your document looks balanced on the page. Compare its parts and format with those of standard documents. If you indent paragraphs, be certain that all are indented.

How to Proofread Routine Documents

5 Most routine documents require a light proofreading. You may be working with a handwritten or a printed copy or on your computer screen. If you wish to print a copy, make it a rough draft (don't print it on letterhead stationery). In time, you may be able to produce a "first-time-final" message, but beginning writers seldom do.

For handwritten or printed messages, read the entire document. Watch for all of the items just described. Use standard proofreading marks, shown on the inside front cover of this book, to indicate changes.

For both routine and complex documents, it's best to proofread from a printed copy, not on a computer screen.

You can read computer messages on the screen using the down arrow to reveal one line at a time. This focuses your attention at the bottom of the screen. A safer proofreading method, however, is reading from a printed copy. You're more likely to find errors and to observe the tone.

How to Proofread Complex Documents

Long, complex, or important documents demand more careful proofreading using the following techniques:

- Print a copy, preferably double-spaced, and set it aside for at least a day. You'll be more alert after a breather.
- Allow adequate time to proofread carefully. A common excuse for sloppy proofreading is lack of time.

TECH TALK

Using Spell Checkers and Grammar/Style Checkers Wisely

Spell-checking and grammar-checking software are two useful tools that can save you from many embarrassing errors. They can also greatly enhance your revision techniques—if you know how to use them wisely.

Spell Checkers

Although some writers dismiss spell checkers as an annoyance, most of us are only too happy to have our typos and misspelled words detected. If you are using Microsoft Word, you need to set the options to "check spelling as you type." (Use the **Tools** menu, click **Options.** On the **Spelling & Grammar** tab choose *Check spelling as you type* and *Always suggest corrections.*) When you see a wavy red line under a word, you are being notified that the highlighted word is not in the computer's dictionary. Right click for a list of suggested replacements and other actions.

Spell checkers are indeed wonderful, but they are far from perfect. If you mistype a word, the spell checker is not sure what you meant and the suggested replacements may be way off target. What's more, a spell checker cannot know when you type *form* that you meant *from.* Lesson: Don't rely totally on spell checkers to find all typos and spelling errors.

Grammar and Style Checkers

Like spell checkers, today's grammar and style checkers are amazingly sophisticated. Microsoft Word marks faults in capitalization, fragments, misused words, double negatives, possessives, plurals, punctuation, subject–verb agreement, gender-specific words, wordiness, and many other problems.

How does a grammar checker work? Let's say you typed the sentence, *The office and its equipment is for sale.* You would see a wavy green line appear under *is.* Right click and a box identifies the subject–verb agreement error and suggests the verb *are* as a correction. When you click *are,* the error is corrected. You can set grammar and style options in the **Grammar Settings** dialogue box (**Tools** menu, **Options** command, **Spelling & Grammar** tab, and **Settings**).

Before you decide that a grammar checker will solve all your writing problems, think again. Even Word's highly developed software misses plenty of errors, and it also mismarks some correct expressions.

- Be prepared to find errors. Psychologically, we don't expect to find errors, and we don't want to find them. You can overcome this obstacle by anticipating errors and congratulating, not criticizing, yourself each time you find one.
- Read the message at least twice—once for word meanings and once for grammar/mechanics. For very long documents (book chapters and long articles or reports), read a third time to verify consistency in formatting.
- Reduce your reading speed. Concentrate on individual words rather than ideas.
- For documents that must be perfect, have someone read the message aloud. Spell names and difficult words, note capitalization, and read punctuation.
- Use standard proofreading marks, shown on the inside front cover of this book, to indicate changes.

WRITING PROCESS PHASE 3: EVALUATE

As part of applying finishing touches, take a moment to evaluate your writing. How successful will this message be? Does it say what you want it to? Will it achieve your purpose? How will you know if it succeeds?

A good way to evaluate messages is through feedback.

As you learned in Chapter 1, the best way to judge the success of your communication is through feedback. Thus, you should encourage the receiver to respond to your message. This feedback will tell you how to modify future efforts to improve your communication technique.

Your instructor will also be evaluating some of your writing. Although any criticism is painful, try not to be defensive. Look on these comments as valuable advice tailored to your specific writing weaknesses—and strengths. Many businesses today spend thousands of dollars bringing in communication consulting companies to improve employee writing skills. You're getting the same training in this course. Take advantage of this chance—one of the few you may have—to improve your skills. The best way to improve your skills, of course, is through instruction, practice, and evaluation.

In this class you have all three elements: instruction in the writing process (summarized in Figure 7.1), practice materials, and someone willing to guide and evaluate your efforts. Those three elements are the reasons that this book and this course may be the most valuable in your entire curriculum.

SUMMARY OF LEARNING OBJECTIVES

1 **Apply Phase 3 of Guffey's 3-×-3 writing process, which begins with techniques to make a message clear, conversational, and concise.** The final phase of the writing process involves revising, proofreading, and evaluating. Clear documents use active-voice sentences and simple words and avoid negative expressions. Clarity is further enhanced by language that sounds like conversation, including occasional contractions and first-person pronouns (*I/we*). Conciseness can be achieved by excluding opening fillers (*There are*), redundancies (*basic essentials*), and compound prepositions (*by means of*).

FIGURE 7.1 The Complete 3-×-3 Writing Process

Prewriting 1

Analyze: Define your purpose. Select the most appropriate form (channel). Visualize the audience.

Anticipate: Put yourself in the reader's position and predict his or her reaction to this message.

Adapt: Consider ways to shape the message to benefit the reader, using his or her language.

Writing 2

Research: Collect data formally and informally. Generate ideas by brainstorming and clustering.

Organize: Group ideas into a list or an outline. Select direct or indirect strategy.

Compose: Write first draft, preferably with a good word processing program.

Revising 3

Revise: Revise for clarity, tone, conciseness, and vigour. Revise to improve readability.

Proofread: Proofread to verify spelling, grammar, punctuation, and format. Check for overall appearance.

Evaluate: Ask yourself whether the final product will achieve the purpose.

2 **Describe revision tactics that make a document vigorous and direct.** Writers can achieve vigour in messages by revising wordy phrases that needlessly convert verbs into nouns. For example, instead of *we conducted a discussion of,* write *we discussed.* To make writing more direct, good writers replace trite business phrases, such as *please do not hesitate to,* with similar expressions, such as *please.*

3 **Discuss revision strategies that improve readability.** One revision technique that improves readability is the use of balanced constructions (*parallelism*). For example, *collecting, analyzing, and illustrating data* is balanced and easy to read. *Collecting, analysis of, and illustration of data* is more difficult to read because it is unbalanced. Parallelism involves matching nouns with nouns, verbs with verbs, phrases with phrases, and clauses with clauses. Other techniques that improve readability are bullets for lists for quick comprehension, headings for visual impact, and graphic techniques such as capital letters, underlining, italics, and bold print to highlight and order ideas. Readability can be measured by formulas that count long words and sentence length.

4 **List problem areas that good proofreaders examine carefully.** Proofreaders must be especially alert to these problem areas: spelling, grammar, punctuation, names, numbers, and document format.

5 **Compare the proofreading of routine and complex documents.** Routine documents may be proofread immediately after completion. They may be read line by line on the computer screen or, better yet, from a printed draft copy. More complex documents, however, should be proofread after a breather. To do a good job, you must read from a printed copy, allow adequate time, reduce your reading speed, and read the document at least three times—for word meanings, for grammar/mechanics, and for formatting.

6 **Evaluate a message to judge its success.** Encourage feedback from the receiver so that you can determine whether your communication achieved its goal. Welcome any advice from your instructor on how to improve your writing skills. Both techniques contribute to helping you evaluate the success of a message.

CHAPTER REVIEW

1. Approximately how much of the total composition time should be spent revising, proofreading, and evaluating? (Obj. 1)
2. What is the KISS method? In what three ways can it apply to business writing? (Obj. 1)
3. What is a redundancy? Give an example. Why should writers avoid redundancies? (Obj. 1)
4. Why should communicators avoid openings such as *there is*? (Obj. 1)
5. What shorter forms could be substituted for the expressions *by means of, despite the fact that,* and *at this point in time*? (Obj. 1)
6. Why should a writer avoid the opening *This memo is to inform you that our next committee meeting is Friday*? (Obj. 1)
7. Why should a writer avoid an expression such as *We hope you will give consideration to our proposal*? (Obj. 2)
8. What's wrong with businesslike expressions such as *enclosed please find* and *as per your request*? (Obj. 2)
9. What is parallelism, and how can you achieve it? (Obj. 3)
10. What is "high skim value," and how can you achieve it? (Obj. 4)
11. Name five specific items to check in proofreading. Be ready to discuss methods you find useful in spotting these errors. (Obj. 4)
12. In proofreading, what major psychological problem do you face in finding errors? How can you overcome this barrier? (Obj. 4)
13. List four or more techniques for proofreading complex documents. (Obj. 5)
14. How can you overcome defensiveness when your writing is criticized constructively? (Obj. 6)

CRITICAL THINKING

1. Why is it difficult to recommend a specific process that all writers can follow in composition? (Obj. 1)
2. Would you agree or disagree with the following statement by writing expert William Zinsser? "Plain talk will not be easily achieved in corporate America. Too much vanity is on the line." (Objs. 1 and 2)
3. Since business writing should have "high skim value," why not write everything in bulleted lists? (Objs. 2 and 4)
4. Why should the proofreading process for routine documents differ from that for complex documents? (Objs. 4 and 5)

ACTIVITIES

7.1 Document for Analysis: Poorly Written Letter (Objs. 1–5)

The following letter suffers from a number of weaknesses discussed in this chapter.

Your Task. Study the letter and analyze its weaknesses. In teams or in a class discussion, list at least five specific weaknesses. Then, revise for clarity, tone, conciseness, readability, and correctness. As your instructor directs, use standard proofreading marks to show corrections or revise at a computer.

As per your request, the undersigned is transmitting to you the attached documents with regard to the improvement of security in your business. To ensure the improvement of your after-hours security, you should initially make a decision with regard to exactly what you contemplate must have protection. You are, in all probability, apprehensive not only about your electronic equipment and paraphernalia but also about your company records, information, and data.

Due to the fact that we feel you will want to obtain protection for both your equipment and data, we will make suggestions for taking a number of judicious steps to inhibit crime. First and foremost, we make a recommendation that you install defensive lighting. A consultant for lighting, currently on our staff, can design both outside and inside lighting, which brings me to my second point. Exhibit security signs, because of the fact that nonprofessional thieves are often as not deterred by posted signs on windows and doors. As my last and final recommendation, you should install space alarms, which are sensors that look down over the areas that are to receive protection, and activate bells or additional lights, thus scaring off intruders.

After reading the materials that are attached, please call me to initiate a verbal discussion regarding protection of your business.

Sincerely,

7.2 Document for Analysis: Weak E-Mail Message (Objs. 1–5)

The following e-mail message suffers from a number of weaknesses discussed in this chapter.

Your Task. Study the message and analyze its weaknesses. In teams or in a class discussion, list at least five specific weaknesses. Then, revise for clarity, tone, conciseness, readability, and correctness. In this message consider using two bulleted lists and headings to improve readability. As your instructor directs, use standard proofreading marks to show corrections or revise at a computer.

TO: Keisha Love, Sales and Marketing Manager <klove@ricco.com>
FROM: Arthur Pentilla, CEO <apentilla@ricco.com>
DATE: Current
SUBJECT: IMPROVING SAFETY AND SECURITY FOR TELECOMMUTERS

This e-mail is to inform you that due to the fact that telecommuting is becoming increasingly popular, we feel that it's important and necessary for us to be more careful in planning for information security as well as for the health and personal safety of our employees.

In view of the fact that many of our employees may be considering telecommuting, we have prepared a complete guide for managers. There are structured agreements in the guide that specify space, equipment, and how you should schedule employees. Please discuss the recommendations that follow for a home workspace as well as recommendations for security with any of your staff members who may be making a consideration of telecommuting.

7.3 Learning About Writing Techniques in Your Field (Objs. 1–6)

How much writing is required by people working in your career area? The best way to learn about on-the-job writing is to talk with someone who has a job similar to one you hope to have some day.

Your Task. Interview someone in your field of study. Ask questions such as these: • *What kind of writing do you do?* • *What kind of planning do you do before writing?* • *Where do you get information? Do you brainstorm? Make lists?* • *Do you compose with pen and paper, a computer, or a dictating machine?* • *How long does it take you to compose a routine one- or two-page memo or letter? Do you revise? How often?* • *Do you have a preferred method for proofreading? When you have questions about grammar and mechanics, what or whom do you consult? Does anyone read your drafts and make suggestions?* • *Can you describe your entire composition process?* • *Do you ever work with others to produce a document? How does this process work?* • *What makes writing easier or harder for you? Have your writing methods and skills changed since you left school?* Your instructor may ask you to present your findings orally or in a written report.

7.4 Clarity (Obj. 1)

Your Task. Revise the following sentences to make them direct, simple, and conversational.

a. In response to your verbal instruction, we will undertake the task of studying your investment program.
b. A request that we are making to managers is that they not spend all their time in their departments and instead visit other departments one hour a month.
c. We in management are of the opinion that employees have not been made sufficiently aware of the problem of computer security.
d. Our organization is honoured to have the pleasure of extending a welcome to you as a new customer.
e. Enclosed herewith please find the proposal which we have the honour to submit to your esteemed organization in regard to the acquisition and purchase of laptop computers.

7.5 Conciseness (Obj. 2)

Your Task. Suggest shorter forms for the following expressions.

a. in the event that
b. a report for which you have no use
c. a project manager who took great care
d. arranged according to numbers
e. a program that is intended to save time

7.6 Conciseness (Obj. 2)

Your Task. Revise and shorten the following sentences.

a. There are only two applicants among all who applied who we think are qualified.
b. As per your recommendation, we will not attempt to make alterations or changes in the proposal at this point in time.
c. Because of the fact that his visit was an unexpected surprise, we were totally unprepared to make a presentation of profit and loss figures.
d. It is perfectly clear that meetings held on a monthly basis are most effective.
e. Despite our supposition that the bill appeared erroneous, we sent a cheque in the amount of $250.

7.7 Vigour (Obj. 2)

Your Task. Revise the following sentences to reduce noun conversions, trite expressions, and other wordiness.

a. It is my understanding that your team shows a preference for bringing its investigation to an end.
b. Please give consideration to our latest proposal, despite the fact that it comes into conflict with the original plan.

c. Our assessment of the damages in the amount of $500 caused us to make a reduction in the amount of the claim.
d. Please give authorization to Human Resources for the conduct of an investigation of employee turnover for the period of January through August.
e. After we engage in the preparation of a report, our recommendations will be presented in their final form before the Executive Committee.

7.8 Parallelism (Obj. 3)

Your Task. Revise the following sentences to improve parallelism. If elements cannot be balanced fluently, use appropriate subordination.

a. Your goal should be to write business messages that are concise, clear, and written with courteousness.
b. Ensuring equal opportunities, the removal of barriers, and elimination of age discrimination are our objectives.
c. Ms. Thomas tries to read all e-mail messages daily, but responses may not be made until the following day.
d. Because of its air conditioning and since it is light and attractive, I prefer this office.
e. For this position we assess oral and written communication skills, how well individuals solve problems, whether they can work with teams, and we're also interested in interpersonal skills, such as cultural awareness and sensitivity.

7.9 Lists, Bullets, and Headings (Obj. 3)

Your Task. Revise the following statements using the suggested highlighting techniques. Improve parallel construction and reduce wordiness if necessary.

a. Revise using letters, such as (a) and (b), within the sentence.

The benefits for employees that our organization offers include annual vacations of two weeks, insurance for group life, provision for insurance coverage of medical expenses for the family, and a private retirement fund.

b. Revise using a vertical list with bullets.

The Canadian Automobile Association makes a provision of the following tips for safe driving. You should start your drive well rested. You should wear sunglasses in bright sunshine. To provide exercise breaks, plan to stop every two hours. Be sure not to drink alcohol or take cold and allergy medications before you drive.

c. Revise using a vertical list with numbers.

Our lawyer made a recommendation that we take several steps to avoid litigation in regard to sexual harassment. The first step we should take involves establishing an unequivocal written statement prohibiting sexual harassment within our organization. The second thing we should do is make sure training sessions are held for supervisors regarding a proper work environment. Finally, some kind of procedure for employees to lodge complaints is necessary. This procedure should include investigation of complaints.

7.10 Proofreading (Obj. 5)

Use proofreading marks to mark spelling, grammar, punctuation, capitalization, and other errors in the following sentences.

a. One of the beautyes of e-mail, is that it enables you to comunicate quick and easy with colleagues, and customers around theGlobe.
b. English maybe the International Language of commerce but that does not mean that every readr will have a trouble-free experience with message writen in english.
c. Be especially carful with dates. For example A message that reads "Our video conference begins at 6 p.m. on 7/8/06" would mean July 8, 2006, to north americans.
d. To europeans the time and date would be written as follows: "The video conference will begin at 18:00 on 7 July 2006.
e. Because europeans use a twenty-four-hour military clock be sure to write int'l messages in that format.

C.L.U.E. REVIEW 7

Edit the following sentences to correct faults in grammar, punctuation, spelling, and word use.

1. Business documents must be written clear to insure that readers comprehend the message quick.
2. The prominant Chairman of Monsanto in europe complained that his managers reports were to long, to frequent and too unread.
3. The report contained so many redundancys that it's main principals requesting Provincial and Federal funding was lost.
4. The information was sited in an recent article entitled "Whats new in grammer-checking softwear, however I can't locate the article now.
5. All 3 of our companys recruiters: Jim Lucus, Doreen Delgado, and Brad Kirby—critisized there poorly-written procedures.
6. To help recievers anticipate and comprehend ideas quick 2 special writing techniques is helpful, parallalism which involves balanced writing and highlighting which makes important points more visible.

7. When you must proof read a important document all ways work from a printed copy.
8. Have you all ready ordered the following? a dictionary a reference manual and a style book.
9. As we completed the final step in the writing process we wondered how feasable it would be to evaluate our message?
10. Its almost impossible to improve your communication skills alone, therefore you should take advantage of this oppertunity.

Unit 3
Business Correspondence

Routine E-Mail Messages and Memos

Routine Letters and Goodwill Messages

Persuasive and Sales Messages

Negative Messages

Chapter 8

Routine E-Mail Messages and Memos

LEARNING OBJECTIVES

1 *Discuss how Guffey's 3-×-3 writing process helps you produce effective e-mail messages and memos.*

2 *Analyze the structure and formatting of e-mail messages and memos.*

3 *Describe smart e-mail practices, including getting started; content, tone, and correctness; netiquette; replying to e-mail; and formatting.*

4 *Write procedure and information e-mail messages and memos.*

5 *Write request and reply e-mail messages and memos.*

6 *Write confirmation e-mail messages and memos.*

APPLYING THE WRITING PROCESS TO PRODUCE EFFECTIVE E-MAIL MESSAGES AND MEMOS

1

E-mail has become the primary communication channel for internal communication.

In most organizations today, an amazing change has taken place in internal communication. In the past, written messages from insiders took the form of hard-copy memorandums. But e-mail is now the communication channel of choice. In a recent survey 85 percent of online Canadians reported that e-mail has made them much more efficient, and nearly two thirds (62 percent) prefer to communicate via e-mail than through other methods.[1]

A primary function of e-mail is exchanging messages within organizations. Such internal communication has taken on increasing importance today. Organizations are downsizing, flattening chains of command, forming work teams, and empowering rank-and-file employees. Given more power in making decisions, employees find that they need more information. They must collect, exchange, and evaluate information about the products and services they offer. Management also needs input from employees to respond rapidly to local and global market changes. This growing demand for information means an increasing use of e-mail, although hard-copy memos are still written.

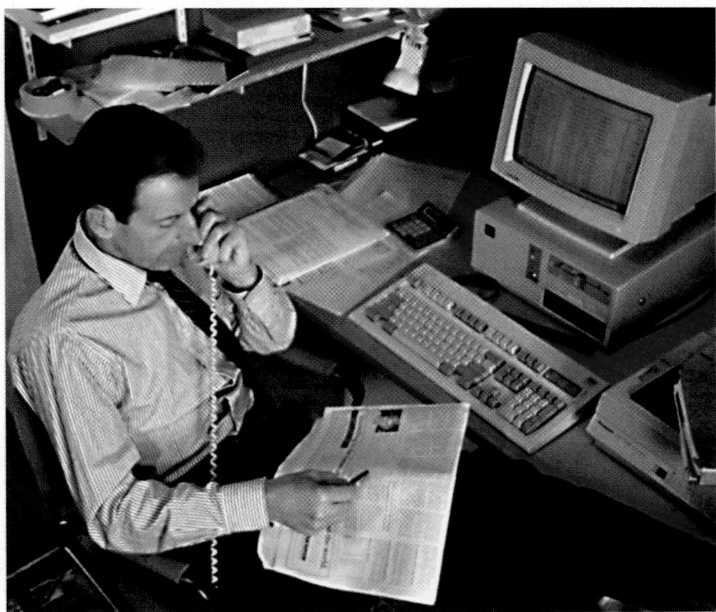

Technology allows increasing numbers of employees to work at home and telecommute to the office. As a result, more and more messages—especially memos—need to be written to keep the lines of communication open between remote employees and the office.

Developing skill in writing e-mail messages and memos brings you two important benefits. First, well-written documents are likely to achieve their goals. They create goodwill by being cautious, caring, and clear. They do not intentionally or unintentionally foment ill feelings. Second, well-written internal messages enhance your image within the organization. Individuals identified as competent, professional writers are noticed and rewarded; most often, they are the ones promoted into management positions.

This chapter concentrates on routine e-mail messages and memos. These straightforward messages open with the main idea because their topics are not sensitive and require little persuasion. You'll study the characteristics, writing process, and organization for e-mail messages and memos. Because e-mail is still a new and powerful channel of communication, we'll devote special attention to using it safely and effectively. Finally, you'll learn to write procedure, information, request, reply, and confirmation memos.

Careful writing takes time—especially at first. By following a systematic plan and practising your skill, however, you can speed up your efforts and greatly improve the product. Bear in mind, moreover, that the effort you make to improve your communication skills can pay big dividends. Frequently, your speaking and writing abilities determine how much influence you'll have in your organization. As with other writing tasks, e-mail and memo writing follow the familiar three-phase writing process.

Analyzing the purpose of a message helps determine whether a permanent record is required.

Phase 1: Analysis, Anticipation, and Adaptation. In Phase 1 (prewriting) you'll need to spend some time analyzing your task. It's amazing how many of us are ready to put our pens or computers into gear before engaging our minds. Ask yourself these important questions:

- **Do I really need to write this e-mail or memo?** A phone call or a quick visit to a nearby coworker might solve the problem—and save the time and expense of a written message. On the other hand, some written messages are needed to provide a permanent record.
- **Why am I writing?** Know why you are writing and what you hope to achieve. This will help you recognize what the important points are and where to place them.
- **How will the reader react?** Visualize the reader and the effect your message will have. Consider ways to shape the message to benefit the reader. Also remember that your message may very well be forwarded to someone else.
- **How can I save my reader's time?** Think of ways that you can make your message easier to comprehend at a glance. Use bullets, asterisks, lists, headings, and white space, discussed in Chapter 7, to improve readability.

Phase 2: Research, Organization, and Composition. In Phase 2 (writing) you'll first want to check the files, gather documentation, and prepare your message. Make an outline of the points you wish to cover. For short messages you can jot down notes on the document you are answering or make a scratch list at your computer. As you compose your message, avoid amassing huge blocks of text. No one wants to read endless lines of type. Instead, group related information into paragraphs, preferably short ones. Paragraphs separated by white space look inviting. Be sure each paragraph begins with the main point and is backed up by details. If you bury the main point in the middle of a paragraph, it may be missed. Be sure to prepare for revision, because excellence is rarely achieved on the first effort.

Phase 3: Revision, Proofreading, and Evaluation. Phase 3, revising, involves putting the final touches on your message. Careful and caring writers will ask a number of questions as they do the following:

- **Revise for clarity.** Viewed from the receiver's perspective, are the ideas clear? Do they need more explanation? If the memo is passed on to others, will they need further explanation? Consider having a colleague critique your message if it is an important one.
- **Proofread for correctness.** Are the sentences complete and punctuated properly? Did you overlook any typos or misspelled words? Remember to use your spell checker and grammar checker to proofread your message before sending it.
- **Plan for feedback.** How will you know whether this message is successful? You can improve feedback by asking questions (such as *Do you agree with these suggestions?*) and by making it easy for the receiver to respond.

Structuring E-Mail Messages and Memos

2

Whether electronic or hard-copy, routine memos generally contain four parts: (1) an informative subject line that summarizes the message, (2) an opening that reveals the main idea immediately, (3) a body that explains and justifies the main idea, and (4) an action closing. Remember that routine messages deliver good news or standard information.

Subject Line. In e-mails and memos a subject line is mandatory. It summarizes the central idea, thus providing quick identification for reading and for filing. In e-mail messages, subject lines are essential. Busy readers glance at a subject line and decide when and whether to read the message. Those without subject lines are automatically deleted.

Direct memos contain a subject line, an opener stating the main idea, a body with explanation and justification, and an action closing.

What does it take to get your message read? For one thing, stay away from meaningless or dangerous words such as *Issue, Problem, Important,* or *Help.* Including a word such as *Free* is dangerous because it may trigger spam filters. Try to make your subject line *talk* by including a verb. Explain the purpose of the message and how it relates to the reader (*Need You to Showcase Two Items at Our Next Trade Show* rather than *Trade Show*). Finally update your subject line to reflect the current message (*Staff Meeting Rescheduled for May 12* rather than *Re: Staff Meeting*). Remember that a subject line is usually written in an abbreviated style often without articles (*a, an, the*). It need not be a complete sentence, and it does not end with a period.

Opening. Most memos and e-mails cover nonsensitive information that can be handled in a straightforward manner. Begin by frontloading; that is, reveal the main idea immediately. Even though the purpose of the memo or e-mail is summarized in the subject line, that purpose should be restated—and amplified—in the first sentence. Some readers skip the subject line and plunge right into the first sentence. Notice how the following indirect opener can be improved by frontloading.

Indirect Opening
For the past six months, the Human Resources Development Department has been considering changes in our employees' benefit plan.

Direct Opening
Please review the following proposal regarding employees' benefits, and let me know by May 20 if you approve these changes.

Body. The body provides more information about the reason for writing. It explains and discusses the subject logically. Good e-mail messages and memos generally discuss only one topic. Limiting the topic helps the receiver act on the subject and respond to it appropriately.

The body explains data and should use graphic devices to improve readability.

Design your data for easy comprehension by using numbered lists, headings, tables, and other graphic highlighting techniques. Compare the following versions of the same message. Observe how the graphic devices of columns, headings, and white space make the main points easy to comprehend.

Hard-to-Read Paragraph Version
Effective immediately are the following air travel guidelines. Between now and December 31, only account executives may take company-approved trips. These individuals will be allowed to take a maximum of two trips, and they are to travel economy or budget class only.

Improved Version With Graphic Highlighting
Effective immediately are the following air travel guidelines:

- Who may travel: Account executives only
- How many trips: A maximum of two trips
- By when: Between now and December 31
- Air class: Economy or budget class only

Memos should close with (1) action information including dates and deadlines, (2) a summary, or (3) a closing thought.

Closing. Generally end with (1) action information, dates, or deadlines; (2) a summary of the message; or (3) a closing thought. Here again the value of thinking through the message before actually writing it becomes apparent. The closing is where readers look for deadlines and action language.

In more complex messages a summary of main points may be an appropriate closing. If no action request is made and a closing summary is unnecessary, you might end with a simple concluding thought. Although you needn't close messages to coworkers with goodwill statements such as those found in letters to customers or clients, some closing thought is often necessary to prevent a feeling of abruptness. Closings can show gratitude or encourage feedback. Other closings look forward to what's next. Avoid closing with trite expressions that sound mechanical and insincere.

Putting It All Together. Now let's put it all together. An e-mail message (see Figure 8.1) was sent by Matt Barnes, marketing manager, to his supervisor, Debbie Pickett.

Notice that it opens directly. Both the subject line and the first sentence explain the purpose for writing. Notice how easy the e-mail is to read. Bullets and headings emphasize the actions necessary to solve the database problems. Notice, too, that the e-mail ends with a deadline and refers to the next action to be taken.

USING E-MAIL SMARTLY AND SAFELY

3

E-mail messages are becoming more proper and more professional.

E-mail messages may be dangerous because they travel long distances and are difficult to erase.

Early e-mail users were encouraged to "ignore stylistic and grammatical considerations." They thought that "words on the fly," as e-mail messages were considered, required little editing or proofing. Correspondents used emoticons (such as sideways happy faces) to express their emotions. And some e-mail today is still quick and dirty. But as this communication channel matures, messages are becoming more proper and more professional. Today more than 31 billion e-mails are sent each day worldwide. E-mail is twice as likely as the telephone to be used to communicate at work. We have become so dependent on e-mail that 53 percent of people using it at work say their productivity drops when they are away from it.[2]

Wise e-mail business communicators are aware of its dangers. They know that thoughtless messages can cause irreparable harm. They know that their messages can travel (intentionally or unintentionally) long distances. A quickly drafted note may end up in the boss's mailbox or be forwarded to an adversary's box.

Getting Started

Because e-mail is now a mainstream communication channel, messages should be well organized, carefully composed, and grammatically correct.

Despite its dangers and limitations, e-mail has definitely become a mainstream channel of communication. That's why it's important to take the time to organize your thoughts, compose carefully, and be concerned with correct grammar and punctuation. The following pointers will help you get off to a good start in using e-mail safely and effectively.

- **Compose offline.** Instead of dashing off hasty messages, consider using your word processing program to write offline. Then upload your message to the e-mail network. This avoids "self destructing" (losing all your writing through some glitch or pressing the wrong key) when working online.
- **Get the address right.** E-mail addresses are sometimes complex, often illogical, and always unforgiving. Omit one character or misread the letter *l* for the number *1*, and your message bounces. Solution: Use your electronic address

FIGURE 8.1 Information E-Mail Message

Prewriting 1

Analyze: The purpose of this memo is to describe database problems and recommend solutions.

Anticipate: The audience is the writer's boss, who is familiar with the topic and who appreciates brevity.

Adapt: Because the reader requested this message, the direct pattern is most appropriate.

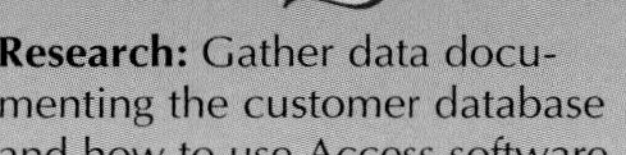

Writing 2

Research: Gather data documenting the customer database and how to use Access software.

Organize: Announce recommendations and summarize problems. In the body, list the three actions for solving the problem. In the closing, describe reader benefits, provide a deadline, and specify the next action.

Compose: Prepare the first draft.

Revising 3

Revise: Highlight the two main problems and the three recommendations. Use asterisks, caps, and headings to improve readability. Make the bulleted ideas parallel.

Proofread: Double-check to see whether *database* is one word or two. Use spell checker.

Evaluate: Does this e-mail supply concise information the boss wants in an easy-to-read form?

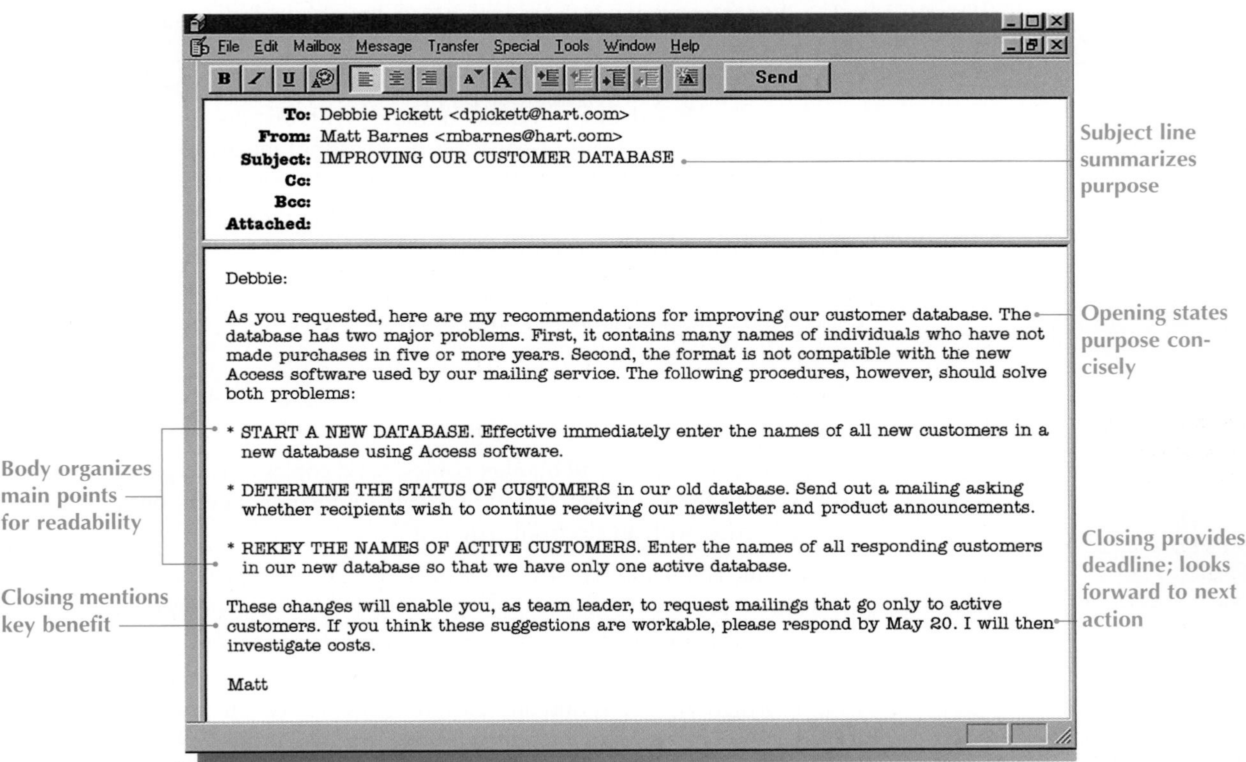
File Edit Mailbox Message Transfer Special Tools Window Help
Send
Subject line summarizes purpose
Opening states purpose concisely
Body organizes main points for readability
Closing mentions key benefit
Closing provides deadline; looks forward to next action

To: Debbie Pickett <dpickett@hart.com>
From: Matt Barnes <mbarnes@hart.com>
Subject: IMPROVING OUR CUSTOMER DATABASE
Cc:
Bcc:
Attached:

Debbie:

As you requested, here are my recommendations for improving our customer database. The database has two major problems. First, it contains many names of individuals who have not made purchases in five or more years. Second, the format is not compatible with the new Access software used by our mailing service. The following procedures, however, should solve both problems:

* START A NEW DATABASE. Effective immediately enter the names of all new customers in a new database using Access software.

* DETERMINE THE STATUS OF CUSTOMERS in our old database. Send out a mailing asking whether recipients wish to continue receiving our newsletter and product announcements.

* REKEY THE NAMES OF ACTIVE CUSTOMERS. Enter the names of all responding customers in our new database so that we have only one active database.

These changes will enable you, as team leader, to request mailings that go only to active customers. If you think these suggestions are workable, please respond by May 20. I will then investigate costs.

Matt

book for people you write frequently. And double-check every address that you key in manually. Also be sure that you don't reply to a group of receivers when you intend to answer only one.

- **Avoid misleading subject lines.** Make sure your subject line is relevant and helpful. Generic tags such as *Hi!* and *Great Deal* may cause your message to be deleted before it is opened.
- **Apply the top-of-screen test.** When readers open your message and look at the first screen, will they see what is most significant? Your subject line and first paragraph should convey your purpose.

Content, Tone, and Correctness. Although e-mail seems as casual as a telephone call, it's not. Because it produces a permanent record, think carefully about what you say and how you say it.

- **Be concise.** Don't burden readers with unnecessary information. Remember that monitors are small and typefaces are often difficult to read. Organize your ideas tightly.
- **Don't send anything you wouldn't want published.** Because e-mail seems like a telephone call or a person-to-person conversation, writers sometimes send sensitive, confidential, inflammatory, or potentially embarrassing messages. Beware! E-mail creates a permanent record that often does not go away even when deleted. And every message is a corporate communication that can be used against you or your employer. Don't write anything that you wouldn't want your boss, your family, or a judge to read.
- **Don't use e-mail to avoid contact.** E-mail is inappropriate for breaking bad news or for resolving arguments. For example, it's improper to fire a person by e-mail. It's also not a good channel for dealing with conflict with supervisors, subordinates, or others. If there's any possibility of hurt feelings, pick up the telephone or pay the person a visit.
- **Care about correctness.** People are still judged by their writing, whether electronic or paper-based. Sloppy e-mail messages (with missing apostrophes, haphazard spelling, and stream-of-consciousness writing) make readers work too hard. They resent not only the information but also the writer.
- **Care about tone.** Your words and writing style affect the reader. Avoid sounding curt, negative, or domineering.
- **Resist humour and tongue-in-cheek comments.** Without the nonverbal cues conveyed by your face and your voice, humour can easily be misunderstood.

Netiquette. Although e-mail is a new communication channel, a number of rules of polite online interaction are emerging.

- **Limit any tendency to send blanket copies.** Send copies only to people who really need to see a message. It is unnecessary to document every business decision and action with an electronic paper trail.
- **Never send "spam."** Forty-three percent of Internet users say that their number one pet peeve of e-mail usage is spam (unsolicited e-mail messages).[3]
- **Consider using identifying labels.** When appropriate, add one of the following labels to the subject line: ACTION (action required, please respond); FYI (for your information, no response needed); RE (this is a reply to another message); URGENT (please respond immediately). Some e-mail programs allow you to flag urgent messages.
- **Use capital letters only for emphasis or for titles.** Avoid writing entire messages in all caps, which is like SHOUTING.
- **Don't forward without permission.** Obtain approval before forwarding a message.
- **Reduce attachments.** Because attachments may carry viruses, some receivers won't open them. Consider including short attachments within an e-mail message. If you must send a longer attachment, explain it.

Reading and Replying to E-Mail. The following tips can save you time and frustration when answering messages.

- **Scan all messages in your inbox before replying to each individually.** Because subsequent messages often affect the way you respond, read them all first (especially all of those from the same individual).
- **Print only when necessary.** Generally, read and answer most messages online without saving or printing. Use folders to archive messages on special topics. Print only those messages that are complex, controversial, or involve significant decisions and follow-up.
- **Don't automatically return the sender's message.** When replying, cut and paste the relevant parts. Avoid irritating your recipients by returning the entire "thread" (sequence of messages) on a topic.
- **Revise the subject line if the topic changes.** When replying or continuing an e-mail exchange, revise the subject line as the topic changes.
- **Provide a clear, complete first sentence.** Avoid fragments such as *That's fine with me* or *Sounds good!* Busy respondents forget what was said in earlier messages, so be sure to fill in the context and your perspective when responding.
- **Never respond when you're angry.** Always allow some time to cool off before shooting off a response to an upsetting message. You often come up with different and better alternatives after thinking about what was said. If possible, iron out differences in person.

Personal Use. Remember that office computers are intended for work-related communication.

- **Don't use company computers for personal matters.** Unless your company specifically allows it, never use your employer's computers for personal messages, personal shopping, or entertainment.
- **Assume that all e-mail is monitored.** Employers legally have the right to monitor e-mail, and many do.

Other Smart E-Mail Practices. Depending on your messages and audience, the following tips promote effective electronic communication.

- **Use design to improve the readability of longer messages.** When a message requires several screens, help the reader with headings, bulleted listings, side headings, and perhaps an introductory summary that describes what will follow. Although these techniques lengthen a message, they shorten reading time.
- **Consider cultural differences.** When using this borderless tool, be especially clear and precise in your language. Remember that figurative clichés (*pull up stakes, playing second fiddle*), sports references (*hit a home run, play by the rules*), and slang (*cool, stoked*) cause confusion abroad.
- **Double-check before hitting the *Send* button.** Have you included everything? Avoid the necessity of sending a second message, which makes you look careless. Use spell check and reread for fluency before sending. It's also a good idea to check your incoming messages before sending, especially if several people are involved in a rapid-fire exchange. This helps avoid "passing"—sending out a message that might be altered depending on an incoming note.

Formatting E-Mail Messages

Because e-mail is a developing communication channel, its formatting and usage conventions are still fluid. Users and authorities, for instance, do not always agree on what's appropriate for salutations and closings. The following suggestions, however, can guide you in formatting most e-mail messages, but always check with your organization to observe its practices.

The position of *To, From, Date,* and *Subject* vary, depending on your e-mail program.

Guide Words. Following the guide word *To*, some writers insert just the recipient's electronic address, such as *ptuckman@accountpro.com.* Other writers prefer to include the receiver's full name plus the electronic address, as shown in Figure 8.2. By including full names in the *To* and *From* slots, both receivers and senders are better able to identify the message. By the way, the order of *Date, To, From, Subject,* and other guide words varies, depending on your e-mail program and whether you are sending or receiving the message.

Most e-mail programs automatically add the current date after *Date.* On the *Cc* line (which stands for *carbon* or *courtesy copy*) you can type the address of anyone who is to receive a copy of the message. Remember, though, to send copies only to those people directly involved with the message. Most e-mail programs also include a line for *Bcc* (*blind carbon copy*). This sends a copy without the addressee's knowledge. Many wise writers today use *Bcc* for the names and addresses of a list of receivers, a technique that avoids revealing the addresses to the entire group. On the subject line, identify the subject of the memo. Be sure to include enough information to be clear and compelling.

Salutations for e-mail messages are optional, and practice is as yet unsettled.

Salutation. What to do about a salutation is sticky. Many writers omit a salutation because they consider the message a memo. In the past, hard-copy memos were sent only to company insiders, and salutations were omitted. However, when e-mail messages travel to outsiders, omitting a salutation seems curt and unfriendly. Because the message is more like a letter, a salutation is appropriate (such as *Dear Jake; Hi, Jake; Greetings;* or just *Jake*). Including a salutation is also a visual cue to where the message begins. Many messages are transmitted or forwarded with such long headers that finding the beginning of the message can be difficult. A salutation helps, as shown in Figure 8.2. Other writers do not use a salutation; instead, they use the name of the recipient in the first sentence.

Body. The body of an e-mail message should be typed with upper- and lowercase characters—never in all uppercase or all lowercase characters. Cover just one topic, and try to keep the total message under three screens in length. To assist you, many e-mail programs have basic text-editing features, such as cut, copy, paste, and word-wrap. However, avoid boldface, italics, graphics, and font changes unless your reader's system can handle them.

Closing lines may include the writer's name, title, and organization.

Closing Lines. Writers of e-mail messages sent within organizations may omit closings and even skip their names at the end of messages. They can omit these items because receivers recognize them from identification in the opening lines. But for outside messages, a writer might include a closing such as *Cheers* or *All the best* followed by the writer's name and e-mail address (because some systems do not transmit your address automatically). If the recipient is unlikely to know you, it's wise to include your title and organization. Some veteran e-mail users include a *signature file* with identifying information embellished with keyboard art. Use restraint, however, because signature files take up precious bandwidth (Internet capacity).

FIGURE 8.2 E-Mail Request

Tips for E-Mail Formatting

- After *To,* type the receiver's electronic address. If you include the receiver's name, enclose the address in angle brackets.
- After *From,* type your name and electronic address, if your program does not insert it automatically.
- After *Subject,* provide a clear description of your message.
- Insert the addresses of anyone receiving carbon or blind copies.
- Include a salutation (such as *Dear Marilyn; Hi, Marilyn; Greetings*) or weave the receiver's name into the first line (see Figure 8.5 on page 167). Some writers omit a salutation.
- Set your line length for no more than 80 characters. If you expect your message to be forwarded, set it for 60 characters.
- Use word-wrap rather than pressing *Enter* at line ends.
- Double-space (press *Enter*) between paragraphs.
- Do not type in all caps or in all lowercase letters.
- Include a complimentary close, your name, and your address if you wish.

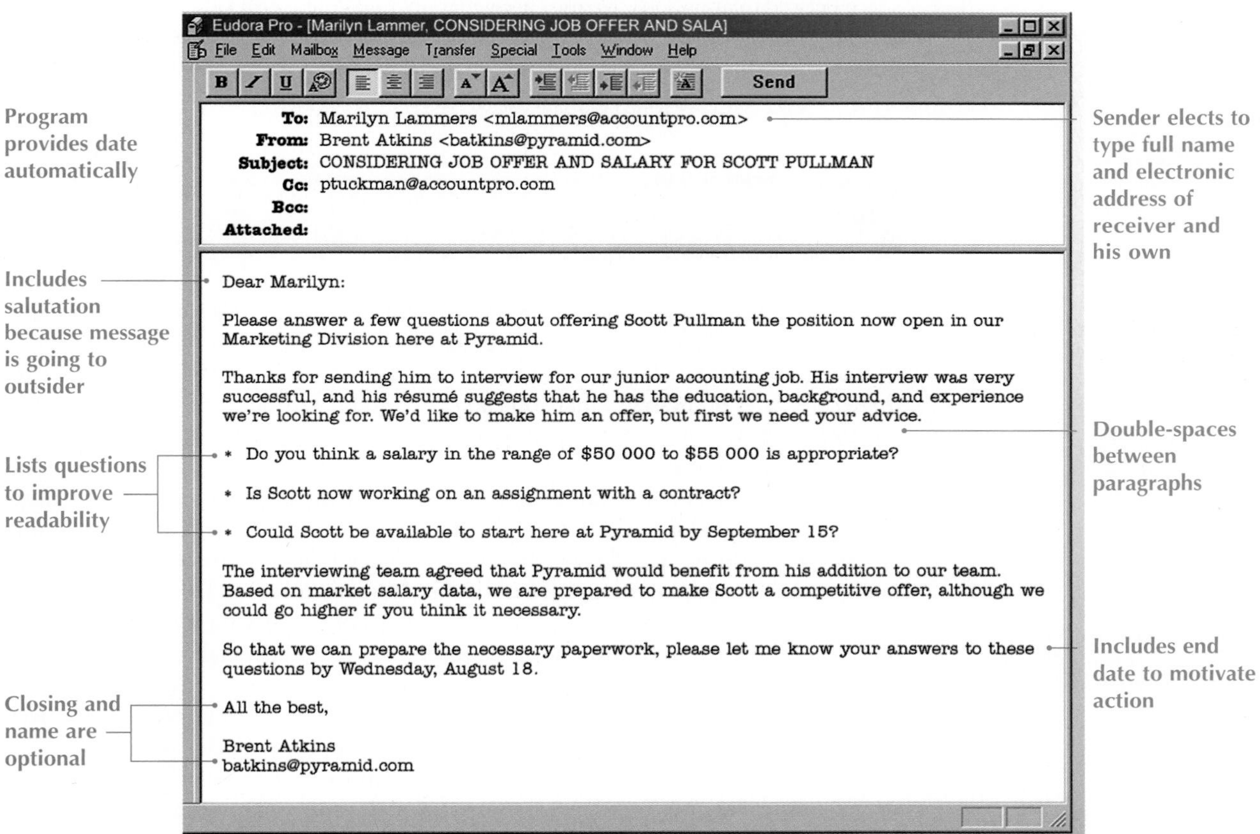
Eudora Pro - [Marilyn Lammer, CONSIDERING JOB OFFER AND SALA]

File Edit Mailbox Message Transfer Special Tools Window Help

Send

To: Marilyn Lammers <mlammers@accountpro.com>
From: Brent Atkins <batkins@pyramid.com>
Subject: CONSIDERING JOB OFFER AND SALARY FOR SCOTT PULLMAN
Cc: ptuckman@accountpro.com
Bcc:
Attached:

Dear Marilyn:

Please answer a few questions about offering Scott Pullman the position now open in our Marketing Division here at Pyramid.

Thanks for sending him to interview for our junior accounting job. His interview was very successful, and his résumé suggests that he has the education, background, and experience we're looking for. We'd like to make him an offer, but first we need your advice.

- Do you think a salary in the range of $50 000 to $55 000 is appropriate?
- Is Scott now working on an assignment with a contract?
- Could Scott be available to start here at Pyramid by September 15?

The interviewing team agreed that Pyramid would benefit from his addition to our team. Based on market salary data, we are prepared to make Scott a competitive offer, although we could go higher if you think it necessary.

So that we can prepare the necessary paperwork, please let me know your answers to these questions by Wednesday, August 18.

All the best,

Brent Atkins
batkins@pyramid.com

Program provides date automatically
Sender elects to type full name and electronic address of receiver and his own
Includes salutation because message is going to outsider
Double-spaces between paragraphs
Lists questions to improve readability
Includes end date to motivate action
Closing and name are optional

Formatting Hard-Copy Memos

Hard-copy memorandums deliver information within organizations. Although e-mail is more often used, hard-copy memos are still useful for important internal messages that require a permanent record or formality. For example, changes in procedures, official instructions, and organization reports are often prepared as hard-copy memos. Because e-mail is still evolving, we examined its formatting carefully in previous paragraphs.

Hard-copy memos require less instruction because formatting is fairly standardized. Some offices use memo forms imprinted with the organization name and, optionally, the department or division names. Although the design and arrangement of memo forms vary, they usually include the basic elements of *Date, To, From,* and *Subject.* Large organizations may include identifying headings, such as *File Number, Floor, Extension, Location,* and *Distribution.* Because of the difficulty of aligning computer printers with preprinted forms, many business writers store memo formats in their computers and call them up when preparing memos. The guide words are then printed with the message, thus eliminating alignment problems.

If no printed or stored computer forms are available, memos may be typed on company letterhead or typed on plain paper. On a full sheet of paper, start the guide word 5 cm from the top; on a half sheet, start 2.5 cm from the top. Double-space and type in all caps the guide words. Align all the fill-in information two spaces after the longest guide word (usually *Subject:*). Leave two blank lines between the last line of the heading and the first line of the memo. Single-space within paragraphs and double-space between paragraphs. Memos are generally formatted with side margins of 3 cm, or they may conform to the printed memo form. Do not justify the right margins. Research has shown that "ragged-right" margins in printed messages are easier to read.

WRITING INFORMATION AND PROCEDURE E-MAIL MESSAGES AND MEMOS

Thus far in this chapter we've reviewed the writing process, analyzed the structure and format of e-mail messages and memos, and presented a number of techniques for using e-mail smartly and safely. Now we're going to apply those techniques to three categories of messages that you can expect to be writing as a business communicator: (1) procedure and information messages, (2) request and reply messages, and (3) confirmation messages.

4

Let's focus first on techniques that will help you write information and procedure messages quickly and efficiently. These messages distribute standard information, describe procedures, and deliver instructions. They typically flow downward from management to employees and relate to the daily operation of an organization. In writing these messages, have one primary function: conveying your idea so clearly that no further explanation (return message, telephone call, or personal visit) is necessary.

As you compose information and procedure messages, follow the writing process and organization plan outlined earlier. That includes an informative subject line, a direct opening, a body that explains, and an appropriate closing.

When writing messages that describe procedures, be particularly careful about clarity and readability. Figure 8.3 shows the first draft of a hard-copy memo written by Troy Bell. His memo was sent to announce a new procedure for employees to follow in advertising open positions. However, the tone was negative, the explanation of the problem rambles, and the new procedure was unclear. Notice, too, that Troy's first draft told readers what they *shouldn't do.* It's more helpful to tell readers what they *should do.* Finally, Troy's memo closed with a threat instead of showing readers how this new procedure will help them.

In the revisions, Troy improved the tone considerably. The subject line contains a please, which is always pleasant to see even if one is giving an order. The subject line also includes a verb and specifies the purpose of the memo. Instead of expressing his ideas with negative words and threats, Troy revised his message to explain objectively and concisely what went wrong.

Troy realized that his original explanation of the new procedure was vague. Messages containing procedures are most readable when instructions are broken down into numbered steps listed chronologically. Each step should begin with an action verb in the command mode. Notice in Troy's revision in Figure 8.3 that numbered items begin with *Write, Bring, Let,* and *Pick up.* It's sometimes difficult to force all the steps in a procedure into this kind of command language.

Why should you go to so much trouble to make lists and achieve parallelism? Parallel language allows readers to comprehend what you have said much more quickly, and it also makes you look professional and efficient.

In writing information and procedure memos, be careful of tone. Today's managers and team leaders seek employee participation and cooperation, but they can't achieve that rapport if they sound like dictators or autocrats. Avoid making accusations and fixing blame. Rather, explain changes, give reasons, and suggest benefits to the reader. Assume that employees want to contribute to the success of the organization and to their own achievement.

Writing Request and Reply E-Mail Messages and Memos

5

Business organizations require information as their fuel. To make operations run smoothly, managers and employees request information from one another and then respond accordingly. Knowing how to write those requests and responses efficiently and effectively can save you time and make you look good.

Request and reply messages follow the direct pattern in seeking or providing information.

Making Requests. If you are requesting routine information or action within an organization, the direct approach works best. Generally, this means asking for information or making the request without first providing elaborate explanations and justifications. Remember that readers are usually thinking, "Why me? Why am I receiving this?" Readers can understand the explanation better once they know what you are requesting.

If you are seeking answers to questions, you have two options for opening the message: (1) ask the most important question first, followed by an explanation and then the other questions, or (2) use a polite command, such as *Please answer the following questions regarding . . . .*

In the body of the memo, you can explain and justify your request or reply. When many questions must be asked, list them, being careful to phrase them similarly. Be courteous and friendly. In the closing include an end date (with a reason, if possible) to promote a quick response. For simple requests some writers encourage their readers to jot responses directly on the request memo.

The e-mail message shown in Figure 8.4 requests information. It opens with a polite command followed by a brief explanation. Notice that the questions are highlighted with asterisks to provide the high "skim value" that is important in business messages. The reader can quickly see what is being asked. The message concludes with an end date and a reason. Providing an end date helps the reader know how to plan a response so that action is completed by the date given. Expressions such as *do it whenever you can* or *complete it as soon as possible* make little impression on procrastinators or very busy people. It's always wise to provide a specific date for completion. Dates can be entered on calendars to serve as reminders.

Replying to Requests. Much business correspondence reacts or responds to previous messages. When responding to an e-mail, memo, or other document, be sure to follow Guffey's 3-×-3 process. Analyze your purpose and audience, collect whatever information is necessary, and organize your thoughts. Make a brief outline of the points you plan to cover.

FIGURE 8.3 Memo That Describes a New Procedure

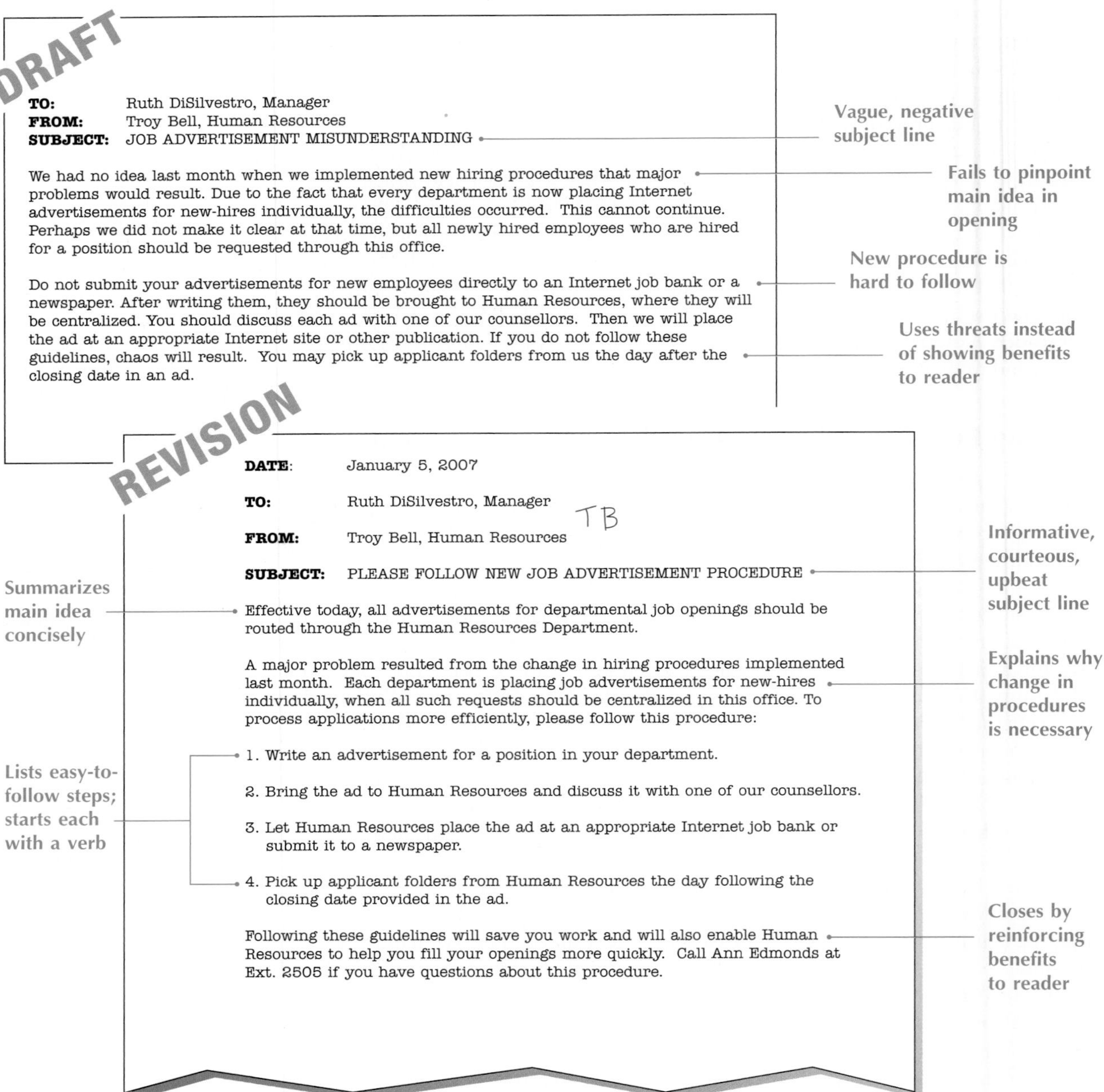

DRAFT

TO: Ruth DiSilvestro, Manager
FROM: Troy Bell, Human Resources
SUBJECT: JOB ADVERTISEMENT MISUNDERSTANDING

We had no idea last month when we implemented new hiring procedures that major problems would result. Due to the fact that every department is now placing Internet advertisements for new-hires individually, the difficulties occurred. This cannot continue. Perhaps we did not make it clear at that time, but all newly hired employees who are hired for a position should be requested through this office.

Do not submit your advertisements for new employees directly to an Internet job bank or a newspaper. After writing them, they should be brought to Human Resources, where they will be centralized. You should discuss each ad with one of our counsellors. Then we will place the ad at an appropriate Internet site or other publication. If you do not follow these guidelines, chaos will result. You may pick up applicant folders from us the day after the closing date in an ad.

REVISION

DATE: January 5, 2007

TO: Ruth DiSilvestro, Manager

FROM: Troy Bell, Human Resources TB

SUBJECT: PLEASE FOLLOW NEW JOB ADVERTISEMENT PROCEDURE

Effective today, all advertisements for departmental job openings should be routed through the Human Resources Department.

A major problem resulted from the change in hiring procedures implemented last month. Each department is placing job advertisements for new-hires individually, when all such requests should be centralized in this office. To process applications more efficiently, please follow this procedure:

1. Write an advertisement for a position in your department.
2. Bring the ad to Human Resources and discuss it with one of our counsellors.
3. Let Human Resources place the ad at an appropriate Internet job bank or submit it to a newspaper.
4. Pick up applicant folders from Human Resources the day following the closing date provided in the ad.

Following these guidelines will save you work and will also enable Human Resources to help you fill your openings more quickly. Call Ann Edmonds at Ext. 2505 if you have questions about this procedure.

Vague, negative subject line
Fails to pinpoint main idea in opening
New procedure is hard to follow
Uses threats instead of showing benefits to reader
Informative, courteous, upbeat subject line
Summarizes main idea concisely
Explains why change in procedures is necessary
Lists easy-to-follow steps; starts each with a verb
Closes by reinforcing benefits to reader

Overused and long-winded openers bore readers and waste their time.

Writers sometimes fall into bad habits in answering memos. Here are some trite and long-winded openers that are best avoided:

In response to your message of the 15th . . . (*States the obvious.*)

Thank you for your memo of the 15th in which you . . . (*Suggests the writer can think of nothing more original.*)

I have before me your memo of the 15th in which you . . . (*Unnecessarily identifies the location of the previous message.*)

Pursuant to your request of the 15th . . . (*Sounds old-fashioned.*)

FIGURE 8.4 E-Mail Message That Makes a Request

Prewriting 1

Analyze: The purpose of this e-mail is to solicit feedback regarding a casual-dress policy.

Anticipate: The message is going to a subordinate who is busy but probably eager to be consulted in this policy matter.

Adapt: Use a direct approach beginning with the most important question. Strive for a positive, professional tone rather than an autocratic, authoritative tone.

Writing 2

Research: Collect secondary information about dress-down days in other organizations. Collect primary information by talking with company managers.

Organize: Begin with the main idea followed by a brief explanation and questions. Conclude with an end date and a reason.

Compose: Prepare the first draft remembering that the receiver is busy and appreciates brevity.

Revising 3

Revise: Rewrite questions to ensure that they are parallel and readable.

Proofread: Decide whether to hyphenate *casual-dress policy* and *dress-down days*. Be sure commas follow introductory clauses. Check question marks.

Evaluate: Does this memo encourage participatory management? Will the receiver be able to answer the questions and respond easily?

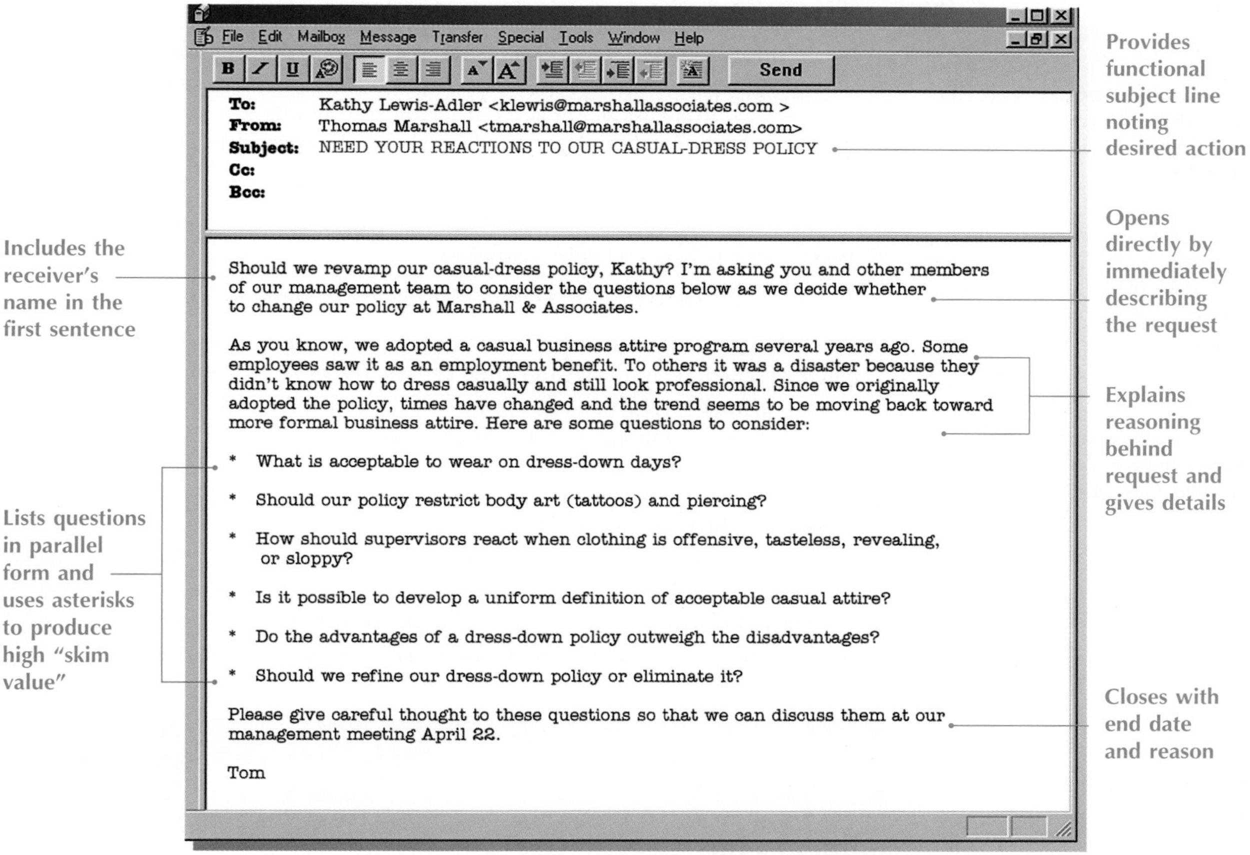

File Edit Mailbox Message Transfer Special Tools Window Help

Send

To: Kathy Lewis-Adler <klewis@marshallassociates.com >
From: Thomas Marshall <tmarshall@marshallassociates.com>
Subject: NEED YOUR REACTIONS TO OUR CASUAL-DRESS POLICY
Cc:
Bcc:

Should we revamp our casual-dress policy, Kathy? I'm asking you and other members of our management team to consider the questions below as we decide whether to change our policy at Marshall & Associates.

As you know, we adopted a casual business attire program several years ago. Some employees saw it as an employment benefit. To others it was a disaster because they didn't know how to dress casually and still look professional. Since we originally adopted the policy, times have changed and the trend seems to be moving back toward more formal business attire. Here are some questions to consider:

* What is acceptable to wear on dress-down days?
* Should our policy restrict body art (tattoos) and piercing?
* How should supervisors react when clothing is offensive, tasteless, revealing, or sloppy?
* Is it possible to develop a uniform definition of acceptable casual attire?
* Do the advantages of a dress-down policy outweigh the disadvantages?
* Should we refine our dress-down policy or eliminate it?

Please give careful thought to these questions so that we can discuss them at our management meeting April 22.

Tom

Provides functional subject line noting desired action

Includes the receiver's name in the first sentence

Opens directly by immediately describing the request

Explains reasoning behind request and gives details

Lists questions in parallel form and uses asterisks to produce high "skim value"

Closes with end date and reason

Instead of falling into the trap of using one of the preceding shopworn openings, start directly by responding to the writer's request. If you agree to the request, show your cheerful compliance immediately. Consider these good-news openers:

Yes, we will be glad to . . . (*Sends message of approval by opening with "Yes."*)

Direct opening statements can also be cheerful and empathic.

Here are answers to the questions you asked about . . . (*Sounds straightforward, businesslike, and professional.*)

You're right in seeking advice about . . . (*Opens with two words that every reader enjoys seeing and hearing.*)

After a direct and empathic opener, provide the information requested in a logical and coherent order. If you're answering a number of questions, arrange your answers in the order of the questions.

In providing additional data, use familiar words, short sentences, short paragraphs, and active-voice verbs. When alternatives exist, make them clear. Consider using graphic highlighting techniques.

If further action is required, be specific in spelling it out. What may be crystal clear to you (because you have been thinking about the problem) is not always immediately apparent to a reader with limited time and interest.

Writing Confirmation E-Mail Messages and Memos

6

Confirmation messages provide a permanent record of oral discussions, decisions, and directives.

Confirmation messages—also called *to-file reports* or *incident reports*—record oral decisions, directives, and discussions. They create a concise, permanent record that could be important in the future. Because individuals may forget, alter, or retract oral commitments, it's wise to establish a written record of significant happenings. Such records are unnecessary, of course, for minor events. The confirmation e-mail message shown in Figure 8.5 reviews the significant points of a sales agreement discussed in a telephone conversation. When you write to confirm an oral agreement, remember these tips:

- Include the names and titles of involved individuals.
- Itemize major issues or points concisely.
- Request feedback regarding unclear or inaccurate points.

Another type of confirmation message simply verifies the receipt of materials or a change of schedule. It is brief and often kept on file to explain your role in a project. Be sure to print a copy if you are using e-mail to have a record.

Confirmation messages can save employees from being misunderstood or blamed unfairly.

Some critics complain that too many "cover-your-tail" messages are written, thus creating excessive and unnecessary paperwork.[4] However, legitimate messages that confirm and clarify events have saved many thoughtful workers from being misunderstood or blamed unfairly.

Sometimes taken lightly, office memos and e-mail messages, like other business documents, should be written carefully. Once they leave the author's hands, they are essentially published. They can't be retrieved, corrected, or revised. Review the following checklist for tips in writing memos that accomplish what you intend.

CHECKLIST FOR WRITING ROUTINE E-MAIL MESSAGES AND MEMOS

Subject Line

- ✓ **Summarize the central idea.** Make the subject line read like a newspaper headline—brief but clear.
- ✓ **Make the subject line talk.** Particularly if action is involved, include a verb.
- ✓ **Avoid empty or dangerous words.** Don't write one-word subject lines such as *Help, Problem,* or *Free.*

FIGURE 8.5 Confirmation E-Mail

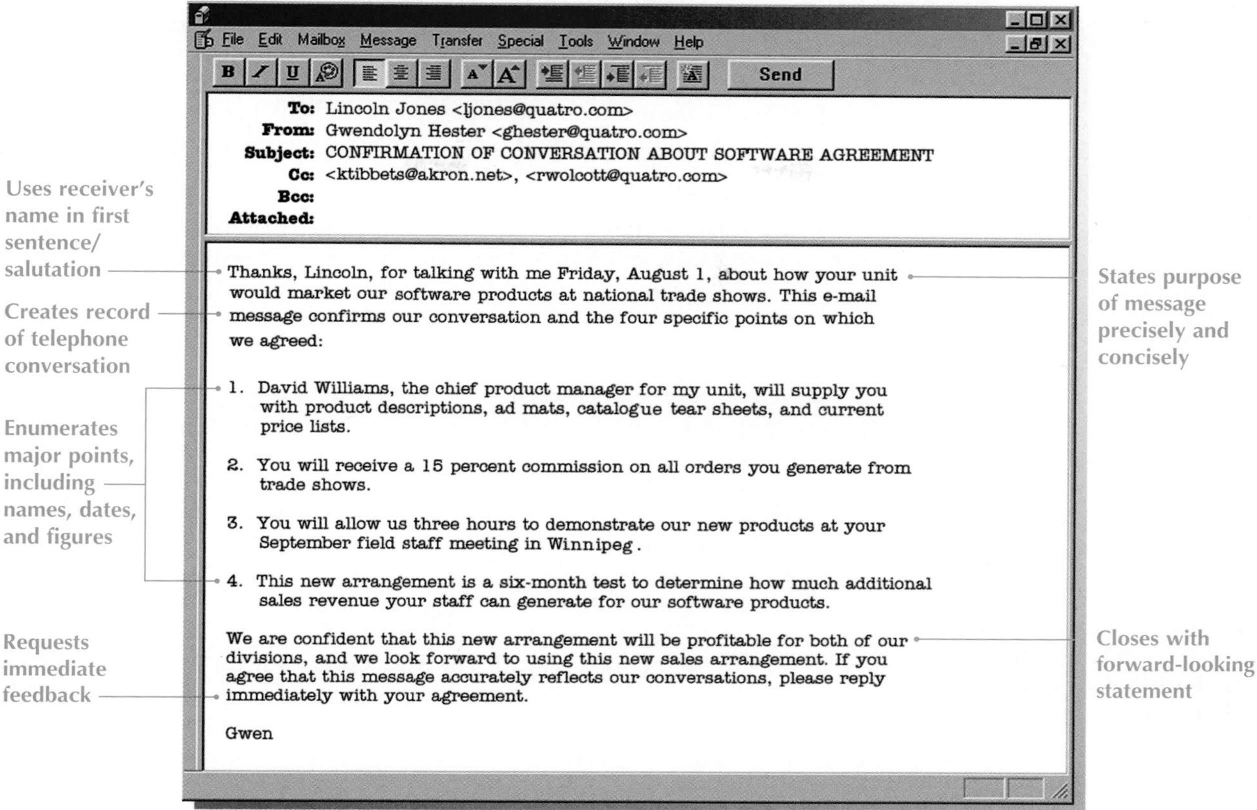

File Edit Mailbox Message Transfer Special Tools Window Help

Send

To: Lincoln Jones <ljones@quatro.com>
From: Gwendolyn Hester <ghester@quatro.com>
Subject: CONFIRMATION OF CONVERSATION ABOUT SOFTWARE AGREEMENT
Cc: <ktibbets@akron.net>, <rwolcott@quatro.com>
Bcc:
Attached:

Thanks, Lincoln, for talking with me Friday, August 1, about how your unit would market our software products at national trade shows. This e-mail message confirms our conversation and the four specific points on which we agreed:

1. David Williams, the chief product manager for my unit, will supply you with product descriptions, ad mats, catalogue tear sheets, and current price lists.

2. You will receive a 15 percent commission on all orders you generate from trade shows.

3. You will allow us three hours to demonstrate our new products at your September field staff meeting in Winnipeg.

4. This new arrangement is a six-month test to determine how much additional sales revenue your staff can generate for our software products.

We are confident that this new arrangement will be profitable for both of our divisions, and we look forward to using this new sales arrangement. If you agree that this message accurately reflects our conversations, please reply immediately with your agreement.

Gwen

Uses receiver's name in first sentence/ salutation
Creates record of telephone conversation
Enumerates major points, including names, dates, and figures
Requests immediate feedback
States purpose of message precisely and concisely
Closes with forward-looking statement

Opening

- **State the purpose for writing.** Include the same information that's in the subject line, but expand it.

- **Highlight questions.** If you are requesting information, begin with the most important question or use a polite command (*Please answer the following questions about . . .*).

- **Supply information directly.** If responding to a request, give the reader the requested information immediately in the opening. Explain later.

Body

- **Explain details.** Arrange information logically. For complex topics use separate paragraphs developed coherently.

- **Enhance readability.** Use short sentences, short paragraphs, and parallel construction for similar ideas.

- **Supply graphic highlighting.** Provide bulleted and/or numbered lists, tables, or other graphic devices to improve readability and comprehension.

- **Be cautious.** Remember that memos and e-mail messages often travel far beyond their intended audiences.

Closing

 **Request action.** If appropriate, state specifically what you want the reader to do. Include a deadline, with reasons, if possible.

 **Summarize the memo or provide a closing thought.** For long memos provide a summary of the important points. If neither an action request nor a summary is necessary, end with a closing thought.

 **Avoid cliché endings.** Use fresh remarks rather than overused expressions such as *If you have additional questions, please do not hesitate to call* or *Thank you for your cooperation.*

SUMMARY OF LEARNING OBJECTIVES

1 **Discuss how Guffey's 3-×-3 writing process helps you produce effective e-mail messages and memos.** The 3-×-3 writing process helps you analyze your purpose and audience before writing. E-mails and memos are appropriate for routine messages, but they shouldn't be used if you need to convey enthusiasm, warmth, or some other emotion; if you need to supply a context; or if you need to smooth over a disagreement. The 3-×-3 process helps you decide how the reader will react and makes you consider how you can save the reader's time. Before writing routine e-mails and memos, collect information and organize your thoughts into a brief outline. After composing the first draft, revise for clarity, proofread for correctness, and plan for feedback.

2 **Analyze the structure and formatting of e-mail messages and memos.** The subject line summarizes the central idea, while the opening repeats that idea and amplifies it. The body explains and provides more information. The closing includes (a) action information, dates, and deadlines; (b) a summary of the memo; and/or (c) a closing thought. E-mail messages should be formatted with a meaningful subject line, an optional salutation, a single-spaced body that is typed with a combination of upper- and lowercase letters, and optional closing lines. Hard-copy memos are formatted similarly but without a salutation or closing. Writers place their initials next to their names on the *From* line.

3 **Describe smart e-mail practices, including getting started; content, tone, and correctness; netiquette; replying to e-mail; and formatting.** Careful e-mail users compose offline, get the address right, avoid misleading subject lines, and are concise. They don't send anything they wouldn't want published, and they don't use e-mail to avoid contact. They care about correctness, resist humour, never send "spam," use identifying labels when appropriate, and use attachments sparingly. In reading and responding, they employ a number of efficient practices such as scanning all incoming messages, limiting printing, and revising the subject line as the message thread changes. They don't use company computers for personal use unless specifically allowed to do so, and they realize that e-mail may be monitored. They strive to improve readability through design, they consider cultural difference, and they double-check before hitting the *Send* button.

QUALITY CHECK (REPRINT)

P.O. #: 531595 **JM**

Pub. Date: Aug 21, 2007

Title: Business Communication: Brief 2e

ISBN: 0176407103

Author: Guffey / Rhodes / Rogin

Filmhouse:

Printer: Quebecor World

Stock: **Text:** New Era Plus

Cover: 12pt C1S

Printing: 02 **Quantity:** 5,264 **Ordered:** Jun 22/07

- [x] P&B Satisfactory
- [ ] Printing Off-Register
- [ ] Hickeys
- [ ] Scuffing
- [ ] Scratching
- [ ] Other
- [ ] Ink Offsetting
- [ ] Trim Rough
- [ ] Minor Inking Variations
- [ ] Major Inking Variations
- [ ] Ghosting

Notes for next reprint:

Distribution:

- [x] Production Library (2)

4 **Write procedure and information e-mail messages and memos.** Messages delivering information or outlining procedures follow the direct memo plan, with the main idea stated immediately. Ideas must be explained so clearly that no further explanation is necessary. The tone of the memo should encourage cooperation.

5 **Write request and reply e-mail messages and memos.** Messages requesting action or information open with a specific request, followed by details. Messages that reply to requests open with information the reader most wants to learn. The body contains details, and the closing may summarize the important points or look forward to a subsequent event or action.

6 **Write confirmation e-mail messages and memos.** Sometimes called "to-file reports" or "incident reports," confirmation messages create a permanent record of oral decisions, directives, and discussions. They should include the names and titles of involved individuals, the major issues discussed, and a request for approval by the receiver.

CHAPTER REVIEW

1. Briefly describe the standard structure for e-mail messages and memos. (Obj. 1)
2. What questions should you ask yourself before writing an e-mail message or memo? (Obj. 1)
3. Name three ways to close a memo or an e-mail message. (Obj. 2)
4. What are some of the dangers for users of e-mail in the workplace? (Obj. 3)
5. Suggest at least ten pointers that you could give to a first-time e-mail user. (Obj. 3)
6. Name at least five rules of e-mail etiquette that show respect for others. (Obj. 3)
7. What are three possibilities in handling the salutation for an e-mail message? (Obj. 3)
8. What tone should managers avoid in writing procedure or information e-mail messages and memos? (Obj. 4)
9. Why should writers of information e-mail messages and memos strive to express ideas positively instead of negatively? (Obj. 4)
10. Should a request e-mail message or memo open immediately with the request or with an explanation? Why? (Obj. 5)
11. What's wrong with a message opener such as *This is to inform you that . . .?* (Obj. 5)
12. What is a confirmation e-mail message or memo? What other names could it be given? (Obj. 6)
13. What three elements should most confirmation e-mail messages and memos include? (Obj. 6)

CRITICAL THINKING

1. How can the writer of a business e-mail message or memo develop a conversational tone and still be professional? Why do e-mail writers sometimes forget to be professional? (Objs. 1–3)
2. What factors would help you decide whether to write a memo, send an e-mail, make a telephone call, leave a voice mail message, or deliver a message in person? (Objs. 1 and 2)
3. Why are lawyers and technology experts warning companies to store, organize, and manage computer data, including e-mail, with sharper diligence? (Obj. 3)
4. Discuss the ramifications of the following statement: Once a memo or any other document leaves your hands, you have essentially published it. (Objs. 2–6)

ACTIVITIES

8.1 Document for Analysis: Information E-Mail (Obj. 4)

Your Task. Analyze the following e-mail message. It suffers from wordiness and lack of graphic highlighting techniques to improve readability. List its weaknesses. If your instructor directs, revise it.

✗ *Poorly Written E-Mail*

To: Todd Shimoyama <todd.shimoyama@chemco.com>

From: Avianca Harper <avianca.harper@chemco.com>

Subject: REPORT

Cc:

Todd:

I went to the Workplace Issues conference on May 2. The topic was how to prevent workplace violence, and I found it very fascinating. Although we have been fortunate to avoid serious incidents at our company, it's better to be safe than sorry. Since I was the representative from our company, I thought you would like me to report about some suggestions for preventing workplace violence. Robert Mather was the presenter, and he made suggestions in three categories, which I will summarize here.

Mr. Mather cautioned organizations to prescreen job applicants. As a matter of fact, wise companies do not offer employment until after a candidate's background has been checked. Just the mention of a background check is enough to make some candidates withdraw. These candidates, of course, are the ones with something to hide.

A second suggestion was that companies should prepare a good employee handbook that outlines what employees should do when they suspect potential workplace violence. This handbook should include a way for informers to be anonymous.

A third recommendation had to do with recognizing red-flag behaviour. This involves having companies train managers to recognize signs of potential workplace violence. What are some of the red flags? One sign is an increasing number of arguments (most of them petty) with coworkers. Another sign is extreme changes in behaviour or statements indicating depression over family or financial problems. Another sign is bullying or harassing behaviour. Bringing a firearm to work or displaying an extreme fascination with firearms is another sign.

By the way, the next Workplace Issues conference is in September, and the topic is the new WSIB standards.

I think that the best recommendation is prescreening job candidates. This is because it is most feasible. If you want me to do more research on prescreening techniques, do not hesitate to let me know. Let me know by May 7 if you want me to make a report at our management meeting, which is scheduled for June.

Avianca

8.2 Document for Analysis: Request Memo (Obj. 5)

Your Task. Analyze the following memo. List its weaknesses. If your instructor directs, revise it.

✗ *Poorly Written Memo*

DATE: Current

TO: All Employees

FROM: Elizabeth Mendoza, Human Resources

SUBJECT: NEW HOLIDAY PLAN

In the past we've offered all employees 11 holidays (starting with New Year's Day in January and proceeding through Christmas Day the following December). Other companies offer similar holiday schedules.

In addition, we've given all employees one floating holiday. As you know, we've determined that day by a companywide vote. As a result, all employees had the same day off. Now, however, management is considering a new plan that we feel would be better. This new plan involves a floating holiday that each individual employee may decide for herself or himself. We've given it considerable thought and decided that such a plan could definitely work. We would allow each employee to choose a day that he or she wants. Of course, we would have to issue certain restrictions. Selections would have to be subject to our staffing needs within individual departments. For example, if everyone wanted the same day, we could not allow everyone to take it. In that case, we would allow the employee with the most seniority to have the day off.

Before we institute the new plan, though, we wanted to see what employees thought about this. Is it better to continue our current companywide uniform floating holiday? Or should we try an individual floating holiday? Please let us know what you think as soon as possible.

8.3 Document for Analysis: Confirmation E-Mail (Obj. 6)

Your Task. Analyze the following e-mail message. List its weaknesses. If your instructor directs, revise it.

✗ *Poorly Written E-Mail Message*

To: William.Morrison@commercial.com
From: TracyAnnPhillips@aol.com
Subject: COMMERCIALS
Cc:

Bill:

It was good to talk to you on the telephone yesterday after exchanging letters with you and after reading so much about Bermuda. I was very interested in learning about the commercials you want me to write. As I understand it, Mr. Morrison, you want a total of 240 one-minute radio commercials. These commercials are intended to rejuvenate the slumping tourist industry in Bermuda. You said that these commercials would be broadcast from March 30 through June 30. You said these commercials would be played on three radio stations. These stations are in the major cities on the East Coast. The commercials would be aimed at morning and evening drive time, for drivers who are listening to their radios, and the campaign would be called "Radio Bermuda."

I am sure I can do as you suggested in reminding listeners that Bermuda is less than three hours away. You expect me to bring to these commercials the colour and character of the island. You want me to highlight the attractions and the civility of Bermuda, at least as much as can be done in one-minute radio commercials. In my notes I wrote that you also mentioned that I should include references to tree frogs and royal palm trees. Another item you suggested that I include in some of the commercials was special Bermuda food, such as delicacies like shark on toast, conch fritters, and mussel stew.

I wanted to be sure to write these points down so that we both agreed on what we said in our telephone conversation. I am eager to begin working on these commercials immediately, but I would feel better if you looked over these points to see if I have it right. I look forward to working with you.

Tracy

8.4 Openers for E-Mail Messages and Memos (Objs. 1 and 3)

Your Task. Revise the following e-mail and memo openers so that they are more direct.

a. I enjoyed talking with you at our last committee meeting. You mentioned a number of new ergonomic products that might solve some of the repetitive stress injuries among our office employees. You said that you had written a report on it, and you said you would be willing to share it with me. I would be very pleased if you would send me a copy of your report.

b. I appreciate your asking me for my ideas on processing data electronically. In the nearly 15 years since EDI (electronic data interchange) was first introduced, large companies have always wanted their smaller suppliers to use it. But now with Internet-based systems, it's much more usable and less expensive. I've worked out six suggestions for how your company can switch to Internet-based EDI. They are discussed below.

c. I have before me your memo of the 16th in which you request permission to attend the Web Site Design Seminar sponsored by Presentation Planners. As I understand it, this is a two-day seminar scheduled for February 25 and 26. Your reasons for attending were well stated and convincing. You have my permission to attend.

d. As you are aware, the document specialists in our department have been unhappy about their chairs and their inability to adjust the back height. The chairs are uncomfortable and cause back fatigue. As a result, I looked into the possibility of purchasing new adjustable chairs that I think will be just right for these employees. New chairs have been ordered for all these employees. The new chairs should be arriving in about three weeks.

8.5 Graphic Highlighting Techniques (Objs. 1 and 3)

Your Task. Revise the following hard-to-read paragraphs. Include an introductory statement or a title before presenting the data in bulleted or numbered lists.

a. A recent survey of car buyers uncovered some very interesting information about what electronic options they really wanted in new cars. Some technology visionaries have been saying that car buyers wanted a lot of fancy electronic gadgets, but the survey showed that only 5.1 percent, for example, wanted a trip computer. Most car buyers mentioned cruise control (79.1 percent). A total of 61.1 percent said that they wanted antilock brakes. A smaller percentage (50.5 percent) wanted keyless entry. Farther down the list we found that buyers wanted CD players (34.1 percent).

b. Our employee leasing program has proven to be an efficient management tool for business owners because we take care of everything. Our program will handle your payroll preparation. Moreover, benefits for employees are covered. We also know what a chore calculating workers' compensation premiums can be, so we do that for you. And we make all the necessary provincial and federal reports that are required today.

c. We are concerned about your safety in using our automated teller machines (ATMs) at night, so we think you should consider the following tips. Users of ATMs are encouraged to look around—especially at night—before using the service. If you notice anything suspicious, the use of another ATM is recommended. Or you could come back later. Another suggestion that we give our customers involves counting your cash. Be sure that the cash you receive is put away quickly. Don't count it as soon as you get it. It's better to check it in the safety of your car or at home. Also, why not take a friend with you if you must use an ATM at night? We also suggest that you park in a well-lighted area as close to the actual location of the ATM as possible.

8.6 Information Memo or E-Mail: Alone in the Office at Night (Obj. 4)

E-MAIL | WEB

After a recent frightening experience, your boss, Beth Meggison, realized that she must draft a memo about office security. Here's why she's concerned. A senior associate, Lisa Taylor, was working overtime cleaning up overdue reports. At about 9 p.m. she heard the office door open, but the intruder quickly left when he found that someone was in the office. Your boss hurriedly put together the following memo to be distributed to office managers in five branch offices. But she was on her way out of town, and she asked you to revise her draft and have it ready for her approval when she returns. One other thing—she wondered whether you would do some research (InfoTrac? Google?) to find other helpful suggestions. Your boss trusts you to totally revise, if necessary.

Your Task. Conduct an InfoTrac or Google search to look for reasonable office security suggestions. Then improve the memo's organization, clarity, conciseness, correctness, and readability. Don't be afraid to do a total overhaul! Bulleted points are a must, and check the correctness, too. Be sure to add an appropriate closing.

DATE: Current
TO: Branch Managers
FROM: Beth Meggison, Vice President
SUBJECT: TERRIFYING EXPERIENCE!

Office security is a topic we have not talked enough about. I was totally terrified recently when a senior associate, who was working late, told me she heard the front door of the branch office open and she thought she heard a person enter. When she called out, the person apparently left. This frightening experience reminded me there are several things that each branch can do to improve it's office security. The following are a few simple things, but we will talk more about this at our next quarterly meeting (June 8?). Please come with additional ideas.

If an office worker is here early or late, then it is your responsibility to talk with them about before and after hours security. When someone comes in early it is not smart to open the doors until most of the rest of the staff arrive. Needless to say, employees working overtime should make sure the door is locked and they should not open their office doors after hours to people they don't know, especially if you are in the office alone. Dark offices are especially attractive to thieves with valuable equipment.

Many branches are turning off lights at points of entry and parking areas to conserve energy. Consider changing this policy or installing lights connected to motion detectors, which is an inexpensive (and easy!) way to discourage burglars and intruders. I also think that "cash-free" decals are a good idea because they make thieves realize that not much is in this office to take. These signs may discourage breaking and entering. On the topic of lighting, we want to be sure that doors and windows that are secluded and not visible to neighbours or passersby is illuminated.

We should also beware of displaying any valuable equipment or other things. When people walk by, they should not be able to look in and see expensive equipment. Notebook computers and small portable equipment is particularly vulnerable at night. It should be locked up. In spite of the fact that most of our branches are guarded by FirstAlert, I'm not sure all branches are displaying the decals prominently—especially on windows and doors. We want people to know that our premises are electronically protected.

8.7 Procedure E-Mail or Memo: Rules for Wireless Phone Use in Sales Reps' Cars (Obj. 4)

E-MAIL	INFOTRAC	TEAM
WEB		

As one of the managers of LaReve, a hair care and skin products company, you are alarmed at a newspaper article you just saw. A stockbroker for was making cold calls on his personal phone while driving. His car hit and killed a motorcyclist. The brokerage firm was sued and accused of contributing to an accident by encouraging employees to use cell phones while driving. To avoid the risk of paying huge damages awarded by an emotional jury, the brokerage firm offered the victim's family a $500 000 settlement.

You begin to worry, knowing that your company has provided its 75 sales representatives with wireless phones to help them keep in touch with the home base while they are in the field. At the next management meeting, other members agreed that you should draft a message detailing some wireless phone safety rules for your sales reps. On the Web you learned that anyone with a wireless phone should get to know its features, including speed dial, automatic memory, and redial. Another suggestion involved using a hands-free device. Management members decided to purchase these for every sales rep and have the devices available within one month. In positioning the wireless phone in a car, it should be within easy reach. It should be where you can grab it without removing your eyes from the road. If you get an incoming call at an inconvenient time, your voice mail should be allowed to pick up the call. You should never talk, of course, during hazardous driving conditions, such as rain, sleet, snow, and ice.

Taking notes or looking up phone numbers is dangerous when driving. You want to warn sales reps not to get into dangerous situations by reading (such as an address book) or writing (such as taking notes) while driving.

The more you think about it, the more you think that sales reps should not use their wireless phones while the car is moving. They really should pull over. But you know that would be hard to enforce.

Your Task. Individually or in teams write a memo or e-mail to LaReve sales reps outlining company suggestions (or should they be rules?) for safe wireless phone use in cars. You may wish to check the Web or InfoTrac for additional safety ideas. Try to suggest receiver benefits in this message. How is safety beneficial to the reader? The message is from you acting as operations manager.

8.8 Procedure E-Mail or Memo: Countdown to Performance Appraisal Deadline (Obj. 4)

It's time to remind all supervisory personnel that they must complete employee performance appraisals by April 15. Your boss, James Robinson, director, Human Resources, asks you to draft a procedure memo announcing the deadline. In talking with Jim, you learn that he wants you to summarize some of the main steps in writing these appraisals. Jim says that the appraisals are really important this year because of changes in work and jobs. Many offices are installing new technologies, and some offices are undergoing reorganization. It's been a hectic year.

Jim also mentions that some supervisors will want to attend a training workshop on February 20 where they can update their skills. Supervisors who want to reserve a space at the training workshop should contact Lynn Jeffers <ljeffers@rainco.com>. When you ask Jim what procedures you should include in the memo, he tells you to consult the employee handbook and pick out the most important steps.

In the handbook you find suggestions that say each employee should have a performance plan with three or four main objectives. In the appraisal the supervisor should mention three strengths the employee has, as well as three areas for improvement. One interesting comment in the handbook indicated that improvements should focus on skills, such as time management, rather than on things like being late frequently. Supervisors are supposed to use a scale of 1 to 5 to assess employees: 1 = consistently exceeds requirements; 5 = does not meet requirements at all. Finally, supervisors should meet with employees to discuss the appraisal. The completed appraisal should be sent to your office.

Your Task. Draft a memo from James Robinson, director, Human Resources, to all department heads, managers, and supervisors. Announce the April 15 deadline for performance appraisals. List five or six steps to be taken by supervisors in completing performance appraisals. If you need more information about writing performance appraisals, search that term on the Web. You'll find many sites with helpful advice.

8.9 Reply Memo or E-Mail: One Sick Day Too Many (Obj. 5)

TEAM | CRITICAL THINKING

As director of Human Resources at a midsize insurance company, you received an inquiry from Suzette Chase, who is supervisor of Legal Support. It seems that one of Suzette's veteran employees recently implemented a four-day workweek for herself. On the fifth morning, the employee calls in with some crisis or sickness that makes it impossible for her to get to work. Suzette asks for your advice in how to handle this situation.

In the past you've told supervisors to keep a written record (a log) of each absence. This record should include the financial and productive impact of the absence. It should include a space where the employee can include her comments and signature. You've found that a written document always increases the significance of the event. You've also told supervisors that they must be objective and professional. It's difficult, but they should not personalize the situation.

Occasionally, of course, an absence is legitimate. Supervisors must know what is unavoidable and what is a lame excuse. In other words, they must know how to separate reasons from excuses. Another thing to consider is how the employee reacts when approached. Is her attitude sincere, or does she automatically become defensive?

You also tell supervisors that "if they talk the talk, they must walk the walk." In other words, they must follow the same policies that are enforced. The best plan, of course, is to clearly define what is and is not acceptable attendance policy and make sure every new hire is informed.

Your Task. In teams discuss what advice to give to Suzette Chase regarding her habitually absent worker. Why is a log important? What other suggestions can you make? How should you conclude this message? Individually or in teams, write a well-organized reply memo or e-mail message to Suzette Chase, supervisor of Legal Support. Remember that bulleted items improve readability.

8.10 Reply Memo or E-Mail: Office Romances Off Limits? (Obj. 5)

CRITICAL THINKING | E-MAIL
INFOTRAC | TEAM

Where can you find the hottest singles scene today? Some would say in your workplace. Because people are working long hours and have little time for outside contacts, relationships often develop at work. Estimates suggest that one third to one half of all romances start at work. Your boss is concerned about possible problems resulting from relationships at work. What happens if a relationship between a superior and subordinate results in perceived favouritism? What happens if a relationship results in a nasty breakup? Your boss would like to simply ban all relationships among employees. But that's not likely to work. He asks you, his assistant, to learn what guidelines could be established regarding office romances.

Your Task. Using InfoTrac, read Timothy Bland's "Romance in the Workplace: Good Thing or Bad?" (Article No. A66460590). From this article select four or five suggestions that you could make to your boss in regard to protecting an employer. Why is it necessary for a company to protect itself? Discuss your findings and reactions with your team. Individually or as a group, submit your findings and reactions in a well-organized, easy-to-read e-mail or memo to your boss (your instructor). You may list main points from the article, but use your own words to write the message.

8.11 Reply Memo: Rescheduling Interviews (Obj. 5)

Your boss, Fred Knox, had scheduled three appointments to interview applicants for an accounting position. All of these appointments were for Friday, October 7. However, he now must travel to Halifax on that weekend. He asks you to reschedule all the appointments for one week later. He also wants a brief summary of the background of each candidate.

You call each person and arrange these times. Paul Scheffel, who has been an accountant for 15 years with Bechtel Corporation, agreed to come at 10:30 a.m. Mark Cunningham, who is a CPA and a consultant to many companies, will come at 11:30. Geraldine Simpson, who has a B.A. degree and eight years of experience in payroll accounting, will come at 9:30 a.m. You're wondering if Mr. Knox forgot to include Don Stastry, operations personnel officer, in these interviews. Mr. Stastry usually is part of the selection process.

Your Task. Write a memo to Mr. Knox including all the vital information he needs.

8.12 Confirmation Memo: Dream Vacation (Obj. 6)

Play the role of Jack Mendoza. You had a vacation planned for September 2 through 16. But yesterday your wife suggested delaying the vacation for several weeks so that you could travel through Quebec's Eastern Townships when the fall colours are most beautiful. She said it would be the vacation of her dreams, and you agree. Perhaps you could change your vacation dates. Unfortunately, you remember that you're scheduled to attend the Winnipeg marketing exhibit September 29–30. But maybe Melanie Grasso would fill in for you and make the presentation of the company's newest product, JuiceMate. You see your boss, Mas Watanabe, in the hall and decide to ask if you can change your vacation to September 28 through October 12. To your surprise, he agrees to the new dates. He also assures you that he will ask Melanie to make the presentation and encourage her to give a special demonstration to the Dana Corporation, which you believe should be targeted.

Your Task. Back in your office, you begin to worry. What if Mas forgets about your conversation? You can't afford to take that chance. Write a confirmation memo that summarizes the necessary facts and also conveys your gratitude.

8.13 Confirmation Memo: Verifying a Job Severance Package (Obj. 6)

You're congratulating yourself on landing a fantastic job. Terrific title. Terrific salary. Terrific boss. You were even smart enough to talk about an exit package during your interviewing. You had read an article in the *National Post* suggesting that the best time to win a generous departure deal is before you accept a position.

Because you knew your skills were in high demand for this position and because you would be giving up a good position, you wanted to know what the typical severance package involved. What would you receive if this job disappeared through a merger or downturn in the economy or similar unforeseen event? The hiring manager told you that the standard severance package includes one week's salary for every year of service, out-placement counselling for up to six months, accrued but unused vacation pay, and extended medical coverage. After a little bargaining, you were able to increase the severance pay to two weeks' salary for each year of service and medical insurance for you and your family up to one year or until you found another position.

Then you begin to worry. You didn't get any of this in writing.

Your Task. You decide to write a confirmation memo outlining the severance package discussed in your interview. The *National Post* says that your memo becomes an enforceable contract. Write a memo to Jefferson Walker, operations manager, describing your understanding of what you were promised.[5] If Mr. Walker doesn't agree with any of the details, ask him to respond immediately. Show your enthusiasm for the job and keep the tone of your message upbeat. Add any necessary details.

C.L.U.E. REVIEW 8

Edit the following sentences to correct all language faults, including grammar, punctuation, spelling, and word use.

1. Todays organizations however are encouraging rank and file employees to share information, and make decisions.
2. Because managers, and employees, are writing more messages then ever before its definitly important that they develop good communication skills.
3. Memos generally contain 4 nesessary parts; subject line, opening, body and action closing.
4. The federal trade commission are holding hearings to illicit information about IBMs request to expand marketing in twenty-one city's.
5. Consumer buying and spending for the past 5 years, is being studied by a Federal team of analysts.
6. When you respond too a e-mail message you should not automaticly return the senders message.
7. Wasnt it Dr Ben Cohen not Mr Temple who allways wrote their e-mails in all capitol letters.
8. A list of the names' and addresses' of e-mail recipients were sent using the "bcc" function.
9. Our human resources department which was formerally in room 35 has moved it's offices to room 5.
10. The Post Dispatch our local newspaper featured as its principle article a story entitled, Smarter E-Mail is here.

Chapter 9

Routine Letters and Goodwill Messages

LEARNING OBJECTIVES

1. *List three characteristics of good letters and describe the direct pattern for organizing letters.*
2. *Write letters requesting information and action.*
3. *Write letters placing orders.*
4. *Write letters making claims.*
5. *Write letters complying with requests.*
6. *Write letters of recommendation.*
7. *Write letters granting claims and making adjustments.*
8. *Write goodwill messages.*

APPLYING GUFFEY'S 3-×-3 WRITING PROCESS TO CREATE SUCCESSFUL LETTERS

1

Letters sent to customers are a primary channel of communication for delivering messages *outside* an organization. Although e-mail is incredibly successful for both internal and external communication, many important messages still require written letters. Business letters are important when a permanent record is required, when formality is necessary, and when a message is sensitive and requires an organized, well-considered presentation. In this book we'll divide letters into three groups: (1) routine letters communicating straightforward requests, replies, and goodwill messages; (2) persuasive messages including sales pitches; and (3) negative messages delivering refusals and bad news.

This chapter concentrates on routine, straightforward letters through which we conduct everyday business and convey goodwill to outsiders. Such letters go to suppliers, government agencies, other businesses, and, most important, customers. The letters to customers receive a high priority because these messages encourage product feedback, project a favourable image of the company, and promote future business.

Routine letters to outsiders encourage product feedback, project a favourable company image, and promote future business.

This chapter teaches you what turns readers on. You'll study the characteristics of good letters, techniques for organizing direct requests and responses, and ways to apply Guffey's 3-×-3 writing process. You'll learn how to write six specific kinds of direct letters, along with special goodwill messages. Finally, you'll study how to modify letters to accommodate other cultures.

Characteristics of Good Letters

Although routine letters deliver straightforward facts, they don't have to sound and look dull or mechanical. At least three characteristics distinguish good business letters: clear content, a tone of goodwill, and correct form.

Clear Content. A clearly written letter separates ideas into paragraphs, uses short sentences and paragraphs, and guides the reader through the ideas with transitional expressions. Moreover, a clear letter uses familiar words and active-voice verbs. In other words, it incorporates the writing techniques you studied in Chapters 5, 6, and 7.

Clear letters feature short sentences and paragraphs, transitional expressions, familiar words, and active-voice verbs.

But many business letters are not written well. As many as one third of business letters do nothing more than seek clarification of earlier correspondence. Clear letters avoid this problem by answering all the reader's questions or concerns so that no further correspondence is necessary. Clear letters also speak the language of the receiver.

Goodwill Tone. Good letters, however, have to do more than deliver clear messages; they also must build goodwill. Goodwill is a positive feeling the reader has toward an individual or an organization. By analyzing your audience and adapting your message to the reader, your letters can establish an overall tone of goodwill.

Letters achieve a tone of goodwill by emphasizing a "you" view and reader benefits.

To achieve goodwill, look for ways to present the message from the reader's perspective. In other words, emphasize the "you" view and point out benefits to the reader. In addition, be sensitive to words that might suggest gender, racial, age, or disability bias. Finally, frame your ideas positively because they will sound more pleasing and will give more information than negative constructions.

Appropriate letter formats send silent but positive messages.

Correct Form. A business letter conveys silent messages beyond that of its printed words. The letter's appearance and format reflect the writer's carefulness and experience. A short letter bunched at the top of a sheet of paper, for example, looks as if it was prepared in a hurry or by an amateur.

For your letters to make a good impression, you need to select an appropriate format. The modified block style shown in Figure 9.1 is a popular format. Other letter formats are illustrated later in this chapter. In the block style, the parts of your letter—dateline, inside address, body, and so on—are set flush left on the page. Also, the letter is formatted so that it is centred on the page and framed by white space. Most letters will have margins of 2.5 to 4 cm.

Finally, be sure to use ragged-right margins; that is, don't allow your computer to justify the right margin and make all lines end evenly. Unjustified margins improve readability, say experts, by providing visual stops and by making it easier to tell where the next line begins. Although book publishers use justified right margins, as you see on this page, your letters should be ragged right. Figure 9.1 illustrates the modified block style and explains how to format business letters. Figure 9.2 illus-

FIGURE 9.1 Business Letter Formatting (Modified Block)

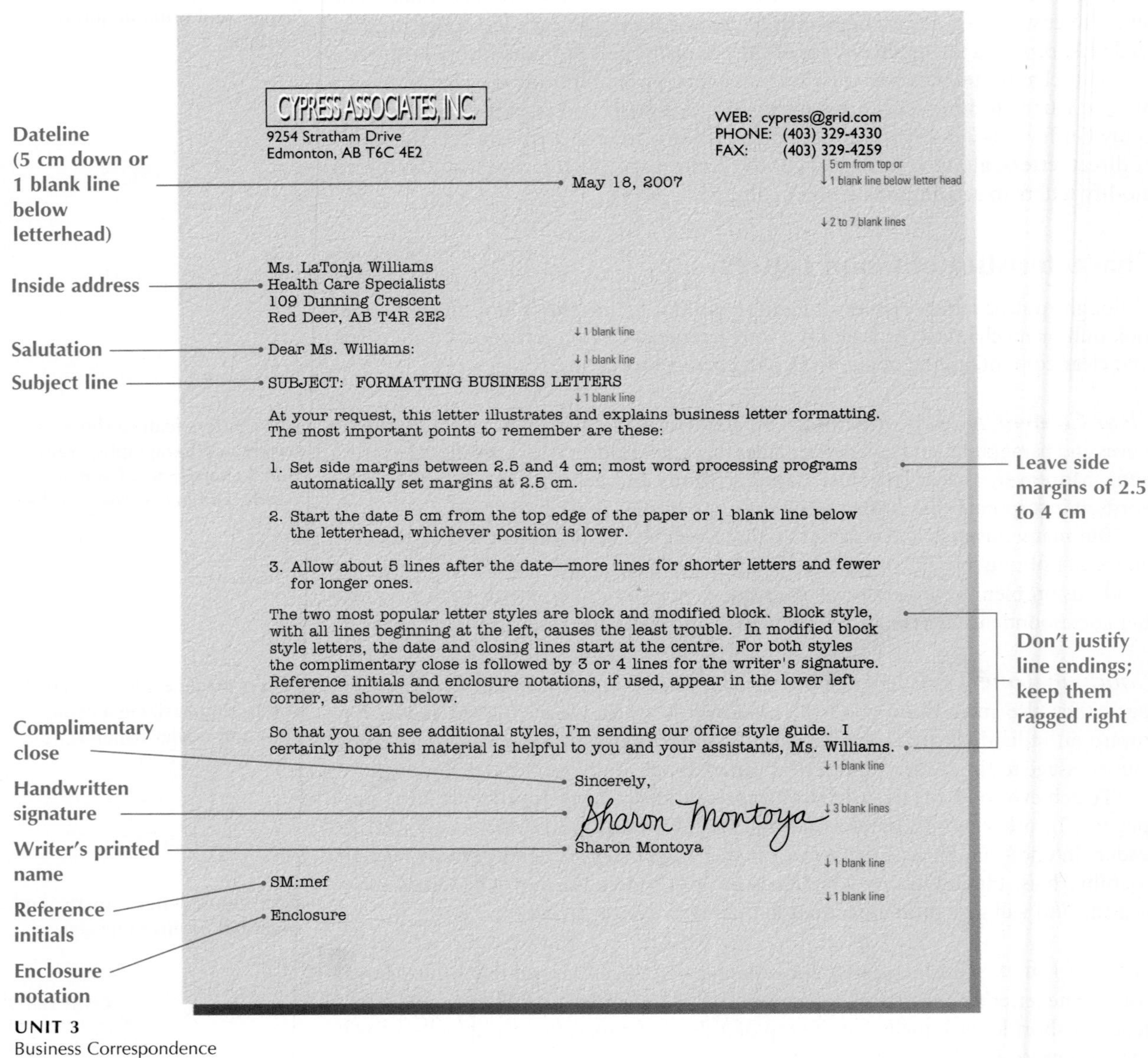

CYPRESS ASSOCIATES, INC.
9254 Stratham Drive
Edmonton, AB T6C 4E2

WEB: cypress@grid.com
PHONE: (403) 329-4330
FAX: (403) 329-4259

May 18, 2007

Ms. LaTonja Williams
Health Care Specialists
109 Dunning Crescent
Red Deer, AB T4R 2E2

Dear Ms. Williams:

SUBJECT: FORMATTING BUSINESS LETTERS

At your request, this letter illustrates and explains business letter formatting. The most important points to remember are these:

1. Set side margins between 2.5 and 4 cm; most word processing programs automatically set margins at 2.5 cm.

2. Start the date 5 cm from the top edge of the paper or 1 blank line below the letterhead, whichever position is lower.

3. Allow about 5 lines after the date—more lines for shorter letters and fewer for longer ones.

The two most popular letter styles are block and modified block. Block style, with all lines beginning at the left, causes the least trouble. In modified block style letters, the date and closing lines start at the centre. For both styles the complimentary close is followed by 3 or 4 lines for the writer's signature. Reference initials and enclosure notations, if used, appear in the lower left corner, as shown below.

So that you can see additional styles, I'm sending our office style guide. I certainly hope this material is helpful to you and your assistants, Ms. Williams.

Sincerely,

Sharon Montoya

Sharon Montoya

SM:mef

Enclosure

trates the block style and provides more information about formatting. Study Figures 9.1 and 9.2 for more tips on making your letters look professional.

Using the Direct Pattern for Routine Letters

The everyday transactions of a business consist mainly of routine requests and responses. Because you expect the reader's response to be positive or neutral, you won't need special techniques to be convincing, to soften bad news, or to be tactful. Thus, in composing routine letters, you can organize your message, as shown in Figure 9.3, into three parts:

Most business messages are routine requests or routine responses.

- **Opening:** A statement that announces the purpose immediately
- **Body:** Details that explain the purpose
- **Closing:** A request for action or a courteous conclusion

FIGURE 9.2 Block Letter Style

Block style
Open punctuation

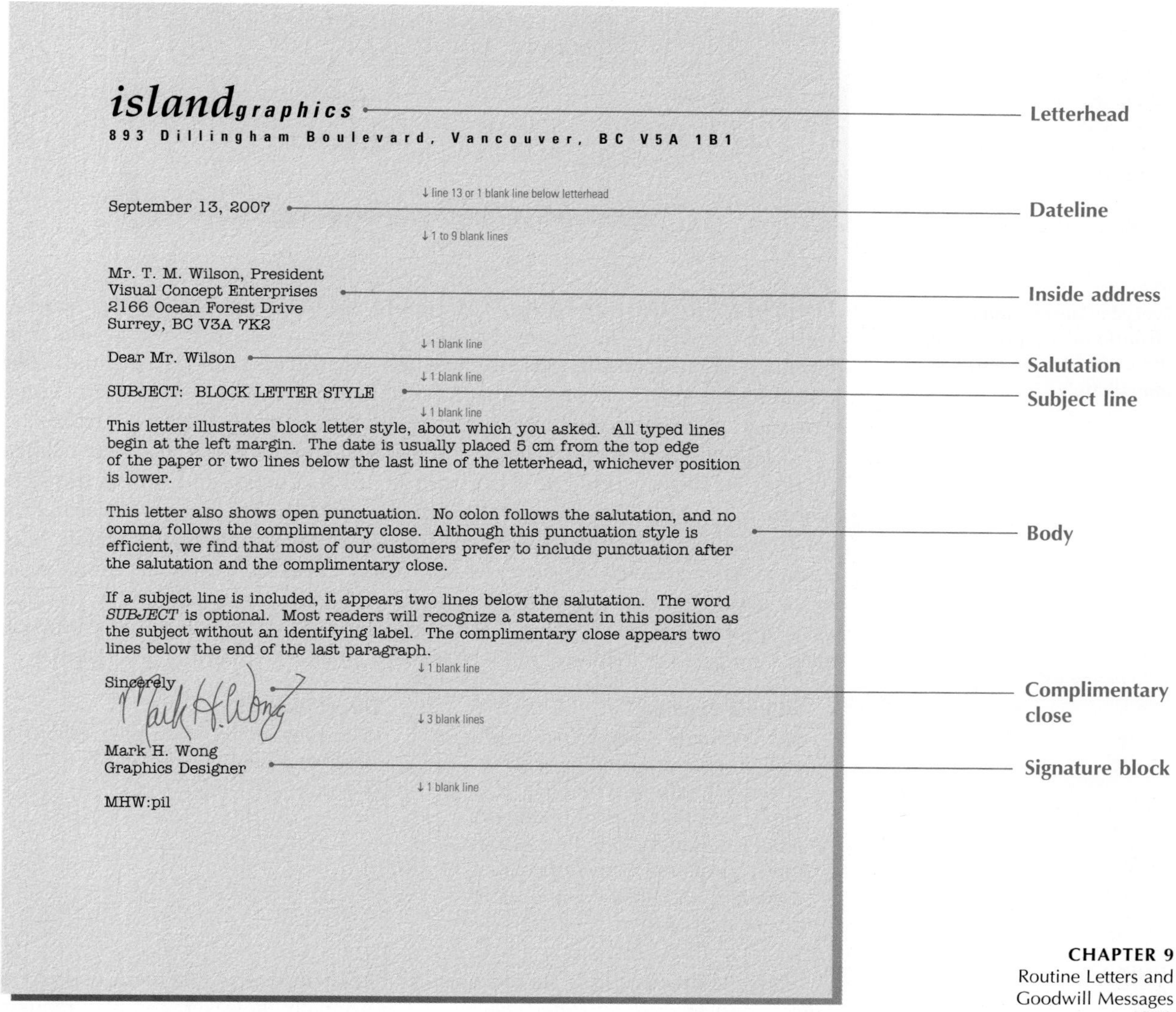

*island*graphics
893 Dillingham Boulevard, Vancouver, BC V5A 1B1

↓ line 13 or 1 blank line below letterhead

September 13, 2007

↓ 1 to 9 blank lines

Mr. T. M. Wilson, President
Visual Concept Enterprises
2166 Ocean Forest Drive
Surrey, BC V3A 7K2

↓ 1 blank line

Dear Mr. Wilson

↓ 1 blank line

SUBJECT: BLOCK LETTER STYLE

↓ 1 blank line

This letter illustrates block letter style, about which you asked. All typed lines begin at the left margin. The date is usually placed 5 cm from the top edge of the paper or two lines below the last line of the letterhead, whichever position is lower.

This letter also shows open punctuation. No colon follows the salutation, and no comma follows the complimentary close. Although this punctuation style is efficient, we find that most of our customers prefer to include punctuation after the salutation and the complimentary close.

If a subject line is included, it appears two lines below the salutation. The word *SUBJECT* is optional. Most readers will recognize a statement in this position as the subject without an identifying label. The complimentary close appears two lines below the end of the last paragraph.

↓ 1 blank line

Sincerely

↓ 3 blank lines

Mark H. Wong
Graphics Designer

↓ 1 blank line

MHW:pil

FIGURE 9.3 Three-Part Direct Pattern for Routine Requests and Responses

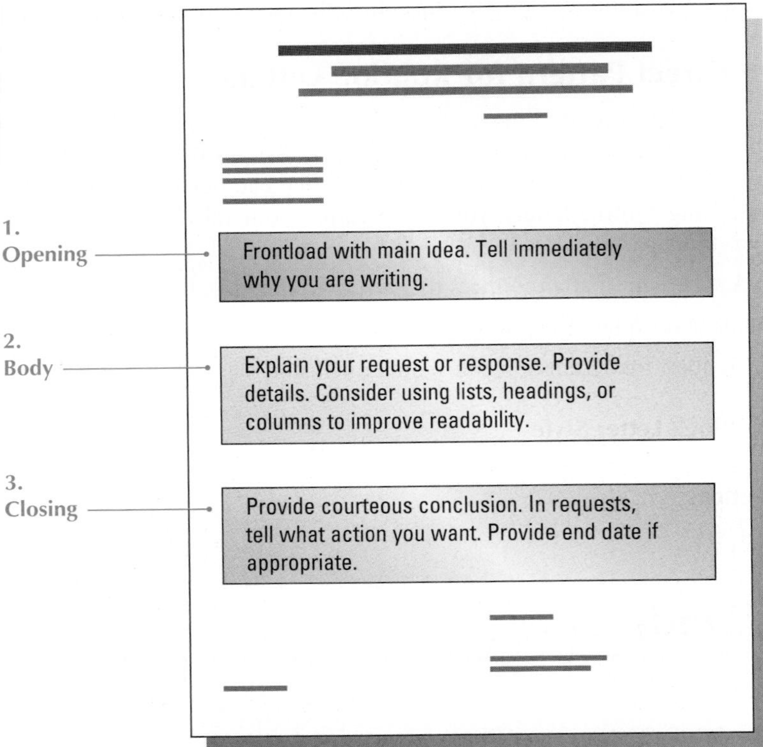
1. Opening
Frontload with main idea. Tell immediately why you are writing.
2. Body
Explain your request or response. Provide details. Consider using lists, headings, or columns to improve readability.
3. Closing
Provide courteous conclusion. In requests, tell what action you want. Provide end date if appropriate.

Everyday business messages "frontload" by presenting the main idea or purpose immediately.

Frontload in the Opening. You should use the direct strategy for routine, everyday messages. This means developing ideas in a straightforward manner by frontloading the main idea. State immediately why you are writing so that the reader can anticipate and comprehend what follows. Remember, every time a reader begins a message, he or she is thinking, "Why was this sent to me?" "What am I to do?"

Some writers make the mistake of organizing a message as if they were telling a story or solving a problem.[1] They start at the beginning and follow the same sequence in which they thought through the problem. This means reviewing the background, discussing the reasons for action, and then requesting an action. Most business letters, though, are better written "backwards." Start with the action desired or the main idea. Don't get bogged down in introductory material, history, justifications, or old-fashioned "business" language.[2] Instead, reveal your purpose immediately. Compare the following indirect and direct openers to see the differences:

Indirect Opening
Our company is experiencing difficulty in retaining employees. We also need help in screening job applicants. Our current testing program is unsatisfactory. I understand that you offer employee testing materials, and I have a number of questions to ask.

Direct Opening
Please answer the following questions about your personnel testing materials.

Most simple requests should open immediately with a statement of purpose (*Please answer these questions about . . .*). Occasionally, however, complex requests may require a sentence or two of explanation or background before the purpose is revealed. What you want to avoid, though, is delaying the purpose of the letter beyond the first paragraph.

Explain in the Body. After a direct opening that tells the reader why you are writing, present details that explain your request or response. This is where your planning pays off, allowing you to structure the information for maximum clarity and readability. Here you should consider using some graphic devices to highlight the details: a numbered or bulleted list, headings, columns, or boldface or italic type.

If you have considerable information, you'll want to develop each idea in a separate paragraph with effective transitions to connect them. The important thing to remember is to keep similar ideas together. The biggest problem in business writing is poor organization, and the body of a letter is where that failure becomes apparent.

The body explains the purpose for writing, perhaps using graphic devices to highlight important ideas.

Be Specific and Courteous in the Closing. In the last paragraph of direct letters, readers look for action information: schedules, deadlines, activities to be completed. Thus, at this point, you should specify what you want the reader to do. If appropriate, include an end date—a date for completion of the action. If possible, give reasons for establishing the deadline. Research shows that people want to know why they should do something—even if the reasons seem obvious. Moreover, people want to be treated courteously (*Please answer these questions before April 1, when we must make a final decision*), not bossed around (*Send this information immediately*).

The closing courteously specifies what the receiver is to do.

Applying Guffey's 3-×-3 Writing Process to Routine Letters

Although routine letters may be short and straightforward, they benefit from attention to the composition process. Here's a quick review of the 3-×-3 writing process to help you think through its application to routine letters.

Before writing routine letters, analyze your purpose and anticipate the audience's response.

Phase 1: Analysis, Anticipation, and Adaptation. Before writing, spend a few moments analyzing your task and audience. Your key goals here are (1) determining your purpose, (2) anticipating the reaction of your audience, and (3) visualizing the audience. Too often, letter writers start a message without enough preparation.

Phase 2: Research, Organization, and Composition. Collect information and make a list of the points you wish to cover. For short messages such as an answer to a customer's inquiry, jot your notes down on the document you are answering. For longer documents that require formal research, use a cluster diagram or the outlining techniques discussed in Chapter 6. When business letters carry information that won't upset the receiver, you can organize them in the direct manner described earlier. And be sure to plan for revision. A writer can seldom turn out an excellent message on the first attempt.

Phase 3: Revision, Proofreading, and Evaluation. When you finish the first draft, revise for clarity. The receiver should not have to read the message twice to grasp its meaning. Proofread for correctness. Check for punctuation irregularities, typos, misspelled words, or other mechanical problems. Also be sure to look for ways to create high "skim value." *Always* take time to examine the words highlighted by your spell checker. Finally, evaluate your product. Before any letter leaves your desk, always reread it and put yourself in the shoes of the reader, asking yourself, "How would I feel if I were receiving it?"

After completing the first draft, revise for clarity, proofread for correctness, and evaluate for effectiveness.

DIRECT REQUEST LETTERS

Many of your routine business letters will fall into one of three categories: (1) asking for information or action, (2) placing orders for products, or (3) making a claim requiring an adjustment when something has gone wrong. In this section you'll learn how to write good letters for each of these circumstances. Before you write any letter, though, consider its costs in terms of your time and workload. Whenever possible, don't write! Instead of asking for information, could you find it yourself? Would a telephone call, an e-mail message, or a brief visit to a coworker solve the problem quickly? If not, use the direct pattern to present your request efficiently.

Direct Requests for Information or Action

2

A direct letter may open with a question or a polite request.

The majority of your business letters will request information or action. For these routine messages put the main idea first. If your request involves several questions, you could open with a polite request, such as *Will you please answer the following questions about your payroll service.* Note that although this request sounds like a question, it's actually a disguised command. Since you expect an action rather than a reply, punctuate this polite command with a period instead of a question mark. To avoid this punctuation problem, just omit *Will you* and start with *Please answer.*

Questions in a direct letter should be parallel (balanced grammatically).

Clarify Requests. In the letter body explain your purpose and provide details. If you have questions, express them in parallel form so that you balance them grammatically. To elicit the most information, pose open-ended questions (*What computer lock-down device can you recommend?*) instead of yes-or-no questions (*Do you carry computer lock-down devices?*). If you are asking someone to do something, be sure your tone is polite. When possible, focus on benefits to the reader (*To ensure that you receive the exact sweater you want, send us your colour choice*). In the closing tell the reader courteously what is to be done. If a date is important, set an end date to take action and explain why. Some careless writers end request letters simply with *Thank you,* forcing the reader to review the contents to determine what is expected and when. You can save the reader time by spelling out the action to be taken. Avoid other overused endings such as *Thank you for your cooperation* (trite), *Thank you in advance for . . .* (trite and presumptuous), and *If you have any questions, do not hesitate to call me* (suggests that you didn't make yourself clear).

Direct request letters maintain a courteous tone, spell out what needs to be done, and focus on reader benefits.

Show Appreciation. It's always appropriate to show appreciation, but try to do so in a fresh and efficient manner. For example, you could hook your thanks to the end date (*Thanks for returning the questionnaire before May 5, when we will begin tabulation*). You might connect your appreciation to a statement developing reader benefits (*We are grateful for the information you will provide because it will help us serve you better*). Or you could describe briefly how the information will help you (*I appreciate this information that will enable me to . . .*). When possible, make it easy for the reader to comply with your request (*Note your answers on this sheet and return it in the postage-paid envelope* or *Here's my e-mail address so that you can reach me quickly*).

A direct request letter written by office manager Melanie Marshall, shown in Figure 9.4, begins directly. The opening sentence introduces the purpose immediately so that the reader quickly knows why the letter was sent. Melanie then provides background information. Most important, she organizes all her requests into specific questions. Study the 3-×-3 writing process outlined in Figure 9.4 to see the plan Melanie followed in writing her letter.

FIGURE 9.4 Direct Request Letter

The Three Phases of the Writing Process

Prewriting 1

Analyze: The purpose of this letter is to gain specific data about devices to lock down computer equipment.

Anticipate: The audience is expected to be a busy but receptive customer service representative.

Adapt: Because the reader will probably react positively to this inquiry, the direct pattern is best.

Writing 2

Research: Determine how much equipment must be locked down and what questions must be answered. Learn the name of the receiver.

Organize: Open with a general inquiry about security devices. In the body give details; arrange any questions logically. Close by courteously providing a specific deadline.

Compose: Draft the first copy on a computer.

Revising 3

Revise: Improve the clarity by grouping similar ideas together. Improve readability by listing and numbering questions. Eliminate wordiness.

Proofread: Look for typos and spelling errors. Check punctuation and placement. Indent the second line of all listed items for a clean look.

Evaluate: Is this message attractive and easily comprehended?

---

inner Circle graphics

32 Hershey Road, Dartmouth, NS B2Y 2H5

(902) 488-3310 phone (902) 488-3319 fax

February 3, 2007

Ms. Sue Ivorson, Customer Service
Micro Supplies and Software
P.O. Box 800
Montreal, QC G5B 2G6

Dear Ms. Ivorson: — *Addresses receiver by name*

Please provide information and recommendations regarding security equipment to prevent the theft of office computers and peripherals. — *Introduces purpose immediately*

Our office now has 18 computer workstations and 6 printers that we must secure to desks or counters. Answers to the following questions will help us select the best devices for our purpose. — *Explains need for information*

1. What device would you recommend that can secure a workstation consisting of a computer, monitor, and keyboard?
2. What expertise and equipment are required to install and remove the security device?
3. How much is each device? Do you offer quantity discounts, and if so, how much?

Groups open-ended questions into list for quick comprehension and best feedback

Your response before February 15 will help us meet an April 1 deadline from our insurance company for locking down this equipment. — *Courteously provides end date and reason*

Sincerely,

Melanie Marshall

Melanie Marshall
Office Manager

Order Letters

3

You may occasionally need to write a letter that orders supplies, merchandise, or services. Generally, such purchases are made by Web page, telephone, catalogue order form, or fax. Sometimes, however, you may not have a telephone number, order form, or Web address—only a street address. To order items by letter, supply the same information that an order blank would require. In the opening let the reader know immediately that this is a purchase authorization and not merely an information inquiry. Instead of *I saw a number of interesting items in your catalogue,* begin directly with order language such as *Please send me by FedEx the following items from your fall merchandise catalogue.*

Letters placing orders specify items or services, quantities, dates, prices, and payment method.

If you're ordering many items, list them vertically in the body of your letter. Include as much specific data as possible: quantity, order number, complete description, unit price, and total price. Show the total amount, and figure the tax and shipping costs if possible. The more information you provide, the less likely that a mistake will be made.

In the closing tell how you plan to pay for the merchandise. Enclose a cheque, provide a credit card number, or ask to be billed. Many business organizations have credit agreements with their regular suppliers that enable suppliers to send goods without prior payment. In addition to payment information, tell when the merchandise should be sent and express appreciation. The order letter from Michael Walker of Wilkenson Industries, shown in Figure 9.5, illustrates the pattern of an order letter.

Direct Claims

In business many things can go wrong—promised shipments are late, warrantied goods fail, or service is disappointing. When you as a customer must write to identify or correct a wrong, the letter is called a *claim.* Straightforward claims are those to which you expect the receiver to agree readily. But even these claims often require a letter. While your first action may be a telephone call or a visit to submit your claim, you may not be satisfied with the result. Written claims are often taken more seriously, and they also establish a record of what happened. Straightforward claims use a direct approach. Claims that require persuasion are presented in Chapter 10.

Claim letters open with a clear problem statement, support the claim with specifics, and close with a statement of goodwill.

Open Directly. When you, as a customer, have a legitimate claim, you can expect a positive response from a company. Smart businesses want to hear from their customers. They know that retaining a customer is far less costly than recruiting a new customer. That's why you should open a claim letter with a clear statement of the problem or with the action you want the receiver to take. You might expect a replacement, a refund, a new order, credit to your account, correction of a billing error, free repairs, free inspection, or cancellation of an order. When the remedy is obvious, state it immediately (*Please send us 24 Royal hot-air popcorn poppers to replace the 24 hot-oil poppers sent in error with our order shipped January 4*). When the remedy is less obvious, you might ask for a change in policy or procedure or simply for an explanation (*Because three of our employees with confirmed reservations were refused rooms September 16 in your hotel, would you please clarify your policy regarding reservations and late arrivals*).

FIGURE 9.5 Order Letter

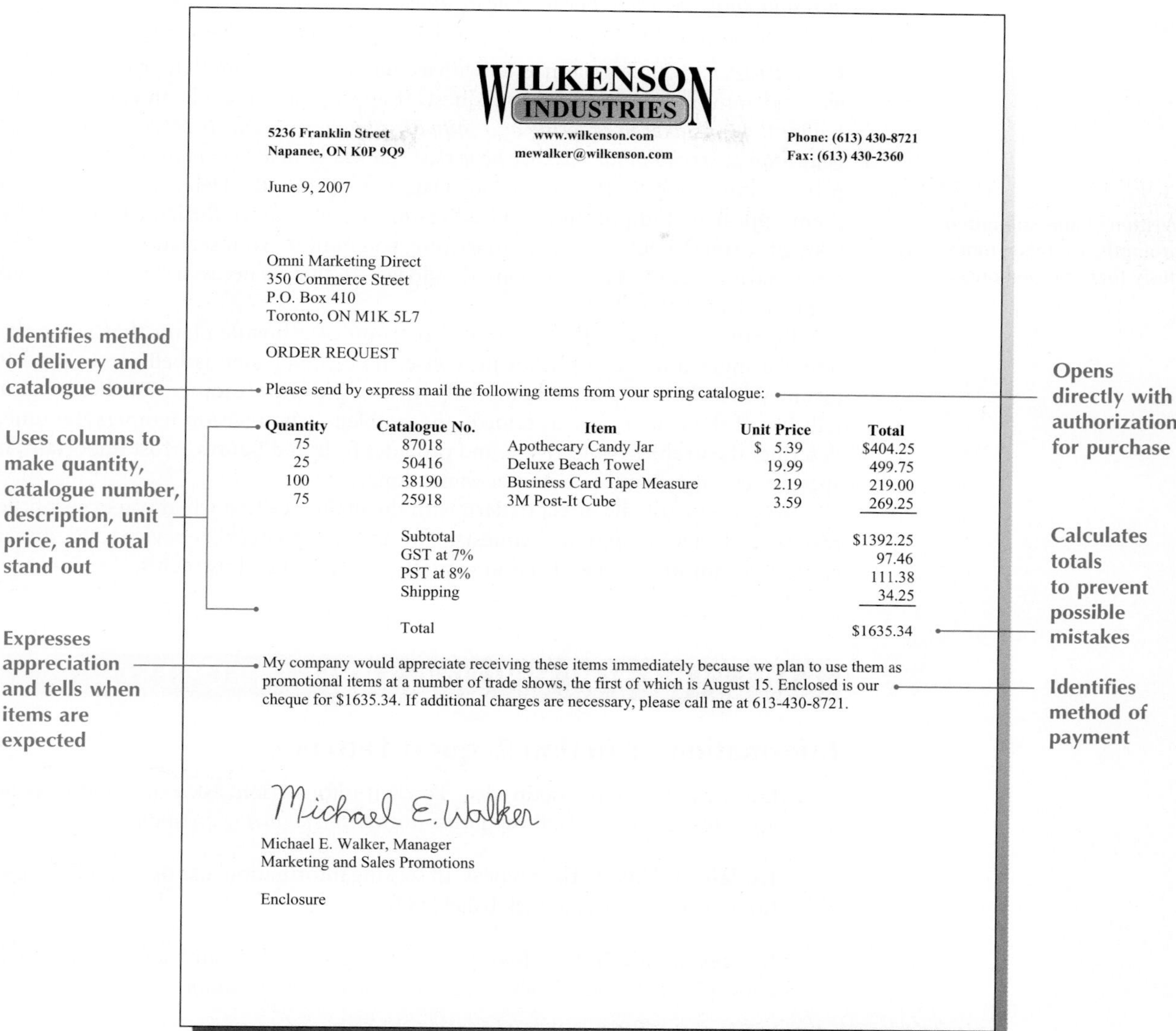

WILKENSON INDUSTRIES

5236 Franklin Street
Napanee, ON K0P 9Q9

www.wilkenson.com
mewalker@wilkenson.com

Phone: (613) 430-8721
Fax: (613) 430-2360

June 9, 2007

Omni Marketing Direct
350 Commerce Street
P.O. Box 410
Toronto, ON M1K 5L7

ORDER REQUEST

Please send by express mail the following items from your spring catalogue:

Quantity	Catalogue No.	Item	Unit Price	Total
75	87018	Apothecary Candy Jar	$ 5.39	$404.25
25	50416	Deluxe Beach Towel	19.99	499.75
100	38190	Business Card Tape Measure	2.19	219.00
75	25918	3M Post-It Cube	3.59	269.25
	Subtotal			$1392.25
	GST at 7%			97.46
	PST at 8%			111.38
	Shipping			34.25
	Total			$1635.34

My company would appreciate receiving these items immediately because we plan to use them as promotional items at a number of trade shows, the first of which is August 15. Enclosed is our cheque for $1635.34. If additional charges are necessary, please call me at 613-430-8721.

Michael E. Walker

Michael E. Walker, Manager
Marketing and Sales Promotions

Enclosure

Identifies method of delivery and catalogue source
Uses columns to make quantity, catalogue number, description, unit price, and total stand out
Expresses appreciation and tells when items are expected
Opens directly with authorization for purchase
Calculates totals to prevent possible mistakes
Identifies method of payment

Explain. In the body of a claim letter, explain the problem and justify your request. Provide the necessary details so that the difficulty can be corrected without further correspondence. Avoid becoming angry or trying to fix blame. Bear in mind that the person reading your letter is seldom responsible for the problem. Instead, state the facts logically, objectively, and unemotionally; let the reader decide on the causes. Include copies of all pertinent documents such as invoices, sales slips, catalogue descriptions, and repair records. (By the way, be sure to send copies and NOT your originals, which could be lost.) When service is involved, cite names of individuals spoken to and dates of calls. Assume that a company honestly wants to satisfy its customers—because most do. When an alternative remedy exists, spell it out (*If you are*

Providing details without getting angry improves the effectiveness of a claim letter.

unable to send 24 Royal hot-air popcorn poppers immediately, please credit our account now and notify us when they become available).

Conclude. Conclude a claim letter with a courteous statement that promotes goodwill and summarizes your action request. If appropriate, include an end date (*We realize that mistakes in ordering and shipping sometimes occur. Because we've enjoyed your prompt service in the past, we hope that you will be able to send us the hot-air poppers by January 15*). Finally, in making claims, act promptly. Delaying claims makes them appear less important. Delayed claims are also more difficult to verify. By taking the time to put your claim in writing, you indicate your seriousness. A written claim starts a record of the problem, should later action be necessary. Be sure to keep a copy of your letter.

Written claims submitted promptly are taken more seriously than delayed ones.

Figure 9.6 shows a first draft and revision of a hostile claim that vents the writer's anger but accomplishes little else. Its original tone is belligerent, and it assumes that the company intentionally mischarged the customer. Furthermore, it fails to tell the reader how to remedy the problem. The revision tempers the tone, describes the problem objectively, and provides facts and figures. Most important, it specifies exactly what the customer wants done.

To sum up, use the direct pattern with the main idea first when you expect little resistance to letters making requests. The following checklist reviews the direct strategy for information and action requests, orders, and adjustments.

CHECKLIST FOR WRITING DIRECT REQUESTS

Information or Action Request Letters

- ✓ **Open by stating the main idea.** To elicit information, ask a question or issue a polite command (*Will you please answer the following questions . . .*).
- ✓ **Explain and justify the request.** In seeking information, use open-ended questions structured in parallel, balanced form.
- ✓ **Request action in the closing.** Express appreciation, and set an end date if appropriate. Avoid clichés (*Thank you for your cooperation*).

Order Letters

- ✓ **Open by authorizing the purchase.** Use order language (*Please send me . . .*), designate the delivery method, and state your information source (such as a catalogue, advertisement, or magazine article).
- ✓ **List items in the body.** Include quantity, order number, description, unit price, extension, tax, shipping, and total costs.
- ✓ **Close with the payment data.** Tell how you are paying and when you expect delivery. Express appreciation.

Direct Claim Letters

- ✓ **Begin with the purpose.** Present a clear statement of the problem or the action requested—such as a refund, replacement, credit, explanation, or correction of an error.

FIGURE 9.6 Direct Claim Letter

First Draft

Dear Premier Quality Systems, Inc.:

You call yourselves Premier Quality, but all I'm getting from your service is garbage! I'm furious that you have your salespeople slip in unwanted service warranties to boost your sales.

When I bought my Panatronic DVD from PQS, Inc., in August, I specifically told the salesperson that I did NOT want a three-year service warranty. But there it is on my VISA statement this month! You people have obviously billed me for a service I did not authorize. I refuse to pay this charge.

How can you hope to stay in business with such fraudulent practices? I was expecting to return this month and look at CD players, but you can be sure I'll find an honest dealer this time.

Sincerely,

Sounds angry; jumps to conclusions

Forgets that mistakes happen

Fails to suggest solution

Revision

2352 Hall Avenue
Windsor, ON N8X 3L9

September 3, 2007

Mr. Sam Lee, Customer Service
Premier Quality Systems, Inc.
41 Bricker Avenue
Waterloo, ON N2L 3B6

Dear Mr. Lee:

Please credit my VISA account, No. 0000-0046-2198-9421, to correct an erroneous charge of $99.

On August 8 I purchased a Panatronic DVD from PQS, Inc. Although the salesperson discussed a three-year extended warranty with me, I decided against purchasing that service for $99. However, when my credit card statement arrived this month, I noticed an extra $99 charge from PQS, Inc. I suspect that this charge represents the warranty I declined.

Enclosed is a copy of my sales invoice along with my VISA statement on which I circled the charge. Please authorize a credit immediately and send a copy of the transaction to me at the above address.

I'm enjoying all the features of my Panatronic DVD and would like to be shopping at PQS for a CD player shortly.

Sincerely,

Keith Cortez

Keith Cortez

Enclosure

Personal business letter style

States simply and clearly what to do

Explains objectively what went wrong

Doesn't blame or accuse

Documents facts

Suggests continued business once problem is resolved

Uses friendly tone

Explain objectively. In the body tell the specifics of the claim. Provide copies of necessary documents.

End by requesting action. Include an end date if important. Add a pleasant, forward-looking statement. Keep a copy of the letter.

DIRECT REPLIES

When you can respond favourably to requests, use the direct pattern.

Often, your messages will respond favourably to requests for information or action. A customer wants information about a product. In complying with such requests, you'll want to apply the same direct pattern you used in making requests.

The opening of a direct reply letter might contain a subject line, as shown in Figure 9.7. A subject line helps the reader recognize the topic immediately. Usually appearing two lines below the salutation, the subject line refers in abbreviated form to previous correspondence and/or summarizes a message (*Subject: Your July 12 Inquiry About WorkZone Software*). It often omits articles (*a, an, the*), is not a complete sentence, and does not end with a period. Knowledgeable business communicators use a subject line to refer to earlier correspondence so that in the first sentence, the most emphatic spot in a letter, they are free to emphasize the main idea.

Open Directly. In the first sentence of a direct reply letter, deliver the information the reader wants. Avoid wordy, drawn-out openings such as *I have before me your letter of August 5, in which you request information about . . . .* More forceful and more efficient is an opener that answers the inquiry (*Here is the information you wanted about . . .*). When agreeing to a request for action, announce the good news promptly (*Yes, I will be happy to speak to your business communication class on the topic of . . .*).

Letters responding to requests may open with a subject line to identify the topic immediately.

In the body of your reply, supply explanations and additional information. Because a letter written on company stationery is considered a legally binding contract, be sure to check facts and figures carefully. If a policy or procedure needs authorization, seek approval from a supervisor or executive before writing the letter.

Responding to customer inquiries provides a good opportunity to promote your business.

Arrange Information Logically. When answering a group of questions or providing considerable data, arrange the information logically and make it readable by using lists, tables, headings, boldface, italics, or other graphic devices. When customers or prospective customers inquire about products or services, your response should do more than merely supply answers. You'll also want to promote your organization and products. Often, companies have particular products and services they want to spotlight. Thus, when a customer writes about one product, provide helpful information that satisfies the inquiry, but consider using the opportunity to introduce another product as well. Be sure to present the promotional material with attention to the "you" view and to reader benefits (*You can use our standardized tests to free you from time-consuming employment screening*). You'll learn more about special techniques for developing sales and persuasive messages in Chapter 10.

In concluding, make sure you are cordial and personal. Refer to the information provided or to its use. If further action is required, describe the procedure and help the reader with specifics.

Emphasize the Positive in Mixed Messages. The direct pattern is also appropriate for messages that are mostly good news but may have some negative elements. For example, a return policy has time limits; an airfare may contain holiday restrictions; a speaker can come but not at the time requested; an appliance can be repaired

FIGURE 9.7 Customer Reply Letter

The Three Phases of the Writing Process

Prewriting 1

Analyze: The purpose of this letter is to provide helpful information and to promote company products.

Anticipate: The reader is the intelligent owner of a small business who needs help with personnel administration.

Adapt: Because the reader requested this data, he will be receptive to the letter. Use the direct pattern.

Writing 2

Research: Gather facts to answer the business owner's questions. Consult brochures and pamphlets.

Organize: Prepare a scratch outline. Plan for a fast, direct opening. Use numbered answers to the business owner's three questions.

Compose: Write the first draft on a computer. Strive for short sentences and paragraphs.

Revising 3

Revise: Eliminate jargon and wordiness. Look for ways to explain how the product fits the reader's needs. Revise for "you" view.

Proofread: Double-check the form of numbers (*July 12, page 6, 8 to 5 PST*).

Evaluate: Does this letter answer the customer's questions and encourage an order?

KELOWNA SOFTWARE, INC.
777 Raymer Road
Kelowna, BC V1W 1H7
www.kelownasoft.ca

July 15, 2007

Mr. Jeffrey M. White
White-Rather Enterprises
220 Telford Court
Leduc, AB T9E 5M6

Dear Mr. White:

SUBJECT: YOUR JULY 12 INQUIRY ABOUT WORKZONE SOFTWARE — **Identifies previous correspondence and subject**

Puts most important information first — Yes, we do offer personnel record-keeping software specially designed for small businesses like yours. Here are answers to your three questions about this software:

Lists answers to sender's questions in order asked / **Emphasizes "you" view**

1. Our WorkZone software provides standard employee forms so that you are always in compliance with current government regulations.
2. You receive an interviewer's guide for structured employee interviews, as well as a scripted format for checking references by telephone.
3. Yes, you can update your employees' records easily without the need for additional software, hardware, or training.

Our WorkZone software was specially designed to provide you with expert forms for interviewing, verifying references, recording attendance, evaluating performance, and tracking the status of your employees. We even provide you with step-by-step instructions and suggested procedures. You can treat your employees as if you had a professional human resources specialist on your staff. — **Links sales promotion to reader benefits**

Helps reader find information by citing page number — On page 6 of the enclosed pamphlet you can read about our WorkZone software. To receive a preview copy or to ask questions about its use, just call 1-800-354-5500. Our specialists are eager to help you weekdays from 8 to 5 PST. If you prefer, visit our Web site to receive more information or to place an order. — **Makes it easy to respond**

Sincerely,

Linda DeLorme

Linda DeLorme
Senior Marketing Representative

Enclosure

In mixed-news messages the good news should precede the bad.

but not replaced. When the message is mixed, emphasize the good news by presenting it first (*Yes, I would be delighted to address your marketing class on the topic of*. . .). Then, explain why a problem exists (*My schedule for the week of October 10 takes me to Calgary and Edmonton, where I am* . . .). Present the bad news in the middle (*Although I cannot meet with your class at that time, perhaps we can schedule a date during the week of*. . .). End the message cordially by returning to the good news (*Thanks for the invitation. I'm looking forward to arranging a date in October when I can talk with your students about careers in marketing*).

Your goal is to present the negative news clearly without letting it become the focus of the message. Thus, you want to spend more time talking about the good news. And by placing the bad news in the middle of the letter, you deemphasize it. You'll learn other techniques for presenting bad news in Chapter 11.

Letters of Recommendation

Letters of recommendation present honest, objective evaluations of individuals and help match candidates to jobs.

Letters of recommendation may be written to nominate people for awards and for membership in organizations. More frequently, though, they are written to evaluate present or former employees. The central concern in these messages is honesty. Thus, you should avoid exaggerating or distorting a candidate's qualifications to cover up weaknesses or to destroy the person's chances. Ethically and legally, you have a duty to the candidate as well as to other employers to describe that person truthfully and objectively. You don't, however, have to endorse everyone who asks. Since recommendations are generally voluntary, you can—and should—resist writing letters for individuals you can't truthfully support. Ask these people to find other recommenders who know them better.

Well-written recommendations do help match candidates with jobs. Hiring companies learn more about a candidate's skills and potential. As a result, they are able to place a candidate properly. Therefore, you should learn to write such letters because you will surely be expected to do so in your future career.

Open With Identification. Begin an employment recommendation by identifying the candidate and the position sought, if you know it. State that your remarks are confidential, and suggest that you are writing at the request of the applicant. Describe your relationship with the candidate, as shown in the first paragraph of the employment recommendation letter in Figure 9.8.

Letters that recommend individuals for awards may open with more supportive statements, such as *I'm very pleased to nominate Robert Walsh for the Employee-of-the-Month award. For the past sixteen months, Mr. Walsh served as staff accountant in my division. During that time he distinguished himself by* . . . .

The body of a letter of recommendation should describe the candidate's job performance and potential in specific terms.

Provide Evidence in the Body. The body of an employment recommendation should describe the applicant's job performance and potential. Employers are particularly interested in such traits as communication skills, organizational skills, people skills, ability to work with a team, ability to work independently, honesty, dependability, ambition, loyalty, and initiative. In describing these traits, be sure to back them up with evidence. One of the biggest weaknesses in letters of recommendation is that writers tend to make global, nonspecific statements (*He was careful and accurate* versus *He completed eight financial statements monthly with about 99 percent accuracy*). Employers prefer definite, task-related descriptions, as shown in the second and third paragraphs in Figure 9.8.

Be especially careful to support any negative comments with verification (not *He was slower than other customer service reps* but *He answered 25 calls per hour, while most service reps average 40 calls per hour*). In reporting deficiencies, be sure to

FIGURE 9.8 Employment Recommendation Letter

Tips for Writing Letters of Recommendation

- Identify the purpose and confidentiality of the message.
- Establish your relationship with the applicant.
- Describe the length of employment and job duties, if relevant.
- Provide specific examples of the applicant's professional and personal skills.
- Compare the applicant with others in his or her field.
- Offer an overall rating of the applicant.
- Summarize the significant attributes of the applicant.
- Draw a conclusion regarding the recommendation.

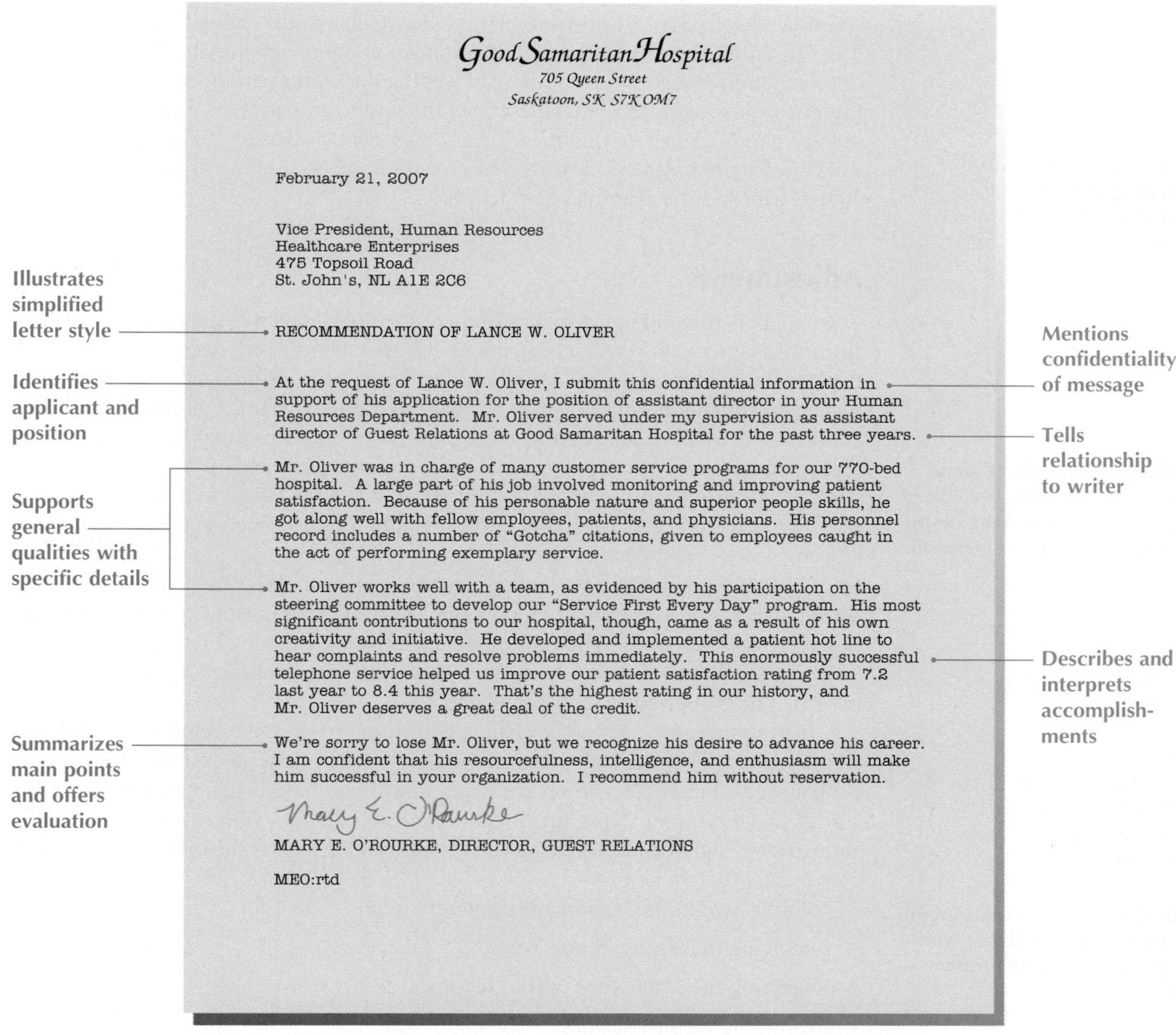

Good Samaritan Hospital
705 Queen Street
Saskatoon, SK S7K 0M7

February 21, 2007

Vice President, Human Resources
Healthcare Enterprises
475 Topsoil Road
St. John's, NL A1E 2C6

RECOMMENDATION OF LANCE W. OLIVER

At the request of Lance W. Oliver, I submit this confidential information in support of his application for the position of assistant director in your Human Resources Department. Mr. Oliver served under my supervision as assistant director of Guest Relations at Good Samaritan Hospital for the past three years.

Mr. Oliver was in charge of many customer service programs for our 770-bed hospital. A large part of his job involved monitoring and improving patient satisfaction. Because of his personable nature and superior people skills, he got along well with fellow employees, patients, and physicians. His personnel record includes a number of "Gotcha" citations, given to employees caught in the act of performing exemplary service.

Mr. Oliver works well with a team, as evidenced by his participation on the steering committee to develop our "Service First Every Day" program. His most significant contributions to our hospital, though, came as a result of his own creativity and initiative. He developed and implemented a patient hot line to hear complaints and resolve problems immediately. This enormously successful telephone service helped us improve our patient satisfaction rating from 7.2 last year to 8.4 this year. That's the highest rating in our history, and Mr. Oliver deserves a great deal of the credit.

We're sorry to lose Mr. Oliver, but we recognize his desire to advance his career. I am confident that his resourcefulness, intelligence, and enthusiasm will make him successful in your organization. I recommend him without reservation.

Mary E. O'Rourke

MARY E. O'ROURKE, DIRECTOR, GUEST RELATIONS

MEO:rtd

Illustrates simplified letter style
Identifies applicant and position
Supports general qualities with specific details
Summarizes main points and offers evaluation
Mentions confidentiality of message
Tells relationship to writer
Describes and interprets accomplish-ments

describe behaviour (*Her last two reports were late and had to be rewritten by her supervisor*) rather than evaluate it (*She is unreliable and her reports are careless*).

The closing of a recommendation presents an overall ranking and may provide an offer to supply more information by telephone.

Evaluate in the Closing. In the final paragraph of a recommendation, you should offer an overall evaluation. Indicate how you would rank this person in relation to others in similar positions. Many managers add a statement indicating whether they would rehire the applicant, given the chance. If you are strongly supportive, summarize the candidate's best qualities. In the closing you might also offer to answer questions by telephone. Such a statement, though, could suggest that the candidate has weak skills and that you will make damaging statements orally but not in print.

General letters of recommendation, written when the candidate has no specific position in mind, often begin with the salutation TO PROSPECTIVE EMPLOYERS. More specific recommendations, to support applications to known positions, address an individual. When the addressee's name is unknown, consider using the simplified letter format, shown in Figure 9.8, which avoids a salutation.

The letter shown in Figure 9.8 illustrates a complete employment letter of recommendation and shows a summary of writing tips. After naming the applicant and the position sought, the letter describes the applicant's present duties. Instead of merely naming positive qualities (*he is personable, possesses superior people skills, works well with a team, is creative, and shows initiative*), these attributes are demonstrated with specific examples and details.

Adjustments

Businesses generally respond favourably to claims because of legal constraints and the desire to maintain customer goodwill.

Even the best-run and best-loved businesses occasionally receive claims or complaints from consumers. When a company receives a claim and decides to respond favourably, the letter is called an *adjustment letter.* Most businesses grant claims and make adjustments promptly—they replace merchandise, refund money, extend discounts, send coupons, and repair goods. Businesses make favourable adjustments to legitimate claims for two reasons. First, consumers are protected by law for recovery of damages. Consumer protection is a joint effort of both federal and provincial legislation.[3] Second, and more obviously, most organizations genuinely want to satisfy their customers and retain their business.

Customer goodwill and retention have an important effect on profits. One study showed that losing a customer reduces profits by $118. Keeping that customer satisfied, however, costs only $20.[4] When customers are unhappy, they don't return. A staggering 91 percent of disgruntled customers swear they will never do business again with a company that does not resolve their complaints.[5]

In responding to customer claims, you must first decide whether to grant the claim. Unless the claim is obviously fraudulent or represents an excessive sum, you'll probably grant it. When you say yes, your adjustment letter will be good news to the reader, so you'll want to use the direct pattern. When your response is no, the indirect pattern might be more appropriate. Chapter 11 discusses the indirect pattern for conveying negative news.

Adjustment letters seek to right wrongs, regain customer confidence, and promote further business.

You'll have three goals in adjustment letters:

- Rectifying the wrong, if one exists
- Regaining the confidence of the customer
- Promoting further business

Open With the Good News. The opening of a positive adjustment letter should approve the customer's claim immediately. Notice how quickly the following openers announce the good news:

Opening sentences tell the good news quickly.

> The enclosed $250 refund cheque demonstrates our desire to satisfy our customers and earn their confidence.

> You will be receiving shortly a new slim Nokia 8860 cell phone to replace the one that shattered when dropped recently.

Occasionally, customers merely want to lodge a complaint and know that something is being done about it. Here's the opening from a bank responding to such a complaint:

> We agree with you completely. Some of our customers have recently spent too much time "on hold" while waiting to speak to a customer service representative. These delays are unacceptable, and we are taking strong measures to eliminate such delays.

In making an adjustment, avoid sounding resentful or grudging. Once you decide to grant a claim, do so willingly. Remember that a primary goal in adjustments is retaining customer loyalty. Statements that sound reluctant (*Although we generally refuse to extend warranties, we're willing to make an exception in this case*) may cause greater dissatisfaction than no response at all.

Explain the Reasons. In the body of an adjustment letter, your goal is to win back the confidence of the customer. You can do this by explaining what caused the problem (if you know) or by describing the measures you are taking to avoid recurrences of the problem, such as in the following:

Explain what caused the problem and the measures taken to avoid future recurrence.

> In preparing our products, we take special care to see that they are wholesome and free of foreign matter. Approved spraying procedures in the field control insects when necessary during the growing season. Our processing plants use screens, air curtains, ultraviolet lights, and other devices to exclude insects. Moreover, we inspect and clean every product to ensure that insects are not present.

Notice that this explanation does not admit error. Many companies sidestep the issue of responsibility because they feel that such an admission damages their credibility or might even encourage legal action. Others admit errors indirectly (*Oversights may sometimes occur*) or even directly (*Once in a while a product that is less than perfect goes out*). The major focus of attention, however, should be on explaining how you are working to prevent recurrence of the problem, as illustrated in the following:

> Waiting "on hold" is as unacceptable to us as it is to you. This delay was brought about when we installed a new automated system. Unfortunately, it took longer than we expected to implement the system and to train our people in their new roles. We are now taking strong measures to eliminate the problem. We have made a significant investment in new technology that will free our customer representatives from routine calls so that they can help you with those banking needs that require personal attention. We are also rerouting calls and modifying the way they are handled.

Explain what went wrong without admitting liability or making excuses.

When an explanation poses no threat of admitting liability, provide details. But don't make your explanation sound like an excuse. Customers resent it when organizations don't take responsibility or try to put the blame elsewhere. The tone of a response is extremely important, and customers expect sincerity.

Decide Whether to Apologize. Another sticky issue is whether to apologize. Studies of adjustment letters received by consumers show that a majority do contain apologies, either in the opening or in the closing.[6] Many business writing experts, however, advise against apologies, contending that they are counterproductive and merely remind the customer of unpleasantness related to the claim. However, if it seems natural to you to apologize, do so. People like to hear apologies. It raises their self-esteem and shows the humility of the writer.[7] Don't, however, fall back on the familiar phrase, "I'm sorry for any inconvenience we may have caused." It sounds mechanical and totally insincere. Instead try something like this: *We understand the frustration our delay has caused you. We're sorry you didn't receive better service,* or *You're right to be disappointed.* If you feel that an apology is appropriate, do it early and briefly. Remember that the primary focus of your letter is on (1) how you are complying with the request, (2) how the problem occurred, and (3) how you are working to prevent its recurrence.

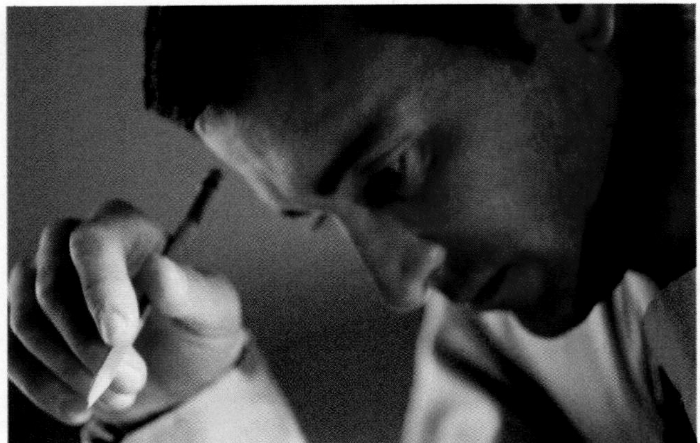

When unhappy customers launch a complaint, 7 of 10 will do business with the company again as long as their concern is handled properly. A staggering 19 of 20 will do business with the company again if the grievance is dealt with swiftly.

Focus on complying with the request, explaining reasons, and preventing recurrence.

Use Sensitive Language. The language of adjustment letters must be particularly sensitive, since customers are already upset. Here are some don'ts:

- Don't use negative words (*trouble, regret, misunderstanding, fault, error, inconvenience, you claim*).
- Don't blame customers—even when they may be at fault.
- Don't blame individuals or departments within your organization; it's unprofessional.
- Don't make unrealistic promises; you can't guarantee that the situation will never recur.

To regain the confidence of your reader, consider including resale information. Describe a product's features and any special applications that might appeal to the reader. Promote a new product if it seems appropriate.

Be Fair But Realistic. If the complaint is justified, offer to solve the problem. Be careful, though, not to "give away the farm." In some instances, all the customer wants is an explanation or an apology. Depending on the product or the damage, consumers might prefer repair or replacement rather than refund. Companies will want to do what is fair. And, within reason, they strive to comply with customers' expectations. Solving a problem, even at a loss to the company, may pay valuable rewards in the form of future sales saved.[8] What is important is responding to complaints sincerely and appropriately.

Close Positively. To close an adjustment letter, assume that the problem has been resolved and that future business will continue. You might express appreciation that the reader wrote, extend thanks for past business, refer to your desire to be of service, or mention a new product. Here are some effective adjustment letter closings for various purposes:

Close an adjustment letter with appreciation, thanks for past business, desire to be of service, or promotion of new product.

> Thanks for writing. Your satisfaction is important to us. We hope that this refund cheque convinces you that service to our customers is our number one priority. Our goals are to earn your confidence and continue to justify that confidence with quality products and excellent service.
>
> Your Nokia 8860 cell phone will come in handy when you're playing and working outside this summer. For additional summer enjoyment take a look at the portable MP3 player on page 37 of the enclosed catalogue. We value your business and look forward to your future orders.

The adjustment letter in Figure 9.9 offers to replace dead rose bushes. It's very possible that grower error caused the plants to die, yet the letter doesn't blame the customer. Notice, too, how resale information and sales promotion material are introduced without seeming pushy. Most important, the tone of the letter suggests that the company is in the customer's corner and wants to do what is right.

Although the direct pattern works for many requests and replies, it obviously won't work for every situation. With more practice and experience, you'll be able to alter the pattern and apply the writing process to other communication problems. The following checklist summarizes the process of writing direct replies.

CHECKLIST FOR WRITING DIRECT REPLIES

Complying With Requests

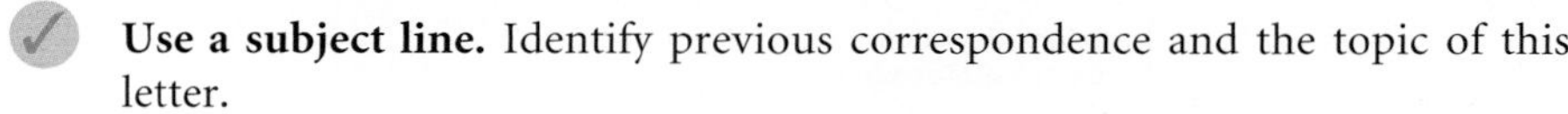

✓ **Use a subject line.** Identify previous correspondence and the topic of this letter.

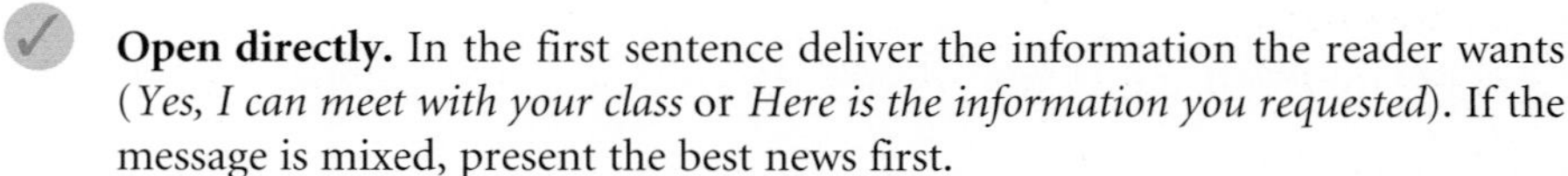

✓ **Open directly.** In the first sentence deliver the information the reader wants (*Yes, I can meet with your class* or *Here is the information you requested*). If the message is mixed, present the best news first.

✓ **In the body provide explanations and additional information.** Arrange this information logically, perhaps using a list, headings, or columns. For prospective customers build your company image and promote your products.

✓ **End with a cordial, personalized statement.** If further action is required, tell the reader how to proceed and give helpful details.

Writing Letters of Recommendation

✓ **Open with identifying information.** Name the candidate, identify the position, and explain your relationship. State that you are writing at the request of the candidate and that the letter is confidential.

FIGURE 9.9 Adjustment Letter

Rose World
Beamsville, ON L0R 1B1
1-800-543-2000

June 3, 2007

Mr. James Bronski
68 Wingate Crescent
Richmond Hill, ON L4B 2Y9

Dear Mr. Bronski:

You may choose six rose bushes as replacements, or you may have a full cash refund for the roses you purchased last year.

The quality of our plants and the careful handling they receive assure you of healthy, viable roses for your garden. Even so, plants sometimes fail without apparent cause. That's why every plant carries a guarantee to grow and to establish itself in your garden.

Along with this letter is a copy of our current catalogue for you to select six new roses or reorder the favourites you chose last year. Two of your previous selections—Red Velvet and Rose Princess—were last season's best-selling roses. For fragrance and old-rose charm, you might like to try the new David Austin English Roses. These enormously popular hybrids resulted from crossing full-petalled old garden roses with modern repeat-flowering shrub roses.

To help you enjoy your roses to the fullest, you'll also receive a copy of our authoritative *Home Gardener's Guide to Roses*. This comprehensive booklet provides easy-to-follow planting tips as well as sound advice about sun, soil, and drainage requirements for roses.

To receive your free replacement order, just fill out the order form inside the catalogue and attach the enclosed certificate. Or return the certificate, and you will receive a full refund of the purchase price.

The quality of Rose World plants reflects the expertise of over a century of hybridizing, growing, harvesting, and shipping top-quality garden stock. Your complete satisfaction is our primary goal. If you're not happy, Mr. Bronski, we're not happy. To ensure your satisfaction and your respect, we maintain our 100 percent guarantee policy.

Sincerely,

Michael Vanderer

Michael Vanderer
General Manager

mv:meg

Enclosures

Tactfully skirts the issue of what caused plant failure

Offers resale information to assure customer of wise choice

Projects personal, conversational tone

Shows pride in the company's products and concern for its customers

Approves customer's claim immediately

Avoids blaming customer

Includes some sales promotion without overkill

Tells reader clearly what to do next

Strives to regain customer's confidence in both products and service

- **In the body add supporting statements.** Describe the applicant's present duties, job performance, skills, and potential. Back up general qualities with specific evidence. Verify any negative statements.

- **Close with an overall ranking of the candidate.** (*Of all the people I have known in this position, Jim ranks . . . .*) Offer to supply more information by telephone.

Granting Claims and Making Adjustments

- **Open with approval.** Comply with the customer's claim immediately. Avoid sounding grudging or reluctant.

In the body win back the customer's confidence. Explain the cause of the problem or describe your ongoing efforts to avoid such difficulties. Focus on your efforts to satisfy customers. If you apologize, do so early and briefly. Avoid negative words, accusations, and unrealistic promises. Consider including resale and sales promotion information.

Close positively. Express appreciation to the customer for writing, extend thanks for past business, anticipate continued patronage, refer to your desire to be of service, and/or mention a new product if it seems appropriate.

GOODWILL MESSAGES

Goodwill messages, which include thanks, recognition, and sympathy, seem to intimidate many communicators. Finding the right words to express feelings is sometimes more difficult than writing ordinary business documents. Writers tend to procrastinate when it comes to goodwill messages, or else they send a ready-made card or pick up the telephone. Remember, though, that the personal sentiments of the sender are always more expressive and more meaningful to readers than are printed cards or oral messages. Taking the time to write gives more importance to our well-wishing. Personal notes also provide a record that can be reread, savoured, and treasured.

In expressing thanks, recognition, or sympathy, you should always do so promptly. These messages are easier to write when the situation is fresh in your mind. They also mean more to the recipient. And don't forget that a prompt thank-you note carries the hidden message that you care and that you consider the event to be important. The best goodwill messages—whether thanks, congratulations, praise, or sympathy—concentrate on the five *S*s. These goodwill messages are

- **Selfless.** Be sure to focus the message solely on the receiver not the sender. Don't talk about yourself; avoid such comments as *I remember when I . . . .*
- **Specific.** Personalize the message by mentioning specific incidents or characteristics of the receiver. Telling a colleague *Great speech* is much less effective than *Great story about McDonald's marketing in Moscow.* Take care to verify names and other facts.
- **Sincere.** Let your words show genuine feelings. Rehearse in your mind how you would express the message to the receiver orally. Then transform that conversational language to your written message. Avoid pretentious, formal, or flowery language (*It gives me great pleasure to extend felicitations on the occasion of your firm's 20th anniversary*).
- **Spontaneous.** Keep the message fresh and enthusiastic. Avoid canned phrases (*Congratulations on your promotion, Good luck in the future*). Strive for directness and naturalness, not creative brilliance.
- **Short.** Although goodwill messages can be as long as needed, try to accomplish your purpose in only a few sentences. What is most important is remembering an individual. Such caring does not require documentation or wordiness. Individuals and business organizations often use special note cards or stationery for brief messages.

Thanks

When someone has done you a favour or when an action merits praise, you need to extend thanks or show appreciation. Letters of appreciation may be written to customers for their orders, to hosts and hostesses for their hospitality, to individuals for kindnesses performed, and especially to customers who complain. After all, complainers are actually providing you with "free consulting reports from the field." Complainers who feel that they were listened to often become the greatest promoters of an organization.[9]

Because the receiver will be pleased to hear from you, you can open directly with the purpose of your message. The letter in Figure 9.10 thanks a speaker who addressed a group of marketing professionals. Although such thank-you notes can be quite short, this one is a little longer because the writer wants to lend importance to the receiver's efforts. Notice that every sentence relates to the receiver and offers enthusiastic praise. And, by using the receiver's name along with contractions and positive words, the writer makes the letter sound warm and conversational.

Written notes that show appreciation and express thanks are significant to their receivers. In expressing thanks, you generally write a short note on special notepaper or heavy card stock. The following messages provide models for expressing thanks for a gift, for a favour, and for hospitality.

Identify the gift, tell why you appreciate it, and explain how you will use it.

To Express Thanks for a Gift

Thanks, Laura, to you and the other members of the department for honouring me with the elegant Waterford crystal vase at the party celebrating my twentieth anniversary with the company.

The height and shape of the vase are perfect to hold roses and other bouquets from my garden. Each time I fill it, I'll remember your thoughtfulness in choosing this lovely gift for me.

Tell what the favour means using sincere, simple statements.

To Send Thanks for a Favour

I sincerely appreciate your filling in for me last week when I was too ill to attend the planning committee meeting for the spring exhibition.

Without your participation much of my preparatory work would have been lost. It's comforting to know that competent and generous individuals like you are part of our team, Mark. Moreover, it's my very good fortune to be able to count you as a friend. I'm grateful to you.

Compliment the fine food, charming surroundings, warm hospitality, excellent host and hostess, and/or good company.

To Extend Thanks for Hospitality

Jeffrey and I want you to know how much we enjoyed the dinner party for our department that you hosted Saturday evening. Your charming home and warm hospitality, along with the lovely dinner and sinfully delicious chocolate dessert, combined to create a truly memorable evening.

Most of all, though, we appreciate your kindness in cultivating togetherness in our department. Thanks, Jennifer, for being such a special person.

Response

Take the time to respond to any goodwill message you may receive.

Should you respond when you receive a congratulatory note or a written pat on the back? By all means! These messages are attempts to connect personally; they are efforts to reach out, to form professional and/or personal bonds. Failing to respond to notes of congratulations and most other goodwill messages is like failing to say "You're welcome" when someone says "Thank you." Responding to such messages is simply the right thing to do. Do avoid, though, minimizing your achievements with comments that suggest you don't really deserve the praise or that the sender is exaggerating your good qualities.

To Answer a Congratulatory Note

Thanks for your kind words regarding my award, and thanks, too, for sending me the newspaper clipping. I truly appreciate your thoughtfulness and warm wishes.

FIGURE 9.10 Thank-You Letter for a Favour

Prewriting 1

Analyze: The purpose of this letter is to express appreciation to a business executive for presenting a talk before professionals.

Anticipate: The reader will be more interested in personalized comments than in general statements showing gratitude.

Adapt: Because the reader will be pleased, use the direct pattern.

Writing 2

Research: Consult notes taken during the talk.

Organize: Open directly by giving the reason for writing. Express enthusiastic and sincere thanks. In the body provide specifics. Refer to facts and highlights in the talk. Supply sufficient detail to support your sincere compliments. Conclude with appreciation. Be warm and friendly.

Compose: Write the first draft.

Revising 3

Revise: Revise for tone and warmth. Use the reader's name. Include concrete detail but do it concisely. Avoid sounding gushy or phony.

Proofread: Check the spelling of the receiver's name; verify facts. Check the spelling of *gratitude, patience, advice, persistence,* and *grateful.*

Evaluate: Does this letter convey sincere thanks?

Hamilton–Wentworth Chapter
North American Marketing Association
P.O. Box 3598
Hamilton, ON L8V 4X2

March 20, 2007

Mr. Bryant Huffman
Marketing Manager, Western Division
Toys "R" Us, Inc.
2777 Langstaff Avenue
Thornhill, ON L3T 3M8

Dear Bryant:

You have our sincere gratitude for providing the Hamilton-Wentworth chapter of the NAMA with one of the best presentations our group has ever heard. — **Tells purpose and delivers praise**

Personalizes the message by using specifics rather than generalities — Your description of the battle Toys "R" Us waged to begin marketing products in Japan was a genuine eye-opener for many of us. Nine years of preparation establishing connections and securing permissions seems an eternity, but obviously such persistence and patience pays off. We now understand better the need to learn local customs and nurture relationships when dealing in Japan.

In addition to your good advice, we particularly enjoyed your sense of humour and jokes—as you must have recognized from the uproarious laughter. What a great routine you do on faulty translations! — **Spotlights the reader's talents**

Concludes with compliments and thanks — We're grateful, Bryant, for the entertaining and instructive evening you provided our marketing professionals. Thanks!

Cordially,

Joyce Barnes

Joyce Barnes
Program Chair, NAMA

JRB:grw

To Respond to a Pat on the Back
Your note about my work made me feel good. I'm grateful for your thoughtfulness.

Sympathy

Sympathy notes should refer to the misfortune sensitively and offer assistance.

Most of us can bear misfortune and grief more easily when we know that others care. Notes expressing sympathy, though, are probably more difficult to write than any other kind of message. Commercial "In sympathy" cards make the task easier—but they are far less meaningful. Grieving friends want to know what you think—not what Hallmark's card writers think. To help you get started, you can always glance through cards expressing sympathy. They will supply ideas about the kinds of thoughts you might wish to convey in your own words. In writing a sympathy note, (1) refer to the death or misfortune sensitively, using words that show you understand what a crushing blow it is; (2) in the case of a death, praise the deceased in a personal way; (3) offer assistance without going into excessive detail; and (4) end on a reassuring, forward-looking note. Sympathy messages may be typed, although handwriting seems more personal. In either case, use notepaper or personal stationery.

To Express Condolences

Mentions the loss tactfully and recognizes good qualities of the deceased.

We are deeply saddened, Gayle, to learn of the death of your husband. Warren's kind nature and friendly spirit endeared him to all who knew him. He will be missed.

Assures receiver of your concern. Offers assistance.

Although words seem empty in expressing our grief, we want you to know that your friends at QuadCom extend their profound sympathy to you. If we may help you or lighten your load in any way, you have but to call.

Concludes on positive, reassuring note.

We know that the treasured memories of your many happy years together, along with the support of your family and many friends, will provide strength and comfort in the months ahead.

CHECKLIST FOR WRITING GOODWILL MESSAGES

General Guidelines: The Five *S*s

- ✓ **Be selfless.** Discuss the receiver, not the sender.
- ✓ **Be specific.** Instead of generic statements (*You did a good job*), include special details (*Your marketing strategy to target key customers proved to be outstanding*).
- ✓ **Be sincere.** Show your honest feelings with conversational, unpretentious language (*We're all very proud of your award*).
- ✓ **Be spontaneous.** Strive to make the message natural, fresh, and direct. Avoid canned phrases (*If I may be of service, please do not hesitate . . .*).
- ✓ **Keep the message short.** Remember that, although they may be as long as needed, most goodwill messages are fairly short.

Giving Thanks

- ✓ **Cover three points in gift thank-yous.** (1) Identify the gift, (2) tell why you appreciate it, and (3) explain how you will use it.

- **Be sincere in sending thanks for a favour.** Tell what the favour means to you. Avoid superlatives and gushiness. Maintain credibility with sincere, simple statements.

- **Offer praise in expressing thanks for hospitality.** Compliment, as appropriate, the (1) fine food, (2) charming surroundings, (3) warm hospitality, (4) excellent host and hostess, and (5) good company.

Answering Congratulatory Messages

- **Respond to congratulations.** Send a brief note expressing your appreciation. Tell how good the message made you feel.

- **Accept praise gracefully.** Don't make belittling comments (*I'm not really all that good!*) to reduce awkwardness or embarrassment.

Extending Sympathy

- **Refer to the loss or tragedy directly but sensitively.** In the first sentence mention the loss and your personal reaction.

- **For deaths, praise the deceased.** Describe positive personal characteristics (*Howard was a forceful but caring leader*).

- **Offer assistance.** Suggest your availability, especially if you can do something specific.

- **End on a reassuring, positive note.** Perhaps refer to the strength the receiver finds in friends, family, colleagues, or religion.

SUMMARY OF LEARNING OBJECTIVES

1 **List three characteristics of good letters and describe the direct pattern for organizing letters.** Good letters are characterized by clear content, a tone of goodwill, and correct form. Letters carrying positive or neutral messages should be organized directly. That means introducing the main idea (the purpose for writing) immediately in the opening. The body of the letter explains and gives details. Letters that make requests close by telling what action is desired and establishing a deadline (end date) for that action.

2 **Write letters requesting information and action.** The opening immediately states the purpose of the letter, perhaps asking a question. The body explains and justifies the request. The closing tells the reader courteously what to do and shows appreciation.

3 **Write letters placing orders.** The opening introduces the order and authorizes a purchase (*Please send me the following items . . .*). The body lists the desired items including quantity, order number, description, unit price, and total price. The closing describes the method of payment, tells when the merchandise should be sent, and expresses appreciation.

4 **Write letters making claims.** The opening describes the problem clearly or tells what action is to be taken. The body explains and justifies the request without anger or emotion. The closing, which might include an end date, describes the desired action.

5 **Write letters complying with requests.** A subject line identifies previous correspondence, while the opening immediately delivers the good news. The body explains and provides additional information. The closing is cordial and personalized.

6 **Write letters of recommendation.** The opening identifies the candidate, the position, your relationship, and the confidentiality of the letter. The body describes the candidate's job duties, performance, skills, and potential. The closing provides an overall ranking of the candidate and offers to give additional information by telephone.

7 **Write letters granting claims and making adjustments.** The opening immediately grants the claim without sounding grudging. To regain the confidence of the customer, the body may explain what went wrong and how the problem will be rectified. However, it may avoid accepting responsibility for any problems. The closing expresses appreciation, extends thanks for past business, refers to a desire to be of service, and/or mentions a new product. An apology is optional.

8 **Write goodwill messages.** Goodwill messages deliver thanks, praise, or sympathy. They should be selfless, specific, sincere, spontaneous, and short. Gift thank-yous should identify the gift, tell why you appreciate it, and explain how you will use it. Thank-yous for favours should tell, without gushing, what they mean to you. Expressions of sympathy should mention the loss tactfully; recognize good qualities in the deceased (in the case of a death); offer assistance; and conclude on a positive, reassuring note.

CHAPTER REVIEW

1. What is goodwill? Briefly describe five ways to develop goodwill in a letter. (Obj. 1)
2. Why is it best to write most business letters "backwards"? (Obj. 1)
3. Under what conditions is it important to send business letters rather than e-mail messages? (Obj. 1)
4. Why is the direct letter strategy appropriate for most business messages? (Obj. 2)
5. What is "frontloading," and why is it useful in routine business letters? (Obj. 2)
6. For order letters what information goes in the opening? In the body? In the closing? (Obj. 3)
7. What is a claim? When is it straightforward? (Obj. 4)
8. Why are most companies today particularly interested in listening to customers? (Obj. 4)
9. In complying with requests, why is it especially important that all facts are correct in letters written on company stationery? (Obj. 5)
10. When answering many questions for a customer, how can the information be grouped to improve readability? (Obj. 5)
11. What information should the opening of a letter of recommendation contain? (Obj. 6)
12. What is an appropriate salutation for a letter of recommendation when the candidate has no specific position in mind? (Obj. 6)
13. What are six guidelines to follow in writing recommendations? (Obj. 6)
14. What is an adjustment letter, and what are a writer's three goals in writing adjustment letters? (Obj. 7)
15. Name five characteristics of goodwill messages. (Obj. 8)

CRITICAL THINKING

1. What's wrong with using the indirect pattern for writing routine requests and replies? If in the end the reader understands the message, why make a big fuss over the organization? (Obj. 1)
2. A recent article in a professional magazine carried this headline: "Is Letter Writing Dead?" How would you respond to such a question? (Obj. 1)
3. Is it insensitive to include resale or sales promotion information in an adjustment letter? Why or why not? (Obj. 7)
4. Why is it important to regain the confidence of a customer in an adjustment letter? How can it be done? (Obj. 7)

ACTIVITIES

9.1 Direct Openings (Objs. 1–8)

Your Task. Revise the following openings so that they are more direct. Add information if necessary.

a. My name is Brandon Brockway, and I am assistant to the manager of Information Services & Technology at HealthCentral, Inc. Our company needs to do a better job of integrating human resources and payroll functions. I understand that you have a software product called "HRFocus" that might do this, and I need to ask you some questions about it.

b. I seem to have lost your order blank, so I have to write this letter. I hope that it is acceptable to place an order this way. I am interested in ordering a number of items from your winter catalogue, which I still have although the order blank is missing.

c. Pursuant to your letter of January 15, I am writing in regard to your inquiry about whether or not we offer our European-style patio umbrella in colours. This unique umbrella receives a number of inquiries. Its 3-m canopy protects you when the sun is directly overhead, but it also swivels and tilts to virtually any angle for continuous sun protection all day long. It comes in two colours: off-white and forest green.

d. I am pleased to receive your inquiry regarding the possibility of my acting as a speaker at the final semester meeting of your business management club on April 30. The topic of online résumés interests me and is one on which I think I could impart helpful information to your members. Therefore, I am responding in the affirmative to your kind invitation.

e. Thank you for your recent order of November 2. We are sure you will enjoy the low-profile, brushed-cotton ball caps that you ordered from our spring catalogue. Your order is currently being processed and should leave our production facility in Montreal early next week. We use UPS for all deliveries in Ontario. Because you ordered caps with your logo embroidered in a two-tone combination, your order cannot be shipped until November 12. You should not expect it until November 15.

9.2 Subject Lines (Objs. 1–8)

Your Task. Write efficient subject lines for each of the messages in Activity 9.1. Add dates and other information if necessary.

9.3 Document for Analysis: Information Request (Obj. 2)

Your Task. Analyze the following letter. List its weaknesses. If your instructor directs, revise the letter.

✗ *Poorly Written Letter*

Dear Sir:

I am a new member of the Corporate Travel Department of my company, QuadCom, and I have been assigned the task of writing to you to inquire about our next sales meeting. We would like to find a resort with conference facilities, which is why I am writing.

We are interested in banquet facilities where we can all be together, but we will also need at least four smaller meeting rooms. Each of these rooms should accommodate about 75. We hope to arrange our conference August 4 through August 9, and we expect about 250 sales associates. Most of our associates will be flying in so I'm interested in what airport is closest and transportation to and from the airport.

Does your hotel have public address systems in the meeting rooms? How about audio-visual equipment and computer facilities for presentations? Thank you for any information you can provide.

Sincerely,

9.4 Document for Analysis: Direct Claim (Obj. 4)

Your Task. Analyze the following letter. List its weaknesses. If your instructor directs, revise the letter.

✗ *Poorly Written Letter*

Dear Customer Service Manager Kent Fowler:

This is to inform you that you can't have it both ways. Either you provide customers with cars with full gas tanks or you don't. And if you don't, you shouldn't charge them when they return with empty tanks!

In view of the fact that I picked up a car in Fredericton August 22 with an empty tank, I had to fill it immediately. Then I drove it until August 25. When I returned to Wolfville, I naturally let the tank go nearly empty, since that is the way I received the car in Fredericton.

But your attendant in Wolfville charged me to fill the tank—$26.50 (premium gasoline at premium prices)! Although I explained to him that I had received it with an empty tank, he kept telling me that company policy required that he charge for a fill-up. My total bill came to $266.50, which, you must agree, is a lot of money for a rental period of only three days. I have the signed rental agreement and a receipt showing that I paid the full amount and that it included $26.50 for a gas fill-up when I returned the car.

Inasmuch as my company is a new customer and inasmuch as we had hoped to use your agency for our future car rentals because of your competitive rates, I trust that you will give this matter your prompt attention.

Disappointedly yours,

9.5 Document for Analysis: Adjustment (Obj. 7)

Your Task. Analyze the following letter. It suffers from many writing faults. List its weaknesses. If your instructor directs, revise the letter.

✗ *Poorly Written Letter*

Dear Mr. Thomas:

Your letter has been referred to me for reply. You claim that the painting recently sent by Central Park Gallery arrived with sags in the canvas and that you are unwilling to hang it in your executive offices.

I have examined your complaint carefully, and, frankly, I find it difficult to believe because we are so careful about shipping, but if what you say is true, I suspect that the shipper may be the source of your problem. We give explicit instructions to our shippers that large paintings must be shipped standing up, not lying down. We also wrap every painting in two layers of convoluted foam and one layer of Perf-Pack foam, which we think should be sufficient to withstand any bumps and scrapes that negligent shipping may cause. We will certainly look into this.

Although it is against our policy, we will in this instance allow you to take this painting to a local framing shop for restretching. We are proud that we can offer fine works of original art at incredibly low prices, and you can be sure that we do not send out sagging canvases.

Sincerely,

9.6 Information Request: Computer Code of Conduct (Obj. 2)

WEB

As an assistant in the campus computer laboratory, you have been asked by your boss to help write a code of conduct for use of the laboratory facilities. This code will spell out what behaviour and activities are allowed in your lab. The first thing you are to do is conduct a search of the Internet to see what other college or university computing labs have written as conduct codes.

Your Task. Using at least two search engines, search the Web employing variations of the keywords "computer code of conduct." Print two or three codes that seem appropriate. Write a letter (or an e-mail message, if your instructor agrees) to the director of an educational computer laboratory asking for further information about its code and its effectiveness. Include at least five significant questions. Attach your printouts to your letter.

9.7 Order Letter: Office Supplies to Go (Obj. 3)

You are Hector Rivera, manager, Lasertronics, Inc., 627 Nordstrum Road, Lethbridge, AB T1R 3L5. You want to order some items from an office supply catalogue, but your catalogue is a year old and you have lost the order form. Because you're in a hurry, you decide to place a fax order. Rather than write for a new catalogue, you decide to take a chance and order items from the old catalogue, realizing that prices may be somewhat different. You want three Panasonic electric pencil sharpeners, Item 22-A, at $19.95 each. You want one steel desktop organizer, 1.5 m long, Item No. 23-K. Its price is $117.50. Order two Roll-a-Flex files for 5- by 10-cm cards at $14.50 each. This is Item 23-G. The next item is No. 29-H, file folders, box of 100, letter size, at $5.29. You need ten boxes. You would like to be invoiced for this purchase, and you prefer UPS delivery. Even though the prices may be somewhat higher, you decide to list the prices shown in your catalogue so that you have an idea of what the total order will cost.

Your Task. Write a letter to Monarch Discount Office Furniture, 2890 Monarch Road, Lethbridge, Alberta T1K 1L6. Between the date and the inside address, type TRANSMITTED BY FAX.

9.8 *Direct Claim: Backing Out of Project Management Seminar* (Obj. 4)

Ace Executive Training Institute offered a seminar titled "Enterprise Project Management Protocol" that sounded terrific. It promised to teach project managers how to estimate work, report status, write work packages, and cope with project conflicts. Because your company often is engaged in large cross-functional projects, it decided to send four key managers to the seminar to be held June 1–2 at the Ace headquarters in Sydney. The fee was $2200 each, and it was paid in advance. About six weeks before the seminar, you learned that three of the managers would be tied up in projects that would not be completed in time for them to attend.

Your Task. On your company letterhead, write a claim letter to Addison O'Neill, Registrar, Ace Executive Training Institute, 49 Harbourview Drive, Sydney, NS B1S 2A8. Ask that the seminar fees for three employees be returned because they cannot attend. Give yourself a title and supply any details necessary.

9.9 *Direct Claim: The Real Thing* (Obj. 4)

Let's face it. Like most consumers, you've probably occasionally been unhappy with service or with a product you have used.

Your Task. Select a product or service that has disappointed you. Write a claim letter requesting a refund, replacement, explanation, or whatever seems reasonable. Generally, such letters are addressed to customer service departments. For claims about food products, be sure to include bar-code identification from the package, if possible. Your instructor may ask you to actually mail this letter. Remember that smart companies want to know what their customers think, especially if a product could be improved. Give your ideas for improvement. When you receive a response, share it with your class.

9.10 *Direct Reply: River Rafting on the Web* (Obj. 5)

WEB

As the program chair for the campus Ski Club, you have been asked by the president to investigate river rafting. The Ski Club is an active organization, and its members want to schedule a summer activity. A majority favoured rafting. Search the Web for relevant information. Select five of the most promising Web sites offering rafting. If possible, print copies of your findings.

Your Task. Summarize your findings in a memo to Brian Krauss, Ski Club president. The next meeting of the Ski Club is May 8, but you think it would be a good idea if you could discuss your findings with Brian before the meeting.

9.11 *Direct Reply: Explaining How to Send Résumés* (Obj. 5)

CRITICAL THINKING | SPEAKING | TEAM | WEB

You've worked at CyberSoft in the Ottawa Valley for a couple of years. It's a great place to work, and it receives many letters from job applicants. Some of them inquire about the company's résumé-scanning techniques. You generally send out the following form letter that has been in the files for some time.

Dear Sir or Madam:

Your letter of April 11 has been referred to me for a response. We are pleased to learn that you are considering employment here at CyberSoft, and we look forward to receiving your résumé, should you decide to send same to us.

You ask if we scan incoming résumés. Yes, we certainly do. Actually, we use SmartTrack, an automated résumé-tracking system. SmartTrack is incredible! We sometimes receive as many as 300 résumés a day, and SmartTrack helps us sort, screen, filter, and separate the résumés. It also processes them, helps us organize them, and keeps a record of all of these résumés. Some of the résumés, however, cannot be scanned, so we have to return those—if we have time.

The reasons that résumés won't scan may surprise you. Some applicants send photocopies or faxed copies, and these can cause misreading, so don't do it. The best plan is to send an original copy. Some people use coloured paper. Big mistake! White paper (8 1/2 x 11-inch) printed on one side is the best bet. Another big problem is unusual type fonts, such as script or fancy gothic or antique fonts. They don't seem to realize that scanners do best with plain, readable fonts such as Arial or Universe in a 10- to 14-point size.

Other problems occur when applicants use graphics, shading, italics, underlining, horizontal and vertical lines, parentheses, and brackets. Scanners like plain "vanilla" résumés! Oh yes, staples can cause misreading. And folding of a résumé can also cause the scanners to foul up. To be safe, don't staple or fold, and be sure to use wide margins and a quality printer.

When a hiring manager within CyberSoft wants to look for an appropriate candidate, he is told to submit keywords to describe the candidate he has in mind for his opening. We tell him (or sometimes her) to zero in on nouns and phrases that best describe what they want. Thus, my advice to you is to try to include those words that highlight your technical and professional areas of expertise.

If you do decide to submit your résumé to CyberSoft, be sure you don't make any of the mistakes described herein that would cause the scanner to misread it.

Sincerely,

Your Task. Your boss saw this letter one day and thought it was miserable. She asks you and your team to produce an informative and effective letter that can be sent to anyone who inquires. As a team, (1) discuss how this letter could be improved; (2) decide what information is necessary to send to potential job applicants; (3) search the Web for additional information that might be helpful; and (4) develop a better letter. Address your first letter to Mr. Michael Madzar, 1101 Copeland Street, Winnipeg, MB R2C 3H8.

9.12 Adjustment: Backing Out of Project Management Seminar (Obj. 7)

Ace Executive Training Institute offered a seminar titled "Enterprise Project Management Protocol" for June 1–2 and was delighted to receive reservations for four attendees (see Activity 9.8). But six weeks before the seminar, Ace received a letter from Raintree Manufacturing asking for a refund because three of the four cannot attend. Ace has already hired the instructor and made arrangements for the seminar based on the projected attendance, so it is disappointed to see this cancellation. Yet, it wants to retain good relations with Raintree in anticipation of future business. It will return the registration fees of $6600. Because Raintree is having difficulty allowing its employees to get away for training, it may be interested in Ace's AccuVision Training Series with on-site training modules. These modules bring the seminar to the client. They teach team building, situational interaction style, initiative, and analysis/problem solving—right on the client's premises. Your Web site provides all the details.

Your Task. As assistant to Addison O'Neill, registrar, write an adjustment letter to Kit Adkins, Raintree Manufacturing, 491 South Emerald Road, St. John's, NL A1N 3Y1. Take advantage of this opportunity to promote your company's on-site programs.

9.13 Letter of Recommendation: Recommending Yourself (Obj. 6)

You are about to leave your present job. When you ask your boss for a letter of recommendation, to your surprise he tells you to write it yourself and then have him sign it. [Actually, this is not an unusual practice today. Many businesspeople find that employees are very perceptive and accurate when they evaluate themselves.]
Your Task. Use specifics from a current or previous job. Describe your duties and skills. Be sure to support general characteristics with specific examples.

9.14 Order Response: Office Supplies to Go (Obj. 7)

As a member of the Order Department at Monarch Discount Office Furniture (2890 Monarch Road, Lethbridge, AB T1K 1L6), respond to the order placed by Hector Rivera at Lasertronics (described in Activity 9.7). Yes, all of the prices listed in your old catalogue have increased. That's the bad news. The good news is that you have in stock nearly everything he ordered. The only item not immediately available is the desktop organizer, Item No. 23-K. That has to be shipped from the manufacturer in Calgary. You've been having trouble with that supplier lately, perhaps because of heavy demand. However, you think that the organizer will be shipped no later than three weeks from the current date. You're pleased to have Lasertronics' order. They might be interested in your new line of office supply products at discount prices. Send Mr. Rivera a new catalogue and call his attention to the low, low price on continuous-form computer paper. It's just $39.95 for a box containing 2700 sheets of 9$\frac{1}{2}$-by 11-inch, 20-pound printout paper. All the items he ordered, except the organizer, are on their way by UPS and should arrive in three days.
Your Task. Respond to Hector Rivera, manager, Lasertronics, Inc., 627 Nordstrum Road, Lethbridge, AB T1R 3L5. Tell him the good and bad news about his order.

9.15 Thanks for a Favour: Got the Job! (Obj. 8)

Congratulations! You completed your degree or diploma and got a terrific job in your field. One of your instructors was especially helpful to you when you were a student. This instructor also wrote an effective letter of recommendation that was instrumental in helping you obtain your job.
Your Task. Write a letter thanking your instructor.

9.16 Sending Good Wishes: Personalizing Group Greeting Cards (Obj. 8)

WEB **TEAM**

When a work colleague has a birthday, gets promoted, or retires, someone generally circulates a group greeting card. In the past it wasn't a big deal. Office colleagues just signed their names and passed the store-bought card along to others. But the current trend is toward personalization with witty, oh-so-clever quips. And that presents a problem. What should you say—or not say? You know that people value special handwritten quips, but you realize that you're not particularly original and you don't have a store of "bon mots" (clever sayings, witticisms). You're tired of the old standbys, such as "This place won't be the same without you" and "You're only as old as you feel."

Your Task. To be prepared for the next greeting card that lands on your desk at work, you decide to work with some friends to make a list of remarks appropriate for business occasions. Use the Web to research witty sayings appropriate for promotions, birthdays, births, weddings, illnesses, or personal losses. Use a search term such as "birthday sayings," "retirement quotes," or "cool sayings." You may decide to assign each category (birthday, retirement, promotion, and so forth) to a separate team. Submit the best sayings in a memo to your instructor.

C.L.U.E. REVIEW 9

Edit the following sentences to correct faults in grammar, punctuation, spelling, and word use.

1. Although we've saw a extrordinary increase in the use of e-mail some business letters must still be wrote.
2. She acts as if she was the only person who ever received a complement about their business writting.
3. Good business letters are distinguished by three characteristics. Clear content, a goodwill tone and correct form.
4. Cynthia Jones whom I think is our newly-appointed Vice President writes many business letters for our Company.
5. After the Office Manager and him returned from their meeting we were able to sort the customer's letters more quick.
6. Even the best run and best loved businesses ocassionaly recieve claims, or complaints from consumers'.
7. On Wenesday we received 2 claims, on Thursday we received 4 more.
8. We enclosed a refund cheque for two hundred dollars, however we worried that it was not enough to regain the confidence of the customer.
9. If you could of saw the customers letter you would have been as upset as Rona and me.
10. To express thanks and show apreciation most people write a short note. On special notepaper or heavy card stock.

Chapter 10

Persuasive and Sales Messages

LEARNING OBJECTIVES

1 *Apply Guffey's 3-×-3 writing process to persuasive messages.*

2 *Explain the components of a persuasive message.*

3 *Request favours and action effectively.*

4 *Write convincing persuasive messages within organizations.*

5 *Request adjustments and make claims successfully.*

6 *Compose successful sales messages.*

7 *Describe the basic elements included in effective news releases.*

STRATEGIES FOR MAKING PERSUASIVE REQUESTS

The ability to persuade is one of life's important skills. *Persuading* means using argument or discussion to change an individual's beliefs or actions. Persuasion, of course, is a very important part of any business that sells goods or services. And selling online is even more challenging than other forms of persuasion because of the technology barrier that must be overcome. However, many of the techniques used online are similar to those you will use in persuasion at home, at school, and on the job.

Successful persuasion results from a reasonable request and a well-presented argument.

Doubtless you've had to be persuasive to convert others to your views or to motivate them to do what you want. The outcome of such efforts depends largely on the reasonableness of your request, your credibility, and the ability to make your request attractive to the receiver. In this chapter you will learn many techniques and strategies to help you be successful in any persuasive effort.

When you think that your listener or reader is inclined to agree with your request, you can start directly with the main idea. But when the receiver is likely to resist, don't reveal the purpose too quickly. Ideas that require persuasion benefit from a slow approach that includes ample preparation. You must gain attention and move to logical reasons supporting your request. This indirect pattern is effective when you must persuade people to grant you favours, accept your recommendations, make adjustments in your favour, or grant your claims.

The same is true for sales messages. Instead of making a sales pitch immediately, smart communicators prepare a foundation by developing credibility and hooking their requests to benefits for the receiver. In persuasive messages other than sales, you must know precisely what you want the receiver to think or do. You must also anticipate what appeals to make or "buttons to push" to motivate action. Achieving these goals in both written and oral messages requires special attention to the initial steps in the process.

Effective sales messages reflect thorough product knowledge, writer credibility, and specific reader benefits.

Applying Guffey's 3-×-3 Writing Process to Persuasive Messages

Persuasion means changing people's views, and that's a difficult task. Pulling it off demands planning and perception. The 3-×-3 writing process provides you with a helpful structure for laying a foundation for persuasion. Of particular importance here are (1) analyzing the purpose, (2) adapting to the audience, (3) collecting information, and (4) organizing the message.

1

The key components of a persuasive request are gaining attention, showing the worth of the proposal, overcoming resistance, and motivating action.

Analyzing the Purpose. The purpose of a persuasive message is to convert the receiver to your ideas or to motivate action. A message without a clear purpose is doomed. Not only must you know what your purpose is and what response you want, but you must know these things when you start writing a letter or planning a presentation. Too often, ineffective communicators reach the end of a message before discovering exactly what they want the receiver to do. Then they must start over, giving the request a different "spin" or emphasis. Because your purpose establishes the strategy of the message, determine it first.

By identifying your purpose up front, you can shape the message to point toward it. This planning effort-saves considerable rewriting time and produces the most successful persuasive messages.

Persuasive messages require careful analysis of the purpose for writing.

Effective persuasive messages focus on audience needs or goals.

Adapting to the Audience. While you're considering the purpose of a persuasive message, you also need to concentrate on the receiver. How can you adapt your request to that individual so that your message is heard? A persuasive message is equally futile unless it meets the needs of its audience. In a broad sense, you'll be seeking to show how your request helps the receiver achieve some of life's major goals or fulfills key needs: money, power, comfort, confidence, importance, friends, peace of mind, and recognition, to name a few.

On a more practical level, you want to show how your request solves a problem, achieves a personal or work objective, or just makes life easier for your audience.

To adapt your request to the receiver, consider these questions that receivers will very likely be asking themselves:

- Why should I?
- What's in it for you?
- What's in it for me?
- Who cares?

Adapting to your audience means being ready to answer these questions. It means learning about audience members and analyzing why they might resist your proposal. It means searching for ways to connect your purpose with their needs. If completed before you begin writing, such analysis goes a long way toward overcoming resistance and achieving your goal. The accompanying Career Coach box presents additional strategies that can make you a successful persuader.

Researching and Organizing Data. Once you've analyzed the audience and considered how to adapt your message to its needs, you're ready to collect data and organize it. You might brainstorm and prepare cluster diagrams to provide a rough outline of ideas.

The next step is organizing your data. Suppose you have already decided that your request will meet with resistance. Thus, you decide not to open directly with your request. Instead, you follow the components of a persuasive message, listed below and shown graphically in Figure 10.1:

- Gain attention
- Build interest
- Reduce resistance
- Motivate action

FIGURE 10.1 Components of a Persuasive Message

GAINING ATTENTION	BUILDING INTEREST	REDUCING RESISTANCE	MOTIVATING ACTION
Summary of problem	Facts, figures	Anticipate objections	Describe specific request
Unexpected statement	Expert opinion	Offer counterarguments	Sound confident
Reader benefit	Examples	Play *What if?* scenarios	Make action easy to take
Compliment	Specific details	Establish credibility	Offer incentive
Related fact	Direct benefits	Demonstrate competence	Don't provide excuses
Stimulating question	Indirect benefits	Show value of proposal	Repeat main benefit

CAREER COACH

Seven Rules Every Persuader Should Know

Successful businesspeople create persuasive memos, letters, reports, and presentations that get the results they want. Yet, their approaches are all different. Some persuaders are gentle, leading readers by the hand to the targeted recommendation. Others are brisk and authoritative. Some are objective, examining both sides of an issue like a judge deciding a difficult case. Some move slowly and carefully toward a proposal, while others erupt like a volcano in their eagerness to announce a recommendation.

Different situations and different goals require different techniques. The following seven rules suggest various strategies—depending on your individual need.

1. **Consider whether your views will create problems for your audience.** If your views make trouble for the audience, think of ways to include the receivers in your recommendation if possible. Whatever your strategy, be tactful and empathic.

2. **Don't offer new ideas, directives, or recommendations for change until your audience is prepared for them.** Receivers are threatened by anything that upsets their values or interests. The greater the change you suggest, the more slowly you should proceed.

3. **Select a strategy that supports your credibility.** If you have great credibility with your audience, you can proceed directly. If not, you might want to establish that credibility first. *Given* credibility results from position or reputation, such as that of the boss of an organization or a highly regarded scientist. *Acquired* credibility is earned.

   To acquire credibility, successful persuaders often identify themselves, early in the message, with the goals and interests of the audience (*As a small business owner myself* . . .). Another way to acquire credibility is to mention evidence or ideas that support the audience's existing views (*We agree that small business owners need more government assistance*). Finally, you can acquire credibility by citing authorities who rate highly with your audience (*Richard Love, recently named Small Businessperson of the Year, supports this proposal*).

4. **If your audience disagrees with your ideas or is uncertain about them, present both sides of the argument.** You might think that you would be most successful by revealing only one side of an issue—your side, of course. But persuasion doesn't work that way. You'll be more successful—particularly if the audience is unfriendly or uncertain—by disclosing *all* sides of an argument. This approach suggests that you are objective. It also helps the receiver remember your view by showing the pros and cons in relation to one another.

5. **Win respect by making your opinion or recommendation clear.** Although you should be truthful in presenting both sides of an argument, don't be shy in supporting your conclusions or final proposals. You will, naturally, have definite views and should persuade your audience to accept them. The two-sided strategy is a means to an end, but it does not mean compromising your argument.

6. **Place your strongest points strategically.** Some experts argue that if your audience is deeply concerned with your subject, you can afford to begin with your weakest points. Because of its commitment, the audience will stay with you until you reach the strongest points at the end of your argument. For an unmotivated audience, begin with your strongest points to get them interested. Other experts feel that a supportive audience should receive the main ideas or recommendations immediately, to avoid wasting time. Whichever position you choose, don't bury your recommendation, strongest facts, or main idea in the middle of your argument.

7. **Don't count on changing attitudes by offering information alone.** "If customers knew the truth about our costs, they would not object to our prices," some companies reason. Well, don't bet on it. Companies have pumped huge sums into advertising and public relations campaigns that provided facts alone. Such efforts often fail because learning something new (that is, increasing the knowledge of the audience) is rarely an effective way to change attitudes. Researchers have found that presentations of facts alone may strengthen opinions—but primarily for people who already agree with the persuader. The added information reassures them and provides ammunition for defending themselves in discussions with others.

Blending the Components of a Persuasive Message

Although the indirect pattern appears to contain separate steps, successful persuasive messages actually blend these steps into a seamless whole. However, the sequence of the components may change depending on the situation and the emphasis. Regardless of where they are placed, the key elements in persuasive requests are (1) gaining the audience's attention, (2) convincing them that your proposal is worthy, (3) overcoming resistance, and (4) motivating action.

Successful openers to persuasive requests should be brief, targeted, and interesting.

Gaining Attention. To grab attention, the opening statement in a persuasive request should be brief, relevant, and engaging. When only mild persuasion is necessary, the opener can be low-key and factual. If, however, your request is substantial and you anticipate strong resistance, provide a thoughtful, provocative opening. The following examples suggest possibilities.

- **Problem description.** In a recommendation to hire temporary employees: *Last month Legal Division staff members were forced to work 120 overtime hours, costing us $6000 and causing considerable employee unhappiness.* With this opener you've presented a capsule of the problem your proposal will help solve.
- **Unexpected statement.** In a memo to encourage employees to attend an optional sensitivity seminar: *Men and women draw the line at decidedly different places in identifying what behaviour constitutes sexual harassment.* Note how this opener gets readers thinking immediately.
- **Reader benefit.** In a proposal offering writing workshops to an organization: *For every letter or memo your employees can avoid writing, your organization saves $78.50.* Companies are always looking for ways to cut costs, and this opener promises significant savings.
- **Compliment.** In a letter inviting a business executive to speak: *Because our members admire your success and value your managerial expertise, they want you to be our speaker.* In offering praise or compliments, however, be careful to avoid obvious flattery.
- **Related fact.** In a memo encouraging employees to start car-pooling: *A car pool is defined as two or more persons who travel to work in one car at least once a week.* An interesting, relevant, and perhaps unknown fact sets the scene for the interest-building section that follows.
- **Stimulating question.** In a plea for funds to support environmental causes: *What do Sum 41, the maple leaf, and hockey have in common?* Readers will be curious to find the answer to this intriguing question.

The body of a persuasive request may require several paragraphs to build interest and reduce resistance.

Building Interest. After capturing attention, a persuasive request must retain that attention and convince the audience that the request is reasonable. To justify your request, be prepared to invest in a few paragraphs of explanation. Persuasive requests are likely to be longer than direct requests because the audience must be convinced rather than simply instructed. You can build interest and conviction through the use of the following:

- Facts, statistics
- Expert opinion
- Direct benefits
- Examples
- Specific details
- Indirect benefits

Showing how your request can benefit the audience directly or indirectly is a key factor in persuasion. A *direct benefit* can be a tax write-off for a contribution. An *indirect benefit* comes from feeling good about helping others who will benefit from the gift. Nearly all charities rely in large part on indirect benefits—the selflessness of givers—to promote their causes.

Reducing Resistance. One of the biggest mistakes in persuasive requests is the failure to anticipate and offset audience resistance. How will the receiver object to your request? In brainstorming for clues, try *What if?* scenarios. For each *What if?* scenario, you need a counterargument.

Persuasive requests reduce resistance by addressing *What if?* questions and establishing credibility.

Unless you anticipate resistance, you give the receiver an easy opportunity to dismiss your request. Countering this resistance is important, but you must do it with finesse. You can minimize objections by presenting your counterarguments in sentences that emphasize benefits. However, don't spend too much time on counterarguments, thus making them overly important. Finally, avoid bringing up objections that may never have occurred to the receiver in the first place.

Another factor that reduces resistance is credibility. Receivers are less resistant if your request is reasonable and if you are believable. When the receiver does not know you, you may have to establish your expertise, refer to your credentials, or demonstrate your competence. Even when you are known, you may have to establish your knowledge in a given area. Some charities establish their credibility by displaying on their stationery the names of famous people who serve on their boards. The credibility of speakers making presentations is usually outlined by someone who introduces them.

Motivating Action. After gaining attention, building interest, and reducing resistance, you'll want to inspire the receiver to act. This is where your planning pays dividends. Knowing exactly what action you favour before you start to write enables you to point your arguments toward this important final paragraph. Here you will make your recommendation as specifically and confidently as possible—without seeming pushy. Compare the following closings for a persuasive memo recommending training seminars in communication skills.

Persuasive requests motivate action by specifying exactly what should be done.

Too General
We are certain we can develop a series of training sessions that will improve the communication skills of your employees.

Too Timid
If you agree that our training proposal has merit, perhaps we could begin the series in June.

Too Pushy
Because we're convinced that you will want to begin improving the skills of your employees immediately, we've scheduled your series to begin in June.

Effective
You will see decided improvement in the communication skills of your employees. Please call me at (613) 439-2201 by May 1 to give your approval so that training sessions may start in June, as we discussed.

Note how the last opening suggests a specific and easy-to-follow action. Figure 10.2 summarizes techniques for overcoming resistance and crafting successful persuasive messages.

FIGURE 10.2 Four-Part Indirect Pattern for Sales or Persuasion

GAINING ATTENTION	BUILDING INTEREST	REDUCING RESISTANCE	MOTIVATING ACTION
Free offer	Rational appeals	Testimonials	Gift
Promise	Emotional appeals	Satisfied users	Incentive
Question	Dual appeals	Guarantee	Limited offer
Quotation	Product description	Free trial	Deadline
Product feature	Reader benefits	Sample	Guarantee
Testimonial	Cold facts mixed with warm feelings	Performance tests	Repetition of selling feature
Action setting		Polls, awards	

Being Persuasive but Ethical

Ethical business communicators maintain credibility and respect by being honest, fair, and objective.

Business communicators may be tempted to make their persuasion even more forceful by fudging on the facts, exaggerating a point, omitting something crucial, or providing deceptive emphasis. A persuader is effective only when he or she is believable. If receivers suspect that they are being manipulated or misled, or if they find any part of the argument untruthful, the total argument fails. Persuaders can also fall into traps of logic without even being aware of it. Avoid the common logical fallacies of circular reasoning, begging the question, and post hoc (after, thus, because).

Persuasion becomes unethical when facts are distorted, overlooked, or manipulated with an intent to deceive. Of course, persuaders naturally want to put forth their strongest case. But that argument must be based on truth, objectivity, and fairness.

In prompting ethical and truthful persuasion, two factors act as powerful motivators. The first is the desire to preserve your reputation and credibility. Once lost, a good name is difficult to regain. An equally important force prompting ethical behaviour, though, is your opinion of yourself.

WRITING SUCCESSFUL PERSUASIVE REQUESTS

3

Convincing someone to change a belief or to perform an action when that individual is reluctant requires planning and skill—and sometimes a little luck. If the request is in writing, rather than face to face, the task is even more difficult. The indirect pattern, though, can help you shape effective persuasive appeals that (1) request favours and action, (2) persuade within organizations, and (3) request adjustments and make claims.

Requesting Favours and Actions

The indirect pattern is appropriate when requesting favours and action, persuading within organizations, and requesting adjustments or making claims.

Persuading someone to do something that largely benefits you is not easy. Fortunately, many individuals and companies are willing to grant requests for time, money, information, special privileges, and cooperation. They grant these favours for a variety of reasons. They may just happen to be interested in your project, or they may see goodwill potential for themselves. Often, though, they comply because they see that others will benefit from the request. Professionals sometimes feel obligated to contribute their time or expertise to "pay their dues."

You may find that you have few direct benefits to offer in your persuasion. Instead, you'll focus on indirect benefits, as the writer does in Figure 10.3. In asking a manager

FIGURE 10.3 Persuasive Favour Request

Prewriting 1

Analyze: The purpose of this letter is to persuade the reader to speak at a dinner meeting.

Anticipate: Although the reader is busy, he may respond to appeals to his ego (describing his successes before an appreciative audience) and to his professionalism.

Adapt: Because the reader will be uninterested at first and require persuasion, use the indirect pattern.

Writing 2

Research: Study the receiver's interests and find ways to relate this request to his interests.

Organize: Gain attention by opening with praise or a stimulating remark. Build interest with explanations and facts. Show how compliance benefits the reader and others. Reduce resistance by providing ideas for the dinner talk.

Compose: Prepare a first draft on a computer.

Revising 3

Revise: Revise to show direct and indirect benefits more clearly.

Proofread: Use quotes around "R" to reflect company usage. In the fourth paragraph, use a semicolon in the compound sentence. Start all lines at the left for block-style letter.

Evaluate: Will this letter convince the reader to accept the invitation?

North American Marketing Association

Hamilton–Wentworth Chapter
1624 Fennell Street
Hamilton, ON
L8V 4X2

(905) 469-8274

January 28, 2007

Mr. Bryant Hoffman
Marketing Manager
Toys "R" Us, Inc.
2777 Langstaff Avenue
Thornhill, ON L3J 3M8

Dear Mr. Hoffman:

One company is legendary for marketing North American products successfully in Japan. ← Piques reader's curiosity; Gains attention

That company, of course, is Toys "R" Us. The triumph of your thriving toy store in Amimachi, Japan, has given other North American marketers hope. But this success story has also raised numerous questions. Specifically, how did Toys "R" Us circumvent local trade restrictions? How did you solve the complex distribution system? And how did you negotiate with all the levels of Japanese bureaucracy? ← Builds interest

The members of the Hamilton-Wentworth chapter of the North American Marketing Association asked me to invite you to speak at our March 19 dinner meeting on the topic of "How Toys 'R' Us Unlocked the Door to Japanese Trade." By describing your winning effort, Mr. Hoffman, you can help launch other North American companies who face the same quagmire of Japanese restrictions and red tape that your organization overcame. Although we can offer you only a small honorarium of $300, we can assure you of a big audience of enthusiastic marketing professionals eager to hear your dramatic story. ← Notes indirect benefit; Notes direct benefit

Our relaxed group doesn't expect a formal address; our members are most interested in what steps Toys "R" Us took to open its Japanese toy outlet. To make your talk easy to organize, I've enclosed a list of questions our members submitted. Most talks are about 45 minutes long. ← Reduces resistance; Offsets reluctance by making the talk informal and easy to organize

Can we count on you to join us for dinner at 7 p.m. on March 19 at the Fisherman's Inn in Hamilton? Just call me at (905) 860-4320 by February 15 to make arrangements. ← Motivates action; Makes acceptance as simple as a telephone call

Sincerely,

Joyce Barnes

Joyce Barnes
Program Chair, NAMA

JCB:grw
Enclosure

to speak before a marketing meeting, the writer has little to offer as a direct benefit other than a $300 honorarium. But indirectly, the writer offers enticements such as an enthusiastic audience and a chance to help other companies solve overseas marketing problems. This persuasive request appeals primarily to the reader's desire to serve his profession—although a receptive audience and an opportunity to talk about one's successes have a certain ego appeal as well. Together, these appeals—professional, egoistic, monetary—make a persuasive argument rich and effective.

An offer to work as an intern, at no cost to a company, would seem to require little persuasion. Actually, though, companies hesitate to participate in internship programs because student interns require supervision, desk space, and equipment. They also pose an insurance liability threat.

In Figure 10.4 college student Melanie Harris seeks to persuade Software Enterprises to accept her as an intern. In the analysis process before writing, Melanie thought long and hard about what benefits she could offer the reader and how she

FIGURE 10.4 Persuasive Action Request

1777 North Dinosaur Trail
Drumheller, AB T0J 0Y1

January 12, 2007

Ms. Nancy Ashley, Director
Human Resources Department
Software Enterprises, Inc.
268 Redmond Avenue
Calgary, AB T3B 6W7

Dear Ms. Ashley:

How often do college-trained specialists offer to work for nothing?

Very infrequently, I imagine. But that's the offer I'm making to Software Enterprises. During the next 14 weeks, could you use the part-time services of a college senior with communication and computer skills?

To gain work experience and to earn three units of credit, I would like to become an intern at Software Enterprises. My skills in Word and Excel, as well as training in letter and report writing, could be put to use in your Customer Service, Human Resources, Legal, Documentation, or other departments.

By granting this internship, your company not only secures the skills of an enthusiastic and well-trained college student, but it also performs a valuable service to your local community college. Your cooperation provides an opportunity for students to acquire the kind of job training that college classrooms simply cannot give.

If equipment and desk space at Software Enterprises are limited, you may want me to fill in for employees who can then be freed up for other projects, training, or release time. In regard to supervision you'll find that I require little direction once I start a project. Moreover, you don't need to worry about insurance, as our college provides liability coverage for all students at internship sites.

Although I'm taking classes in the mornings, I'm available to work afternoons for 15 hours per week. Please examine the enclosed résumé to confirm my education and qualifications.

Do you have any questions about my proposal to become an intern? To talk with me about it, please call 893-2155. I could begin working for you as early as February 1. You gain a free employee, and you also provide an appreciative local college student with much-needed job training.

Sincerely,

Melanie E. Harris

Melanie E. Harris

Enclosure

Starts with date and address in personal business style

Uses strongest benefit for stimulating opener

Introduces request after presenting main benefit

Notes direct benefit

Notes indirect benefit

Anticipates three obstacles and answers each

Introduces a negative in a positive way

Refers to enclosure only after presenting main points

Couples action request with reference to direct and indirect benefits could present them strategically. She decided that the offer of a trained college student's free labour was her strongest benefit. Thus, she opens with it, as well as mentioning the same benefit in the letter body and in the closing. After opening with the main audience benefit, she introduces the actual request ("Could you use the part-time services of a college senior . . . ?").

In the interest section, Melanie tells why she is making the request and describes its value in terms of direct and indirect benefits. Notice how she transforms obstacles (lack of equipment or desk space) into helpful suggestions about how her services would free up other staff members to perform more important tasks. She delays mentioning a negative (being able to work only 15 hours per week and only in the afternoon) until she builds interest and reduces resistance. And she closes confidently and motivates action with reference to both direct and indirect benefits.

Persuading Within Organizations

Internal persuasive memos present honest arguments detailing specific reader benefits.

Instructions or directives moving downward from superiors to subordinates usually require little persuasion. Employees expect to be directed in how to perform their jobs. These messages (such as information about procedures, equipment, or customer service) follow the direct pattern, with the purpose immediately stated. However, employees are sometimes asked to perform in a capacity outside their work roles or to accept changes that are not in their best interests (such as pay cuts, job transfers, or reduced benefits). In these instances, a persuasive memo using the indirect pattern may be most effective.

The goal is not to manipulate employees or to seduce them with trickery. Rather, the goal is to present a strong but honest argument, emphasizing points that are important to the receiver. In business, honesty is not just the best policy—it's the *only* policy. Especially within your own organization, people see right through puffery and misrepresentation. For this reason, the indirect pattern is effective only when supported by accurate, honest evidence.

Another form of persuasion within organizations centres on suggestions made by subordinates. Convincing management to adopt a procedure or invest in a product or new equipment generally requires skillful communication. Managers are just as resistant to change as others. Providing evidence is critical when subordinates submit recommendations to their bosses.

In Figure 10.5, you see the draft copy of a persuasive memo that needs revision. The writer lacked organization and did not sell the benefits. When revising, it was apparent a little more time spent on developing the persuasive argument would increase the chance of approval. Notice that although the revision is longer, it is far more effective. Remember that a persuasive message will typically take more space than a direct message because proving a case requires evidence. Notice that the subject line in Figure 10.5 tells the purpose of the memo without disclosing the actual request. By delaying the request until she's had a chance to describe the problem and discuss a solution, the writer prevents the reader's premature rejection.

The strength of this revision, though, is in the clear presentation of comparison figures showing how much money can be saved by purchasing a remanufactured copier. Although the organization pattern is not obvious, the revised memo begins with an attention-getter (frank description of problem), builds interest (with easy-to-read facts and figures), provides benefits, and reduces resistance. Notice that the conclusion tells what action is to be taken, makes it easy to respond, and repeats the main benefit to motivate action.

FIGURE 10.5 Persuasive Memo

DRAFT

TO: Kenneth Richardson, Vice President

Although you've opposed the purchase of additional copiers in the past, I think I've found a great deal on a copier that's just too good to pass up but we must act before May 1! Copy City has reconditioned copiers that are practically being given away. If we move fast, they will provide many free incentives—like a free copier stand, free starter supplies, free delivery, and free installation.

We must find a way to reduce copier costs in my department. Our current copier can't keep up with our demand. We're sending secretaries or sales reps to Copy Quick for an average of 10 000 copies a month. These copies cost 7 cents a page and waste a lot of time. We're making at least eight trips a week, adding up to a considerable expense in travel time and copy costs.

Please give this matter your immediate attention and get back to me as soon as possible. We don't want to miss this great deal!

Begins poorly with reminder of past negative feelings

Sounds high-pressured

Fails to compare costs and emphasize savings in logical, coherent presentation

Does not request or motivate specific action

REVISION

DATE: April 18, 2007

TO: Kenneth Richardson, Vice President

FROM: Mona Massey, Marketing

SUBJECT: SAVING TIME AND MONEY ON COPYING

Describes topic without revealing request

Summarizes problem

We're losing money on our current copy services and wasting the time of employees as well. Because our Canon copier is in use constantly, we find it increasingly necessary to send major jobs out to Copy Quick. Just take a look at how much we spend each month for outside copy service:

Copy Costs: Outside Service

10 000 copies/month made at Copy Quick	$700.00
Salary costs for assistants to make 32 trips to drop off originals and pick up copies	384.00
Total	$1084.00

Uses headings and columns for easy comparison

When sales reps make the trips, the costs are even greater. Because this expense must be reduced, I've been considering alternatives. New copiers with collating capability and automatic multidrawer paper feeding are very expensive. But reconditioned copiers with all the features we need are available—and at attractive prices and terms. From Copy City we can get a fully remanufactured copier that is guaranteed to work like new. After we make an initial payment of $219, our monthly costs would look like this:

Proves credibility of request with facts and figures

Copy Costs: Remanufactured Copier

Paper supplies for 10 000 copies	$130.00
Toner and copy supplies	95.00
Labour of assistants to make copies	130.00
Monthly financing charge for copier (purchase price of $1105 amortized at 10% with 29 payments)	34.52
Total	$389.52

As you can see, **a remanufactured copier saves us nearly $700 per month.**

Highlights most important benefit

Provides more benefits

For a limited time Copy City is offering a free 15-day trial offer, a free copier stand (worth $165), free starter supplies, and free delivery and installation. We have office space available, and my staff is eager to add a second machine.

Counters possible resistance

Makes it easy to grant approval

Call me at Ext. 630 if you have questions. This copier is such a good opportunity that I've attached a purchase requisition authorizing the agreement with Copy City. With your approval before May 1, we can have our machine by May 10 and start saving time and nearly $700 every month. Fast action will also take advantage of Copy City's free start-up incentives.

Repeats main benefit with motivation to act quickly

Attachment

Complaint Letters: Writing Persuasive Claims

Persuasive adjustment letters make claims about damaged products, mistaken billing, inaccurate shipments, warranty problems, return policies, insurance mix-ups, faulty merchandise, and so on. Generally, the direct pattern is best for requesting straightforward adjustments (see Chapter 9). When you feel your request is justified and will be granted, the direct strategy is most efficient. But if a past request has been refused or ignored or if you anticipate reluctance, then the indirect pattern is appropriate.

5

Effective complaint/adjustment letters make reasonable claims backed by solid evidence.

In a sense, a claim letter is a complaint letter. Someone is complaining about something that went wrong. Some complaint letters just vent anger; the writers are mad, and they want to tell someone about it. But if the goal is to change something (and why bother to write except to motivate change?), then persuasion is necessary. Effective adjustment letters make a reasonable claim, present a logical case with clear facts, and adopt a moderate tone. Anger and emotion are not effective persuaders.

Logical Development

Strive for logical development in an adjustment letter. You'll want to open with sincere praise, an objective statement of the problem, a point of agreement, or a quick review of what you have done to resolve the problem. Then you can explain precisely what happened or why your claim is legitimate. Don't provide a blow-by-blow chronology of details; just hit the highlights. Be sure to enclose copies of relevant invoices, shipping orders, warranties, and payments. And close with a clear statement of what you want done: refund, replacement, credit to your account, or other action. Be sure to think through the possibilities and make your request reasonable.

Moderate Tone

The tone of the letter is important. You should never suggest that the receiver intentionally deceived you or intentionally created the problem. Rather, appeal to the receiver's sense of responsibility and pride in its good name. Calmly express your disappointment in view of your high expectations of the product and of the company. Communicating your feelings, without bitterness, is often your strongest appeal.

Adjustment requests should adopt a moderate tone, appeal to the receiver's sense of responsibility, and specify needed actions.

Janet Walker's letter, shown in Figure 10.6, follows the persuasive pattern as she seeks to return three answering machines. Notice that she uses simplified letter style (skipping the salutation and complimentary close) because she doesn't have a person's name to use in addressing the letter. Note also her positive opening; her calm, well-documented claims; and her request for specific action.

The following checklist reviews pointers for helping you make persuasive requests of all kinds.

CHECKLIST FOR MAKING PERSUASIVE REQUESTS

Gain attention. In requesting favours, begin with a compliment, statement of agreement, unexpected fact, stimulating question, reader benefit, summary of the problem, or candid plea for help. For claims and complaints, also consider opening with a review of action you have taken to resolve the problem.

Build interest. Prove the accuracy and merit of your request with solid evidence, including facts, figures, expert opinion, examples, and details. Suggest

FIGURE 10.6 Request for Adjustment (Complaint Letter)

Tips for Requesting Adjustments and Making Complaints

- Begin with a compliment, point of agreement, statement of the problem, or brief review of action you have taken to resolve the problem.
- Provide identifying data.
- Prove that your claim is valid; explain why the receiver is responsible.
- Enclose document copies supporting your claim.
- Appeal to the receiver's fairness, ethical and legal responsibilities, and desire for customer satisfaction.
- Describe your feelings and your disappointment.
- Avoid sounding angry, emotional, or irrational.
- Close by telling exactly what you want done.

CHAMPLAIN AUTOMOTIVES
141 Rue Champlain, Gatineau, QC J8T 3H9 (819) 690-3500

November 21, 2007

Customer Service
Raytronic Electronics
57 Émile Simard Avenue
Edmunston, NB E3V 3N9

SUBJECT: CODE-A-PHONE MODEL 100S

Uses simplified letter style when name of receiver is unknown

Begins with compliment

Your Code-A-Phone Model 100S answering unit came well recommended. We liked our neighbour's unit so well that we purchased three for different departments in our business.

Describes problem calmly

After the three units were unpacked and installed, we discovered a problem. Apparently our office fluorescent lighting interferes with the electronics in these units. When the lights are on, heavy static interrupts every telephone call. When the lights are off, the static disappears.

We can't replace the fluorescent lights, so we tried to return the Code-A-Phones to the place of purchase (Office Mart, 479 Pleasant Street, Truro, NS B2N 3J9). A salesperson inspected the units and said they could not be returned since they were not defective and they had been used.

Suggests responsibility

Stresses disappointment

Because the descriptive literature and instructions for the Code-A-Phones say nothing about avoiding use in rooms with fluorescent lighting, we expected no trouble. We were quite disappointed that this well-engineered unit—with its time/date stamp, room monitor, and auto-dial features—failed to perform as we hoped it would.

Tells what action to take

Appeals to company's desire to preserve good reputation

If you have a model with similar features that would work in our offices, give me a call. Otherwise, please authorize the return of these units and refund the purchase price of $519.45 (see enclosed invoice). We're confident that a manufacturer with your reputation for excellent products and service will want to resolve this matter quickly.

Janet Walker

JANET WALKER, PRESIDENT

JPW:ett
Enclosure

direct and indirect benefits for the receiver. Avoid sounding high-pressured, angry, or emotional.

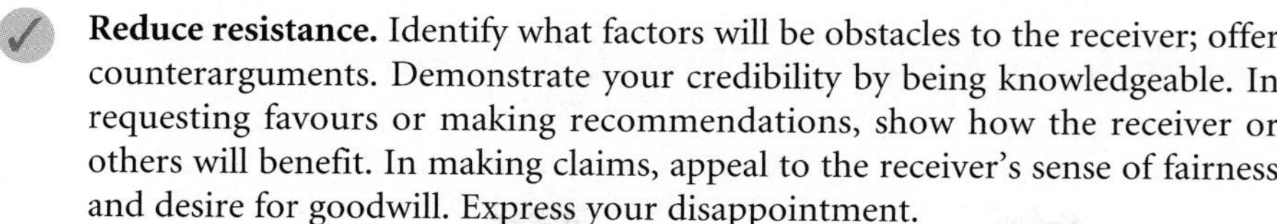

- **Reduce resistance.** Identify what factors will be obstacles to the receiver; offer counterarguments. Demonstrate your credibility by being knowledgeable. In requesting favours or making recommendations, show how the receiver or others will benefit. In making claims, appeal to the receiver's sense of fairness and desire for goodwill. Express your disappointment.

- **Motivate action.** Confidently ask for specific action. For favours include an end date (if appropriate) and try to repeat a key benefit.

PLANNING AND COMPOSING SALES MESSAGES

Sales messages involve using persuasion to promote specific products and services. In our coverage we will be most concerned with sales messages delivered by mail or e-mail. Many of the concepts you will learn about sales persuasion can be applied to radio, TV, print, online, and wireless media. The best sales messages, whether delivered by e-marketing or direct mail, have much in common. In this section we'll look at the changing world of direct marketing. We'll study how to apply Guffey's 3-×-3 writing process to sales messages. Then you'll learn techniques developed by experts to draft outstanding sales messages.

The Changing World of Direct Marketing

Traditional direct-mail marketing involves messages delivered by land mail.

Traditional direct-mail marketing involves the sale of goods and services through letters, catalogues, brochures, envelope stuffers, and other messages delivered by land mail. But today's powerful communication technologies present advertisers with exciting new ways to reach target audiences. As discussed in Chapter 1, the whole communication infrastructure has changed in the past decade. Companies employing direct marketing may now turn to electronic marketing, which involves sales messages delivered by e-mail, Web sites, and even wireless devices. To some marketers, e-mail sounds like a promised land, guaranteeing instant delivery at pennies per message. However, unsolicited commercial e-mail, or "spam," has generated an incredible backlash from recipients. They want their e-mail addresses to remain private and unviolated.

Effective marketing strategies balance traditional direct mail and e-marketing.

E-Marketing. Although many consumers object to unsolicited e-mail sales messages, others don't mind receiving helpful information about services or new products they can use. This kind of e-marketing is rapidly gaining acceptance because it is efficient, cheap, easily tracked, and faster than direct mail.

E-marketing, however, is limited to tech-savvy audiences. Smart companies will strive to develop a balanced approach to their overall marketing strategy, including both e-marketing and direct mail when appropriate. "Even when e-commerce is exploding, every marketing plan should include a direct-mail component in order to communicate a company's message," insists marketing expert John R. Graham. To enforce his point, Graham points out that "if you want proof of the power of direct mail, notice how Internet companies rely on direct mail to promote their Web sites."[1] You can learn what successful e-mail marketing messages have in common in the accompanying Tech Talk box.

TECH TALK

What Successful Online Sales Messages Have in Common

To make the best use of limited advertising dollars, many businesses are turning to e-mail marketing campaigns instead of traditional direct mailings. E-mail marketing can attract new customers, keep existing ones, upsell, cross-sell, and cut costs. As consumers feel more comfortable and secure with online advertising, they will be receiving more e-mail sales messages. If your organization requires an online sales message, try using the following techniques gleaned from the best-performing e-mails:

- **Communicate only with those who have given permission!** By sending messages only to "opt-in" folks, you greatly increase your "open rate"—those e-mail messages that will be opened. E-mail users detest spam. However, receivers are surprisingly receptive to offers specifically for them. Remember that today's customer is *somebody*—not *anybody*.
- **Craft a catchy subject line.** Offer discounts or premiums. Promise solutions to everyday work-related problems. Highlight hot new industry topics. Invite readers to scan a top-10 list, such as issues, trends, or people.
- **Keep the main information "above the fold."** E-mail messages should be top heavy. Primary points should appear early in the message so that they capture the reader's attention.
- **Keep the message short, conversational, and focused.** Because on-screen text is taxing to read, be brief. Focus on one or two central selling points only.
- **Convey urgency.** Top-performing e-mail messages state an offer deadline or demonstrate why the state of the industry demands action on the reader's part. Good messages also tie the product to relevant current events.
- **Sprinkle testimonials throughout the copy.** Consumers' own words are the best sales copy. These comments can serve as callouts or be integrated into the copy.
- **Provide a means for opting out.** It's polite and a good business tactic to include a statement that tells receivers how to be removed from the sender's mailing database.

Professional direct mailers study the product, target an audience, and prepare a complete package.

Direct-Mail Marketing. Our main focus in this chapter will be on writing sales letters as part of direct-mail marketing. Traditional sales letters are a powerful means to make sales, generate leads, boost retail traffic, solicit donations, and direct consumers to Web sites. Mail allows a personalized, tangible, three-dimensional message that is less invasive than telephone solicitations and less reviled than unsolicited e-mail.

Professionals who specialize in traditional direct-mail services have made a science of analyzing a market, developing an effective mailing list, studying the product, preparing a sophisticated campaign aimed at a target audience, and motivating the reader to act. You've probably received many direct-mail packages, often called "junk" mail. These packages typically contain a sales letter, a brochure, a price list, illustrations of the product, testimonials, and other persuasive appeals.

We're most concerned here with the sales letter: its strategy, organization, and evidence. Because sales letters are generally written by specialists, you may never write one on the job. Why, then, learn how to write a sales letter? In many ways, every letter we create is a form of sales letter. We sell our ideas, our organizations, and ourselves. Learning the techniques of sales writing will help you be more successful in any communication that requires persuasion and promotion. Furthermore, you'll recognize sales strategies, thus enabling you to become a more perceptive consumer of ideas, products, and services.

Applying Guffey's 3-×-3 Writing Process to Sales Messages

Marketing professionals analyze every aspect of a sales message because consumers reject most direct-mail offers. Like the experts, you'll want to pay close attention to the preparatory steps of analysis and adaptation before writing the actual message.

Successful sales messages require research on the product or service offered and analysis of the purpose for writing.

Analyzing the Product and Purpose. Before writing a sales letter, you should study the product carefully. What can you learn about its design, construction, raw materials, and manufacturing process? About its ease of use, efficiency, durability, and applications? Be sure to consider warranties, service, price, and special appeals. At the same time, evaluate the competition so that you can compare your product's strengths against the competitor's weaknesses.

Now you're ready to identify your central selling points. Analyzing your product and studying the competition help you determine what to emphasize in your sales letter.

Another important decision in the preparatory stage involves the specific purpose of your letter. Before you write the first word of your message, know what features of the product you will emphasize and what response you want.

Adapting to the Audience. Blanket mailings sent "cold" to occupants generally produce low responses—typically only 2 percent. That means that 98 percent of us usually toss direct-mail sales letters directly into the garbage. But the response rate can be increased dramatically by targeting the audience through database mailing lists. These lists can be purchased or compiled. By directing your message to a selected group, you can make certain assumptions about the receivers. You would expect similar interests, needs, and demographics (age, income, and other characteristics). With this knowledge you can adapt the sales letter to a specific audience.

Crafting a Winning Sales Message

Your primary goal in writing a sales message is to get someone to devote a few moments of attention to it.[2] You may be promoting a product, a service, an idea, or yourself. In each case the most effective messages will (1) gain attention, (2) build interest, (3) reduce resistance, and (4) motivate action. This is the same recipe we studied earlier, but the ingredients are different.

Gaining Attention. One of the most critical elements of a sales letter is its opening paragraph. This opener should be short (one to five lines), honest, relevant, and stimulating. Marketing pros have found that eye-catching typographical arrangements or provocative messages, such as the following, can hook a reader's attention:

Openers for sales messages should be brief, honest, relevant, and provocative.

- **Offer:** *A free trip to Hawaii is just the beginning!*
- **Promise:** *Now you can raise your sales income by 50 percent or even more with the proven techniques found in . . . .*
- **Question:** *Do you yearn for an honest, fulfilling relationship?*
- **Quotation or proverb:** *Necessity is the mother of invention.*
- **Fact:** *The Greenland Eskimos ate more fat than anyone in the world. And yet . . . they had virtually no heart disease.*
- **Product feature:** *Volvo's snazzy new convertible ensures your safety with a roll bar that pops out when the car tips 40 degrees to the side.*

- **Testimonial:** *"It is wonderful to see such a well-written and informative piece of work." (Thomas J. Bata, chairman, Bata Ltd., about* Secrets of Power Presentations*)*
- **Startling statement:** *Let the poor and hungry feed themselves! For just $100 they can.*
- **Personalized action setting:** *It's 4:30 p.m. and you've got to make a decision. You need everybody's opinion, no matter where they are. Before you pick up your phone to call them one at a time, pick up this card: Bell Canada Teleconference Services.*

Other openings calculated to capture attention might include a solution to a problem, an anecdote, a personalized statement using the receiver's name, or a relevant current event.

Building Interest. In this phase of your sales message, you should describe clearly the product or service. In simple language emphasize the central selling points that you identified during your prewriting analysis. Those selling points can be developed using rational or emotional appeals.

Rational appeals are associated with reason and intellect. They translate selling points into references to making or saving money, increasing efficiency, or making the best use of resources. In general, rational appeals are appropriate when a product is expensive, long-lasting, or important to health, security, and financial success. Emotional appeals relate to status, ego, and sensual feelings. Appealing to the emotions is sometimes effective when a product is inexpensive, short-lived, or nonessential. Many clever sales messages, however, combine emotional and rational strategies for a dual appeal. Consider the following examples.

Rational Appeal
You can buy the things you need and want, pay household bills, pay off higher-cost loans and credit cards—as soon as you're approved and your Credit-Line account is opened.

Emotional Appeal
Leave the urban bustle behind and escape to sun-soaked Bermuda! To recharge your batteries with an injection of sun and surf, all you need is your bathing suit, a little suntan lotion, and your Credit-Line card.

Dual Appeal
New Credit-Line cardholders are immediately eligible for a $100 travel certificate and additional discounts at fun-filled resorts. Save up to 40 percent while lying on a beach in picturesque, sun-soaked Bermuda, the year-round resort island.

A physical description of your product is not enough, however. Zig Ziglar, thought by some to be America's greatest salesperson, points out that no matter how well you know your product, no one is persuaded by cold, hard facts alone. In the end, he contends, "People buy because of the product benefits."[3] Your job is to translate those cold facts into warm feelings and reader benefits.

Techniques for reducing resistance include testimonials, guarantees, warranties, samples, and performance polls.

Reducing Resistance. Marketing pros use a number of techniques to overcome resistance and build desire. When price is an obstacle, consider these suggestions:

- Delay mentioning price until after you've created a desire for the product.
- Show the price in small units, such as the price per issue of a magazine.
- Demonstrate how the reader saves money by, for instance, subscribing for two or three years.
- Compare your prices with those of a competitor.

In addition, you need to anticipate other objections and questions the receiver may have. When possible, translate these objections into selling points (*If you've never ordered software by mail, let us send you our demonstration disks at no charge*). Other techniques to overcome resistance and prove the credibility of the product include the following:

- **Testimonials:** *"I learned so much in your language courses that I began to dream in French." —Holly Franker, Woodstock, Ontario*
- **Names of satisfied users** (with permission, of course): *Enclosed is a partial list of private pilots who enthusiastically subscribe to our service.*
- **Money-back guarantee or warranty:** *We offer the longest warranties in the business—all parts and service on-site for two years!*
- **Free trial or sample:** *We're so confident that you'll like our new accounting program that we want you to try it absolutely free.*
- **Performance tests, polls, or awards:** *Our TP-3000 was named Best Web Phone, and Etown.com voted it Cell Phone of the Year.*

Motivating Action. All the effort put into a sales message is wasted if the reader fails to act. To make it easy for readers to act, you can provide a reply card, a stamped and preaddressed envelope, a toll-free telephone number, an easy Web site, or a promise of a follow-up call. Because readers often need an extra push, consider including additional motivators, such as the following:

Techniques for motivating action include offering a gift or incentive, limiting an offer, and guaranteeing satisfaction.

- **Offer a gift:** *You'll receive a free cell phone with the purchase of any new car.*
- **Promise an incentive:** *With every new, paid subscription, we'll plant a tree in one of Canada's national parks.*
- **Limit the offer:** *Only the first 100 customers receive free cheques.*
- **Set a deadline:** *You must act before June 1 to get these low prices.*
- **Guarantee satisfaction:** *We'll return your full payment if you're not entirely satisfied—no questions asked.*

The final paragraph of the sales letter carries the punch line. This is where you tell readers what you want done and give them reasons for doing it. Most sales letters also include postscripts because they make irresistible reading. Even readers who might skim over or bypass paragraphs are drawn to a P.S. Therefore, use a postscript to reveal your strongest motivator, to add a special inducement for a quick response, or to reemphasize a central selling point.

Putting It All Together. Sales letters are a preferred marketing medium because they can be personalized, directed to target audiences, and filled with a more complete message than other advertising media. But direct mail is expensive. That's why the total sales message is crafted so painstakingly.

Because direct mail is an expensive way to advertise, messages should present complete information in a personalized tone for specific audiences.

Let's examine a sales letter, shown in Figure 10.7, addressed to a target group of small-business owners. To sell the new magazine *Small Business Monthly*, the letter incorporates all four components of an effective persuasive message. Notice that the personalized action-setting opener places the reader in a familiar situation (getting into an elevator) and draws an analogy between failing to reach the top floor and failing to achieve a business goal. The writer develops a rational central selling point (a magazine that provides valuable information for a growing small business) and repeats this selling point in all the components of the letter. Notice, too, how a testimonial from a small-business executive lends support to the sales message, and how the closing pushes for action. Since the price of the magazine is not a selling feature,

FIGURE 10.7 Sales Letter

Prewriting 

Analyze: The purpose of this letter is to persuade the reader to return the reply card and subscribe to *Small Business Monthly*.

Anticipate: The targeted audience consists of small-business owners. The central selling point is providing practical data to help their businesses grow.

Adapt: Because readers will be reluctant, use the indirect pattern.

Writing 2

Research: Gather facts to promote your product, including testimonials.

Organize: Gain attention by opening with a personalized action picture. Build interest with an analogy and a description of magazine features. Use a testimonial to reduce resistance. Motivate action with a free booklet and an easy-reply card.

Compose: Prepare a first draft for a pilot study.

Revising 

Revise: Use short paragraphs and short sentences. Replace words like *malfunction* with words like *glitch*.

Proofread: Indent long quotations on the left and right sides. Italicize or underscore titles of publications. Hyphenate *first-of-its-kind* and *hard-headed*.

Evaluate: Monitor the response rate to this letter to assess its effectiveness.

---

small business monthly
160 Duncan Mills Road • Toronto ON M3B 1Z5

April 15, 2007

Mr. James Wehrley
1608 Davidson Avenue North
Listowel, ON N4W 3A2

Dear Mr. Wehrley:

You walk into the elevator and push the button for the top floor. The elevator glides upward. You step back and relax. *(Puts reader into action setting; Gains attention)*

But the elevator never reaches the top. A glitch in its electronics prevents it from processing the information it needs to take you to your destination.

Do you see a similarity between your growing company and this elevator? You're aiming for the top, but a lack of information halts your progress. Now you can put your company into gear and propel it toward success with a new publication—*Small Business Monthly*. *(Suggests analogy; Builds interest)*

This first-of-its-kind magazine brings you marketing tips, hard-headed business pointers, opportunities, and inspiration. This is the kind of current information you need today to be where you want to be tomorrow. One executive wrote: *(Emphasizes central selling point)*

> As president of a small manufacturing company, I read several top business publications, but I get my "bread and butter" from *Small Business Monthly*. I'm not interested in a lot of "pie in the sky" and theory. I find practical problems and how to solve them in *SBM*.
> —Mitchell M. Perry, Oshawa, Ontario

(Uses testimonial for credibility; Reduces resistance)

Mr. Perry's words are the best recommendation I can offer you to try *SBM*. In less time than you might spend on an average business lunch, you learn the latest in management, operations, finance, taxes, business law, compensation, and advertising.

To evaluate *Small Business Monthly* without cost or obligation, let me send you a free issue. Just initial and return the enclosed card to start receiving a wealth of practical information that could keep your company travelling upward to its goal. *(Repeats central sales pitch in last sentence; Motivates action)*

Cordially,

Cheryl Owings

Cheryl Owings
Vice President, Circulation

P.S. Act before May 15 and I'll send you our valuable booklet *Managing for Success*, revealing more than 100 secrets for helping small businesses grow. *(Spotlights free offer in P.S. to prompt immediate reply)* it's mentioned only on the reply card. This sales letter saves its strongest motivator—a free booklet—for the high-impact P.S. line.

Whether you actually write sales letters on the job or merely receive them, you'll better understand their organization and appeals by reviewing this chapter and the tips in the following checklist.

CHECKLIST FOR WRITING SALES LETTERS

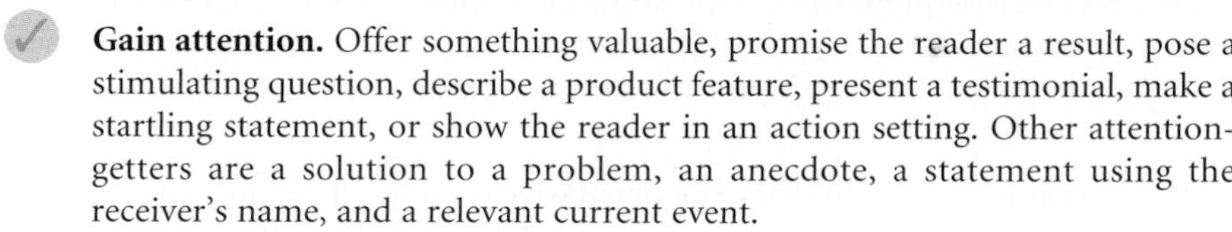

- **Gain attention.** Offer something valuable, promise the reader a result, pose a stimulating question, describe a product feature, present a testimonial, make a startling statement, or show the reader in an action setting. Other attention-getters are a solution to a problem, an anecdote, a statement using the receiver's name, and a relevant current event.
- **Build interest.** Describe the product in terms of what it does for the reader: save or make money, reduce effort, improve health, produce pleasure, boost status. Connect cold facts with warm feelings and needs.
- **Reduce resistance.** Counter reluctance with testimonials, money-back guarantees, attractive warranties, trial offers, or free samples. Build credibility with results of performance tests, polls, or awards. If price is not a selling feature, describe it in small units (*only 99 cents an issue*), show it as savings, or tell how it compares favourably with the competition.
- **Motivate action.** Close with a repetition of the central selling point and clear instructions for an easy action to be taken. Prompt the reader to act immediately with a gift, incentive, limited offer, deadline, and/or guarantee of satisfaction. Put the strongest motivator in a postscript.

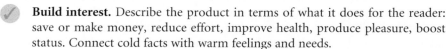

DEVELOPING PERSUASIVE NEWS RELEASES

News (media) releases announce information about your company: new products, new managers, new facilities, participation in community projects, awards given or received, joint ventures, donations, or seminars and demonstrations. Naturally, you hope that this news will be published and provide good publicity for your company. But this kind of largely self-serving information is not always appealing to magazine and newspaper editors or to TV producers. To get them to read beyond the first sentence, try these suggestions:

Effective news releases feature an attention-getting opener, place key information up front, appeal to the target audience, and maintain visual interest.

- Open with an attention-getting lead or a summary of the important facts.
- Include answers to the five Ws and one H (who, what, when, where, why, and how) in the article—but not all in the first sentence!
- Appeal to the audience of the target media. Emphasize reader benefits written in the style of the focus publication or newscast.
- Present the most important information early, followed by supporting information. Don't put your best ideas last because they may be chopped off or ignored.
- Make the release visually appealing. Limit the text to one or two double-spaced pages with attractive formatting.
- Look and sound credible—no typos, no imaginative spelling or punctuation, no factual errors.

The most important ingredient of a press release, of course, is *news.* Articles that merely plug products end up in the circular file.

SUMMARY OF LEARNING OBJECTIVES

1 **Apply Guffey's 3-×-3 writing process to persuasive messages.** The first step in the writing process for a persuasive message is analysis of the audience and purpose. Writers must know exactly what they want the receiver to do or think. The second step involves thinking of ways to adapt the message to the audience. Particularly important is expressing the request so that it may benefit the reader. Next, the writer must collect data and organize it into an appropriate strategy. An indirect strategy is probably best if the audience will resist the request.

2 **Explain the components of a persuasive message.** The most effective persuasive messages gain attention by opening with a problem, unexpected statement, reader benefit, compliment, related fact, stimulating question, or similar device. They build interest with facts, expert opinions, examples, details, and additional reader benefits. They reduce resistance by anticipating objections and presenting counterarguments. They conclude by motivating a specific action and making it easy for the reader to respond. Skilled communicators avoid distortion, exaggeration, and deception when making persuasive arguments.

3 **Request favours and action effectively.** When writing to ask for a favour, the indirect pattern is appropriate. This means delaying the request until after logical reasons have been presented. Such memos should emphasize, if possible, benefits to the reader. Appeals to professionalism are often a useful technique. Writers can counter any anticipated resistance with explanations and motivate action in the closing.

4 **Write convincing persuasive messages within organizations.** In writing internal messages that require persuasion, the indirect pattern is appropriate. These messages might begin with a frank discussion of a problem. They build interest by emphasizing points that are important to the readers. They support the request with accurate, honest evidence.

5 **Request adjustments and make claims successfully.** When writing about damaged products, mistaken billing, or other claims, the indirect pattern is appropriate. These messages might begin with a sincere compliment or an objective statement of the problem. They explain concisely why a claim is legitimate. Copies of relevant documents should be enclosed. The message should conclude with a clear statement of the action to be taken.

6 **Compose successful sales messages.** Before writing a sales message, it's necessary to analyze the product and purpose carefully. The letter begins with an attention-getting statement that is short, honest, relevant, and stimulating. It builds interest by describing the product or service clearly in simple language, incorporating appropriate appeals. Testimonials, a money-back guarantee, a free trial, or some other device can reduce resistance. A gift, incentive, deadline, or other device can motivate action.

7 **Describe the basic elements included in effective news releases.** Effective news releases usually open with an attention-getting lead or summary of the important facts. They attempt to answer the questions who, what, when, where, why, and how. They are written carefully to appeal to the audience of the target media. The best news releases present the most important information early, make the release visually appealing, and look and sound credible.

CHAPTER REVIEW

1. List the four steps in the indirect pattern for persuasive messages. (Objs. 1 and 2)
2. List six or more techniques for opening a persuasive request for a favour. (Obj. 3)
3. List techniques for building interest in a persuasive request for a favour. (Obj. 3)
4. Describe ways to reduce resistance in persuasive requests. (Obj. 3)
5. How should a persuasive request end? (Objs. 2 and 3)
6. When does persuasion become unethical? (Obj. 2)
7. What are the differences between direct and indirect reader benefits? Give an original example of each (other than those described). (Obj. 3)
8. When would persuasion be necessary in messages moving downward in organizations? (Obj. 4)
9. Why are persuasive messages usually longer than direct messages? (Objs. 1–4)
10. When is it necessary to use the indirect pattern in requesting adjustments or making claims? (Obj. 5)
11. What is an appropriate tone for a letter requesting an adjustment? (Obj. 5)
12. Name eight or more ways to attract attention in opening a sales message. (Obj. 6)
13. How do rational appeals differ from emotional appeals? Give an original example of each. (Obj. 6)
14. Name five or more ways to motivate action in closing a sales message. (Obj. 6)
15. List five or more topics that an organization might feature in a press release. (Obj. 7)

CRITICAL THINKING

1. How are requests for action and sales letters similar and how are they different? (Objs. 3 and 6)
2. What are some of the underlying motivations that prompt individuals to agree to requests that do not directly benefit themselves or their organizations? (Objs. 2–7)
3. In view of the burden that "junk" mail places on society (depleted landfills, declining timber supplies, overburdened postal system), how can "junk" mail be justified? (Obj. 6)
4. Why is it important to know your needs and have documentation when you make requests of superiors? (Obj. 4)

ACTIVITIES

10.1 Document for Analysis: Weak Persuasive Invitation (Obj. 3)

Your Task. Analyze the following document. List its weaknesses. If your instructor directs, revise it.

✗ *Ineffective Letter*

Dear Dr. Thomas:

Because you're a local Guelph author, we thought it might not be too much trouble for you to speak at our U of G banquet May 5.

Some of us business students here at Guelph University admired your book *Beyond Race and Gender*, which appeared last spring and became such a hit across the nation. One of our professors said you were now the nation's diversity management guru. What exactly did you mean when you said that Canada is no longer a blend of two cultures—that it's now a "smorgasbord of multicultural expectations"?

Because we have no funds for honoraria, we have to rely on local speakers. The Reverend James R. Jones and Vice Mayor Rebecca A. Timmons were speakers in the past. Our banquets usually begin at 6:30 with a social hour, followed by dinner at 7:30 and the speaker from 8:30 until 9:00 or 9:15. We can arrange transportation for you and your wife if you need it.

We realize that you must be very busy, but we hope you'll agree. Please let our advisor, Professor Alexa North, have the favour of an early response.

Cordially,

10.2 Document for Analysis: Weak Persuasive Memo (Obj. 4)

Your Task. Analyze the following document. List its weaknesses. If your instructor directs, revise it.

✗ *Poorly Written Memo*

TO: Jennifer Ritter, VP, Media Relations
FROM: Phillip Pitino, Product Manager
SUBJECT: OUR TRADE BOOTH

We have all enjoyed attending the many trade shows where we exhibit our products. I particularly look forward to the Toronto Comdex show, which, as you know, is the biggest software and hardware trade show in the country.

My fellow product managers and I try to get visitors to come to our booth, but it's not easy. In the past we've tried promotions with T-shirts, coffee mugs, and pens all sporting our company logo. We also tried "freemiums," but we lost a bundle on these $50 coupons. You will recall that they were supposed to be used toward future software purchases, but we learned too late that they could be easily photocopied and multiple copies printed out. What a bummer!

But here's a promotion idea that is not going to lose us a lot of money. Digital Equipment Corporation, at its exhibit at Networld a couple of months ago in Toronto, had a way of making personalized Web pages for visitors. They used a template, took a picture of the visitor with a digital camera, and made a Web page for each visitor. They then gave a disk to the visitor with the page in HTML format, ready to upload to their personal Web sites. It was a huge hit! The great part about this is that visitors have to leave their names, addresses, and contact information to insert into their Web pages. We get all this great information—they get a free disk. Doesn't this sound like a winner? About all we have to do in the way of preparation is have our Web design team make a Web page template. This shouldn't be too difficult.

Let me know what you think. Our next big trade show is June 10 in Vancouver.

10.3 Document for Analysis: Poor Claim Letter (Obj. 5)

Your Task. Analyze the following poorly written claim letter. List its weaknesses. If your instructor directs, revise it.

Dear Sir:

Three months ago we purchased four of your E-Studio 120 photocopiers, and we've had nothing but trouble ever since.

Our salesperson, Julia Franks, assured us that the E-Studio 120 could easily handle our volume of 3000 copies a day. This seemed strange since the sales brochure said that the E-Studio 120 was meant for 500 copies a day. But we believed Ms. Franks. Big mistake! Our four E-Studio 120 copiers are down constantly; we can't go on like this. Because they're still under warranty, they eventually get repaired. But we're losing considerable business in downtime.

Your Ms. Franks has been less than helpful, so I telephoned the district manager, Ron Rivera. I suggested that we trade in our E-Studio 120 copiers (which we got for $2500 each) on two E-Studio 600 models (at $13 500 each). However, Mr. Rivera said he would have to charge 50 percent depreciation on our E-Studio 120 copiers. What a ripoff! I think that 20 percent depreciation is more reasonable since we've had the machines only three months. Mr. Rivera said he would get back to me, and I haven't heard from him since.

I'm writing to your headquarters because I have no faith in either Ms. Franks or Mr. Rivera, and I need action on these machines. If you understood anything about business, you would see what a sweet deal I'm offering you. I'm willing to stick with your company and purchase your most expensive model—but I can't take such a steep loss on the E-Studio 120 copiers. The E-Studio 120 copiers are relatively new; you should be able to sell them with no trouble. And think of all the money you'll save by not having your repair technicians making constant trips to service our 120 copiers! Please let me hear from you immediately.

10.4 Sales Letter Analysis (Obj. 6)

Your Task. Select a one- or two-page sales letter received by you or a friend. Study the letter and then answer these questions:

a. What techniques capture the reader's attention?
b. Is the opening effective? Explain.
c. What are the central selling points?
d. Does the letter use rational, emotional, or a combination of appeals? Explain.
e. What reader benefits are suggested?
f. How does the letter build interest in the product or service?
g. How is price handled?
h. How does the letter anticipate reader resistance and offer counterarguments?
i. What action is the reader to take? How is the action made easy?
j. What motivators spur the reader to act quickly?

10.5 Persuasive Favour/Action Request: PDAs Lighten Realtors' Load (Obj. 3)

TEAM | CRITICAL THINKING | SPEAKING | WEB

As a staffer at one of Vancouver's top realty agencies, you recently attended an Association of Realtors meeting and talked with fellow agent Bob Drewisch. He showed you his new personal digital assistant (PDA) and said, "Watch this." He accessed listing after listing of homes for sale by his company and others. You couldn't believe your eyes. You saw island properties, historic homes, beachfront condos—all with pictures and complete listing information. In this little device, which could easily fit into a pocket (or purse), you could carry six months of active, pending, and closed listings, along with contact details for agents and other valuable information.

You thought about the size of your multiple listing books and how often you had to trudge back to the office when a home buyer wanted to see a market listing. "Looks terrific," you said to Bob. "But what about new listings? And how much does this thing cost? And I bet it has a steep learning curve." Eager to show off his new toy, Bob demonstrated its user-friendly interface that follows intuitive prompts such as *price, area,* and *number of bedrooms.* He explained that his agency bought the software for $129. For a monthly fee of $19, he downloads updates as often as he likes. In regard to ease of use, Bob said that even his fellow agent Emily, notoriously computer challenged, loved it. None of the staff found it confusing or difficult to operate.

You decide that the agency where you work should provide this service to all 18 full-time staff agents. Assume that multiple listing software is available for the greater Vancouver area.

Your Task. With other staff members (your classmates), decide how to approach the agency owner, who is "old school" and shuns most technology. Decide what you want to request. Do you merely want the owner to talk with you about the service? Should you come right out and ask for PDAs and the service for all 18 staff members? Should you expect staff members to provide the hardware (a basic PDA at about $200) and the agency to purchase the service and individual updates for each full-time agent? Or should you ask for the service plus a top-of-the-line device that combines PDA/phone, GPS (global positioning system), and other capabilities? Learn more about PDA possibilities on the Web. Explore this information with your team. Once you decide on a course of action, what appeals would be most persuasive? Discuss how to handle price in your persuasive argument. Individually or as a group, prepare a persuasive message to George R. Hollings, president, Hollings Vancouver Realty. Decide whether you should deliver your persuasive message as a hard-copy memo or an e-mail.[4]

10.6 Persuasive Internal Memo or E-Mail: We Need a Change (Obj. 4)

CRITICAL THINKING

In your own work or organization experience, identify a problem for which you have a solution. Should a procedure be altered to improve performance? Would a new or different piece of equipment help you perform your work better? Could some tasks be scheduled more efficiently? Are employees being used most effectively? Could customers be better served by changing something? Do you want to work other hours or perform other tasks? Do you deserve a promotion? Do you have a suggestion to improve profitability?

Your Task. Once you have identified a situation requiring persuasion, write a memo or an e-mail to your boss or organization head. Use actual names and facts. Employ the concepts and techniques in this chapter to help you convince your boss that your idea should prevail. Include concrete examples, anticipate objections, emphasize reader benefits, and end with a specific action to be taken.

10.7 Persuasive Internal Request: Overusing Overnight Shipments (Obj. 4)

As office manager of Cupertino Software, write a memo persuading technicians, engineers, programmers, and other employees to reduce the number of overnight or second-day mail shipments. Your Federal Express and other shipping bills have been sky high, and you feel that staff members are overusing these services.

You think employees should send messages by fax. Sending a fax costs only about 35 cents a page to most long-distance areas and nothing to local areas. There's a whopping difference between 35 cents and $12 to $18 for FedEx service! Whenever possible, staff members should obtain the FedEx account number of the recipient and use it for charging the shipment. If staff members plan ahead and allow enough time, they can use Canada Post ground service, which takes three to five days. You wonder whether staff members consider whether the recipient is *really* going to use the message as soon as it arrives. Does it justify an overnight shipment? You'd like to reduce overnight delivery services voluntarily by 50 percent over the next two months. Unless a sizable reduction occurs, the CEO threatens severe restrictions in the future.

Your Task. Address your memo to all employees. Include any other ways in which employees could reduce shipping costs.

10.8 Persuasive Claim: Please Remove This "Technology" Fee From My Bill (Obj. 3)

LISTENING SPEAKING

As they check out, hotel guests are increasingly being hit with unexpected charges such as energy surcharges, technology fees, and Internet connection fees. At one major hotel, Jeff Wansley dialled a local number from his computer to check his e-mail and stayed connected for hours. When he checked out, he was handed a bill for more than $200. Nothing on the desk in his room indicated he would be charged by the minute for local phone calls. He did, however, persuade the hotel to halve the bill.

When Anthony Marshall checked out of his hotel recently he was upset by a $3-per-night "technology fee" that popped up on his bill. The technology fee covered wireless access in the atriums and Internet bar, plus free local phone calls. Because Marshall did not bring his laptop on the trip and used his cell phone to place all his calls, he did not use these hotel services. The fee was never mentioned when he was first quoted a room rate. Although receptionists were trained to tell guests about the technology charge at check-in, Marshall's receptionist apparently did not tell him. He noticed later, however, that the fee was explained in fine print on the key envelope he received at check-in.

Anthony Marshall was totally steamed at the charge, and his angry reaction to the extra charge was not motivated by the money involved. Instead, he was upset by the deceptive way the charge was added to his bill. Along with a growing number of other travellers, Marshall believes that hotel room rate quotes should include all mandatory charges. All other charges should be user-based or voluntary.[5]

Your Task. Form groups of three to four students. One will role-play Anthony Marshall; one will role-play the hotel's customer service representative that Anthony calls. The remaining group members are observers. Anthony's goal is removal of the technology fee from his bill. The customer service rep's goal is to keep Anthony's goodwill while supporting the hotel's policy. The hotel will not remove the charge. The goal of the remaining group members is to analyze Anthony's request to determine how well he followed the chapter's persuasive claim principles. As a group, discuss what you learned from this exercise to help you get the results you want the next time you're trying to persuade someone in a spoken claim situation.

10.9 Claim Request: Outrageous Charge for Pancake Breakfast (Obj. 5)

As regional manager for an electronics parts manufacturer, you and two other employees attended a conference in Montreal. You stayed at the Excelsior Hotel because your company recommends that employees use it. Generally, your employees have liked their accommodations, and the rates have been within your company's budget. The hotel's service has been excellent.

Now, however, you're unhappy with the charges you see on your company's credit statement from the Excelsior. When your department's administrative assistant made the reservations, she was assured that you would receive the weekend rates and that a hot breakfast—in the hotel restaurant, the Atrium—would be included in the rate. You hate those cold sweet rolls and instant coffee "continental" breakfasts, especially when you have to leave early and won't get another meal until afternoon. So you and the other two employees went to the restaurant and ordered a hot meal from the menu.

When you received the credit card statement, though, you see a charge for $79 for three champagne buffet breakfasts in the Atrium. You hit the ceiling! For one thing, you didn't have a buffet breakfast and certainly no champagne. The three of you got there so early that no buffet had been set up. You ordered pancakes and sausage, and for this you were billed $25 each. You're outraged! What's worse, your company may charge you personally for exceeding the expected rates.

In looking back at this event, you remembered that other guests on your floor were having a "continental" breakfast in a lounge on your floor. Perhaps that's where the hotel expected all guests on the weekend rate to eat. However, your administrative assistant had specifically asked about this matter when she made the reservations, and she was told that you could order breakfast from the menu at the hotel's restaurant.

Your Task. You want to straighten out this matter, and you can't do it by telephone because you suspect that you will need a written record of this entire mess. Write a claim request to Customer Service, Montreal Excelsior Hotel, 1221 22nd Street, Montreal, QC J1M 1R7. Decide whether you should include a copy of the credit card statement showing the charge.

10.10 Sales Letter: Fitness at Crowne Pizza (Obj. 6)

The Canadian Council on Integrated Healthcare reports that employee absences cost Canadian employers an estimated $8.6 billion a year. Many of these absences are related to employee fitness (or lack of it). Dofasco in Hamilton, Ontario, found in an employee audit that obese nonsmokers lost an average of 72 hours per year and obese smokers lost an average of 106 hours per year. Many companies are responding to these concerns by offering wellness programs such as weight loss (Dofasco's Big Steel Men and Women; the Kitchener, Ontario Home & Park Motorhomes' Fat Cat Club) and smoking cessation (Home & Park's Kick Ash Club), and on-site fitness facilities.[6]

As a sales representative for Fitness Associates, you think your fitness equipment and programs could be instrumental in helping people lose weight. With regular exercise at an on-site fitness centre, employees lose weight and improve their overall health. As employee health improves, absenteeism is reduced and overall productivity increases. And employees love working out before or after work. They make the routine part of their workday, and they often have work buddies who share their fitness regimen.

Although many companies resist spending money to save money, fitness centres need not be large or expensive to be effective. Studies show that moderately sized centres coupled with motivational and training programs yield the greatest success. For just $30 000, Fitness Associates (FA) will provide exercise equipment including stationary bikes, weight machines, and treadmills. Their fitness experts will design a fitness room, set up the fitness equipment, and design appropriate programs. Best of all, the one-time cost is usually offset by cost savings within one year of centre installation. For additional fees FA can also provide fitness consultants for employee fitness assessments. FA specialists will also train employees on proper use of equipment and clean and manage the facility—for an extra charge, of course.

Your Task. Write a sales letter to Ms. Kathleen Stewart, Human Resources Vice President, Crowne Pizza, 3939 West Highland Blvd., Fredericton, NB E3A 8T4. Assume you are writing on company letterhead paper. Ask for an appointment to meet with her. Send her a brochure detailing the products and services that Fitness Associates provides. As an incentive offer a free fitness assessment for all employees if Crowne Pizza installs a fitness facility by December 1.

10.11 Sales Letter: Promoting Your Product or Service (Obj. 6)

Identify a situation in your current job or a previous one in which a sales letter is (was) needed. Using suggestions from this chapter, write an appropriate sales letter that promotes a product or service. Use actual names, information, and examples. If you have no work experience, imagine a business you'd like to start: word processing, student typing, pet grooming, car detailing, tutoring, specialty knitting, balloon decorating, delivery service, child care, gardening, lawn care, or something else. Write a letter selling your product or service to be distributed to your prospective customers. Be sure to tell them how to respond.

10.12 News Release: EarthShell Wants You (Obj. 7)

INFOTRAC | WEB

You have been interviewed for a terrific job in corporate communications at EarthShell, which produces biodegradable packaging materials for traditional food service items. Its clamshell sandwich containers are made from potato starch and have been approved for 300 McDonald's stores. The best part of the job offer is that you could work in Victoria, one of BC's most beautiful cities. However, EarthShell wants you to submit a news release as a writing sample. EarthShell features a number of news releases at its Web site, and many articles about its products have appeared in periodicals. The EarthShell recruiter wants you to submit a news release that would appeal to the publisher of your local newspaper.

Your Task. Using InfoTrac, search for EarthShell information. Read several articles. Also go to its Web site (use a search engine to find it) and look at its current news releases. Select one event or product that you think would be of interest to your local newspaper. Although you can use the information from current EarthShell news releases, don't copy the exact wording because it will be obvious to EarthShell. As a contact person to be named in your news release, use a name from a current EarthShell news release.

10.13 News Release: It's New! (Obj. 7)

Your Task. In a company where you now work or for an organization you belong to, identify a product or service that could be publicized. Consider writing a press release announcing a new course at your school, a new president, new equipment, or a campaign to raise funds. Write the press release for your local newspaper.

C.L.U.E. REVIEW 10

Edit the following sentences to correct faults in grammar, punctuation, spelling, and word use.

1. Sucessful persuasion results from 2 important elements; a reasonable request, and a well presented argument.
2. If we wanted to persuade a bank to lend you and I ten thousand dollars we would probibly use rational appeals.
3. Our Senior Marketing Director and the sales manager wants to send a sales letter to our current customers therefore they analyzed the product, purpose and audience.
4. 4 important parts of a persuasive message are: (1) Gaining the audiences attention (2) Convincing them that your purpose is worthy (3) Overcoming resistance and (4) Motivating action.
5. One of the most biggest mistakes in persuasive request's are the failure to anticipate, and off set audience resistance.
6. If the CEO and him had behaved more professional the chances of a practicle settlement would be considerably greater.
7. A adjustment letter is a form of complaint consequently its wise to use the indirect strategy.
8. Anger and emotion is not effective in persuasion but many writers cannot controll there tempers.
9. When we open our office in Montreal we will need at least 3 people whom are fluent in french and english.
10. A good news release looks and sound credible that is it has no typos no imaginative spelling and no factual errors.

Chapter 11
Negative Messages

LEARNING OBJECTIVES

1 Describe the goals and strategies of business communicators in delivering bad news.

2 Explain techniques for delivering bad news sensitively.

3 Identify routine requests and describe a strategy for refusing such requests.

4 Explain techniques for delivering bad news to customers.

5 Explain techniques for delivering bad news within organizations.

6 Compare strategies for revealing bad news in different cultures.

STRATEGIES FOR DELIVERING BAD NEWS

1

The sting of bad news can be reduced by giving reasons and communicating sensitively.

Breaking bad news is a fact of business life for nearly every business communicator. In all businesses, things occasionally go wrong. Because bad news disappoints, irritates, and sometimes angers the receiver, such messages must be written carefully. The bad feelings associated with disappointing news can generally be reduced if (1) the reader knows the reasons for the rejection and (2) the bad news is revealed with sensitivity. You've probably heard people say, "It wasn't so much the bad news that I resented. It was the way I was told!"

The direct strategy, which you learned to apply in earlier chapters, frontloads the main idea, even when it's bad news. This direct strategy appeals to efficiency-oriented writers who don't want to waste time with efforts to soften the effects of bad news.[1] Many business writers, however, prefer to use the indirect pattern in delivering negative messages. The indirect strategy is especially appealing to relationship-oriented writers. They care about how a message will affect its receiver.

In this chapter you'll learn when to use the direct or indirect pattern to deliver bad news. You'll study the goals of business communicators in working with bad news, and you'll examine three causes for legal concerns. The major focus of this chapter, however, is on developing the indirect strategy and applying it to situations in which you must refuse routine requests, decline invitations, and deliver negative news to employees and customers. You'll also learn how bad news is handled in other cultures.

Goals in Communicating Bad News

In communicating bad news, key goals include getting the receiver to accept it, maintaining goodwill, and avoiding legal liability.

As a business communicator working with bad news, you will have many goals, the most important of which are these:

- **Acceptance.** Make sure the reader understands and *accepts* the bad news. The indirect pattern helps in achieving this objective.
- **Positive image.** Promote and maintain a good image of yourself and your organization. Realizing this goal assumes that you will act ethically.
- **Message clarity.** Make the message so clear that additional correspondence is unnecessary.
- **Protection.** Avoid creating legal liability or responsibility for you or your organization.

These are ambitious goals, and we're not always successful in achieving them all. The patterns you're about to learn, however, provide the beginning communicator with strategies and tactics that many writers have found successful in conveying disappointing news sensitively and safely. With experience, you'll be able to vary these patterns and adapt them to your organization's specific writing tasks.

Using the Indirect Pattern to Prepare the Reader

The indirect pattern softens the impact of bad news by giving reasons and explanations first.

Revealing bad news slowly and indirectly shows sensitivity to your reader. By preparing the reader, you tend to soften the impact. A blunt announcement of disappointing news might cause the receiver to stop reading and toss the message aside. The indirect strategy enables you to keep the reader's attention until you have been able to explain the reasons for the bad news. In fact, the most important part of a bad-news letter is the explanation, which you'll learn about shortly. The indirect plan consists of four parts, as shown in Figure 11.1.

FIGURE 11.1 Four-Part Indirect Pattern for Bad News

Buffer		Reasons		Bad News		Closing
Open with a neutral but meaningful statement that does not mention the bad news.	➤	Explain the causes of the bad news before disclosing it.	➤	Reveal the bad news without emphasizing it. Provide an alternative or compromise, if possible.	➤	End with a personalized, forward-looking, pleasant statement. Avoid referring to the bad news.

When to Use the Direct Pattern

Many bad-news letters are best organized indirectly, beginning with a buffer and reasons. The direct pattern, with the bad news first, may be more effective, though, in situations such as the following.

The direct pattern is appropriate when the receiver might overlook the bad news, when directness is preferred, when firmness is necessary, when the bad news is not damaging, or when the goodwill of the receiver is unimportant.

- **When the receiver may overlook the bad news.** With the crush of mail today, many readers skim messages, looking only at the opening. If they don't find substantive material, they may discard the message. Rate increases, changes in service, new policy requirements—these critical messages may require boldness to ensure attention.
- **When organization policy suggests directness.** Some companies expect all internal messages and announcements—even bad news—to be straightforward and presented without frills.
- **When the receiver prefers directness.** Busy managers may prefer directness. Such shorter messages enable the reader to get in the proper frame of mind immediately. If you suspect that the reader prefers that the facts be presented straightaway, use the direct pattern.
- **When firmness is necessary.** Messages that must demonstrate determination and strength should not use delaying techniques. For example, the last in a series of collection letters that seek payment of overdue accounts may require a direct opener.
- **When the bad news is not damaging.** If the bad news is insignificant (such as a small increase in cost) and doesn't personally affect the receiver, then the direct strategy certainly makes sense.
- **When the receiver's goodwill is not an issue.** Rarely, a business may have to send a message rejecting a customer's business. For instance, a chain of bargain retail stores sent letters to two sisters announcing that their business was no longer welcome. The sisters had a history of returning items and making complaints about service.[2]

Applying Guffey's 3-×-3 Writing Process

Thinking through the entire process is especially important in bad-news letters. Not only do you want the receiver to understand and accept the message, but you want to be careful that your words say only what you intend. Thus, you'll want to apply the familiar 3-×-3 writing process to bad-news letters.

The 3-×-3 writing process is especially important in crafting bad-news messages because of the potential consequences of poorly written messages.

Analysis, Anticipation, and Adaptation. In Phase 1 (prewriting) you need to analyze the bad news so that you can anticipate its effect on the receiver. If the disappointment will be mild, announce it directly. If the bad news is serious or personal, consider techniques to reduce the pain. Adapt your words to protect the receiver's ego. Choose words that show you respect the reader as a responsible, valuable person.

Research, Organization, and Composition. In Phase 2 (writing) you can gather information and brainstorm for ideas. Jot down all the reasons you have that explain the bad news. If four or five reasons prompted your negative decision, concentrate on the strongest and safest ones. Avoid presenting any weak reasons; readers may seize on them to reject the entire message. After selecting your best reasons, outline the four parts of the bad-news pattern: buffer, reasons, bad news, closing. Flesh out each section as you compose your first draft.

Revision, Proofreading, and Evaluation. In Phase 3 (revising) you're ready to switch positions and put yourself into the receiver's shoes. Have you looked at the problem from the receiver's perspective? Is your message too blunt? Too subtle? Does the message make the refusal, denial, or bad-news announcement clear? Prepare the final version, and proofread for format, punctuation, and correctness.

Avoiding Three Causes of Legal Problems

Before we examine the components of a bad-news message, let's look more closely at how you can avoid exposing yourself and your employer to legal liability in writing negative messages. Although we can't always anticipate the consequences of our words, we should be alert to three causes of legal difficulties: (1) abusive language, (2) careless language, and (3) the "good-guy syndrome."

Abusive language becomes legally actionable when it is false, harmful to the person's good name, and "published."

Abusive Language. Calling people names (such as *deadbeat, crook,* or *quack*) can get you into trouble. *Defamation* is the legal term for any false statement that harms an individual's reputation. When the abusive language is written, it's called *libel*; when spoken, it's *slander.*

To be actionable (likely to result in a lawsuit), abusive language must be (1) false, (2) damaging to one's good name, and (3) "published"—that is, spoken within the presence of others or written. Thus, if you were alone with Jane Doe and accused her of accepting bribes and selling company secrets to competitors, she couldn't sue because the defamation wasn't published. Her reputation was not damaged. But if anyone heard the words or if they were written, you might be legally liable.

In a new wrinkle, you may now be prosecuted if you transmit a harassing or libelous message by e-mail or on a computer bulletin board. Such electronic transmission is considered to be "published." Moreover, a company may incur liability for messages sent through its computer system by employees. That's why many companies are increasing their monitoring of both outgoing and internal messages. "Off-the-cuff, casual e-mail conversations among employees are exactly the type of messages that tend to trigger lawsuits and arm litigators with damaging evidence," says e-mail guru Nancy Flynn.[3] Instant messaging adds another danger for companies. Its use continues to increase, and it's largely an unmonitored channel.[4]

Whether in print or electronically, competent communicators avoid making unproven charges and letting their emotions prompt abusive language.

Careless Language. As the marketplace becomes increasingly litigious, we must be certain that our words communicate only what we intend. First, be careful in making statements that are potentially damaging or that could be misinterpreted. Be wary of explanations that convey more information than you intend. Second, be careful about what documents you save. Lawyers may demand, in pursuing a lawsuit, all company files pertaining to a case. Even documents marked "Confidential" or "Personal" may be used.

Careless language includes statements that could be damaging or misinterpreted.

Remember, too, that e-mail messages are especially risky. You may think that a mere tap of the *Delete* key makes a file disappear; however, messages continue to exist on backup storage devices in the files of the sender and the recipient.

The Good-Guy Syndrome. Most of us hate to have to reveal bad news—that is, to be the bad guy. To make ourselves look better, to make the receiver feel better, and to maintain good relations, we are tempted to make statements that are legally dangerous.

Avoid statements that make you feel good but may be misleading or inaccurate.

Business communicators act as agents of their organizations. Their words, decisions, and opinions are assumed to represent those of the organization. If you want to communicate your personal feelings or opinions, use your home computer or write on plain paper (rather than company letterhead) and sign your name without title or affiliation. Volunteering extra information can lead to trouble. Thus, avoid supplying data that could be misused, and avoid making promises that can't be fulfilled. Don't admit or imply responsibility for conditions that caused damage or injury. Even apologies (*We're sorry that a faulty bottle cap caused damage to your carpet*) may suggest liability.

Use organizational stationery for official business only, and beware of making promises that can't be fulfilled.

In Chapter 5 we discussed four information areas that generate the most lawsuits: investments, safety, marketing, and human resources. In this chapter we'll make specific suggestions for avoiding legal liability in writing responses to claim letters, credit letters, and personnel documents. You may find that in the most critical areas (such as collection letters or hiring/firing messages) your organization provides language guidelines and form letters approved by legal counsel. As the business environment becomes more perilous, we must not only be sensitive to receivers but also keenly aware of risks to ourselves and to the organizations we represent.

TECHNIQUES FOR DELIVERING BAD NEWS SENSITIVELY

2

Legal matters aside, let's now study specific techniques for using the indirect pattern in sending bad-news messages. In this pattern the bad news is delayed until after explanations have been given. The four components of the indirect pattern, shown in Figure 11.2, include buffer, reasons, bad news, and closing.

Buffering the Opening

A buffer is a device to reduce shock or pain. To buffer the pain of bad news, begin with a neutral but meaningful statement that makes the reader continue reading. The buffer should be relevant and concise and provide a natural transition to the explanation that follows. The individual situation, of course, will help determine what you should put in the buffer. Avoid trite buffers such as *Thank you for your letter.* Here are some possibilities for opening bad-news messages.

To reduce negative feelings, use a buffer opening for sensitive bad-news messages.

- **Best news.** Start with the part of the message that represents the best news.
- **Compliment.** Praise the receiver's accomplishments, organization, or efforts. But do so with honesty and sincerity.

FIGURE 11.2 Delivering Bad News Sensitively

Buffer		Reasons		Bad News		Closing
Best news Compliment Appreciation Agreement Facts Understanding Apology	➤	Cautious explanation Reader or other benefits Company policy explanation Positive words Evidence that matter was considered fairly and seriously	➤	Embedded placement Passive voice Implied refusal Compromise Alternative	➤	Forward look Information about alternative Good wishes Freebies Resale Sales promotion

Hotel giant Starwood accidentally listed exclusive bungalows at a Bora Bora resort in the South Pacific for $85 instead of $850 a night over the Internet. The deal was pounced on by 136 people who booked thousands of nights. Honouring the rate, however, would have cost the company $2 million in lost revenue. When companies are forced to deliver bad news, they generally begin with a buffer and reasons before announcing the bad news.

- **Appreciation.** Convey thanks to the reader for doing business, for sending something, for conveying confidence in your organization, for expressing feelings, or simply for providing feedback. Avoid thanking the reader, however, for something you are about to refuse.
- **Agreement.** Make a relevant statement with which both reader and receiver can agree.
- **Facts.** Provide objective information that introduces the bad news.
- **Understanding.** Show that you care about the reader. You might want to express concern.
- **Apology.** As you learned in Chapter 9, a carefully worded apology may be appropriate. If you do apologize, do it early, briefly, and sincerely.

Good buffers avoid revealing the bad news immediately. Moreover, they do not convey a false impression that good news follows. Additionally, they provide a natural transition to the next bad-news letter component—the reasons.

Presenting the Reasons

Bad-news messages should explain reasons before stating the negative news.

The most important part of a bad-news letter is the section that explains why a negative decision is necessary. Without sound reasons for denying a request or refusing a claim, a letter will fail, no matter how cleverly it is organized or written. As part of your planning before writing, you analyzed the problem and decided to refuse a request for specific reasons. Before disclosing the bad news, try to explain those reasons. Providing an explanation reduces feelings of ill will and improves the chances that the reader will accept the bad news.

Being Cautious in Explaining. If the reasons are not confidential and if they will not create legal liability, you can be specific. Don't, however, make unrealistic or dangerous statements in an effort to be the "good guy."

Citing Reader or Other Benefits if Plausible. Readers are more open to bad news if in some way, even indirectly, it may help them. Readers also accept bad news better if they recognize that someone or something else benefits, such as other workers or the environment.

Readers accept bad news more readily if they see that someone benefits.

Explaining Company Policy. Readers resent blanket policy statements prohibiting something: *Company policy prevents us from making cash refunds* or *Contract bids may be accepted from local companies only* or *Company policy requires us to promote from within.* Instead of hiding behind company policy, gently explain why the policy makes sense: *We prefer to promote from within because it rewards the loyalty of our employees. In addition, we've found that people familiar with our organization make the quickest contribution to our team effort.* By offering explanations, you demonstrate that you care about readers and are treating them as important individuals.

Choosing Positive Words. Because the words you use can affect a reader's response, choose carefully. Remember that the objective of the indirect pattern is holding the reader's attention until you've had a chance to explain the reasons justifying the bad news. To keep the reader in a receptive mood, avoid expressions with punitive, demoralizing, or otherwise negative connotations. Stay away from such words as as *cannot, claim, denied, error, failure, fault, impossible, mistaken, misunderstand, never, regret, rejected, unable, unwilling, unfortunately,* and *violate.*

Don't use expressions with punitive, demoralizing, or other negative meanings.

Showing That the Matter Was Treated Seriously and Fairly. In explaining reasons, demonstrate to the reader that you take the matter seriously, have investigated carefully, and are making an unbiased decision. Consumers are more accepting of disappointing news when they feel that their requests have been heard and that they have been treated fairly. Avoid blaming others within your organization. Such unprofessional behaviour makes the reader lose faith in you and your company.

Cushioning the Bad News

Although you can't prevent the disappointment that bad news brings, you can reduce the pain somewhat by breaking the news sensitively. Be especially considerate when the reader will suffer personally from the bad news. A number of thoughtful techniques can cushion the blow.

Positioning the Bad News Strategically. Instead of spotlighting it, sandwich the bad news between other sentences, perhaps among your reasons. Don't let the refusal begin or end a paragraph—the reader's eye will linger on these high-visibility spots. Another technique that reduces shock is putting a painful idea in a subordinate clause, which often begins with words like *although, as, because, if,* and *since.*

Techniques for cushioning bad news include positioning it strategically, and using the passive voice.

Using the Passive Voice. Passive-voice verbs enable you to depersonalize an action. Whereas the active voice focuses attention on a person, the passive voice highlights the action. Use the passive voice for the bad news. In some instances you can combine passive-voice verbs and a subordinate clause.

Accentuating the Positive. As you learned earlier, messages are far more effective when you describe what you can do instead of what you can't do.

Implying the refusal and offering alternatives or compromises help to soften bad news.

Implying the Refusal. It's sometimes possible to avoid a direct statement of refusal. Often, your reasons and explanations leave no doubt that a request has been denied. Explicit refusals may be unnecessary and at times cruel. The danger of an implied refusal, of course, is that it is so subtle that the reader misses it. Be certain that you make the bad news clear, thus preventing the need for further correspondence.

Suggesting a Compromise or an Alternative. A refusal is not so depressing—for the sender or the receiver—if a suitable compromise, substitute, or alternative is available. You can further reduce the impact of the bad news by refusing to dwell on it. Present it briefly (or imply it), and move on to your closing.

Closing Pleasantly

Closings to bad-news messages might include a forward look, an alternative, good wishes, freebies, and resale or sales promotion information.

After explaining the bad news sensitively, close the message with a pleasant statement that promotes goodwill. The closing should be personalized and may include a forward look, an alternative, good wishes, freebies, resale information, or an off-the-subject remark.

Forward Look. Anticipate future relations or business.

Alternative. If an alternative exists, end your letter with follow-through advice.

Good Wishes. A letter rejecting a job candidate may conclude with good luck wishes.

Freebies. When customers complain—primarily about food products or small consumer items—companies often send coupons, samples, or gifts to restore confidence and to promote future business.

Resale or Sales Promotion. When the bad news is not devastating or personal, references to resale information or promotion may be appropriate.

Avoid endings that sound canned, insincere, inappropriate, or self-serving. Don't invite further correspondence (*If you have any questions, do not hesitate . . .*), and don't refer to the bad news. To review these suggestions for delivering bad news sensitively, take another look at Figure 11.2.

REFUSING ROUTINE REQUESTS

3

Every business communicator will occasionally have to say no to a request. Depending on how you think the receiver will react to your refusal, you can use the direct or the indirect pattern. If you have any doubt, use the indirect pattern.

Most of us prefer to be let down gently when we're being refused something we want. That's why the reasons-before-refusal pattern works well when you must turn down requests for favours, money, information, action, and so forth.

Saying No to Requests From Outsiders

Requests for contributions to charity are common. Many large and small companies receive requests for contributions of money, time, equipment, and support. Although the causes may be worthy, resources are usually limited. In a letter from Forest Financial Services, shown in Figure 11.3, the company must refuse a request for a donation to a charity. Following the indirect strategy, the letter begins with a buffer acknowledging the request. It also praises the good work of the charity and uses those words as a transition to the second paragraph. In the second paragraph, the writer explains why the company cannot donate, using a gentle refusal, thereby making it unnecessary to be blunter in stating the denial. In the letter shown in Figure 11.3, the writer felt a connection to the charity. Thus, he wanted to provide a full explanation.

The reasons-before-refusal pattern works well when turning down requests for favours, money, information, or action.

Refusing Internal Requests

Just as managers must refuse requests from outsiders, they must also occasionally refuse requests from employees. In Figure 11.4 you see the first draft and revision of a message responding to a request from a key manager, Mark Stevenson. He wants permission to attend a conference. However, he can't attend the conference because the timing is bad; he must be present at budget planning meetings scheduled for the same two weeks. Normally, this matter would be discussed in person. But Mark has been travelling among branch offices, and he just hasn't been in the office recently.

The vice president's first inclination was to send a quick memo, as shown in Figure 11.4, and "tell it like it is." In revising, the vice president realized that this message was going to hurt and that it had possible danger areas. Moreover, the memo misses a chance to give Mark positive feedback. An improved version of the memo starts with a buffer that delivers honest praise. By the way, don't be stingy with compliments; they cost you nothing. The buffer also includes the date of the meeting, used strategically to connect the reasons that follow. You will recall from Chapter 6 that repetition of a key idea is an effective transitional device to provide smooth flow between components of a message.

The middle paragraph provides reasons for the refusal. Notice that they focus on positive elements: Mark is the specialist; the company relies on his expertise; and everyone will benefit if he passes up the conference. In this section it becomes obvious that the request will be refused. The writer is not forced to say, *No, you may not attend.* Although the refusal is implied, the reader gets the message.

The closing suggests a qualified alternative (*if our workloads permit, we'll try to send you then*). It also ends positively with gratitude for Mark's contributions to the organization and with another compliment (*you're a valuable player*). Notice that the improved version focuses on explanations and praise rather than on refusals and apologies.

The success of this message depends on attention to the entire writing process, not just on using a buffer or scattering a few compliments throughout.

Declining Invitations

When we must decline an invitation to speak or attend a program, we generally try to provide a response that says more than *I can't* or *I don't want to.* Unless the reasons are confidential or business secrets, try to explain them. Because responses to invitations are often taken personally, make a special effort to soften the refusal. In

FIGURE 11.3 Refusing Donation Request

Prewriting 1

Analyze: The purpose of this letter is to reject the request for a monetary donation without causing bad will.

Anticipate: The reader is proud of his or her organization and the good work it pursues.

Adapt: The writer should strive to cushion the bad news and explain why it is necessary.

Writing 2

Research: Collect information about the receiver's organization as well as reasons for the refusal.

Organize: Use the indirect strategy. Begin with complimentary comments, present reasons, reveal the bad news gently, and close pleasantly.

Compose: Write the message and consider keeping a copy to serve as a form letter.

Revising 3

Revise: Be sure that the tone of the message is positive and that it suggests that the matter was taken seriously.

Proofread: Check the receiver's name and address to be sure they are accurate. Check the letter's format.

Evaluate: Will this message retain the goodwill of the receiver despite its bad news?

FOREST FINANCIAL SERVICES
3410 Oxford Road
London, ON N5V 2Z7
519.593.4400
www.forestfinancial.com

November 14, 2007

Mr. Alan Gee, Chair
Oxford-Wellington County Chapter
National Reye's Syndrome Foundation
RR # 2
Kerwood, ON N0M 2B0

Dear Mr. Gee:

[Opens with praise and compliments] *[Doesn't say yes or no]*

We appreciate your letter describing the good work your Oxford-Wellington County chapter of the National Reye's Syndrome Foundation is doing in preventing and treating this serious affliction. Your organization is to be commended for its significant achievements resulting from the efforts of dedicated members.

[Transitions with repetition of key idea (good work)] *[Explains sales decline and cutback in gifts]* *[Reveals refusal without actually stating it]*

Supporting the good work of your organization and others, although unrelated to our business, is a luxury we have enjoyed in past years. Because of sales declines and organizational downsizing, we're forced to take a much harder look at funding requests that we receive this year. We feel that we must focus our charitable contributions on areas that relate directly to our business.

[Closes graciously with forward look]

We're hopeful that the worst days are behind us and that we'll be able to renew our support for worthwhile projects like yours next year.

Sincerely,

Paul Rosenberg

Paul Rosenberg
Vice President

FIGURE 11.4 Refusing an Internal Request

DRAFT

DATE: July 2, 2007

TO: Mark Stevenson
Manager, Telecommunications

FROM: Ann Wells-Freed AWF
VP, Management Information Systems

SUBJECT: CONFERENCE REQUEST

We can't allow you to attend the conference in September, Mark. Perhaps you didn't know that budget planning meetings are scheduled for that month.

Your expertise is needed here to help keep our telecommunications network on schedule. Without you, the entire system—which is shaky at best—might fall apart. I'm sorry to have to refuse your request to attend the conference. I know this is small thanks for the fine work you have done for us. Please accept our humble apologies.

In the spring I'm sure your work schedule will be lighter, and we can release you to attend a conference at that time.

Announces the bad news too quickly and painfully

Gives reasons, but includes a dangerous statement

Makes a promise that might be difficult to keep

REVISION

DATE: July 2, 2007

TO: Mark Stevenson
Manager, Telecommunications

FROM: Ann Wells-Freed AWF
VP, Management Information Systems

SUBJECT: REQUEST TO ATTEND SEPTEMBER CONFERENCE

The Management Council and I are extremely pleased with the leadership you have provided in setting up live video transmission to our regional offices. Because of your genuine professional commitment, Mark, I can understand your desire to attend the conference of the Telecommunication Specialists of North America September 23 to 28 in Kelowna.

The last two weeks in September have been set aside for budget planning. As you and I know, we've only scratched the surface of our teleconferencing projects for the next five years. Since you are the specialist and we rely heavily on your expertise, we need you here for those planning sessions.

If you're able to attend a similar conference in the spring and if our workloads permit, we'll try to send you then. You're a valuable player, Mark, and I'm grateful you're on our MIS team.

Buffer: Includes sincere praise

Transition: Uses date to move smoothly from buffer to reasons

Reasons: Tells why refusal is necessary

Bad news: Implies refusal

Closing: Contains realistic alternative, praise, and appreciation

the letter shown in Figure 11.5, an accountant must say no to the invitation from a friend's son to speak before the young man's college business club. The refusal is embedded in a long paragraph and deemphasized in a subordinate clause (*Although your invitation must be declined*). The reader naturally concentrates on the main clause that follows. In this case that main clause contains an alternative that draws attention away from the refusal.

Notice that the tone of a refusal is warm, upbeat, and positive. This refusal starts with conviviality and compliments.

The following checklist reviews the steps in composing a letter refusing a routine request.

FIGURE 11.5 Refusing an Invitation

GALLAGHER, BRACIO, CASAGRANDE, L.L.P.
Certified Public Accountants
942 Savin Boulevard
Toronto, ON M4P 2A9
(416) 435-9800
E-mail: cpa@gbcllp.com www.gbcllp.com

April 14, 2007

Mr. Tyler Simpson
4208 Eastern Avenue
Toronto, ON M5A 1H5

Dear Tyler:

News of your leadership position in your campus student association fills me with delight and pride. Your father must be proud also of your educational and extracurricular achievements.

You honour me by asking me to speak to your group in the spring about codes of ethics in the accounting field. Because our firm has not yet adopted such a code, we have been investigating the codes developed by other accounting firms. I am decidedly not an expert in this area, but I have met others who are. Although your invitation must be declined, I would like to recommend Dr. Carolyn S. Marshall, who is a member of the ethics subcommittee of the Institute of Internal Auditors. Dr. Marshall is a professor who often addresses groups on the subject of ethics in accounting. I spoke with her about your club, and she indicated that she would be happy to consider your invitation.

It's good to learn that you are guiding your organization toward such constructive and timely program topics. Please call Dr. Marshall at (416) 389-2210 if you would like to arrange for her to address your club.

Sincerely,

Joan F. Gallagher

Joan F. Gallagher, CPA

JFG:mhr

Opens cordially with praise

Focuses attention on alternative

Reduces impact of refusal by placing it in subordinate clause

Ends positively with compliments and offer of assistance

CHECKLIST FOR REFUSING ROUTINE REQUESTS

- **Open indirectly with a buffer.** Pay a compliment to the reader, show appreciation for something done, or mention some mutual understanding. Avoid raising false hopes or thanking the reader for something you will refuse.

- **Provide reasons.** In the body explain why the request must be denied—without revealing the refusal. Avoid negativity (*unfortunately, unwilling,* and *impossible*) and potentially damaging statements. Show how your decision benefits the reader or others, if possible.

- **Soften the bad news.** Reduce the impact of bad news by using (1) a subordinate clause, (2) the passive voice, (3) a long sentence, or (4) a long paragraph. Consider implying the refusal, but be certain it is clear. Suggest an alternative, if a suitable one exists.

Close pleasantly. Supply more information about an alternative, look forward to future relations, or offer good wishes and compliments. Maintain a bright, personal tone. Avoid referring to the refusal.

DELIVERING BAD NEWS TO CUSTOMERS

Businesses must occasionally respond to disappointed customers. In Chapter 9 you learned to use the direct strategy in granting claims and making adjustments because these were essentially good-news messages. But in some situations you have little good news to share. Sometimes your company is at fault, in which case an apology is generally in order. Other times the problem is with product orders you can't fill, claims you must refuse, or credit that you must deny. Messages with bad news for customers generally follow the same pattern as other negative messages. Customer letters, though, differ in one major way: they usually include resale or sales promotion emphasis.

Damage Control: Dealing With Disappointed Customers

When a customer problem arises and the company is at fault, many businesspeople call and apologize, explain what happened, and follow up with a goodwill letter.

All companies occasionally disappoint their customers. Merchandise is not delivered on time, a product fails to perform as expected, service is deficient, charges are erroneous, or customers are misunderstood. All businesses offering products or services must sometimes deal with troublesome situations that cause unhappiness to customers. Whenever possible, these problems should be dealt with immediately and personally. One study found that a majority of business professionals strive to control the damage and resolve such problems in the following manner:[5]

- Call the individual involved.
- Describe the problem and apologize.
- Explain why the problem occurred, what you are doing to resolve it, and how you will prevent it from happening again.
- Follow up with a letter that documents the phone call and promotes goodwill.

Dealing with problems immediately is very important in resolving conflict and retaining goodwill. Written correspondence is generally too slow for problems that demand immediate attention. But written messages are important (1) when personal contact is impossible, (2) to establish a record of the incident, (3) to formally confirm follow-up procedures, and (4) to promote good relations.

A bad-news follow-up letter is shown in Figure 11.6. Consultant Maris Richfield found herself in the embarrassing position of explaining why she had given out the name of her client to a salesperson. The client, Data.com, Inc., had hired her firm, Richfield Consulting Services, to help find an appropriate service for outsourcing its payroll functions. Without realizing it, Maris had mentioned to a potential vendor (Payroll Services, Inc.) that her client was considering hiring an outside service to handle its payroll. An overeager salesperson from Payroll Services immediately called on Data.com, thus angering the client. The client had hired the consultant to avoid this very kind of intrusion. Data.com did not want to be hounded by vendors selling their payroll services.

When she learned of the problem, the first thing consultant Maris Richfield did was call her client to explain and apologize. But she also followed up with the letter shown in Figure 11.6. The letter not only confirms the telephone conversation but

FIGURE 11.6 Bad-News Follow-Up Message

Tips for Resolving Problems and Following Up

- Whenever possible, call or see the individual involved.
- Describe the problem and apologize.
- Explain why the problem occurred.
- Describe what you are doing to resolve it.
- Explain how it will not happen again.
- Follow up with a letter that documents the personal message.
- Look forward to positive future relations.

Richfield Consulting Services

1642 Sherbrooke St. West
Montreal, QC H3G 1H6

Voice: 514.499.8224
Web: www.richfieldconsulting.ca

October 23, 2007

Ms. Angela Ranier
Vice President, Human Resources
Data.com, Inc.
21067 Lacombe Avenue
Montreal, QC H5B 2G6

Dear Angela:

Opens with agreement and apology

You have every right to expect complete confidentiality in your transactions with an independent consultant. As I explained in yesterday's telephone call, I am very distressed that you were called by a salesperson from Payroll Services, Inc. This should not have happened, and I apologize to you again for inadvertently mentioning your company's name in a conversation with a potential vender, Payroll Services, Inc.

Explains what caused problem and how it was resolved

Promises to prevent recurrence

All clients of Richfield Consulting are assured that their dealings with our firm are held in the strictest confidence. Because your company's payroll needs are so individual and because you have so many contract workers, I was forced to explain how your employees differed from those of other companies. The name of your company, however, should never have been mentioned. I can assure you that it will not happen again. I have informed Payroll Services that it had no authorization to call you directly and its actions have forced me to reconsider using its services for my future clients.

Closes with forward look

A number of other payroll services offer excellent programs. I'm sure we can find the perfect partner to enable you to outsource your payroll responsibilities, thus allowing your company to focus its financial and human resources on its core business. I look forward to our next appointment when you may choose from a number of excellent payroll outsourcing firms.

Sincerely yours,

Maris Richfield

Maris Richfield

also adds the right touch of formality. It sends the nonverbal message that the matter is being taken seriously and that it is important enough to warrant a written letter.

When situations involve many unhappy customers, companies may need to write personalized form letters. The following specific strategies are effective in dealing with unhappy customers.

Personalized form letters may be necessary when delivering bad news to large groups of customers.

- Apologize if your organization is to blame.
- Identify the problem and take responsibility.
- Explain the steps being taken to prevent recurrence.
- Offer gifts, benefits, or bonuses to offset disappointment and to reestablish the relationship.
- Thank customers for their past business and patience.
- Look forward to future warm relations.

Handling Problems With Orders

Not all customer orders can be filled as received. Suppliers may be able to send only part of an order or none at all. Substitutions may be necessary, or the delivery date may be delayed. Suppliers may suspect that all or part of the order is a mistake; the customer may actually want something else. In writing to customers about problem orders, it's generally wise to use the direct pattern if the message has some good-news elements. But when the message is disappointing, the indirect pattern is more appropriate.

In handling problems with orders, the indirect pattern is appropriate unless the message has some good-news elements.

Let's say you represent Live and Learn Toys, a large West Coast toy manufacturer, and you're scrambling for business in a slow year. A big customer, Child Land, calls in August and asks you to hold a block of your best-selling toy, the Space Station. Like most vendors, you require a deposit on large orders. September rolls around, and you still haven't received any money from Child Land. You must now write a tactful letter asking for the deposit—or else you will release the toy to other buyers. The problem, of course, is delivering the bad news without losing the customer's order and goodwill. Another challenge is making sure the reader understands the bad news. An effective letter might begin with a positive statement that also reveals the facts.

✓ *Effective Letter*

> Dear Mr. Ronzelli:
>
> You were smart to reserve a block of 500 Space Stations, which we have been holding for you since August. As the holidays approach, the demand for all our learning toys, including Space Station, is rapidly increasing.

Next, the letter should explain why the payment is needed and what will happen if it is not received:

> Toy stores from St. John's to Victoria are asking us to ship these Space Stations. One reason the Space Station is moving out of our warehouses so quickly is its assortment of gizmos that children love, including a land rover vehicle, a shuttle craft, a hovercraft, astronauts, and even a robotic arm. As soon as we receive your deposit of $4000, we'll have this popular item on its way to your stores. Without a deposit by September 20, though, we must release this block to other retailers.

The closing makes it easy to respond and motivates action:

> Use the enclosed envelope to send us your cheque immediately. You can begin showing this fascinating Live and Learn toy in your stores by November 1.

Denying Claims

In denying claims, the reasons-before-refusal pattern sets an empathic tone and buffers the bad news.

Customers occasionally want something they're not entitled to or that you can't grant. They may misunderstand warranties or make unreasonable demands. Because these customers are often unhappy with a product or service, they are emotionally involved. Letters that say no to emotionally involved receivers will probably be your most challenging communication task.

Fortunately, the reasons-before-refusal plan helps you be empathic and artful in breaking bad news. Obviously, in denial letters you'll need to adopt the proper tone. Don't blame customers, even if they are at fault. Avoid *you* statements that sound preachy (*You would have known that cash refunds are impossible if you had read your contract*). Use neutral, objective language to explain why the claim must be refused. Consider offering resale information to rebuild the customer's confidence in your products or organization. In Figure 11.7 the writer denies a customer's claim for the difference between the price the customer paid for speakers and the price he saw advertised locally (which would have resulted in a cash refund of $151). While the catalogue service does match any advertised lower price, the price-matching policy applies only to exact models. This claim must be rejected because the advertisement the customer submitted showed a different, older speaker model.

The letter to Matthew Tyson opens with a buffer that agrees with a statement in the customer's letter. It repeats the key idea of product confidence as a transition to the second paragraph. Next comes an explanation of the price-matching policy. The writer does not assume that the customer is trying to pull a fast one. Nor does he suggest that the customer is a dummy who didn't read or understand the price-matching policy. The safest path is a neutral explanation of the policy along with precise distinctions between the customer's speakers and the older ones. The writer also gets a chance to resell the customer's speakers and demonstrate what a quality product they are. By the end of the third paragraph, it's evident to the reader that his claim is unjustified.

Refusing Credit

Goals when refusing credit include maintaining customer goodwill and avoiding actionable language.

As much as companies want business, they can extend credit only when payment is likely to follow. Credit applications, from individuals or from businesses, are generally approved or disapproved on the basis of the applicant's credit history. This record is supplied by a credit-reporting agency, such as Equifax. After reviewing the applicant's record, a credit manager applies the organization's guidelines and approves or disapproves the application.

If you must deny credit to prospective customers, you have four goals in conveying the refusal:

- Avoiding language that causes hard feelings
- Retaining customers on a cash basis
- Preparing for possible future credit without raising false expectations
- Avoiding disclosures that could cause a lawsuit

Because credit applicants are likely to continue to do business with an organization even if they are denied credit, you'll want to do everything possible to encourage that patronage. Thus, keep the refusal respectful, sensitive, and upbeat. A letter to a customer denying her credit application might begin as follows:

> We genuinely appreciate your application of January 12 for a Fashion Express credit account.

FIGURE 11.7 Denying a Claim

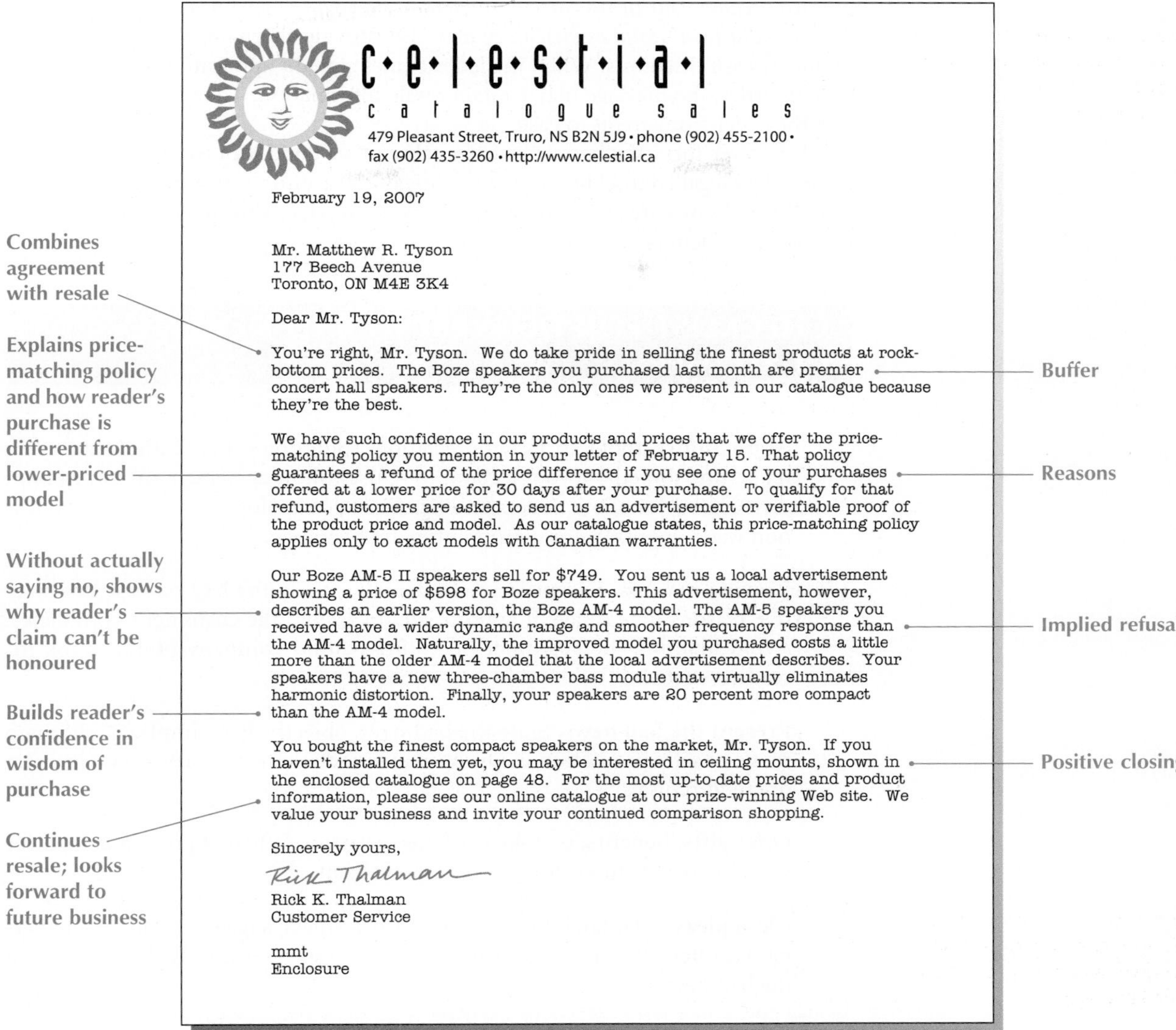

c•e•l•e•s•t•i•a•l
c a t a l o g u e s a l e s
479 Pleasant Street, Truro, NS B2N 5J9 • phone (902) 455-2100 •
fax (902) 435-3260 • http://www.celestial.ca
Combines agreement with resale
Explains price-matching policy and how reader's purchase is different from lower-priced model
Without actually saying no, shows why reader's claim can't be honoured
Builds reader's confidence in wisdom of purchase
Continues resale; looks forward to future business
Buffer
Reasons
Implied refusal
Positive closing

February 19, 2007

Mr. Matthew R. Tyson
177 Beech Avenue
Toronto, ON M4E 3K4

Dear Mr. Tyson:

You're right, Mr. Tyson. We do take pride in selling the finest products at rock-bottom prices. The Boze speakers you purchased last month are premier concert hall speakers. They're the only ones we present in our catalogue because they're the best.

We have such confidence in our products and prices that we offer the price-matching policy you mention in your letter of February 15. That policy guarantees a refund of the price difference if you see one of your purchases offered at a lower price for 30 days after your purchase. To qualify for that refund, customers are asked to send us an advertisement or verifiable proof of the product price and model. As our catalogue states, this price-matching policy applies only to exact models with Canadian warranties.

Our Boze AM-5 II speakers sell for $749. You sent us a local advertisement showing a price of $598 for Boze speakers. This advertisement, however, describes an earlier version, the Boze AM-4 model. The AM-5 speakers you received have a wider dynamic range and smoother frequency response than the AM-4 model. Naturally, the improved model you purchased costs a little more than the older AM-4 model that the local advertisement describes. Your speakers have a new three-chamber bass module that virtually eliminates harmonic distortion. Finally, your speakers are 20 percent more compact than the AM-4 model.

You bought the finest compact speakers on the market, Mr. Tyson. If you haven't installed them yet, you may be interested in ceiling mounts, shown in the enclosed catalogue on page 48. For the most up-to-date prices and product information, please see our online catalogue at our prize-winning Web site. We value your business and invite your continued comparison shopping.

Sincerely yours,

Rick Thalman

Rick K. Thalman
Customer Service

mmt
Enclosure

To avoid possible litigation, some organizations give no explanation of the reasons for the refusal. Instead, they provide the name of the credit-reporting agency and suggest that inquiries be directed to it. In the following example, notice the use of the passive voice (*credit cannot be extended*) and a long sentence to deemphasize the bad news.

> After we received a report of your current credit record from Equifax, it is apparent that credit cannot be extended at this time. To learn more about your record, you may call an Equifax credit counsellor at (800) 356-0922.

The cordial close looks forward to the possibility of future reapplication:

> Thanks, Ms. Love, for the confidence you've shown in Fashion Express. We invite you to continue shopping at our stores, and we look forward to your reapplication in the future.

Some businesses do provide reasons explaining credit denials (*Credit cannot be granted because your firm's current and long-term credit obligations are nearly twice as great as your firm's total assets*). They may also provide alternatives, such as deferred billing or cash discounts. When the letter denies a credit application that accompanies an order, the message may contain resale information. The writer tries to convert the order from credit to cash.

Whatever form the bad-news letter takes, it's a good idea to have the message reviewed by legal counsel because of the litigation landmines awaiting unwary communicators in this area. The following checklist provides tips on how to craft effective bad-news letters.

CHECKLIST FOR DELIVERING BAD NEWS TO CUSTOMERS

- ✓ **Begin indirectly.** Express appreciation (but don't thank the reader for requesting something you're about to refuse), show agreement on some point, review facts, or show understanding. Consider apologizing if your organization was responsible for disappointing its customers.
- ✓ **Provide reasons.** Except in credit denials, justify the bad news with objective reasons. Use resale, if appropriate, to restore the customer's confidence. Avoid blaming the customer or hiding behind company policy. Look for reader benefits.
- ✓ **Present the bad news.** State the bad news objectively or imply it. Although resale or sales promotion is appropriate in order letters, it may offend in claim or credit refusals.
- ✓ **Offer gifts, benefits, or tokens of appreciation.** When appropriate, look for ways to offset your customers' disappointment.
- ✓ **Close pleasantly.** Look forward to future business, suggest action on an alternative, offer best wishes, refer to gifts, or use resale sensitively. Don't mention the bad news.

DELIVERING BAD NEWS WITHIN ORGANIZATONS

5 A tactful tone and a reasons-first approach help preserve friendly relations with customers. These same techniques are useful when delivering bad news within organizations. Interpersonal bad news might involve telling the boss that something went wrong or confronting an employee about poor performance. Organizational bad news might involve declining profits, lost contracts, harmful lawsuits, public relations controversies, and changes in policy. Whether you use a direct or an indirect pattern in delivering that news depends primarily on the anticipated reaction of the audience. Generally, bad news is better received when reasons are given first. Within organizations, you may find yourself giving bad news in person or in writing.

Giving Bad News Personally

Whether you are an employee or a supervisor, you may have the unhappy responsibility of delivering bad news. First, decide whether the negative information is newsworthy. For example, trivial, noncriminal mistakes or one-time bad behaviours are best left alone. But fraudulent travel claims, consistent hostile behaviour, or failing projects must be reported.[6] For example, you might have to tell the boss that the team's computer crashed with all its important files. As a team leader or supervisor, you might be required to confront an underperforming employee. If you know that the news will upset the receiver, the reasons-first strategy is most effective. When the bad news involves one person or a small group nearby, you should generally deliver that news in person. Here are pointers on how to do so tactfully, professionally, and safely:[7]

When delivering bad news within organizations, strive to do so tactfully, professionally, and safely.

- **Gather all the information.** Cool down and have all the facts before marching in on the boss or confronting someone. Remember that every story has two sides.
- **Prepare and rehearse.** Outline what you plan to say so that you are confident, coherent, and dispassionate.
- **Explain: past, present, future.** If you are telling the boss about a problem such as the computer crash, explain what caused the crash, the current situation, and how and when you plan to fix it.
- **Consider taking a partner.** If you fear a "shoot the messenger" reaction, especially from your boss, bring a colleague with you. Each person should have a consistent and credible part in the presentation. If possible, take advantage of your organization's internal resources. To lend credibility to your view, call on auditors, inspectors, or human resources experts.
- **Think about timing.** Don't deliver bad news when someone is already stressed or grumpy. Experts also advise against giving bad news on Friday afternoon when people have the weekend to dwell on it.
- **Be patient with the reaction.** Give the receiver time to vent, think, recover, and act wisely.

Delivering Workplace Bad News

Organizations can sustain employee morale by communicating bad news openly and honestly.

Many of the same techniques used to deliver bad news personally are useful when organizations face a crisis or must deliver bad news in the workplace. Smart organizations involved in a crisis prefer to communicate the news openly to employees, customers, and stockholders. A crisis might involve serious performance problems, a major relocation, massive layoffs, a management shakeup, or public controversy. Instead of letting rumours distort the truth, they explain the organization's side of the story honestly and early. Morale can be destroyed when employees learn of major events affecting their jobs through the grapevine or from news accounts—rather than from management.

When routine bad news must be delivered to employees, management may want to deliver the news personally. But with large groups this is generally impossible. Instead, organizations deliver bad news through hard-copy memos. Organizations are experimenting with other delivery channels such as e-mail, videos, webcasts, and voice mail. Still, hard-copy memos seem to function most effectively because they are more formal and make a permanent record.

The draft of the memo shown in Figure 11.8 announces a substantial increase in the cost of employee health care benefits. However, the memo suffers from many problems. It announces jolting news bluntly in the first sentence. Worse, it offers little or no explanation for the steep increase in costs. It also sounds insincere (*We did everything possible . . .*) and arbitrary. In a final miscue, the writer fails to give credit to the company for absorbing previous health cost increases.

The revision of this bad-news memo uses the indirect pattern and improves the tone considerably. Notice that it opens with a relevant, upbeat buffer regarding health care—but says nothing about increasing costs. For a smooth transition, the second paragraph begins with a key idea from the opening (*comprehensive package*). The reasons section discusses rising costs with explanations and figures. The bad news (*you will be paying $119 a month*) is clearly presented but embedded within the paragraph. Throughout, the writer strives to show the fairness of the company's position. The ending, which does not refer to the bad news, emphasizes how much the company is paying and what a wise investment it is. Notice that the entire memo demonstrates a kinder, gentler approach than that shown in the first draft. Of prime importance in breaking bad news to employees is providing clear, convincing reasons that explain the decision.

Saying No to Job Applicants

Being refused a job is one of life's major rejections. The blow is intensified by tactless letters (*Unfortunately, you were not among the candidates selected for . . .*).

You can reduce the receiver's disappointment somewhat by using the indirect pattern—with one important variation. In the reasons section it's wise to be vague in explaining why the candidate was not selected. First, giving concrete reasons may be painful to the receiver (*Your grade point average of 2.7 was low compared with GPAs of other candidates*). Second, and more important, providing extra information may prove fatal in a lawsuit. Hiring and firing decisions generate considerable litigation today. To avoid charges of discrimination or wrongful actions, legal advisors warn organizations to keep employment rejection letters general, simple, and short.

Letters that deny applications for employment should be courteous and tactful but free of specifics that could trigger lawsuits.

The following checklist gives tips on how to communicate bad news within an organization.

CHECKLIST FOR DELIVERING NEGATIVE NEWS WITHIN ORGANIZATIONS

- ✓ **Start with a relevant, upbeat buffer.** Open with a small bit of good news, praise, appreciation, agreement, understanding, or a discussion of facts leading to the reasons section.
- ✓ **Discuss reasons.** Except in job refusal letters, explain what caused the decision necessitating the bad news. Use objective, nonjudgmental, and nondiscriminatory language. Show empathy and fairness.
- ✓ **Reveal the bad news.** Make the bad news clear but don't accentuate it. Avoid negative language.
- ✓ **Close harmoniously.** End on a positive, friendly note. For job refusals, extend good wishes.

FIGURE 11.8 Announcing Bad News to Employees

Prewriting 1

Analyze: The purpose of this memo is to tell employees that they must share with the company the increasing costs of health care.

Anticipate: The audience will be employees who are unaware of health care costs and, most likely, reluctant to pay more.

Adapt: Because the readers will probably be unhappy and resentful, use the indirect pattern.

Writing 2

Research: Collect facts and statistics that document health care costs.

Organize: Begin with a buffer describing the company's commitment to health benefits. Provide an explanation of health care costs. Announce the bad news. In the closing, focus on the company's major share of the cost.

Compose: Draft the first version on a computer.

Revising 3

Revise: Remove negativity (*unfortunately, we can't, was forced, inadvisable*). Explain the increase with specifics.

Proofread: Use quotes around *defensive* to show its special sense. Spell out *percent* after *300.*

Evaluate: Is there any other way to help readers accept this bad news?

DRAFT

Beginning January 1 your monthly payment for supplementary health care benefits will be increased to $119 (up from $52 last year). — *Hits readers with bad news without any preparation*

Every year supplementary health care costs go up. Although we considered dropping other benefits, Midland decided that the best plan was to keep the present comprehensive package. Unfortunately, we can't do that unless we pass along some of the extra cost to you. Last year the company was forced to absorb the total increase in health care premiums. However, such a plan this year is inadvisable. — *Offers no explanation*

We did everything possible to avoid the sharp increase in costs to you this year. A rate schedule describing the increases in payments for your family and dependants is enclosed. — *Fails to take credit for absorbing previous increases*

REVISION

DATE: October 2, 2007

TO: Fellow Employees

FROM: Lawrence R. Romero, President LRR

SUBJECT: MAINTAINING QUALITY HEALTH CARE

Begins with positive buffer — Supplementary health care programs have always been an important part of our commitment to employees at Midland, Inc. We're proud that our total benefits package continues to rank among the best in the country.

Offers reasons explaining why costs are rising — Such a comprehensive package does not come cheaply. In the last decade supplementary health care costs alone have risen over 300 percent. We're told that several factors fuel the cost spiral: inflation, technology improvements, increased cost of outpatient services, and "defensive" medicine practised by doctors to prevent lawsuits.

Reveals bad news clearly but embeds it in paragraph — Just two years ago our monthly health care cost for each employee was $515. It rose to $569 last year. We were able to absorb that jump without increasing your contribution. But this year's hike to $639 forces us to ask you to share the increase. To maintain your current health care benefits, you will be paying $119 a month. The enclosed rate schedule describes the costs for families and dependants.

Ends positively by stressing the company's major share of the costs — Midland continues to pay the major portion of your health care program ($520 each month). We think it's a wise investment.

Enclosure

PRESENTING BAD NEWS IN OTHER CULTURES

Communicating bad news in other cultures may require different strategies.

To minimize disappointment, Westerners generally prefer to present negative messages indirectly. Other cultures may treat bad news differently.

In Germany, for example, business communicators occasionally use buffers but tend to present bad news directly. British writers also tend to be straightforward with bad news, seeing no reason to soften its announcement. In Latin countries the question is not how to organize negative messages but whether to present them at all. It's considered disrespectful and impolite to report bad news to superiors. Thus, reluctant employees may fail to report accurately any negative messages to their bosses.

In Asian cultures, harmony and peace are sought in all relationships. Disrupting the harmony with bad news is avoided. To prevent discord, Japanese communicators use a number of techniques to indicate *no*—without being forced to say it. In conversation they may respond with silence or with a counter question, such as "Why do you ask?" They may change the subject or tell a white lie to save face for themselves and for the questioner. Sometimes the answer sounds like a qualified *yes*: "I will do my best, but if I cannot, I hope you will understand," "Yes, but . . . ," or "yes" followed by an apology. All of these responses should be recognized as *no*.

In China, Westerners often have difficulty understanding the "hints" given by communicators.

> "I agree" might mean "I agree with 15 percent of what you say."
> "We might be able to" could mean "Not a chance."
> "We will consider" could mean "WE will, but the real decision maker will not."
> "That is a little too much" might equate to "That is outrageous."[8]

In Thailand the negativism represented by a refusal is completely alien; the word *no* does not exist. In many cultures negative news is offered with such subtleness or in such a positive light that it may be overlooked or misunderstood by literal-minded low-context cultures. To understand the meaning of what's really being communicated, we must look beyond an individual's actual words, considering the communication style, the culture, and especially the context.

You've now studied the indirect method for revealing bad news and analyzed many examples of messages applying this method. As you observed, business writers generally try to soften the blow; however, they do eventually reveal the bad news. No effort is made to sweep it under the carpet or ignore it totally.

SUMMARY OF LEARNING OBJECTIVES

1 **Describe the goals and strategies of business communicators in delivering bad news.** All businesses will occasionally deal with problems. Good communicators have several goals in delivering bad news: (a) making the reader understand and accept the bad news, (b) promoting and maintaining a good image of themselves and their organizations, (c) making the message so clear that additional correspondence is unnecessary, and (d) avoiding creating legal liability or responsibility. The indirect pattern involves delaying the bad news until reasons have been presented. The direct pattern reveals the main idea immediately. The direct pattern is preferable when (a) the receiver may overlook the bad news, (b) organization policy suggests directness, (c) the receiver prefers directness, (d) firmness is neces-

sary, and (e) the bad news is not damaging. Careful communicators will avoid careless and abusive language, which is actionable when it is false, damages a person's reputation, and is "published" (spoken within the presence of others or written). Messages written on company stationery represent that company and can be legally binding.

2 **Explain techniques for delivering bad news sensitively.** Begin with a buffer, such as a compliment, appreciation, a point of agreement, objective information, understanding, or some part of the message that represents good news. Then explain the reasons that necessitate the bad news, trying to cite benefits to the reader or others. Choose positive words, and clarify company policy if necessary. Announce the bad news strategically, mentioning a compromise or alternative if possible. Close pleasantly with a forward-looking goodwill statement.

3 **Identify routine requests and describe a strategy for refusing such requests.** Routine requests ask for favours, money, information, action, and other items. When the answer will be disappointing, use the reasons-before-refusal pattern. Open with a buffer; provide reasons; announce the refusal sensitively; suggest possible alternatives; and end with a positive, forward-looking comment.

4 **Explain techniques for delivering bad news to customers.** When a company disappoints its customers, most organizations (a) call the individual involved, (b) describe the problem and apologize (when it is to blame), (c) explain why the problem occurred and what is being done to prevent its recurrence, and (d) follow up with a letter that documents the phone call and promotes goodwill. Some organizations also offer gifts or benefits to offset customers' disappointment and to reestablish the business relationship. In denying claims or refusing credit, begin indirectly, provide reasons for the refusal, and close pleasantly, looking forward to future business. When appropriate, resell a product or service.

5 **Explain techniques for delivering bad news within organizations.** When breaking bad news to employees, use the indirect pattern but be sure to provide clear, convincing reasons that explain the decision. In refusing job applicants, however, keep letters short, general, and tactful.

6 **Compare strategies for revealing bad news in different cultures.** North American communicators often prefer to break bad news slowly and indirectly. In other low-context cultures, such as Germany and Britain, however, bad news is revealed directly. In high-context cultures, straightforwardness is avoided. In Latin cultures bad news may be totally suppressed. In Asian cultures negativism is avoided and hints may suggest bad news. Subtle meanings must be interpreted carefully.

CHAPTER REVIEW

1. Discuss four goals of a business communicator who must deliver bad news. (Obj. 1)
2. How can business documents in an organization's files become part of a lawsuit? (Obj. 1)
3. Describe the four parts of the indirect message pattern. (Obj. 1)
4. Name five situations in which the direct pattern should be used for bad news. (Obj. 1)
5. Name five or more techniques to buffer the opening of a bad-news message. (Obj. 2)
6. Name four or more techniques to deemphasize bad news when it is presented. (Obj. 2)
7. Name four kinds of routine requests that businesses must frequently refuse. (Obj. 3)
8. Why should you be especially careful in cushioning the refusal to an invitation? (Obj. 3)
9. What is the major difference between bad-news messages for customers and those for other people? (Obj. 4)
10. Identify a process used by many business professionals in resolving problems with disappointed customers. (Obj. 4)
11. List four goals a writer seeks to achieve in writing messages that deny credit to prospective customers. (Obj. 4)
12. Why should a writer be somewhat vague in the reasons section of a letter rejecting a job applicant? (Obj. 4)
13. When organizations must reveal a crisis, how should they communicate the news to employees, customers, shareholders, and the public? (Objs. 4 and 5)
14. Why is the reasons-before-refusal strategy appropriate for customers who are unhappy with a product or service? (Obj. 4)
15. What actions are tactful, professional, and safe when a subordinate must personally deliver upsetting news to a superior? (Obj. 5)

CRITICAL THINKING

1. Does bad news travel faster and farther than good news? Why? What implications would this have for companies responding to unhappy customers? (Objs. 1–5)
2. Some people feel that all employee news, good or bad, should be announced directly. Do you agree or disagree? Why? (Objs. 1–5)
3. Consider times when you have been aware that others have used the indirect pattern in writing or speaking to you. How did you react? (Objs. 1–5)
4. In considering negative organization news, should companies immediately reveal grave illnesses of key executives? Or should executives be entitled to keep their health a private matter? Does it matter if the company is public or private? (Objs. 4 and 5)

ACTIVITIES

11.1 Organizational Patterns (Objs. 1–5)

Your Task. Identify which organizational pattern you would use for the following messages: direct or indirect.

a. A letter from an amusement park refusing the request of a customer who was unhappy with a substitute concert performer.
b. The last in a series of letters from a collection agency demanding payment of a long-overdue account. The next step will be hiring a lawyer.
c. A letter from a computer company refusing to authorize repair of a customer's computer on which the warranty expired six months ago.
d. A memo from an executive refusing a manager's plan to economize by purchasing reconditioned computers. The executive and the manager both appreciate efficient, straightforward messages.
e. A letter informing a customer that the majority of the customer's recent order will not be available for six weeks.

11.2 Passive-Voice Verbs (Obj. 2)

Your Task. Revise the following sentences to present the bad news with passive-voice verbs.

a. We will no longer be accepting credit cards for purchases under $5.
b. Company policy forbids us to give performance reviews until an employee has been on the job for 12 months.
c. Because management now requires more stringent security, we are postponing indefinitely requests for company tours.
d. Your car rental insurance coverage does not cover large SUVs.

11.3 Subordinating Bad News (Obj. 2)

Your Task. Revise the following sentences to position the bad news in a subordinate clause. (**Hint:** Consider beginning the clause with *Although.*) Use passive-voice verbs for the bad news.

a. Unfortunately, we no longer print a complete catalogue. However, we now offer all of our catalogue choices at our Web site, which is always current.

b. We appreciate your interest in our organization, but we are unable to extend an employment offer to you at this time.

c. It is impossible for us to ship your complete order at this time. However, we are able to send the four oak desks now; you should receive them within five days.

d. Provincial law does not allow smoking within 1.5 metres of a public building. But the college has set aside 16 outdoor smoking areas.

11.4 Implying Bad News (Obj. 2)

Your Task. Revise the following statements to *imply* the bad news. If possible, use passive-voice verbs and subordinate clauses to further deemphasize the bad news.

a. Unfortunately, we find it impossible to contribute to the fund-raising campaign this year. At present all the funds of my organization are needed to lease new equipment and offices for our new branch in Richmond. We hope to be able to support this endeavour in the future.

b. Because of the holiday period, all our billboard space was used this month. Therefore, we are sorry to say that we could not give your charitable group free display space. However, next month, after the holidays, we hope to display your message as we promised.

c. We cannot ship our fresh fruit baskets c.o.d. Your order was not accompanied by payment, so we are not shipping it. We have it ready, though, and will rush it to its destination as soon as you call us with your credit card number.

11.5 Evaluating Bad-News Statements (Obj. 2)

Your Task. Discuss the strengths or weaknesses of the following bad-news statements.

a. It's impossible for us to ship your order before May 1.

b. Frankly, we like your résumé, but we were hoping to hire someone a little younger who might be able to stay with us longer.

c. I'm thoroughly disgusted with this entire case, and I will never do business with shyster lawyers like you again.

d. We can assure you that on any return visit to our hotels, you will not be treated so poorly.

e. We must deny your credit application because your record shows a history of late payments, nonpayment, and irregular employment.

f. *(In a confidential company memo:)* I cannot recommend that we promote this young lady into any position where she will meet the public. Her colourful facial decoration, as part of her religion, may offend our customers.

11.6 Document for Analysis: Request Refusal (Objs. 1–3)

Your Task. Analyze the following letter. List its weaknesses. If your instructor directs, revise it.

✗ *Ineffective Letter*

Dear Mr. Waters:

Unfortunately, we cannot permit you to apply the lease payments you've been making for the past ten months toward the purchase of your Sako 600 copier.

Company policy does not allow such conversion. Have you ever wondered why we can offer such low leasing and purchase prices? Obviously, we couldn't stay in business long if we agreed to proposals such as yours.

You've had the Sako 600 copier for ten months now, Mr. Waters, and you say you like its versatility and reliability. Perhaps we could interest you in another Sako model—one that's more within your price range. Do give us a call.

11.7 Document for Analysis: Bad News for Customers (Objs. 1–4)

Your Task. Analyze the following letter. List its weaknesses. If your instructor directs, revise it.

✗ *Ineffective Letter*

Dear Charge Customers:

This letter is being sent to you to announce the termination of in-house charge accounts at Golden West Print and Frame Shop. We are truly sorry that we can no longer offer this service.

Because some customers abused the privilege, we must eliminate local charge accounts. We regret that we must take this action, but we found that carrying our own credit had become quite costly. To continue the service would have meant raising our prices. As a small but growing business, we decided it was more logical to drop the in-house charges. As a result, we are forced to begin accepting bank credit cards, including VISA and MasterCard.

Please accept our apologies and deepest regrets in reducing our services. We hope to see you soon when we can show you our new collection of museum-quality gilded wood frames.

11.8 Document for Analysis: Saying No to a Job Applicant (Objs. 1, 2, and 5)

Your Task. Analyze the following letter. List its weaknesses. If your instructor directs, revise it.

✗ *Ineffective Letter*

Dear Mr. Franklin:

Ms. Sievers and I wish to thank you for the pleasure of allowing us to interview you last Thursday. We were delighted to learn about your superb academic record, and we also appreciated your attentiveness in listening to our description of the operations of the Maxwell Corporation.

However, we had many well-qualified applicants who were interested in the advertised position of human resources assistant. As you may have guessed, we were particularly eager to find a minority individual who could help us fill out our employment equity goals. Although you did not fit one of our goal areas, we enjoyed talking with you. We hired a female graduate of Ryerson Polytechnic University who had most of the qualities we sought.

Although we realize that the job market is difficult at this time, you have our heartfelt wishes for good luck in finding precisely what you are looking for.

11.9 Request Refusal: Thumbs Down on PDAs for Vancouver Agents (Objs. 1–3)

George R. Hollings, president of Hollings Vancouver Realty, is not keen on using technology to sell real estate. As you learned in **Chapter 10, Activity 10.5**, he was asked to purchase PDAs plus software plus monthly updates for all 18 staff members of his firm. He did the math, and it figures out to be something like $6000 for the initial investment plus $4000 per year for updates. That's a lot of money for technology that he's not convinced is needed. He appreciated the tactful, logical, and persuasive memo that he received from a talented agent requesting this PDA support. He wants to respond in writing because he can control exactly what he says and a written response is more forceful. His memo will also make a permanent record of this decision, in case agents make similar requests in the future. The more he ponders the request, the more Mr. Hollings thinks that this kind of investment in software and hardware should be made by agents themselves—not by the agency.

Your Task. Put yourself in the place of Mr. Hollings and write a refusal that retains the goodwill of the agent yet makes it clear that this request cannot be granted.

11.10 Request Refusal: Saying No to Under-21 Crowd on Carnival Cruises (Obj. 3)

WEB

The world's largest cruise line finds itself in a difficult position. Carnival climbed to the number one spot by promoting fun at sea and pitching its appeal to younger customers who were drawn to on-board discos, swim-up bars, and hassle-free partying. But apparently the partying of high school and college students went too far. Roving bands of teens had virtually taken over some cruises in recent years. Travel agents complained of "drunken, loud behaviour," as reported by Mike Driscall, editor of *Cruise Week.*

To crack down, Carnival raised the drinking age from 18 to 21 and required more chaperoning of school groups. But young individual travellers were still unruly and disruptive. Thus, Carnival instituted a new policy, effective immediately. No one under 21 may travel unless accompanied by an adult over 25. Says Vicki Freed, Carnival's vice president for marketing, "We will turn them back at the docks, and they will not get refunds." As Eric Rivera, a Carnival marketing manager, you must respond to the inquiry of April Corcoran of Counsellor Travel, a travel agency that features special spring- and summer-break packages for college and high school students.

Counsellor Travel has been one of Carnival's best customers. However, Carnival no longer wants to encourage unaccompanied young people. You must refuse the request of Ms. Corcoran to help set up student tour packages. Carnival discourages even chaperoned tours. Its real market is now family packages. You must write to Counsellor and break the bad news. Try to promote fun-filled, carefree cruises destined for sunny, exotic ports of call that remove guests from the stresses of everyday life. By the way, Carnival attracts more passengers than any other cruise line—over a million people a year from all over the world. And over 98 percent of Carnival's guests say that they were well satisfied. For more information about Carnival, visit its Web site: **<www.carnival.com>**. There's no need to register; simply click "About Carnival."

Your Task. Write your letter to April Corcoran, Counsellor Travel Agency, 103 Juniper Crescent, Eastern Passage, NS B3G 1M1. Send her a schedule for spring and summer Caribbean cruises. Tell her you will call during the week of January 5 to help her plan special family tour packages.[9]

11.11 Damage Control for Disappointed Customers: Late Delivery of Printing Order (Obj. 4)

LISTENING SPEAKING

Kevin Kearns, a printing company sales manager, must tell one of his clients that the payroll cheques his company ordered are not going to be ready by the date Kearns had promised. The printing company's job scheduler overlooked the job and didn't get the cheques into production in time to meet the deadline. As a result, Kearns' client, a major insurance company, is going to miss its pay run.

Kearns meets with internal department heads. They decide on the following plan to remedy the situation: (1) move the cheque order to the front of the production line; (2) make up for the late production date by shipping some of the cheques—enough to meet their client's immediate payroll needs—by air freight; (3) deliver the remaining cheques by truck.[10]

Your Task. Form groups of three to four students. Discuss the following issues about how to present the bad news to Andrew Tyra, Kearns' contact person at the insurance company.

a. Should Kearns call Tyra directly or delegate the task to his assistant?
b. When should Tyra be informed of the problem?
c. What is the best procedure for delivering the bad news?
d. What follow-up would you recommend to Kearns?

Be prepared to share your group's responses during a class discussion. Your instructor may ask two students to role-play the presentation of the bad news.

11.12 Damage Control for Disappointed Customers: J. Crew Goofs on Cashmere Turtleneck (Obj. 4)

Who wouldn't want a cashmere zip turtleneck sweater for $18? At the J. Crew Web site, **<www.jcrew.com>**, many delighted shoppers scrambled to order the bargain cashmere. Unfortunately, the price should have been $218! Before J. Crew officials could correct the mistake, several hundred e-shoppers had bagged the bargain sweater for their digital shopping carts.

When the mistake was discovered, J. Crew immediately sent an e-mail message to the soon-to-be disappointed shoppers. The subject line shouted "Big Mistake!" Emily Woods, chairwoman of J. Crew, began her message with this statement: "I wish we could sell such an amazing sweater for only $18. Our price mistake on your new cashmere zip turtleneck probably went right by you, but rather than charge you such a large difference, I'm writing to alert you that this item has been removed from your recent order."

As an assistant in the communication department at J. Crew, you saw the e-mail message that was sent to customers and you tactfully suggested that the bad news might have been broken differently. Your boss says, "Okay, hot stuff. Give it your best shot."

Your Task. Although you have only a portion of the message, analyze the customer bad news message sent by J. Crew. Using the principles suggested in this chapter, write an improved e-mail message. In the end, J. Crew decided to allow customers who ordered the sweater at $18 to reorder it for $118.80 to $130.80, depending on the size. Customers were given a special Web site to reorder (make up an address). Remember that J. Crew customers are youthful and hip. Keep your message upbeat.[11]

11.13 Claim Denial: Depressed Mattress (Obj. 4)

TEAM

The following letter was sent in response to a customer's complaint about depressions in your company's BeautyTest mattress. Your company receives enough of these kinds of letters to warrant preparation of a standard response.

✗ *Ineffective Letter*

Dear Mrs. Kearney:

We have received your letter of May 23 demanding repair or replacement of your newly purchased BeautyTest mattress. You say that you enjoy sleeping on it; however, in the morning when you and your husband get up, you claim that the mattress has body impressions that remain all day.

Unfortunately, Mrs. Kearney, we can neither repair nor replace your mattress because those impressions are perfectly normal. If you will read your warranty carefully, you will find this statement: "Slight body impressions will appear with use and are not indicative of structural failure. The body-conforming coils and comfort cushioning materials are beginning to work for you and impressions are caused by the natural settling of these materials."

When you purchased your mattress, I'm sure your salesperson told you that the BeautyTest mattress has a unique, scientifically designed system of individually pocketed coils that provide separate support for each person occupying the bed. This unusual construction, with those hundreds of independently operating coils, reacts to every body contour, providing luxurious comfort. At the same time, this system provides firm support. It is this unique design that's causing the body impressions that you see when you get up in the morning.

Although we never repair or replace a mattress when it merely shows slight impressions, we will send our representative out to inspect your mattress, if it would make you feel better. Please call for an appointment at (800) 322-9800. Remember, on a BeautyTest mattress you get the best night's rest possible.

Your Task. To evaluate your writing skills, your boss asks you and some other interns to come up with a better response. If your letter is better, he may begin using it as a pattern for similar responses. The problem seems to be that customers don't understand how the unique coil system works. And they have not read the mattress warranty. Get together with your intern team and discuss the faults in this letter before generating a new, more effective letter. Write to the same customer.

11.14 Claim Denial: Long, Hot Summer (Obj. 4)

As Kissandra Powell, owner of Town & Country Landscaping, you must refuse the following request. Mr. and Mrs. Paul Alexander have asked that you replace the landscaping of the home they recently purchased in Regina. You had landscaped that home nearly a year ago for the former owner, Mrs. Hunter, installing a sod lawn and many shrubs, trees, and flowers. It looked beautiful when you finished, but six months later, Mrs. Hunter sold the property and moved to Summerville. Four months elapsed before the new owners moved in. After four months of neglect and a hot, dry summer, the newly installed landscaping suffered.

You guarantee all your work and normally would replace any plants that do not survive. Under these circumstances, however, you do not feel justified in making any refund because your guarantee necessarily presumes proper maintenance on the part of the property owner. Moreover, your guarantee is made only to the individual who contracted with you—not to subsequent owners. You would like to retain the goodwill of the new owners, since this is an affluent neighbourhood and you hope to attract additional work here. On the other hand, you can't afford to replace the materials invested in this job. You believe that the lawn could probably be rejuvenated with deep watering and fertilizer.

Your Task. Write to Mr. and Mrs. Paul Alexander, 3318 Clearview Drive, Regina, SK S4R 7W4 refusing their claim. You would be happy to inspect the property and offer suggestions to the Alexanders. In reality, you wonder if the Alexanders might not have a claim against the former owner or the escrow agency for failing to maintain the property. Clearly, however, the claim is not against you.

11.15 Credit Refusal: Risky Order for Cool Camera Phones (Obj. 4)

As a CellCity sales manager, you are delighted to land a sizable order for your new T-Mobile Nokia digital video camera phone. This great phone is too cool with its full-colour LCD, multimedia player, speaker phone, and voice dialling.

The purchase order comes from Beech Grove Electronics, a retail distributor in Regina, SK. You send the order on to Pat Huckabee, your credit manager, for approval of the credit application attached. To your disappointment, Pat tells you that Beech Grove doesn't qualify for credit. Equifax Credit Services reports that credit would be risky for Beech Grove.

Because you think you can be more effective in writing than on the telephone, you decide to write to Beech Grove with the bad news and offer an alternative. Suggest that Beech Grove order a smaller number of the camera phones. If it pays cash, it can receive a 2 percent discount. After Beech Grove has sold these fast-moving units, it can place another cash order through your toll-free order number. With your fast delivery system, its inventory will never be depleted. Beech Grove can get the camera phones it wants now and can replace its inventory almost overnight. Credit Manager Huckabee tells you that your company generally reveals to credit applicants the name of the credit reporting service it used and encourages them to investigate their credit record.

Your Task. Write a credit refusal to Jacob Jackson, Beech Grove Electronics, 3590 Plainfield Road, Regina, SK S4V 6W3.

11.16 Employee Bad News: Strikeout for Expanded Office Teams (Obj. 5)

Assume you are Hank James, vice president of Human Resources at Tissue Mills Paper Co. in Kingston, Ontario. Recently several of your employees requested that their spouses or friends be allowed to participate in Tissue Mills' intramural sports teams. Although the teams play only once a week during the season, these employees claim that they can't afford more time away from friends and family. Over 100 employees currently participate in the eight coed volleyball, softball, and tennis teams, which are open to company employees only. The teams were designed to improve employee friendships and to give employees a regular occasion to have fun together.

If nonemployees were to participate, you're afraid that employee interaction would be limited. And while some team members might have fun if spouses or friends were included, you're not so sure all employees would enjoy it. You're not interested in turning intramural sports into "date night." Furthermore, the company would have to create additional teams if many nonemployees joined, and you don't want the administrative or equipment costs of more teams. Adding teams also would require changes to team rosters and game schedules, which could be a problem for some employees. You do understand the need for social time with friends and families, but guests are welcome as spectators at all intramural games. Besides, the company already sponsors a family holiday party and an annual company picnic.

Your Task. Write an e-mail or hard-copy memo to the staff denying the request of several employees to include nonemployees on Tissue Mills' intramural sports teams.

C.L.U.E. REVIEW 11

Edit the following sentences to correct all language faults, including grammar, punctuation, spelling, and word confusions.

1. When delivering bad news you can reduce the disappointment by: (1) telling the reasons for the rejection, and (2) reveal the news with sensitivity.
2. Its important that you make sure the reciever understands the bad news, and excepts it.
3. The indirect pattern consists of 4 parts, buffer, reasons, bad news, and close.
4. Undoubtlessly the indirect pattern can not be used in every situation, however, it is often better than a blunt announcement of bad news.
5. When the bad news is not devastating references to re-sale, or promotion may be apropriate.
6. If the Vice President of our Company must announce a big increase in each employees contributions to health benefits should he use the indirect strategy.
7. Most of us prefer to be let down gently when were being refused something, thats why the reasons before refusal pattern is effective.
8. Publisher Malcolm Forbes said "To be agreeable while disagreeing—thats an art.
9. When a well known Tire company recalled 100s of thousands of tires it's President issued an apology to all injured customers'.
10. If I was you I would be more concerned with long term not short term returns on the invested capitol.

Unit 4

Reports and Proposals

Preparing to Write Business Reports

Organizing and Writing Typical Business Reports

Proposals and Formal Reports

Chapter 12

Preparing to Write Business Reports

LEARNING OBJECTIVES

1 *Describe business report basics, including functions, patterns, formats, and writing style.*

2 *Apply Guffey's 3-×-3 writing process to business reports.*

3 *Understand where to find and how to use print and electronic sources of secondary data.*

4 *Understand where to find and how to use sources of primary data.*

5 *Illustrate reports with graphics that create meaning and interest.*

6 *Recognize the purposes and techniques of documentation in business reports.*

UNDERSTANDING REPORT BASICS

1

Reports are common in North American business. In a low-context culture such as North America, our values and attitudes seem to prompt us to write reports. We analyze the pros and cons of problems, studying alternatives and assessing facts, figures, and details. We pride ourselves on being practical and logical. We solve problems by applying scientific procedures. When we must persuade management to support a project, we generally write a report laying out the case.

Management decisions in many organizations are based on information submitted in the form of reports. This chapter examines the functions, patterns, formats, and writing styles of typical reports. It also introduces the report-writing process and discusses methods of collecting, illustrating, and documenting data.

Effective business reports solve problems and answer questions systematically.

Business reports may range from informal half-page trip reports to formal 200-page financial forecasts. Reports may be presented orally in front of a group or electronically on a computer screen. Some reports appear as words on paper in the form of memos and letters. Others are primarily numerical data, such as tax reports or profit-and-loss statements. Some seek to provide information only; others aim to analyze and make recommendations. Although reports vary greatly in length, content, form, and formality level, they all have one common purpose: *Business reports are systematic attempts to answer questions and solve problems.*

Functions

In terms of what they do, most reports can be placed in two broad categories: informational reports and analytical reports.

Informational reports simply present data without analysis or recommendations.

Informational Reports. Reports that present data without analysis or recommendations are primarily informational. For such reports, writers collect and organize facts, but they do not analyze the facts for readers. A trip report describing an employee's visit to a trade show, for example, simply presents information. Other reports that present information without analysis involve routine operations, compliance with regulations, and company policies and procedures.

Analytical reports provide data, analyses, conclusions, and, if requested, recommendations.

Analytical Reports. Reports that provide data, analyses, and conclusions are analytical. If requested, writers also supply recommendations. Analytical reports may intend to persuade readers to act or to change their beliefs. Assume you're writing a feasibility report that compares several potential locations for a workout/fitness club. After analyzing and discussing alternatives, you might recommend one site, thus attempting to persuade readers to accept this choice.

Organizational Patterns

Like letters and memos, reports may be organized directly or indirectly. The reader's expectations and the content of a report determine its pattern of development, as illustrated in Figure 12.1. In long reports, such as corporate annual reports, some parts may be developed directly while other parts are arranged indirectly.

The direct pattern places conclusions and recommendations near the beginning of a report.

Direct Pattern. When the purpose for writing is presented close to the beginning, the organizational pattern is direct. Informational reports, such as the letter report shown in Figure 12.2, are usually arranged directly. They open with an introduction, followed by the facts and a summary. In Figure 12.2 the writer explains a legal services

FIGURE 12.1 Audience Analysis and Report Organization

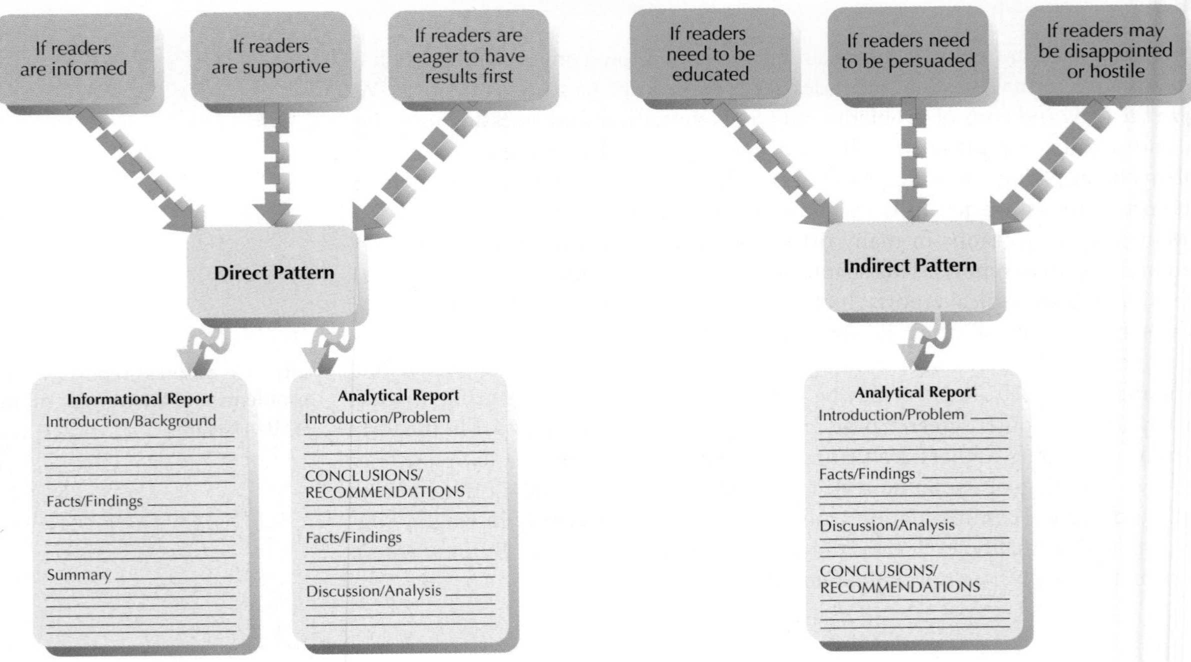

plan. The letter report begins with an introduction. Then it presents the facts, which are divided into three subtopics identified by descriptive headings. The letter ends with a summary and a complimentary close.

Analytical reports may also be organized directly, especially when readers are supportive or are familiar with the topic. Many busy executives prefer this pattern because it gives them the results of the report immediately. They don't have to spend time wading through the facts, findings, discussion, and analyses to get to the two items they are most interested in—conclusions and recommendations. Figure 12.3 illustrates such an arrangement. This analytical memo report describes environmental hazards of a property that a realtor has just listed. The realtor is familiar with the investigation and eager to find out the recommendations. Therefore, the memo is organized directly. You should be aware, though, that unless readers are familiar with the topic, they may find the direct pattern confusing. Many readers prefer the indirect pattern because it seems logical and mirrors the way we solve problems.

The indirect pattern is appropriate for analytical reports that seek to persuade or that convey bad news.

Indirect Pattern. When the conclusions and recommendations, if requested, appear at the end of the report, the organizational pattern is indirect. Such reports usually begin with an introduction or description of the problem, followed by facts and interpretation from the writer. They end with conclusions and recommendations. This pattern is helpful when readers are unfamiliar with the problem. It's also useful when readers must be persuaded or when they may be disappointed in or hostile toward the report's findings. The writer is more likely to retain the reader's interest by first explaining, justifying, and analyzing the facts and then making recommendations. This pattern also seems most rational to readers because it follows the normal thought process: problem, alternatives (facts), solution.

FIGURE 12.2 Informational Report—Letter Format

Tips for Letter Reports

- Use letter format for short informal reports sent to outsiders.
- Organize the facts section into logical divisions identified by consistent headings.
- Single-space the body.
- Double-space between paragraphs.
- Leave two blank lines above each side heading.
- Create side margins of 2.5 to 3 cm.
- Add a second-page heading, if necessary, consisting of the addressee's name, the date, and the page number.

Centre for Consumers of Legal Services
P.O. Box 260
Kitchener, ON N2K 2V5

Uses letterhead stationery for an informal report addressed to an outsider

September 7, 2007

Ms. Lisa Burgess, Secretary
Westwood Homeowners
3902 Westwood Drive
Guelph, ON N1H 6Y7

Dear Ms. Burgess:

As executive director of the Centre for Consumers of Legal Services, I'm pleased to send you this information describing how your homeowners' association can sponsor a legal services plan for its members. After an introduction with background data, this report will discuss three steps necessary for your group to start its plan.

Presents introduction and facts without analysis or recommendations

Introduction

A legal services plan promotes preventive law by letting members talk to lawyers whenever problems arise. Prompt legal advice often avoids or prevents expensive litigation. Because groups can supply a flow of business to the plan's lawyers, groups can negotiate free consultation, follow-up, and discounts.

Two kinds of plans are commonly available. The first, a free plan, offers free legal consultation along with discounts for services when the participating groups are sufficiently large to generate business for the plan's lawyers. These plans actually act as a substitute for advertising for the lawyers. The second common type is the prepaid plan. Prepaid plans provide more benefits, but members must pay annual fees, usually of $200 or more per year.

Since you inquired about a free plan for your homeowners' association, the following information describes how to set up such a program.

Arranges facts of report into sections with descriptive headings

Determine the Benefits Your Group Needs

The first step in establishing a free legal services plan is to meet with the members of your group to decide what benefits they want. Typical benefits include the following:

Free consultation. Members may consult a participating lawyer—by phone or in the lawyer's office—to discuss any matter. The number of consultations is unlimited, provided each is about a separate matter. Consultations are generally limited to 30 minutes, but they include substantive analysis and advice.

Emphasizes benefits in paragraph headings with boldface type

Free document review. Important papers—such as leases, insurance policies, and instalment sales contracts—may be reviewed with legal counsel. Members may ask questions and receive an explanation of terms.

Continued

FIGURE 12.2 Continued

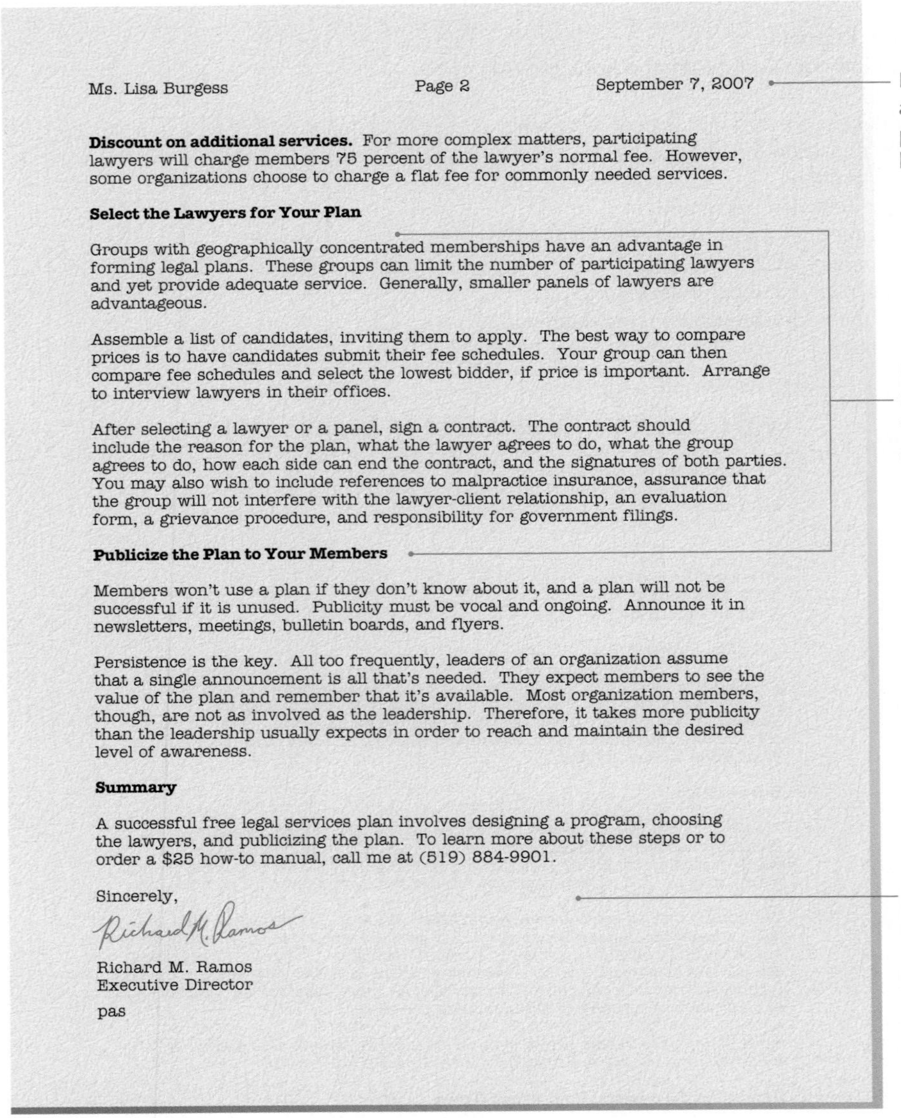

Ms. Lisa Burgess Page 2 September 7, 2007

Identifies second and succeeding pages with headings

Discount on additional services. For more complex matters, participating lawyers will charge members 75 percent of the lawyer's normal fee. However, some organizations choose to charge a flat fee for commonly needed services.

Select the Lawyers for Your Plan

Groups with geographically concentrated memberships have an advantage in forming legal plans. These groups can limit the number of participating lawyers and yet provide adequate service. Generally, smaller panels of lawyers are advantageous.

Assemble a list of candidates, inviting them to apply. The best way to compare prices is to have candidates submit their fee schedules. Your group can then compare fee schedules and select the lowest bidder, if price is important. Arrange to interview lawyers in their offices.

After selecting a lawyer or a panel, sign a contract. The contract should include the reason for the plan, what the lawyer agrees to do, what the group agrees to do, how each side can end the contract, and the signatures of both parties. You may also wish to include references to malpractice insurance, assurance that the group will not interfere with the lawyer-client relationship, an evaluation form, a grievance procedure, and responsibility for government filings.

Uses parallel side headings for consistency and readability

Publicize the Plan to Your Members

Members won't use a plan if they don't know about it, and a plan will not be successful if it is unused. Publicity must be vocal and ongoing. Announce it in newsletters, meetings, bulletin boards, and flyers.

Persistence is the key. All too frequently, leaders of an organization assume that a single announcement is all that's needed. They expect members to see the value of the plan and remember that it's available. Most organization members, though, are not as involved as the leadership. Therefore, it takes more publicity than the leadership usually expects in order to reach and maintain the desired level of awareness.

Summary

A successful free legal services plan involves designing a program, choosing the lawyers, and publicizing the plan. To learn more about these steps or to order a $25 how-to manual, call me at (519) 884-9901.

Sincerely,

Richard M. Ramos

Richard M. Ramos
Executive Director

pas

Includes complimentary close and signature

Formats

A report's format depends on its length, topic, audience, and purpose.

The format of a report is governed by its length, topic, audience, and purpose. After considering these elements, you'll probably choose from among the following four formats:

Letter Format. Use letter format for short (usually eight or fewer pages) informal reports addressed outside an organization. Prepared on office stationery, a letter report contains a date, inside address, salutation, and complimentary close, as shown in Figure 12.2. Although they may carry information similar to that found in correspondence, letter reports usually are longer and show more careful organization than most letters. They also include headings.

Memo Format. For short informal reports that stay within organizations, memo format is appropriate. Memo reports begin with *Date, To, From* and *Subject*, as shown in Figure 12.3. Like letter reports, memo reports differ from regular memos in length, use of headings, and deliberate organization.

Manuscript Format. For longer, more formal reports, use manuscript format. These reports are usually printed on plain paper instead of letterhead stationery or memo forms. They begin with a title followed by systematically displayed headings and subheadings. You will see examples of proposals and formal reports using manuscript formats in Chapter 14.

Printed Forms. Prepared forms are often used for repetitive data, such as monthly sales reports, performance appraisals, merchandise inventories, and personnel and financial reports. Standardized headings on these forms save time for the writer. Preprinted forms also make similar information easy to locate and ensure that all necessary information is provided.

Writing Style

Like other business messages, reports can range from informal to formal, depending on their purpose, audience, and setting. Research reports from consultants to their clients tend to be rather formal. Such reports must project an impression of objectivity, authority, and impartiality. But a report to your boss describing a trip to a conference would probably be informal.

Reports can be formal or informal depending on the purpose, audience, and setting.

Figure 12.4, which compares characteristics of formal and informal report-writing styles, can help you decide the writing style that is appropriate for your reports.

APPLYING GUFFEY'S 3-×-3 WRITING PROCESS TO REPORTS

2

Because business reports are systematic attempts to answer questions and solve problems, the best reports are developed methodically. The same 3-×-3 writing process that guided memo and letter writing can be applied to reports. Let's channel the writing process into seven specific steps:

The best reports grow out of a seven-step process beginning with analysis and ending with proofreading and evaluation.

- **Step 1:** Analyze the problem and purpose.
- **Step 2:** Anticipate the audience and issues.
- **Step 3:** Prepare a work plan.
- **Step 4:** Implement your research strategy.
- **Step 5:** Organize, analyze, interpret, and illustrate the data.
- **Step 6:** Compose the first draft.
- **Step 7:** Revise, proofread, and evaluate.

How much time you spend on each step depends on your report task. A short informational report on a familiar topic might require a brief work plan, little research, and no data analysis. A complex analytical report, on the other hand, might demand a comprehensive work plan, extensive research, and careful data analysis.

FIGURE 12.3 Analytical Report—Memo Format

Tips for Memo Reports

- Use memo format for most short (eight or fewer pages) informal reports within an organization.
- Leave side margins of 2.5 to 3 cm.
- Sign your initials on the *From* line.
- Use an informal, conversational style.
- For direct analytical reports, put recommendations first.
- For indirect analytical reports, put recommendations last.

Atlantic Environmental, Inc.

Interoffice Memo

Applies memo format for short, informal internal report

DATE: March 7, 2007

TO: Kermit Fox, President

FROM: Cynthia M. Rashid, Environmental Engineer CMR

SUBJECT: INVESTIGATION OF MOUNTAIN PARK COMMERCIAL SITE

For Laurentian Realty, Inc., I've completed a preliminary investigation of its Mountain Park property listing. The following recommendations are based on my physical inspection of the site, official records, and interviews with officials and persons knowledgeable about the site.

Uses first paragraph as introduction

Presents recommendations first (direct pattern) because reader is supportive and familiar with topic

Recommendations

To reduce its potential environmental liability, Laurentian Realty should take the following steps in regard to its Mountain Park listing:

- Conduct an immediate asbestos survey at the site, including inspection of ceiling insulation material, floor tiles, and insulation around a gas-fired heater vent pipe at 2539 Mountain View Drive.
- Prepare an environmental audit of the generators of hazardous waste currently operating at the site, including Mountain Technology.
- Obtain lids for the dumpsters situated in the parking areas and ensure that the lids are kept closed.

Combines findings and analyses in short report

Findings and Analyses

My preliminary assessment of the site and its immediate vicinity revealed rooms with damaged floor tiles on the first and second floors of 2539 Mountain View Drive. Apparently, in recent remodelling efforts, these tiles had been cracked and broken. Examination of the ceiling and attic revealed further possible contamination from asbestos. The insulation for the hot-water tank was in poor condition.

Located on the property is Mountain Technology, a possible hazardous waste generator. Although I could not examine its interior, this company has the potential for producing hazardous material contamination.

In the parking area large dumpsters collect trash and debris from several businesses. These dumpsters were uncovered, thus posing a risk to the general public.

In view of the construction date of the structures on this property, asbestos-containing building materials might be present. Moreover, this property is located in an industrial part of the city, further prompting my recommendation for a thorough investigation. Laurentian Realty can act immediately to eliminate one environmental concern: covering the dumpsters in the parking area.

FIGURE 12.4 Report-Writing Styles

	FORMAL WRITING STYLE	INFORMAL WRITING STYLE
Use	Theses Research studies Controversial or complex reports (especially to outsiders)	Short, routine reports Reports for familiar audiences Noncontroversial reports Most reports for company insiders
Effect	Impression of objectivity, accuracy, professionalism, fairness Distance created between writer and reader	Feeling of warmth, personal involvement, closeness
Characteristics	Absence of first-person pronouns; use of third-person *(the researcher, the writer)*	Use of first-person pronouns *(I, we, me, my, us, our)*
	Absence of contractions *(can't, don't)*	Use of contractions
	Use of passive-voice verbs *(the study was conducted)*	Emphasis on active-voice verbs *(I conducted the study)*
	Complex sentences; long words	Shorter sentences; familiar words
	Absence of humour and figures of speech	Occasional use of humour, metaphors
	Reduced use of colourful adjectives and adverbs	Occasional use of colourful speech
	Elimination of "editorializing" (author's opinions, perceptions)	Acceptance of author's opinions and ideas

To illustrate the planning stages of a report, we'll watch Diane Camas develop a report she's preparing for her boss, Mike Rivers, at Mycon Pharmaceutical Laboratories. Mike asked Diane to investigate the problem of transportation for sales representatives. Currently, some Mycon reps visit customers (mostly doctors and hospitals) using company-leased cars. A few reps drive their own cars, receiving reimbursements for use. In three months Mycon's leasing agreement for 14 cars expires, and Mike is considering a major change. Diane's task is to investigate the choices and report her findings to Mike.

Analyzing the Problem and Purpose

Before beginning a report, identify the problem to be solved in a clear statement.

The first step in writing a report is understanding the problem or assignment clearly. For complex reports it's wise to prepare a written problem statement. In analyzing her report task, Diane had many questions. Is the problem that Mycon is spending too much money on leased cars? Does Mycon wish to invest in owning a fleet of cars? Is Mike unhappy with the paperwork involved in reimbursing sales reps when they use their own cars? Does he suspect that reps are submitting inflated kilometre figures? Before starting research for the report, Diane talked with Mike to define the problem. She learned several dimensions of the situation and wrote the following statement to clarify the problem—both for herself and for Mike.

> **Problem Statement:** The leases on all company cars will be expiring in three months. Mycon must decide whether to renew them or develop a new policy regarding transportation for sales reps. Expenses and paperwork for employee-owned cars seem excessive.

Diane further defined the problem by writing a specific question that she would try to answer in her report:

Problem Question: What plan should Mycon follow in providing transportation for its sales reps?

Now Diane was ready to concentrate on the purpose of the report. Again, she had questions. Exactly what did Mike expect? Did he want a comparison of costs for buying cars and leasing cars? Should she conduct research to pinpoint exact reimbursement costs when employees drive their own cars? Did he want her to do all the legwork, present her findings in a report, and let him make a decision? Or did he want her to evaluate the choices and recommend a course of action? After talking with Mike, Diane was ready to write a simple purpose statement for this assignment.

A simple purpose statement defines the focus of a report.

Simple Statement of Purpose: To recommend a plan that provides sales reps with cars to be used in their calls.

Preparing a written purpose statement is a good idea because it defines the focus of a report and provides a standard that keeps the project on target. In writing useful purpose statements, choose active verbs telling what you intend to do: *analyze, choose, investigate, compare, justify, evaluate, explain, establish, determine,* and so on. Notice that Diane's statement begins with the active verb *recommend.*

Some reports require only a simple statement of purpose: *to investigate expanded teller hours, to select a manager from among four candidates, to describe the position of accounts supervisor.* Many assignments, though, demand additional focus to guide the project. An expanded statement of purpose considers three additional factors:

Setting boundaries on a project helps determine its scope.

- **Scope.** What issues or elements will be investigated? To determine the scope, Diane brainstormed with Mike and others to pin down her task. She learned that Mycon currently had enough capital to consider purchasing a fleet of cars outright. Mike also told her that employee satisfaction was almost as important as cost-effectiveness. Moreover, he disclosed his suspicion that employee-owned cars were costing Mycon more than leased cars. Diane had many issues to sort out in setting the boundaries of her report.
- **Significance.** Why is the topic worth investigating at this time? Some topics, after initial examination, turn out to be less important than originally thought. Others involve problems that cannot be solved, making a study useless. For Diane and Mike the problem had significance because Mycon's leasing agreement would expire shortly and decisions had to be made about a new policy for transportation of sales reps.
- **Limitations.** What conditions affect the generalizations and utility of a report's findings? In Diane's case her conclusions and recommendations might apply only to reps in her Edmonton sales district. Her findings would probably not be reliable for reps in Rimouski, Windsor, or Brandon. Another limitation for Diane is time. She must complete the report in four weeks, thus restricting the thoroughness of her research.

Diane decided to expand her statement of purpose to define the scope, significance, and limitations of the report.

Expanded Statement of Purpose: The purpose of this report is to recommend a plan that provides sales reps with cars to be used in their calls. The report will compare costs for three plans: outright ownership, leasing, and compensation for employee-owned cars. It will also measure employee reaction to each plan. The report is significant because Mycon's current leasing agreement expires April 1 and an improved plan could reduce costs and paperwork. The study is limited to costs for sales reps in the Edmonton district.

An expanded purpose statement considers scope, significance, and limitations.

After preparing a statement of purpose, Diane checked it with Mike Rivers to be sure she was on target.

Anticipating the Audience and Issues

Report writers must take into account both primary and secondary readers.

After defining the purpose of a report, a writer must think carefully about who will read it. Concentrating solely on a primary reader is a major mistake. Although one individual may have solicited the report, others within the organization may eventually read it, including upper management and people in other departments. A report to an outside client may first be read by someone who is familiar with the problem and then be distributed to others less familiar with the topic. Moreover, candid statements to one audience may be offensive to another audience. Diane could make a major blunder, for instance, if she mentioned Mike's suspicion that sales reps were padding their kilometre statements. If the report were made public—as it probably would be to explain a new policy—the sales reps could feel insulted that their integrity was questioned.

As Diane considered her primary and secondary readers, she asked herself these questions:

- *What do my readers need to know about this topic?*
- *What do they already know?*
- *What is their education level?*
- *How will they react to this information?*
- *Which sources will they trust?*
- *How can I make this information readable, believable, and memorable?*

Answers to these questions help writers determine how much background material to include, how much detail to add, whether to include jargon, what method of organization and presentation to follow, and what tone to use.

Major report problems should be broken into subproblems—or factored—to highlight possible solutions.

In the planning stages a report writer must also break the major investigative problem into subproblems. This process, sometimes called factoring, identifies issues to be investigated or possible solutions to the main problem. In this case Mycon must figure out the best way to transport sales reps. Each possible "solution" or issue that Diane considers becomes a factor or subproblem to be investigated. Diane came up with three tentative solutions to provide transportation to sales reps: (1) purchase cars outright, (2) lease cars, or (3) compensate employees for using their own cars. These three factors form the outline of Diane's study.

Diane continued to factor these main points into the following subproblems for investigation:

What plan should Mycon use to transport its sales reps?

I. Should Mycon purchase cars outright?
   A. How much capital would be required?
   B. How much would it cost to insure, operate, and maintain company-owned cars?
   C. Do employees prefer using company-owned cars?

II. Should Mycon lease cars?
   A. What is the best lease price available?
   B. How much would it cost to insure, operate, and maintain leased cars?
   C. Do employees prefer using leased cars?
III. Should Mycon compensate employees for using their own cars?
   A. How much has it cost in the past to operate employee-owned cars?
   B. How much paperwork is involved in reporting expenses?
   C. Do employees prefer being compensated for using their own cars?

Each subproblem would probably be further factored into additional subproblems. These issues may be phrased as questions, as Diane's are, or as statements. In factoring a complex problem, prepare an outline showing the initial problem and its breakdown into subproblems. Make sure your divisions are consistent (don't mix issues), exclusive (don't overlap categories), and complete (don't skip significant issues).

Preparing a Work Plan

A good work plan provides an overview of a project: resources, priorities, course of action, and schedule.

After analyzing the problem, anticipating the audience, and factoring the problem, you're ready to prepare a work plan. A good work plan includes the following:

- Statement of the problem (based on key background/contextual information)
- Statement of the purpose including scope, significance, and limitations
- Research strategy including description of the sources and methods of collecting data
- Tentative outline that factors the problem into manageable chunks
- Work schedule

Preparing a plan forces you to evaluate your resources, set priorities, outline a course of action, and establish a time schedule. Such a plan keeps you on schedule and also gives management a means of measuring your progress.

A work plan gives a complete picture of a project. Because the usefulness and quality of any report rest primarily on its data, you'll want to allocate plenty of time to locate sources of information. For firsthand information you might interview people, prepare a survey, or even conduct a scientific experiment. For secondary information you'll probably search printed materials such as books and magazines as well as electronic materials on the Internet and Web. Your work plan describes how you expect to generate or collect data. Since data collection is a major part of report writing, the next section of this chapter treats the topic more fully.

Figure 12.5 shows a complete work plan for a proposal to Lee Jeans. This work plan is particularly useful because it outlines the issues to be investigated. Notice that considerable thought and discussion—and even some preliminary research—are necessary to be able to develop a useful work plan.

Although this tentative outline guides investigation, it does not determine the content or order of the final report. You may, for example, study five possible solutions to a problem. If two prove to be useless, your report may discuss only the three winners. Moreover, you will organize the report to accomplish your goal and satisfy the audience. Remember that a busy executive who is familiar with a topic may prefer to read the conclusions and recommendations before a discussion of the findings. If the report is authorized by someone, be sure to review the work plan with that individual (your manager, client, or professor, for example) before proceeding with the project.

FIGURE 12.5 Work Plan for a Formal Report

Tips for Preparing a Work Plan

- Start early; allow plenty of time for brainstorming and preliminary research.
- Describe the problem motivating the report.
- Write a purpose statement that includes the report's scope, significance, and limitations.
- Describe the research strategy including data collection sources and methods.
- Divide the major problem into subproblems stated as questions to be answered.
- Develop a realistic work schedule citing dates for completion of major tasks.
- Review the work plan with whoever authorized the report.

Statement of Problem

Many women between the ages of 22 and 35 have trouble finding jeans that fit. Lee Jeans hopes to remedy that situation with its One True Fit line. We want to demonstrate to Lee that we can create a word-of-mouth campaign that will help it reach its target audience.

Defines purpose, scope, limits, and significance of report

Statement of Purpose

The purpose of this report is to secure an advertising contract from Lee Jeans. We will examine published accounts about the jeans industry and Lee Jeans in particular. In addition, we will examine published results of Lee's current marketing strategy. We will conduct focus groups of women in our company to generate campaign strategies for our pilot study of 100 BzzAgents. The report will persuade Lee Jeans that word-of-mouth advertising is an effective strategy to reach women in this demographic group and that BzzAgent is the right company to hire. The report is significant because an advertising contract with Lee Jeans would help our company grow significantly in size and stature.

Describes primary and secondary data

Research Strategy (Sources and Methods of Data Collection)

We will gather information about Lee Jeans and the product line by examining published marketing data and conducting focus group surveys of our employees. In addition, we will gather data about the added value of word-of-mouth advertising by examining published accounts and interpreting data from previous marketing campaigns, particularly those with similar age groups. Finally, we will conduct a pilot study of 100 BzzAgents in the target demographic.

Factors problem into manageable chunks

Tentative Outline

I. How effectively has Lee Jeans marketed to the target population (women, ages 22 to 35)?
   A. Historically, who has typically bought Lee Jeans products? How often? Where?
   B. How effective are the current marketing strategies for the One True Fit line?
II. Is this product a good fit for our marketing strategy and our company?
   A. What do our staff members and our sample survey of BzzAgents say about this product?
   B. How well does our pool of BzzAgents correspond to the target demography in terms of age and geographic distribution?
III. Why should Lee Jeans engage BzzAgent to advertise its One True Fit line?
   A. What are the benefits of word of mouth in general and for this demographic in particular?
   B. What previous campaigns have we engaged in that demonstrate our company's credibility?
   C. What are our marketing strategies, and how well did they work in the pilot study?

Estimates time needed to complete report tasks

Work Schedule

Investigate Lee Jeans and the One True Fit line's current marketing strategy	July 15–25
Test product using focus groups	July 15–22
Create campaign materials for BzzAgents	July 18–31
Run a pilot test with a selected pool of 100 BzzAgents	August 1–21
Evaluate and interpret findings	August 22–25
Compose draft of report	August 26–28
Revise draft	August 28–30
Submit final report	September 1

GATHERING INFORMATION FROM SECONDARY SOURCES

3

A report is only as good as its data.

One of the most important steps in the process of writing a report is that of gathering information (research). Because a report is only as good as its data, the remainder of this chapter describes finding, documenting, and illustrating data. As you analyze a report's purpose and audience, you'll assess the kinds of data needed to support your argument or explain your topic. Do you need statistics, background data, expert opinions, group opinions, or organizational data? Figure 12.6 lists five forms of data and provides questions to guide you in making your research accurate and productive.

Data fall into two broad categories, primary and secondary. Primary data result from firsthand experience and observation. Secondary data come from reading what

FIGURE 12.6 Gathering and Selecting Report Data

FORM OF DATA	QUESTIONS TO ASK
Background or historical	How much do my readers know about the problem? Has this topic/issue been investigated before? Are those sources current, relevant, and/or credible? Will I need to add to the available data?
Statistical	What or who is the source? How recent are the data? How were the figures derived? Will these data be useful in this form?
Expert opinion	Who are the experts? What are their biases? Are their opinions in print? Are they available for interviewing? Do we have in-house experts?
Individual or group opinion	Whose opinion(s) would the readers value? Have surveys or interviews been conducted on this topic? If not, do questionnaires or surveys exist that I can modify and/or use? Would focus groups provide useful information?
Organizational	What are the proper channels for obtaining in-house data? Are permissions required? How can I learn about public and private companies?

others have experienced and observed. Secondary data are easier and cheaper to develop than primary data, which might involve interviewing large groups or sending out questionnaires.

Primary data come from first-hand experience and observation; secondary data, from reading.

We're going to discuss secondary data first because that's where nearly every research project should begin. Often, something has already been written about your topic. Reviewing secondary sources can save time and effort and prevent you from "reinventing the wheel." Most secondary material is available either in print or electronically.

Print Resources

Although we're seeing a steady movement away from print to electronic data, print sources are still the most visible part of nearly all libraries. Much information is available only in print, and you may want to use some of the following print resources.

Print sources are still the most visible part of libraries.

By the way, if you are an infrequent library user, begin your research by talking with a reference librarian about your project. These librarians won't do your research for you, but they will steer you in the right direction. Many libraries help you understand their computer, cataloguing, and retrieval systems by providing advice, brochures, handouts, and workshops.

Books. Although quickly outdated, books provide excellent historical, in-depth data on subjects. Books can be located through print or computer listings.

Books provide historical, in-depth data.

- **Card catalogue.** Some libraries still maintain card catalogues with all books indexed on 3- by 5-inch cards alphabetized by author, title, or subject.
- **Online catalogue.** Most libraries today have computerized their card catalogues. Some systems are fully automated, thus allowing users to learn not only whether a book is located in the library but also whether it is currently available.

Periodicals. Magazines, pamphlets, and journals are called *periodicals* because of their recurrent or periodic publication. Journals, by the way, are compilations of scholarly articles. Articles in journals and other periodicals will be extremely useful to you because they are concise, limited in scope, current, and can supplement information in books.

Exploration of secondary data includes searching periodicals both in print and electronic forms.

- **Print indexes.** The *Readers' Guide to Periodical Literature* is a valuable index of general-interest magazine article titles. It includes such magazines as *Time, Newsweek, Maclean's,* and *The Canadian Forum.* More useful to business writers, though, will be the titles of articles appearing in business and industrial magazines (such as *Canadian Business, Canadian Banker,* and *Business Quarterly*). For an index of these publications, consult the *Business Periodicals Index.* The *Canadian Business Index* can be very useful too, listing articles from more than 200 Canadian business periodicals. Many of these indexes are also available in computerized form.
- **CD-ROM and Web-based bibliographic indexes.** Automated indexes similar to the print indexes just described are stored in CD-ROM and online databases. Many libraries now provide such bibliographic databases for computer-aided location of references and abstracts from magazines, journals, and newspapers, such as *The Globe and Mail.* When using CD-ROM and Web-based online indexes, follow the on-screen instructions or ask for assistance from a librarian.

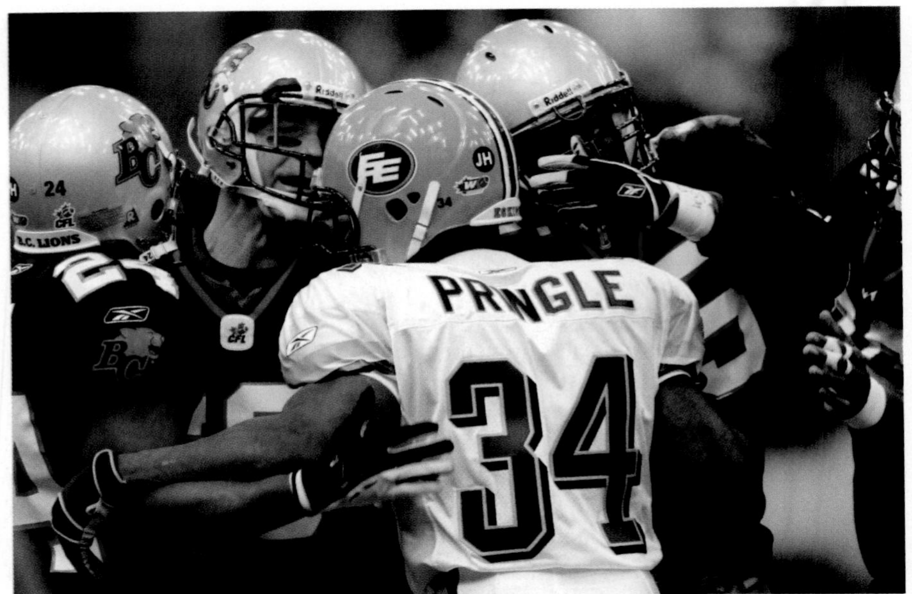

Investors in sports teams, equipment, broadcasting, sponsorship, and marketing require a steady stream of information, much of which comes from electronic databases. For example, the Sports Business Research Network offers a fee-based electronic database with information gathered from various sports governing bodies, magazines, newsletters, and the government. Sports investors and product developers use this electronic database to study leagues and teams, operating results, legal issues, and trends in major market segments, such as youth sports, women's sports, and extreme sports.

It's a good idea to begin with a subject search because it generally turns up more relevant citations than keyword searches (especially when searching for names of people or companies). Once you locate usable references, print a copy of your findings and then check the shelf listings to see if the publications are available.

Electronic Databases

Many researchers today begin by looking in electronic databases.

As a writer of business reports today, you will probably begin your secondary research with electronic resources. Most writers turn to them first because they are fast, cheap, and easy to use. This means that you can conduct detailed searches without ever leaving your office, home, or dorm room. Although some databases are still presented on CD-ROMs, information is increasingly available in online databases. They have become the staple of secondary research.

A database is a collection of information stored electronically so that it is accessible by computer and is digitally searchable. Databases provide both bibliographic (titles of documents and brief abstracts) and full-text documents. Most researchers today, however, prefer full-text documents. Various databases contain a rich array of magazine, newspaper, and journal articles, as well as newsletters, business reports, company profiles, government data, reviews, and directories. Provided with this textbook is access to InfoTrac, a Web-centred database that is growing rapidly. Web-based documents are enriched with charts, graphs, bold and italic fonts, colour, and pictures. Other well-known databases are Ingenta, ABI Inform, and Lexis Nexis.

Developing a search strategy and narrowing your search can save time. As you develop your strategy, think about the time frame for your search, the language of publication, and the types of materials you will need. One of the advantages of databases is the ability to focus a search easily. In addition, don't constrain yourself to English-language articles only; some Web sites offer translation services, and some of these services are free.

Although well stocked and well organized, specialized commercial databases are indeed expensive to use. Many also involve steep learning curves. While learning how to select *keywords* (or *descriptors*) and how to explore the database, you can run up quite a bill.

The World Wide Web

After e-mail, the most-used function of the Internet is the World Wide Web.[1] According to the federal government, Canadians surf the Internet more than any other people in the world.[2] To a business researcher, the Web offers a wide range of organizational and commercial information. You can expect to find such items as product and service facts, public relations material, mission statements, staff directories, press releases, current company news, government information, selected article reprints, collaborative scientific project reports, and employment information.

The Web offers trillions of pages of information.

Although a wealth of information is available, finding what you need can be frustrating and time-consuming. The constantly changing contents of the Web and its lack of organization make it more problematic for research than searching commercial databases such as InfoTrac. Moreover, Web content is uneven and often the quality is questionable.

The problem of gathering information is complicated by the fact that the total amount of information on the Web grows daily at the rate of over 7 million pages.[3] In addition, what is now being called the "deep" or "invisible" Web is 400 to 500 times larger than that of the "surface" Web, which is the part of the Web indexed by the most familiar search tools, such as Google.[4] Thus, to succeed in your search for information and answers, you need to understand the search tools. You also need to understand how to evaluate the information you find.

Search Tools. Finding what you are looking for on the Web is hopeless without powerful, specialized search tools, such as Google, AskJeeves, and Yahoo! These search tools can be divided into three types: subject directories, search engines, and search engine partners. Early in the history of the Internet, search tools usually were classified in only one category. Today, larger tools such as Yahoo! are actually search engines and subject directories combined. Subject directories fall into two categories—commercial ones (e.g., Yahoo!) and academic ones (e.g., Infomine). Organized into subject categories, these directories contain a collection of links to Internet resources submitted by site creators or evaluators. The best are excellent; the worst can be misleading or out-of-date.

Search tools such as Google, Yahoo!, and AskJeeves help you locate specific Web sites and information.

Search engines and search engine partners, sometimes referred to as second-generation search tools, are gaining popularity and becoming more sophisticated. Search engines such as Google use automated software "spiders" that crawl through the Web at regular intervals to collect and index the information from each location visited. Search engine partners, such as AskJeeves, use natural language processing technology to enable you to ask questions to gather information. Both tools will help you search for specific information.

Even though search engines such as Google boast about the numbers of items they have indexed (e.g., close to 6 billion),[5] no single search engine or directory can come close to indexing all of the pages on the Internet. In fact, according to the NEC Research Institute, these engines index less than 16 percent of the surface Web, or what we commonly call the World Wide Web, and only about 0.03 percent of the total pages available on the surface and invisible Webs combined.[6]

No search engine or directory indexes all Web pages.

The invisible Web is considerably different from the surface Web. Some researchers claim that it has 500 times more data than the surface Web.[7] Much of that information is dynamic and changing constantly (e.g., data in job banks, flight information, geographical and company information), and some is accessible only through paid subscription sites such as Hoover's. Other information such as that contained in many government databases is free, but often it too is not easily accessed. To help you search for data on both the visible and invisible Webs, consider using the search tools listed in Figure 12.7.

FIGURE 12.7 Visible and Invisible Web Search Tools

VISIBLE WEB		
SEARCH ENGINES	**SIZE AND TYPE**	**KEY FEATURES**
Google <www.google.com> <www.google.ca>	Nearly 6 billion pages—over 4 billion fully indexed	Relevance ranking Advanced search options
Yahoo! Search <search.yahoo.com> <ca.yahoo.com>	Over 3 billion pages fully indexed	Relevance ranking Advanced search options (includes options for different languages)
MSN Search <search.msn.com>	Over 3 billion pages fully indexed	Advanced search options (including international search sites)
Teoma <www.teoma.com>	Over 1 billion pages fully indexed and 1 billion partially indexed	Subject-specific rankings Advanced search options (ten languages) "Refine" feature—suggests topics to explore after initial search
AskJeeves <www.askjeeves.com>	Over 1 billion pages fully indexed and 1 billion partially indexed	Natural language questions Relies on Teoma.com's technology Binoculars tool (preview search results)
Infospace <www.infospace.com>	N/A; relies on other search engines for data	Metasearch technology: searches Google, FAST, Yahoo!, About, AskJeeves, FindWhat, LookSmart, Inktomi
Vivisimo <www.vivisimo.com>	Slightly less than 1 billion pages indexed	Metasearch function clusters results into categories Advanced search options and help
LookSmart <search.looksmart.com>	Over 2.3 billion pages indexed	Primarily a human-compiled directory Articles tab provides access to thousands of periodicals Uses textual analysis of hyperlinks, Web page popularity, and user feedback
HotBot <www.hotbot.com>	N/A; relies on other search engines for data	Quick check of three major search engine databases (Google, Yahoo!, AskJeeves/Teoma) Advanced search options and help
Open Directory Project <http://dmoz.org>	Over 3 billion pages indexed	Comprehensive human-edited directory (59 000+ editors)

INVISIBLE OR DEEP WEB	
InfoMine <http://infomine.ucr.edu>	Directory of nearly 120 000 sites, grouped into nine indexed and annotated categories for scholarly research
About <http://www.about.com>	Directory that organizes content from over 1 million sites with commentary from chosen experts
Librarian's Index to the Internet <http://lii.org/>	Directory of 14 000 well-chosen and annotated sites of use for academic research
ProFusion <http://www.profusion.com>	Updated, metasearch engine that offers access to subject categories 21+ categories; option to create new categories
CompletePlanet <http://www.completeplanet.com/>	Directory with over 70 000 searchable databases and specialty search engines

Internet Search Tips and Techniques. To conduct a thorough search for information you need, build a (re)search strategy by understanding the tools available.

You must know how to use search engines to make them most effective.

- **Use two or three search tools.** Begin by conducting a topic search. Use a subject directory such as Yahoo! or UK's BUBL link at <**http://bubl.ac.uk/link/**>. Once you have narrowed your topic, switch to a search engine or search engine partner.
- **Understand case-sensitivity.** Generally use lowercase for your searches, unless you are searching for a term that is usually written in upper and lowercase, such as a person's name.
- **Use nouns as search words and up to six or eight words in a query.** The right keywords—and more of them—can narrow the search effectively.
- **Combine keywords into phrases.** Phrases, marked by the use of quotation marks (e.g., "business ethics") will limit results to specific matches.
- **Omit articles and prepositions.** These are known as "stop words," and they do not add value to a search. Instead of *request for proposal*, use *proposal request.*
- **Use wild cards.** Most search engines support wild cards, such as asterisks. For example, the search term *cent** will retrieve *cents*, while *cent*** will retrieve both *centre* and *center.*
- **Know your search tool.** When connecting to a search service for the first time, always read the description of its service, including its FAQs (Frequently Asked Questions), Help, and How to Search sections. Often there are special features (e.g., News Category on AskJeeves) that can speed up the search process.

Effective Web searches use two or more tools and precise, uncommon keywords.

- **Learn basic Boolean search strategies.** You can save yourself a lot of time and frustration by narrowing your search with the following Boolean operators:

  AND — Identifies only documents containing all of the specified words: **employee AND productivity AND morale**

  OR — Identifies documents containing at least one of the specified words: **employee OR productivity OR morale**

  NOT — Excludes documents containing the specified word: **employee productivity NOT morale**

  NEAR — Finds documents containing target words or phrases within a specified distance, for instance, within ten words: **employee NEAR productivity**

- **Bookmark the best.** To keep track of your favourite Internet sites, save them as bookmarks or favourites.
- **Keep trying.** If a search produces no results, check your spelling. If you are using Boolean operators, check the syntax of your queries. Try synonyms and variations on words. Try to be less specific in your search term. If your search produces too many hits, try to be more specific. Think of words that uniquely identify what you're looking for. Use as many relevant keywords as possible.
- **Repeat your search a week later.** For the best results, return to your search a couple of days or a week later. The same keywords will probably produce additional results. That's because millions of new pages are being added to the Web every day.

Remember, subject directories and search engines vary in their contents, features, selectivity, accuracy, and retrieval technologies. Only through clever cybersearching can you uncover the jewels hidden on the Internet.

Evaluate the currency, authority, content, and accuracy of Web sites carefully.

Evaluating Web Sources. Most of us using the Web have a tendency to assume that any information turned up via a search engine has somehow been evaluated as part of a valid selection process.[8] Wrong! The truth is that the Internet is rampant with unreliable sites that reside side by side with reputable sites. Anyone with a computer and an Internet connection can publish anything on the Web. Unlike library-based research, information at many sites has not undergone the editing or scrutiny of scholarly publication procedures. The information we read in journals and most reputable magazines is reviewed, authenticated, and evaluated. That's why we have learned to trust these sources as valid and authoritative. But information on the Web is much less reliable. Some sites exist to distribute propaganda; others want to sell you something. To use the Web meaningfully, you must scrutinize what you find. Here are specific questions to ask as you examine a site.

- **Currency.** What is the date of the Web page? When was it last updated? Is some of the information obviously out of date? If the information is time-sensitive and the site has not been updated recently, the site is probably not reliable.
- **Authority.** Who publishes or sponsors this Web page? What makes the presenter an authority? Is a contact address available for the presenter? Learn to be skeptical about data and assertions from individuals whose credentials are not verifiable.
- **Content.** Is the purpose of the page to entertain, inform, convince, or sell? How would you classify this page (e.g., news, personal, advocacy, reference)? Who is the intended audience, based on content, tone, and style? Can you judge the overall value of the content compared with the other resources on this topic? Web presenters with a slanted point of view cannot be counted on for objective data.
- **Accuracy.** Do the facts that are presented seem reliable to you? Do you find errors in spelling, grammar, or usage? Do you see any evidence of bias? Are footnotes provided? If you find numerous errors and if facts are not referenced, you should be alerted that the data may be questionable.

GATHERING INFORMATION FROM PRIMARY SOURCES

4

Business reports often rely on primary data.

Up to this point, we've been talking about secondary data. You should begin nearly every business report assignment by evaluating the available secondary data. However, you'll probably need primary data to give a complete picture. Business reports that solve specific current problems typically rely on primary, firsthand data. Providing answers to business problems often means generating primary data through surveys, interviews, observation, or experimentation.

Surveys

Surveys yield efficient and economical primary data for reports.

Surveys collect data from groups of people. When companies develop new products, for example, they often survey consumers to learn their needs. The advantages of surveys are that they gather data economically and efficiently. Mailed surveys reach big groups nearby or at great distances. Moreover, people responding to mailed surveys have time to consider their answers, thus improving the accuracy of the data.

Mailed questionnaires, of course, have disadvantages. Most of us rank them with junk mail, so response rates may be no higher than 15 percent. Furthermore, those who do respond may not represent an accurate sample of the overall population, thus invalidating generalizations from the group. A final problem with surveys has to do with truthfulness. Some respondents exaggerate their incomes or distort other facts, thus causing the results to be unreliable. Nevertheless, surveys may be the best way to generate data for business and student reports. In preparing print or electronic surveys, consider these pointers:

Although mailed surveys may suffer low response rates, they are still useful in generating primary data.

- **Explain why the survey is necessary.** In a cover letter or an opening paragraph, describe the need for the survey. Suggest how someone or something other than you will benefit. If appropriate, offer to send recipients a copy of the findings.
- **Consider incentives.** If the survey is long, persuasive techniques may be necessary. Response rates can be increased by offering money (such as a loonie), coupons, gift certificates, free books, or other gifts.
- **Limit the number of questions.** Resist the temptation to ask for too much. Request only information you will use. Don't, for example, include demographic questions (income, gender, age, and so forth) unless the information is necessary to evaluate responses.
- **Use questions that produce quantifiable answers.** Check-off, multiple-choice, yes-no, and scale (or rank-order) questions (illustrated in Figure 12.8) provide quantifiable data that are easily tabulated. Responses to open-ended questions (*What should the bookstore do about plastic bags?*) reveal interesting, but difficult-to-quantify, perceptions.[9] To obtain workable data, give interviewees a list of possible responses (as shown in items 5–8 of Figure 12.8). For scale and multiple-choice questions, try to present all the possible answer choices. To be safe, add an "Other" or "Don't know" category in case the choices seem insufficient to the respondent. Many surveys use scale questions because they capture degrees of feelings. Typical scale headings are "agree strongly," "agree somewhat," "neutral," "disagree somewhat," and "disagree strongly."

Effective surveys target appropriate samples and ask a limited number of specific questions with quantifiable answers.

- **Avoid leading or ambiguous questions.** The wording of a question can dramatically affect responses to it. Because words have different meanings for different people, you must strive to use objective language and pilot test your questions with typical respondents. Stay away from questions that suggest an answer (*Don't you agree that the salaries of CEOs are obscenely high?*). Instead, ask neutral questions (*Do CEOs earn too much, too little, or about the right amount?*). Also avoid queries that really ask two or more things (*Should the salaries of CEOs be reduced or regulated by government legislation?*). Instead, break them into separate questions (*Should the salaries of CEOs be regulated by government legislation? Should the salaries of CEOs be reduced by government legislation?*).

The way a question is stated influences its response.

- **Select the survey population carefully.** Many surveys question a small group of people (a sample) and project the findings to a larger population. To be able to generalize from a survey, you need to make the sample as large as possible. In addition, you need to determine whether the sample is like the larger population. For important surveys you will want to consult books on or experts in sampling techniques.

The larger the sample, the more accurate the resulting data is likely to be.

- **Make it easy for respondents to return the survey.**
- **Conduct a pilot study.** Try the questionnaire with a small group so that you can remedy any problems. For example, in the survey shown in Figure 12.8, a pilot study revealed that female students generally favoured cloth book bags and were willing to pay for them. Male students opposed purchasing cloth bags. By adding a gender category, researchers could verify this finding. The pilot study also revealed the need to ensure an appropriate representation of male and female students in the survey.

FIGURE 12.8 Preparing a Survey

Prewriting 1

Analyze: The purpose is to help the bookstore decide whether it should replace plastic bags with cloth bags for customer purchases.

Anticipate: The audience will be busy students who will be initially uninterested.

Adapt: Because students will be unwilling to participate, the survey must be short and simple. Its purpose must be significant and clear.

Writing 2

Research: Ask students how they would react to cloth bags. Use their answers to form response choices.

Organize: Open by explaining the survey's purpose and importance. In the body ask clear questions that produce quantifiable answers. Conclude with appreciation and instructions.

Compose: Write the first draft of the questionnaire.

Revising 3

Revise: Try out the questionnaire with a small, representative group. Revise unclear questions.

Proofread: Read for correctness. Be sure that answer choices do not overlap and that they are complete. Provide "other" category if appropriate (as in No. 9).

Evaluate: Is the survey clear, attractive, and easy to complete?

North Shore College Bookstore
STUDENT SURVEY

The North Shore College Bookstore wants to do its part in protecting the environment. Each year we give away 45 000 plastic bags for students to carry off their purchases. We are considering changing from plastic to cloth bags or some other alternative, but we need your views.

Explains need for survey (use cover letter for longer surveys)

Please place checks below to indicate your responses.

Uses groupings that do not overlap (not 9 to 15 and 15 or more)

1. How many units are you presently carrying?
   ___ 15 or more units
   ___ 9 to 14 units
   ___ 8 or fewer units

   ___ Male
   ___ Female

2. How many times have you visited the bookstore this semester?
   ___ 0 times ___ 1 time ___ 2 times ___ 3 times ___ 4 or more times

3. Indicate your concern for the environment.
   ___ Very concerned ___ Concerned ___ Unconcerned

4. To protect the environment, would you be willing to change to another type of bag when buying books?
   ___ Yes
   ___ No

Indicate your feeling about the following alternatives.

Uses scale questions to channel responses into quantifiable alternatives, as opposed to open-ended questions

For major purchases the bookstore should	Agree	Undecided	Disagree
5. Continue to provide plastic bags.	___	___	___
6. Provide no bags; encourage students to bring their own bags.	___	___	___
7. Provide no bags; offer cloth bags at reduced price (about $3).	___	___	___
8. Give a cloth bag with each major purchase, the cost to be included in registration fees.	___	___	___
9. Consider another alternative, such as			

Allows respondent to add an answer in case choices provided seem insufficient

____

Please return the completed survey form to your instructor or to the survey box at the North Shore College Bookstore exit. Your opinion counts.

Tells how to return survey form

Thanks for your help!

Interviews

Some of the best report information, particularly on topics about which little has been written, comes from individuals. These individuals are usually experts or veterans in their fields. Consider both in-house and outside experts for business reports. Tapping these sources will call for in-person, telephone, or online interviews. To elicit the most useful data, try these techniques:

Interviews with experts yield useful report data, especially when little has been written about a topic.

- **Locate an expert.** Ask managers and individuals working in an area whom they consider to be most knowledgeable in their areas. Check membership lists of professional organizations, and consult articles about the topic or related topics. Most people enjoy being experts or at least recommending them. You could also post an inquiry to an Internet *newsgroup.* An easy way to search newsgroups in a topic area is through the browse groups now indexed by the popular search tool Google <**http://groups.google.com**>.
- **Prepare for the interview.** Learn about the individual you're interviewing as well as the background and terminology of the topic. Let's say you're interviewing a corporate communication expert about producing an in-house newsletter. You ought to be familiar with terms like *font* and software like QuarkXpress, Adobe Pagemaker, and Ventura Publisher. In addition, be prepared by making a list of questions that pinpoint your focus on the topic. Ask the interviewee if you may record the talk.
- **Maintain a professional attitude.** Call before the interview to confirm the arrangements and then arrive on time. Be prepared to take notes if your recorder fails (and remember to ask permission beforehand if you want to record). Use your body language to convey respect.
- **Make your questions objective and friendly.** Adopt a courteous and respectful attitude. Don't get into a debating match with the interviewee. And remember that you're there to listen, not to talk! Use open-ended, rather than yes-or-no, questions to draw experts out.
- **Watch the time.** Tell interviewees in advance how much time you expect to need for the interview. Don't overstay your appointment.
- **End graciously.** Conclude the interview with a general question, such as "Is there anything you'd like to add?" Express your appreciation, and ask permission to telephone later if you need to verify points.

Observation and Experimentation

Some kinds of primary data can be obtained only through firsthand observation and investigation. If you determine that the questions you have require observational data, then you need to plan the observations carefully. One of the most important questions is to ask what or whom you're observing and how often those observations are necessary to provide reliable data.

Some of the best report data come from firsthand observation and investigation.

When you observe, plan ahead. Arrive early enough to introduce yourself and set up whatever equipment you think is necessary. Make sure that you've received permission beforehand, particularly if you are recording. In addition, take notes, not only of the events or actions but also of the settings. Changes in environment often have an effect on actions.

Experimentation produces data suggesting causes and effects. Informal experimentation might be as simple as a pretest and posttest in a college course. Did students expand their knowledge as a result of the course? More formal experimentation is undertaken by scientists and professional researchers who control variables to test their effects. Assume, for example, that Cadbury Chocolate Canada Inc. wants to test the hypothesis (which is a tentative assumption) that chocolate lifts people out of the doldrums. An experiment testing the hypothesis would separate depressed individuals into two groups: those who ate chocolate (the experimental group) and those who did not (the control group). What effect did chocolate have? Such experiments are not done haphazardly, however. Valid experiments require sophisticated research designs and careful attention to matching the experimental and control groups.

ILLUSTRATING DATA

5 After collecting and interpreting information, you need to consider how best to present it. If your report contains complex data and numbers, you may want to consider using graphics such as tables and charts. These graphics clarify data, create visual interest, and make numerical data meaningful. By simplifying complex ideas and emphasizing key data, well-constructed graphics make key information easier to remember. However, the same data can be shown in many different forms, for example, in a chart, table, or graph. That's why you need to recognize how to match the appropriate graphics with your objective and incorporate it into your report.

Effective graphics clarify numerical data and simplify complex ideas.

Matching Graphics and Objectives

In developing the best graphics, you must first decide what data you want to highlight. Chances are you will have many points you would like to show in a table or chart. But which graphics are most appropriate for your objectives? Tables? Bar charts? Pie graphs? Line charts? Flow charts? Organization charts? Pictures? Figure 12.9 summarizes appropriate uses for each type of graphic. The following text discusses each visual in more detail.

Tables permit the systematic presentation of large amounts of data, while charts enhance visual comparisons.

Tables. Probably the most frequently used graphic in reports is the table. Because a table presents quantitative or verbal information in systematic columns and rows, it can clarify large quantities of data in small spaces. You may have made rough tables to help you organize the raw data collected from literature, questionnaires, or interviews. In preparing tables for your readers or listeners, though, you'll need to pay more attention to clarity and emphasis. Here are tips for making good tables.

- Provide clear headings for the rows and columns.
- Identify the units in which figures are given (percentages, dollars, units per worker hour, and so forth) in the table title, in the column or row head, with the first item in a column, or in a note at the bottom.
- Provide titles and labels at the top of the table.
- Arrange items in a logical order (alphabetical, chronological, geographical, highest to lowest) depending on what you need to emphasize.
- Use *N/A* (not available) for missing data.
- Make long tables easier to read by shading alternate lines or by leaving a blank line after groups of five.
- Place tables as close as possible to the place where they are mentioned in the text.

Bar Charts. Although they lack the precision of tables, bar charts enable you to make emphatic visual comparisons. Bar charts can be used to compare related items, illustrate changes in data over time, and show segments as part of a whole.

FIGURE 12.9 Matching Graphics to Objectives

Graphics	Objective
Table	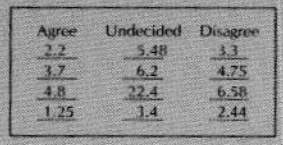 To show exact figures and values
Bar chart	 To compare one item with others
Line chart	 To demonstrate changes in quantitative data over time
Pie graph	 To visualize a whole unit and the proportions of its components
Flow chart	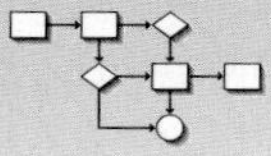 To display a process or procedure
Organization chart	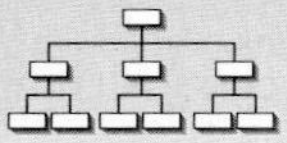 To define a hierarchy of elements
Photograph, map, illustration	 To create authenticity, to spotlight a location, and to show an item in use

Selecting an appropriate graphic form depends on the purpose that it serves.

Many techniques for constructing tables also hold true for bar charts. Here are a few additional tips:

- Keep the length of each bar and segment proportional.
- Include a total figure in the middle of a bar or at its end if the figure helps the reader and does not clutter the chart.
- Start dollar or percentage amounts at zero.
- Avoid showing too much information, thus producing clutter and confusion.
- Place the first bar at some distance (usually half the amount of space between bars) from the *y* axis.

Line Charts. The major advantage of line charts is that they show changes over time, thus indicating trends. The vertical axis is typically the dependent variable, and the horizontal axis the independent one. Simple line charts show just one variable. Multiple-line charts combine several variables. Segmented line charts, also called surface charts, illustrate how the components of a whole change over time.

Line charts illustrate trends and changes in data over time.

Here are tips for preparing a line chart:

- Begin with a grid divided into squares.
- Arrange the time component (usually years) horizontally across the bottom; arrange values for the other variable vertically.

- Draw small dots at the intersections to indicate each value at a given year.
- Connect the dots and add colour if desired.
- To prepare a segmented (surface) chart, plot the first value (say, video income) across the bottom; add the next item (say, motion picture income) to the first figures for every increment; for the third item (say, theme park income) add its value to the total of the first two items. The top line indicates the total of the three values.

Pie graphs are most useful in showing the proportion of parts to a whole.

Pie Graphs. Pie, or circle, graphs enable readers to see a whole and the proportion of its components, or wedges. Although less flexible than bar or line charts, pie graphs are useful in showing percentages. They are very effective for nonexpert audiences. A wedge can be "exploded" or popped out for special emphasis.

For the most effective pie graphs, follow these suggestions:

- Begin at the 12 o'clock position, drawing the largest wedge first. (Computer software programs don't always observe this advice, but if you're drawing your own graphs, you can.)
- Include, if possible, the actual percentage or absolute value for each wedge.
- Use four to eight segments for best results; if necessary, group small portions into one wedge called "Other."
- Draw radii from the centre.
- Distinguish wedges with colour, shading, or crosshatching.
- Keep all the labels horizontal.

Many software programs help you prepare professional-looking graphs with a minimum of effort.

Flow Charts. Procedures are simplified and clarified by diagramming them in a flow chart. Whether you need to describe the procedure for handling a customer's purchase order or outline steps in solving a problem, flow charts help the reader visualize the process. Traditional flow charts use the following symbols:

- Ovals to designate the beginning and end of a process
- Diamonds to denote decision points
- Rectangles to represent major activities or steps

Organization charts show the line of command and thus the flow of official communication from management to employees.

Organization Charts. Many large organizations are so complex that they need charts to show the chain of command, from the boss down to line managers and employees. Organization charts provide such information as who reports to whom, how many subordinates work for each manager (the span of control), and what channels of official communication exist. They may also illustrate a company's structure (by function, customer, or product, for example), the work being performed in each job, and the hierarchy of decision making.

Computer technology permits photographs, maps, and illustrations to be scanned directly into a report.

Photographs, Maps, and Illustrations. Some business reports include photographs, maps, and illustrations to serve specific purposes. Photos, for example, add authenticity and provide a visual record. Maps enable report writers to depict activities or concentrations geographically, such as dots indicating sales reps in provinces across the country. Illustrations and diagrams are useful in indicating how an object looks or operates. With today's computer technology, photographs, maps, and illustrations can be scanned directly into business reports.

Incorporating Graphics Into Reports

Used appropriately, graphics make reports more interesting and easier to understand. In putting graphics into your reports, follow these suggestions for best effects.

Effective graphics are accurate and ethical, avoid overuse of colour or decorations, and include titles.

- **Evaluate the audience.** Evaluate the reader, the content, your schedule, and your budget (graphics take time and money to prepare) in deciding how many graphics to use. Six charts in an internal report to an executive may seem like overkill; but in a long technical report to outsiders, six may be too few.
- **Use restraint.** Don't overuse colour or decorations. Although colour can effectively distinguish bars or segments in charts, too much colour can be distracting and confusing. Remember, too, that colours themselves sometimes convey meaning: reds suggest deficits or negative values, blues suggest coolness, and yellow may suggest warning.
- **Be accurate and ethical.** Double-check all graphics for accuracy of figures and calculations. Be certain that your visuals aren't misleading—either accidentally or intentionally. Manipulation of a chart scale can make trends look steeper and more dramatic than they really are. Also, be sure to cite sources when you use someone else's facts.

Textual graphics should be introduced by statements that help readers interpret them.

- **Introduce a graphic meaningfully.** Refer to every graphic in the text, and place the graphic close to the point where it is mentioned. Most important, though, help the reader understand the significance of a graphic. You can do this by telling the reader what to look for or by summarizing the main point of a graphic. Don't assume the reader will automatically draw the same conclusions you reached from a set of data. Instead of *The findings are shown in Figure 3*, tell the reader what to look for: *Two thirds of the responding employees, as shown in Figure 3, favour a flextime schedule.* The best introductions for graphics interpret them for readers.
- **Choose an appropriate caption or title style.** Like reports, graphics may use "talking" titles or generic, descriptive titles. "Talking" titles are more persuasive; they tell the reader what to think. Descriptive titles describe the facts more objectively.

Talking Title	**Descriptive Title**
Average Annual Health Care Costs per Worker Rise Steeply as Workers Grow Older	Average Annual Health Care Costs per Worker as Shown by Age Groups

Judge the style you should use by your audience and your company's preferences. Regardless of the style, make the titles consistent and specific.

DOCUMENTING DATA

In writing business and other reports, you will often build on the ideas and words of others. In Western culture whenever you "borrow" the ideas of others, you must give credit to your information sources. This is called *documentation.*

Purposes of Documentation

As a careful writer, you should take pains to properly document report data for the following reasons:

Documenting data lends credibility, protects the writer from plagiarism, and aids the reader.

- **To strengthen your argument.** Including good data from reputable sources will convince readers of your credibility and the logic of your reasoning.
- **To protect you from charges of plagiarism.** Acknowledging your sources keeps you honest. Plagiarism, which is illegal and unethical, is the act of using others' ideas without proper documentation.
- **To instruct the reader.** Citing references enables readers to pursue a topic further and make use of the information themselves.

Academic Documentation vs. Business Documentation

In the academic world documentation is critical. Especially in the humanities and sciences, students are taught to cite sources by using quotation marks, parenthetical citations, footnotes, and bibliographies. Academic term papers require full documentation to demonstrate that a student has become familiar with respected sources and can cite them properly in developing an argument. Giving credit to the author is extremely important. Students who plagiarize risk a failing grade in a class and even expulsion from school.

Business writers may not follow the same strict documentation standards as academic writers.

In the business world, however, documentation is often viewed differently. Business communicators on the job may find that much of what is written does not follow the standards they learned in school.[10] In many instances, individual authorship is unimportant. For example, employees may write for the signature of their bosses. The writer receives no credit. Similarly, team projects turn out documents written by many people, none of whom receives individual credit. Internal business reports, which often include chunks of information from previous reports, also fail to acknowledge sources or give credit. Even information from outside sources may lack proper documentation. Yet, if facts are questioned, business writers must be able to produce their source materials.

Although both internal and external business reports are not as heavily documented as school assignments or term papers, business communication students are well-advised to learn proper documentation methods. Your instructor may use a commercial plagiarism detection service, which can cross-reference much of the information on the Web, looking for documents with similar phrasing. The result, an "originality report," will provide the instructor with a clear idea of whether you've been accurate and honest.

Plagiarism of words or ideas is a serious charge, which can lead to academic penalties or loss of a job. You can avoid charges of plagiarism as well as add clarity to your work by knowing what to document and developing good research habits.

Learning What to Document

When you write reports, especially in college or university, you are continually dealing with other people's ideas. You are expected to conduct research, synthesize ideas, and build on the work of others. But you are also expected to give proper credit for borrowed material. To avoid plagiarism, you must give credit whenever you use the following:[11]

Give credit when you use another's ideas, when you borrow facts that are not common knowledge, and when you quote or paraphrase another's words.

- Another person's ideas, opinions, examples, or theory
- Any facts, statistics, graphs, and drawings that are not common knowledge
- Quotations of another person's actual spoken or written words
- Paraphrases of another person's spoken or written words

Information that is common knowledge requires no documentation. For example, the statement *The Globe and Mail is a popular business newspaper* would require no citation. Statements that are not common knowledge, however, must be documented. For example, *The Globe and Mail is the largest daily newspaper in Canada* would require a citation because most people do not know this fact. Cite sources for proprietary information such as statistics organized and reported by a newspaper or magazine. Also use citations to document direct quotations and ideas that you summarize in your own words.

Developing Good Manual and Electronic Research Habits

Report writers who are gathering information have two methods available for recording the information they find. The time-honoured manual method of note-taking works well because information is recorded on separate cards, which can then be arranged in the order needed to develop a thesis or argument. Today, though, writers rely heavily on electronic researching. Traditional notetaking methods may seem antiquated and laborious in comparison. Let's explore both methods.

Handwritten note cards help writers identify sources and organize ideas.

Manual Notetaking. To make sure you know whose ideas you are using, train yourself to take excellent notes. If possible, know what you intend to find before you begin your research so that you won't waste time on unnecessary notes. Here are some pointers on taking good notes:

- Record all major ideas from various sources on separate note cards.
- Include all publication data along with precise quotations.
- Consider using one card colour for direct quotes and a different colour for your paraphrases and summaries.
- Put the original source material aside when you are summarizing or paraphrasing.

Set up a folder for electronic notes, but be careful not to cut-and-paste excessively in writing reports.

Electronic Notetaking. Instead of recording facts on note cards, smart researchers today take advantage of electronic tools, as noted in the accompanying Tech Talk box. Here are some pointers on taking good electronic notes:

- Begin your research by setting up a folder on your hard drive or on a storage device (zip disk, USB pen, etc.). Create subfolders for major topics, such as introduction, body, and closing.
- When you find facts on the Web or in electronic databases, highlight the material you want to record, copy it, and paste it into a document in an appropriate folder.
- Be sure to include all publication data.
- Consider archiving on a zip disk those Web pages or articles used in your research in case the data must be verified.

Developing the Fine Art of Paraphrasing

Paraphrasing involves putting an original passage into your own words.

In writing reports and using the ideas of others, you will probably rely heavily on *paraphrasing,* which means restating an original passage in your own words and in your own style. To do a good job of paraphrasing, follow these steps:

- Read the original material intently to comprehend its full meaning.
- Write your own version without looking at the original.
- Do not repeat the grammatical structure of the original, and do not merely replace words with synonyms.

TECH TALK

Managing Your Electronic Research Data Like a Pro

In amassing electronic data, you can easily lose track of Web sites and articles you quoted. To document Web data that may change as well as to manage all of your electronic data, you need a specific plan for saving sources. At the very least, you will want to create a *working bibliography* in which you record the URL of each electronic source and its access date. Here are techniques that can help you build your bibliography as well as manage your electronic data like a pro:

- **Saving sources to disk** has advantages, including being able to open the document in a browser even if you don't have access to the Internet. More important, saving sources to disk ensures that you will have access to information that may or may not be available later. Using either the *File* and *Save As* or the *File* and *Save Page As* menu command in your browser, you will be able to store the information permanently. Saving images and other kinds of media can be accomplished with your mouse by either right-clicking or command-clicking on the item, followed by a command such as *Save Picture As* or *Save Image As* from a pop-up window.
- **Copying and pasting** information you find on the Web into word processing documents is an easy way to save and store it. Remember to also copy and paste the URL into the file as well, and record the URL in your working bibliography.
- **Printing** pages is a handy way to gather and store information. Doing so enables you to have copies of important data that you can annotate or highlight. Make sure the URL prints with the document (usually on the bottom of the page). If not, write it on the page.
- **Favourites lists and bookmarks** are options within browsers to enable users to record and store the URLs for important sources. The key to using these options is learning to create folders with names that are relevant and to use names for bookmarks that make sense and are not redundant. Pay attention or the browser will provide the information for you, relying on the name the Web page creator gave it. If no name is provided, the browser will default to the URL.
- **E-mailing** documents, URLs, or messages to yourself is another useful strategy. Many databases and online magazines permit you to e-mail information and sometimes the entire article to your account. If you combine the copy-and-paste function with e-mail, you can send yourself nearly any information you find on the Web.

- Reread the original to be sure you covered the main points but did not borrow specific language.

To better understand the difference between plagiarizing and paraphrasing, study the following passages. Notice that the writer of the plagiarized version uses the same grammatical construction as the source and often merely replaces words with synonyms. Even the acceptable version, however, requires a reference to the source author.

Source
The collapse in the cost of computing has made cellular communication economically viable. Worldwide, one in two new phone subscriptions is cellular. The digital revolution in telephony is most advanced in poorer countries because they have been able to skip an outdated technological step relying on land lines.

The plagiarized version uses the same sentence structure as the original and makes few changes other than replacing some words.

Plagiarized version
The drop in computing costs now makes cellular communication affordable around the world. In fact, one out of every two new phones is cellular. The digital revolution in cellular telephones is developing faster in poorer countries because they could skip an outdated technological process using land lines.

Acceptable paraphrase

Cellular phone use around the world is increasing rapidly as a result of decreasing computing costs. Half of all new phones are now wireless. Poorer countries are experiencing the most rapid development because they can move straight to cellular without focusing on outdated technology using land lines (Henderson 44).

The acceptable paraphrase presents ideas from a different perspective and uses a different sentence structure than the original.

Knowing When and How to Quote

On occasion you will want to use the exact words of a source. But beware of overusing quotations. Documents that contain pages of spliced-together quotations suggest that writers have few ideas of their own. Wise writers and speakers use direct quotations for three purposes only:

- To provide objective background data and establish the severity of a problem as seen by experts
- To repeat identical phrasing because of its precision, clarity, or aptness
- To duplicate exact wording before criticizing

Use quotations only to provide background data, to cite experts, to repeat precise phrasing, or to duplicate exact wording before criticizing.

When you must use a long quotation, try to summarize and introduce it in your own words. Readers want to know the gist of a quotation before they tackle it. For example, to introduce a quotation discussing the shrinking staffs of large companies, you could precede it with your words: *In predicting employment trends, Charles Waller believes the corporation of the future will depend on a small core of full-time employees.* To introduce quotations or paraphrases, use wording such as the following:

- According to Waller, ...
- Waller argues that . . . .
- In his recent study, Waller reported . . . .

Use quotation marks to enclose exact quotations, as shown in the following: "*The current image,*" *says Charles Waller,* "*of a big glass-and-steel corporate headquarters on landscaped grounds directing a worldwide army of tens of thousands of employees may soon be a thing of the past.*"

Using Citation Formats

You can direct readers to your sources with parenthetical notes inserted into the text and with bibliographies. The most common citation formats are those presented by the Modern Language Association (MLA) and the American Psychological Association (APA). Learn more about how to use these formats in Appendix B.

Guidelines for MLA and APA citation formats can be found in Appendix B; guidelines for electronic citations are at this book's Web site.

SUMMARY OF LEARNING OBJECTIVES

1 **Describe business report basics, including functions, patterns, formats, and writing style.** Business reports generally function either as informational reports (without analysis or recommendations) or as analytical reports (with analysis, conclusions, and possibly recommendations). Reports organized directly present the purpose immediately. This pattern is appropriate when receivers are supportive and are familiar with the topic. Reports organized indirectly provide the conclusions and recommendations last. This pattern is helpful when

receivers are unfamiliar with the problem or when they may be disappointed or hostile. Reports may be formatted as letters, memos, manuscripts, or prepared forms. Reports written in a formal style use third-person constructions, avoid contractions, and include many passive-voice verbs, complex sentences, and long words. Reports written informally use first-person constructions, contractions, shorter sentences, familiar words, and active-voice verbs.

2 **Apply Guffey's 3-×-3 writing process to business reports.** Report writers begin by analyzing a problem and writing a problem statement, which may include the scope, significance, and limitations of the project. Writers then analyze the audience and define major issues. They prepare a work plan, including a tentative outline and work schedule. They collect, organize, interpret, and illustrate their data. Then they compose the first draft. Finally, they revise (perhaps many times), proofread, and evaluate.

3 **Understand where to find and how to use print and electronic sources of secondary data.** Secondary data may be located by searching for books, periodicals, and newspapers through print or electronic indexes. Much report information today is located in electronic databases that are generally offered through professional information services such as Ingenta, ABI Inform, and Lexis Nexis. Much information is also available on the Internet, but searching for it requires knowledge of search tools and techniques. Popular search tools are Google and Yahoo! Search. Information obtained on the Internet should be scrutinized for currency, authority, content, and accuracy.

4 **Understand where to find and how to use sources of primary data.** Researchers generate firsthand, primary data through surveys (in-person, print, and online), interviews, observation, and experimentation. Surveys are most economical and efficient for gathering information from large groups of people. Interviews are useful when working with experts in a field. Firsthand observation can produce rich data, but it must be objective. Experimentation produces data suggesting causes and effects. Valid experiments require sophisticated research designs and careful attention to matching the experimental and control groups.

5 **Illustrate reports with graphics that create meaning and interest.** Good graphics improve reports by clarifying, simplifying, and emphasizing data. Tables organize precise data into rows and columns. Bar and line charts enable data to be compared visually. Line charts are especially helpful in showing changes over time. Pie graphs show a whole and the proportion of its components. Organization charts, pictures, maps, and illustrations serve specific purposes. In choosing or crafting graphics, smart communicators evaluate their audience, purpose, topic, and budget to determine the number and kind of graphics. They are consistent in writing "talking" titles (telling readers what to think about the graphic) or "descriptive" titles (summarizing the topic objectively).

6 **Recognize the purposes and techniques of documentation in business reports.** Documentation means giving credit to information sources. Careful writers document data to strengthen an argument, protect against charges of plagiarism, and instruct readers. Although documentation in business reports is less stringent than in academic reports, business writers should learn

proper techniques to be able to verify their sources and to avoid charges of plagiarism. Report writers should document others' ideas, facts that are not common knowledge, quotations, and paraphrases. Good notetaking, either manual or electronic, enables writers to give accurate credit to sources. Paraphrasing involves putting another's ideas into your own words. Quotations may be used to provide objective background data, to repeat identical phrasing, and to duplicate exact wording before criticizing.

CHAPTER REVIEW

1. What purpose do most reports serve? (Obj. 1)
2. How do informational and analytical reports differ? (Obj. 1)
3. How do the direct and indirect patterns of development differ? (Obj. 1)
4. Identify four common report formats. (Obj. 1)
5. List the seven steps in the report-writing process. (Obj. 2)
6. What is factoring? (Obj. 2)
7. How do primary data differ from secondary data? Give an original example of each. (Obj. 3)
8. What should a research strategy include? (Obj. 3)
9. Discuss five techniques that you think are most useful in enhancing a Web search. (Obj. 3)
10. What are four major sources of primary information? (Obj. 4)
11. Why is a pilot study necessary before conducting a survey? (Obj. 4)
12. Briefly compare the advantages and disadvantages of illustrating data with charts (bar and line) versus tables. (Obj. 5)
13. What is the major advantage of using a pie graph to illustrate data? (Obj. 5)
14. What is documentation, and why is it necessary in reports? (Obj. 6)
15. List two strategies for managing your research data. (Obj. 6)

CRITICAL THINKING

1. Discuss this statement made by three well-known professional business writers: "Nothing you write will be completely new."[12] (Objs. 1–4)
2. For long reports, why is a written work plan a wise idea? (Obj. 2)
3. Is information obtained on the Web as reliable as information obtained from journals, newspapers, and magazines? (Obj. 3)
4. Some people say that business reports never contain footnotes. If you were writing your first report for a business and you did considerable research, what would you do about documenting your sources? (Obj. 6)

ACTIVITIES

12.1 Report Functions, Writing Styles, and Formats (Obj. 1)

Your Task. For the following reports, (1) name the report's primary function (informational or analytical), (2) recommend a direct or indirect pattern of development, and (3) select a report format (memo, letter, or manuscript).

a. A persuasive proposal from a construction firm to the Ontario College of Art and Design describing the contractor's bid to construct the Sharp Pavilion, a controversial 15-storey table-top structure.
b. A report submitted by a sales rep to her manager describing her attendance at a sports products trade show, including the reactions of visitors to a new noncarbonated sports drink.
c. A recommendation report from a special review team (composed of members of the board of directors and staff) to the executive director of a major nonprofit organization to outline the necessary computer and phone system upgrades for the organization's headquarters building.
d. A progress report from a location manager to a Hollywood production company describing safety, fire, and environmental precautions taken for the shooting of a stunt involving blowing up a boat off the Toronto Islands.
e. A report prepared by an outside consultant examining whether a company should invest in a health and fitness centre for its employees.

12.2 Collaborative Project: Report Portfolio (Obj. 1)

TEAM

Your Task. In teams of three or four, collect four or more sample business reports illustrating various types of business reports. Don't forget corporate annual reports. For each report identify and discuss the following characteristics:

a. Function (informational or analytical)
b. Pattern (primarily direct or indirect)
c. Writing style (formal or informal)
d. Format (memo, letter, manuscript, preprinted form)
e. Effectiveness (clarity, accuracy, expression)

In an informational memo report to your instructor, describe your findings.

12.3 Data Forms and Questions (Obj. 3)

Your Task. In conducting research for the following reports, name at least one form of data you will need and the questions you should ask to determine whether that set of data is appropriate (see Figure 12.6).

a. A report evaluating the relocation of a Montreal company to Toronto. You find figures in a *Toronto Life* article showing the average cost of housing for 60 cities, including Montreal and Toronto.

b. A report by provincial investigators analyzing the causes of a massive power-grid failure.

c. A report examining the effectiveness of ethics codes in Canadian businesses.

12.4 Problem and Purpose Statements (Obj. 2)

Your Task. The following situations require reports. For each situation write (1) a concise problem question and (2) a simple statement of purpose.

a. Last winter a severe ice storm damaged well over 50 percent of the pear trees lining the main street in the small town of Somerset. The local university's experts believe that well over 70 percent of the damaged trees will die in the next two years and that this variety is not the best one for providing shade (one of the major goals behind planting them eight years ago).

b. New federal regulations have changed the definitions of common terms such as *fresh, fat free, low in cholesterol,* and *light.* The Big Deal Bakery worries that it must rewrite all its package labels. Big Deal doesn't know whether to hire a laboratory or a consultant for this project.

c. Customers placing telephone orders for clothing with James River Enterprises typically order only one or two items. JRE wonders whether it can train telephone service reps to motivate customers to increase the number of items ordered per call.

12.5 Problem and Purpose Statements (Obj. 2)

Your Task. Identify a problem in your current job or a previous job (such as inadequate equipment, inefficient procedures, poor customer service, poor product quality, or personnel problems). Assume your boss agrees with your criticism and asks you to prepare a report. Write (a) a two- or three-sentence statement describing the problem, (b) a problem question, and (c) a simple statement of purpose for your report.

12.6 Factoring and Outlining a Problem (Obj. 2)

CRITICAL THINKING

Japan Airlines has asked your company, Connections International, to prepare a proposal for a training school for tour operators. JAL wants to know whether Victoria would be a good spot for its school. Victoria interests JAL but only if nearby entertainment facilities can be used for tour training. JAL also needs an advisory committee consisting, if possible, of representatives of the travel community and perhaps executives of other major airlines. The real problem is how to motivate these people to cooperate with JAL.

You've heard that CBC Studios in Victoria offers training seminars, guest speakers, and other resources for tour operators. You wonder whether Magic Mountain in Vancouver would also be willing to cooperate with the proposed school. And you remember that Griffith Park is nearby and might make a good tour training spot. Before JAL will settle on Victoria as its choice, it wants to know whether access to air travel is adequate. It's also concerned about available school building space. Moreover, JAL wants to know whether city officials in Victoria would be receptive to this tour training school proposal.

Your Task. To guide your thinking and research, factor this problem into an outline with several areas to investigate. Further divide the problem into subproblems, phrasing each entry as a question. For example, *Should the JAL tour training program be located in Victoria?* (See the work plan model in Figure 12.5.)

12.7 Developing a Work Plan (Obj. 2)

Your Task. Select a report topic from those listed at this book's Student Resources Web site. Click on "Web Links by Chapter," "Chapter 12," and "Report Topics." For that report prepare a work plan that includes the following:

a. Statement of the problem

b. Expanded statement of purpose (including scope, limitations, and significance)

c. Sources and methods

d. Tentative outline

e. Work schedule (with projected completion dates)

12.8 Using Secondary Sources (Obj. 3)

Secondary sources can provide quite different information depending on your mode of inquiry.

Your Task. Select a topic in your field and conduct research in your school's library. Then research the same topic using the Internet. Write a short memo to your instructor comparing the results, focusing on the strengths and weaknesses of each search strategy.

12.9 Documenting the Best Resources in Your Field (Obj. 3)

Business and professional people should know what publications are most significant in their career fields.

Your Task. Prepare a bibliography of the most important magazines and professional journals in your major field of study. Your instructor may ask you to list the periodicals and briefly describe their content, purpose, and audience. In a cover memo to your instructor, describe your bibliography and your research sources (manual or electronic indexes, Web, databases, CD-ROM, and so on).

12.10 Developing Primary Data: Collaborative Survey (Obj. 4)

TEAM

Parking on campus has always been a problem. Students complain bitterly about the lack of spaces for them, the distance of parking lots from classrooms, and the poor condition of some of the lots. Some solutions have been proposed: limiting parking to full-time students, using auxiliary parking lots farther away and offering a shuttle bus to campus, encouraging bicycle and moped use, and reducing the number of spaces for visitors.

Your Task. In teams of three to five, design a survey for your associated student body council. The survey seeks student feedback in addressing the parking problem on campus. Discuss these solutions and add at least three other possibilities. Then prepare a questionnaire to be distributed on campus. If possible, pilot-test the questionnaire before submitting it to your instructor. Be sure to consider how the results will be tabulated and interpreted.

12.11 Researching Data: Zellers Wants to Know What's Happening South of the Border (Objs. 3 and 4)

INFOTRAC TEAM

With U.S. retailers, such as Wal-Mart, capturing much of the Canadian market, stores such as Zellers need to be proactive. The casualties of retailers such as Bi-Way and Eaton's have had a major impact on the retail landscape.

Looking to the south, some of the U.S. competition may provide some insightful information. Target, the U.S. discount retailer, piles it high and sells it cheap. Lauren Bacall and Robert Redford have promoted it. Oprah Winfrey thinks it is so chic that she pronounces its name in mock French ("Tar-Jay"). Despite its celebrity shoppers, Target still lags behind Wal-Mart, which stands out as the gold standard of retailing. The two companies are similar in net margins and cost structures, but Wal-Mart is way ahead in sales per square metre.

Target has indicated that it wants to narrow the gap through the sincerest form of flattery: imitation. Gerald Storch, Target's vice chairman, says his company is "the world's premier student of Wal-Mart." If it works well for Wal-Mart it might work for Target.[13]

Your Task. As one of several interns working in the office of Zellers' vice chairman, you have been given the task of learning about Wal-Mart and Target activities and reporting on trends, techniques, procedures, or new marketing plans that might be interesting to Zellers. For example, Wal-Mart has been experimenting with the idea of adding gas stations to more of its stores. Perhaps Zellers should consider this. You're not expected to conduct extensive research or write a long report. Your boss just wants you to think about what is happening south of the border and whether any policies or practices might be worth imitating at Zellers. Using InfoTrac, read a number of articles about Wal-Mart and/or Target. Your team should develop three to ten ideas to present to Gerry Stanton, your supervisor. Write individual informative memos or one collaborative memo.

12.12 Selecting Graphics (Obj. 5)

Your Task. Identify the best kind of graphic to illustrate the following data.

a. Instructions for workers telling them how to distinguish between worker accidents that must be reported to provincial and federal agencies and those that need not be reported.

b. Figures showing what proportion of every provincial tax dollar is spent on education, social services, transportation, debt, and other expenses.

c. Figures comparing the sales of PDAs (personal data assistants), cell phones, and laptop computers over the past five years.

d. Data showing areas in Canada most likely to have earthquakes.

e. Percentages showing the causes of forest fires (lightning, 73 percent; arson, 5 percent; campfires, 9 percent; and so on) in the Rocky Mountains.

12.13 Evaluating Graphics (Obj. 5)

Your Task. Select four graphics from newspapers or magazines. Look in *The Globe and Mail, The Economist, Canadian Business, Financial Post,* or other business news publications. In a memo to your instructor, critique each graphic based on what you have learned in this chapter. What is correctly shown? What is incorrectly shown? How could the graphic be improved?

12.14 Drawing a Bar Chart (Obj. 5)

Your Task. Prepare a bar chart comparing the tax rates of eight industrial countries in the world: Canada, 34 percent; France, 42 percent; Germany, 39 percent; Japan, 26 percent; Netherlands, 48 percent; Sweden, 49 percent; United Kingdom, 37 percent; United States, 28 percent. These figures represent a percentage of the gross domestic product for each country. The sources of the figures are the International Monetary Fund and the Japanese Ministry of Finance. Arrange the entries logically. Write two titles: a talking title and a descriptive title. What should be emphasized in the graph and title?

12.15 Drawing a Line Chart (Obj. 5)

Your Task. Prepare a line chart showing the sales of Sidekick Athletic Shoes, Inc., for these years: 2005, $6.7 million; 2004, $5.4 million; 2003, $3.2 million; 2002, $2.1 million; 2001, $2.6 million; 2000, $3.6 million. In the chart title, highlight the trend you see in the data.

12.16 Studying Graphics in Annual Reports (Obj. 5)

Your Task. In a memo to your instructor, evaluate the effectiveness of graphics in three to five corporation annual reports. Critique their readability, clarity, and effectiveness in visualizing data. How were they introduced in the text? What suggestions would you make to improve them?

C.L.U.E. REVIEW 12

On a separate sheet edit the following sentences to correct faults in grammar, punctuation, spelling, numbers, proofreading, and word use.

1. In a low context culture, such as north America our values and attitudes prompts us to write many reports.
2. A readers expectations and the content of a report determines it's pattern of development.
3. The format of a report is governed by it's length, topic, audience and purpose.
4. If a report has 10 or less pages, it's generally considered an short informal report.
5. Research reports from consultants to there clients tend to be formal, however a conference report to your boss would be informal.
6. My colleague and me followed step by step instructions in preparing a workplan for our report.
7. If your report is authorized by someone be sure to review it's workplan with them before proceding.
8. Eric was offerred one thousand dollars to finish Roberts report but he said it was "to little and to late."
9. To search the internet you need a browser such as netscape navigator, or microsoft internet explorer.
10. To illustrate report data you may chose from among following visual aids, tables, charts, graphs and pictures.

Chapter 13
Organizing and Writing Typical Business Reports

LEARNING OBJECTIVES

1. *Use tabulating and statistical techniques to sort and interpret report data.*

2. *Draw meaningful conclusions and make practical report recommendations.*

3. *Organize report data logically and provide cues to aid comprehension.*

4. *Prepare typical informational reports.*

5. *Prepare typical analytical reports.*

INTERPRETING DATA

1

Organizations need information to stay abreast of what's happening inside and outside of their firms. Much of that information will be presented to decision makers in the form of reports.

Unprocessed data become meaningful information through sorting, analysis, combination, and recombination. You'll be examining each item to see what it means by itself and what it means when connected with other data. You're looking for meanings, relationships, and answers to the research questions posed in your work plan. This chapter will focus on interpreting and organizing data, drawing conclusions, providing reader cues, and writing typical business reports.

Tabulating and Analyzing Responses

Interpreting data means sorting, analyzing, combining, and recombining to yield meaningful information.

If you've collected considerable numerical and other information, you must tabulate and analyze it. Fortunately, several tabulating and statistical techniques can help you create order from the chaos. These techniques simplify, summarize, and classify large amounts of data into meaningful terms. From the condensed data you're more likely to be able to draw valid conclusions and make reasoned recommendations. The most helpful summarizing techniques include tables, statistical concepts (mean, median, and mode), correlations, and grids.

Tables. Numerical data from questionnaires or interviews are usually summarized and simplified in tables. Using systematic columns and rows, tables make quantitative information easier to comprehend. After assembling your data, you'll want to prepare preliminary tables to enable you to see what the information means.

Sometimes data become more meaningful when cross-tabulated. This process allows analysis of two or more variables together. By cross-tabulating the findings, you sometimes uncover data that may help answer your problem question or that may prompt you to explore other possibilities. Don't, however, undertake cross-tabulation unless it serves more than mere curiosity.

Tables also help you compare multiple data collected from questionnaires and surveys. Figure 13.1 shows, in raw form, responses to several survey items. To convert these data into a more usable form, you need to calculate percentages for each item. Then you can arrange the responses in some rational sequence, such as largest percentage to smallest.

Once the data are displayed in a table, you can more easily draw conclusions. As Figure 13.1 shows, Midland College students apparently are not interested in public transportation or shuttle buses from satellite lots. They want to park on campus, with restricted visitor parking; only half are willing to pay for new parking lots.

Three statistical concepts—mean, median, and mode—help you describe data.

The Three Ms: Mean, Median, Mode. Tables help you organize data, and the three Ms help you describe it. These statistical terms—mean, median, and mode—are all occasionally used loosely to mean "average." To be safe, though, you should learn to apply these statistical terms precisely.

When people say *average*, they usually intend to indicate the *mean*, or arithmetic average.

The *median* represents the midpoint in a group of figures arranged from lowest to highest (or vice versa).

FIGURE 13.1 Converting Survey Data Into Finished Tables

Tips for Converting Raw Data

- Tabulate the responses on a copy of the survey form.
- Calculate percentages (divide the score for an item by the total for all responses to that item; for example, for item 1, divide 331 by 663).
- Round off figures to one decimal point or to whole numbers.
- Arrange items in a logical order, such as largest to smallest percentage.
- Prepare a table with a title that tells such things as who, what, when, where, and why.
- Include the total number of respondents.

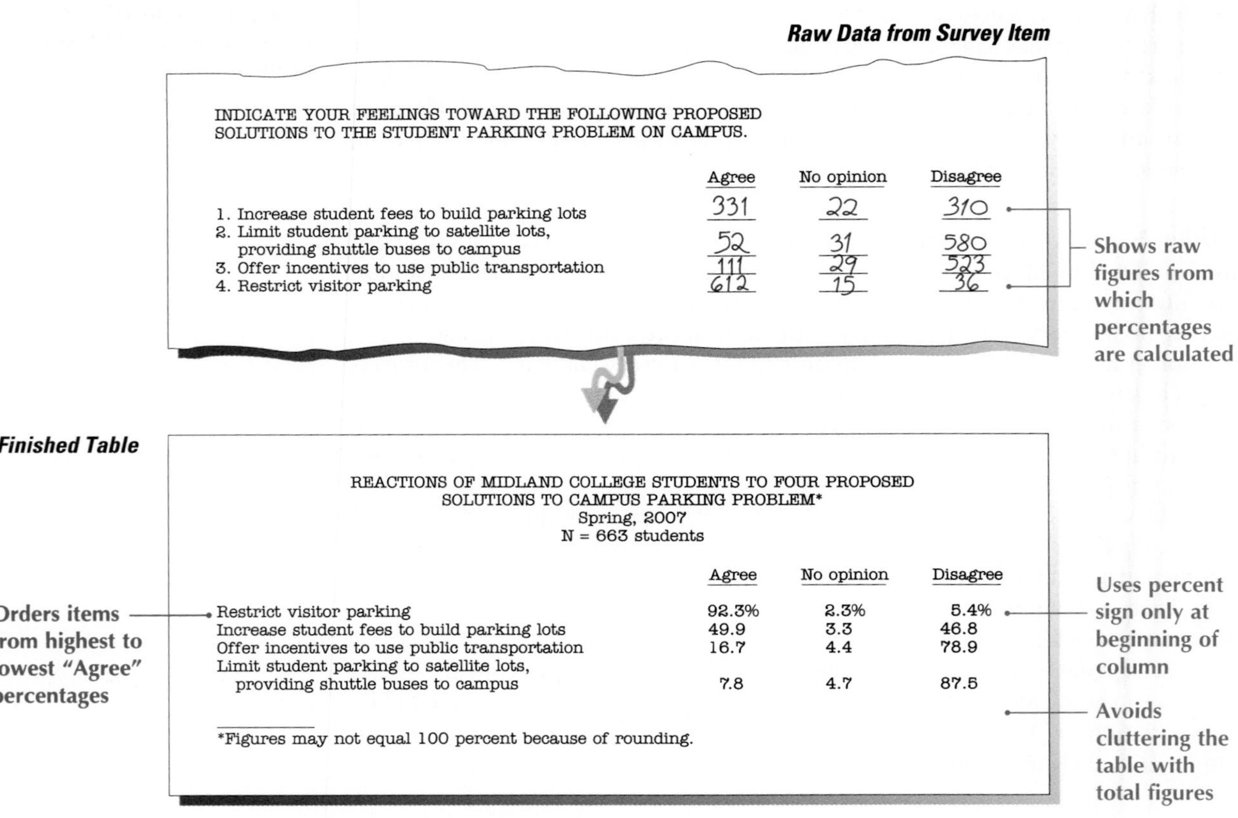

Raw Data from Survey Item

INDICATE YOUR FEELINGS TOWARD THE FOLLOWING PROPOSED SOLUTIONS TO THE STUDENT PARKING PROBLEM ON CAMPUS.

	Agree	No opinion	Disagree
1. Increase student fees to build parking lots	331	22	310
2. Limit student parking to satellite lots, providing shuttle buses to campus	52	31	580
3. Offer incentives to use public transportation	111	29	523
4. Restrict visitor parking	612	15	36

Shows raw figures from which percentages are calculated

Finished Table

REACTIONS OF MIDLAND COLLEGE STUDENTS TO FOUR PROPOSED SOLUTIONS TO CAMPUS PARKING PROBLEM*
Spring, 2007
N = 663 students

	Agree	No opinion	Disagree
Restrict visitor parking	92.3%	2.3%	5.4%
Increase student fees to build parking lots	49.9	3.3	46.8
Offer incentives to use public transportation	16.7	4.4	78.9
Limit student parking to satellite lots, providing shuttle buses to campus	7.8	4.7	87.5

*Figures may not equal 100 percent because of rounding.

Orders items from highest to lowest "Agree" percentages
Uses percent sign only at beginning of column
Avoids cluttering the table with total figures

The mean is the arithmetic average; the median is the midpoint in a group of figures; the mode is the most frequently occurring figure.

The *mode* is simply the value that occurs most frequently. Although mode is infrequently used by researchers, knowing the mode is useful in some situations. To remember the meaning of *mode*, think about fashion; the most frequent response, the mode, is the most fashionable.

Mean, median, and mode figures are especially helpful when the range of values is also known. Range represents the span between the highest and lowest values. To calculate the range, you simply subtract the lowest figure from the highest. Knowing the range enables readers to put mean and median figures into perspective. This knowledge also prompts researchers to wonder why such a range exists, thus stimulating hunches and further investigation to solve problems.

Correlations. In tabulating and analyzing data, you may see relationships among two or more variables that help explain the findings. Intuition suggests correlations that may or may not prove to be accurate. Although one event may not be said to cause another, the business researcher who sees a correlation begins to ask why and how the two variables are related. In this way, apparent correlations stimulate investigation and present possible problem solutions to be explored.

Correlations between variables suggest possible relationships that will explain research findings.

In reporting correlations, you should avoid suggesting that a cause-and-effect relationship exists when none can be proved. Only sophisticated research methods can statistically prove correlations. Instead, present a correlation as a possible relationship. Cautious statements followed by explanations gain you credibility and allow readers to make their own decisions.

Grids. Another technique for analyzing raw data—especially verbal data—is the grid. Complex verbal information is transformed into concise, manageable data; readers can see immediately which points are supported and opposed.

Grids permit analysis of raw verbal data by grouping and classifying.

Arranging data in a grid also works for projects such as feasibility studies that compare many variables. *Consumer Reports* often uses grids to show information; additionally, grids help classify employment data.

DRAWING CONCLUSIONS AND MAKING RECOMMENDATIONS

2

The most widely read portions of a report are the sections devoted to conclusions and recommendations. Knowledgeable readers go straight to the conclusions to see what the report writer thinks the data mean. Because conclusions summarize and explain the findings, they represent the heart of a report. Your value in an organization rises considerably if you can draw conclusions that analyze information logically and show how the data answer questions and solve problems.

Analyzing Data to Arrive at Conclusions

Any set of data can produce a variety of conclusions. Always bear in mind, though, that the audience for a report wants to know how these data relate to the problem being studied. What do the findings mean in terms of solving the original report problem?

Conclusions summarize and explain the findings in a report.

For example, the Marriott Corporation recognized a serious problem among its employees. Conflicting home and work requirements seemed to be causing excessive employee turnover and decreased productivity. To learn the extent of the problem and to consider solutions, Marriott surveyed its staff.[1] It learned, among other things, that nearly 35 percent of its employees had children under age twelve, and 15 percent had children under age five. Other findings, shown in Figure 13.2, indicated that one third of its staff with young children took time off because of child-care difficulties. Moreover, many current employees left previous jobs because of work and family conflicts. The survey also showed that managers did not consider child-care or family problems to be appropriate topics for discussion at work.

FIGURE 13.2 Report Conclusions and Recommendations

Tips for Writing Conclusions

- Interpret and summarize the findings; tell what they mean.
- Relate the conclusions to the report problem.
- Limit the conclusions to the data presented; do not introduce new material.
- Number the conclusions and present them in parallel form.
- Be objective; avoid exaggerating or manipulating the data.
- Use consistent criteria in evaluating options.

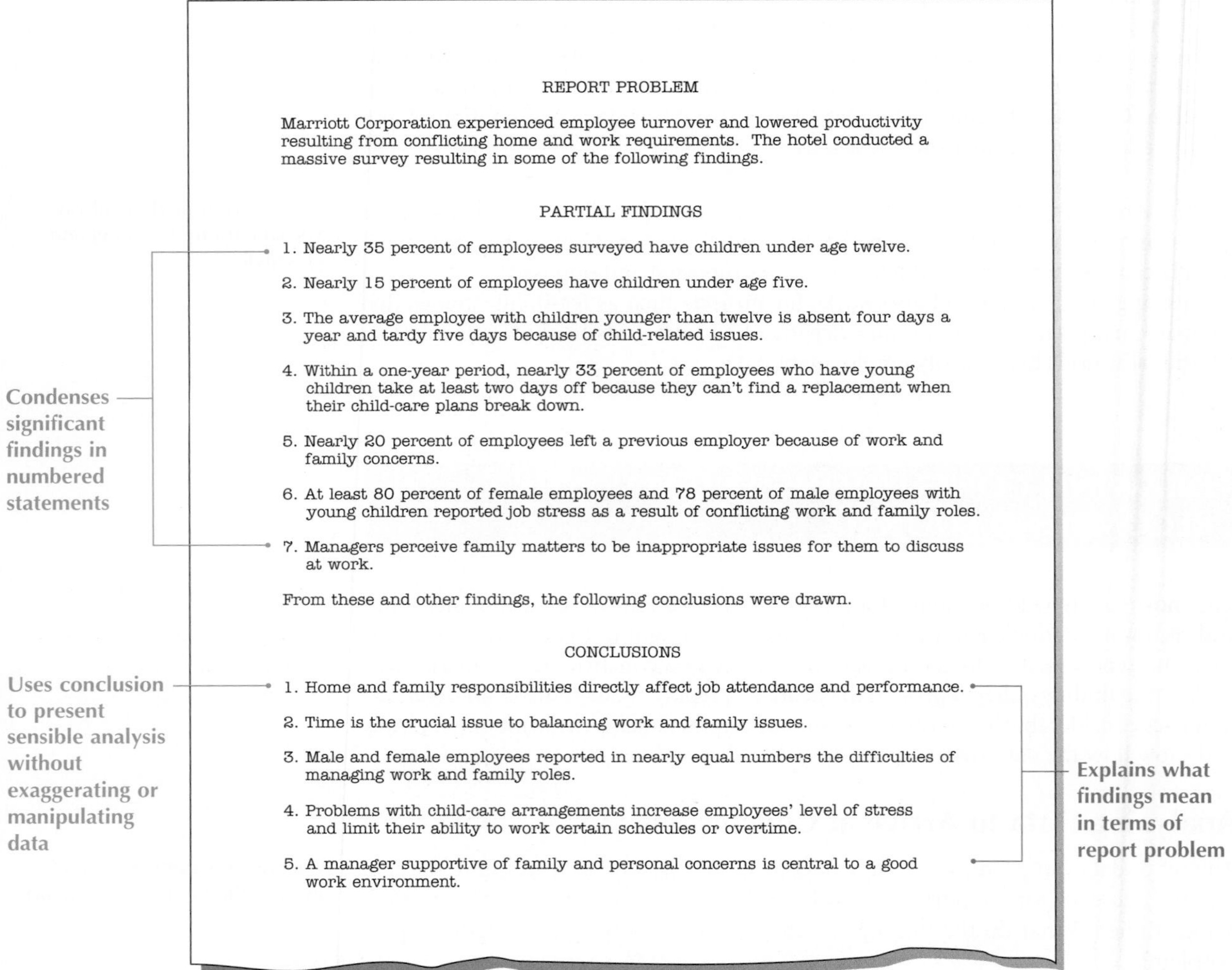

REPORT PROBLEM

Marriott Corporation experienced employee turnover and lowered productivity resulting from conflicting home and work requirements. The hotel conducted a massive survey resulting in some of the following findings.

PARTIAL FINDINGS

1. Nearly 35 percent of employees surveyed have children under age twelve.
2. Nearly 15 percent of employees have children under age five.
3. The average employee with children younger than twelve is absent four days a year and tardy five days because of child-related issues.
4. Within a one-year period, nearly 33 percent of employees who have young children take at least two days off because they can't find a replacement when their child-care plans break down.
5. Nearly 20 percent of employees left a previous employer because of work and family concerns.
6. At least 80 percent of female employees and 78 percent of male employees with young children reported job stress as a result of conflicting work and family roles.
7. Managers perceive family matters to be inappropriate issues for them to discuss at work.

From these and other findings, the following conclusions were drawn.

CONCLUSIONS

1. Home and family responsibilities directly affect job attendance and performance.
2. Time is the crucial issue to balancing work and family issues.
3. Male and female employees reported in nearly equal numbers the difficulties of managing work and family roles.
4. Problems with child-care arrangements increase employees' level of stress and limit their ability to work certain schedules or overtime.
5. A manager supportive of family and personal concerns is central to a good work environment.

Condenses significant findings in numbered statements
Uses conclusion to present sensible analysis without exaggerating or manipulating data
Explains what findings mean in terms of report problem

A sample of possible conclusions that could be drawn from these findings is shown in Figure 13.2. Notice that each conclusion relates to the initial report problem. Although only a few possible findings and conclusions are shown here, you can see that the conclusions try to explain the causes for the home/work conflict among employees. Many report writers would expand the conclusion section by explaining each item and citing supporting evidence. Even for simplified conclusions, such as those shown in Figure 13.2, you will want to number each item separately and use parallel construction (balanced sentence structure).

FIGURE 13.2 Continued

Tips for Writing Recommendations

- Make specific suggestions for actions to solve the report problem.
- Prepare practical recommendations that will be agreeable to the audience.
- Avoid conditional words such as *maybe* and *perhaps*.
- Present each suggestion separately as a command beginning with a verb.
- Number the recommendations for improved readability.
- If requested, describe how the recommendations may be implemented.
- When possible, arrange the recommendations in an announced order, such as most important to least important.

RECOMMENDATIONS

1. Provide managers with training in working with personal and family matters.
2. Institute a flextime policy that allows employees to adapt their work schedules to home responsibilities.
3. Investigate opening a pilot child development centre for preschool children of employees at company headquarters.
4. Develop a child-care resource program to provide parents with professional help in locating affordable child care.
5. Offer a child-care discount program to help parents pay for services.
6. Authorize weekly payroll deductions, using tax-free dollars, to pay for child care.
7. Publish a quarterly employee newsletter devoted to family and child-care issues.

Arranges actions to solve problems from most important to least important

Effective report conclusions are objective and bias-free.

Although your goal is to remain objective, drawing conclusions naturally involves a degree of subjectivity. Your goals, background, and frame of reference all colour the inferences you make. Findings will be interpreted from the writer's perspective, but they should not be manipulated to achieve a preconceived purpose.

You can make your report conclusions more objective if you use consistent evaluation criteria. Let's say you are comparing computers for an office equipment purchase. If you evaluate each by the same criteria (such as price, specifications, service, and warranty), your conclusions are more likely to be bias-free.

You also need to avoid the temptation to sensationalize or exaggerate your findings or conclusions. Be careful of words like *many*, *most*, and *all*. Instead of *many of the respondents felt . . .*, you might more accurately write *some of the respondents . . . .* Examine your motives before drawing conclusions. Don't let preconceptions or wishful thinking colour your reasoning.

Preparing Report Recommendations

Conclusions explain a problem; recommendations offer specific suggestions for solving the problem.

Recommendations, unlike conclusions, make specific suggestions for actions that can solve the report problem. Typically, readers prefer specific recommendations. They want to know exactly how to implement the suggestions. The specificity of your recommendations depends on your authorization. What are you commissioned to do, and what does the reader expect? In the planning stages of your report project, you anticipate what the reader wants in the report. Your intuition and your knowledge of the audience indicate how far your recommendations should be developed.

In the recommendations section of the Marriott employee survey, shown in the continuation of Figure 13.2, many of the suggestions are summarized. In the actual report each recommendation could have been backed up with specifics and ideas for implementing them. For example, the child-care resource recommendation would be explained: it provides parents with names of agencies and professionals who specialize in locating child care across the country.

The best recommendations offer practical suggestions that are feasible and agreeable to the audience.

A good report provides practical recommendations that are agreeable to the audience. In the Marriott survey, for example, report researchers knew that the company wanted to help employees cope with conflicts between family and work obligations. Thus, the report's conclusions and recommendations focused on ways to resolve the conflict. If Marriott's goal had been merely to reduce employee absenteeism and save money, the recommendations would have been quite different.

If possible, make each recommendation a command. Note in Figure 13.2 that each recommendation begins with a verb. This structure sounds forceful and confident and helps the reader comprehend the information quickly. Avoid words such as *maybe* and *perhaps*; they suggest conditional statements that reduce the strength of recommendations.

Experienced writers may combine recommendations and conclusions. And in short reports, writers may omit conclusions and move straight to recommendations. The important thing about recommendations, though, is that they include practical suggestions for solving the report problem.

Moving From Findings to Recommendations

Recommendations evolve from interpretation of the findings and conclusions. Consider the following examples from the Marriott survey:

Finding
A majority of managers perceive family matters to be inappropriate issues for them to discuss at work.

Conclusion
Managers are neither willing nor trained to discuss family troubles that may cause employees to miss work.

Recommendation
Provide managers with training in recognizing and working with personal and family troubles that affect work.

Finding
Within a one-year period, nearly 33 percent of employees who have young children take at least two days off because they can't find a replacement when their child-care plans break down.

Conclusion
Problems with child-care arrangements increase employees' level of stress and create absenteeism.

Recommendation
Develop a child-care resource program to provide parents with professional help in locating affordable child care.

ORGANIZING DATA

3

After collecting sets of data, interpreting them, drawing conclusions, and thinking about the recommendations you will make, you're ready to organize the parts of the report into a logical framework. Poorly organized reports lead to frustration. Readers will not understand, remember, or be persuaded. Wise writers know that reports rarely "just organize themselves." Instead, organization must be imposed on the data.

The direct pattern is appropriate for informed or receptive readers; the indirect pattern is appropriate when educating or persuading.

Informational reports, as you learned in Chapter 12, generally present data without interpretation. As shown in Figure 13.3, informational reports are typically organized in three parts: (1) introduction/background, (2) facts/findings, and (3) summary/conclusion. Analytical reports, which generally analyze data and draw conclusions, typically contain four parts: (1) introduction/problem, (2) facts/findings, (3) discussion/analysis, and (4) conclusions/recommendations. However, the parts in analytical reports do not always follow the same sequence. For readers who know about the project, are supportive, or are eager to learn the results quickly, the direct method is appropriate. Conclusions and recommendations, if requested, appear up front. For readers who must be educated or persuaded, the indirect method works better. Conclusions/recommendations appear last, after the findings have been presented and analyzed.

Although every report is different, the overall organizational patterns described here typically hold true. The real challenge, though, lies in (1) organizing the facts/findings and discussion/analysis sections and (2) providing reader cues.

Ordering Information Logically

Organization by time, component, importance, criteria, or convention helps readers comprehend data.

Whether you're writing informational or analytical reports, the data you've collected must be structured coherently. Five common organizational methods are by time, component, importance, criteria, or convention. Regardless of the method you choose, be sure that it helps the reader understand the data. Reader comprehension, not writer convenience, should govern organization.

Time. Ordering data by time means establishing a chronology of events. Agendas, minutes of meetings, progress reports, and procedures are usually organized by time. Beware of overusing time chronologies, however. Although this method is easy and often mirrors the way data are collected, chronologies tend to be boring, repetitious, and lacking in emphasis. Readers can't always pick out what's important.

FIGURE 13.3 Organizing Informational and Analytical Reports

	Analytical Reports	
Informational Reports	**Direct Pattern**	**Indirect Pattern**
I. Introduction/background II. Facts/findings III. Summary/conclusion	I. Introduction/problem II. Conclusions/recommendations III. Facts/findings IV. Discussion/analysis	I. Introduction/problem II. Facts/findings III. Discussion/analysis IV. Conclusions/recommendations

Component. Especially for informational reports, data may be organized by components such as location, geography, division, product, or part. Organization by components works best when the classifications already exist.

Organizing by level of importance saves the time of busy readers and increases the odds that key information will be retained.

Importance. Organization by importance involves beginning with the most important item and proceeding to the least important—or vice versa. The Marriott report describing work/family conflicts might begin by discussing child care, if the writer considered it the most important issue. Using importance to structure findings involves a value judgment. The writer must decide what is most important, always keeping in mind the readers' priorities and expectations. Busy readers appreciate seeing important points first; they may skim or skip other points. On the other hand, building to a climax by moving from least important to most important enables the writer to focus attention at the end. Thus, the reader is more likely to remember the most important item. Of course, the writer also risks losing the attention of the reader along the way.

Criteria. Establishing criteria by which to judge helps writers to treat topics consistently. Organizing a report around criteria helps readers make comparisons, instead of forcing them to search through the report for similar data.

Organizing by convention simplifies the organizational task and yields easy-to-follow information.

Convention. Many operational and recurring reports are structured according to convention. That is, they follow a prescribed plan that everyone understands.

Like operating reports, proposals are often organized conventionally. They might use such groupings as background, problem, proposed solution, staffing, schedule, costs, and authorization. As you might expect, reports following these conventional, prescribed structures greatly simplify the task of organization.

Providing Reader Cues

When you finish organizing a report, you probably see a neat outline in your mind: major points, supported by subpoints and details. However, readers don't know the material as well as you; they cannot see your outline. To guide them through the data, you need to provide the equivalent of a map and road signs. For both formal and informal reports, devices such as introductions, transitions, and headings prevent readers from getting lost.

Good openers tell readers what topics will be covered in what order and why.

Introduction. The best way to point a reader in the right direction is to provide an introduction that does three things:

- Tells the purpose of the report
- Describes the significance of the topic
- Previews the main points and the order in which they will be developed

The following paragraph includes all three elements in introducing a report on computer security:

> The purpose of this report is to examine the security of our current computer operations and present suggestions for improving security. Lax computer security could mean loss of information, loss of business, and damage to our equipment and systems. Because many former employees, released during recent downsizing efforts, know our systems, major changes must be made. To improve security, I will present three recommendations: (1) begin using smart cards that limit access to our computer system, (2) alter sign-on and log-off procedures, (3) move central computer operations to a more secure area.

This opener tells the purpose (examining computer security), describes its significance (loss of information and business, damage to equipment and systems), and outlines how the report is organized (three recommendations). Good openers in effect set up a contract with the reader. The writer promises to cover certain topics in a specified order. Readers expect the writer to fulfill the contract. They want the topics to be developed as promised—using the same wording and presented in the order mentioned. For example, if in your introduction you state that you will discuss the use of *smart cards*, don't change the heading for that section to *access cards*. Remember that the introduction provides a map to a report; switching the names on the map will ensure that readers get lost. To maintain consistency, delay writing the introduction until after you have completed the report. Long, complex reports may require introductions for each section.

Like tourists who need a map to reach their destination, report readers need the equivalent of a map and road signs to find their way through a report. Introductions, transitions, and headings provide cues so that readers know where they've been and where they are headed.

Transitions. Expressions such as *on the contrary*, *at the same time*, and *however* show relationships and help reveal the logical flow of ideas in a report. These transitional expressions enable writers to tell readers where ideas are headed and how they relate.

The following expressions enable you to show readers how you are developing your ideas.

To Present Additional Thoughts: additionally, again, also, moreover, furthermore

To Suggest Cause and Effect: accordingly, as a result, consequently, therefore

To Contrast Ideas: at the same time, but, however, on the contrary, though, yet

To Show Time and Order: after, before, first, finally, now, previously, then, to conclude

To Clarify Points: for example, for instance, in other words, that is, thus

In using these expressions, recognize that they don't have to sit at the head of a sentence. Listen to the rhythm of the sentence, and place the expression where a natural pause occurs. Used appropriately, transitional expressions serve readers as guides; misused or overused, they can be as distracting and frustrating as too many road signs on a highway.

Transitional expressions inform readers where ideas are headed and how they relate.

Headings. Good headings are another structural cue that assist readers in comprehending the organization of a report. They highlight major ideas, allowing busy readers to see the big picture in a glance. Moreover, headings provide resting points for the mind and for the eye, breaking up large chunks of text into manageable and inviting segments.

Report writers may use functional or talking heads. Functional heads (for example, *Background*, *Findings*, *Personnel*, and *Production Costs*) describe functions

Good headings provide organizational cues and spotlight key ideas.

or general topics. They show the outline of a report but provide little insight for readers. Functional headings are useful for routine reports. They're also appropriate for sensitive topics that might provoke emotional reactions. By keeping the headings general, experienced writers hope to minimize reader opposition or response to controversial subjects. Talking heads (for example, *Two Sides to Campus Parking Problem* or *Survey Shows Support for Parking Fees*) provide more information and interest. Unless carefully written, however, talking heads can fail to reveal the organization of a report. With some planning, though, headings can be both functional and talking, such as *Parking Recommendations: Shuttle and New Structures.* To create the most effective headings, follow a few basic guidelines:

- **Use appropriate heading levels.** The position and format of a heading indicate its level of importance and relationship to other points. Figure 13.4 both illustrates and discusses a commonly used heading format for business reports.
- **Capitalize and underline carefully.** Most writers use all capital letters (without underlines) for main titles, such as the report, chapter, and unit titles. For first- and second-level headings, they capitalize only the first letter of main words. For additional emphasis, they use a bold font, as shown in Figure 13.4.
- **Balance headings within levels.** All headings at a given level should be grammatically similar. For example, *Developing Product Teams* and *Presenting Plan to Management* are balanced, but *Development of Product Teams* and *Presenting Plan to Management* are not.
- **For short reports use first- or second-level headings.** Many business reports contain only one or two levels of headings. For such reports use first-level headings (centred, bolded) and/or second-level headings (flush left, bolded). See Figure 13.4.
- **Include at least one heading per report page.** Headings increase the readability and attractiveness of report pages. Use at least one per page to break up blocks of text.
- **Keep headings short but clear.** One-word headings are emphatic but not always clear. For example, the heading *Budget* does not adequately describe figures for a summer project involving student interns for an oil company in Alberta. Try to keep your headings brief (no more than eight words), but make sure they are understandable. Experiment with headings that concisely tell who, what, when, where, and why.

Headings should be brief, parallel, and ordered in a logical hierarchy.

WRITING INFORMATIONAL REPORTS

4

Informational reports provide data on periodic and situational activities for readers who do not need to be persuaded.

Now that we've covered the basics of gathering, interpreting, and organizing data, we are ready to put it all together into typical informational or analytical reports. Informational reports often describe periodic, recurring activities (such as monthly sales or weekly customer calls) as well as situational, nonrecurring events (such as trips, conferences, and progress on special projects). What they have in common is delivering information to readers who do not have to be persuaded. Informational report readers usually are neutral or receptive.

You can expect to write many informational reports as an entry-level or middle-management employee. Because these reports generally deliver nonsensitive data and thus will not upset the reader, they are organized directly. Often they need little background material or introductory comments since readers are familiar with the topics. Although they're generally conversational and informal, informational

FIGURE 13.4 Levels of Headings in Reports

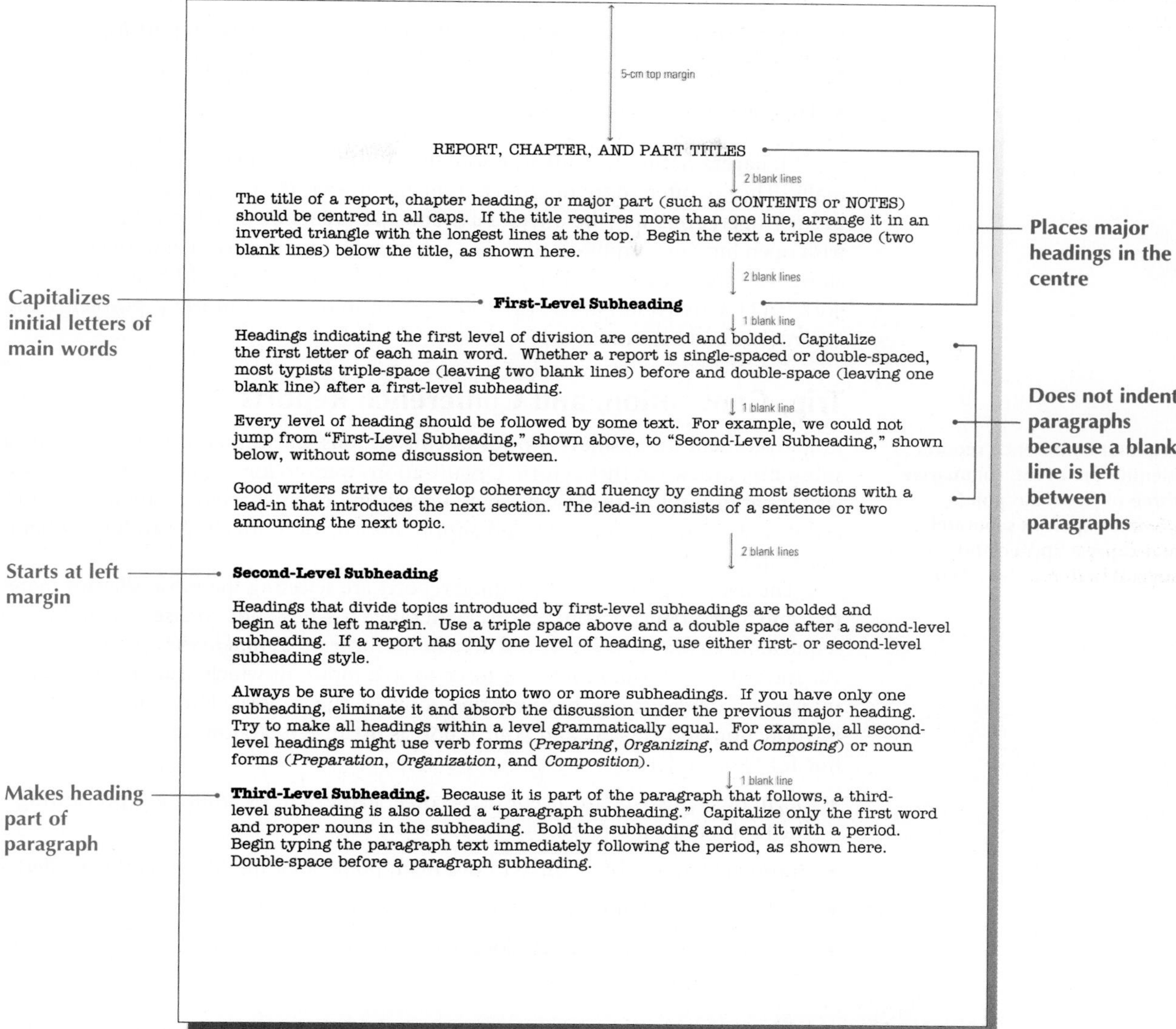

reports should not be so casual that the reader struggles to find the important points. Main points must be immediately visible. Headings, lists, bulleted items, and other graphic highlighting, as well as clear organization, enable readers to grasp major ideas immediately.

5-cm top margin
REPORT, CHAPTER, AND PART TITLES
2 blank lines
The title of a report, chapter heading, or major part (such as CONTENTS or NOTES) should be centred in all caps. If the title requires more than one line, arrange it in an inverted triangle with the longest lines at the top. Begin the text a triple space (two blank lines) below the title, as shown here.
2 blank lines
First-Level Subheading
1 blank line
Headings indicating the first level of division are centred and bolded. Capitalize the first letter of each main word. Whether a report is single-spaced or double-spaced, most typists triple-space (leaving two blank lines) before and double-space (leaving one blank line) after a first-level subheading.
1 blank line
Every level of heading should be followed by some text. For example, we could not jump from "First-Level Subheading," shown above, to "Second-Level Subheading," shown below, without some discussion between.
Good writers strive to develop coherency and fluency by ending most sections with a lead-in that introduces the next section. The lead-in consists of a sentence or two announcing the next topic.
2 blank lines
Second-Level Subheading
Headings that divide topics introduced by first-level subheadings are bolded and begin at the left margin. Use a triple space above and a double space after a second-level subheading. If a report has only one level of heading, use either first- or second-level subheading style.
Always be sure to divide topics into two or more subheadings. If you have only one subheading, eliminate it and absorb the discussion under the previous major heading. Try to make all headings within a level grammatically equal. For example, all second-level headings might use verb forms (Preparing, Organizing, and Composing) or noun forms (Preparation, Organization, and Composition).
1 blank line
Third-Level Subheading. Because it is part of the paragraph that follows, a third-level subheading is also called a "paragraph subheading." Capitalize only the first word and proper nouns in the subheading. Bold the subheading and end it with a period. Begin typing the paragraph text immediately following the period, as shown here. Double-space before a paragraph subheading.
Capitalizes initial letters of main words
Starts at left margin
Makes heading part of paragraph
Places major headings in the centre
Does not indent paragraphs because a blank line is left between paragraphs

Periodic/Activity Reports

Periodic reports keep management informed of operations and activities.

Most businesses—especially larger ones—require periodic reports (sometimes called activity reports) to keep management informed of operations. These recurring reports are written at regular intervals—weekly, monthly, yearly—so that management can monitor and, if necessary, remedy business strategies. Some periodic reports simply contain figures, such as sales volume, number and kind of customer service calls, shipments delivered, accounts payable, and personnel data. More challenging periodic reports require description and discussion of activities. In preparing a narrative description of their activities, employees writing periodic reports usually do the following:

- Summarize regular activities and events performed during the reporting period
- Describe irregular events deserving the attention of management
- Highlight special needs and problems

Managers naturally want to know that routine activities are progressing normally. They're often more interested, though, in what the competition is doing and in how operations may be affected by unusual events or problems. In companies with open lines of communication, managers expect to be informed of the bad news along with the good news. The periodic report shown in Figure 13.5 uses four categories: (1) activity summary, (2) competition update, (3) product problems and comments, and (4) needs.

Trip, Convention, and Conference Reports

Trip and conference reports identify the event, summarize three to five main points, itemize expenses separately, and express appreciation or suggest action to be taken.

Employees sent on business trips or to conventions and conferences typically must submit reports when they return. Organizations want to know that their money was well spent in funding the travel. These reports inform management about new procedures, equipment, and laws and supply information affecting products, operations, and service.

The hardest parts of writing these reports are selecting the most relevant material and organizing it coherently. Generally, it's best not to use chronological sequencing (*in the morning we did X, at lunch we heard Y, and in the afternoon we did Z*). Instead, you should focus on three to five topics in which your reader will be interested. These items become the body of the report. Then simply add an introduction and closing, and your report is organized. Following is a general outline for trip, conference, and convention reports.

- Begin by identifying the event (exact date, name, and location) and previewing the topics to be discussed.
- Summarize in the body three to five main points that might benefit the reader.
- Itemize your expenses, if requested, on a separate sheet.
- Close by expressing appreciation, suggesting action to be taken, or synthesizing the value of the trip or event.

Jeff Marchant was recently named employment coordinator in the Human Resources Department of an electronics appliance manufacturer headquartered in Windsor, Ontario. Recognizing his lack of experience in interviewing job applicants, he asked permission to attend a one-day conference on the topic. His boss, Angela Taylor, encouraged Jeff to attend, saying, "We all need to brush up on our interviewing techniques." The conference report shown in Figure 13.6 discusses three topics that the writer felt would be important to his reader.

Progress and Interim Reports

Progress and interim reports describe ongoing projects to both internal and external readers.

Continuing projects often require progress or interim reports to describe their status. These reports may be external (advising customers regarding the headway of their projects) or internal (informing management of the status of activities). Progress reports typically follow this pattern of development:

- Specify in the opening the purpose and nature of the project.
- Provide background information if the audience requires filling in.

FIGURE 13.5 Periodic Report

Prewriting 1

Analyze: The purpose of this report is to inform management of the week's activities, customer reactions, and the rep's needs.

Anticipate: The audience is a manager who wants to be able to pick out the report highlights quickly. His reaction will probably be neutral or positive.

Adapt: Introduce the report data in a direct, straightforward manner.

Writing 2

Research: Verify data for the landscape judging test. Collect facts about competitors. Double-check problems and needs.

Organize: Make lists of items for each of the four report categories. Be sure to distinguish between problems and needs. Emphasize needs.

Compose: Write and print first draft on a computer.

Revising 3

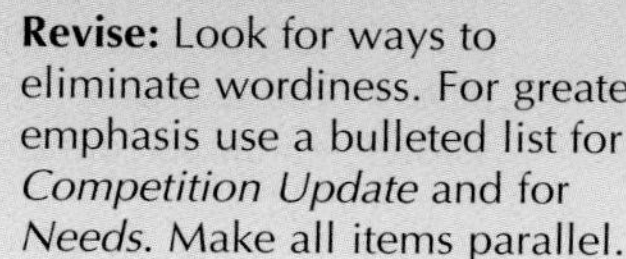

Revise: Look for ways to eliminate wordiness. For greater emphasis use a bulleted list for *Competition Update* and for *Needs.* Make all items parallel.

Proofread: Run spell checker. Adjust white space around headings.

Evaluate: Does this report provide significant data in an easy-to-read format?

DATE: March 15, 2007

TO: Steve Schumacher

FROM: Jim Chrisman JC

SUBJECT: WEEKLY ACTIVITY REPORT

Presents internal informational report in memo format

Activity Summary

Highlights of my activities for the week ending March 14 follow:

Sherbrooke. On Thursday and Friday I demonstrated our new Rain Stream drip systems at a vendor fair at Benbrook Farm Supply, where more than 500 people walked through.

Frontenac. Over the weekend I was a judge for the Quebec Landscape Technician test given at the college. This certification program ensures potential employers that a landscaper is properly trained. Applicants are tested in such areas as irrigation theory, repair, trouble-shooting, installation, and controller programming. The event proved to be very productive, I was able to talk to my distributors and to several important contractors whose crews were taking the tests.

Condenses weekly activity report into topics requested by management

Competition Update

- Toronado can't seem to fill its open sales position in the Eastern Townships.
- RainCo tried to steal the Trinity Country Club golf course contract from us by waiting until the job was spec'd our way and then submitting a lower bid. Fortunately, the Trinity people saw through this ploy and awarded us the contract nevertheless.
- Atlas has a real warranty problem with its 500 series in this area. One distributor had over 200 controllers returned in a seven-week period.

Product Problems, Comments

A contractor in Drummondville told me that our Rain Stream No. 250 valves do not hold the adjustment screw in the throttled-down position. Are they designed to do so?

Our Remote Streamer S-100 is generating considerable excitement. Every time I mention it, people are very interested and request demos. I gave four demos last week and have three more scheduled this week. I'm not sure, though, how quickly these demos will translate into sales because contractors are waiting for our six-month special prices.

Needs

- More information on xerigation training.
- French training videos showing our products.
- Spray nozzle to service small planter areas, say 2 to 4 m.

Summarizes needs in abbreviated, easy-to-read form

FIGURE 13.6 Conference Report

DATE: April 22, 2007

TO: Angela Taylor

FROM: Jeff Marchant JM

SUBJECT: TRAINING CONFERENCE ON EMPLOYMENT INTERVIEWING

I enjoyed attending the "Interviewing People" training conference sponsored by the National Business Foundation. This one-day meeting, held in Toronto on April 19, provided excellent advice that will help us strengthen our interviewing techniques. Although the conference covered many topics, this report concentrates on three areas: structuring the interview, avoiding common mistakes, and responding to new legislation.

Identifies topic and previews how the report is organized

Structuring the Interview

Job interviews usually have three parts. The opening establishes a friendly rapport with introductions, a few polite questions, and an explanation of the purpose for the interview. The body of the interview consists of questions controlled by the interviewer. The interviewer has three goals: (a) educating the applicant about the job, (b) eliciting information about the applicant's suitability for the job, and (c) promoting goodwill about the organization. In closing, the interviewer should encourage the applicant to ask questions, summarize main points, and indicate what actions will follow.

Sets off major topics with centred headings

Avoiding Common Mistakes

Probably the most interesting and practical part of the conference centred on common mistakes made by interviewers, some of which I summarize here:

1. Not taking notes at each interview. Recording important facts enables you to remember the first candidate as easily as you remember the last—and all those in between.
2. Losing control of the interview. Keep control of the interview by digging into the candidate's answers to questions. Probe for responses of greater depth. Don't move on until a question has been satisfactorily answered.
3. Not testing the candidate's communication skills. To be able to evaluate a candidate's ability to express ideas, ask the individual to explain some technical jargon from his or her current position.
4. Having departing employees conduct the interviews for their replacements. Departing employees may be unreliable as interviewers because they tend to hire candidates not quite as strong as they are.
5. Failing to check references. As many as 15 percent of all résumés may contain falsified data. The best way to check references is to network: ask the person whose name has been given to suggest the name of another person.

Covers facts that will most interest and help reader

Angela Taylor Page 2 April 22, 2007

Responding to New Legislation

Recently enacted provisions of the Human Rights Code prohibit interviewers from asking candidates—or even their references—about candidates' disabilities. A question we frequently asked ("Do you have any physical limitations that would prevent you from performing the job for which you are applying?") would now break the law. Interviewers must also avoid asking about medical history; prescription-drug use; prior workers' compensation claims; work absenteeism due to illness; and past treatment for alcoholism, drug use, or mental illness.

Conclusion

This conference provided me with valuable training that I would like to share with other department members at a future staff meeting. Let me know when it can be scheduled.

- Describe the work completed.
- Explain the work currently in progress, including personnel, activities, methods, and locations.
- Anticipate problems and possible remedies.
- Discuss future activities and provide the expected completion date.

Progress reports, such as the one shown in Figure 13.7, include background information to hit the high points of what has been completed, outline what the writer plans to do next, and avoid minute details.

Investigative Reports

Investigative or informational reports deliver data for a specific situation—without offering interpretation or recommendations. These nonrecurring reports are generally arranged in a direct pattern with three segments: introduction, body, and summary. The body—which includes the facts, findings, or discussion—may be organized by time, component, importance, criteria, or convention. What's important is dividing the topic into logical segments, say, three to five areas that are roughly equal and don't overlap. The subject matter of the report usually suggests the best way to divide or organize it.

Investigative reports provide information without interpretation or recommendations.

Whether you are writing a periodic, trip, conference, progress, or investigative report, you'll want to review the suggestions found in the following checklist.

CHECKLIST FOR WRITING INFORMATIONAL REPORTS

Introduction

- ✓ **Begin directly.** Identify the report and its purpose.
- ✓ **Provide a preview.** If the report is over a page long, give the reader a brief overview of its organization.
- ✓ **Supply background data selectively.** When readers are unfamiliar with the topic, briefly fill in the necessary details.
- ✓ **Divide the topic.** Strive to group the facts or findings into three to five roughly equal segments that do not overlap.

Body

- ✓ **Arrange the subtopics logically.** Consider organizing by time, component, importance, criteria, or convention.
- ✓ **Use clear headings.** Supply functional or talking heads (at least one per page) that describe each important section.

FIGURE 13.7 Progress Report

Tips for Writing Progress Reports

- Identify the purpose and the nature of the project immediately.
- Supply background information only if the reader must be educated.
- Describe the work completed.
- Discuss the work in progress, including personnel, activities, methods, and locations.
- Identify problems and possible remedies.
- Consider future activities.
- Close by telling the expected date of completion.

QuaStar Productions

Interoffice Memo

DATE: January 7, 2007

TO: Rick Willens, Executive Producer

FROM: Sheila Ryan, Location Manager *SR*

SUBJECT: SITES FOR "BODEGA BAY" TELEFILM

Identifies project and previews report

This memo describes the progress of my search for an appropriate rustic home, villa, or ranch to be used for the wine country sequences in the telefilm "Bodega Bay." Three sites will be available for you to inspect on January 21, as you requested.

Background: In preparation for this assignment, I consulted Director Dave Durslag, who gave me his preferences for the site. He suggested a picturesque ranch home situated near vineyards, preferably with a scenic background. I also consulted Producer Teresa Silva, who told me that the site must accommodate 55 to 70 production crew members for approximately three weeks of filming. Ben Waters, telefilm accountant, requested that the cost of the site not exceed $24 000 for a three-week lease.

Saves space by integrating headings into paragraphs

Work Completed: For the past eight days I have searched the Niagara Escarpment area in Southern Ontario's wine country. Possible sites include turn-of-the-century estates, Victorian mansions, and rustic farmhouses in the Welland/St. Catharines area. One exceptional site is the Country Meadow Inn, a 97-year-old farmhouse nestled among vineyards with a breathtaking view of valleys and distant hills.

Work To Be Completed: In the next five days, I'll search the Niagara countryside. Many wineries contain charming structures that may present exactly the degree of atmosphere and mystery we need. These wineries have the added advantage of easy access. I will also inspect possible structures in and around Niagara-on-the-Lake. Finally, I've made an appointment with the director of provincial parks to discuss our project, use of provincial lands, restrictions, and costs.

Tells the bad news as well as the good

Anticipated Problems: You should be aware of two complications for filming in this area:

1. Property owners seem unfamiliar with the making of films and are suspicious of short-term leases.
2. Many trees won't have leaves again until May. You may wish to change the filming schedule somewhat.

Concludes by giving completion date and describing what follows

By January 14 you'll have my final report describing the three most promising locations. Arrangements will be made for you to visit these sites January 21.

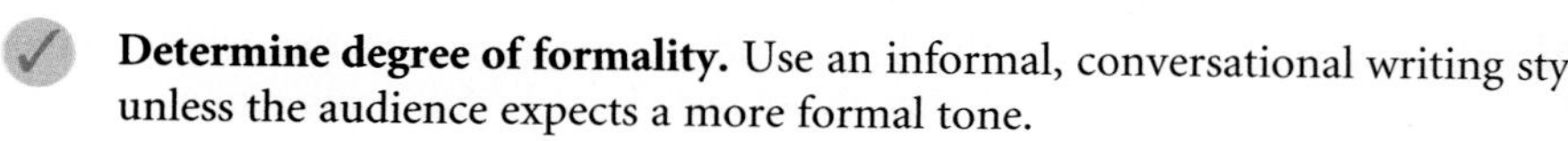

- **Determine degree of formality.** Use an informal, conversational writing style unless the audience expects a more formal tone.

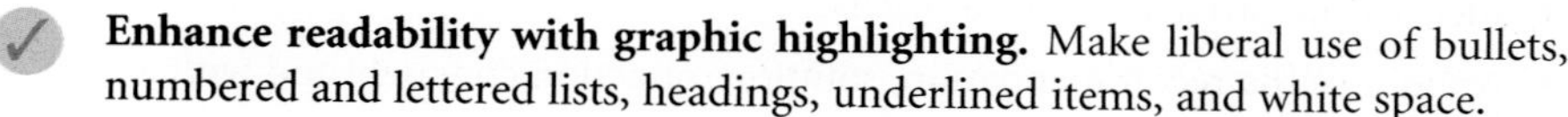

- **Enhance readability with graphic highlighting.** Make liberal use of bullets, numbered and lettered lists, headings, underlined items, and white space.

Summary/Conclusion

- **When necessary, summarize the report.** Briefly review the main points and discuss what action will follow.
- **Offer a concluding thought.** If relevant, express appreciation or describe your willingness to provide further information.

WRITING ANALYTICAL REPORTS

5

Analytical reports present information but emphasize reasoning, conclusions, and recommendations.

Analytical reports differ significantly from informational reports. Although both seek to collect and present data clearly, analytical reports also analyze the data and typically try to persuade the reader to accept the conclusions and act on the recommendations. Informational reports emphasize facts; analytical reports emphasize reasoning and conclusions.

For some readers analytical reports may be organized directly with the conclusions and recommendations near the beginning. Directness is appropriate when the reader has confidence in the writer, based on either experience or credentials. Frontloading the recommendations also works when the topic is routine or familiar and the reader is supportive.

Directness can backfire, though. If you announce the recommendations too quickly, the reader may immediately object to a single idea, one that you had no suspicion would trigger a negative reaction. Once the reader is opposed, changing an unfavourable mind-set may be difficult or impossible. A reader may also think you have oversimplified or overlooked something significant if you lay out all the recommendations before explaining how you arrived at them. When the reader must be led through the process of discovering the solution or recommendation, use the indirect method: present conclusions and recommendations last.

Most analytical reports answer questions about specific problems. Three typical analytical reports answer business questions: justification/recommendation reports, feasibility reports, and yardstick reports. Because these reports all solve problems, the categories are not mutually exclusive. What distinguishes them are their goals and organization.

Justification/Recommendation Reports

Justification/recommendation reports follow the direct or indirect pattern depending on the audience and the topic.

Both managers and employees must occasionally write reports that justify or recommend something, such as buying equipment, changing a procedure, hiring an employee, consolidating departments, or investing funds. Large organizations sometimes prescribe how these reports should be organized; they use forms with conventional headings. When you are free to select an organizational plan yourself, however, let your audience and topic determine your choice of direct or indirect structure.

The direct pattern is appropriate for justification/recommendation reports on nonsensitive topics and for receptive audiences.

Direct Pattern. For nonsensitive topics and recommendations that will be agreeable to readers, you can organize directly according to the following sequence:

- Identify the problem or need briefly.
- Announce the recommendation, solution, or action concisely and with action verbs.
- Explain more fully the benefits of the recommendation or steps to be taken to solve the problem.
- Include a discussion of pros, cons, and costs.
- Conclude with a summary specifying the recommendation and action to be taken.

The justification/recommendation report shown in Figure 13.8 concentrates on four separate benefits of the writer's recommendation.

The indirect pattern is appropriate for justification/recommendation reports on sensitive topics and for potentially unreceptive audiences.

Indirect Pattern. When a reader may oppose a recommendation or when circumstances suggest caution, don't be in a hurry to reveal your recommendation. Consider using the following sequence for an indirect approach to your recommendations:

- Make a general reference to the problem, not to your recommendation, in the subject line.
- Describe the problem or need your recommendation addresses. Use specific examples, supporting statistics, and authoritative quotes to lend credibility to the seriousness of the problem.
- Discuss alternative solutions, beginning with the least likely to succeed.
- Present the most promising alternative (your recommendation) last.
- Show how the advantages of your recommendation outweigh its disadvantages.
- Summarize your recommendation. If appropriate, specify the action it requires.
- Ask for authorization to proceed if necessary.

Footnoting sources lends added credibility to justification/recommendation reports.

The report shown in Figure 13.9 is single-spaced because that's the company's preference. Some companies prefer the readability of double spacing. Be sure to check with your organization for its preference before printing your reports.

Feasibility Reports

Feasibility reports analyze whether a proposal or plan will work.

Feasibility reports examine the practicality and advisability of following a course of action. They answer this question: Will this plan or proposal work? Feasibility reports typically are internal reports written to advise on matters such as consolidating departments, offering a wellness program to employees, or hiring an outside firm to handle a company's accounting or computing operations. These reports may also be written by consultants called in to investigate a problem. The focus in these reports is on the decision to stop or proceed with the proposal. Since your role is not to persuade the reader to accept the decision, you'll want to present the decision immediately. In writing feasibility reports, consider these suggestions:

- Announce your decision immediately.
- Provide a description of the background and problem necessitating the proposal.
- Discuss the benefits of the proposal.
- Describe the problems that may result.
- Calculate the costs associated with the proposal, if appropriate.
- Show the time frame necessary for implementation of the proposal.

FIGURE 13.8 Justification/Recommendation Report: Direct Pattern

Prewriting 1

Analyze: The purpose of this report is to persuade the manager to authorize the purchase and pilot testing of smart tires.

Anticipate: The audience is a manager who is familiar with operations but not with this product. He will probably be receptive to the recommendation.

Adapt: Present the report data in a direct, straightforward manner.

Writing 2

Research: Collect data on how smart tires could benefit operations.

Organize: Discuss the problem briefly. Introduce and justify the recommendation by noting its cost-effectiveness and paperwork benefits. Explain the benefits of smart tires. Describe the action to be taken.

Compose: Write and print first draft.

Revising 3

Revise: Revise to break up long paragraphs about benefits. Isolate each benefit in an enumerated list with headings.

Proofread: Double-check all figures. Be sure all headings are parallel.

Evaluate: Does this report make its request concisely but emphatically? Will the reader see immediately what action is required?

DATE: July 19, 2007
TO: Bill Montgomery, Vice President
FROM: Justin Brown, Operations Manager *JB*
SUBJECT: PILOT TESTING SMART TIRES

Next to fuel, truck tires are our biggest operating cost. Last year we spent $211 000 replacing and retreading tires for 495 trucks. This year the costs will be greater because prices have jumped at least 12 percent and because we've increased our fleet to 550 trucks. Truck tires are an additional burden since they require labour-intensive paperwork to track their warranties, wear, and retread histories. To reduce our long-term costs and to improve our tire tracking system, I recommend that we do the following:

Introduces problem briefly

- Purchase 24 Goodyear smart tires.
- Begin a one-year pilot test on six trucks.

Presents recommendations immediately

How Smart Tires Work

Smart tires have an embedded computer chip that monitors wear, performance, and durability. The chip also creates an electronic fingerprint for positive identification of a tire. By passing a hand-held sensor next to the tire, we can learn where and when a tire was made (for warranty and other identification), how much tread it had originally, and its serial number.

How Smart Tires Could Benefit Us

Although smart tires are initially more expensive than other tires, they could help us improve our operations and save us money in four ways:

Justifies recommendation by explaining product and benefits

1. **Retreads.** Goodyear believes that the wear data is so accurate that we should be able to retread every tire three times, instead of our current two times. If that's true, in one year we could save at least $27 000 in new tire costs.
2. **Safety.** Accurate and accessible wear data should reduce the danger of blowouts and flat tires. Last year, drivers reported six blowouts.
3. **Record keeping and maintenance.** Smart tires could reduce our maintenance costs considerably. Currently, we use an electric branding iron to mark serial numbers on new tires. Our biggest headache is manually reading those serial numbers, decoding them, and maintaining records to meet safety regulations. Reading such data electronically could save us thousands of dollars in labour.
4. **Theft protection.** The chip can be used to monitor each tire as it leaves or enters the warehouse or yard, thus discouraging theft.

Enumerates items for maximum impact and readability

Summary and Action

Specifically, I recommend that you do the following:

- Authorize the special purchase of 24 Goodyear smart tires at $450 each, plus one electronic sensor at $1200.
- Approve a one-year pilot test in our Quebec territory that equips six trucks with smart tires and tracks their performance.

FIGURE 13.9 Justification/Recommendation Report: Indirect Pattern

1

DATE: October 11, 2007

TO: Damon Moore, Director, Human Resources

FROM: Diane Andreas, Executive Assistant *DA*

SUBJECT: MEASURES TO HELP EMPLOYEES STOP SMOKING

At your request, I have examined measures that encourage employees to quit smoking. As company records show, approximately 23 percent of our employees still smoke, despite the antismoking and clean-air policies we adopted in 1995. To collect data for this report, I studied professional and government publications; I also inquired at companies and clinics about stop-smoking programs.

Introduces purpose of report, tells method of data collection, and previews organization

Avoids revealing recommendation immediately

This report presents data describing the significance of the problem, three alternative solutions, and a recommendation based on my investigation.

Uses headings that combine function and description

Significance of Problem: Health Care and Productivity Losses

Employees who smoke are costly to any organization. The following statistics show the effects of smoking for workers and for organizations:

- Absenteeism is 40 to 50 percent greater among smoking employees.
- Accidents are two to three times greater among smokers.
- Bronchitis, lung and heart disease, cancer, and early death are more frequent among smokers (Johns, 2005, p. 14).

Documents data sources for credibility; uses APA style citing author, date, and page number in the text

Although our clean-air policy prohibits smoking in the building, shop, and office, we have done little to encourage employees to stop smoking. Many workers still go outside to smoke at lunch and breaks. Other companies have been far more proactive in their attempts to stop employee smoking. Many companies have found that persuading employees to stop smoking was a decisive factor in reducing their supplementary health insurance premiums. Below is a discussion of three common stop-smoking measures tried by other companies, along with a projected cost factor for each.

Discusses least effective alternative first

Alternative 1: Literature and Events

The least expensive and easiest stop-smoking measure involves the distribution of literature, such as "The Ten-Step Plan" from Smokefree Enterprises and government pamphlets citing smoking dangers. Some companies have also sponsored events such as Weedless Wednesday, a one-day occasion intended to develop group spirit in spurring smokers to quit. "Studies show, however," says one expert, "that literature and company-sponsored events have little permanent effect in helping smokers quit" (Woo, 2004, p. 107).

Cost: Negligible

A typical feasibility report presents the decision, background information, benefits, problems, costs, and a schedule.

The feasibility report shown in Figure 13.10 examines the feasibility of a consultant's plan and provides all necessary information: background, benefits, problems, costs, and time frame.

Yardstick Reports

Yardstick reports consider alternative solutions to a problem by establishing criteria against which to weigh options.

"Yardstick" reports examine problems with two or more solutions. To evaluate the best solution, the writer establishes criteria by which to compare the alternatives. The criteria then act as a yardstick against which all the alternatives are measured. This yardstick approach is effective when companies establish specifications for equipment purchases, and then compare each manufacturer's product with the established specs. The yardstick approach is also effective when exact specifications cannot be established.

FIGURE 13.9 Continued

Damon Moore Page 2 October 11, 2007

Alternative 2: Stop-Smoking Programs Outside the Workplace

Local clinics provide treatment programs in classes at their centres. Here in Calgary we have Smokers' Treatment Centre, ACC Motivation Centre, and the New-Choice Program for Stopping Smoking. These behaviour-modification stop-smoking programs are acknowledged to be more effective than literature distribution or incentive programs. However, studies of companies using off-workplace programs show that many employees fail to attend regularly and do not complete the programs.

Cost: $750 per employee, three-month individual program (New-Choice Program)
$500 per employee, three-month group sessions

Highlights costs for easy comparison

Alternative 3: Stop-Smoking Programs at the Workplace

Many clinics offer workplace programs with counsellors meeting employees in company conference rooms. These programs have the advantage of keeping a firm's employees together so that they develop a group spirit and exert pressure on each other to succeed. The most successful programs are on company premises and also on company time. Employees participating in such programs had a 72 percent greater success record than employees attending the same stop-smoking program at an outside clinic (Manley, 2003, p. 35). A disadvantage of this arrangement, of course, is lost work time—amounting to about two hours per week for three months.

Arranges alternatives so that most effective is last

Cost: $500 per employee, three-month program two hours per week release time for three months

Conclusions and Recommendation

Summarizes findings and ends with specific recommendation

Smokers seem to require discipline, counselling, and professional assistance in kicking the nicotine habit. Workplace stop-smoking programs, on company time, are more effective than literature, incentives, and off-workplace programs. If our goal is to reduce supplementary health care costs and lead our employees to healthful lives, we should invest in a workplace stop-smoking program with release time for smokers. Although the program temporarily reduces productivity, we can expect to recapture that loss in lower health care premiums and healthier employees.

Therefore, I recommend that we begin a stop-smoking treatment program on company premises with two hours per week of release time for participants for three months.

Reveals recommendation only after discussing all alternatives

Lists all references in APA style

References

Magazine
Journal
Book

Johns, K. (2005, May). No smoking in your workplace. *Business Times*, 14–16.

Manley, D. (2003). Up in smoke: A case study of one company's proactive stance against smoking. *Management Review, 14*, 33–37.

Woo, N. A. (2004). *The last gasp*. New York: Field Publishers.

The real advantage to yardstick reports is that alternatives can be measured consistently using the same criteria. Reports using a yardstick approach typically are organized this way:

- Begin by describing the problem or need.
- Explain possible solutions and alternatives.

FIGURE 13.10 Feasibility Report

DATE: November 11, 2007

TO: Shauna Clay-Taylor, Vice President

FROM: Elizabeth W. Webb, Customer Service Manager *E.W.W.*

SUBJECT: FEASIBILITY OF PROGRESSION SCHEDULE FOR CSRs

The plan calling for a progression schedule for our customer service representatives is workable, and I think it could be fully implemented by April 1. This report discusses the background, benefits, problems, costs, and time frame involved in executing the plan.

Background: Training and Advancement Problems for CSR Reps. Because of the many insurance policies and agents we service, new customer service representatives require eight weeks of intensive training. Even after this thorough introduction, CSRs are overwhelmed. They take about eight more months before feeling competent on the job. Once they reach their potential, they often look for other positions in the company because they see few advancement possibilities in customer service. These problems were submitted to an outside consultant, who suggested a CSR progression schedule.

Benefits of Plan: Career Progression and Incremental Training. The proposed plan sets up a schedule of career progression, including these levels: (1) CSR trainee, (2) CSR Level I, (3) CSR Level II, (4) CSR Level III, (5) Senior CSR, and (6) CSR supervisor. This program, which includes salary increments with each step, provides a career ladder and incentives for increased levels of expertise and achievement. The plan also facilitates training. Instead of overloading a new trainee with an initial eight-week training program, we would train CSRs slowly with a combination of classroom and on-the-job experiences. Each level requires additional training and expertise.

Problems of Plan: Difficulty in Writing Job Descriptions and Initial Confusion. One of the biggest problems will be distinguishing the job duties at each level. However, I believe that, with the help of our consultant, we can sort out the tasks and expertise required at each level. Another problem will be determining appropriate salary differentials. Attached is a tentative schedule showing proposed wages at each level. We expect to encounter confusion and frustration in implementing this program at first, particularly in placing our current CSRs within the structure.

Costs. Implementing the progression schedule involves two direct costs. The first is the salary of a trainer, at about $40 000 a year. The second cost derives from increased salaries of upper-level CSRs, shown on the attached schedule. I believe, however, that the costs involved are within the estimates planned for this project.

Time Frame. Developing job descriptions should take us about three weeks. Preparing a training program will require another three weeks. Once the program is started, I expect a breaking-in period of at least three months. By April 1 the progression schedule will be fully implemented and showing positive results in improved CSR training, service, and retention.

Attachment

Reveals decision immediately

Outlines organization of the report

Describes problem and background

Evaluates positive and negative aspects of proposal objectively

Presents costs and schedule; omits unnecessary summary

- Establish criteria for comparing the alternatives; tell how the criteria were selected or developed.
- Discuss and evaluate each alternative in terms of the criteria.
- Draw conclusions and make recommendations.

The report shown in Figure 13.11 compares three outplacement agencies and recommends one of them.

FIGURE 13.11 Yardstick Report

DATE: April 28, 2007

TO: George O. Dawes, Vice President

FROM: Kelly Linden, Benefits Administrator *KL*

SUBJECT: CHOICE OF OUTPLACEMENT SERVICES

Here is the report you requested April 1 investigating the possibility of CompuTech's use of outplacement services. It discusses the problem of counselling services for discharged staff and establishes criteria for selecting an outplacement agency. It then evaluates three prospective agencies and presents a recommendation based on that evaluation.

Introduces purpose and gives overview of report organization

Problem: Counselling Discharged Staff

Discusses background briefly because reader already knows the problem

In an effort to reduce costs and increase competitiveness, CompuTech will begin a program of staff reduction that will involve releasing up to 20 percent of our work force over the next 12 to 24 months. Many of these employees have been with us for ten or more years, and they are not being released for performance faults. These employees deserve a severance package that includes counselling and assistance in finding new careers.

Uses dual headings, giving function and description

Solution and Alternatives: Outplacement Agencies

Numerous outplacement agencies offer discharged employees counselling and assistance in locating new careers. This assistance minimizes not only the negative feelings related to job loss but also the very real possibility of litigation. Potentially expensive lawsuits have been lodged against some companies by unhappy employees who felt they were unfairly released.

In seeking an outplacement agency, we should find one that offers advice to the sponsoring company as well as to dischargees. Frankly, many of our managers need help in conducting termination sessions. A suitable outplacement agency should be selected soon so that we can learn about legal termination procedures and also have an agency immediately available when employees are discharged. Here in the metropolitan area, I have located three potential outplacement agencies appropriate to serve our needs: Gray & Associates, Right Access, and Careers Plus.

Announces solution and the alternatives it presents

Establishing Criteria for Selecting Agency

Tells how criteria were selected

In order to choose among the three agencies, I established criteria based on professional articles, discussions with officials at other companies using outplacement agencies, and interviews with agencies. Here are the four groups of criteria I used in evaluating the three agencies:

1. Counselling services—including job-search advice, résumé help, crisis management, corporate counselling, and availability of full-time counsellors
2. Secretarial and research assistance—including availability of secretarial staff, librarian, and personal computers
3. Reputation—based on a telephone survey of former clients and listing with a professional association
4. Costs—for both group programs and executive services

Creates four criteria to use as yardsticks in evaluating alternatives

CHECKLIST FOR WRITING ANALYTICAL REPORTS

Introduction

- ✓ Identify the purpose of the report. Explain why the report is being written.
- ✓ Preview the organization of the report. Especially for long reports, explain to the reader how the report will be organized.
- ✓ Summarize the conclusions and recommendations for receptive audiences. Use the direct pattern only if you have the confidence of the reader.

FIGURE 13.11 Continued

Vice President Dawes Page 2 April 28, 2007

Discussion: Evaluating Agencies by Criteria

Each agency was evaluated using the four criteria just described. Data comparing the first three criteria are summarized in Table 1.

Table 1

A COMPARISON OF SERVICES AND REPUTATIONS FOR THREE LOCAL OUTPLACEMENT AGENCIES

	Gray & Associates	Right Access	Careers Plus
Counselling services			
Résumé advice	Yes	Yes	Yes
Crisis management	Yes	No	Yes
Corporate counselling	Yes	No	No
Full-time counsellors	Yes	No	Yes
Secretarial, research assistance			
Secretarial staff	Yes	Yes	Yes
Librarian, research library	Yes	No	Yes
Personal computers	Yes	No	Yes
Listed by National Association of Career Consultants	Yes	No	Yes
Reputation (telephone survey of former clients)	Excellent	Good	Excellent

Places table close to spot where it is first mentioned

Summarizes complex data in table for easy reading and reference

Counselling Services

All three agencies offered similar basic counselling services with job-search and résumé advice. They differed, however, in three significant areas.

Right Access does not offer crisis management, a service that puts the discharged employee in contact with a counsellor the same day the employee is released. Experts in the field consider this service especially important to help the dischargee begin "bonding" with the counsellor immediately. Immediate counselling also helps the dischargee through the most traumatic moments of one of life's great disappointments and helps him or her learn how to break the news to family members. Crisis management can be instrumental in reducing lawsuits because dischargees immediately begin to focus on career planning instead of concentrating on their pain and need for revenge. Moreover, Right Access does not employ full-time counsellors; it hires part-timers according to demand. Industry authorities advise against using agencies whose staff members are inexperienced and employed on an "as-needed" basis.

Highlights the similarities and differences among the alternatives

In addition, neither Right Access nor Careers Plus offers regular corporate counselling, which I feel is critical in training our managers to conduct exit interviews. Careers Plus, however, suggested that it could schedule special workshops if desired.

Secretarial and Research Assistance

Both Gray & Associates and Careers Plus offer complete secretarial services and personal computers. Dischargees have access to staff and equipment to assist them in their job searches. These agencies also provide research libraries, librarians, and databases of company information to help in securing interviews.

Does not repeat obvious data from table

Findings

Discuss pros and cons. In recommendation/justification reports, evaluate the advantages and disadvantages of each alternative. For unreceptive audiences consider placing the recommended alternative last.

Establish criteria to evaluate alternatives. In "yardstick" studies, create criteria to use in measuring each alternative consistently.

Support the findings with evidence. Supply facts, statistics, expert opinion, survey data, and other proof from which you can draw logical conclusions.

FIGURE 13.11 Continued

Vice President Dawes Page 3 April 28, 2007

Reputation

Discusses objectively how each agency meets criteria

To assess the reputation of each agency, I checked its listing with the National Association of Career Consultants. This is a voluntary organization of outplacement agencies that monitors and polices its members. Gray & Associates and Careers Plus are listed; Right Access is not.

For further evidence I conducted a telephone survey of former agency clients. The three agencies supplied me with names and telephone numbers of companies and individuals they had served. I called four former clients for each agency. Most of the individuals were pleased with the outplacement services they had received. I asked each client the same questions so that I could compare responses.

Costs

All three agencies have two separate fee schedules, summarized in Table 2. The first schedule is for group programs intended for lower-level employees. These include off-site or on-site single-day workshop sessions, and the prices range from $1000 per session (at Right Access) to $1500 per session (at Gray & Associates). An additional fee of $40 to $50 is charged for each participant.

The second fee schedule covers executive services. This counselling is individual and costs from 10 percent to 18 percent of the dischargee's previous year's salary. Since CompuTech will be forced to release numerous managerial staff members, the executive fee schedule is critical. Table 2 shows fees for a hypothetical case involving a manager who earns $60 000 per year.

Selects most important data from table to discuss

Table 2

A COMPARISON OF COSTS FOR THREE AGENCIES

	Gray & Associates	Right Access	Careers Plus
Group programs	$1500/session, $45/participant	$1000/session, $40/participant	$1400/session, $50/participant
Executive services	15% of previous year's salary	10% of previous year's salary	18% of previous year's salary plus $1000 fee
Manager at $60 000/year	$9000	$6000	$11 800

Conclusions and Recommendations

Gives reasons for making recommendation

Although Right Access has the lowest fees, it lacks crisis management, corporate counselling, full-time counsellors, library facilities, and personal computers. Moreover, it is not listed by the National Association of Career Consultants. Therefore, the choice is between Gray & Associates and Careers Plus. Since they have similar services, the deciding factor is cost. Careers Plus would charge nearly $3000 more for counselling a manager than would Gray & Associates. Although Gray & Associates has fewer computers available, all other elements of its services seem good. Therefore, I recommend that CompuTech hire Gray & Associates as an outplacement agency to counsel discharged employees.

Narrows choice to final alternative

✓ Organize the findings for logic and readability. Arrange the findings around the alternatives or the reasons leading to the conclusion. Use headings, enumerations, lists, tables, and graphics to focus emphasis.

Conclusions/Recommendations

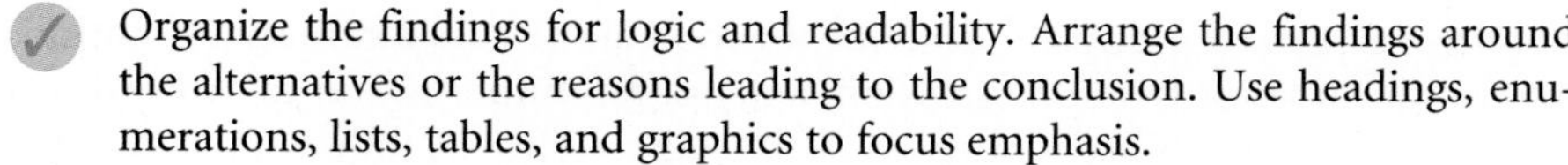

✓ Draw reasonable conclusions from the findings. Develop conclusions that answer the research question. Justify the conclusions with highlights from the findings.

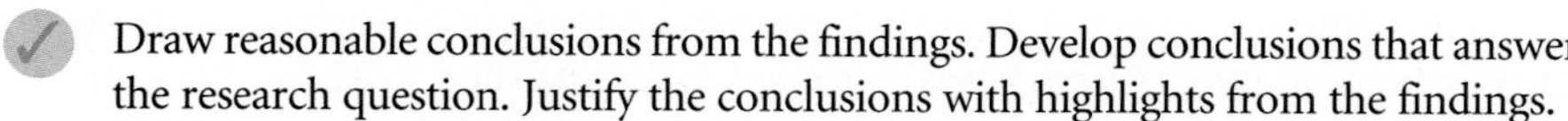

✓ Make recommendations, if asked. For multiple recommendations prepare a list. Use action verbs. Explain needed action.

SUMMARY OF LEARNING OBJECTIVES

1 **Use tabulating and statistical techniques to sort and interpret report data.** Report data are more meaningful when sorted into tables or when analyzed by mean (the arithmetic average), median (the midpoint in a group of figures), and mode (the most frequent response). Range represents a span between the highest and lowest figures. Grids help organize complex data into rows and columns.

2 **Draw meaningful conclusions and make practical report recommendations.** Conclusions tell what the survey data mean—especially in relation to the original report problem. They summarize key findings and may attempt to explain what caused the report problem. They are usually enumerated. In reports that call for recommendations, writers make specific suggestions for actions that can solve the report problem. Recommendations should be feasible and potentially agreeable to the audience. They should all relate to the initial problem. Recommendations may be combined with conclusions.

3 **Organize report data logically and provide cues to aid comprehension.** Reports may be organized in many ways, including by (1) time (establishing a chronology or history of events), (2) component (discussing a problem by geography, division, or product), (3) importance (arranging data from most important to least important, or vice versa), (4) criteria (comparing items by standards), or (5) convention (using an already established grouping).

4 **Prepare typical informational reports.** Periodic, trip, convention, progress, and investigative reports are examples of typical informational reports. Such reports include an introduction that may preview the report purpose and supply background data if necessary. The body of the report is generally divided into three to five segments that may be organized by time, component, importance, criteria, or convention. The body should include clear headings and may use an informal, conversational style unless the audience expects a more formal tone. The summary or conclusion reviews the main points and discusses what action will follow. The conclusion may offer a final thought, express appreciation, or express willingness to provide further information.

5 **Prepare typical analytical reports.** Typical analytical reports include justification/recommendation reports, feasibility reports, and yardstick reports. Justification/recommendation reports organized directly identify a problem, immediately announce a recommendation or solution, explain and discuss its merits, and summarize the action to be taken. Justification/recommendation reports organized indirectly describe a problem, discuss alternative solutions, prove the superiority of one solution, and ask for authorization to proceed with that solution. Feasibility reports study the advisability of following a course of action. They generally announce the author's proposal immediately. Then they describe the background, advantages and disadvantages, costs, and time frame for implementing the proposal. Yardstick reports compare two or more solutions to a problem by measuring each against a set of established criteria. They usually describe a problem, explain possible solutions, establish criteria for comparing alternatives, evaluate each alternative in terms of the criteria, draw conclusions, and make recommendations. The advantage to yardstick reports is consistency in comparing various alternatives.

CHAPTER REVIEW

1. What is data tabulation? Provide an original example. Why is tabulation necessary for a researcher who has collected large amounts of data? (Obj. 1)
2. Forms that use systematic columns and rows to enable you to summarize and simplify numerical data from questionnaires and interviews are called what? (Obj. 1)
3. What is cross-tabulation? Give an example. (Obj. 1)
4. How can a grid help classify material? (Obj. 1)
5. What are the two most widely read sections of a report? (Obj. 2)
6. How do conclusions differ from recommendations? (Obj. 2)
7. When reports have multiple recommendations, how should they be presented? (Obj. 2)
8. Name five methods for organizing report data. Be prepared to discuss each. (Obj. 3)
9. What three devices can report writers use to prevent readers from getting lost in the text? (Obj. 3)
10. Informational reports typically are organized into what three parts? (Obj. 4)
11. Describe periodic reports and what they generally contain. (Obj. 4)
12. What should a progress report include? (Obj. 4)
13. What sequence should a direct recommendation/justification report follow? (Obj. 5)
14. What is a feasibility report? Are they generally intended for internal or external audiences? (Obj. 5)
15. What is a yardstick report? (Obj. 5)

CRITICAL THINKING

1. Researchers can draw various conclusions from a set of data. How do you know how to shape conclusions and recommendations? (Obj. 2)
2. Why is audience analysis particularly important in making report recommendations? (Obj. 2)
3. Should all reports be organized so that they follow the sequence of investigation—that is, describing for the reader the initial problem, analysis of issues, data collection, data analysis, and conclusions? Why or why not? (Obj. 3)
4. What are the major differences between informational and analytical reports? (Objs. 4 and 5)

ACTIVITIES

13.1 Tabulation and Interpretation of Survey Results (Obj. 1)

TEAM | CRITICAL THINKING | LISTENING | SPEAKING

Your business communication class at North Shore College was asked by the college bookstore manager, Larry Krause, to conduct a survey. Concerned about the environment, Krause wants to learn students' reactions to eliminating plastic bags, of which 45 000 are given away annually by the bookstore. Students were questioned about a number of proposals, resulting in the following raw data.

For major purchases the bookstore should:

	Agree	**Undecided**	**Disagree**
5. Continue to provide plastic bags	132	17	411
6. Provide no bags; encourage students to bring their own bags	414	25	121
7. Provide no bags; offer cloth bags at reduced price (about $3)	357	19	184
8. Give a cloth bag with each major purchase, the cost to be included in registration fees	63	15	482

Your Task. In groups of four or five, do the following:

- **a.** Convert the data into a table with a descriptive title. Arrange the items in a logical sequence.
- **b.** How could these survey data be cross-tabulated? Would cross-tabulation serve any purpose?
- **c.** Given the conditions of this survey, name at least three conclusions that could be drawn from the data.
- **d.** Prepare three to five recommendations to be submitted to Mr. Krause. How could they be implemented?

13.2 Evaluating Conclusions (Obj. 2)

E-MAIL

Your Task. Read an in-depth article (800 or more words) in *Business Week, Fortune, Forbes, Canadian Business* or

Financial Post Magazine. What conclusions does the author draw? Are the conclusions valid, based on the evidence presented? In an e-mail message to your instructor, summarize the main points in the article and analyze the conclusions. What conclusions would you have drawn from the data?

13.3 Distinguishing Between Conclusions and Recommendations (Obj. 2)

Your Task. For each of the following statements, indicate whether it could be classified as a conclusion or a recommendation.

a. In times of recession, individuals spend less money on meals away from home.
b. Our restaurant should offer a menu featuring a variety of low-priced items in addition to the regular menu.
c. Absenteeism among employees with families decreases when they have adequate child care.
d. Nearly 80 percent of our business comes from only 20 percent of our customers.
e. Datatech Company should concentrate its major sales effort on its largest accounts.
f. The length of vacations for employees across the country is directly correlated with their length of employment.
g. The employee vacation schedule of Datatech Company compares favourably with the averages of other similar Canadian companies.
h. Offering outplacement service (assistance in finding jobs) tends to defuse the anger that goes with involuntary separation (being released from a job).

13.4 Organizing Data (Obj. 3)

LISTENING SPEAKING

Your Task. How could the findings in the following reports be best organized? Consider these methods: time, component, importance, criteria, and convention.

a. An informational brochure for job candidates that describes your company's areas of employment: accounting, finance, information systems, operations management, marketing, production, and computer-aided design.
b. A monthly sales report submitted to the sales manager.
c. A recommendation report to be submitted to management presenting four building plans to improve access to your building, in compliance with federal regulations. The plans range considerably in feasibility and cost.
d. A progress report submitted six months into the process of planning the program for your organization's convention.
e. An informational report describing a company's expansion plans in South America, Europe, Australia, and Southeast Asia.

13.5 Evaluating Headings and Titles (Obj. 3)

Your Task. Identify the following report headings and titles as "talking" or "functional/descriptive." Discuss the usefulness and effectiveness of each.

a. Need for Tightening Computer ID System
b. Annual Budget
c. Case History: Liberty Regency Hotel Focuses on Improving Service to Customers
d. Solving Our Records Management Problems
e. Alternatives

13.6 Periodic Report: Filling in the Boss (Obj. 4)

E-MAIL

You work hard at your job, but you rarely see your boss and it's hard to keep him informed of your activities and accomplishments.
Your Task. For a job that you currently hold or a previous one, describe your regular activities, discuss irregular events that management should be aware of, and highlight any special needs or problems. Use a memo format in writing a periodic report to your boss.

13.7 Progress Report: Checking In (Obj. 4)

E-MAIL

Students writing a long report described in Chapter 14 must keep their instructors informed of their progress.
Your Task. Write a progress report informing your instructor of your work. Briefly describe the project (its purpose, scope, limitations, and methodology), work you have completed, work yet to be completed, problems encountered, future activities, and expected completion date. Address the e-mail memo report to your instructor.

13.8 Investigative Report: Studying the Journals in Your Field (Obj. 4)

Your campus library has limited funds for the purchase of print journals, and you have been assigned the task of examining journals in your field. Your report to the head librarian will help the library decide which journals are most helpful to students.

Your Task. Prepare an informational letter or memo report that identifies three journals in your field. Discuss the format, tone, and readability of each journal. What kinds of articles are presented? Which journals would be most useful to students in your field? Why? Select one article from each journal to critique as part of your report. Address your report to the head librarian on your campus. Remember that your goal is to investigate and inform, not necessarily to promote and recommend.

13.9 *Investigative Report: Marketing Abroad* (Obj. 4)

WEB

You have been asked to prepare a training program for Canadian companies doing business outside Canada.
Your Task. Select a country to investigate (other than the United States and preferably one for which your library has *Culturgram* materials). Collect data from Culturgram files and from the country's embassy in Ottawa. Interview on-campus international students. Use the Web to discover data about the country. Collect information about formats for written communication, observance of holidays, customary greetings, business ethics, and other topics of interest to businesspeople. Remember that your report should promote business, not tourism. Prepare a memo report addressed to Kelly Jazork, editor for the training program materials.

13.10 *Progress Report: Heading Toward That Degree* (Obj. 4)

You have made an agreement with your parents (or spouse, relative, or significant friend) that you would submit a progress report at this time.
Your Task. Prepare a progress report in letter format. Describe your headway toward your educational goal (such as employment, degree, diploma, or certificate). List your specific achievements, and outline what you have left to complete.

13.11 *Conference or Trip Report: In Your Dreams* (Obj. 4)

You have been sent to a meeting, conference, or seminar in an exotic spot at company expense.
Your Task. From a business periodical select an article describing a conference or meeting connected with your major area of study. The article must be at least 500 words long. Assume you attended the meeting. Prepare a memo report to your supervisor.

13.12 *Justification/Recommendation Report: We Need It* (Obj. 5)

Your office needs a piece of equipment, such as a photocopier, fax, VCR, computer, printer, digital camera, or the like.
Your Task. Select a piece of equipment and do the research necessary to write a convincing report to your boss. Although your boss did not request this report, you feel that he or she will be receptive to your request. Assume that you can be direct and straightforward in your report.

13.13 *Justification/Recommendation Report: Solving a Campus Problem* (Obj. 5)

TEAM

Your Task. In groups of three to five, investigate a problem on your campus, such as inadequate parking, slow registration, poor class schedules, inefficient bookstore, weak job-placement program, unrealistic degree or diploma requirements, or lack of internship programs. Within your group develop a solution to the problem. If possible, consult the officials involved to ask for their input in arriving at a feasible solution. After reviewing persuasive techniques discussed in Chapter 10, write a group or individual justification/recommendation report(s). Address it to the proper campus official or to your instructor.

13.14 *Feasibility Report: International Organization* (Obj. 5)

CRITICAL THINKING

To fulfill a senior project in your department, you have been asked to submit a letter report to the dean evaluating the feasibility of starting an organization of international students on campus.
Your Task. Find out how many international students are on your campus, what nations they represent, how one goes about starting an organization, and whether a faculty sponsor is needed. Assume that you conducted an informal survey of international students. Of the 39 who filled out the survey, 31 said they would be interested in joining.

13.15 *Feasibility Report: Improving Employee Fitness* (Obj. 5)

CRITICAL THINKING

Your company is considering ways to promote employee fitness and morale.

Your Task. Select a possible fitness program that seems reasonable for your company. Consider a softball league, bowling teams, basketball league, lunchtime walks, lunchtime fitness speakers and demos, company-sponsored health club membership, workout room, fitness centre, fitness director, and so on. Assume that your boss has tentatively agreed to one of the programs and has asked you to write a memo report investigating its feasibility.

13.16 Yardstick Report: Evaluating Equipment (Obj. 5)

CRITICAL THINKING

You recently complained to your boss that you were unhappy with a piece of equipment that you use (printer, computer, copier, fax, or the like). After some thought, the boss decided you were right and told you to go shopping.

Your Task. Compare at least three different manufacturers' models and recommend one. Since the company will be purchasing ten or more units and since several managers must approve the purchase, write a careful report documenting your findings. Establish at least five criteria for comparing the models. Submit a memo report to your boss.

13.17 Yardstick Report: Measuring the Alternatives (Obj. 5)

CRITICAL THINKING

Your Task. Consider a problem where you work or in an organization you know. Select a problem with several alternative solutions or courses of action (retaining the present status could be one alternative). Develop criteria that could be used to evaluate each alternative. Write a report measuring each alternative by the yardstick you have created. Recommend a course of action to your boss or to the organization head.

C.L.U.E. REVIEW 13

On a separate sheet edit the following sentences to correct faults in grammar, punctuation, spelling, numbers, proofreading, and word use.

1. If you are conducting research for a report you will probibly face a jumble of data including: printouts, note cards, copies of articles, inter view notes, questionaire results and statistics.
2. Numerical information from surveys are usally summarized, and simplified in tables.
3. Researchers use 3 statistical terms to describe data; mean, median and mode.
4. When my boss and me use the word *average* we are refering to the mean which is the arithmetic average.
5. Readers' of reports often turn right to the conclusions and reccommendations, therefore these section must be written vary carefully.
6. Report Conclusions explain what the problem is, Recommendations tell how to solve it.
7. In writing reports you will probably organize you're data using 1 of the following 5 methods, time, component, importance, criteria or convention.
8. The Introduction to a report should tell it's purpose and significance, it should also preview the main points.
9. You should however delay writing the introduction, until after you complete the report.
10. To turn out professional looking documents be sure to design attractive pages, and avoid using to many typefaces and graphics.

Chapter 14

Proposals and Formal Reports

LEARNING OBJECTIVES

1 *Discuss the components of informal proposals.*

2 *Discuss the special components in formal proposals.*

3 *Identify formal report components that precede its introduction.*

4 *Outline topics that might be covered in the introduction of a formal report.*

5 *Describe the components of a formal report that follow the introduction.*

6 *Specify tips that aid writers of formal reports.*

PREPARING FORMAL AND INFORMAL PROPOSALS

Proposals are persuasive offers to solve problems, provide services, or sell equipment.

Proposals are written offers to solve problems, provide services, or sell equipment. Although some proposals are internal, often taking the form of justification and recommendation reports, most proposals are external. External proposals are an important means of generating income for many organizations.

Because proposals are vital to their success, some businesses hire consultants or maintain specialists who do nothing but write proposals. Such proposals typically tell how a problem can be solved, what procedure will be followed, who will do it, how long it will take, and how much it will cost.

Government agencies and large companies use requests for proposals (RFPs) to solicit competitive bids on projects.

Proposals may be divided into two categories: solicited or unsolicited. When firms know exactly what they want, they prepare a request for proposal (RFP) specifying their requirements. Government agencies and large companies are likely to use RFPs to solicit competitive bids from vendors. Companies today want to be able to compare "apples with apples," and they also want the protection offered by proposals, which are legal contracts. Unsolicited proposals are written when an individual or firm sees a problem to be solved and offers a proposal to do so.

The most important point to remember about proposals—whether solicited or unsolicited—is that they are sales presentations. They must be persuasive, not merely mechanical descriptions of what you can do. Among other things, you may recall, effective persuasive sales messages (1) emphasize benefits for the reader, (2) "toot

FIGURE 14.1 Components of Formal and Informal Proposals

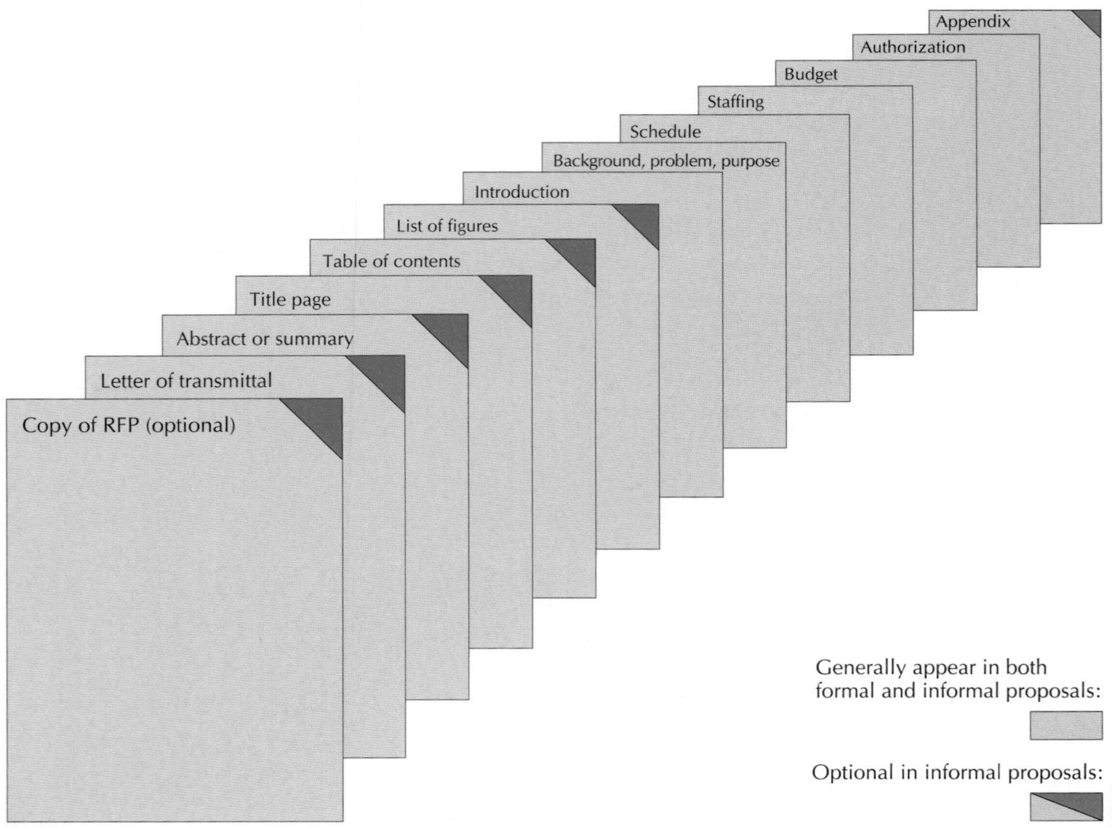

your horn" by detailing your expertise and accomplishments, and (3) make it easy for the reader to understand and respond.

Proposals may be informal or formal; they differ primarily in length and format. Notice in Figure 14.1 that formal proposals, described shortly, have many more components than informal proposals.

Components of Informal Proposals

Informal proposals may be presented in short (two- to four-page) letters. Sometimes called *letter proposals*, they may contain six principal components: introduction, background, proposal, staffing, budget, and authorization request. As you can see in Figure 14.1, both informal and formal proposals contain these six basic parts.

1

Informal proposals may contain an introduction, background information, the proposal, staffing requirements, a budget, and an authorization request.

Introduction. Most proposals begin by briefly explaining the reasons for the proposal and by highlighting the writer's qualifications. To make your introduction more persuasive, you need to provide a "hook" to capture the reader's interest. One proposal expert suggests these possibilities:[1]

- Hint at extraordinary results with details to be revealed shortly.
- Promise low costs or speedy results.
- Mention a remarkable resource (well-known authority, new computer program, well-trained staff) available exclusively to you.
- Identify a serious problem (worry item) and promise a solution, to be explained later.
- Specify a key issue or benefit that you feel is the heart of the proposal.

Although writers may know what goes into the proposal introduction, many face writer's block before they can get started. It's often a good idea to put off writing the proposal introduction until after you have completed other parts. For longer proposals the introduction also describes the scope and limitations of the project, as well as outlining the organization of the material to come.

Background, Problem, Purpose. The background section identifies the problem and discusses the goals or purposes of the project. In an unsolicited proposal your goal is to convince the reader that a problem exists. Thus, you must present the problem in detail, discussing such factors as monetary losses, failure to comply with government regulations, or loss of customers. In a solicited proposal your aim is to persuade the reader that you understand the problem completely. Thus, if you are responding to an RFP, this means repeating its language.

Proposal, Plan, Schedule. In the proposal section itself, you should discuss your plan for solving the problem. In some proposals this is tricky because you want to disclose enough of your plan to secure the contract without giving away so much information that your services aren't needed. Without specifics, though, your proposal has little chance, so you must decide how much to reveal. Tell what you propose to do and how it will benefit the reader. Remember, too, that a proposal is a sales presentation. Sell your methods, product, and "deliverables"—items that will be left with the client. In this section some writers specify how the project will be managed and how its progress will be audited. Most writers also include a schedule of activities or timetable showing when events will take place.

The actual proposal section must give enough information to secure the contract but not so much detail that the services are no longer needed.

Staffing. The staffing section of a proposal describes the credentials and expertise of the project leaders. It may also identify the size and qualifications of the support

The staffing section promotes the credentials and expertise of the project leaders and support staff.

staff, along with other resources such as computer facilities and special programs for analyzing statistics. The staffing section is a good place to endorse and promote your staff.

Because a proposal is a legal contract, the budget must be carefully researched.

Budget. A central item in most proposals is the budget, a list of proposed project costs. You need to prepare this section carefully because it represents a contract; you can't raise the price later—even if your costs increase. You can—and should—protect yourself with a deadline for acceptance. In the budget section some writers itemize hours and costs; others present a total sum only. Your analysis of the project will help you decide what kind of budget to prepare.

Authorization Request. Informal proposals often close with a request for approval or authorization. In addition, the closing should remind the reader of key benefits and motivate action. It might also include a deadline date beyond which the offer is invalid. In some organizations, authorization to proceed is not part of the proposal. Instead, it is usually discussed after the customer has received the proposal. In this way the customer and the sales account manager are able to negotiate terms before a formal agreement is drawn.

Special Components of Formal Proposals

2

Formal proposals differ from informal proposals not in style but in size and format. Formal proposals respond to big projects and may range from 5 to 200 or more pages. To facilitate comprehension and reference, they are organized into many parts, as shown in Figure 14.1. In addition to the six basic components just described, formal proposals may contain some or all of the following front and end parts.

Formal proposals might also contain a copy of the RFP, a letter of transmittal, an abstract, a title page, a table of contents, a list of figures, and an appendix.

Copy of RFP. A copy of the RFP may be included in the opening parts of a formal proposal. Large organizations may have more than one RFP circulating, and identification is necessary.

Letter of Transmittal. A letter of transmittal, usually bound inside formal proposals, addresses the person who is designated to receive the proposal or who will make the final decision. The letter describes how you learned about the problem or confirms that the proposal responds to the enclosed RFP. This persuasive letter briefly presents the major features and benefits of your proposal. Here, you should assure the reader that you are authorized to make the bid and mention the time limit for which the bid stands. You may also offer to provide additional information and ask for action, if appropriate.

An abstract summarizes a proposal's highlights for specialists; an executive summary does so for managers.

Abstract or Executive Summary. An abstract is a brief summary (typically one page) of a proposal's highlights intended for specialists or for technical readers. An executive summary also reviews the proposal's highlights, but it is written for managers and so should be less technically oriented. Formal proposals may contain one or both summaries.

Title Page. The title page includes the following items, generally in this order: title of proposal, name of client organization, RFP number or other announcement, date of submission, author's name, and/or her or his organization.

Table of Contents. Because most proposals don't contain an index, the table of contents becomes quite important. Tables of contents should include all headings and their beginning page numbers. Items that appear before the table of contents (copy of RFP, letter of transmittal, abstract, and title page) typically are not listed in the contents. However, any appendixes should be listed.

List of Figures. Proposals with many tables and figures often contain a list of figures. This list includes each figure or table title and its page number. If you have just a few figures or tables, however, you may omit this list.

Appendix. Ancillary material of interest to some readers goes in appendixes. Appendix A might include résumés of the principal investigators or testimonial letters. Appendix B might include examples or a listing of previous projects. Other appendixes could include audit procedures, technical graphics, or professional papers cited in the body of the proposal.

Proposals in the past were always paper-based and delivered by mail or special messenger. Today, however, companies increasingly prefer *online proposals.* Receiving companies may transmit the electronic proposal to all levels of management without ever printing a page, thus appealing to many environmentally conscious organizations.

Well-written proposals win contracts and business for companies and individuals. Many companies depend entirely on proposals to generate their income, so proposal writing becomes critical. For more information about industry standards and resources, visit the Web site of the Association of Proposal Management Professionals at <**www.apmp.org**>.

Another form of proposal is a business plan. Entrepreneurs who want to start a business or expand an existing business often must ask for funding. To secure financial backing, these budding businesspeople write business plans to submit to potential backers. To learn more about preparing a business plan, see the accompanying Career Coach box.

CHECKLIST FOR WRITING PROPOSALS

Introduction

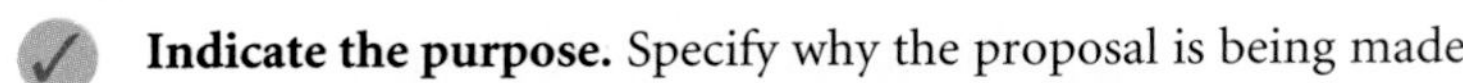

- ✓ **Indicate the purpose.** Specify why the proposal is being made.
- ✓ **Develop a persuasive "hook."** Suggest excellent results, low costs, or exclusive resources. Identify a serious problem or name a key issue or benefit.

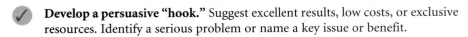

Background, Problem

- ✓ **Provide necessary background.** Discuss the significance of the proposal and its goals or purposes.
- ✓ **Introduce the problem.** For unsolicited proposals convince the reader that a problem exists. For solicited proposals show that you fully understand the problem and its ramifications.

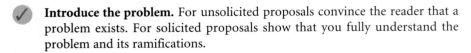

Proposal, Plan

- ✓ **Explain the proposal.** Present your plan for solving the problem or meeting the need.

CAREER COACH

Preparing an Effective Business Plan

Let's say you want to start your own business. Unless you can count on the Bank of Mom and Dad, you will need financial backing (called *venture capital*). A business plan is critical for securing financial support of any kind. Such a plan also ensures that you have done your homework and know what you are doing in launching your business. It provides you with a detailed road map to chart a course to success. Here are suggestions for preparing an effective business plan:

- **Letter of transmittal and/or executive summary.** Explain your reason for writing. Provide your name, address, and telephone number, along with contact information for all principals. Include a concise mission statement that describes your business and explains the reasons it will succeed. Because potential investors will be looking for this mission statement, consider highlighting it with a paragraph heading (*Mission statement*), or use bolding or italics. Some consultants say that you should be able to write your mission statement on the back of a business card. Others think that one or two short paragraphs might be more realistic. To give it special treatment, you could make the mission statement a section of its own following the table of contents. Your executive summary should conclude by introducing the parts of the following plan and asking for support.

- **Table of contents.** List the page numbers and topics included in your plan.

- **Company description.** Identify the form of your business (proprietorship, partnership, or corporation) and its business type (merchandising, manufacturing, or service). For existing companies, describe the company's founding, growth, sales, and profit.

- **Product/service description.** In jargon-free language, explain what you are providing, how it will benefit customers, and why it is better than existing products or services. For start-ups, explain why the business will be profitable. Investors aren't always looking for a unique product or service. Instead, they are searching for a concept whose growth potential distinguishes it from other proposals competing for funds.

- **Market analysis.** Discuss market characteristics, trends, projected growth, customer behaviour, complementary products and services, and barriers to entry. Identify your customers and how you will attract, hold, and increase your market share. Discuss the strengths and weaknesses of your direct and indirect competitors.

- **Operations and management.** Explain specifically how you will run your business, including location, equipment, personnel, and management. Highlight experienced and well-trained members of the management team and your advisors. Many investors consider this the most important factor in assessing business potential. Can your management team implement this business plan?

- **Financial analysis.** Outline a realistic start-up budget that includes fees for legal/professional services, occupancy, licences/permits, equipment, insurance, supplies, advertising/promotions, salaries/wages, accounting, income, and utilities. Also present an operating budget that projects costs for personnel, insurance, rent, depreciation, loan payments, salaries, taxes, repairs, and so on. Explain how much money you have, how much you will need to start up, and how much you will need to stay in business.

- **Appendixes.** Provide necessary extras such as managers' résumés, promotional materials, and product photos.

Seeing Sample Business Plans on the Web

Writing a business plan is easier if you can see examples and learn from experts' suggestions. On the Web you will find many sites devoted to business plans. Some sites want to sell you something; others offer free advice. One of the best sites **<www.bplans.com>** does try to sell business plans. But the site also provides 60 free samples of business plans ranging from aircraft rental to wedding consultant businesses.

- **Discuss plan management and evaluation.** If appropriate, tell how the plan will be implemented and evaluated.

- **Outline a timetable.** Provide a schedule showing what will be done and when.

Staffing

- **Promote the qualifications of your staff.** Explain the specific credentials and expertise of the key personnel for the project.

- **Mention special resources or equipment.** Show how your support staff and resources are superior to those of the competition.

Budget

- **Show project costs.** For most projects itemize costs. Remember, however, that proposals are contracts.

- **Include a deadline.** Here or in the conclusion present a date beyond which the bid figures are no longer valid.

Authorization

- **Ask for approval.** Make it easy for the reader to authorize the project (for example, *Sign and return the duplicate copy*).

WRITING FORMAL REPORTS

Formal reports are similar to formal proposals in length, organization, and serious tone. Instead of making an offer, however, formal reports represent the end product of thorough investigation and analysis. They present ordered information to decision makers in business, industry, government, and education. In many ways formal reports are extended versions of the analytical business reports presented in Chapter 13. Figure 14.2 shows the components of typical formal reports, their normal sequence, and parts that might be omitted in informal reports. 3

Components of Formal Reports

Formal reports discuss the results of a process of thorough investigation and analysis.

A number of front and end items lengthen formal reports but enhance their professional tone and serve their multiple audiences. Formal reports may be read by many levels of managers, along with technical specialists and financial consultants. Therefore, breaking a long, formal report into small segments makes its information more accessible and easier to understand for all readers. These segments are discussed here and also illustrated in the model report shown in Figure 14.3. This analytical report studies the recycling program at West Coast College and makes recommendations for improving its operation.

FIGURE 14.2 Components of Formal and Informal Reports

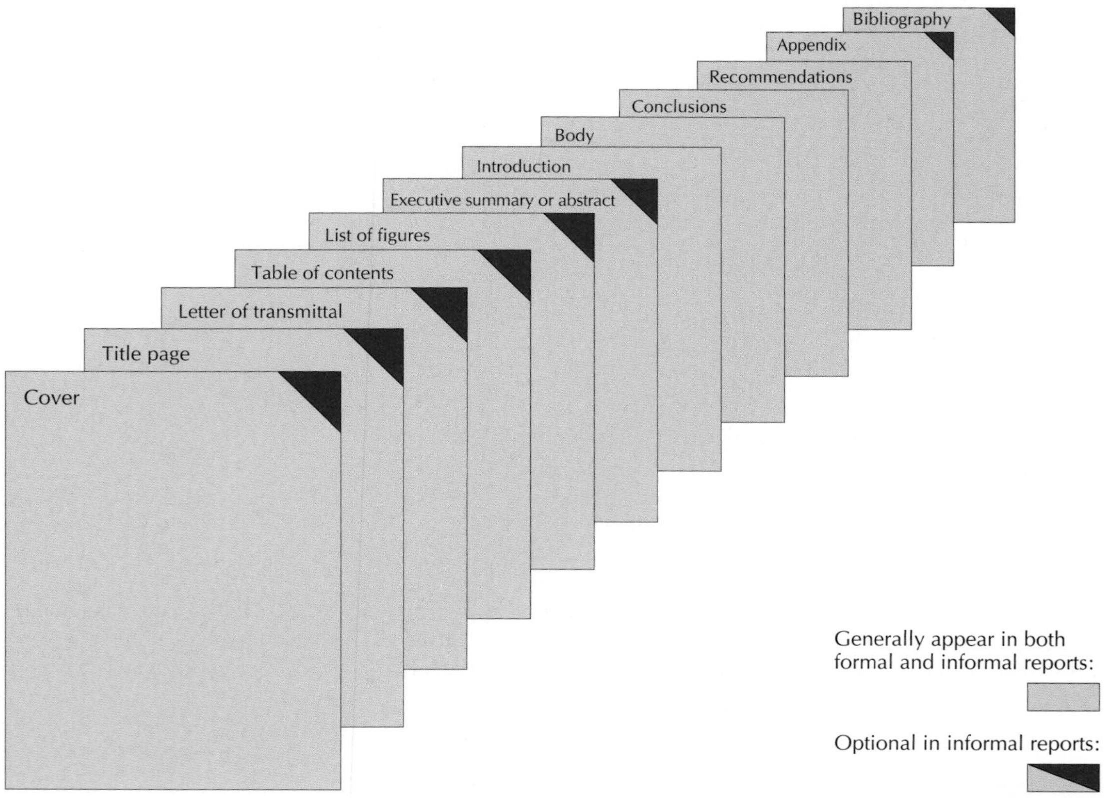

Like proposals, formal reports are divided into many segments to make information comprehensible and accessible.

Cover. Formal reports are usually enclosed in vinyl or heavy paper binders to protect the pages and to give a professional, finished appearance. Some companies have binders imprinted with their name and logo. The title of the report may appear through a cut-out window or may be applied with an adhesive label. Good stationery and office supply stores usually stock an assortment of report binders and labels.

Title Page. A report title page, as illustrated in the Figure 14.3 model report, begins with the name of the report typed in uppercase letters (no underscore and no quotation marks). Next comes *Presented to* (or *Submitted to*) and the name, title, and organization of the individual receiving the report. Lower on the page is *Prepared by* (or *Submitted by*) and the author's name plus any necessary identification. The last item on the title page is the date of submission. All items after the title are typed in a combination of upper- and lowercase letters.

A letter or memo of transmittal gives a personalized overview of a formal report.

Letter or Memo of Transmittal. Generally written on organization stationery, a letter or memorandum of transmittal introduces a formal report. You will recall that letters are sent to outsiders and memos to insiders. A transmittal letter or memo follows the direct pattern and is usually less formal than the report itself (for example, the letter or memo may use contractions and the first-person pronouns *I* and *we*). The transmittal letter or memo typically (1) announces the topic of the report and tells how it was authorized; (2) briefly describes the project; (3) highlights the report's findings, conclusions, and recommendations, if the reader is expected to be supportive; and (4) closes with appreciation for the assignment, instruction for the reader's follow-up actions, acknowledgment of help from others, or offers of assistance in answering questions. If a report is going to different readers, a special transmittal letter or memo should be prepared for each, anticipating what each reader needs to know in using the report.

Table of Contents. The table of contents shows the headings in a report and their page numbers. It gives an overview of the report topics and helps readers locate them. You should wait to prepare the table of contents until after you've completed the report. For short reports you should include all headings. For longer reports you might want to list only first- and second-level headings. Leaders (spaced or unspaced dots) help guide the eye from the heading to the page number. Items may be indented in outline form or typed flush with the left margin.

List of Figures. For reports with several figures or illustrations, you may wish to include a list of figures to help readers locate them. This list may appear on the same page as the table of contents, space permitting. For each figure or illustration, include a title and page number. Some writers distinguish between tables and all other illustrations, which are called figures. If you make this distinction, you should also prepare separate lists of tables and figures. Because the model report in Figure 14.3 has few illustrations, the writer labelled them all "figures," a method that simplifies numbering (see page 349).

An executive summary supplies an overview of a longer report.

Executive Summary. The purpose of an executive summary is to present an overview of a longer report to people who may not have time to read the entire document. Generally, an executive summary is prepared by the author who is writing about his or her own report. But occasionally you may be asked to write an executive summary of a published report or article written by someone else. In either case you will probably perform the following activities:

- **Summarize key points.** Your goal is to summarize the important points including the purpose of the report; the problem addressed; and the findings, conclusions, and recommendations. You might also summarize the research methods, if they can be stated concisely.
- **Look for strategic words and sentences.** Read the completed report carefully. Pay special attention to first and last sentences of paragraphs, which often contain summary statements. Look for words that enumerate (*first, next, finally*) and words that express causation (*therefore, as a result*). Also look for words that signal essentials (*basically, central, leading, principal, major*) and words that contrast ideas (*however, consequently*).
- **Prepare an outline with headings.** At a minimum include headings for the purpose, findings, and conclusions/recommendations. What kernels of information would your reader want to know about these topics?
- **Fill in your outline.** Some writers use their computers to cut and paste important parts of the text. Then they condense with careful editing. Others find it most efficient to create new sentences as they prepare the executive summary.
- **Begin with the purpose.** The easiest way to begin an executive summary is with the words "The purpose of this report is to . . . ." Experienced writers may be more creative.
- **Follow the report order.** Present all your information in the order in which it is found in the report.
- **Eliminate nonessential details.** Include only main points. Don't include anything not in the original report. Use minimal technical language.

- **Control the length.** An executive summary is usually no longer than 10 percent of the original document. Thus, a 100-page report might require a 10-page summary. A 10-page report might need only a 1-page summary—or no summary at all. The executive summary for a long report may also include graphics to adequately highlight main points.

To see a representative executive summary, look at Figure 14.3 on page 350. Although it is only one page long, this executive summary includes headings to help the reader see the main divisions immediately. Let your organization's practices guide you in determining the length and form of an executive summary.

Introduction. Formal reports begin with an introduction that sets the scene and announces the subject. Because they contain many parts serving different purposes, formal reports have a degree of redundancy. The same information may be included in the letter of transmittal, summary, and introduction. To avoid sounding repetitious, try to present the data slightly differently. But don't skip the introduction because you've included some of its information elsewhere. You can't be sure that your reader saw the information earlier. A good report introduction typically covers the following elements, although not necessarily in this order:

- **Background.** Describe events leading up to the problem or need.
- **Problem or purpose.** Explain the report topic and specify the problem or need that motivated the report.
- **Significance.** Tell why the topic is important. You may wish to quote experts or cite newspapers, journals, books, and other secondary sources to establish the importance of the topic.
- **Scope.** Clarify the boundaries of the report, defining what will be included or excluded.
- **Organization.** Launch readers by giving them a road map that previews the structure of the report.

Beyond these minimal introductory elements, consider adding any of the following information that is relevant for your readers:

- **Authorization.** Identify who commissioned the report. If no letter of transmittal is included, also tell why, when, by whom, and to whom the report was written.
- **Literature review.** Summarize what other authors and researchers have published on this topic, especially for academic and scientific reports.
- **Sources and methods.** Describe your secondary sources (periodicals, books, databases). Also explain how you collected primary data, including survey size, sample design, and statistical programs used.
- **Definitions of key terms.** Define words that may be unfamiliar to the audience. Also define terms with special meanings, such as *small business* when it specifically means businesses with fewer than 30 employees.

Body. The principal section in a formal report is the body. It discusses, analyzes, interprets, and evaluates the research findings or solution to the initial problem. This is where you show the evidence that justifies your conclusions. Organize the body into main categories following your original outline or using one of the patterns described earlier (such as time, component, importance, criteria, or convention).

Although we refer to this section as the body, it doesn't carry that heading. Instead, it contains clear headings that explain each major section. Headings may be functional or talking. Functional heads (such as *Results of the Survey, Analysis of Findings,* or *Discussion*) help readers identify the purpose of the section but don't reveal what's in it. Such headings are useful for routine reports or for sensitive topics that may upset readers. Talking heads (for example, *Recycling Habits of Campus Community*) are more informative and interesting, but they don't help readers see the organization of the report. The model report in Figure 14.3 uses functional heads for organizational sections requiring identification (*Introduction, Conclusions,* and *Recommendations*) and talking heads to divide the body.

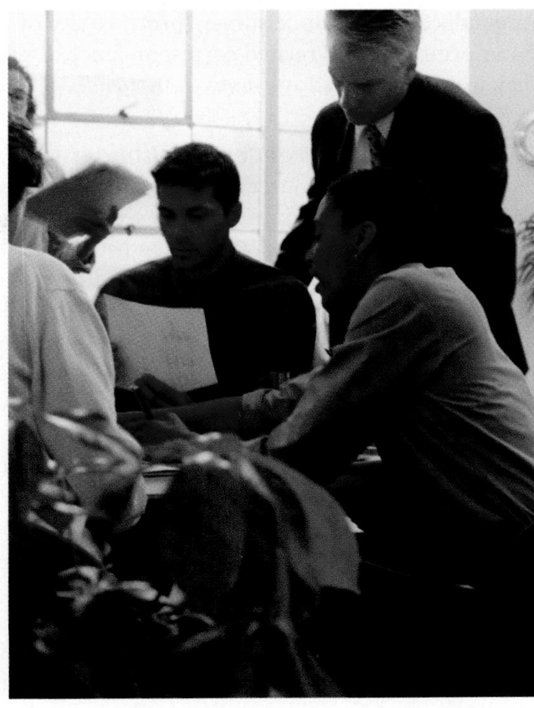

Keep in mind the following important piece of business advice: Start with a statement of purpose. If you can't explain your idea in 25 words or less, it's probably not a good idea.

Conclusions. This important section tells what the findings mean, particularly in terms of solving the original problem. Some writers prefer to intermix their conclusions with the analysis of the findings—instead of presenting the conclusions separately. Other writers place the conclusions before the body so that busy readers can examine the significant information immediately. Still others combine the conclusions and recommendations. Most writers, though, present the conclusions after the body because readers expect this structure. In long reports this section may include a summary of the findings. To improve comprehension, you may present the conclusions in a numbered or bulleted list. See Chapter 13 for more suggestions on drawing conclusions.

The recommendations section of a formal report offers specific suggestions for solving a problem.

Recommendations. When requested, you should submit recommendations that make precise suggestions for actions to solve the report problem. Recommendations are most helpful when they are practical and reasonable. Naturally, they should evolve from the findings and conclusions. Don't introduce new information in the conclusions or recommendations. As with conclusions, the position of recommendations is somewhat flexible. They may be combined with conclusions, or they may be presented before the body, especially when the audience is eager and supportive. Generally, though, in formal reports they come last.

Recommendations require an appropriate introductory sentence, such as *The findings and conclusions in this study support the following recommendations.* When making many recommendations, number them and phrase each as a command, such as *Begin an employee fitness program with a workout room available five days a week.* If appropriate, add information describing how to implement each recommendation. Some reports include a timetable describing the who, what, when, where, and how for putting each recommendation into operation. Chapter 13 provides more information about writing recommendations.

Appendix. Incidental or supporting materials belong in appendixes at the end of a formal report. These materials are relevant to some readers but not to all.

Appendixes may include survey forms, copies of other reports, tables of data, computer printouts, and related correspondence. If additional appendixes are necessary, they would be named *Appendix A, Appendix B,* and so forth.

The bibliography section of a formal report identifies sources of ideas mentioned in the report.

Works Cited, References, or Bibliography. Readers look in the bibliography section to locate the sources of ideas mentioned in a report. Your method of report documentation determines how this section is developed. If you use the MLA referencing format, all citations would be listed alphabetically in the "Works Cited." If you use the APA format, your list would be called "References." Regardless of the format, you must include the author, title, publication, date of publication, page number, and other significant data for all ideas or quotations used in your report. For electronic references include the preceding information plus a description of the electronic address or path leading to the citation. Also include the date on which you located the electronic reference. To see electronic and other citations, examine the list of references at the end of Figure 14.3. Appendix B of the text contains additional documentation information.

Final Writing Tips

6

Formal reports require careful attention to all phases of Guffey's 3-×-3 writing process.

Formal reports are not undertaken lightly. They involve considerable effort in all three phases of writing, beginning with analysis of the problem and anticipation of the audience. Researching the data, organizing it into a logical presentation, and composing the first draft make up the second phase of writing. Revising, proofreading, and evaluating are the third phase. Although everyone approaches the writing process somewhat differently, the following tips offer advice in problem areas faced by most formal report writers.

Smart report writers allow themselves plenty of time, research thoroughly, draw up a useful outline, and work on a computer.

Effective formal reports maintain parallelism in verb tenses, avoid first-person pronouns, and use the active voice.

- **Allow sufficient time.** Develop a realistic timetable and stick to it.
- **Finish data collection.** Don't begin writing until you've collected all the data and drawn the primary conclusions. Starting too early often means backtracking. For reports based on survey data, compile the tables and figures first.
- **Work from a good outline.** A clear outline provides the necessary order and direction.
- **Provide a proper writing environment.** You'll need a quiet spot where you can spread out your materials and work without interruption.
- **Use a computer.** Preparing a report on a computer enables you to keyboard quickly; revise easily; and check spelling, grammar, and synonyms readily.
- **Write rapidly; revise later.** Some experts advise writers to record their ideas quickly and save revision until after the first draft is completed.
- **Save difficult sections.** If some sections are harder to write than others, save them until you've developed confidence and rhythm working on easier topics.
- **Be consistent in verb tense.** Use past-tense verbs to describe completed action, use present-tense verbs to explain current actions, and use past-tense verbs when citing references.
- **Generally avoid *I* and *we* and write in the third person.** This formal style sometimes results in the overuse of passive-voice verbs so look for alternative constructions.
- **Let the first draft sit and return to it with the expectation of revising and improving it.**
- **Revise for clarity, coherence, and conciseness.** Make sure that your writing is so clear that a busy manager does not have to reread any part.

- **Proofread the final copy three times.** First, read a printed copy slowly for word meanings and content. Then read the copy again for spelling, punctuation, grammar, and other mechanical errors. Finally, scan the entire report to check its formatting and consistency.

Putting It All Together

Formal reports in business generally aim to study problems and recommend solutions. Alan Christopher, business senator to the Office of Associated Students (OAS) at West Coast College, was given a campus problem to study, resulting in the formal report shown in Figure 14.3, which begins on page 347.

The campus recycling program, under the direction of Cheryl Bryant and supported by the OAS, was not attracting the anticipated level of participation. As the campus recycling program began its second year of operation, Cheryl and the OAS wondered whether campus community members were sufficiently aware of the program. They also wondered how participation could be increased. Alan volunteered to investigate the problem because of his strong support for environmental causes. He also needed to conduct a research project for one of his business courses, and he had definite ideas for improving the campus OAS recycling program.

Alan's report illustrates many of the points discussed in this chapter. Although it's a good example of typical report format and style, it should not be viewed as the only way to present a report. Wide variation exists in reports.

The following checklist summarizes the report process and report components in one handy list.

CHECKLIST FOR PREPARING FORMAL REPORTS

Report Process

- ✓ **Analyze the report problem and purpose.** Develop a problem question (*Is sexual harassment affecting employees at DataTech?*) and a purpose statement (*The purpose of this report is to investigate sexual harassment at DataTech and recommend remedies*).

- ✓ **Anticipate the audience and issues.** Consider primary and secondary audiences. What do they already know? What do they need to know? Divide the major problem into subproblems for investigation.

- ✓ **Prepare a work plan.** Include problem and purpose statements, as well as a description of the sources and methods of collecting data. Prepare a tentative project outline and a work schedule with anticipated dates of completion for all segments of the project.

- ✓ **Collect data.** Begin by searching secondary sources (electronic databases, books, magazines, journals, newspapers) for information on your topic. Then, if necessary, gather primary data by surveying, interviewing, observing, and experimenting.

- ✓ **Document data sources.** Prepare note cards or separate sheets of paper citing all references (author, date, source, page, and quotation). Select a documentation format (Chapter 12) and use it consistently.

- ✓ **Interpret and organize the data.** Arrange the collected information in tables, grids, or outlines to help you visualize relationships and interpret meanings. Organize the data into an outline (Chapter 6).

- **Prepare graphics.** Make tables, charts, graphs, and illustrations—but *only* if they serve a function. Use graphics to help clarify, condense, simplify, or emphasize your data.
- **Compose the first draft.** At a computer write the first draft from your outline. Use appropriate headings as well as transitional expressions (such as *however, on the contrary,* and *in addition*) to guide the reader through the report.
- **Revise and proofread.** Revise to eliminate wordiness, ambiguity, and redundancy. Look for ways to improve readability, such as bulleted or numbered lists. Proofread three times for (1) word and content meaning, (2) grammar and mechanical errors, and (3) formatting.
- **Evaluate the product.** Examine the final report. Will it achieve its purpose? Encourage feedback so that you can learn how to improve future reports.

Report Components

- **Title page.** Balance the following lines on the title page: (1) name of the report (in all caps); (2) name, title, and organization of the individual receiving the report; (3) author's name, title, and organization; and (4) date submitted.
- **Letter of transmittal.** Announce the report topic and explain who authorized it. Briefly describe the project and preview the conclusions, if the reader is supportive. Close by expressing appreciation for the assignment, suggesting follow-up actions, acknowledging the help of others, or offering to answer questions.
- **Table of contents.** Show the beginning page number where each report heading appears in the report. Connect the page numbers and headings with leaders (spaced dots).
- **List of illustrations.** Include a list of tables, illustrations, or figures showing the title of the item and its page number. If space permits, put these lists on the same page with the table of contents.
- **Executive summary.** Summarize the report purpose, findings, conclusions, and recommendations. Gauge the length of the summary by the length of the report and by your organization's practices.
- **Introduction.** Explain the problem motivating the report; describe its background and significance. Clarify the scope and limitations of the report. Optional items include a review of relevant literature and a description of data sources, methods, and key terms. Close by previewing the report's organization.
- **Body.** Discuss, analyze, and interpret the research findings or the proposed solution to the problem. Arrange the findings in logical segments following your outline. Use clear, descriptive headings.
- **Conclusions and recommendations.** Explain what the findings mean in relation to the original problem. If requested, make enumerated recommendations that suggest actions for solving the problem.
- **Appendix.** Include items of interest to some, but not all, readers, such as a data questionnaire or computer printouts.
- **References and bibliography.** If footnotes are not provided in the text, list all references in a bibliographical section called "Works Cited," or "References."

FIGURE 14.3 Model Formal Report With MLA Citation Style

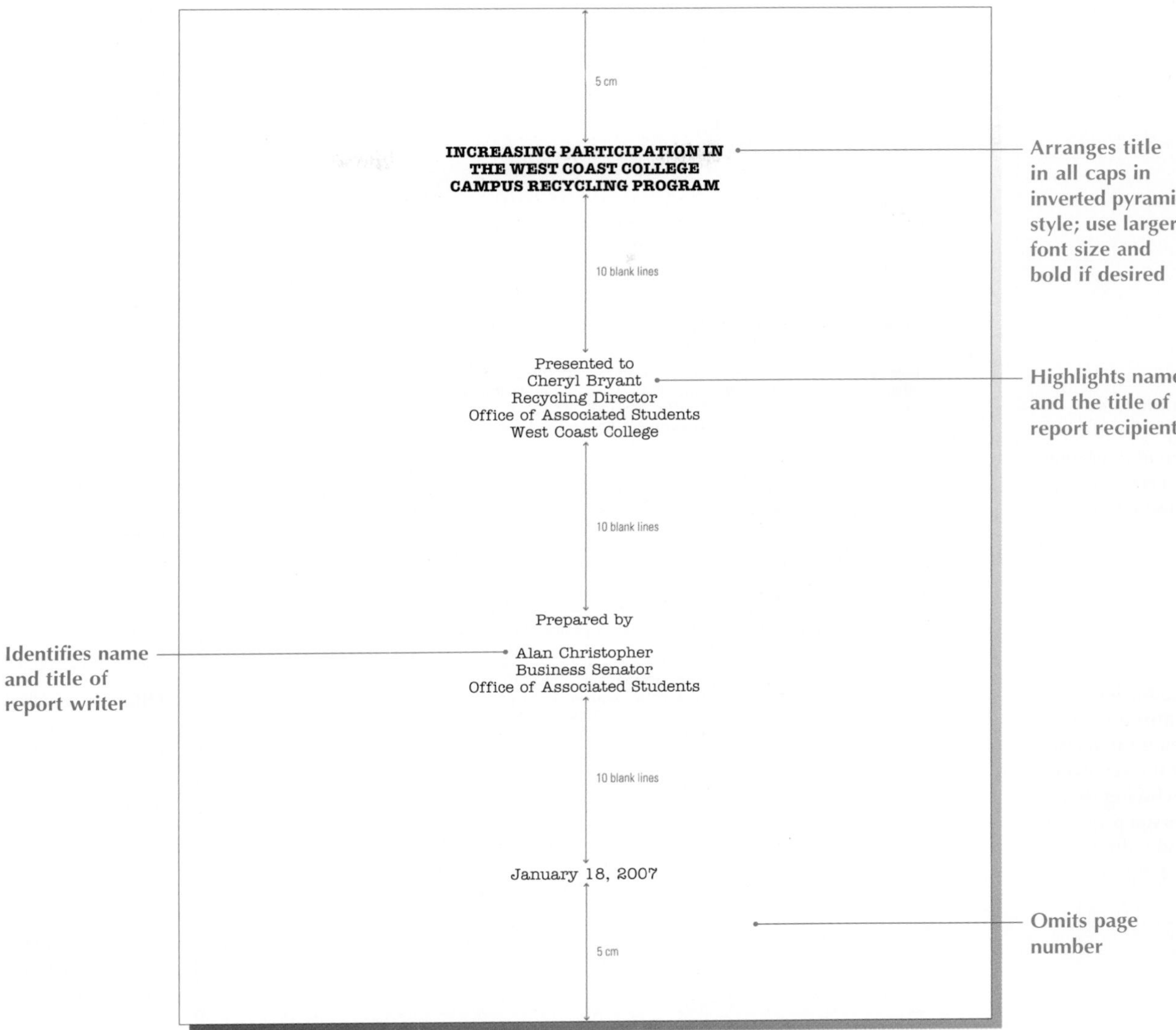

5 cm
INCREASING PARTICIPATION IN
THE WEST COAST COLLEGE
CAMPUS RECYCLING PROGRAM
Arranges title in all caps in inverted pyramid style; use larger font size and bold if desired
10 blank lines
Presented to
Cheryl Bryant
Recycling Director
Office of Associated Students
West Coast College
Highlights name and the title of report recipient
10 blank lines
Prepared by
Alan Christopher
Business Senator
Office of Associated Students
Identifies name and title of report writer
10 blank lines
January 18, 2007
5 cm
Omits page number

Alan arranges the title page so that the amount of space above the title is equal to the space below the date. If a report is to be bound on the left, move the left margin and centre point approximately 0.5 cm to the right. Notice that no page number appears on the title page, although it is counted as page i.

If you use scalable fonts, word processing capabilities, or a laser printer to enhance your report and title page, be careful to avoid anything unprofessional (such as too many type fonts, oversized print, and inappropriate graphics).

FIGURE 14.3 Continued

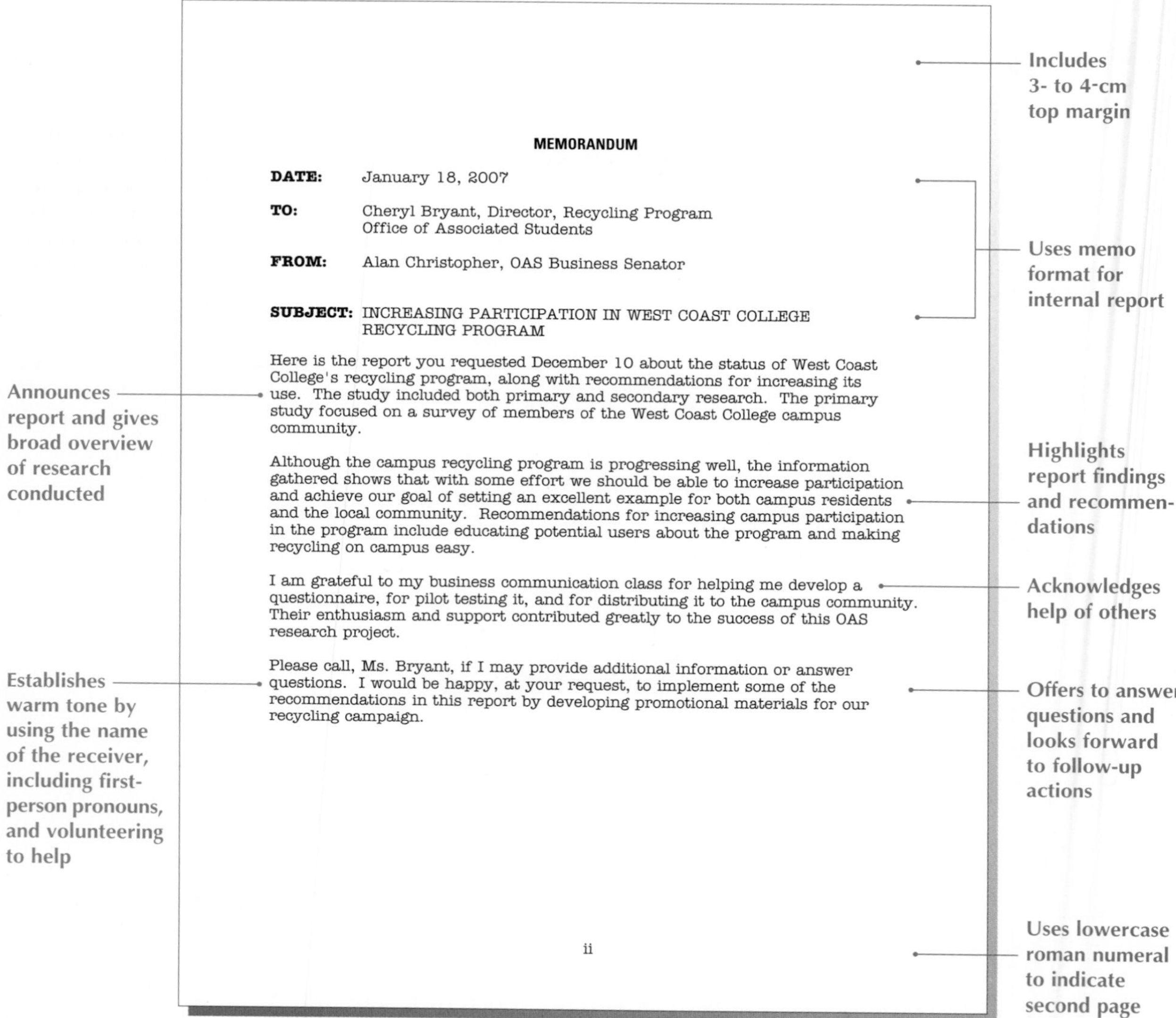
MEMORANDUM

DATE: January 18, 2007

TO: Cheryl Bryant, Director, Recycling Program
Office of Associated Students

FROM: Alan Christopher, OAS Business Senator

SUBJECT: INCREASING PARTICIPATION IN WEST COAST COLLEGE RECYCLING PROGRAM

Here is the report you requested December 10 about the status of West Coast College's recycling program, along with recommendations for increasing its use. The study included both primary and secondary research. The primary study focused on a survey of members of the West Coast College campus community.

Although the campus recycling program is progressing well, the information gathered shows that with some effort we should be able to increase participation and achieve our goal of setting an excellent example for both campus residents and the local community. Recommendations for increasing campus participation in the program include educating potential users about the program and making recycling on campus easy.

I am grateful to my business communication class for helping me develop a questionnaire, for pilot testing it, and for distributing it to the campus community. Their enthusiasm and support contributed greatly to the success of this OAS research project.

Please call, Ms. Bryant, if I may provide additional information or answer questions. I would be happy, at your request, to implement some of the recommendations in this report by developing promotional materials for our recycling campaign.

ii

Includes 3- to 4-cm top margin
Uses memo format for internal report
Announces report and gives broad overview of research conducted
Highlights report findings and recommendations
Acknowledges help of others
Establishes warm tone by using the name of the receiver, including first-person pronouns, and volunteering to help
Offers to answer questions and looks forward to follow-up actions
Uses lowercase roman numeral to indicate second page

Because this report is being submitted within his own organization, Alan uses a memorandum of transmittal. Formal organization reports submitted to outsiders would carry a letter of transmittal printed on company stationery.

The margins for the transmittal should be the same as for the report, about 3 cm on all sides. If a report is to be bound, add an extra 0.5 cm to the left margin. Because the report is single-spaced, the paragraphs are not indented. When a report is double-spaced, paragraphs are indented. A page number is optional.

FIGURE 14.3 Continued

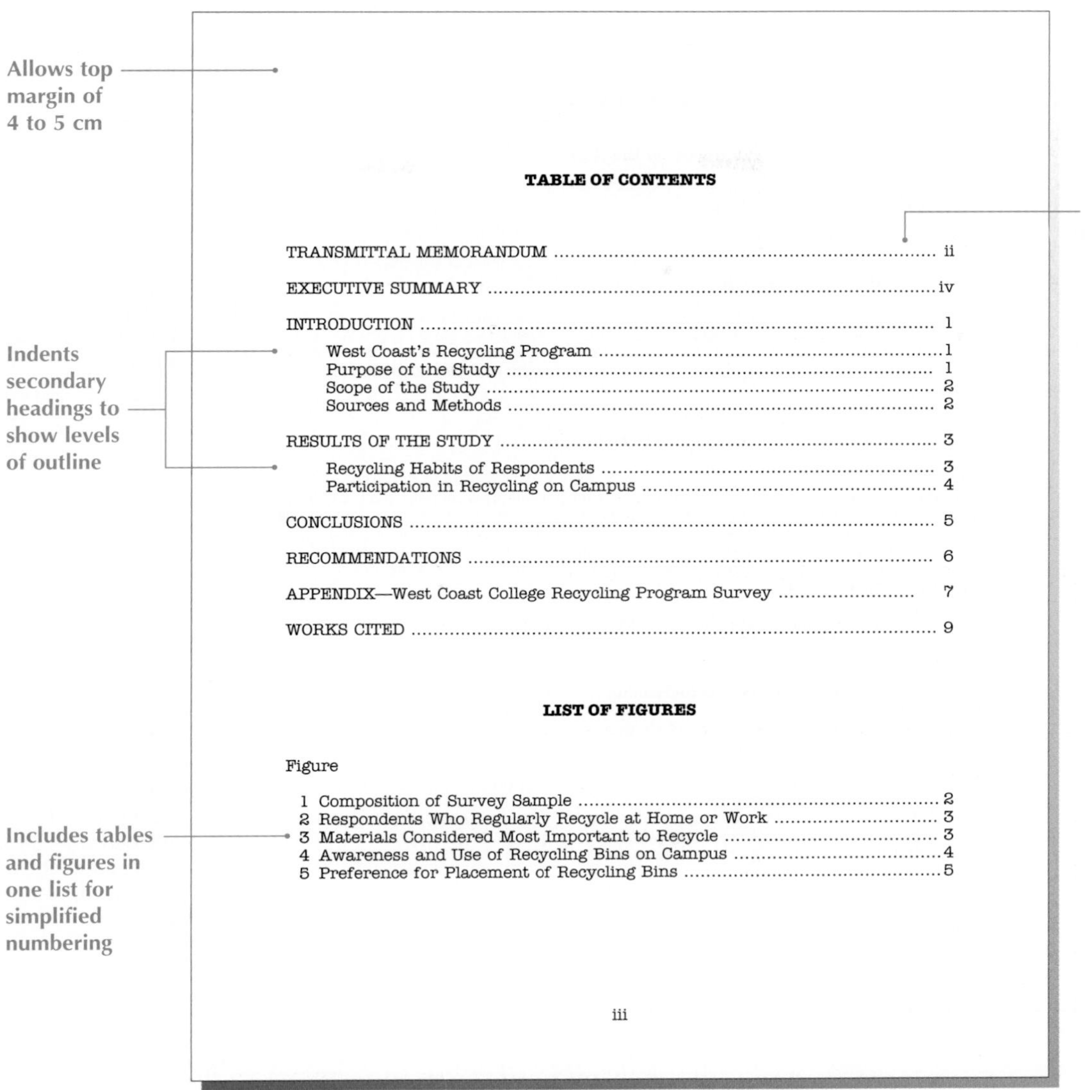

Allows top margin of 4 to 5 cm
Uses leaders to guide eye from heading to page number
Indents secondary headings to show levels of outline
Includes tables and figures in one list for simplified numbering

TABLE OF CONTENTS

LIST OF FIGURES

Figure

iii

Because Alan's table of contents and list of figures are small, he combines them on one page. Notice that he uses all caps for the titles of major report parts and a combination of upper- and lowercase letters for first-level headings. This duplicates the style within the report.

Advanced word processing capabilities enable you to generate a contents page automatically, including leaders and accurate page numbering—no matter how many times you revise!

FIGURE 14.3 Continued

EXECUTIVE SUMMARY

Purposes of the Report

The purposes of this report are to (1) determine the West Coast College campus community's awareness of the campus recycling program and (2) recommend ways to increase participation. West Coast's recycling program was intended to respond to the increasing problem of waste disposal, to fulfill its social responsibility as an educational institution, and to meet the demands of legislation requiring individuals and organizations to recycle.

A questionnaire survey was conducted to learn about the campus community's recycling habits and to assess participation in the current recycling program. A total of 220 individuals responded to the survey. Since West Coast College's recycling program includes only aluminum, glass, paper, and plastic at this time, these were the only materials considered in this study.

Tells purpose of report and briefly describes survey

Recycling at West Coast

Most survey respondents recognized the importance of recycling and stated that they do recycle aluminum, glass, paper, and plastic on a regular basis either at home or at work. However, most respondents displayed a low level of awareness and use of the on-campus program. Many of the respondents were unfamiliar with the location of the bins around campus and, therefore, had not participated in the recycling program. Other responses indicated that the bins were not conveniently located.

Summarizes findings of survey

The results of this study show that more effort is needed to increase participation in the campus recycling program.

Draws primary conclusion

Recommendations for Increasing Recycling Participation

Recommendations for increasing participation in the program include the following:

1. Relocate the recycling bins for greater visibility
2. Develop incentive programs to gain the participation of individuals and on-campus student groups
3. Train student volunteers to give on-campus presentations explaining the benefits of using the recycling program
4. Increase advertising about the program

Concisely enumerates four recommendations using parallel (balanced) phrasing

iv

Numbers pages that precede the body with lowercase roman numerals

For readers who want a quick picture of the report, the executive summary presents its most important elements. Alan has divided the summary into three sections for increased readability.

Executive summaries focus on the information the reader requires for making a decision related to the issues discussed in the report. The summary may include some or all of the following elements: purpose, scope, research methods, results, conclusions, and recommendations. In jargon-free language, a good executive summary condenses what management needs to know about a problem and its study.

FIGURE 14.3 Continued

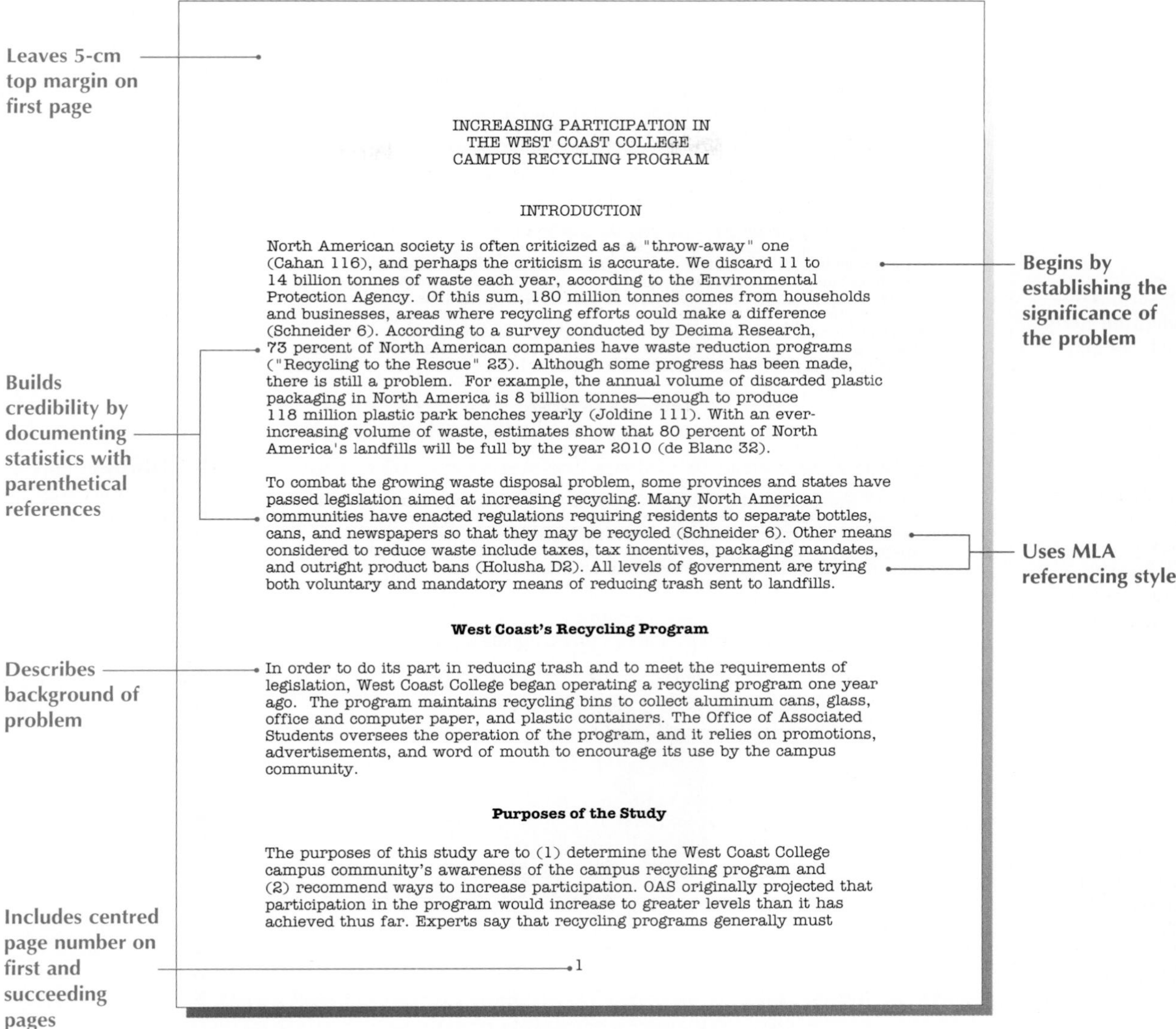

Leaves 5-cm top margin on first page
INCREASING PARTICIPATION IN
THE WEST COAST COLLEGE
CAMPUS RECYCLING PROGRAM
INTRODUCTION
North American society is often criticized as a "throw-away" one (Cahan 116), and perhaps the criticism is accurate. We discard 11 to 14 billion tonnes of waste each year, according to the Environmental Protection Agency. Of this sum, 180 million tonnes comes from households and businesses, areas where recycling efforts could make a difference (Schneider 6). According to a survey conducted by Decima Research, 73 percent of North American companies have waste reduction programs ("Recycling to the Rescue" 23). Although some progress has been made, there is still a problem. For example, the annual volume of discarded plastic packaging in North America is 8 billion tonnes—enough to produce 118 million plastic park benches yearly (Joldine 111). With an ever-increasing volume of waste, estimates show that 80 percent of North America's landfills will be full by the year 2010 (de Blanc 32).
To combat the growing waste disposal problem, some provinces and states have passed legislation aimed at increasing recycling. Many North American communities have enacted regulations requiring residents to separate bottles, cans, and newspapers so that they may be recycled (Schneider 6). Other means considered to reduce waste include taxes, tax incentives, packaging mandates, and outright product bans (Holusha D2). All levels of government are trying both voluntary and mandatory means of reducing trash sent to landfills.
West Coast's Recycling Program
In order to do its part in reducing trash and to meet the requirements of legislation, West Coast College began operating a recycling program one year ago. The program maintains recycling bins to collect aluminum cans, glass, office and computer paper, and plastic containers. The Office of Associated Students oversees the operation of the program, and it relies on promotions, advertisements, and word of mouth to encourage its use by the campus community.
Purposes of the Study
The purposes of this study are to (1) determine the West Coast College campus community's awareness of the campus recycling program and (2) recommend ways to increase participation. OAS originally projected that participation in the program would increase to greater levels than it has achieved thus far. Experts say that recycling programs generally must
1
Begins by establishing the significance of the problem
Builds credibility by documenting statistics with parenthetical references
Uses MLA referencing style
Describes background of problem
Includes centred page number on first and succeeding pages

The first page of a report generally contains the title printed 5 cm from the top edge. Titles for major parts of a report (such as *Introduction, Results, Conclusion,* and so forth) are centred in all caps. First-level headings are bold and printed with upper- and lowercase letters. Second-level headings begin at the side. For illustration of heading formats, see Figure 13.4.

Notice that Alan's report is single-spaced. Many businesses prefer this space-saving format. However, some organizations prefer double-spacing, especially for preliminary drafts. Page numbers may be centred 2.5 cm from the bottom of the page or placed 2.5 cm from the upper right corner at the margin.

FIGURE 14.3 Continued

operate at least a year before results become apparent (de Blanc 33). The OAS program has been in operation one year, yet gains are disappointing. Therefore, OAS authorized this study to determine the campus community's awareness and use of the program. Recommendations for increasing participation in the campus recycling program will be made to the OAS based on the results of this study.

Scope of the Study

Describes what the study includes and excludes

This study investigates potential participants' attitudes toward recycling in general, their awareness of the campus recycling program, their willingness to recycle on campus, and the perceived convenience of the recycling bins. Only aluminum, glass, paper, and plastic are considered in this study, as they are the only materials being recycled on campus at this time. The costs involved in the program were not considered in this study, since a recycling program generally does not begin to pay for itself during the first year. After the first year, the financial benefit is usually realized in reduced disposal costs (Steelman, Desmond, and Johnson 145).

Sources and Methods

Discusses how the study was conducted

Current business periodicals and newspapers were consulted for background information and to learn how other organizations are encouraging use of in-house recycling programs. In addition, a questionnaire survey (shown in the appendix) of administrators, faculty, staff, and students at West Coast College campus was conducted to learn about this group's recycling habits. In all, a convenience sample of 220 individuals responded to the self-administered survey. The composition of the sample closely resembles the makeup of the campus population. Figure 1 shows the percentage of students, faculty, staff, and administrators who participated in the survey.

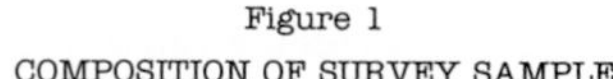

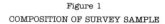

Figure 1
COMPOSITION OF SURVEY SAMPLE

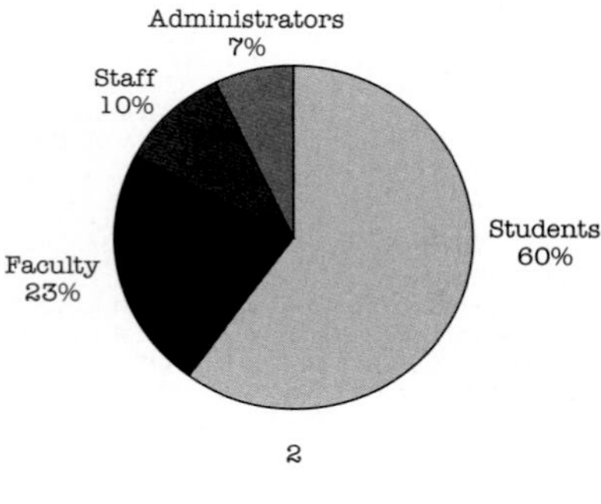

Uses computer-generated pie graph to illustrate makeup of survey

2

Because Alan wants this report to be formal in tone, he avoids *I* and *we.* Notice, too, that he uses present-tense verbs to describe his current writing (*this study investigates*), but past-tense verbs to indicate research completed in the past (*newspapers were consulted*).

If you use figures or tables, be sure to introduce them in the text. Although it's not always possible, try to place them close to the spot where they are first mentioned. If necessary to save space, you can print the title of a figure at its side.

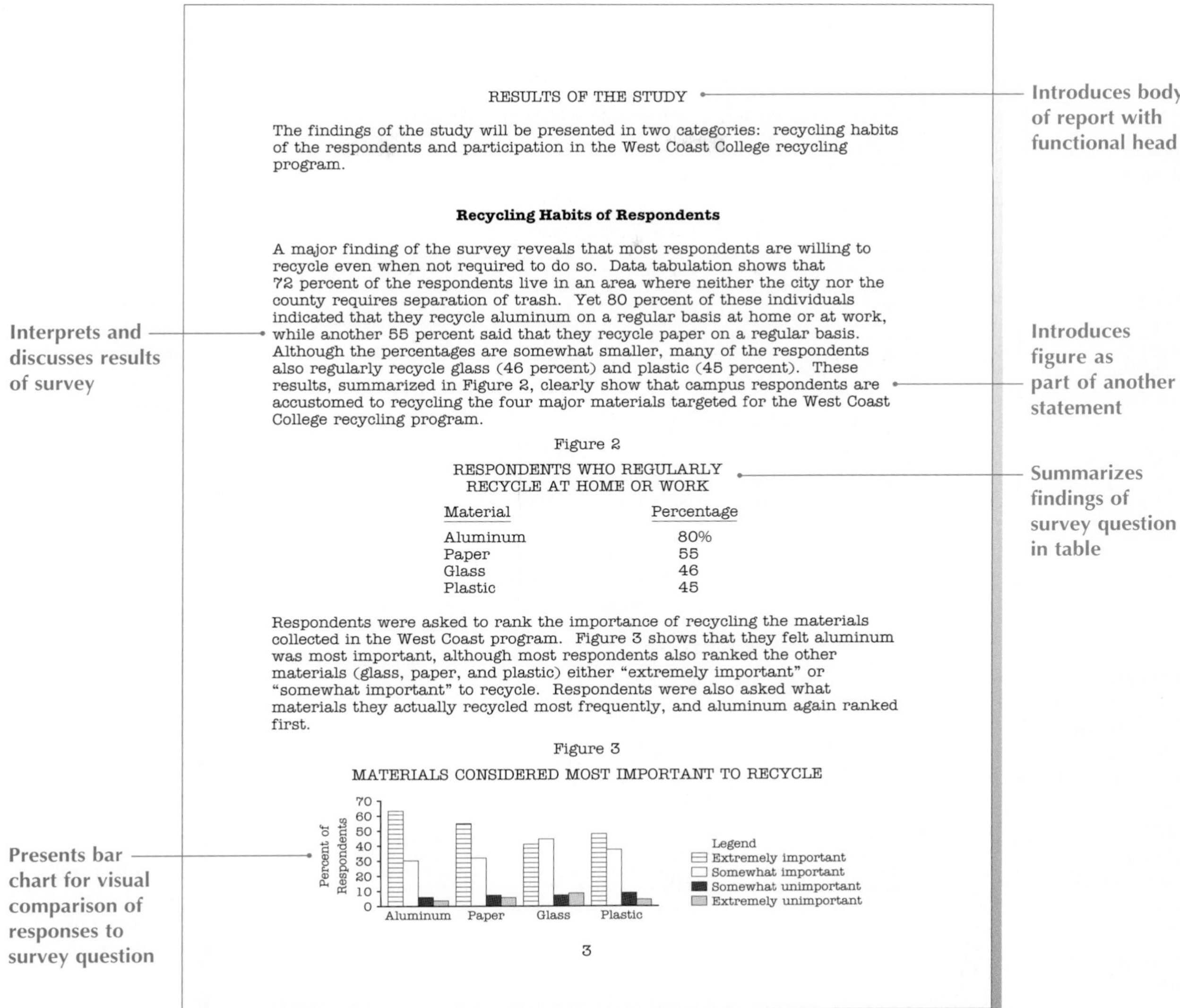

RESULTS OF THE STUDY

The findings of the study will be presented in two categories: recycling habits of the respondents and participation in the West Coast College recycling program.

Recycling Habits of Respondents

A major finding of the survey reveals that most respondents are willing to recycle even when not required to do so. Data tabulation shows that 72 percent of the respondents live in an area where neither the city nor the county requires separation of trash. Yet 80 percent of these individuals indicated that they recycle aluminum on a regular basis at home or at work, while another 55 percent said that they recycle paper on a regular basis. Although the percentages are somewhat smaller, many of the respondents also regularly recycle glass (46 percent) and plastic (45 percent). These results, summarized in Figure 2, clearly show that campus respondents are accustomed to recycling the four major materials targeted for the West Coast College recycling program.

Figure 2

RESPONDENTS WHO REGULARLY RECYCLE AT HOME OR WORK

Material	Percentage
Aluminum	80%
Paper	55
Glass	46
Plastic	45

Respondents were asked to rank the importance of recycling the materials collected in the West Coast program. Figure 3 shows that they felt aluminum was most important, although most respondents also ranked the other materials (glass, paper, and plastic) either "extremely important" or "somewhat important" to recycle. Respondents were also asked what materials they actually recycled most frequently, and aluminum again ranked first.

Figure 3

MATERIALS CONSIDERED MOST IMPORTANT TO RECYCLE

3

Introduces body of report with functional head

Interprets and discusses results of survey

Introduces figure as part of another statement

Summarizes findings of survey question in table

Presents bar chart for visual comparison of responses to survey question

Alan selects the most important survey findings to interpret and discuss for readers. Notice that he continues to use present-tense verbs *(the survey reveals* and *these results clearly show)* to discuss the current report.

Because he has few tables and charts, he labels them all as "Figures." Notice that he numbers them consecutively and places the label above each figure. Report writers with a great many tables, charts, and illustrations may prefer to label and number them separately. Tables are labelled as such; everything else is generally called a figure. When tables and figures are labelled separately, tables may be labelled above the table and figures below the figure.

FIGURE 14.3 Continued

Adds personal interpretation

When asked how likely they would be to go out of their way to deposit an item in a recycling bin, 29 percent of the respondents said "very likely," and 55 percent said "somewhat likely." Thus, respondents showed a willingness—at least on paper—to recycle even if it means making a special effort to locate a recycling bin.

Participation in Recycling on Campus

For any recycling program to be successful, participants must be aware of the location of recycling centres and must be trained to use them (de Blanc 33). Another important ingredient in thriving programs is convenience to users. If recycling centres are difficult for users to reach, these centres will be unsuccessful. To collect data on these topics, the survey included questions assessing awareness and use of the current bins. The survey also investigated reasons for not participating and the perceived convenience of current bin locations.

Introduces more findings and relates them to the report's purpose

Student Awareness and Use of Bins

Two of the most significant questions in the survey asked whether respondents were aware of the OAS recycling bins on campus and whether they had used the bins. Responses to both questions were disappointing, as Figure 4 illustrates.

Figure 4

AWARENESS AND USE OF RECYCLING BINS ON CAMPUS

Location	Awareness of bins at this location	Use of bins at this location
Social sciences building	38%	21%
Bookstore	29	12
Administration building	28	12
Computer labs	16	11
Library	15	7
Student union	9	5
Department offices	6	3
Campus dormitories	5	3
Unaware of any bins; have not used any bins	20	7

Arranges responses from highest to lowest with "unaware" category placed last

Only 38 percent of the respondents, as shown in Figure 4, were aware of the bins located outside the social sciences building. Even fewer were aware of the bins outside the bookstore (29 percent) and outside the administration building (28 percent). Equally dissatisfying, only 21 percent of the respondents had used the most visible recycling bins outside the social sciences

4

Clarifies and emphasizes meaning of findings

In discussing the results of the survey, Alan highlights those that have significance for the purpose of the report.

As you type a report, avoid widows and orphans (ending a page with the first line of a paragraph or carrying a single line of a paragraph to a new page). Strive to start and end pages with at least two lines of a paragraph, even if a slightly larger bottom margin results.

FIGURE 14.3 Continued

building. Other recycling bin locations were even less familiar to the survey respondents and, of course, were little used. These responses plainly show that the majority of the respondents in the West Coast campus community have a low awareness of the recycling program and an even lower record of participation.

Reasons for Not Participating

Respondents offered several reasons for not participating in the campus recycling program. Forty-five percent said that the bins are not convenient to use. Thirty percent said that they did not know where the bins were located. Another 25 percent said that they are not in the habit of recycling. Although many reasons for not participating were listed, the primary one appears to centre on convenience of bin locations.

Location of Recycling Bins

When asked specifically how they would rate the location of the bins currently in use, only 13 percent of the respondents felt that the bins were extremely convenient. Another 35 percent rated the locations as somewhat convenient. Over half of the respondents felt that the locations of the bins were either somewhat inconvenient or extremely inconvenient. Recycling bins are currently located outside nearly all of the major campus buildings, but respondents clearly considered these locations inconvenient or inadequate.

Discusses results of other survey questions not represented in tables or charts

In indicating where they would like recycling bins placed (see Figure 5), 42 percent of the respondents felt that the most convenient locations would be outside each building on campus. Placing recycling bins near the food service facilities on campus seemed most convenient to another 33 percent of those questioned, while 15 percent stated that they would like to see the bins placed near the vending machines. Ten percent of the individuals responding to the survey did not seem to think that the locations of the bins would matter to them.

Clarifies results of another survey question with textual discussion accompanied by table

Figure 5

PREFERENCE FOR PLACEMENT OF RECYCLING BINS

Outside each building on campus	42%
Near food service facilities	33
Near vending machines	15
Does not matter	10

CONCLUSIONS

Based on the findings of the recycling survey of members of the West Coast College campus community, the following conclusions are drawn:

1. Most members of the campus community are already recycling at home or at work without being required to do so.

5

After completing a discussion of the survey results, Alan lists what he considers the five most important conclusions to be drawn from this survey. Some writers combine the conclusions and recommendations, particularly when they are interrelated. Alan separated them in his study because the survey findings were quite distinct from the recommendations he would make based on them.

Notice that it is unnecessary to start a new page for the conclusions.

FIGURE 14.3 Continued

Draws conclusions based on survey findings; summarizes previous discussion

2. Over half of the respondents recycle aluminum and paper on a regular basis; most recycle glass and plastic to some degree.
3. Most of the surveyed individuals expressed a willingness to participate in a recycling program. Many, however, seem unwilling to travel very far to participate; 42 percent would like recycling bins to be located outside every campus building.
4. Awareness and use of the current campus recycling program are low. Only a little over one third of the respondents knew of any recycling bin locations on campus, and only one fifth had actually used them.
5. Respondents considered the locations of the campus bins inconvenient. This perceived inconvenience was given as the principal reason for not participating in the campus recycling program.

RECOMMENDATIONS

Supported by the findings and conclusions of this study, the following recommendations are offered in an effort to improve the operations and success of the West Coast recycling program:

Lists specific actions to help solve report problem; suggests practical ways to implement recommendations

1. Increase on-campus awareness and visibility by designing an eye-catching logo that represents the campus recycling program for use in promotions.
2. Enhance comprehension of recycling procedures by training users how to recycle. Use posters to explain the recycling program and to inform users of recycling bin locations. Label each bin clearly as to what materials may be deposited.
3. Add bins in several new locations, particularly in the food service and vending machine areas.
4. Recruit student leaders to promote participation in the recycling program by giving educational talks to classes and other campus groups, informing them of the importance of recycling.
5. Develop an incentive program for student organizations. Offer incentives for meeting recycling goals as determined by OAS. On-campus groups could compete in recycling drives designed to raise money for the group, the college, or a charity. Money from the proceeds of the recycling program could be used to fund the incentive program.

6

The most important parts of a report are its conclusions and recommendations. To make them especially clear, Alan enumerated each conclusion and recommendation. Notice that each recommendation starts with a verb and is stated in command language for emphasis and readability.

Report recommendations are most helpful to readers when they not only make suggestions to solve the original research problem but also describe specific actions to be taken. Notice that Alan goes beyond merely listing ideas; instead, he provides practical suggestions for ways to implement the recommendations.

FIGURE 14.3 Continued

Includes copy of survey questionnaire so that report readers can see actual questions

APPENDIX

WEST COAST COLLEGE RECYCLING PROGRAM SURVEY

West Coast College recently implemented a recycling program on campus. Please take a few minutes to answer the following questions so that we can make this program as convenient and helpful as possible for you to use.

Explains why survey is necessary, emphasizing "you" view

1. Please indicate which items you recycle on a regular basis at home or at work. (Check *all* that apply.)
   - ☐ Aluminum
   - ☐ Glass
   - ☐ Paper
   - ☐ Plastic
2. Do you live in an area where the city/municipality requires separation of trash?
   ☐ Yes ☐ No
3. How important is it to you to recycle each of the following:

	Extremely Important	Somewhat Important	Somewhat Unimportant	Extremely Unimportant
Aluminum				
Glass				
Paper				
Plastic				

4. How likely would it be for you to go out of your way to put something in a recycling bin?

Very Likely	Somewhat Likely	Somewhat Unlikely	Very Unlikely

Provides range of answers that will be easy to tabulate

5. Which of the following items do you recycle *most* often? (Choose *one* item only.)
   - ☐ Aluminum
   - ☐ Glass
   - ☐ Paper
   - ☐ Plastic
   - ☐ Other
6. The following are locations of the recycling bins on campus. (Check *all* those of which you are aware.)
   - ☐ Administration building
   - ☐ Bookstore
   - ☐ Campus dorms
   - ☐ Computer labs
   - ☐ Engineering building
   - ☐ Library
   - ☐ Social sciences building
   - ☐ Student union
   - ☐ I'm unaware of any of these recycling bins.

7

Alan had space to add the word "Appendix" to the top of the survey questionnaire. If space were not available, he could have typed a separate page with that title on it. If more than one item were included, he would have named them Appendix A, Appendix B, and so on.

Notice that the appendix continues the report pagination.

FIGURE 14.3 Continued

7. Which of the following recycling bins have you actually used? (Check *all* that you have used.)
   - ☐ Administration building
   - ☐ Bookstore
   - ☐ Campus dorms
   - ☐ Computer labs
   - ☐ Engineering building
   - ☐ Library
   - ☐ Social sciences building
   - ☐ Student union
   - ☐ I've not used any of these recycling bins.

8. If you don't recycle on campus, why don't you participate?
   - ☐ I'm not in the habit of recycling.
   - ☐ I don't know where the bins are.
   - ☐ The bins aren't convenient for me.
   - ☐ Other ______________________

9. How do you rate the convenience of the bins' locations?
   - ☐ Extremely convenient
   - ☐ Somewhat convenient
   - ☐ Somewhat inconvenient
   - ☐ Extremely inconvenient

10. Which of the following possible recycling bin locations would be most convenient for you to use? (Check *one* only.)
    - ☐ Outside each building
    - ☐ Near the food service facilities
    - ☐ Near the vending machines
    - ☐ Does not matter
    - ☐ Other ______________________

11. Please indicate:
    - ☐ Student
    - ☐ Faculty
    - ☐ Administrator
    - ☐ Staff

COMMENTS:

Thank you for your responses! Please return the questionnaire in the enclosed, stamped envelope to West Coast College, School of Business, Rm. 321. If you have any questions, please call (555) 450-2391.

8

Anticipates responses but also supplies "Other" category

Uses scale questions to capture degrees of feeling

Requests little demographic data to keep survey short

Offers comment section for explanations and remarks

Concludes with appreciation and instructions

FIGURE 14.3 Continued

Works Cited

Cahan, Vicky. "Waste Not, Want Not? Not Necessarily." Business Week 17 July 2005: 116. — Magazine

de Blanc, Susan. "Paper Recycling: How to Make It Effective." The Office Dec. 2004: 32.

Foster, David. "Recycling: A Green Idea Turns to Gold." Los Angeles Times 5 Mar. 2006. Retrieved 7 Mar. 2006 <http://www.latimes.com/library/cyber/week/y05dat.html>. — Online Newspaper

Freeman, Monique M. Personal interview. 2 Nov. 2006. — Interview

Holusha, John. "Mixed Benefits from Recycling." New York Times on the Web 26 July 2004. Retrieved 26 Oct. 2005 <http://www.nytimes.com/2004/07/26/science/recycling.html>. — Online Newspaper

Joldine, Lee. Spirit of the Wolf: The Environment and Canada's Future. Ed. Jo Davis. Waterloo: Turnaround Decade Ecological Communications, 2000. — Book—author with an editor

Landsburg, Steven E. "Who Shall Inherit the Earth?" Slate 1 May 2005. Retrieved 2 May 2006 <http://www.slate.com/Economics/05-05-01/Economics.asp>. — Online Magazine

Schneider, Keith. "As Recycling Becomes a Growth Industry, Its Paradoxes Also Multiply." The New York Times 20 Jan. 2006, sec. 4: 6. — Newspaper

Steelman, James W., Shirley Desmond, and LeGrand Johnson. Facing Global Limitations. New York: Rockford Press, 2003. — Book

Steuteville, Robert. "The State of Garbage in America." Part 1. BioCycle Apr. 2002. Retrieved 30 Nov. 2005 <http://www.biocycle/recycle/guid.html>. — Online Magazine

"Tips to Reduce, Reuse, and Recycle." Environmental Recycling Hotline May 2003. Retrieved 8 July 2006 <http://www.primenet.com/cgi-bin/erh.pl>. — World Wide Web

Weddle, Bruce, and Edward Klein. "A Strategy to Control the Garbage Glut." EPA Journal 12.2 (2004): 28–34. — Journal

9

On this page Alan lists all the references cited in the text as well as others that he examined during his research. (Some authors list only those works cited in the report.) Alan formats his citations following the MLA referencing style. Notice that all entries are arranged alphabetically. He underlines book and periodical titles, but italics could be used. When referring to online items, he shows the full name of the citation and then identifies the path leading to that reference as well as the date on which he accessed the electronic reference. "Retrieved" or "Accessed" should be added to distinguish the retrieval date from the document date, although the MLA style does not include this.

Most word processing software today automatically updates citation references within the text and prints a complete list for you. For more information about documentation styles, see Chapter 12 and Appendix B.

SUMMARY OF LEARNING OBJECTIVES

1 **Discuss the components of informal proposals.** Most informal proposals contain (1) a persuasive introduction that explains the purpose of the proposal and qualifies the writer; (2) background material identifying the problem and project goals; (3) a proposal, plan, or schedule outlining the project; (4) a section describing staff qualifications; (5) a budget showing expected costs; and (6) a request for approval or authorization.

2 **Discuss the special components in formal proposals.** Beyond the six components generally contained in informal proposals, formal proposals may include these additional parts: (1) copy of the RFP (request for proposal), (2) letter of transmittal, (3) executive summary or abstract, (4) title page, (5) table of contents, (6) list of illustrations, and (7) appendix.

3 **Identify formal report components that precede its introduction.** Formal reports may include these beginning components: (1) vinyl or heavy paper cover, (2) title page, (3) letter of transmittal, (4) table of contents, (5) list of illustrations, and (6) executive summary.

4 **Outline topics that might be covered in the introduction of a formal report.** The introduction to a formal report sets the scene by discussing some or all of the following topics: background material, problem or purpose, significance of the topic, scope and organization of the report, authorization, review of relevant literature, sources and methods, and definitions of key terms.

5 **Describe the components of a formal report that follow the introduction.** The body of a report discusses, analyzes, interprets, and evaluates the research findings or solution to a problem. The conclusion tells what the findings mean and how they relate to the report's purpose. The recommendations tell how to solve the report problem. The last portions of a formal report are the appendix, references, and bibliography.

6 **Specify tips that aid writers of formal reports.** Before writing, develop a realistic timetable and collect all necessary data. During the writing process, work from a good outline, work in a quiet place, and use a computer. Also, try to write rapidly, revising later. While writing, use verb tenses consistently, and avoid *I* and *we.* A few days after completing the first draft, revise to improve clarity, coherence, and conciseness. Proofread the final copy three times.

CHAPTER REVIEW

1. What is a proposal? (Obj. 1)
2. What is the difference between solicited and unsolicited proposals? (Obj. 1)
3. What are the six principal components in an informal letter proposal? (Obj. 1)
4. How is a formal proposal different from an informal proposal? (Obj. 2)
5. Why does an entrepreneur need to write a business plan? (Obj. 2)
6. Discuss eight components of typical business plans. (Obj. 2)
7. What does a mission statement cover, and why is it so important in a business plan? (Obj. 2)
8. Why are formal reports written in business? Give an original example of a business-related formal report. (Obj. 3)
9. What is a table of contents, and when should it be written? (Obj. 3)
10. What should be included in the executive summary of a formal report? (Obj. 3)
11. What should be included in the introduction to a formal report? (Obj. 4)
12. What should the writer strive to do in the body of a formal report? (Obj. 5)
13. What is the purpose of a bibliography? (Obj. 5)
14. In your view, what are six of the most important tips for the writer of a formal report? Explain each of your choices. (Obj. 6)
15. What are first-person pronouns, and why do most writers of formal reports avoid them? (Obj. 6)

CRITICAL THINKING

1. Why are proposals important to many businesses? (Obj. 1)
2. How do formal reports differ from informal reports? (Objs. 1 and 2)
3. Discuss the three phases of the writing process in relation to formal reports. What activities take place in each phase? (Objs. 3–5)
4. Compare and contrast proposals and business plans. (Objs. 1 and 2)

ACTIVITIES

14.1 Proposal: Looking for Clients for Your Business

TEAM | CRITICAL THINKING

A new medical clinic, ProMed Institute, is opening its doors in your hometown, and a mutual friend has recommended your small business to the administrator of the clinic. You have received a letter asking you to provide information about your service. The new medical clinic specializes in sports medicine, physical therapy, and cardiac rehabilitation services. It is interested in retaining your company, rather than hiring its own employees to perform the service your company offers.

Your Task. Working in teams, first decide what service you will offer. It could be landscaping, uniform supply, laundry of uniforms, general cleaning, computerized no-paper filing systems, online medical supplies, patient transportation, supplemental hospice care, temporary office support, or food service. As a team, develop a letter proposal outlining your plan, staffing, and budget. Use persuasion to show why contracting your services is better than hiring in-house employees. In the proposal letter, request a meeting with the administrative board. In addition to a written proposal, you may be expected to make an oral presentation that includes visual aids and/or handouts. Send your proposal to Mr. Jack Dawson, Director, ProMed Institute. Supply a local address.

14.2 Proposal and Grant Writing: Learning From the Nonprofits (Objs. 1 and 2)

INFOTRAC

You'd like to learn more about writing business proposals and especially about writing grants. The latter involves funding supplied by an institution, foundation, or the government. You might one day even decide to become a professional grant/proposal writer. But first you need experience.

Your Task. Volunteer your services for a local nonprofit organization, such as a United Way <**www.unitedway.ca**> member agency, an educational institution, or your local place of worship. To learn more about writing grants, complete an InfoTrac subject guide search for "proposal." Click on articles under the categories of "business proposal writing" and "grant proposal writing." Your instructor may ask you to submit a preliminary memo report outlining ten or more pointers you learned about writing proposals and grants for nonprofit organizations.

14.3 *Unsolicited Proposal: Thwarting Dorm Room Thievery* (Objs. 1 and 2)

WEB | **CRITICAL THINKING** | **TEAM**

As an enterprising college student, you recognized a problem as soon as you arrived on campus. Dorm rooms filled with pricey digital gadgets were very attractive to thieves. Some students move in with more than $3000 in gear, including laptop computers, digital cameras, MP3 players, PDAs, and DVD players. You solved the problem by buying an extra-large steel footlocker to lock away your valuables. But shipping the footlocker was expensive (nearly $100), and you had to wait for it to arrive from a catalogue company. Your bright idea is to propose to the Student Organization that it allow you to offer these steel footlockers to students at a reduced price and with campus delivery. Your footlocker, which you found by searching the Web, is extremely durable and works great as a coffee table, nightstand, or card table. It comes with a smooth interior liner and two compartments.

Your Task. Working individually or with a team, imagine that you have made arrangements with a manufacturer to act as a middleman selling footlockers on your campus at a reduced price. Consult the Web for manufacturers and make up your own figures. But how can you get the SO's permission to proceed? Give that organization a cut? Use your imagination in deciding how this plan might work on a college campus. Then prepare an unsolicited proposal to your SO. Outline the problem and your goals of protecting students' valuables and providing convenience. Check the Web for statistics regarding on-campus burglaries. Such figures should help you develop one or more persuasive "hooks." Then explain your proposal, project possible sales, discuss a timetable, and describe your staffing. Submit your proposal to Toni Bell, president, Student Organization.

14.4 *Executive Summary: Keeping the Boss Informed* (Objs. 5 and 6)

INFOTRAC

Many managers and executives are too rushed to read long journal articles, but they are eager to keep up with developments in their fields. Assume your boss has asked you to help him stay abreast of research in his field. He asks you to submit to him one executive summary every month on an article of interest.

Your Task. In your field of study, select a professional journal, such as the *Journal of Management.* Using InfoTrac Power search, look for articles in your targeted journal. Select an article that is at least five pages long and is interesting to you. Write an executive summary in a memo format. Include an introduction that might begin with *As you requested, I am submitting this executive summary of* . . . . Identify the author, article name, journal, and date of publication. Explain what the author intended to do in the study or article. Summarize three or four of the most important findings of the study or article. Use descriptive rather than functional headings. Summarize any recommendations made. Your boss would also like a concluding statement indicating your reaction to the article. Address your memo to Matthew R. Ferranto.

14.5 *Proposal, Business Plan, and Report Topics* (Objs. 1–6)

A list with over 70 report topics is available on this book's Student Resources Web site. Click "Web Links by Chapter" and go to Chapter 12. The topics are divided into the following categories: accounting, finance, personnel/human resources, marketing, information systems, management, and general business/education/campus issues. You can collect information for many of these reports by using InfoTrac and the Web. Your instructor may assign them as individual or team projects. All involve critical thinking in organizing information, drawing conclusions, and making recommendations. The topics include assignments appropriate for proposals, business plans, and formal reports.

C.L.U.E. REVIEW 14

On a separate sheet edit the following sentences to correct faults in grammar, punctuation, spelling, numbers, proofreading, and word use.

1. Proposals are writen offers to do the following, solve problems, provide services or sell equippment.
2. Our company President and Vice President worked together in developing 2 RFP's to solicit competitive bids.
3. To make a introduction to a proposal interesting, a "hook" should be provided by the writer to capture a readers attention.
4. A central item in most Proposals, is the budget which is a list of proposed project costs.
5. Any proposal delivered to the Manager or I should definitly explain the specific credentials and expertise of key personal for the project.
6. Lisa and him wanted to start there own business, therefore they wrote a business plan, that included a detailed market analysis.
7. Nicolas Scott who is a member of our research and development department presented a formal report based on through investigation and analysis.
8. The principle sections of the report is the body, it discusses the research findings.
9. If a report is one hundred pages long it may require a ten page Executive Summary.
10. Only 1 of the executives were present at the June 10th meeting, when the report was presented.

Unit 5
Presentations

Speaking Skills

Employment Communication

Chapter 15
Speaking Skills

LEARNING OBJECTIVES

1. *Discuss two important first steps in preparing effective oral presentations.*

2. *Explain the major elements in organizing the content of a presentation, including the introduction, body, and conclusion.*

3. *Identify techniques for gaining audience rapport, including using effective imagery, providing verbal signposts, and sending appropriate nonverbal messages.*

4. *Discuss designing and using effective visual aids, handouts, and multimedia presentation materials.*

5. *Specify delivery techniques for use before, during, and after a presentation.*

6. *Explain effective techniques for adapting oral presentations to cross-cultural audiences.*

7. *List techniques for improving telephone, voice mail, and remote conferencing effectiveness.*

PREPARING EFFECTIVE ORAL PRESENTATIONS

According to Canadian speaker and author Peter Urs Bender, the greatest fear of most people is not death, but public speaking.[1] While this may seem extreme, most of us feel great stress when faced with making a speech. The physiological responses that you experience are much like those triggered by a car accident or a narrow escape from a dangerous situation.[2] Regardless, *at some point, everyone in business has to sell an idea, and such persuasion is often done in person.* 1

Many businesspeople must make presentations as part of their careers.

Many future businesspeople, however, fail to take advantage of opportunities in university or college to develop speaking skills. Yet, such skills often play an important role in a successful career. This chapter prepares you to use speaking skills in making oral presentations and in using the telephone, voice mail, and conferencing to advantage.

For any presentation, you can reduce your fears and lay the foundation for a professional performance by focusing on five areas: preparation, organization, audience rapport, visual aids, and delivery.

Knowing Your Purpose

The most important part of your preparation is deciding what you want to accomplish. Whether your goal is to persuade or to inform, you must have a clear idea of where you are going. At the end of your presentation, what do you want your listeners to remember or do?

Preparing for an oral presentation means identifying the purpose and knowing the audience.

Eric Evans, a loan officer at Dominion Trust, faced such questions as he planned a talk for a class in small business management. Eric's former business professor had asked him to return to campus and give the class advice about borrowing money from banks in order to start new businesses. Because Eric knew so much about this topic, he found it difficult to extract a specific purpose statement for his presentation. After much thought he narrowed his purpose to this: *To inform potential entrepreneurs about three important factors that loan officers consider before granting start-up loans to launch small businesses.* His entire presentation focused on ensuring that the class members understood and remembered three principal ideas.

Knowing Your Audience

Audience analysis issues include size, age, gender, experience, attitude, and expectations.

A second key element in preparation is analyzing your audience, anticipating its reactions, and making appropriate adaptations. By anticipating your audience, you have a better idea of how to organize your presentation. Other elements, such as age, gender, education, experience, and size of audience will affect your style and message content. Analyze the following questions to help you determine your organizational pattern, delivery style, and supporting material.

- *How will this topic appeal to this audience?*
- *How can I relate this information to their needs?*
- *How can I earn respect so that they accept my message?*
- *What would be most effective in making my point? Facts? Statistics? Personal experiences? Expert opinion? Humour? Cartoons? Graphic illustrations? Demonstrations? Case histories? Analogies?*
- *What measures must I take to ensure that this audience remembers my main points?*

ORGANIZING THE CONTENT FOR A POWERFUL IMPACT

Once you have determined your purpose and analyzed the audience, you're ready to collect information and organize it logically. Good organization and conscious repetition are the two most powerful keys to audience comprehension and retention. In fact, many speech experts recommend the following admittedly repetitious, but effective, plan:

- **Step 1:** Tell them what you're going to say.
- **Step 2:** Say it.
- **Step 3:** Tell them what you've just said.

Capturing Attention in the Introduction

Attention-grabbing openers include questions, startling facts, jokes, anecdotes, and quotations.

The opening of your presentation should strive to accomplish three specific goals:

- Capture listeners' attention and get them involved.
- Identify yourself and establish your credibility.
- Preview your main points.

If you're able to appeal to listeners and involve them in your presentation right from the start, you're more likely to hold their attention until the finish. Consider some of the same techniques that you used to open sales letters: a question, a startling fact, a joke, a story, or a quotation. Some speakers achieve involvement by opening with a question or command that requires audience members to raise their hands or stand up. Additional techniques to gain and keep audience attention are presented in the accompanying Career Coach box.

To establish your credibility, you need to describe your position, knowledge, or experience—whatever qualifies you to speak. Try also to connect with your audience. Listeners are particularly drawn to speakers who reveal something of themselves and identify with them.

After capturing attention and establishing yourself, you'll want to preview the main points of your topic, perhaps with a visual aid. You may wish to put off actually writing your introduction, however, until after you have organized the rest of the presentation and crystallized your principal ideas.

Take a look at Eric Evans' introduction, shown in Figure 15.1, to see how he integrated all the elements necessary for a good opening.

Organizing the Body

The best oral presentations focus on a few key ideas.

The biggest problem with most oral presentations is a failure to focus on a few principal ideas. Thus, the body of your short presentation (20 or fewer minutes) should include a limited number of main points, say, two to four. Develop each main point with adequate, but not excessive, explanation and details. Too many details can obscure the main message, so keep your presentation simple and logical. Remember, listeners have no pages to leaf back through should they become confused.

When Eric Evans began planning his presentation, he realized immediately that he could talk for hours on his topic. He also knew that listeners are not good at separating major and minor points. So, instead of submerging his listeners in a sea of information, he sorted out a few principal ideas. In the mortgage business, loan

CAREER COACH

Nine Techniques for Gaining and Keeping Audience Attention

Experienced speakers know how to capture the attention of an audience and how to maintain that attention during a presentation. Here are nine proven techniques.

1. **A promise.** Begin with a promise that keeps the audience expectant (for example, "By the end of this presentation I will have shown you how you can increase your sales by 50 percent").
2. **Drama.** Open by telling an emotionally moving story or by describing a serious problem that involves the audience. Throughout your talk include other dramatic elements, such as a long pause after a key statement. Change your vocal tone or pitch. Professionals use high-intensity emotions such as anger, joy, sadness, and excitement.
3. **Eye contact.** As you begin, command attention by surveying the entire audience to take in all listeners. Take two to five seconds to make eye contact with as many people as possible.
4. **Movement.** Leave the lectern area whenever possible. Walk around the conference table or between the aisles of your audience. Try to move toward your audience, especially at the beginning and end of your talk.
5. **Questions.** Keep listeners active and involved with rhetorical questions. Ask for a show of hands to get each listener thinking. The response will also give you a quick gauge of audience attention.
6. **Demonstrations.** Include a member of the audience in a demonstration (for example, "I'm going to show you exactly how to implement our four-step customer courtesy process, but I need a volunteer from the audience to help me").
7. **Samples/gimmicks.** If you're promoting a product, consider using items to toss out to the audience or to award as prizes to volunteer participants. You can also pass around product samples or promotional literature. Be careful, though, to maintain control of the audience.
8. **Visuals.** Give your audience something to look at besides yourself. Use a variety of visual aids in a single session. Also consider writing the concerns expressed by your listeners on a flipchart or white board as you go along.
9. **Self-interest.** Review your entire presentation to ensure that it meets the critical "What's-in-it-for-me?" audience test. Remember that people are most interested in things that benefit them.

officers generally ask the following three questions of each applicant for a small business loan: (1) Are you ready to "hit the ground running" in starting your business? (2) Have you done your homework? and (3) Have you made realistic projections of potential sales, cash flow, and equity investment? These questions would become his main points, but Eric wanted to streamline them further so that his audience would be sure to remember them. He summarized the questions in three words: *experience, preparation,* and *projection.* As you can see in Figure 15.1, Eric prepared a sentence outline showing these three main ideas. Each is supported by examples and explanations.

How to organize and sequence main ideas may not be immediately obvious when you begin working on a presentation. The following methods, which review those discussed in Chapter 12, provide many possible strategies and examples to help you organize a presentation.

- **Chronology.** Example: A presentation describing the history of a problem, organized from the first sign of trouble to the present.
- **Geography/space.** Example: A presentation about the changing diversity of the work force, organized by regions in the country (East Coast, West Coast, and so forth).

FIGURE 15.1 Oral Presentation Outline

Prewriting 1

Analyze: The purpose of this report is to inform listeners of three critical elements in securing business loans.

Anticipate: The audience members are aspiring businesspeople who are probably unfamiliar with loan operations.

Adapt: Because the audience will be receptive but uninformed, explain terms and provide examples. Repeat the main ideas to ensure comprehension.

Writing 2

Research: Analyze previous loan applications; interview other loan officers. Gather critical data.

Organize: Group the data into three major categories. Support with statistics, details, and examples. Plan visual aids.

Compose: Prepare a sentence outline. Consider using presentation software to outline your talk.

Revising 3

Revise: Develop transitions between topics. Prepare note cards or speaker's notes.

Practise: Rehearse the entire talk and time it. Practise enunciating words and projecting your voice. Practise using your visual aids. Develop natural hand motions.

Evaluate: Tape-record or videotape a practice session to evaluate your movements, voice tone, enunciation, and timing.

What Makes a Loan Officer Say "Yes"?

I. INTRODUCTION

A. How many of you expect one day to start your own businesses? How many of you have all the cash available to capitalize that business when you start? — **Captures attention**

B. Like you, nearly every entrepreneur needs cash to open a business, and I promise you that by the end of this talk you will have inside information on how to make a loan application that will be successful. — **Involves audience**

C. As a loan officer at Dominion Trust, which specializes in small-business loans, I make decisions on requests from entrepreneurs like you applying for start-up money. — **Identifies speaker**

Transition: Your professor invited me here today to tell you how you can improve your chances of getting a loan from us or from any other lender. I have suggestions in three areas: experience, preparation, and projection. — **Previews three main points**

II. BODY — **Establishes main points**

A. First, let's consider experience. You must show that you can hit the ground running.
   1. Demonstrate what experience you have in your proposed business.
   2. Include your résumé when you submit your business plan.
   3. If you have little experience, tell us whom you would hire to supply the skills that you lack.

Transition: In addition to experience, loan officers will want to see that you have researched your venture thoroughly.

B. My second suggestion, then, involves preparation. Have you done your homework?
   1. Talk to local businesspeople, especially those in related fields.
   2. Conduct traffic counts or other studies to estimate potential sales.
   3. Analyze the strengths and weaknesses of the competition.

Transition: Now that we've discussed preparation, we're ready for my final suggestion.

C. My last tip is the most important one. It involves making a realistic projection of your potential sales, cash flow, and equity.
   1. Present detailed monthly cash-flow projections for the first year.
   2. Describe "what-if" scenarios indicating both good and bad possibilities.
   3. Indicate that you intend to supply at least 25 percent of the initial capital yourself.

Transition: The three major points I've just outlined cover critical points in obtaining start-up loans. Let me review them for you.

— **Develops coherence with planned transitions**

III. CONCLUSION

A. Loan officers are most likely to say "yes" to your loan application if you do three things: (1) prove that you can hit the ground running when your business opens; (2) demonstrate that you've researched your proposed business seriously; and (3) project a realistic picture of your sales, cash flow, and equity. — **Summarizes main points**

B. Experience, preparation, and projection, then, are the three keys to launching your business with the necessary start-up capital so that you can concentrate on where your customers, not your funds, are coming from. — **Provides final focus**

- **Topic/function/conventional grouping.** Example: A report discussing mishandled airline baggage, organized by names of airlines.
- **Comparison/contrast (pro/con).** Example: A report comparing organic farming methods with those of modern industrial farming.
- **Journalism pattern.** Example: A report describing how identity thieves can ruin your good name. Organized by *who, what, when, where, why,* and *how.*
- **Value/size.** Example: A report describing fluctuations in housing costs, organized by prices of homes.
- **Importance.** Example: A report describing five reasons that a company should move its headquarters to a specific city, organized from the most important reason to the least important.
- **Problem/solution.** Example: A company faces a problem such as declining sales. A solution such as reducing the staff is offered.
- **Simple/complex.** Example: A report explaining genetic modification of plants such as corn, organized from simple seed production to complex gene introduction.
- **Best case/worst case.** Example: A report analyzing whether two companies should merge, organized by the best case result (improved market share, profitability, employee morale) opposed to the worse case result (devalued stock, lost market share, employee malaise).

Main ideas can be organized according to chronology, geography/space, topic/function/conventional grouping, comparison/contrast, journalism pattern, value/size, importance, problem/solution, simple/complex, and best case/worst case.

In his presentation, Eric arranged the main points by importance, placing the most important point last where it had maximum effect. When organizing any presentation, prepare a little more material than you think you will actually need. Skilled speakers always have something useful in reserve (such as an extra handout, transparency, or idea)—just in case they finish early.

Summarizing in the Conclusion

Nervous speakers often rush to wrap up their presentations because they can't wait to flee the stage. But listeners will remember the conclusion more than any part of a speech. That's why you should spend some time to make it most effective. Strive to achieve two goals:

Effective conclusions summarize main points and allow the speaker to exit gracefully.

- Summarize the main themes of the presentation.
- Include a statement that allows you to leave the podium gracefully.

Don't end limply with comments such as "I guess that's about all I have to say." Skilled speakers alert the audience that they are finishing. They use phrases such as, *In conclusion, As I end this presentation,* or *It's time for me to stop.* Then they proceed immediately to the conclusion. Audiences become justly irritated with a speaker who announces the conclusion but then digresses with one more story or talks on for ten more minutes.

A straightforward summary should review major points and focus on what you want the listeners to do, think, or remember. Notice how Eric Evans, in the conclusion shown in Figure 15.1, summarized his three main points and provided a final focus to listeners.

In your conclusion you might want to use an anecdote, an inspiring quotation, or a statement that ties in the opener and offers a new insight. Whatever you choose, be sure to include a closing thought that indicates you are finished.

HOW THE BEST SPEAKERS BUILD AUDIENCE RAPPORT

3

Good speakers are adept at building audience rapport. They form a bond with the audience; they entertain as well as inform. How do they do it? Based on observations of successful and unsuccessful speakers, we learn that the good ones use a number of verbal and nonverbal techniques to connect with the audience. Helpful techniques include providing effective imagery, supplying verbal signposts, and using body language strategically.

Effective Imagery

Use analogies, metaphors, similes, personal anecdotes, personalized statistics, and worst- and best-case scenarios instead of dry facts.

You'll lose your audience quickly if your talk is filled with abstractions, generalities, and dry facts. To enliven your presentation and enhance comprehension, try using some of these techniques:

- **Analogies.** A comparison of similar traits between dissimilar things can be effective in explaining and drawing connections.
- **Metaphors.** A comparison between otherwise dissimilar things without using the words *like* or *as* results in a metaphor.
- **Similes.** A comparison that includes the words *like* or *as* is a simile.
- **Personal anecdotes.** Nothing connects you faster or better with your audience than a good personal story.
- **Personalized statistics.** Although often misused, statistics stay with people—particularly when they relate directly to the audience.
- **Worst- and best-case scenarios.** Hearing the worst that could happen can be effective in driving home a point.

Verbal Signposts

Knowledgeable speakers provide verbal signposts to spotlight organization and key ideas.

Speakers must remember that listeners, unlike readers of a report, cannot control the rate of presentation or flip back through pages to review main points. As a result, listeners get lost easily. Knowledgeable speakers help the audience recognize the organization and main points in an oral message with verbal signposts. They keep listeners on track by including helpful previews, summaries, and transitions, such as these:

- **Previewing**
  The next segment of my talk presents three reasons for . . . .
  Let's now consider the causes of . . . .
- **Summarizing**
  Let me review with you the major problems I've just discussed . . . .
  You see, then, that the most significant factors are . . . .
- **Switching directions**
  Thus far we've talked solely about . . . ; now let's move to . . . .
  I've argued that . . . and . . . , but an alternative view holds that . . . .

You can further improve any oral presentation by including appropriate transitional expressions such as *first, second, next, then, therefore, moreover, on the other hand, on the contrary,* and *in conclusion.* These expressions lend emphasis and tell listeners where you are headed. Notice in Eric Evans' outline, in Figure 15.1, the specific transitional elements designed to help listeners recognize each new principal point.

Nonverbal Messages

Although what you say is most important, the nonverbal messages you send can also have a powerful effect on how well your message is received. How you look, how you move, and how you speak can make or break your presentation. The following suggestions focus on nonverbal tips to ensure that your verbal message is well received.

The way you look, how you move, and how you speak affect the success of your presentation.

- **Look terrific.** Like it or not, you will be judged by your appearance. For everything but small in-house presentations, be sure you dress professionally. The rule of thumb is that you should dress at least as well as the best-dressed person in the audience.
- **Animate your body.** Be enthusiastic and let your body show it. Emphasize ideas to enhance points about size, number, and direction. Use a variety of gestures, but don't consciously plan them in advance.
- **Punctuate your words.** You can keep your audience interested by varying your tone, volume, pitch, and pace. Use pauses before and after important points. Allow the audience to take in your ideas.
- **Get out from behind the podium.** Avoid being planted to the podium. Movement makes you look natural and comfortable. You might pick a few places in the room to walk to. Even if you must stay close to your visual aids, make a point of leaving them occasionally so that the audience can see your whole body.
- **Vary your facial expression.** Begin with a smile, but change your expressions to correspond with the thoughts you are voicing. You can shake your head to show disagreement, roll your eyes to show disdain, look heavenward for guidance, or wrinkle your brow to show concern or dismay. To see how speakers convey meaning without words, mute the sound on your TV and watch the facial expressions of a talk show personality.

PLANNING VISUAL AIDS, HANDOUTS, AND MULTIMEDIA PRESENTATIONS

Before you make a business presentation, consider this wise Chinese proverb: "Tell me, I forget. Show me, I remember. Involve me, I understand." Your goals as a speaker are to make listeners understand, remember, and act on your ideas. To get them interested and involved, include effective visual aids. Some experts say that we acquire 85 percent of all our knowledge visually. Therefore, an oral presentation that incorporates visual aids is far more likely to be understood and retained than one lacking visual enhancement.

Good visual aids have many purposes. They emphasize and clarify main points, thus improving comprehension and retention. They increase audience interest, and they make the presenter appear more professional, better prepared, and more persuasive. Furthermore, research shows that the use of visual aids actually shortens meetings.[3] Visual aids are particularly helpful for inexperienced speakers because the audience concentrates on the aid rather than on the speaker. Good visuals also serve to jog the memory of a speaker, thus improving self-confidence, poise, and delivery.

Visual aids clarify points, improve comprehension, and aid retention.

Types of Visual Aids

Fortunately for today's speakers, many forms of visual media are available to enhance a presentation. Figure 15.2 describes the pros and cons for a number of

FIGURE 15.2 Consider the Pros and Cons for Visual Aid Options

MEDIUM	PROS	CONS
Multimedia slides	Creates professional appearance with many colour, art, graphic, and font options. Easy to use and transport via removable disk, Web download, or e-mail attachment. Inexpensive to update.	Presents potential incompatibility issues. Requires costly projection equipment and practice for smooth delivery. Tempts user to include razzle-dazzle features that may fail to add value.
Transparencies	Gives professional appearance with little practice. Easy to (1) prepare, (2) update and maintain, (3) locate reliable equipment, and (4) limit information shown at one time.	Appears to some as an outdated presentation method. Holds speaker captive to the machine. Provides poor reproduction of photos and some graphics.
Handouts	Encourages audience participation. Easy to maintain and update. Enhances recall because audience keeps reference material.	Increases risk of unauthorized duplication of speaker's material. Can be difficult to transport. May cause speaker to lose audience's attention.
Flipcharts or whiteboards	Provides inexpensive option available at most sites. Easy to (1) create, (2) modify or customize on the spot, (3) record comments from the audience, and (4) combine with more high-tech visuals in the same presentation.	Requires graphics talent. Difficult for larger audiences to see. Prepared flipcharts are cumbersome to transport and easily worn with use.
Video	Gives an accurate representation of the content; strong indication of forethought and preparation.	Creates potential for compatibility issues related to computer video formats. Expensive to create and update.
Objects for demonstration	Offers a realistic reinforcement of message content. Increases audience participation with close observation.	Leads to extra work and expense in transporting and replacing worn objects. Limited use with larger audiences.

visual aids that can guide you in selecting the best visual for any speaking occasion. Three of the most popular visuals are overhead transparencies, handouts, and multimedia slides.

Overhead Transparencies. Student and professional speakers alike rely on the overhead projector for many reasons. Most meeting areas are equipped with projectors and screens. Moreover, acetate transparencies for the overhead are cheap, easily prepared on a computer or copier, and simple to use. And, because rooms need not be darkened, a speaker using transparencies can maintain eye contact with the audience. A word of caution, though: stand to the side of the projector so that you don't obstruct the audience's view.

Handouts. You can enhance and complement your presentations by distributing pictures, outlines, brochures, articles, charts, summaries, or other supplements. Speakers who use computer presentation programs often prepare a set of their slides along with notes to hand out to viewers. Timing the distribution of any handout, though, is tricky. If given out during a presentation, your handouts tend to distract the audience, causing you to lose control. Thus, it's probably best to discuss most handouts during the presentation but delay distributing them until after you finish.

To maintain control, distribute handouts after you finish speaking.

Multimedia Slides. With today's excellent software programs—such as Microsoft PowerPoint, Apple Keynote, Lotus Freelance Graphics, and Corel Presentations—you can create dynamic, colourful presentations with your PC. The output from these programs is generally shown on a PC monitor, a TV monitor, an LCD (liquid crystal display) panel, or a screen. With a little expertise and advanced equipment, you can create a multimedia presentation that includes stereo sound, videos, and hyperlinks, as described in the following discussion of multimedia presentations.

Designing a Multimedia Presentation

Computer-aided presentations are economical, flexible, professional, and easy to prepare.

Whether making a presentation to a dozen people sitting around a conference table or speaking to an audience of 500 in a large auditorium, smart speakers choose to put their key points on-screen to underscore and reinforce them. As a result, computer programs such as PowerPoint have become the business standard for presenting, defending, and selling ideas most effectively. Business speakers use computer presentations because they are economical, flexible, and easy to prepare. Changes can be made right up to the last minute. Most important, though, such presentations, when well done, make even amateurs look like real pros.

Critics say that PowerPoint is too regimented and detracts attention from the speaker.

Yet, PowerPoint has its critics. They charge that the program dictates the way in which information is structured and presented. PowerPoint stifles "the storyteller, the poet, the person whose thoughts cannot be arranged in the shape of an AutoContent slide."[4] PowerPoint, say its detractors, when utilized poorly can isolate and diminish the speaker in the eyes of the audience. Some speakers choose to minimize their fear by hiding behind the slides. In such a case, PowerPoint is a misused technology. Successful business speakers, on the other hand, use PowerPoint because it increases audience enjoyment, comprehension, and retention. PowerPoint speakers, however, are effective only when they are skillful. To be effective, you must learn about using templates, working with colour, building bullet points, and adding multimedia effects.

Creating Your Presentation

All presentation programs require you to (1) select or create a template that will serve as the background for your presentation and (2) make each individual slide by selecting a layout that best conveys your message. You can use one of the templates provided with the program, download one from many Web sites, or create one from scratch.

Novice and even advanced users choose existing templates because they are designed by professionals who know how to combine harmonious colours, borders, and fonts for pleasing visual effect. If you prefer, you can alter existing templates so they better suit your needs. Adding a corporate logo, adjusting the colour scheme to better match the colours used on your organization's Web site, or selecting a different font are just some of the ways you can customize existing templates.

Be careful, though, of what one expert labels "visual clichés."[5] Overused templates and even clip art that ship with PowerPoint can weary viewers who have seen them repeatedly in presentations. Instead of using a standard template, key in "PowerPoint template" in your favourite search engine. You will see hundreds of template options available as free downloads. Unless your employer requires that presentations all have the same look, your audience will most likely appreciate fresh templates that complement the purpose of your presentation and provide visual variety.

Background and text colours depend on the lightness of the room.

Whether you create your own template or choose one designed by professionals, consider these principles when evaluating your colour options. Warm colours—reds, oranges, and yellows—are best to highlight important elements. Blue is associated with calmness; yellow signals caution; red can mean stop, financial loss, or danger; and green relates to nature, go, and money. The colour for backgrounds and text depends on where the presentation will be given. Use light text on a dark background for presentations in darkened rooms. Use dark text on a light background for computer presentations in lighted rooms.

In selecting the best slide layout for each slide, you again can choose from the layout options that are part of your presentation program, or you can create a layout from scratch by adding your own elements to each slide. You can alter layouts by repositioning, resizing, or changing the fonts for the placeholders in which your title, bulleted list, organization chart, video clip, photograph, or other elements appear.

When team members are working together to prepare a slide presentation, be sure that each member is using the same template. That way, when they merge their individual sections into one presentation file, no one will be surprised about how the slides look. To maintain a consistent look throughout the presentation, only one team member should be in charge of making colour, font, or other global formatting changes to the slide and title masters. Team members should be encouraged to follow the global formatting established by the master slides. In addition, team members should understand that making global changes one time using the master slides is a definite plus. It prevents the problems associated with changing many individual slides.

Building Bullet Points

Bullet points should be short phrases that are parallel.

When you prepare your slides, translate the major headings in your presentation outline into titles for slides. Then build bullet points using short phrases. In Chapter 5 you learned to improve readability by using listing techniques, including bullets, numbers, and headings. In preparing a PowerPoint presentation, you will use those same techniques.

Text can be converted into bullet points by experimenting with key phrases that are concise and balanced grammatically.

To convert text into bullet points, start with a title and then list the main ideas that relate to that title. Work with the list until all the items are parallel. They should be key phrases, not complete sentences. Finally, you may add a photo or graphic to illustrate a point or add interest.

Incremental bullet points enable a speaker to animate the presentation and control the flow of ideas.

PowerPoint's animation feature can focus the viewer's attention on each point of a bulleted slide. By choosing from a variety of effects, such as "fly" in from the top or "wipe" right, each bullet point can be displayed to coordinate with the speaker's comments.

Text Converted to Bullet Points

Voice Mail Can Make Your Calls More Efficient

- *Eliminates telephone tag*
- *Reduces callbacks*
- *Improves timely communication*
- *Shortens "hold" times*

When moving from one slide to the next, you can use *slide transition* elements, such as venetian blinds or spinning like spokes on a wheel. But don't overdo it. Experts suggest choosing one transition effect and applying it consistently.[6]

FIGURE 15.3 Preparing a PowerPoint Presentation

Tips for Preparing and Using Slides

- Keep all visuals simple; spotlight major points only.
- Use the same font size and style for similar headings.
- Apply the Rule of Seven: No more than seven words on a line, seven total lines, and 7 × 7 or 49 total words.
- Be sure that everyone in the audience can see the slides.
- Show a slide, allow the audience to read it, then paraphrase it. Do NOT read from a slide.
- Rehearse by practising talking to the audience, not to the slides.
- Bring backup transparencies in case of equipment failure.

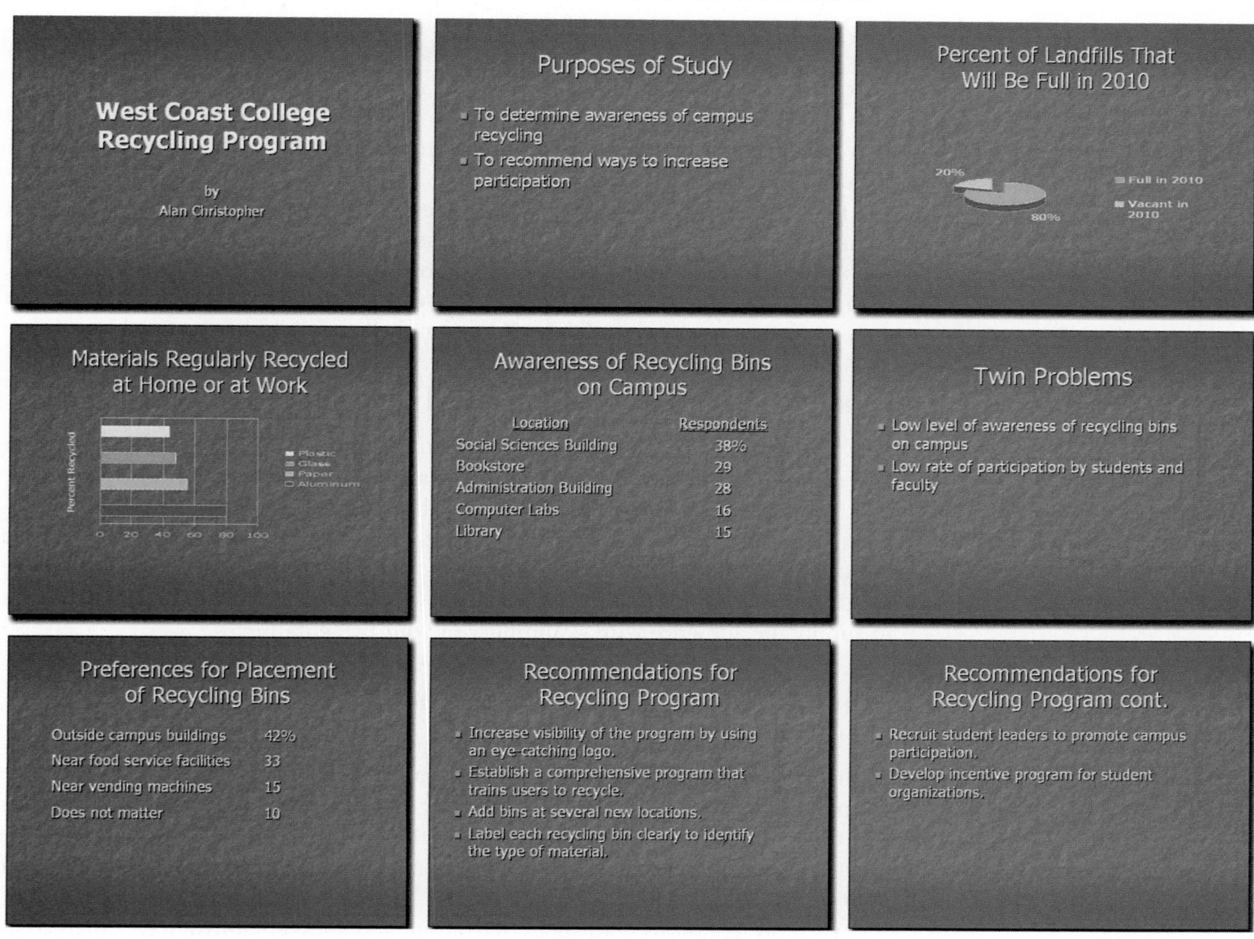

For the most readable slides, apply the *Rule of Seven.* Each slide should include no more than seven words in a line, no more than seven total lines, and no more than 7 × 7 or 49 total words. If possible, use fewer words. Remember that presentation slides summarize; they don't tell the whole story. That's the job of the presenter.

Adding Multimedia Elements

Multimedia elements include sound, animation, and video features.

Few approaches are more mind numbing to your audience than displaying endless slides of bulleted lists. Thanks to the multimedia features available on presentation programs, you can include sound, animation, video, and other visual elements to enhance your content. For example, video clips can add excitement and depth to a presentation.

Another way to enliven a presentation is with photographic images. These images are easy to obtain thanks to stock photos that can be purchased online and to the prevalence of low-cost scanners and digital cameras. Furthermore, presenting processes, operations, and sequences in an animated flowchart format reflects the information more accurately than the same data presented in a bulleted list.

Numeric information is more easily grasped in charts or graphs than in a listing of numbers. Moreover, in most programs, you can animate your graphs and charts.

Most programs are also capable of generating hyperlinks ("hot" spots on the screen) that allow you to jump instantly to sources outside your presentation. With a click of your mouse, you could take your audience "live" to a Web site that contains up-to-the-minute data related to your presentation. Hyperlinks can enhance interest in your presentation by adding interactive features and a wide variety of multimedia elements.

Be warned, though, that using multimedia effects or visual enhancements just because you can is never a good enough reason to include them. Every multimedia and visual effect you use should enhance your message and engage your audience. Using too many "bells and whistles" is annoying and may cause your audience to remember the entertaining slides rather than the key points.

Producing Speaker's Notes and Handouts

You also have a variety of options for printing hard-copy versions of your presentation. You can make speaker's notes that are a wonderful aid for practising your talk. Beneath the miniature image of each slide is space for you to key in your supporting comments for the abbreviated material in your slides. You can also include up to nine miniature versions of your slides per printed page. These miniatures are handy if you want to preview your talk to a sponsoring organization or if you wish to supply the audience with a summary of your presentation.

Moving Your Presentation to the Internet

Web presentations are less expensive than videoconferencing.

You have a range of alternatives, from simple to complex, for moving your multimedia presentation to the Internet. The simplest option is posting your slides online for others to access. Even if you are giving a face-to-face presentation, attendees appreciate these *electronic handouts* because they don't have to carry them home. The most complex option for moving your multimedia presentation to the Internet involves a Web conference or broadcast.

Web presentations with slides, narration, and speaker control have emerged as a way for anyone who has access to the Internet to attend your presentation without leaving the office. For example, you could initiate a meeting via a conference call, narrate using a telephone, and have participants see your slides from the browsers on their computers. If you prefer, you could skip the narration and provide a prerecorded presentation. Web-based presentations have many applications, including providing access to updated training or sales data whenever needed.[7]

Avoiding Being Upstaged by Multimedia Slides

One expert urges speakers to "use their PowerPresence in preference to their PowerPoint."[8] Although multimedia presentations can provide great impact, they shouldn't carry the show. Your goal is to avoid letting PowerPoint "steal your thunder." Here are suggestions for keeping control in your slide presentation:

- Use your slide primarily to summarize important points. For each slide have one or more paragraphs of narration to present to your audience.
- Remember that your responsibility is to *add value* to the information you present. Explain the analyses leading up to the major points and what each point means.
- Look at the audience, not the screen.
- As you show new elements on a slide, allow the audience time to absorb the information, and then paraphrase and elaborate on what they have seen. Do *not* read verbatim from a slide.
- Leave the lights as bright as you can. Make sure the audience can see your face and eyes.
- Use a radio remote control (not infrared) so you can stand near the screen rather than remain tethered to your computer. Radio remotes will allow you to be up to 15 metres away from your laptop.
- Maintain a connection with the audience by using a laser pointer to highlight slide items to discuss.
- Darken the screen while you discuss points, tell a story, give an example, or involve the audience.
- Don't rely totally on PowerPoint. Help the audience visualize your points by using other techniques. Drawing a diagram on a whiteboard or flipchart can be more engaging than showing slide after slide of static drawings. Showing real objects is a welcome relief from slides.
- In case of equipment failure, bring backups of your presentation. Overhead transparencies or handouts of your presentation would provide good substitutes. Transferring your presentation to a CD or a USB flash drive that could run from any available laptop might prove useful as well.

Keep in mind that your slides and transparencies merely supply a framework for your presentation. Your audience came to see and hear *you.*

POLISHING YOUR DELIVERY AND FOLLOWING UP

Once you've organized your presentation and prepared visuals, you're ready to practise delivering it. Here are suggestions for selecting a delivery method, along with specific techniques to use before, during, and after your presentation. 5

Delivery Method

Inexperienced speakers often feel that they must memorize an entire presentation to be effective. Unless you're an experienced performer, however, you will sound

Novice speakers often speed up their delivery, perhaps out of nervousness or eagerness to sit down. Preparation and practice are keys to improving presentation skills.

wooden and unnatural. Moreover, forgetting your place can be disastrous! Therefore, memorizing an entire oral presentation is not recommended. However, memorizing significant parts—the introduction, the conclusion, and perhaps a meaningful quotation—can be dramatic and impressive.

If memorizing won't work, is reading your presentation the best plan? Definitely not! Reading to an audience is boring and ineffective. Because reading suggests that you don't know your topic very well, the audience loses confidence in your expertise. Reading also prevents you from maintaining eye contact. You can't see audience reactions; consequently, you can't benefit from feedback.

Neither the memorizing nor the reading method creates very convincing presentations. The best plan, by far, is a "notes" method. Plan your presentation carefully and talk from note cards or an outline containing key sentences and major ideas. By preparing and then practising with your notes, you can talk to your audience in a conversational manner. Your notes should be neither entire paragraphs nor single words. Instead, they should contain a complete sentence or two to introduce each major idea. Under the topic sentence(s), outline subpoints and illustrations. Note cards will keep you on track and prompt your memory, but only if you have rehearsed the presentation thoroughly.

Delivery Techniques

Stage fright is both natural and controllable.

Nearly everyone experiences some degree of stage fright when speaking before a group. "If you hear someone say he or she isn't nervous before a speech, you're talking either to a liar or a very boring speaker," says corporate speech consultant Dianna Booher.[9] Being afraid is quite natural and results from actual physiological changes occurring in your body. Faced with a frightening situation, your body responds with the fight-or-flight response, discussed more fully in the accompanying Career Coach box. You can learn to control and reduce stage fright, as well as to incorporate techniques for effective speaking, by using the following strategies and techniques before, during, and after your presentation.

Before Your Presentation

- **Prepare thoroughly.** One of the most effective strategies for reducing stage fright is knowing your subject thoroughly. Research your topic diligently and prepare a careful sentence outline. Those who try to "wing it" usually suffer the worst butterflies—and make the worst presentations.

Thorough preparation, extensive rehearsal, and stress-reduction techniques can lessen stage fright.

- **Rehearse repeatedly.** When you rehearse, practise your entire presentation, not just the first half. Place your outline sentences on separate cards. You may also wish to include transitional sentences to help you move to the next topic. Use these cards as you practise, and include your visual aids in your rehearsal. Rehearse alone or before friends and family. Also try rehearsing on audio- or videotape so that you can evaluate your effectiveness.
- **Time yourself.** Most audiences tend to get restless during longer talks. Thus, try to complete your presentation in no more than 20 minutes. Set a timer during your rehearsal to measure your speaking time.
- **Request a lectern.** Every beginning speaker needs the security of a high desk or lectern from which to deliver a presentation. It serves as a note holder and a convenient place to rest wandering hands and arms.

CAREER COACH

How to Avoid Stage Fright

Ever get nervous before giving a speech? Everyone does! And it's not all in your head, either. When you face something threatening or challenging, your body reacts in what psychologists call the *fight-or-flight* response. This response provides your body with increased energy to deal with threatening situations. It also creates those sensations—dry mouth, sweaty hands, increased heartbeat, and stomach butterflies—that we associate with stage fright. The fight-or-flight response arouses your body for action—in this case, making a presentation.

Because everyone feels some form of apprehension before speaking, it's impossible to eliminate the physiological symptoms altogether. But you can help reduce their effects with the following techniques:

- **Breathe deeply.** Use deep breathing to ease your fight-or-flight symptoms. Inhale to a count of ten, hold this breath to a count of ten, and exhale to a count of ten. Concentrate on your counting and your breathing; both activities reduce your stress.
- **Convert your fear.** Don't view your sweaty palms and dry mouth as evidence of fear. Interpret them as symptoms of exuberance, excitement, and enthusiasm to share your ideas.
- **Know your topic.** Feel confident about your topic. Select a topic that you know well and that is relevant to your audience.
- **Use positive self-talk.** Remind yourself that you know your topic and are prepared. Tell yourself that the audience is on your side—because it is!
- **Shift the spotlight to your visuals.** At least some of the time the audience will be focusing on your slides, transparencies, handouts, or whatever you have prepared—and not totally on you.
- **Ignore any stumbles.** Don't apologize or confess your nervousness. If you keep going, the audience will forget any mistakes quickly.
- **Feel proud when you finish.** You'll be surprised at how good you feel when you finish. Take pride in what you've accomplished, and your audience will reward you with applause and congratulations. And, of course, your body will call off the fight-or-flight response and return to normal!

- **Check the room.** Before you talk, make sure that a lectern has been provided. If you are using a computer, sound equipment, or a projector, be certain they are operational. Check electrical outlets and the position of the viewing screen. Ensure that the seating arrangement is appropriate to your needs.
- **Greet members of the audience.** Try to make contact with a few members of the audience when you enter the room, while you are waiting to be introduced, or when you walk to the podium. Your body language should convey friendliness, confidence, and enjoyment.
- **Practise stress reduction.** If you feel tension and fear while you are waiting your turn to speak, use stress-reduction techniques, such as deep breathing. Additional techniques to help you conquer stage fright are presented in the accompanying Career Coach box.

During Your Presentation

Eye contact, a moderate tone of voice, and natural movements enhance a presentation.

- **Begin with a pause.** When you first approach the audience, take a moment to adjust your notes and make yourself comfortable. Establish your control of the situation.
- **Present your first sentence from memory.** By memorizing your opening, you can immediately establish rapport with the audience through eye contact. You'll also sound confident and knowledgeable.

- **Maintain eye contact.** If the size of the audience overwhelms you, pick out two individuals on the right and two on the left. Talk directly to these people.
- **Control your voice and vocabulary.** This means speaking in moderated tones but loudly enough to be heard. Eliminate verbal static, such as *ah, er, you know,* and *um.* Silence is preferable to meaningless fillers when you are thinking of your next idea.
- **Put the brakes on.** Many novice speakers talk too rapidly, displaying their nervousness and making it very difficult for audience members to understand their ideas. Slow down and listen to what you are saying.
- **Move naturally.** You can use the lectern to hold your notes so that you are free to move about casually and naturally. Avoid fidgeting with your notes, your clothing, or items in your pockets. Learn to use your body to express a point.
- **Use visual aids effectively.** You should discuss and interpret each visual aid for the audience. Move aside as you describe it so that it can be seen fully. Use a pointer if necessary.
- **Avoid digressions.** Stick to your outline and notes. Don't suddenly include clever little anecdotes or digressions that occur to you on the spot. If it's not part of your rehearsed material, leave it out so that you can finish on time. Remember, too, that your audience may not be as enthralled with your topic as you are.
- **Summarize your main points.** Conclude your presentation by reiterating your main points or by emphasizing what you want the audience to think or do. Once you have announced your conclusion, proceed to it directly.

After Your Presentation

The time to answer questions, distribute handouts, and reiterate main points is after a presentation.

- **Distribute handouts.** If you prepared handouts with data the audience will need, pass them out when you finish.
- **Encourage questions.** If the situation permits a question-and-answer period, announce it at the beginning of your presentation. Then, when you finish, ask for questions. Set a time limit for questions and answers.
- **Repeat questions.** Although the speaker may hear the question, audience members often do not. Begin each answer with a repetition of the question. This also gives you thinking time. Then, direct your answer to the entire audience.
- **Reinforce your main points.** You can use your answers to restate your primary ideas ("I'm glad you brought that up because it gives me a chance to elaborate on . . ."). In answering questions, avoid becoming defensive or debating the questioner.
- **Keep control.** Don't allow one individual to take over. Keep the entire audience involved.
- **Avoid *Yes, but* answers.** The word *but* immediately cancels any preceding message. Try replacing it with *and.* For example, *Yes, X has been tried. And Y works even better because . . . .*
- **End with a summary and appreciation.** To signal the end of the session before you take the last question, say something like *We have time for just one more question.* As you answer the last question, try to work it into a summary of your main points. Then, express appreciation to the audience for the opportunity to talk with them.

ADAPTING TO INTERNATIONAL AND CROSS-CULTURAL AUDIENCES

Every good speaker adapts to the audience, and cross-cultural presentations call for special adjustments and sensitivity. When working with an interpreter or speaking before individuals whose English is limited, you'll need to be very careful about your language.

Beyond these basic language adaptations, however, more fundamental sensitivity is often necessary. In organizing a presentation for a cross-cultural audience, think twice about delivering your main idea up front. Many people (notably those in Japanese, Latin American, and Arabic cultures) consider such directness to be brash and inappropriate. Remember that others may not share our cultural emphasis on straightforwardness.[10]

Addressing cross-cultural audiences requires a speaker to consider audience expectations and cultural conventions.

Also consider breaking your presentation into short, discrete segments. In the Middle East, for example, Arab speakers "mix circuitous, irrelevant (by North American standards) conversations with short dashes of information that go directly to the point." Presenters who are patient, tolerant, and "mature" (in the eyes of the audience) will make the sale or win the contract.[11]

Remember, too, that some cultures prefer greater formality than Westerners exercise. Writing on a flipchart or transparency seems natural and spontaneous in this country. Abroad, though, such informal techniques may suggest that the speaker does not value the audience enough to prepare proper visual aids in advance.[12]

This caution aside, you'll still want to use visual aids to communicate your message. These visuals should be written in both languages, so that you and your audience understand them. Never use numbers without writing them out for all to see. If possible, say numbers in both languages. Distribute translated handouts, summarizing your important information, when you finish. Finally, be careful of your body language. Looking people in the eye suggests intimacy and self-confidence in this country, but in other cultures such eye contact may be considered disrespectful.

Whether you are speaking to a familiar or cross-cultural audience, your presentation requires attention to content and strategy. The following checklist summarizes suggestions for preparing, organizing, and illustrating an oral presentation.

CHECKLIST FOR PREPARING AND ORGANIZING ORAL PRESENTATIONS

Getting Ready to Speak

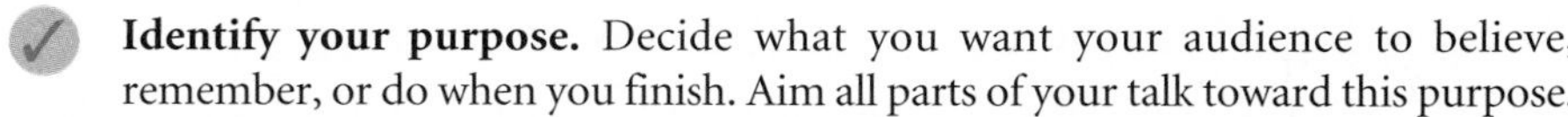

✓ **Identify your purpose.** Decide what you want your audience to believe, remember, or do when you finish. Aim all parts of your talk toward this purpose.

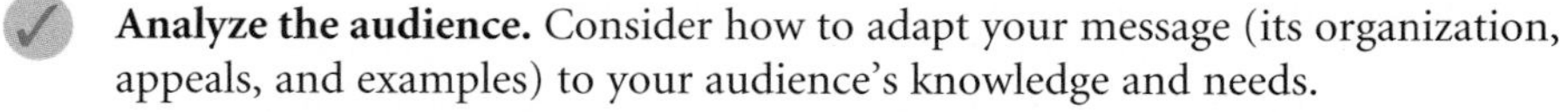

✓ **Analyze the audience.** Consider how to adapt your message (its organization, appeals, and examples) to your audience's knowledge and needs.

Organizing the Introduction

✓ **Get the audience involved.** Capture the audience's attention by opening with a promise, story, startling fact, question, quote, relevant problem, or self-effacing joke.

- **Establish yourself.** Demonstrate your credibility by identifying your position, expertise, knowledge, or qualifications.
- **Preview your main points.** Introduce your topic and summarize its principal parts.

Organizing the Body

- **Develop two to four main points.** Streamline your topic so that you can concentrate on its major issues.
- **Arrange the points logically.** Sequence your points chronologically, from most important to least important, by comparison and contrast, or by some other strategy.
- **Prepare transitions.** Between each major point write "bridge" statements that connect the previous item to the next one. Use transitional expressions as verbal signposts (*first, second, then, however, consequently, on the contrary,* and so forth).
- **Have extra material ready.** Be prepared with more information and visuals in case you have additional time to fill.

Organizing the Conclusion

- **Review your main points.** Emphasize your main ideas in your closing so that your audience will remember them.
- **Provide a final focus.** Tell how your listeners can use this information, why you have spoken, or what you want them to do.

Designing Visual Aids

- **Select your medium carefully.** Consider the size of your audience, degree of formality desired, cost and ease of preparation, and potential effectiveness.
- **Highlight main ideas.** Use visual aids to illustrate major concepts only. Keep them brief and simple.
- **Use aids skillfully.** Talk to the audience, not to the visuals. Paraphrase their contents.

Developing Multimedia Presentations

- **Learn to use your software program.** Study template and slide layout designs to see how you can adapt them to your purposes.
- **Select colours based on the light level in the room.** Consider how mixing light and dark fonts and backgrounds affects their visibility.
- **Use bulleted points for major ideas.** Make sure your points are all parallel and observe the Rule of Seven.
- **Make speaker's notes.** Jot down the narrative supporting each slide and use these notes to practise your presentation.

 **Maintain control.** Don't let your slides upstage you. Engage your audience by using additional techniques to help them visualize your points.

IMPROVING TELEPHONE, VOICE MAIL, AND REMOTE CONFERENCING SKILLS

Telephone calls and voice mail should promote goodwill and increase productivity.

Despite the heavy reliance on e-mail, the telephone is still an extremely important piece of equipment in offices. With the addition of today's wireless technology, it doesn't matter whether you are in or out of the office. You can be reached by phone. In the Career Coach box on page 13 of Chapter 1, you learned some specific techniques for being courteous in using cell phones. In this chapter we'll focus on traditional telephone techniques as well as voice mail and remote conferencing efficiency. As a business communicator, you can be more productive, efficient, and professional by following some simple suggestions.

Making Telephone Calls Efficiently

Making productive telephone calls means planning an agenda, identifying the purpose, being courteous and cheerful, and avoiding rambling.

Before making a telephone call, decide whether the intended call is really necessary. Could you find the information yourself? If you wait a while, would the problem resolve itself? Perhaps your message could be delivered more efficiently by some other means. Some companies have found that telephone calls are often less important than the work they interrupted. Alternatives to telephone calls include instant messaging, e-mail, memos, or calls to voice mail systems. If a telephone call must be made, consider using the following suggestions to make it fully productive.

- **Plan a mini-agenda.** Have you ever been embarrassed when you had to make a second telephone call because you forgot an important item the first time? Before placing a call, jot down notes regarding all the topics you need to discuss. Following an agenda guarantees not only a complete call but also a quick one. You'll be less likely to wander from the business at hand while rummaging through your mind trying to remember everything.
- **Use a three-point introduction.** When placing a call, immediately (1) name the person you are calling, (2) identify yourself and your affiliation, and (3) give a brief explanation of your reason for calling.
- **Be brisk if you are rushed.** For business calls when your time is limited, avoid questions such as "How are you?" Instead, say, "Lisa, I knew you'd be the only one who could answer these two questions for me." Another efficient strategy is to set a "contract" with the caller: "Look, Lisa, I have only ten minutes, but I really wanted to get back to you."
- **Be cheerful and accurate.** Let your voice show the same kind of animation that you radiate when you greet people in person. In your mind try to envision the individual answering the telephone. A smile can certainly affect the tone of your voice, so smile at that person. Moreover, be accurate about what you say. "Hang on a second; I'll be right back" rarely is true. Better to say, "It may take me two or three minutes to get that information. Would you prefer to hold or have me call you back?"
- **Bring it to a close.** The responsibility for ending a call lies with the caller. This is sometimes difficult to do if the other person rambles on. You may need to use suggestive closing language, such as "I've certainly enjoyed talking with you," "I've learned what I needed to know, and now I can proceed with my work."

- **Avoid telephone tag.** If you call someone who's not in, ask when it would be best for you to call again. State that you will call at a specific time—and do it. If you ask a person to call you, give a time when you can be reached—and then be sure you are in at that time.
- **Leave complete voice mail messages.** Remember that there's no rush when you leave a voice mail message. Always enunciate clearly. And be sure to provide a complete message, including your name, telephone number, and the time and date of your call. Explain your purpose so that the receiver can be ready with the required information when returning your call.

Receiving Telephone Calls Professionally

With a little forethought you can make your telephone a productive, efficient work tool. Developing good telephone manners also reflects well on you and on your organization.

Receiving productive telephone calls means identifying oneself, acting responsive, being helpful, and taking accurate messages.

- **Identify yourself immediately.** In answering your telephone or someone else's, provide your name, title or affiliation, and, possibly, a greeting. Force yourself to speak clearly and slowly. Remember that the caller may be unfamiliar with what you are saying and fail to recognize slurred syllables.
- **Be responsive and helpful.** If you are in a support role, be sympathetic to callers' needs. Instead of "I don't know," try "That's a good question; let me investigate." Instead of "We can't do that," try "That's a tough one; let's see what we can do." Avoid "No" at the beginning of a sentence. It sounds especially abrasive and displeasing because it suggests total rejection.
- **Practise telephone confidentiality.** Be courteous and helpful, but don't give out confidential information. Better to say, "She's away from her desk" or "He's out of the office" than to report a colleague's exact whereabouts.
- **Take messages carefully.** Few things are as frustrating as receiving a potentially important phone message that is illegible. Repeat the spelling of names and verify telephone numbers. Write messages legibly and record their time and date. Promise to give the messages to intended recipients, but don't guarantee return calls.
- **Explain what you're doing when transferring calls.** Give a reason for transferring, and identify the extension to which you are directing the call in case the caller is disconnected.

Making the Best Use of Voice Mail

Voice mail eliminates telephone tag, inaccurate message-taking, and time-zone barriers; it also allows communicators to focus on essentials.

Because telephone calls can be disruptive, many businesspeople are making extensive use of voice mail to intercept and screen incoming calls. Voice mail links a telephone system to a computer that digitizes and stores incoming messages. Some systems also provide functions such as automated attendant menus, allowing callers to reach any associated extension by pushing specific buttons on a touch-tone telephone.

Voice mail is quite efficient for message storage. Because as many as half of all business calls require no discussion or feedback, the messaging capabilities of voice mail can mean huge savings for businesses. Incoming information is delivered without interrupting potential receivers and without all the niceties that most two-way conversations require. Stripped of superfluous chitchat, voice mail messages allow communicators to focus on essentials. Voice mail also eliminates telephone tag, inaccurate message-taking, and time-zone barriers.

However, voice mail should not be overused. Individuals who screen all incoming calls cause irritation, resentment, and needless telephone tag. Here are some ways that you can make voice mail work more effectively for you.

- **Announce your voice mail.** If you rely principally on a voice mail message system, identify it on your business stationery and cards. Then, when people call, they will be ready to leave a message.
- **Prepare a warm and informative greeting.** Make your mechanical greeting sound warm and inviting, both in tone and content. Identify yourself and your organization so that callers know they have reached the right number. Thank the caller and briefly explain that you are unavailable. Invite the caller to leave a message or, if appropriate, call back.
- **Test your message.** Call your number and assess your message. Does it sound inviting? Sincere? Understandable? Are you pleased with your tone? If not, says one consultant, have someone else, perhaps a professional, record a message for you.

Getting Together Through Remote Conferencing

Tightened airport security and trimmed travel budgets have created a boon for remote conferencing. As discussed in Chapter 2, collaborative technology can take many forms. It typically uses three media alone or in combination: (1) Participants in *teleconferences*, also known as *conference calls*, communicate by telephone. (2) Participants in *Web conferences* are linked by their Web browsers and can view presentations, documents, and live or recorded video. They usually talk to one another by telephone. (3) Participants in *videoconferences* see live images carried over digital telephone networks or the Internet.

Those using these remote conferencing options are quick to point out the benefits and drawbacks of staying at the office instead of travelling. Benefits include saving time and money, increasing productivity, avoiding airport hassles, and having more time at home with families. Drawbacks include untimely technology breakdowns, fewer opportunities to build relationships, and limitations in gauging audience reactions and body language.

Of the three remote-conferencing options, teleconferencing is the most widely used. These calls are easy to coordinate and require the least expense related to equipment and preparation time. The Tech Talk box provides suggestions for helping you be comfortable and effective when you participate in conference calls.

TECH TALK

Making Effective Conference Calls

Teleconferencing allows participants to participate in a group telephone call. However, conference calls cannot replicate the experience of meeting in person. Participants, therefore, need to make the most of this communication medium by *capitalizing* on its efficiencies and *compensating* for the lack of face-to-face interactions. The guidelines that follow will help you accomplish both of these goals.

As a conference leader, you should do the following:

- Choose equipment that provides excellent audio quality and user-friendly features.
- Select carefully who should be invited to participate.
- Establish a clear list of desired outcomes.
- Create and distribute an agenda. Include directions for dialling into the call and attach visual aids that are numbered for easy reference during the call.
- Greet participants as they "check in," engaging in small talk those who are waiting until everyone is online.
- Encourage the silent members to participate.
- Poll each member each time a decision point is reached.
- Acknowledge when an issue cannot be resolved during that call or when it may require a second call or a different medium to resolve.
- Review conclusions reached and assignments made, and end the call on a positive note.
- Prepare and send out immediately the to-do list with the deadlines and designees.
- Request feedback on how to improve future conference calls.

As a conference participant, you should do the following:

- Compensate for the shortcomings of this medium by (1) weighing carefully what you say and how you say it and (2) listening with concentration and focus.
- Place your call in a quiet room to minimize the interference of background noise.
- Identify yourself each time you speak.
- Remember that communication is two-way and that this medium requires extra effort to make that happen.

SUMMARY OF LEARNING OBJECTIVES

1 **Discuss two important first steps in preparing effective oral presentations.** First, identify what your purpose is and what you want the audience to believe or do so that you can aim the entire presentation toward your goal. Second, know your audience so that you can adjust your message and style to its knowledge and needs.

2 **Explain the major elements in organizing the content of a presentation, including the introduction, body, and conclusion.** The introduction of a good presentation should capture the listener's attention, identify the speaker, establish credibility, and preview the main points. The body should discuss two to four main points, with appropriate explanations, details, and verbal signposts to guide listeners. The conclusion should review the main points, provide a final focus, and allow the speaker to leave the podium gracefully.

3 **Identify techniques for gaining audience rapport, including using effective imagery, providing verbal signposts, and sending appropriate nonverbal messages.** You can improve audience rapport by using effective imagery including analogies, metaphors, similes, personal anecdotes, statistics, and worst/best-case scenarios. Rapport is also gained by including verbal signposts that tell the audience when you are previewing, summarizing, and switching directions. Nonverbal messages have a powerful effect on the way your message is received. You should look terrific, animate your body, punctuate your words, get out from behind the podium, and vary your facial expressions.

4 **Discuss designing and using effective visual aids, handouts, and multimedia presentation materials.** Use simple, easily understood visual aids to emphasize and clarify main points. Choose multimedia slides, flipcharts, or other visuals depending on audience size, degree of formality desired, and budget. Generally, it's best to distribute handouts after a presentation. Speakers employing a program such as PowerPoint use templates, layout designs, and bullet points to produce effective slides. A presentation may be enhanced with slide transitions, sound, animation, video elements, and other multimedia effects.

5 **Specify delivery techniques for use before, during, and after a presentation.** Before your talk prepare a sentence outline on note cards or speaker's notes and rehearse repeatedly. Check the room, lectern, and equipment. During the presentation consider beginning with a pause and presenting your first sentence from memory. Make eye contact, control your voice, speak and move naturally, and avoid digressions. After your talk distribute handouts and answer questions. End gracefully and express appreciation.

6 **Explain effective techniques for adapting oral presentations to cross-cultural audiences.** In presentations before groups whose English is limited, speak slowly, use simple English, avoid jargon and clichés, and use short sentences. Consider building up to your main idea rather than announcing it immediately. Also consider breaking the presentation into short segments to allow participants to ask questions and digest small parts separately. Beware of appearing too spontaneous and informal. Use visual aids to help communicate your message, but also distribute translated handouts summarizing the most important information.

7 **List techniques for improving telephone, voice mail, and remote conferencing effectiveness.** You can improve your telephone calls by planning a mini-agenda and using a three-point introduction (name, affiliation, and purpose). Be cheerful and responsive, and use closing language to end a conversation. Avoid telephone tag by leaving complete messages. In answering calls, identify yourself immediately, avoid giving out confidential information when answering for others, and take careful messages. In setting up an automated-attendant voice mail menu, limit the number of choices. For your own message prepare a warm and informative greeting. Tell when you will be available. Evaluate your message by calling it yourself. Remote conferencing uses three media alone or in combination: *teleconferencing*, *Web conferencing*, and *videoconferencing*. Teleconferencing is the most widely used remote conferencing option.

CHAPTER REVIEW

1. In preparing an oral presentation, you can reduce your fears and lay a foundation for a professional performance by focusing on what five areas? (Obj. 1)
2. Name three goals to be achieved in the introduction of an oral presentation. (Obj. 2)
3. For a 20-minute presentation, how many main points should be developed? (Obj. 2)
4. Which part of a speech—the introduction, body, or conclusion—will listeners most remember? (Obj. 2)
5. List six techniques for creating effective imagery in a presentation. Be prepared to discuss each. (Obj. 3)
6. Name three ways for a speaker to use verbal signposts in a presentation. Illustrate each. (Obj. 3)
7. Why are visual aids particularly useful to inexperienced speakers? (Obj. 4)
8. Why are transparencies a favourite visual aid? (Obj. 4)
9. Name specific advantages and disadvantages of multimedia presentation software. (Obj. 4)
10. How is the Rule of Seven applied in preparing bulleted points? (Obj. 4)
11. What delivery method is most effective for speakers? (Obj. 5)
12. Why should speakers deliver the first sentence from memory? (Obj. 5)
13. How might presentations before international or cross-cultural audiences be altered to be most effective? (Obj. 6)
14. What is a three-point introduction for a telephone call? (Obj. 7)
15. Name two benefits and two drawbacks to remote conferencing. (Obj. 7)

CRITICAL THINKING

1. Why is it necessary to repeat key points in an oral presentation? (Objs. 2 and 5)
2. How can a speaker make the most effective use of visual aids? (Obj. 4)
3. How can speakers prevent multimedia presentation software from stealing their thunder? (Obj. 4)
4. Discuss effective techniques for reducing stage fright. (Obj. 5)

ACTIVITIES

15.1 Outlining an Oral Presentation (Objs. 1 and 2)

One of the hardest parts of preparing an oral presentation is developing the outline.

Your Task. Select an oral presentation topic from the list in Activity 15.4 or suggest an original topic. Prepare an outline for your presentation using the following format.

Title	
Purpose	
	I. INTRODUCTION
Gain attention of audience	A.
Involve audience	B.
Establish credibility	C.
Preview main points	D.
Transition	
	II. BODY
Main point	A.
Illustrate, clarify, contrast	1.
	2.
	3.
Transition	
Main point	B.
Illustrate, clarify, contrast	1.
	2.
	3.
Transition	
Main point	C.
Illustrate, clarify, contrast	1.
	2.
	3.
Transition	
	III. CONCLUSION
Summarize main points	A.
Provide final focus	B.
Encourage questions	C.

15.2 Overcoming Stage Fright (Obj. 5)

What makes you most nervous when making a presentation before class? Being tongue-tied? Fearing all eyes on you? Messing up? Forgetting your ideas and looking silly?

Your Task. Discuss the previous questions as a class. Then, in groups of three or four talk about ways to overcome these fears. Your instructor may ask you to write a memo (individual or collective) summarizing your suggestions, or you may break out of your small groups and report your best ideas to the entire class.

15.3 Exploring the New World of Web Conferencing (Objs. 2–5)

INFOTRAC	LISTENING
SPEAKING	WEB

Your boss at the Home Realty Company is interested in learning more about Web conferencing but doesn't have time to do the research herself. She asks you to find out the following:

a. In terms of revenue, how big is the Web conferencing industry?

b. Who are the leading providers of Web conferencing tools?
c. What are the typical costs associated with holding a Web conference?
d. How are other realtors using Web conferencing?

Your Task. Using InfoTrac and the Internet, locate articles and Web sites that will provide the information your boss has outlined. Be prepared to role-play an informal presentation to your boss in which you begin with an introduction, answer the four questions in the body, and present a conclusion.

15.4 Choosing a Topic for an Oral Presentation (Objs. 1–5)

Your Task. Select a topic from the list below or from the report topics on this book's Web site: "Student Resources," "Web Links by Chapter," "Chapter 12." Prepare a five- to ten-minute oral presentation. Consider yourself an expert who has been called in to explain some aspect of the topic before a group of interested people. Since your time is limited, prepare a concise yet forceful presentation with effective visual aids.

a. What are the top five career opportunities for your field of study? Consider job growth, compensation, and benefits. What kind of academic and other experience is typically required to apply for each?
b. What information and tools are available at Web job banks to students searching for full-time employment after graduation? Consider Monster.ca and other job banks.
c. How can attendance be improved in a minor sports field (your choice) at your school?
d. What simple computer security tips can your company employ to avoid problems?
e. What is telecommuting, and for what kinds of workers is it an appropriate work alternative?
f. What travel location would you recommend for college students at Christmas or another holiday or in the summer?
g. What is the economic outlook for a given product, such as domestic cars, laptop computers, digital cameras, fitness equipment, or a product of your choice?
h. How can your organization or institution improve its image?
i. What brand and model of computer and printer represent the best buy for college students today?
j. What franchise would offer the best investment opportunity for an entrepreneur in your area?
k. What should a guide to proper cell phone use include?
l. What risks are involved for companies without written rules for e-mail and instant messaging?
m. What is the outlook for real estate (commercial or residential) investment in your area?

C.L.U.E. REVIEW 15

On a separate sheet edit the following sentences to correct faults in grammar, punctuation, spelling, and word use.

1. The CEOs assistant asked my colleague and I to explain why our proposed method was better then the one previously used.
2. My friend and me were definitly inexperienced in making presentations, therefore him and I decided to learn more about public speaking.
3. We learned that the introduction to a presentation should accomplish 3 goals (a) capture attention, (b) establish credibility and (c) preview main points.
4. In the body of a short presentation which is usually 20 or less minutes we should focus on 2 to 4 principle points.
5. One of the most important ways to end a presentation are focusing on what you want the audience to do think or remember.
6. Speakers must remember that listeners unlike readers' can not controll the rate of presentation, or flip back thorough pages to review main points.
7. In working with electronic presentation softwear experts suggest chosing 1 transition effect, and using it consistantly.
8. The range of effects are staggering but presenters using electronic slides must control there urge to pile on to many dazzling features.
9. Every good speaker adapt to his audience and cross cultural presentations call for special adjustments and sensitivity.
10. One study found that 2/3 of telephone calls were less important then the work it interupted.

Chapter 16

Employment Communication

LEARNING OBJECTIVES

1 *Prepare for employment by identifying your interests, evaluating your assets, recognizing the changing nature of jobs, choosing a career path, and studying traditional and electronic job search techniques.*

2 *Compare and contrast chronological, functional, and combination résumés.*

3 *Organize, format, and produce a persuasive résumé.*

4 *Identify techniques that optimize a résumé for today's technologies, including preparing a scannable résumé, an inline résumé, and an e-portfolio.*

5 *Write a persuasive cover letter to accompany your résumé.*

6 *Write effective employment follow-up letters and other messages.*

7 *Evaluate successful job interview strategies.*

PREPARING FOR EMPLOYMENT

One day you may be sending your résumé to a recruiting specialist who reads thousands of such résumés annually. What can you do to make your résumé and cover letter stand out? This chapter provides many tips for writing dynamite résumés and cover letters, as well as suggestions for successful interviewing. But the job search process actually begins long before you are ready to write a résumé. Whether you are looking for an internship, applying for a full-time position, searching for a part-time job, competing for a promotion, or changing careers, you must invest time and effort preparing yourself. You can't hope to find the position of your dreams without first (1) knowing yourself, (2) knowing the job market, and (3) knowing the employment process. 1

Finding a satisfying career means learning about oneself, the job market, and the employment process.

One of the first things you should do is obtain career information and choose a specific job objective. At the same time, you should be studying the job market and becoming aware of substantial changes in the nature of work. You'll want to understand how to use the latest Internet resources in your job search. Finally, you'll need to design a persuasive résumé and letter of application appropriate for small businesses as well as for larger organizations that may be using résumé-scanning programs. Following these steps, summarized in Figure 16.1 and described in this chapter, gives you a master plan for landing a job you really want.

Identifying Your Interests

Answer specific questions to help yourself choose a career.

The employment process begins with introspection. This means looking inside yourself to analyze what you like and dislike so that you can make good employment choices. Career counsellors charge large sums for helping individuals learn about themselves. You can do the same kind of self-examination—without spending a

FIGURE 16.1 The Employment Search

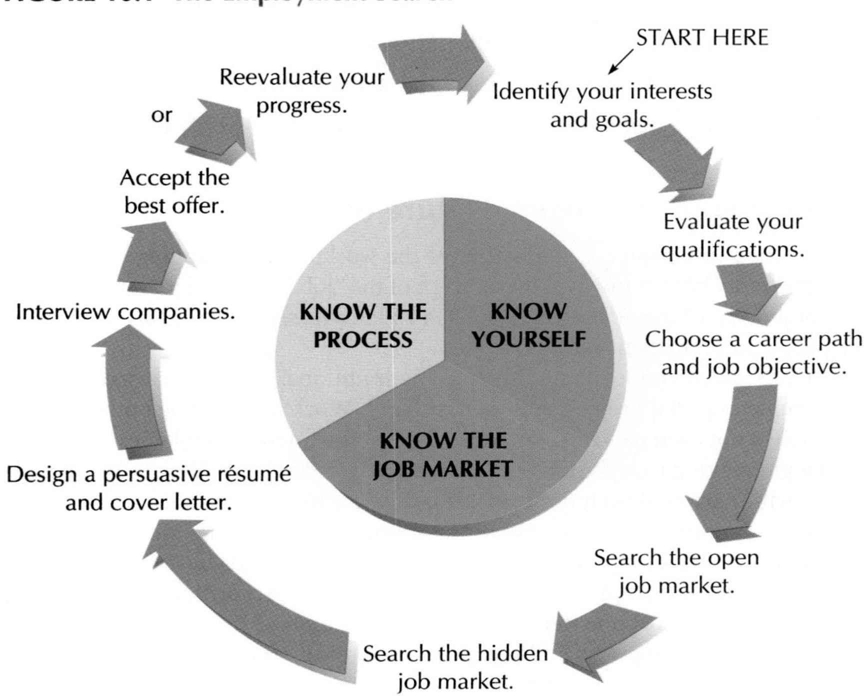

dime. For guidance in choosing a field that eventually proves to be satisfying, answer the following questions. If you have already chosen a field, think carefully about how your answers relate to that choice.

- *Do I enjoy working with people, data, or things?*
- *How important is it to be my own boss?*
- *How important are salary, benefits, technology support, and job stability?*
- *How important are working environment, colleagues, and job stimulation?*
- *Would I rather work for a large or small company?*
- *Must I work in a specific city, geographical area, or climate?*
- *Am I looking for security, travel opportunities, money, power, or prestige?*
- *How would I describe the perfect job, boss, and coworkers?*

Evaluating Your Qualifications

In addition to your interests, assess your qualifications. Employers today want to know what assets you have to offer them. Your responses to the following questions will target your thinking as well as prepare a foundation for your résumé. Remember, though, that employers seek more than empty assurances; they will want proof of your qualifications.

- *What computer skills can I offer?* Employers are often interested in specific software programs.
- *What other skills have I acquired in school, on the job, or through activities?* How can I demonstrate these skills?
- *Do I work well with people?* What proof can I offer? Consider extracurricular activities, clubs, and jobs.
- *Am I a leader, self-starter, or manager?* What evidence can I offer?
- *Do I speak, write, or understand another language?*
- *Do I learn quickly? Am I creative?* How can I demonstrate these characteristics?
- *Do I communicate well in speech and in writing?* How can I verify these talents?

Recognizing the Changing Nature of Jobs

People feel less job security after downsizing and movement to flatter organizations.

As you learned in Chapter 1, the nature of the workplace is changing. One of the most significant changes involves the concept of the "job." Following the downsizing of corporations and the offshoring of jobs in recent years, companies are employing fewer people in permanent positions.

Other forms of employment are replacing traditional jobs. In many companies teams complete special projects and then disband. Work may also be outsourced to a group that's not even part of an organization. Because new technologies can spring up overnight making today's skills obsolete, employers are less willing to hire people into jobs with narrow descriptions. Instead, they are hiring contingency employees who work temporarily and then leave. What's more, big companies are no longer the main employers. In fact, over 78 percent of businesses in Canada have fewer than five employees,[1] and self-employment is growing rapidly. According to a Statistics Canada manager, almost one in five workers is self-employed.[2]

"Jobs" are becoming more flexible and less permanent.

What do these changes mean for you? For one thing, you should probably forget about a lifelong career with a single company. Don't count on regular pay raises, promotions, and a comfortable retirement income. You should also become keenly aware that a career that relies on yesterday's skills is headed for trouble. You're going to need updated, marketable skills that serve you well as you move from job to job. Upgrading your skills and retraining yourself constantly is the best career strategy for the twenty-first century.

You should be prepared for constant retraining to update your skills. People who learn quickly and adapt to change are "high-value-added" individuals who will always be in demand even in a climate of surging change.[3]

Choosing a Career Path

The employment picture today is much different from that of a decade or two ago. By the time you are 30, you can expect to have had five to seven jobs. The average employee will have worked at 12 to 15 jobs over the course of a career, staying an average of 3.6 years at each job.[4] Some of you probably have not yet settled on your first career choice; others are returning to college to retrain for a new career. Although you may be changing jobs in the future, you still need to train for a specific career area now. In choosing an area, you'll make the best decisions when you can match your interests and qualifications with the requirements and rewards in specific careers. But where can you find career data? Here are some suggestions:

- Visit your campus career centre.
- Search the Web.
- Use your library.
- Take a summer job, internship, or part-time position in your field.
- Interview someone in your chosen field.
- Monitor the classified ads.
- Join professional organizations in your field.

Searching for a Job Using Traditional Techniques

A traditional job search campaign might include checking classified ads and announcements in professional publications, contacting companies, and developing a network of contacts.

Finding the perfect job requires an early start and a determined effort. Whether you use traditional or online job search techniques, you should be prepared to launch an aggressive campaign. And you can't start too early. Here are some traditional steps that job candidates take:

- Check classified ads in local and national newspapers.
- Check announcements in publications of professional organizations.
- Contact companies in which you're interested, even if you know of no current opening.
- Sign up for campus interviews with visiting company representatives.
- Ask for advice from your professors.
- Develop your own network of contacts.

Searching for a Job Electronically

An electronic job search campaign includes searching career and company Web sites for job listings.

Another significant change in the workplace involves the way we find jobs. Searching for a job electronically has become a common, but not always fruitful, approach. In fact, according to an Ipsos-Reid poll, nearly 8.5 million Canadians have used the Internet to hunt for jobs on Internet sites.[5] With all the publicity given to Internet job boards, you might think that electronic job searching has totally replaced traditional methods. However, although various Web sites list millions of jobs, actually landing a job is much harder than just clicking a mouse.

There are benefits for recruiters using this tool, such as "decreased paper work and advertising costs, access to a wider pool of qualified candidates, and quicker fill times. Studies show that online recruitment can cost 30% to 90% less than using a headhunter or classified advertising in a newspaper."[6] The five most common Canadian sites are as follows:[7]

Workopolis.ca
Monster.ca
Careerclick.com
Jobshark.ca
HotJobs.ca

Beyond the Big Job Boards. Disillusioned job-seekers increasingly turn their backs on job boards but not on electronic job-searching tactics. Skilled candidates know how to use their computers to search for jobs at Web sites such as corporate and association Web sites.

Thousands of job boards listing millions of jobs now flood the Internet. However, the harsh reality is that landing a job still depends largely on personal contacts.

THE PERSUASIVE RÉSUMÉ

2

After using both traditional and online resources to learn about the employment market and to develop job leads, you'll focus on writing a persuasive résumé. Such a résumé does more than merely list your qualifications. It packages your assets into a convincing advertisement that sells you for a specific job. The goal of a persuasive résumé is winning an interview. Even if you are not in the job market at this moment, preparing a résumé now has advantages. Having a current résumé makes you look well organized and professional should an unexpected employment opportunity arise. Moreover, preparing a résumé early helps you recognize weak qualifications and gives you two or three years in which to bolster them.

Choosing a Résumé Style

Your qualifications and career goal will help you choose from among three résumé styles: chronological, functional, and combination.

Chronological résumés focus on past employment; functional résumés focus on skills.

Chronological. Most popular with recruiters is the chronological résumé, shown in Figure 16.2. It lists work history job by job, starting with the most recent position. Many recruiters favour the chronological style because such résumés quickly reveal a candidate's education and experience record. The chronological style works well for candidates who have experience in their field of employment and for those who show steady career growth. But for many college and university students and others who lack extensive experience, the functional résumé format may be preferable.

Functional. The functional résumé, shown in Figure 16.3, focuses attention on a candidate's skills rather than on past employment. Like a chronological résumé, the functional résumé begins with the candidate's name, address, telephone number, job objective, and education. Instead of listing jobs, though, the functional résumé

FIGURE 16.2 Chronological Résumé

Prewriting 1

Analyze: The purpose is to respond to a job advertisement and win an interview.

Anticipate: The reader probably sees many résumés and will skim this one quickly. He or she will be indifferent and must be persuaded to read on.

Adapt: Emphasize the specific skills that the targeted advertisement mentions.

Writing 2

Research: Investigate the targeted company and its needs. Find the name of the person who will be receiving this résumé.

Organize: Make lists of all accomplishments and skills. Select those items most appropriate for the targeted job.

Compose: Experiment with formats to achieve readability, emphasis, and attractiveness.

Revising 3

Revise: Use present-tense verbs to describe current experience. Bullet experience items. Check for parallel phrasing. Adjust spacing for best effect.

Proofread: Run spell checker. Read for meaning. Have a friend proofread and critique.

Evaluate: Will this résumé impress a recruiter in 30 seconds?

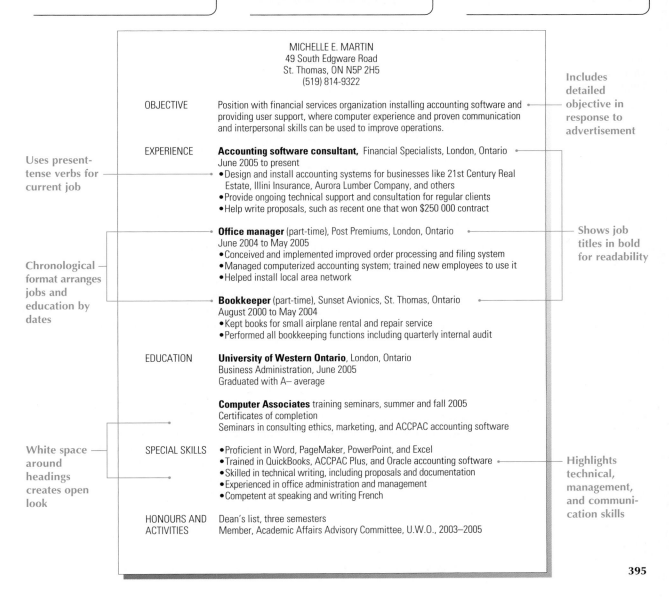

MICHELLE E. MARTIN
49 South Edgware Road
St. Thomas, ON N5P 2H5
(519) 814-9322

OBJECTIVE — Position with financial services organization installing accounting software and providing user support, where computer experience and proven communication and interpersonal skills can be used to improve operations.

EXPERIENCE

Accounting software consultant, Financial Specialists, London, Ontario
June 2005 to present
- Design and install accounting systems for businesses like 21st Century Real Estate, Illini Insurance, Aurora Lumber Company, and others
- Provide ongoing technical support and consultation for regular clients
- Help write proposals, such as recent one that won $250 000 contract

Office manager (part-time), Post Premiums, London, Ontario
June 2004 to May 2005
- Conceived and implemented improved order processing and filing system
- Managed computerized accounting system; trained new employees to use it
- Helped install local area network

Bookkeeper (part-time), Sunset Avionics, St. Thomas, Ontario
August 2000 to May 2004
- Kept books for small airplane rental and repair service
- Performed all bookkeeping functions including quarterly internal audit

EDUCATION

University of Western Ontario, London, Ontario
Business Administration, June 2005
Graduated with A– average

Computer Associates training seminars, summer and fall 2005
Certificates of completion
Seminars in consulting ethics, marketing, and ACCPAC accounting software

SPECIAL SKILLS
- Proficient in Word, PageMaker, PowerPoint, and Excel
- Trained in QuickBooks, ACCPAC Plus, and Oracle accounting software
- Skilled in technical writing, including proposals and documentation
- Experienced in office administration and management
- Competent at speaking and writing French

HONOURS AND ACTIVITIES
Dean's list, three semesters
Member, Academic Affairs Advisory Committee, U.W.O., 2003–2005

Includes detailed objective in response to advertisement

Uses present-tense verbs for current job

Shows job titles in bold for readability

Chronological format arranges jobs and education by dates

White space around headings creates open look

Highlights technical, management, and communication skills

Because functional résumés focus on skills, they may be more advisable for graduates with little experience.

groups skills and accomplishments in special categories, such as *Supervisory and Management Skills* or *Retailing and Marketing Experience.* This résumé style highlights accomplishments and can deemphasize a negative employment history. People who have changed jobs frequently or who have gaps in their employment records may prefer the functional résumé. Recent graduates with little employment experience often find the functional résumé useful. Be aware, though, that job boards may insist on chronological format. What's more, some recruiters are suspicious of functional résumés, thinking the candidate is hiding something.

Combination résumés present capabilities along with a complete job history.

Combination. The combination résumé style, shown in Figure 16.4, draws on the best features of the chronological and functional résumés. It emphasizes a candidate's capabilities while also including a complete job history. For recent graduates the combination résumé is a good choice because it enables them to profile what they can do for a prospective employer. If the writer has a specific job in mind, the items should be targeted to that job description.

Deciding on Its Length

Recruiters may *say* they prefer one-page résumés, but many *choose* to interview those with longer résumés.

Experts simply do not agree on how long a résumé should be. Conventional wisdom has always held that recruiters prefer one-page résumés. However, a recent carefully controlled study of 570 recruiters revealed that they *claimed* they preferred one-page résumés. However, the recruiters actually *chose* to interview the applicants with two-page résumés.[8] Apparently, recruiters who are serious about candidates often prefer a full picture with the kinds of details that can be provided in a two-page résumé.

The entire question may become moot as recruiters increasingly encourage online résumés, which are not restricted by page lengths. Perhaps the best advice is to make your résumé as long as needed to sell your skills. Individuals with more experience will naturally have longer résumés.

Arranging the Parts

3

The parts of résumés should be arranged with the most important qualifications first.

Although résumés have standard parts, their arrangement and content should be strategically planned. The most persuasive résumés emphasize skills and achievements aimed at a particular job or company. They show a candidate's most important qualifications first, and they deemphasize any weaknesses. In arranging the parts, try to create as few headings as possible; more than six generally looks cluttered. No two résumés are ever exactly alike, but most writers consider including all or some of these items: main heading, career objective, education, experience, capabilities and skills, awards and activities, personal information, and references.

Main Heading. Your résumé should always begin with your name, address, and telephone number. If possible, include a number where messages may be left for you. Prospective employers tend to call the next applicant when no one answers. Avoid showing both permanent and temporary addresses; some specialists say that dual addresses immediately identify about-to-graduate college students. Keep the main heading as uncluttered and simple as possible. And don't include the word *résumé*; it's like putting the word *letter* above correspondence.

FIGURE 16.3 Functional Résumé

Recent graduate Kevin Touhy chose this functional format to deemphasize his meagre work experience and emphasize his potential in sales and marketing. This version of his résumé is more generic than one targeted for a specific position. Yet, it emphasizes his strong points with specific achievements and includes an employment section to satisfy recruiters.

The functional format presents ability-focused topics. It illustrates what the job-seeker can do for the employer instead of narrating a history of previous jobs. Although recruiters prefer chronological résumés, the functional format is a good choice for new graduates, career changers, and those with employment gaps.

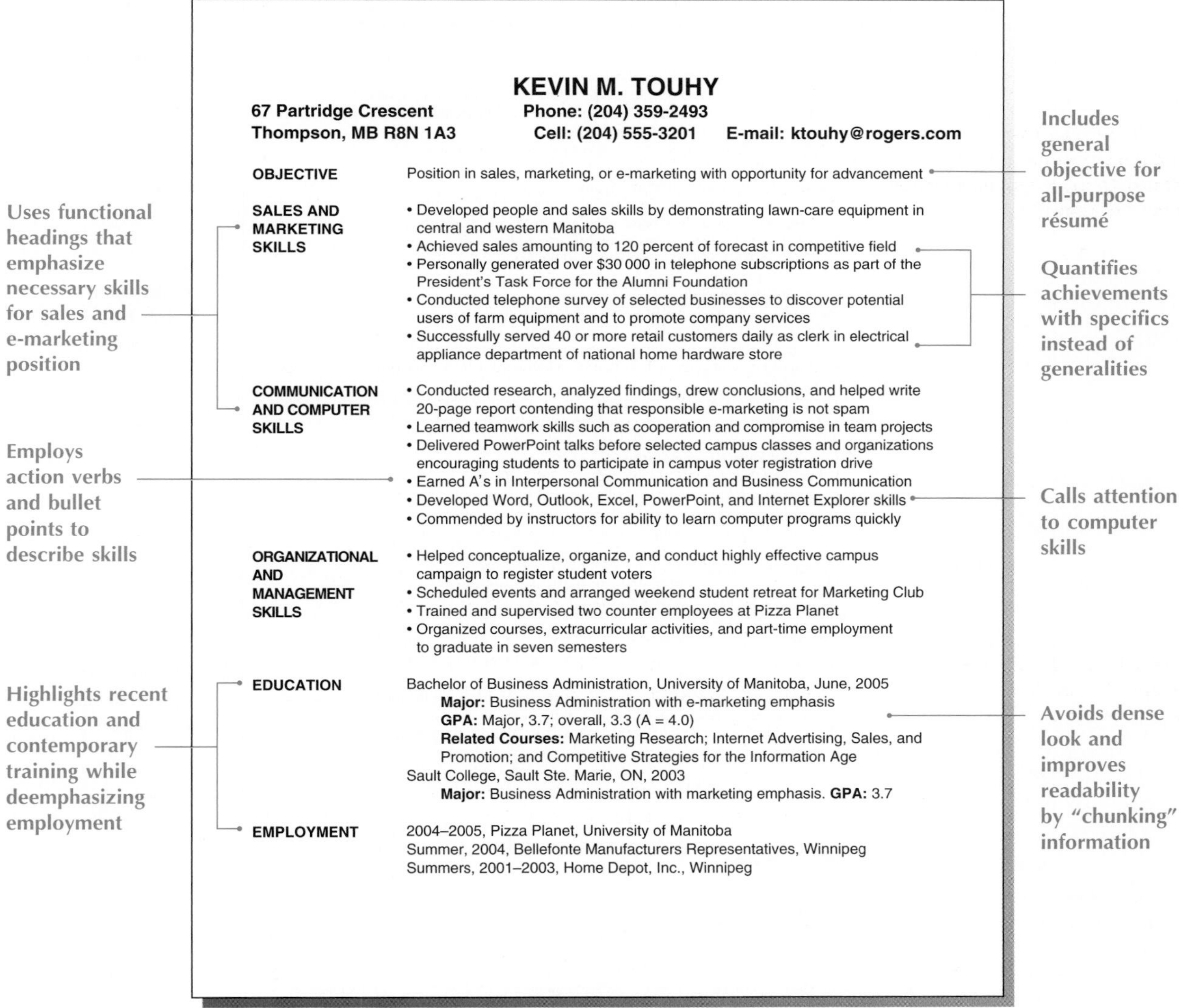

KEVIN M. TOUHY

67 Partridge Crescent **Phone: (204) 359-2493**
Thompson, MB R8N 1A3 **Cell: (204) 555-3201** **E-mail: ktouhy@rogers.com**

OBJECTIVE Position in sales, marketing, or e-marketing with opportunity for advancement

SALES AND MARKETING SKILLS

- Developed people and sales skills by demonstrating lawn-care equipment in central and western Manitoba
- Achieved sales amounting to 120 percent of forecast in competitive field
- Personally generated over $30 000 in telephone subscriptions as part of the President's Task Force for the Alumni Foundation
- Conducted telephone survey of selected businesses to discover potential users of farm equipment and to promote company services
- Successfully served 40 or more retail customers daily as clerk in electrical appliance department of national home hardware store

COMMUNICATION AND COMPUTER SKILLS

- Conducted research, analyzed findings, drew conclusions, and helped write 20-page report contending that responsible e-marketing is not spam
- Learned teamwork skills such as cooperation and compromise in team projects
- Delivered PowerPoint talks before selected campus classes and organizations encouraging students to participate in campus voter registration drive
- Earned A's in Interpersonal Communication and Business Communication
- Developed Word, Outlook, Excel, PowerPoint, and Internet Explorer skills
- Commended by instructors for ability to learn computer programs quickly

ORGANIZATIONAL AND MANAGEMENT SKILLS

- Helped conceptualize, organize, and conduct highly effective campus campaign to register student voters
- Scheduled events and arranged weekend student retreat for Marketing Club
- Trained and supervised two counter employees at Pizza Planet
- Organized courses, extracurricular activities, and part-time employment to graduate in seven semesters

EDUCATION Bachelor of Business Administration, University of Manitoba, June, 2005
Major: Business Administration with e-marketing emphasis
GPA: Major, 3.7; overall, 3.3 (A = 4.0)
Related Courses: Marketing Research; Internet Advertising, Sales, and Promotion; and Competitive Strategies for the Information Age
Sault College, Sault Ste. Marie, ON, 2003
Major: Business Administration with marketing emphasis. **GPA:** 3.7

EMPLOYMENT 2004–2005, Pizza Planet, University of Manitoba
Summer, 2004, Bellefonte Manufacturers Representatives, Winnipeg
Summers, 2001–2003, Home Depot, Inc., Winnipeg

Uses functional headings that emphasize necessary skills for sales and e-marketing position
Employs action verbs and bullet points to describe skills
Highlights recent education and contemporary training while deemphasizing employment
Includes general objective for all-purpose résumé
Quantifies achievements with specifics instead of generalities
Calls attention to computer skills
Avoids dense look and improves readability by "chunking" information

FIGURE 16.4 Combination Résumé

Because Casey wanted to highlight her skills and capabilities along with her experience, she combined the best features of functional and traditional résumés. She used the tables feature of her word processing program to help her format. Casey's résumé required part of a second page because she included references, a practice preferred by some employers who say it saves time.

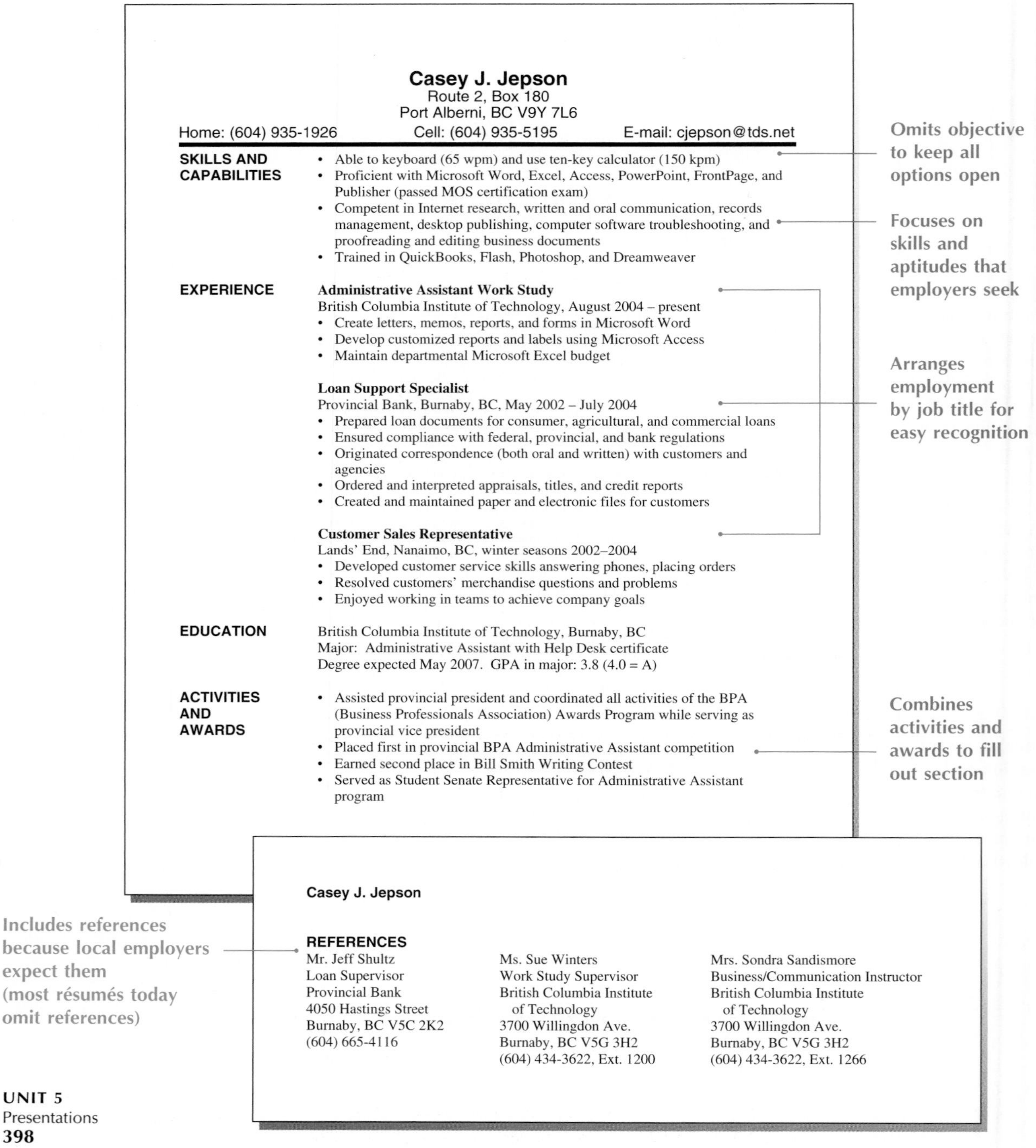

Casey J. Jepson
Route 2, Box 180
Port Alberni, BC V9Y 7L6
Home: (604) 935-1926 Cell: (604) 935-5195 E-mail: cjepson@tds.net

SKILLS AND CAPABILITIES

- Able to keyboard (65 wpm) and use ten-key calculator (150 kpm)
- Proficient with Microsoft Word, Excel, Access, PowerPoint, FrontPage, and Publisher (passed MOS certification exam)
- Competent in Internet research, written and oral communication, records management, desktop publishing, computer software troubleshooting, and proofreading and editing business documents
- Trained in QuickBooks, Flash, Photoshop, and Dreamweaver

EXPERIENCE

Administrative Assistant Work Study
British Columbia Institute of Technology, August 2004 – present
- Create letters, memos, reports, and forms in Microsoft Word
- Develop customized reports and labels using Microsoft Access
- Maintain departmental Microsoft Excel budget

Loan Support Specialist
Provincial Bank, Burnaby, BC, May 2002 – July 2004
- Prepared loan documents for consumer, agricultural, and commercial loans
- Ensured compliance with federal, provincial, and bank regulations
- Originated correspondence (both oral and written) with customers and agencies
- Ordered and interpreted appraisals, titles, and credit reports
- Created and maintained paper and electronic files for customers

Customer Sales Representative
Lands' End, Nanaimo, BC, winter seasons 2002–2004
- Developed customer service skills answering phones, placing orders
- Resolved customers' merchandise questions and problems
- Enjoyed working in teams to achieve company goals

EDUCATION

British Columbia Institute of Technology, Burnaby, BC
Major: Administrative Assistant with Help Desk certificate
Degree expected May 2007. GPA in major: 3.8 (4.0 = A)

ACTIVITIES AND AWARDS

- Assisted provincial president and coordinated all activities of the BPA (Business Professionals Association) Awards Program while serving as provincial vice president
- Placed first in provincial BPA Administrative Assistant competition
- Earned second place in Bill Smith Writing Contest
- Served as Student Senate Representative for Administrative Assistant program

Casey J. Jepson

REFERENCES

Mr. Jeff Shultz
Loan Supervisor
Provincial Bank
4050 Hastings Street
Burnaby, BC V5C 2K2
(604) 665-4116

Ms. Sue Winters
Work Study Supervisor
British Columbia Institute of Technology
3700 Willingdon Ave.
Burnaby, BC V5G 3H2
(604) 434-3622, Ext. 1200

Mrs. Sondra Sandismore
Business/Communication Instructor
British Columbia Institute of Technology
3700 Willingdon Ave.
Burnaby, BC V5G 3H2
(604) 434-3622, Ext. 1266

Omits objective to keep all options open
Focuses on skills and aptitudes that employers seek
Arranges employment by job title for easy recognition
Combines activities and awards to fill out section
Includes references because local employers expect them (most résumés today omit references)

Career Objective. Opinion is divided about the effect of including a career objective on a résumé. Recruiters think such statements indicate that a candidate has made a commitment to a career. Moreover, career objectives make the recruiter's life easier by quickly classifying the résumé.

Career objectives are most appropriate for specific, targeted openings, but they may limit a broader job search.

You have three choices regarding career objectives. The first is to omit the objective, which makes sense if it is an all-purpose résumé. A second possibility involves using a general statement, such as *Objective: Challenging position in urban planning* or *Job Goal: Position in sales/marketing.* The third, and probably the most effective plan, is to write a specific career objective when applying for a targeted position. Match the objective to the job description—for example, *Objective: To work in the health care industry as a human resources trainee with exposure to recruiting, training, and benefit administration.* With today's word processing capabilities, you can easily change the objective for each application. You should write a separate résumé for each job.

Some consultants warn against using the words *entry-level* in your objective, as these words emphasize lack of experience. Because companies generally prefer individuals with experience, it's smart to get all the experience you can while in school. It's also wise to prepare individual résumés that are targeted for each company or position sought.

Education. The next component is your education—if it is more noteworthy than your work experience. In this section you should include the name and location of schools, dates of attendance, major fields of study and diplomas or degrees received. Your grade-point average and/or class ranking are important to prospective employers. One way to enhance your GPA is to calculate it in your major courses only (for example, 3.6 in major, A = 4.0). By the way, it is not unethical to showcase your GPA in your major—as long as you clearly indicate what you are doing.

Some applicants want to list all their courses, but such a list makes for very dull reading. It's better to refer to courses only if you can relate them to the position sought. When relevant, include certificates earned, seminars attended, and workshops completed. Because employers are interested in your degree of self-sufficiency, you might wish to indicate the percentage of your education for which you paid. If your education is incomplete, include such statements as *B.S.C. degree expected 6/08* or *80 units completed in 120-unit program.* Entitle this section *Education, Academic Preparation,* or *Professional Training.*

Work Experience or Employment History. If your work experience is significant and relevant to the position sought, this information should appear before education. List your most recent employment first and work backward, including only those jobs that you think will help you win the targeted position. A job application form may demand a full employment history, but your résumé may be selective. (Be aware, though, that time gaps in your employment history will probably be questioned in the interview.) For each position show the following:

- Employer's name, city, and province
- Dates of employment
- Most important job title
- Significant duties, activities, accomplishments, and promotions

Describe your employment achievements concisely but concretely. Avoid generalities like *Worked with customers.* Be more specific, with statements such as *Served 40 or more retail customers a day, Successfully resolved problems about custom stationery orders,* or *Acted as intermediary among customers, printers, and suppliers.* If possible, quantify

The work experience section of a résumé should list specifics and quantify achievements.

your accomplishments, such as *Conducted study of equipment needs of 100 small businesses in Halifax, Personally generated orders for sales of $90 000 annually, Keyboarded all the production models for a 250-page employee procedures manual,* or *Assisted editor in layout, design, and news writing for 12 issues of division newsletter.* One professional recruiter said, "I spend a half hour every day screening 50 résumés or more, and if I don't spot some [quantifiable] results in the first 10 seconds, the résumé is history."[9]

In addition to technical skills, employers seek individuals with communication, management, and interpersonal capabilities. This means you'll want to select work experiences and achievements that illustrate your initiative, dependability, responsibility, resourcefulness, and leadership. Employers also want people who can work together in teams. Thus, include statements like *Collaborated with interdepartmental task force in developing ten-page handbook for temporary workers* and *Headed student government team that conducted most successful voter registration in campus history.*

Statements describing your work experience can be made forceful and persuasive by using action verbs, such as those listed in Figure 16.5 and demonstrated in Figure 16.6. You'll also want to include plenty of solid nouns, which we'll present shortly.

Emphasize the skills and aptitudes that recommend you for a specific position.

Capabilities and Skills. Recruiters want to know specifically what you can do for their companies. Therefore, list your special skills, such as *Proficient in preparing correspondence and reports using Word ME.* Include your ability to use computer programs, office equipment, foreign languages, or sign language. Describe proficiencies you have acquired through training and experience, such as *Trained in computer accounting, including general ledger, accounts receivable, accounts payable, and payroll.* Use expressions like *competent in, skilled in, proficient with, experienced in,* and *ability to;* for example, *Competent in keyboarding, editing, and/or proofreading reports, tables, letters, memos, manuscripts, and business forms.*

You'll also want to highlight exceptional aptitudes, such as working well under stress and learning computer programs quickly. If possible, provide details and evidence that back up your assertions; for example, *Mastered PhotoShop in 25 hours with little instruction.* Search for examples of your writing, speaking, management, organizational, and interpersonal skills—particularly those talents that are relevant to your targeted job.

For recent graduates, this section can be used to give recruiters evidence of your potential. Instead of *Capabilities,* the section might be called *Skills and Abilities.*

Awards, honours, and activities are appropriate for résumés; most personal data are not.

Awards, Honours, and Activities. If you have three or more awards or honours, highlight them by listing them under a separate heading. If not, put them with activities. Include awards, scholarships (financial and other), fellowships, honours, recognition, commendations, and certificates. Be sure to identify items clearly. Your reader may be unfamiliar with scholarships and awards; tell what they mean. Instead of saying *Recipient of Star award,* give more details: *Recipient of Star award given by Mount Allison University to outstanding graduates who combine academic excellence and extracurricular activities.*

It's also appropriate to include postsecondary, community, and professional activities. (High school activities and accomplishments are not generally included.) Employers are interested in evidence that you are a well-rounded person. This section provides an opportunity to demonstrate leadership and interpersonal skills. Strive to use action statements. For example, instead of saying *Treasurer of business club,* explain more fully: *Collected dues, kept financial records, and paid bills while serving as treasurer of 35-member business management club.*

FIGURE 16.5 Strengthen Your Résumé With Action Verbs

accelerated	constructed	encouraged	facilitated	organized	resolved	spearheaded
achieved	converted	engineered	improved	originated	restructured	spurred
analyzed	designed	established	increased	overhauled	reviewed	strengthened
collaborated	directed	expanded	introduced	pioneered	revitalized	targeted
conceptualized	enabled	expedited	managed	reduced	screened	transformed

FIGURE 16.6 Use Action Verbs in Statements That Quantify Results

Identified weaknesses in internships and **researched** five alternative programs

Reduced delivery delays by an average of three days per order

Streamlined filing system, thus reducing 400-item backlog to 0

Organized holiday awards program for 1200 attendees and 140 awardees

Created a 12-point checklist for use when requesting temporary workers

Designed five posters announcing new employee suggestion program

Calculated shipping charges for overseas deliveries and **recommended** most economical rates

Managed 24-station computer network linking data in three departments

Distributed and **explained** voter registration forms to over 500 prospective student voters

Praised by top management for enthusiastic teamwork and achievement

Secured national recognition from Communities in Bloom Foundation for tree project

Personal Data. Today's résumés omit personal data, such as birth date, marital status, height, weight, and religious affiliation. Such information doesn't relate to genuine occupational qualifications, and recruiters are legally barred from asking for such information. Some job-seekers do, however, include hobbies or interests (such as skiing or photography) that might grab the recruiter's attention or serve as conversation starters. Naturally, you wouldn't mention dangerous pastimes (such as bungee jumping or sports car racing) or time-consuming interests. But you should indicate your willingness to travel or to relocate, since many companies will be interested.

Omit personal data not related to job qualifications.

References. Listing references on a résumé is favoured by some recruiters and opposed by others.[10] Such a list takes up valuable space. Moreover, references are not normally instrumental in securing an interview—few companies check them before the interview. Instead, recruiters prefer that a candidate bring to the interview a list of individuals willing to discuss her or his qualifications. If you do list them, use parallel form as shown in Figure 16.4. Include land addresses, telephone numbers, and e-mail addresses.

References are unnecessary for the résumé, but they should be available for the interview.

Whether or not you include references on your résumé, you should have their names available when you begin your job search. Ask three to five instructors or previous employers whether they will be willing to answer inquiries regarding your qualifications for employment. Be sure, however, to provide them with an opportunity to refuse. No reference is better than a negative one. Do not include personal or character references, such as friends, family, or neighbours, because recruiters rarely consult them. Companies are more interested in the opinions of objective individuals.

One final note: personnel officers see little reason for including the statement *References furnished upon request.* "It's like saying the sun comes up every morning," remarked one human resources professional.[11]

OPTIMIZING YOUR RÉSUMÉ FOR TODAY'S TECHNOLOGIES

Because résumés are increasingly becoming part of searchable databases, you may need three versions.

Thus far we've aimed our résumé advice at human readers. However, the first reader of your résumé may well be a computer. Hiring organizations today use a variety of methods to process incoming résumés. Some organizations still welcome traditional print-based résumés that may include attractive formatting. Larger organizations, however, must deal with thousands of incoming résumés. Increasingly, they are placing those résumés directly into searchable databases. So that you can optimize your chances, you may need three versions of your résumé: (1) a traditional print-based résumé, (2) a scannable résumé, and (3) an inline résumé for e-mailing. You should also be aware of the significant role of résumé keywords.

Designing a Traditional Print-Based Résumé

A traditional print-based résumé is attractive, readable, and outlined with headings in an orderly, uncluttered format.

Traditional print-based résumés are attractively formatted to maximize readability. You can create a professional-looking résumé by using your word processing program to highlight your qualifications. You can examine template résumés for styling ideas. Their inflexibility, however, leads to frustration as you try to force your skills and experience into a predetermined template sequence. What's more, recruiters who read hundreds of résumés can usually spot a template-based résumé. Instead, create your own original résumé that fits your unique qualifications. Your print-based résumé should use an outline format with headings and bulleted points to present information in an orderly, uncluttered format. An attractive print-based résumé is necessary (1) when you compete for a job that does not require electronic submission, (2) to present in addition to an electronic submission, and (3) to distribute when you are interviewed. Even if a résumé is submitted electronically, nearly every job candidate will want to have an attractive traditional résumé handy for human readers.

Preparing a Scannable Résumé

Applicant-tracking software scans incoming résumés searching for keywords.

To screen incoming résumés, many mid- and large-sized companies use automated applicant-tracking software. These systems scan an incoming résumé with optical character recognition (OCR) looking for keywords. The most sophisticated programs enable recruiters and hiring managers to search for keywords, rank résumés based on the number of "hits," and generate reports. Information from your résumé is stored, usually from six months to a year.

Before sending your résumé, find out whether the recipient uses scanning software. If you can't tell from the job announcement, call the company to ask whether it scans résumés electronically. If you don't get a clear answer and you have even the slightest suspicion that your résumé might be read electronically, you'll be smart to prepare a plain, scannable version.

Tips for Maximizing Scannability. A scannable résumé must sacrifice many of the graphic enhancements you might have used to dress up your traditional print résumé. To maximize scannability:

Scannable résumés use plain formatting, large font, quality printing, and white space.

- **Avoid unusual typefaces, underlining, and italics.** Moreover, don't use boxing, shading, or other graphics to highlight text. These features don't scan well. Most applicant-tracking programs, however, can accurately read bold print, solid bullets, and asterisks.
- **Use 10- to 14-point type.** Because touching letters or unusual fonts are likely to be misread, it's safest to use a large, well-known font, such as 12-point Times Roman or Helvetica. This may mean that your résumé will require two pages. After printing, inspect your résumé to see whether any letters touch—especially in your name.
- **Use smooth white paper, black ink, and quality printing.** Avoid coloured or textured paper, and use a good printer.
- **Be sure that your name is the first line on the page.** Don't use fancy layouts that may confuse a scanner.
- **List each phone number on its own line.** Your land and cell phone numbers should appear on separate lines to improve recognition.
- **Provide white space.** To ensure separation of words and categories, leave plenty of white space. For example, instead of using parentheses to enclose a telephone area code, insert blank spaces, such as 416 799-2415. Leave blank lines around headings.
- **Avoid double columns.** When listing job duties, skills, computer programs, and so forth, don't tabulate items into two- or three-column lists. Scanners read across and may convert tables into gobbledygook.
- **Don't fold or staple your résumé.** Send it in a large envelope so that you can avoid folds. Words that appear on folds may not be scanned correctly.

Tips for Maximizing "Hits." In addition to paying attention to the physical appearance of your résumé, you must also be concerned with keywords that produce "hits" or recognition by the scanner. To maximize hits:

Scanners produce "hits" when they recognize targeted keywords such as nouns describing skills, traits, tasks, and job titles.

- **Focus on specific keywords.** Study carefully any advertisements and job descriptions for the position you want. Select keywords that describe skills, traits, tasks, and job titles.
- **Incorporate words from the advertisement or job description.** Describe your experience, education, and qualifications in terms associated with the job advertisement or job description for this position.
- **Use typical headings.** Include expected categories such as Objective, Experience, Employment, Work History, Skills, Summary of Qualifications, and Accomplishments. Scanning software looks for such headings.
- **Use accurate names.** Spell out complete names of schools, degrees, and dates.
- **Be careful of abbreviations.** Minimize unfamiliar abbreviations, but maximize easily recognized abbreviations—especially those within your field, such as CAD, COBRA, or JIT. When in doubt, though, spell out! Computers are less addled by whole words.

FIGURE 16.7 Interpersonal Keywords Most Requested by Employers Using Résumé-Scanning Software*

Ability to delegate	Creative	Leadership	Self-accountable
Ability to implement	Customer oriented	Multitasking	Self-managing
Ability to plan	Detail minded	Open communication	Setting priorities
Ability to train	Ethical	Open minded	Supportive
Accurate	Flexible	Oral communication	Takes initiative
Adaptable	Follow instructions	Organizational skills	Team building
Aggressive worker	Follow through	Persuasive	Team player
Analytical ability	Follow up	Problem solving	Tenacious
Assertive	High energy	Public speaking	Willing to travel
Communication skills	Industrious	Results oriented	
Competitive	Innovative	Safety conscious	

*Reported by Resumix, a leading producer of résumé-scanning software.

Source: Joyce Lain Kennedy and Thomas J. Morrow, *Electronic Résumé Revolution* (New York: John Wiley & Sons), 70. Reprinted by permission of John Wiley & Sons, Inc.

- **Describe interpersonal traits and attitudes.** Hiring managers look for keywords and phrases such as *time management skills, dependability, high energy, leadership, sense of responsibility,* and *team player.*
- **Use more than one page if necessary.** Computers can easily handle more than one page so include as much as necessary to describe your qualifications and maximize hits.
- **Consider adding a keyword summary.** Some authorities recommend adding a special paragraph loaded with keywords. Others think it is unnecessary and clutters a résumé.

If you decide to include a keyword summary, go through your traditional résumé and mark all relevant nouns. Also try to imagine what eight to ten words an employer might use to describe the job you want. Then select the 25 best words for your summary. Because interpersonal traits are often requested by employers, consult Figure 16.7. It shows the most frequently requested interpersonal traits, as reported by Resumix, one of the leaders in résumé-scanning software. You may entitle your list *Keyword Summary*, *Keyword Profile*, or *Keyword Index*. Here's an example of a possible keyword summary for a junior accountant:

A computer-friendly résumé may contain a keyword summary filled with words (usually nouns) that describe the job or candidate.

KEYWORD SUMMARY

Accountant: Public. Junior. Staff. AA, Durham College—Business Administration. BA, York University—Accounting. Payables. Receivables. Payroll Experience. Quarterly Reports. Unemployment Reports. Communication Skills. Computer Skills. Excel. Word. PCs. Mainframes. Internet. Web. Networks. J. D. Edwards Software. Ability to learn software. Accurate. Dean's List. Award of Merit. Team player. Willing to travel. Relocate.

Preparing an Inline Résumé for E-Mailing

An *inline* résumé is one that is stripped of formatting and embedded within an e-mail message. An inline résumé may also be called an *ASCII* résumé, a *plain text* résumé, or an *electronic* résumé. Regardless of its name, this format is increasingly requested because employers worry about viruses and word processing incompatibilities in attachments. Employers don't want to open attachments. They prefer inline résumés that are immediately searchable and avoid the scanning step.[12] Many job boards also require inline résumés. Thus, you should be prepared with an inline résumé that can be imported directly into an e-mail message. To create an inline résumé:

Employers prefer inline résumés because these plain-text documents are immediately searchable and avoid viruses and software incompatibilities.

- **Follow all the tips for a scannable résumé.** An inline résumé requires the same attention to content, formatting, and keywords as that recommended for a scannable résumé.
- **Consider reformatting with shorter lines.** Many e-mail programs wrap lines longer than 60 characters. To avoid having your résumé look as if a chain saw attacked it, use a short line length (such as 10 cm).
- **Think about using keyboard characters to enhance format.** In addition to using capital letters and asterisks, you might use spaced equals signs (= = =) and tildes (~ ~ ~) to create separating lines that highlight résumé categories.
- **Move all text to the left.** Do not centre items; start all text at the left margin. Remove tabs.
- **Save your résumé in plain text (.txt) or rich text format (.rtf).** After saving it as a text file, send your résumé to yourself and check to see whether any non-ASCII characters appear. They may show up as question marks, square blocks, or other odd characters.

Creating an E-Portfolio

As the workplace becomes increasingly digitized, you have yet another way to display your qualifications to prospective employers—the digitized e-portfolio. Resourceful job candidates in other fields—particularly writers, models, artists, and graphic artists—created print portfolios to illustrate their qualifications and achievements. Now business and professional job candidates are using electronic portfolios to show off their talents.

An e-portfolio offers links to examples of a job candidate's performance, talents, and accomplishments in digitized form.

An *e-portfolio* is a collection of digitized materials that provides viewers with a snapshot of a candidate's performance, talents, and accomplishments. It may include a copy of your résumé, reference letters, special achievements, awards, certificates, work samples, a complete list of your courses, thank-you letters, and anything else that touts your accomplishments. An advanced portfolio might include links to electronic copies of your artwork, film projects, blueprints, and photographs of classwork that might otherwise be difficult to share with potential employers. Moreover, you can include impressive effects such as colour, animation, sound, and graphics.

E-portfolios are generally presented at Web sites, where they are available 24/7 to employers. Some colleges and universities not only make Web site space available for student e-portfolios but also provide instruction and resources for scanning photos, digitizing images, and preparing graphics. E-portfolios may also be burned onto CDs that you mail to prospective employers.

Job candidates generally offer e-portfolios at Web sites, but they may also burn them onto a CD.

E-portfolios have many advantages. At Web sites they can be viewed whenever convenient for an employer. Let's say you are talking on the phone with an employer in another city who wants to see a copy of your résumé. You can simply refer the employer to the Web address where your résumé resides. E-portfolios can also be seen by many individuals in an organization without circulating a paper copy. But the real reason for preparing an e-portfolio is that it shows off your talents and qualifications more thoroughly than a print résumé.

Applying the Final Touches to Your Résumé

Because your résumé is probably the most important message you will ever write, you'll revise it many times. With so much information in concentrated form and with so much riding on its outcome, your résumé demands careful polishing, proofreading, and critiquing.

In addition to being well written, a résumé must be carefully formatted and meticulously proofread.

As you revise, be certain to verify all the facts, particularly those involving your previous employment and education. Don't be caught in a mistake, or worse, distortion of previous jobs and dates of employment. These items likely will be checked. And the consequences of puffing up a résumé with deception or flat-out lies are simply not worth the risk. Other ethical traps you'll want to avoid are described in the accompanying Ethical Insights box.

Polishing. As you continue revising, look for other ways to improve your résumé. For example, consider consolidating headings. By condensing your information into as few headings as possible, you'll produce a clean, professional-looking document. Study other résumés for valuable formatting ideas. Ask yourself what graphics highlighting techniques you can use to improve readability: capitalization, underlining, indenting, and bulleting. Experiment with headings and styles to achieve a pleasing, easy-to-read message. Moreover, look for ways to eliminate wordiness. For example, instead of *Supervised two employees who worked at the counter*, try *Supervised two counter employees.* Review Chapter 7 for more tips.

Above all, make your résumé look professional. Avoid anything humorous or "cute," such as a help-wanted poster with your name or picture inside. Eliminate the personal pronoun *I.* The abbreviated, objective style of a résumé precludes the use of personal pronouns. Use good-quality white, off-white, or buff-coloured heavy bond paper (24-pound) and a first-rate printer. Be prepared with a résumé for people to read as well as one for a computer to read.

Because résumés must be perfect, they should be proofread many times.

Proofreading. After revising, proofread, proofread, and proofread again: for spelling and mechanics, for content, and for format. Then, have a knowledgeable friend or relative proofread it again. This is one document that must be perfect.

By now you may be thinking that you'd like to hire someone to write your résumé. Don't. First, you know yourself better than anyone else could know you. Second, you'll end up with either a generic or a one-time résumé. A generic résumé in today's highly competitive job market will lose out to a targeted résumé nine times out of ten. Equally useless is a one-time résumé aimed at a single job. What if you don't get that job? Because you will need to revise your résumé many times as you seek a variety of jobs, be prepared to write (and rewrite) it yourself.

A final word about résumé-writing services. Some tend to produce eye-catching, elaborate documents with lofty language, fancy borders, and fuzzy thinking. Here's an example of empty writing: "Seeking a position which will utilize academic achievements and hands-on experience while providing for career-development opportunities."[13] Save your money and buy a good interview suit instead.

CHECKLIST FOR WRITING A PERSUASIVE RÉSUMÉ

Preparation

Research the job market. Learn about available jobs, common qualifications, and potential employers. The best résumés are targeted for specific jobs with specific companies.

ETHICAL INSIGHTS

Are Inflated Résumés Worth the Risk?

A résumé is expected to showcase a candidate's strengths and minimize weaknesses. For this reason, recruiters expect a certain degree of self-promotion. But some résumé writers step over the line that separates honest self-marketing from deceptive half-truths and flat-out lies. Distorting facts on a résumé is unethical; lying is illegal. And either practice can destroy a career.

Given the competitive job market, it might be tempting to puff up your résumé. And you wouldn't be alone in telling fibs or outright whoppers. One study found that one in seven job applicants makes false claims about education.[14] Although recruiters can't check everything, most will verify previous employment and education before hiring candidates. Over half will require official transcripts.

After hiring, the checking process may continue. At one of the nation's top accounting firms, the human resources director described the posthiring routine: "If we find a discrepancy in GPA or prior experience due to an honest mistake, we meet with the new hire to hear an explanation. But if it wasn't a mistake, we terminate the person immediately. Unfortunately, we've had to do that too often."[15]

No job-seeker wants to be in the unhappy position of explaining résumé errors or defending misrepresentation. Avoiding the following common problems can keep you off the hot seat:

- **Inflated education, grades, or honours.** Some job candidates claim diplomas or degrees from colleges or universities when in fact they merely attended classes. Others increase their grade-point averages or claim fictitious honours. Any such dishonest reporting is grounds for dismissal when discovered.
- **Enhanced job titles.** Wishing to elevate their status, some applicants misrepresent their titles. For example, one technician called himself a "programmer" when he had actually programmed only one project for his boss. A mail clerk who assumed added responsibilities conferred upon herself the title of "supervisor." Even when the description seems accurate, it's unethical to list any title not officially granted.
- **Puffed-up accomplishments.** Some job-seekers inflate their employment experience or achievements. One clerk, eager to make her photocopying duties sound more important, said that she assisted the *vice president in communicating and distributing employee directives.* One graduate who spent the better part of six months watching rented videos on his VCR described the activity as *Independent Film Study*. The latter statement may have helped win an interview, but it lost him the job.[16] In addition to avoiding puffery, guard against taking sole credit for achievements that required many people. When recruiters suspect dubious claims on résumés, they nail applicants with specific—and often embarrassing—questions during their interviews.[17]
- **Altered employment dates.** Some candidates extend the dates of employment to hide unimpressive jobs or to cover up periods of unemployment and illness. Let's say that several years ago Cindy was unemployed for 14 months between working for Company A and being hired by Company B. To make her employment history look better, she adds seven months to her tenure with Company A and seven months to Company B. Now her employment history has no gaps, but her résumé is dishonest and represents a potential landmine for her.

The employment process can easily lure you into ethical traps, such as those described in Chapter 1. Beware of these specific temptations:

- **The relative-filth trap:** "A little fudging on my GPA is nothing compared with the degrees that some people buy in degree mills."
- **The rationalization trap:** "I deserve to call myself 'manager' because that's what I really did."
- **The self-deception trap:** "Giving myself a certificate from the institute is OK because I really intended to finish the program, but I got sick."

Falling into these ethical traps risks your entire employment future. If your honest qualifications aren't good enough to get you the job you want, start working now to improve them.

- ✓ **Analyze your strengths.** Determine what aspects of your education, experience, and personal characteristics will be assets to prospective employers.
- ✓ **Study models.** Look at other résumés for formatting and element placement ideas. Experiment with headings and styles to achieve an artistic, readable product.

Heading and Objective

- ✓ **Identify yourself.** List your name, address, and telephone number. Skip the word *résumé.*
- ✓ **Include a career objective for a targeted job.** If this résumé is intended for a specific job, include a statement tailored to it (*Objective: Cost accounting position in the petroleum industry*).

Education

- ✓ **Name your diploma or degree, date of graduation, and institution.** Emphasize your education if your experience is limited.
- ✓ **List your major and GPA.** Give information about your studies, but don't inventory all your courses.

Work Experience

- ✓ **Itemize your jobs.** Start with your most recent job. Give the employer's name and city, dates of employment (month, year), and most significant job title.
- ✓ **Describe your experience.** Use action verbs to summarize achievements and skills relevant to your targeted job.
- ✓ **Promote your "soft" skills.** Give evidence of communication, management, and interpersonal talents. Employers want more than empty assurances; try to quantify your skills and accomplishments (*Collaborated with six-member task force in producing 20-page mission statement*).

Special Skills, Achievements, and Awards

- ✓ **Highlight computer skills.** Remember that nearly all employers seek employees who are proficient in using the Internet, e-mail, word processing, databases, and spreadsheets.
- ✓ **Show that you are a well-rounded individual.** List awards, experiences, and extracurricular activities—particularly if they demonstrate leadership, teamwork, reliability, loyalty, industry, initiative, efficiency, and self-sufficiency.

Final Tips

- ✓ **Consider omitting references.** Have a list of references available for the interview, but don't include them or refer to them unless you have a specific reason to do so.

- **Look for ways to condense your data.** Omit all street addresses except your own. Consolidate your headings. Study models and experiment with formats to find the most readable and efficient groupings.

- **Double-check for parallel phrasing.** Be sure that all entries have balanced construction, such as similar verb forms (*Organized files, trained assistants, scheduled events*).

- **Make your résumé scannable.** If there's a chance it will be read by a computer, use a common font, remove graphics, and consider adding a keyword summary.

- **Project professionalism and quality.** Avoid personal pronouns and humour. Use 24-pound bond paper and a high-quality printer.

- **Proofread, proofread, proofread.** Make this document perfect by proofreading at least three times.

THE PERSUASIVE COVER LETTER

5

Cover letters introduce résumés, relate writer strengths to reader benefits, and seek an interview.

Job candidates often slave over their résumés but treat the cover letter as an afterthought. This critical mistake could sink a job search. Even if an advertisement doesn't request one, be sure to distinguish your application with a persuasive cover letter (also called a *letter of application*). It has three purposes: (1) introducing the résumé, (2) highlighting your strengths in terms of benefits to the reader, and (3) gaining an interview.

Recruiting professionals disagree on how long to make a cover letter. Many prefer short letters with no more than three paragraphs. Others desire longer letters that supply more information, thus giving them a better opportunity to evaluate a candidate's qualifications. These recruiters argue that hiring and training new employees is expensive and time-consuming; therefore, they welcome extra data to guide them in making the best choice the first time. Follow your judgment in writing a brief or a longer cover letter. If you feel, for example, that you need space to explain in more detail what you can do for a prospective employer, do so.

Regardless of its length, a cover letter should have three primary parts: (1) an opening that gains attention, (2) a body that builds interest and reduces resistance, and (3) a closing that motivates action.

Gaining Attention in the Opening

The opener in a cover letter gains attention by addressing the receiver by name.

The first step in gaining the interest of your reader is addressing that individual by name. Rather than sending your letter to the "Personnel Manager" or "Human Resources Department," try to identify the name of the appropriate individual. Make it a rule to call the organization for the correct spelling and the complete address. This personal touch distinguishes your letter and demonstrates your serious interest.

How you open your cover letter depends largely on whether the application is solicited or unsolicited. If an employment position has been announced and applicants are being solicited, you can use a direct approach. If you do not know whether a position is open and you are prospecting for a job, use an indirect approach. Whether direct or indirect, the opening should attract the attention of the reader. Strive for openings that are more imaginative than *Please consider this letter an application for the position of. . .* or *I would like to apply for . . . .*

Openings for Solicited Jobs.

Here are some of the best techniques to open a cover letter for a job that has been announced:

Openers for solicited jobs refer to the source of the information, the job title, and qualifications for the position.

- **Refer to the name of an employee in the company.** Remember that employers always hope to hire known quantities rather than complete strangers:

  Mitchell Sims, a member of your Customer Service Department, told me that IntriPlex is seeking an experienced customer service representative. The attached summary of my qualifications demonstrates my preparation for this position.

- **Refer to the source of your information precisely.** If you are answering an advertisement, include the exact position advertised and the name and date of the publication. For large organizations it's also wise to mention the section of the newspaper where the ad appeared:

  The September 10 issue of *The Globe and Mail* reports that you are seeking a mature, organized, and reliable administrative assistant with excellent communication skills.

  Susan Butler, placement director at Durham College, told me that DataTech has an opening for a technical writer with knowledge of Web design and graphics.

- **Refer to the job title and describe how your qualifications fit the requirements.** Personnel directors are looking for a match between an applicant's credentials and the job needs:

  Will an honours graduate with a degree in recreation and two years of part-time experience organizing social activities for a convalescent hospital qualify for your position of activity director?

Openings for Unsolicited Jobs.

Openers for unsolicited jobs show interest in and knowledge of the company, as well as spotlighting reader benefits.

If you are unsure whether a position actually exists, you may wish to use a more persuasive opening. Since your goal is to convince this person to read on, try one of the following techniques:

- **Demonstrate interest in and knowledge of the reader's business.** Show the personnel director that you have done your research and that this organization is more than a mere name to you:

  Since Signa HealthNet, Inc., is organizing a new information management team for its recently established group insurance division, could you use the services of a well-trained information systems graduate who seeks to become a professional systems analyst?

- **Show how your special talents and background will benefit the company.** Personnel directors need to be convinced that you can do something for them:

  Could your rapidly expanding publications division use the services of an editorial assistant who offers exceptional language skills, an honours degree from the University of Prince Edward Island, and two years' experience in producing a campus literary publication?

In applying for an advertised job, Nancy Sullivan James wrote the solicited cover letter shown in Figure 16.8. Notice that her opening identifies the position and the newspaper completely so that the reader knows exactly what advertisement Nancy means.

FIGURE 16.8 Solicited Cover Letter

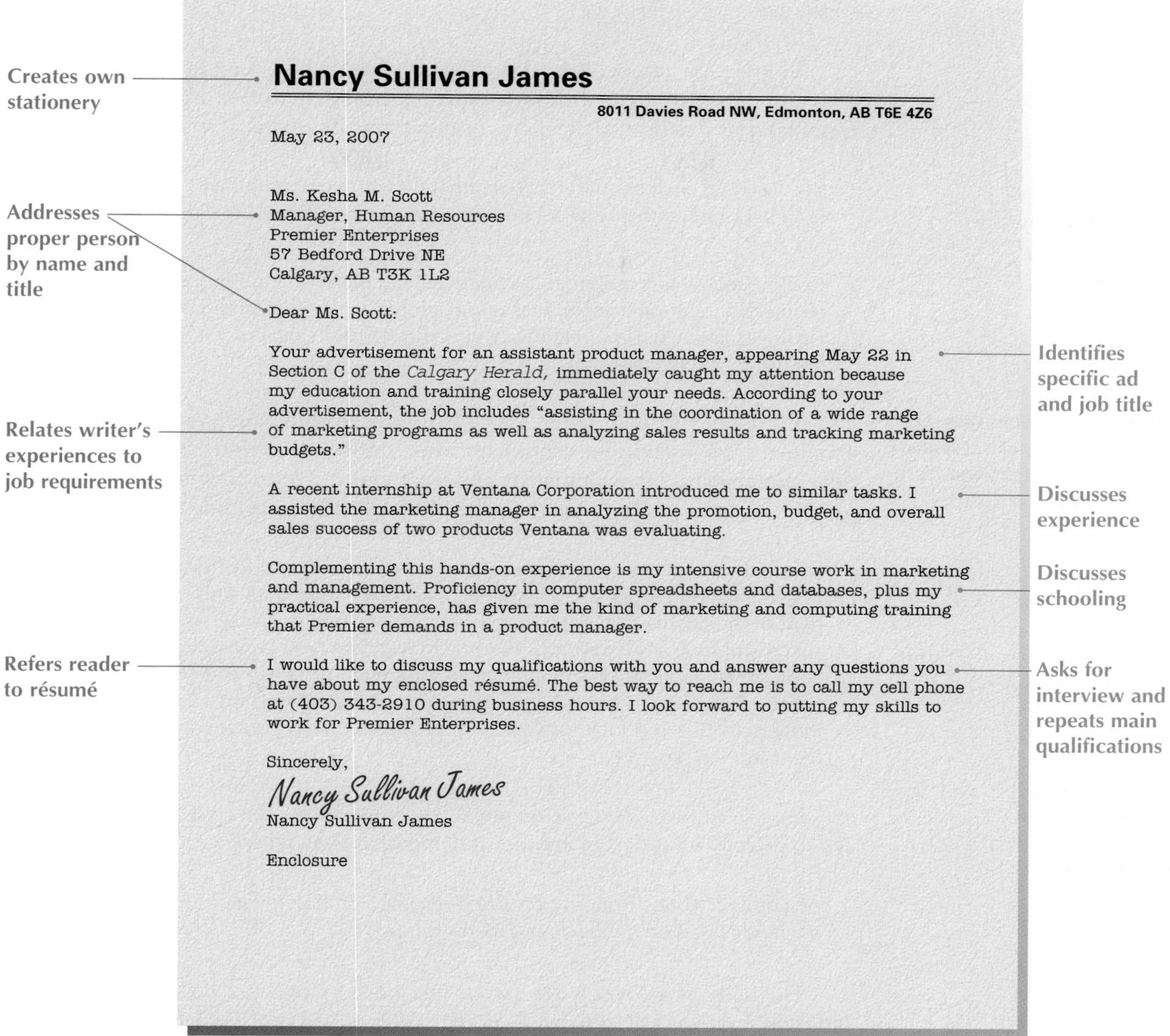

Creates own stationery
Addresses proper person by name and title
Relates writer's experiences to job requirements
Refers reader to résumé
Identifies specific ad and job title
Discusses experience
Discusses schooling
Asks for interview and repeats main qualifications

Nancy Sullivan James

8011 Davies Road NW, Edmonton, AB T6E 4Z6

May 23, 2007

Ms. Kesha M. Scott
Manager, Human Resources
Premier Enterprises
57 Bedford Drive NE
Calgary, AB T3K 1L2

Dear Ms. Scott:

Your advertisement for an assistant product manager, appearing May 22 in Section C of the *Calgary Herald,* immediately caught my attention because my education and training closely parallel your needs. According to your advertisement, the job includes "assisting in the coordination of a wide range of marketing programs as well as analyzing sales results and tracking marketing budgets."

A recent internship at Ventana Corporation introduced me to similar tasks. I assisted the marketing manager in analyzing the promotion, budget, and overall sales success of two products Ventana was evaluating.

Complementing this hands-on experience is my intensive course work in marketing and management. Proficiency in computer spreadsheets and databases, plus my practical experience, has given me the kind of marketing and computing training that Premier demands in a product manager.

I would like to discuss my qualifications with you and answer any questions you have about my enclosed résumé. The best way to reach me is to call my cell phone at (403) 343-2910 during business hours. I look forward to putting my skills to work for Premier Enterprises.

Sincerely,

Nancy Sullivan James

Nancy Sullivan James

Enclosure

Building Interest in the Body

The body of a cover letter should build interest, reduce resistance, and discuss relevant personal traits.

Once you have identified your purpose in the letter opening, you should use the body of the letter to promote your qualifications for this position.

If you are responding to an advertisement, you'll want to explain how your preparation and experience fill the stated requirements. If you are prospecting for a job, you may not know the exact requirements. Your employment research and knowledge of your field, however, should give you a reasonably good idea of what is expected for this position.

It's also important to emphasize reader benefits. In other words, you should describe your strong points in relation to the needs of the employer. Instead of *I have completed courses in business communication, report writing, and technical writing,* try this:

Courses in business communication, report writing, and technical writing have helped me develop the research and writing skills required of your technical writers.

Choose your strongest qualifications and show how they fit the targeted job. And remember, students with little experience are better off spotlighting their education and its practical applications, as these candidates did:

Because you seek an architect's apprentice with proven ability, I submit a drawing of mine that won second place in the Sinclair College drafting contest last year.

Composing e-mail messages, business letters, memos, and reports in my communication and microcomputer application courses helped me develop the writing, language, proofreading, and computer skills mentioned in your ad for an administrative assistant.

Employers seek employees who are team players, take responsibility, show initiative, and learn easily.

In the body of your letter, you'll also want to discuss relevant personal traits. Employers are looking for candidates who, among other things, are team players, take responsibility, show initiative, and learn easily. Notice how the following paragraph uses action verbs to paint a picture of a promising candidate:

In addition to developing technical and academic skills at Dalhousie University, I have gained interpersonal, leadership, and organizational skills. As vice president of the business students' organization, I helped organize and supervise two successful fundraising events. These activities involved conceptualizing the tasks, motivating others to help, scheduling work sessions, and coordinating the efforts of 35 diverse students in reaching our goal. I enjoyed my success with these activities and look forward to applying such experience in your management trainee program.

Finally, in this section or the next, you should refer the reader to your résumé. Do so directly or as part of another statement, as shown here:

As you will notice from my enclosed résumé, I will graduate in June with a bachelor's degree in business administration.

The body of a cover letter can be expanded or contracted depending on how long you want your letter to be. As noted earlier, experts are divided on length. If you prefer a shorter cover letter, reduce the size of the body.

Motivating Action in the Closing

The closing of a cover letter should motivate action and include a request for an interview.

After presenting your case, you should conclude by asking for an interview. However, never ask for the job. To do so would be presumptuous and naive. In requesting an interview, suggest reader benefits or review your strongest points. Sound sincere and appreciative. Remember to make it easy for the reader to agree by supplying your telephone number and the best times to call you. And keep in mind that some personnel directors prefer that you take the initiative to call them. Here are possible endings:

I hope this brief description of my qualifications and the additional information in my résumé indicate to you my genuine desire to put my skills in accounting to work for you. Please call me at (604) 655-4455 before 10 a.m. or after 3 p.m. to arrange an interview.

Next week, after you have examined the attached résumé, I will call you to discuss the possibility of arranging an interview.

Sending Your Cover Letter by E-Mail

Serious job candidates will send a professional cover letter even if a résumé is submitted by e-mail.

It sounds like a "no brainer," but many applicants using the Internet don't include cover letters with their résumés submitted online. A résumé that arrives without a cover letter makes the receiver wonder what it is and why it was sent. Recruiters want you to introduce yourself, and they also are eager to see some evidence that you can write. Because it's only e-mail, some candidates either skip the cover letter or think they can get by with one-line cover letters such as this: *Please see attached résumé, and thanks for your consideration.*

If you are serious about landing the job, take the time to prepare a professional cover letter. You may use the same cover letter you would send by land mail but shorten it a bit. As illustrated in Figure 16.9, don't include an inside address for the e-mail recipient. Also move your return address from the top of the letter to just below your name. Include your e-mail address and phone number. Remove tabs, bullets, underlining, and italics that might be problematic in e-mail messages.

Be careful when sending e-mail cover letters. One widespread error involves mismerging. Let's say you send the same cover letter to different companies. Unless you're alert, you might send a letter to Fed-Ex that says, "I'm eager to put my skills to work for you at UPS."[18] Also be mindful of the impression your e-mail address makes. Avoid addresses such as *hotbabe@hotmail.com* or *buffedguy@aol.com.* Moreover, don't include anything unbusinesslike, such as your favourite inspirational quotation, in your signature block.

FIGURE 16.9 E-Mail Cover Letter

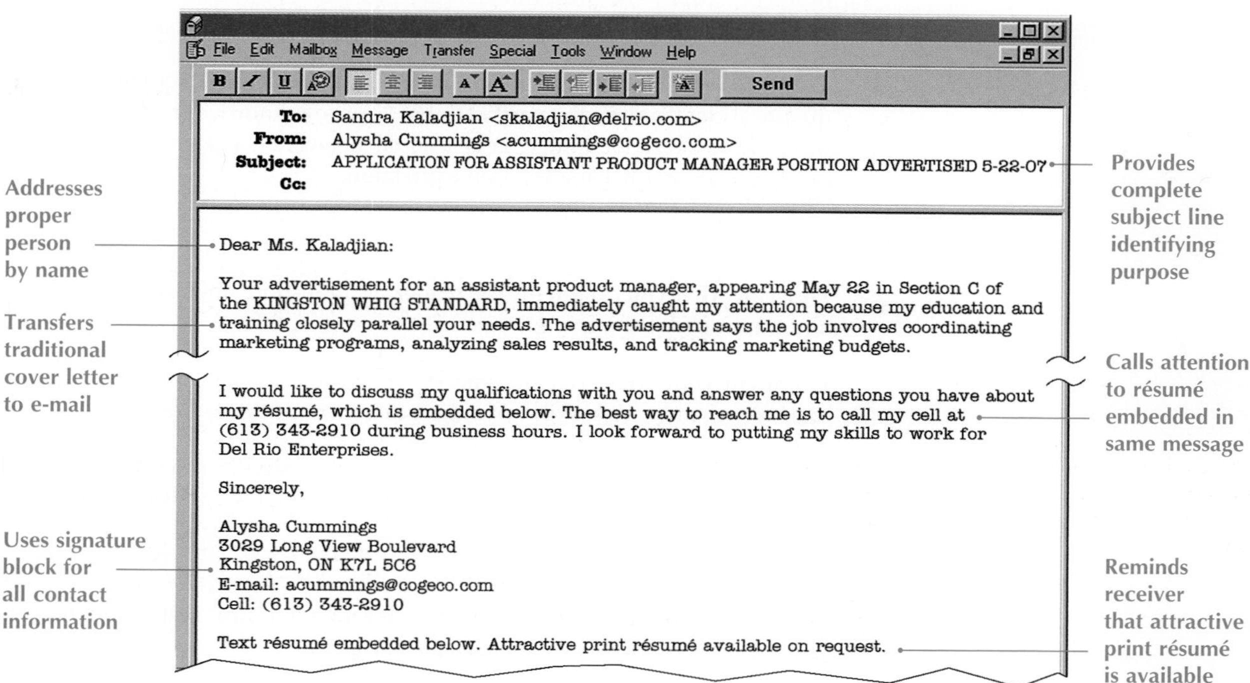

Final Tips

Look for ways to reduce the overuse of "I."

As you revise your cover letter, notice how many sentences begin with *I.* Although it's impossible to talk about yourself without using *I,* you can reduce "I" domination with this writing technique. Make activities and outcomes, and not yourself, the subjects of sentences. For example, rather than *I took classes in business communication and computer applications,* say *Classes in business communication and computer applications prepared me to . . . .* Instead of *I enjoyed helping customers,* say *Helping customers was a real pleasure.*

A cover letter should look professional and suggest quality.

Like the résumé, your cover letter must look professional and suggest quality. This means using a traditional letter style, such as block or modified block. Also, be sure to print it on the same bond paper as your résumé. And, as with your résumé, proofread it several times yourself; then, have a friend read it for content and mechanics. The following checklist provides a quick summary of suggestions to review when you compose and proofread your cover letter.

CHECKLIST FOR WRITING A PERSUASIVE COVER LETTER

Opening

- ✓ **Use the receiver's name.** Whenever possible, address the proper individual by name.
- ✓ **Identify your information source, if appropriate.** In responding to an advertisement, specify the position advertised as well as the date and publication name. If someone referred you, name that person.
- ✓ **Gain the reader's attention.** Use one of these techniques: (1) tell how your qualifications fit the job specifications, (2) show knowledge of the reader's business, (3) describe how your special talents will be assets to the company, or (4) use an original and relevant expression.

Body

- ✓ **Describe what you can do for the reader.** Demonstrate how your background and training fill the job requirements.
- ✓ **Highlight your strengths.** Summarize your principal assets from education, experience, and special skills. Avoid repeating specific data from your résumé.
- ✓ **Refer to your résumé.** In this section or the closing, direct the reader to the attached or enclosed résumé. Do so directly or incidentally as part of another statement.

Closing

- ✓ **Ask for an interview.** Also consider reviewing your strongest points or suggesting how your assets will benefit the company.
- ✓ **Make it easy to respond.** Tell when you can be reached during office hours or announce when you will call the reader. Note that some recruiters prefer that you call them.

E-Mailing

 **Include a cover letter with your résumé.** Send the same letter that might go by land mail except remove the formatting.

 **Put your contact information in the signature area.** Move your return address from the top of the letter to the signature block. Include your phone number and e-mail address.

FOLLOW-UP LETTERS AND OTHER EMPLOYMENT DOCUMENTS

Although the résumé and cover letter are your major tasks, other important letters and documents are often required during the employment process. You may need to make requests, write follow-up letters, or fill out employment applications. Because each of these tasks reveals something about you and your communication skills, you'll want to put your best foot forward. These documents often subtly influence company officials to arrange an interview or offer a job.

Reference Request

Most employers expect job candidates at some point to submit names of individuals who are willing to discuss the candidates' qualifications. Before you list anyone as a reference, however, be sure to ask permission. Try to do this in person. Ask an instructor, for example, if he or she would be willing and has the time to act as your recommender. If you detect any sign of reluctance, don't force the issue. Your goal is to find willing individuals who think well of you.

To get good letters of recommendation, find willing people and provide ample data about yourself.

What your recommenders need most is information about you. What should they stress to prospective employers? Let's say you're applying for a specific job that requires a letter of recommendation. Professor Orenstein has already agreed to be a reference for you. To get the best letter of recommendation from Professor Orenstein, help her out. Write a letter telling her about the position, its requirements, and the recommendation deadline. Include a copy of your résumé. You might remind her of a positive experience with you (*You said my report was well organized*) that she could use in the recommendation. Remember that recommenders need evidence to support generalizations. Give them appropriate ammunition, as the student has done in the following request:

Dear Professor Orenstein:

Recently I applied for the position of administrative assistant in the Human Resources Department of Host International. Because you kindly agreed to help me, I am now asking you to write a letter of recommendation to Host.

Identify the target position and company. Tell immediately why you are writing.

The position calls for good organizational, interpersonal, and writing skills, as well as computer experience. To help you review my skills and training, I enclose my résumé. As you may recall, I earned an *A* in your business communication class, and you commended my long report for its clarity and organization.

Specify the job requirements so that the recommender knows what to stress in the letter. Also, supply data to jog the memory of the writer.

Please send your letter before July 1 in the enclosed stamped, addressed envelope. I'm grateful for your support, and I promise to let you know the results of my job search.

Provide a stamped, addressed envelope.

Application or Résumé Follow-Up Letter

If your letter or application generates no response within a reasonable time, you may decide to send a short follow-up letter like the one shown here. Doing so (1) jogs the memory of the personnel officer, (2) demonstrates your serious interest, and (3) allows you to emphasize your qualifications or to add new information.

Dear Ms. Farmer:

Open by reminding the reader of your interest.

Please know I am still interested in becoming an administrative support specialist with Quad, Inc.

Substitute *letter* or *résumé* if appropriate. Use this opportunity to review your strengths or to add new qualifications.

Since I submitted an application in May, I have completed my schooling and have been employed as a summer replacement for office workers in several downtown offices. This experience has honed my word processing and communication skills. It has also introduced me to a wide range of office procedures.

Close by looking forward positively; avoid accusations that make the reader defensive.

Please keep my application in your active file and let me know when I may put my formal training, technical skills, and practical experience to work for you.

Interview Follow-Up Letter

After a job interview you should always send a brief letter of thanks. This courtesy sets you apart from other applicants (most of whom will not bother). Your letter also reminds the interviewer of your visit as well as suggesting your good manners and genuine enthusiasm for the job. Follow-up letters are most effective if sent immediately after the interview. In your letter refer to the date of the interview, the exact job title for which you were interviewed, and specific topics discussed. Avoid worn-out phrases, such as *Thank you for taking the time to interview me.* Be careful, too, about overusing *I*, especially to begin sentences. Most important, show that you really want the job and that you are qualified for it. Notice how the following letter conveys enthusiasm and confidence:

Dear Ms. Ouchi:

Mention the interview date and specific position.

Talking with you Thursday, May 23, about the graphic designer position was both informative and interesting.

Show appreciation, good manners, and perseverance—traits that recruiters value.

Thanks for describing the position in such detail and for introducing me to Ms. Thomas, the senior designer. Her current project designing the annual report in four colours on a Macintosh sounds fascinating as well as quite challenging.

Personalize your letter by mentioning topics discussed in the interview. Highlight a specific skill you have for the job.

Now that I've learned in greater detail the specific tasks of your graphic designers, I'm more than ever convinced that my computer and creative skills can make a genuine contribution to your graphic productions. My training in Macintosh design and layout ensures that I could be immediately productive on your staff.

Remind the reader of your interpersonal skills as well as your enthusiasm and eagerness for this job.

You will find me an enthusiastic and hard-working member of any team effort. I'm eager to join the graphics staff at your Kitchener headquarters, and I look forward to hearing from you soon.

Rejection Follow-Up Letter

If you didn't get the job and you think it was perfect for you, don't give up. Employment specialists encourage applicants to respond to a rejection. The candidate who was offered the position may decline, or other positions may open up. In a rejection follow-up letter, it's okay to admit you're disappointed. Be sure to add, however, that you're still interested and will contact them again in a month in case a job opens up. Then follow through for a couple of months—but don't overdo it. You should be professional and persistent, but not a pest. Here's an example of an effective rejection follow-up letter:

> Dear Mr. O'Neal:
>
> Although I'm disappointed that someone else was selected for your accounting position, I appreciate your promptness and courtesy in notifying me.
>
> Because I firmly believe that I have the technical and interpersonal skills needed to work in your fast-paced environment, I hope you will keep my résumé in your active file. My desire to become a productive member of your Trillium staff remains strong.
>
> I enjoyed our interview, and I especially appreciate the time you and Mr. Samson spent describing your company's expansion into international markets. To enhance my qualifications, I've enrolled in a course in International Accounting at NBU.
>
> Should you have an opening for which I am qualified, you may reach me at (506) 719-3901. In the meantime, I will call you in a month to discuss employment possibilities.

Subordinate your disappointment to your appreciation at being notified promptly and courteously.

Emphasize your continuing interest. Express confidence in meeting the job requirements.

Refer to specifics of your interview. If possible, tell how you are improving your skills.

Take the initiative; tell when you will call for an update.

Application Form

Some organizations require job candidates to fill out job application forms instead of submitting résumés. This practice permits them to gather and store standardized data about each applicant. Here are some tips for filling out such forms:

- Carry a card summarizing those vital statistics not included on your résumé. If you are asked to fill out an application form in an employer's office, you will need a handy reference to the following data: social insurance number; graduation dates; beginning and ending dates of all employment; salary history; full names, titles, and present work addresses of former supervisors; and full names, occupational titles, occupational addresses, and telephone numbers of persons who have agreed to serve as references.
- Look over all the questions before starting. Fill out the form neatly, printing if your handwriting is poor.
- Answer all questions. Write *Not applicable* (*N.A.*) if appropriate.
- Be prepared for a salary question. Unless you know what comparable employees are earning in the company, the best strategy is to suggest a salary range or to write in *Negotiable* or *Open.*
- Ask if you may submit your résumé in addition to the application form.

INTERVIEWING FOR EMPLOYMENT

7

Job interviews, for most of us, are intimidating; no one enjoys being judged and, possibly, rejected. You can overcome your fear of the interview process by knowing how it works and how to prepare for it.

Trained recruiters generally structure the interview in three separate activities: (1) establishing a cordial relationship, (2) eliciting information about the candidate, and (3) giving information about the job and company. During the interview its participants

A job interview gives you a chance to explain your résumé and sell your technical expertise as well as your communication and interpersonal skills. But the interview also allows the recruiter to promote the company and explain the duties of the position. Be prepared to ask meaningful questions.

have opposing goals. The interviewer tries to uncover any negative information that would eliminate a candidate. The candidate, of course, tries to minimize faults and emphasize strengths to avoid being eliminated. You can become a more skillful player in the interview game if you know what to do before, during, and after the interview.

Before the Interview

- **Research the organization.** Never enter an interview cold. Visit the library or use your computer to search for information about the target company or its field, service, or product. Visit the company's Web site and read everything. Call the company to request annual reports, catalogues, or brochures. Ask about the organization and possibly the interviewer. Learn something about the company's size, number of employees, competitors, reputation, and strengths and weaknesses.
- **Learn about the position.** Obtain as much specific information as possible. What are the functions of an individual in this position? What is the typical salary range? What career paths are generally open to this individual? What did the last person in this position do right or wrong?
- **Plan to sell yourself.** Identify three to five of your major selling points regarding skills, training, personal characteristics, and specialized experience. Memorize them; then in the interview be certain to find a place to insert them.
- **Prepare answers to possible questions.** Imagine the kinds of questions you may be asked and work out sample answers. Although you can't anticipate precise questions, you can expect to be asked about your education, skills, experience, and availability. The accompanying Career Coach box shows ten of the most common questions and suggests responses.
- **Prepare success stories.** Rehearse two or three incidents that you can relate about your accomplishments. These may focus on problems you have solved, promotions you have earned, or recognition or praise you have received.
- **Arrive early.** Get to the interview five or ten minutes early. If you are unfamiliar with the area where the interview is to be held, you might visit it before the scheduled day. Locate the building, parking facilities, and office. Time yourself.
- **Dress appropriately.** Don't overdo perfume, jewellery, or after-shave lotion. Avoid loud colours; strive for a coordinated, natural appearance. Favourite "power" colours for interviews are grey and dark blue. It's a good idea to check your appearance in a restroom before entering the office.

During the Interview

- **Establish the relationship.** Shake hands firmly. Don't be afraid to offer your hand first. Address the interviewer formally ("Hello, Mrs. Jones"). Allow the interviewer to put you at ease with small talk.

CAREER COACH

Answering Ten Frequently Asked Interview Questions

Interviewers want to learn about your job experiences and education so that they can evaluate who you are and predict how you might perform on the job. Study each of the following frequently asked interview questions and the strategies for answering them successfully.

- **Why do you want to work for us?** Questions like this illustrate the need for you to research an organization thoroughly before the interview. Go to the company's Web site, read its annual report, conduct library research, ask friends, and read the company's advertisements and other printed materials to gather data. Describe your desire to work for them not only from your perspective but also from their point of view. What have you to offer them?
- **Why should we hire you?** Here is an opportunity for you to sell your strong points in relation to this specific position. Describe your skills, academic preparation, and relevant experience. If you have little experience, don't apologize—the interviewer has read your résumé. Emphasize strengths as demonstrated in your education, such as initiative and persistence in completing assignments, ability to learn quickly, self-sufficiency, and excellent attendance.
- **What can you tell me about yourself?** Use this chance to promote yourself. Stick to professional or business-related strengths; avoid personal or humorous references. Be ready with at least three success stories illustrating characteristics important to this job. Demonstrate responsibility you have been given; describe how you contributed as a team player.
- **What are your strongest (or weakest) personal qualities?** Stress your strengths, such as "I believe I am conscientious, reliable, tolerant, patient, and thorough." Add examples that illustrate these qualities: "My supervisor said that my research was exceptionally thorough." If pressed for a weakness, give a strength disguised as a weakness: "Perhaps my greatest fault is being too painstaking with details." Or, "I am impatient when tasks are not completed on time." Don't admit weaknesses, not even to sound human. You'll be hired for your strengths, not your weaknesses.
- **What do you expect to be doing ten years from now?** Formulate a realistic plan with respect to your present age and situation. The important thing is to be prepared for this question.
- **Do you prefer working with others or by yourself?** This question can be tricky. Provide a middle-of-the-road answer that not only suggests your interpersonal qualities but also reflects an ability to make independent decisions and work without supervision.
- **Have you ever changed your major during your education? Why?** Another tricky question. Don't admit weaknesses or failures. In explaining changes, suggest career potential and new aspirations awakened by your expanding education, experience, or maturity.
- **What have been your most rewarding or disappointing work (or school) experiences?** If possible, concentrate on positive experiences such as technical and interpersonal skills you acquired. Avoid dwelling on negative or unhappy topics. Never criticize former employers. If you worked for an ungrateful, penny-pinching slave driver in a dead-end position, say that you learned all you could from that job. Move the conversation to the prospective position and what attracts you to it.
- **Have you established any new goals lately?** Watch out here. If you reveal new goals, you may inadvertently admit deficiencies. Instead of "I've resolved to finally learn something about graphics design," try "Although I'm familiar with simple graphics programs, I decided to get serious about graphics design by mastering the tools of Adobe PhotoShop and Illustrator."
- **What are your long- and short-term goals?** Suggest realistic goals that you have consciously worked out before the interview. Know what you want to do with your future. To admit to an interviewer that you're not sure what you want to do is a sign of immaturity, weakness, and indecision.

During an interview, applicants should act confident, focus on their strengths, and sell themselves.

- **Act confident but natural.** Establish and maintain eye contact, but don't get into a staring contest. Sit up straight, facing the interviewer. Don't cross your arms and legs at the same time (review body language cues in Chapter 3). Don't manipulate objects, like a pencil or keys, during the interview. Try to remain natural and at ease.
- **Don't criticize.** Avoid making negative comments about previous employers, instructors, or others. Such criticism may be taken to indicate a negative personality. Employers are not eager to hire complainers. Moreover, such criticism may suggest that you would do the same to this organization.
- **Stay focused on your strengths.** Be prepared to answer questions such as those shown in the Career Coach box. If the interviewer asks a question that does not help you promote your strongest qualifications, answer briefly. Alternatively, try to turn your response into a positive selling point.

Asking questions about the job helps applicants learn whether this position is right for them.

- **Find out about the job early.** Because your time will be short, try to learn all you can about the target job early in the interview. Ask about its responsibilities and the kinds of people who have done well in the position before. Inquiring about the company's culture will help you decide if your personality fits with this organization.
- **Prepare for behavioural questions.** Instead of traditional interview questions, you may be asked to tell stories. The interviewer may say, *Describe a time when* or *Give me an example….* To respond effectively, learn to use the storytelling or STAR technique. Ask yourself, what the **S**ituation or **T**ask was, what **A**ction you took, and what the **R**esults were.[19] Practise using this method to recall specific examples of your skills and accomplishments. Examples of behavioural questions: (1) *Tell me about a problem you solved in a unique way,* (2) *Describe a time when you had to analyze information and make a recommendation,* and (3) *Give me an example of a time when you were under stress to meet several deadlines.* To be fully prepared, develop a coherent and articulate STAR narrative for every bullet point on your résumé.
- **Prepare for salary questions.** Remember that nearly all salaries are negotiable, depending on your qualifications. Knowing the typical salary range for the target position helps. The recruiter can tell you the salary ranges—but you will have to ask. If you've had little experience, you will probably be offered a salary somewhere between the low point and the midpoint in the range. With more experience you can negotiate for a higher figure. A word of caution, though. One personnel manager warns that candidates who emphasize money are suspect because they may leave if offered a few thousand dollars more elsewhere.
- **Be ready for inappropriate questions.** If you are asked a question that you think is illegal, politely ask the interviewer how that question is related to this job. Ask the purpose of the question. Perhaps valid reasons exist that are not obvious.
- **Ask your own questions.** Often, the interviewer concludes an interview with "Do you have any questions about the position?" Inquire about career paths, orientation or training for new employees, or the company's promotion policies. Have a list of relevant questions prepared. If the interview has gone well, ask the recruiter about his or her career in the company.
- **Conclude positively.** Summarize your strongest qualifications, show your enthusiasm for obtaining this position, and thank the interviewer for a constructive interview. Be sure you understand the next step in the employment process.

After the Interview

- **Make notes on the interview.** While the events are fresh in your mind, jot down the key points—good and bad.
- **Write a thank-you letter.** Immediately write a letter thanking the interviewer for a pleasant and enlightening discussion. Be sure to spell her or his name correctly.

Keeping notes of the meeting helps candidates remember what happened.

SUMMARY OF LEARNING OBJECTIVES

1 **Prepare for employment by identifying your interests, evaluating your assets, recognizing the changing nature of jobs, choosing a career path, and studying traditional and electronic job search techniques.** The employment process begins with an analysis of your likes and your qualifications. Because the nature of jobs is changing, your future work may include flexible work assignments, multiple employers, and constant retraining. You can learn more about career opportunities through your campus career centre, the Web, your library, internships, part-time jobs, interviews, classified ads, and professional organizations. Traditional job search techniques range from newspaper ads to developing your own network of friends and relatives. Electronic job search techniques include visiting Internet job sites and company Web sites.

2 **Compare and contrast chronological, functional, and combination résumés.** Chronological résumés, listing work and education by dates, rank highest with recruiters. Functional résumés, highlighting skills instead of jobs, appeal to people changing careers or those having negative employment histories. Combination résumés, including a complete job history along with skill areas, are increasingly popular.

3 **Organize, format, and produce a persuasive résumé.** Target your résumé for a specific job. Study models to arrange most effectively your main heading, career objective (optional), education, work experience, capabilities, awards and activities, personal data, and references (optional). Use action verbs to show how your assets will help the target organization.

4 **Identify techniques that prepare a résumé for today's technologies, including preparing a scannable résumé, an inline résumé, and an e-portfolio.** In addition to a print-based traditional résumé, candidates should consider preparing a scannable résumé that limits formatting and emphasizes keywords. Keywords are nouns that an employer might use to describe a position and its requirements. Inline résumés (also called *ASCII*, *plain text*, or *electronic résumés*) are stripped of all formatting and prepared as a text file so that they may be embedded within e-mail messages. An e-portfolio is a collection of digitized materials that illustrate a candidate's performance, talents, and accomplishments. E-portfolios may be posted at Web sites or burned onto CDs.

5 **Write a persuasive cover letter to accompany your résumé.** Gain attention in the opening by mentioning the job or a person who referred you. Build interest in the body by stressing what you can do for the targeted company. Refer to your résumé, request an interview, and make it easy for the receiver to reach you. If you send your cover letter by e-mail, shorten it a bit and include complete contact information in the signature block. Remove tabs, bullets, underlining, and italics that could be problematic in e-mail.

6 **Write effective employment follow-up letters and other messages.** Follow up all your employment activities with appropriate messages. After submitting your résumé, after an interview—even after being rejected—follow up with letters that express your appreciation and continuing interest.

7 **Evaluate successful job interview strategies.** Learn about the job and the organization. Prepare answers to possible questions and be ready with success stories. Act confident and natural. Be prepared to ask or answer salary questions. Have a list of your own questions, summarize your key strengths, and stay focused on your strong points. Afterward, send a thank-you letter.

CHAPTER REVIEW

1. List at least five questions that you should ask yourself to identify your employment qualifications. (Obj. 1)
2. List five sources of career information. (Obj. 1)
3. How are most jobs likely to be found? Through classified ads? The Internet? Employment agencies? Networking? (Obj. 1)
4. What is the goal of your résumé? (Obj. 2)
5. Describe a chronological résumé and discuss its advantages. (Obj. 2)
6. Describe a functional résumé and discuss its advantages. (Obj. 2)
7. What are the disadvantages of a functional résumé? (Obj. 2)
8. When does it make sense to include a career objective on your résumé? (Obj. 3)
9. On a chronological résumé what information should you include for the jobs you list? (Objs. 2 and 3)
10. In addition to technical skills, what traits and characteristics do employers seek? (Objs. 2 and 3)
11. What changes must be made in a typical résumé to make it effective for computer scanning? (Obj. 4)
12. What information goes into the body of a cover letter? (Obj. 5)
13. Other than a cover letter, name three kinds of letters you might need to write in the employment process. (Obj. 6)
14. What information should a candidate gather in preparing for a job interview? (Obj. 7)
15. How are behavioural interview questions different from traditional questions? Give an example that would be appropriate for your career field. (Obj. 7)

CRITICAL THINKING

1. How has the concept of the "job" changed, and how will it affect your employment search? (Obj. 1)
2. How is a résumé different from a company employment application? (Objs. 1 and 2)
3. Some job candidates think that applying for unsolicited jobs can be more fruitful than applying for advertised openings. Discuss the advantages and disadvantages of letters that "prospect" for jobs. (Obj. 5)
4. How do the interviewer and interviewee play opposing roles during job interviews? What strategies should the interviewee prepare in advance? (Obj. 7)

ACTIVITIES

16.1 Identifying Your Employment Interests (Obj. 1)

Your Task. In an e-mail or a memo addressed to your instructor, answer the questions in the section "Identifying Your Interests" at the beginning of the chapter. Draw a conclusion from your answers. What kind of career, company, position, and location seem to fit your self-analysis?

16.2 Evaluating Your Qualifications (Objs. 1, 2, and 3)

Your Task. Prepare four worksheets that inventory your qualifications in these areas: employment, education, capabilities and skills, and honours and activities. Use active verbs when appropriate.

a. **Employment.** Begin with your most recent job or internship. For each position list the following information: employer; job title; dates of employment; and three to five duties, activities, or accomplishments. Emphasize activities related to your job goal. Strive to quantify your achievements.
b. **Education.** List degrees, diplomas, certificates, and training accomplishments. Include courses, seminars, or skills that are relevant to your job goal. Calculate your grade-point average in your major.
c. **Capabilities and skills.** List all capabilities and skills that recommend you for the job you seek. Use words like *skilled, competent, trained, experienced,* and *ability to.* Also list five or more qualities or interpersonal skills necessary for a successful individual in your chosen field. Write action statements demonstrating that you possess some of these qualities. Empty assurances aren't good enough; try to show evidence (*Developed teamwork skills by working with a committee of eight to produce a . . .*).
d. **Awards, honours, and activities.** Explain any awards so that the reader will understand them. List campus, community, and professional activities that suggest you are a well-rounded individual or possess traits relevant to your target job.

16.3 Choosing a Career Path (Obj. 1)

WEB

Many people know amazingly little about the work done in various occupations and the training requirements.
Your Task. Visit your institution's library, local library, or campus career centre. Consult the National Occupational Classification (NOC) binder and guide, published by Human Resources Development Canada, or the latest release of Job Futures <**www.jobfutures.ca**>. From either of the two

sources, print or photocopy the pages that describe the employment area in which you are interested. If your instructor directs, attach these copies to the cover letter you will write in Activity 16.9.

16.4 Searching the Job Market (Obj. 1)

Your Task. Clip a job advertisement from the classified section of a newspaper or print one from a career site on the Web. Select an ad describing the kind of employment you are seeking now or plan to seek when you graduate. Save this advertisement to attach to the résumé you will write in Activity 16.8.

16.5 Posting a Résumé on the Web (Obj. 4)

WEB

Your Task. List at least three Web sites where you could post your résumé. Describe the procedure involved and the advantages for each site.

16.6 Draft Document: Résumé (Objs. 2 and 3)

Your Task. Analyze the following résumé. Discuss its strengths and weaknesses. Your instructor may ask you to revise sections of this résumé before showing you an improved version.

Wendy Lee Cox
9 Franklin Terrace
Timmins, Ontario

Phone: (d) (705) 834-4583 (n) (705) 594-2985
E-mail: wendycox22@aol.com

Seeking to be hired at Mead Products as an intern in Accounting

SKILLS: Accounting, Internet, Windows 98, Excel, PowerPoint, Freelance Graphics

EDUCATION
Now working on diploma in Business Administration.
Major, Management and Accounting; GPA is 3.5.
Expect to graduate in June 2007.

EXPERIENCE
Assistant Accountant, 2002 to present. March and McLennan, Inc., Bookkeeping/Tax Service, Timmins. I keep accounting records for several small businesses accurately. I prepare 150 to 200 individual income tax returns each year. At the same time for Hill and Hill Truck Line I maintain accurate and up-to-date A/R records. And I prepare payroll records for 16 employees at three other firms.

Peterson Controls Inc., Timmins. Data Processing Internship, 2006 to present. I design and maintain spreadsheets and also process weekly and monthly information for production uptime and downtime. I prepare graphs to illustrate uptime and downtime data.

Timmins Country Club. Accounts Payable Internship, 2005 to 2005. Took care of accounts payable including filing system for the club. Responsible for processing monthly adjusting entries for general ledger. Worked closely with treasurer to give the Board budget/disbursement figures regularly.

Northern College, Timmins. I marketed the VITA program to Northern students and organized volunteers and supplies. Official title: Coordinator of Volunteer Income Tax Assistance Project. I did this for three years.

COMMUNITY SERVICE: Canadian Cancer Society, Central Park High School; All Souls Unitarian Church, assistant director of Children's Choir

16.7 Draft Document: Cover Letter (Obj. 5)

Your Task. Analyze each section of the following cover letter written by an accounting major about to graduate.

Dear Human Resources Director:

Please consider this letter as an application for the position of staff accountant that I saw advertised in the *Whig-Standard.* Although I have had no paid work experience in this field, accounting has been my major in college and I'm sure I could be an asset to your company.

For four years I have studied accounting, and I am fully trained for full-charge bookkeeping as well as electronic accounting. I have taken 36 units of college accounting and courses in business law, economics, statistics, finance, management, and marketing.

In addition to my course work, during the tax season I have been a student volunteer for VITA. This is a project to help individuals in the community prepare their income tax returns, and I learned a lot from this experience. I have also received some experience in office work and working with figures when I was employed as an office assistant for Copy Quick, Inc.

I am a competent and responsible person who gets along pretty well with others. I have been a member of some college and social organizations and have even held elective office.

I feel that I have a strong foundation in accounting as a result of my course work and my experience. Along with my personal qualities and my desire to succeed, I hope that you will agree that I qualify for the position of staff accountant with your company.

16.8 Résumé (Objs. 2 and 3)

Your Task. Using the data you developed in Activity 16.2, write your résumé. Aim it at a full-time job, part-time position, or internship. Attach a job listing for a specific position (from Activity 16.4). Use a computer. Revise your résumé until it is perfect.

16.9 Cover Letter (Obj. 5)

Your Task. Write a cover letter introducing your résumé. Again, use a computer. Revise your cover letter until it is perfect.

16.10 Interview Follow-Up Letter (Obj. 6)

Your Task. Assume you were interviewed for the position you seek. Write a follow-up thank-you letter.

16.11 Reference Request (Obj. 6)

Your Task. Your favourite professor has agreed to recommend you. Write to the professor and request that he or she send a letter of recommendation to a company where you are applying for a job. Provide data about the job description and about yourself so that the professor can target its content.

16.12 Résumé Follow-Up Letter (Obj. 6)

Your Task. A month has passed since you sent your résumé and cover letter in response to a job advertisement. Write a follow-up letter that doesn't offend the reader or damage your chances of employment.

16.13 Interview Cheat Sheet (Obj. 7)

Even the best-rehearsed applicants sometimes forget to ask the questions they prepared, or they fail to stress their major accomplishments in job interviews. Sometimes applicants are so rattled they even forget the interviewer's name. To help you keep your wits during an interview, make a "cheat sheet." It summarizes key facts, answers, and questions. Use it before the interview and also review it as the interview is ending to be sure you have covered everything that is critical.
Your Task. Prepare a cheat sheet with the following information:

Day and time of interview:

Meeting with: (Name of interviewer, title, company, city, province, postal code, telephone, fax, pager, e-mail)

Major accomplishments: (four to six)

Management or work style: (four to six)

Things you need to know about me: (three to four items)

Reason I left my last job:

Answers to difficult questions: (four to five answers)

Questions to ask interviewer:

Things I can do for you:

16.14 Developing Skill With Behavioural Interview Questions (Obj. 7)

LISTENING | SPEAKING | WEB

Behavioural interview questions are increasingly popular, and they take a little practicing before you can answer them easily. **Your Task.** Use your favourite search engine to locate lists of behavioural questions on the Web. Select five skills areas such as communication, teamwork, and decision making. For each skill area find three behavioural questions that you think would be effective in an interview. In pairs of two students, role-play interviewer and interviewee alternating with your listed questions. Your goal is to answer effectively in one or two minutes. Remember to use the STAR method when answering.

C.L.U.E. REVIEW 16

On a separate sheet edit the following sentences to correct faults in grammar, punctuation, numbers, spelling, proofreading, and word use.

1. You cant hope to find the job of your dreams' without first: (1) Knowing yourself; (2) knowing the job market and (3) know the employment process.
2. Only about 1/3 of the people currently employed works for companys with more then five hundred employees.
3. If your looking for a job you should check classified ads, as well as online job banks.
4. Preparing a résumé while you are still in school, help you recognize week qualifications, and give you 2 or 3 years in which to bolster it.
5. Recruiters like to see career objectives on résumés, however it may restrict a candidates chances.
6. Todays résumés omit personel data such as birth date, martial status, hite, weigt, and religious affiliation.
7. When listing job duties, skills, computer skills, and so forth; don't tabulate them into 2 or 3 colume tables.
8. Did you see the article entitled Which is better—A functional or a chronologial résumé? in the latest issue of Canadian Business.
9. Although its impossable to talk about your self without using *I* you should try to reduce *I* domination in your cover letter.
10. Before going to a job interview learn something about the: companies size, number of employees, competitors, reputation, and strengths, and weakness.

Appendix A

Competent Language Usage Essentials (C.L.U.E.)

A BUSINESS COMMUNICATOR'S GUIDE

In the business world, people are often judged by the way they speak and write. Using the language competently can mean the difference between individual success and failure. Often a speaker sounds accomplished; but when that same individual puts ideas in print, errors in language usage destroy his or her credibility.

What C.L.U.E. Is

This appendix provides a condensed guide to competency in language usage essentials (C.L.U.E.). Fifty-four guidelines review sentence structure, grammar, usage, punctuation, capitalization, number style, and abbreviations. These guidelines focus on the most frequently used—and abused—language elements. Presented from a business communicator's perspective, the guidelines also include realistic tips for application. And frequent checkpoint exercises enable you to try out your skills immediately.

The concentrated materials in this guide will help novice business communicators focus on the major areas of language use. The guide is not meant to teach or review *all* the principles of English grammar and punctuation.

How to Use C.L.U.E.

Your instructor may give you a language diagnostic test to help you assess your competency. After taking this test, read and work your way through the 54 guidelines. Concentrate on areas where you are weak.

Guidelines: Competent Language Usage Essentials

Sentence Structure

GUIDE 1: Express ideas in complete sentences. You can recognize a complete sentence because it (a) includes a subject (a noun or pronoun that interacts with a verb), (b) includes a verb (a word expressing action or describing a condition), and (c) makes sense (comes to a closure). A complete sentence is an independent clause.

One of the most serious errors a writer can make is punctuating a fragment as if it were a complete sentence. A fragment is a broken-off part of a sentence.

Fragment	**Improved**
Because 90 percent of all business transactions involve written messages. Good writing skills are critical.	Because 90 percent of all business transactions involve written messages, good writing skills are critical.
The recruiter requested a writing sample. Even though the candidate seemed to communicate well.	The recruiter requested a writing sample, even though the candidate seemed to communicate well.

Tip. Fragments often can be identified by the words that introduce them—words like *although, as, because, even, except, for example, if, instead of, since, so, such as, that, which,* and *when.* These words introduce dependent clauses. Make sure such clauses are always connected to independent clauses.

DEPENDENT CLAUSE — INDEPENDENT CLAUSE

Since she became supervisor, she had to write more memos and reports.

GUIDE 2: Avoid run-on (fused) sentences. A sentence with two independent clauses must be joined by a coordinating conjunction (*and, or, nor, but*) or by a semicolon (;). Without a conjunction or a semicolon, a run-on sentence results.

Run-on	**Improved**
Robin visited resorts of the rich and the famous he also dropped in on luxury spas.	Robin visited resorts of the rich and famous, and he also dropped in on luxury spas.
	Robin visited resorts of the rich and famous; he also dropped in on luxury spas.

GUIDE 3: Avoid comma-splice sentences. A comma splice results when a writer joins (splices together) two independent clauses—without using a coordinating conjunction (*and, or, nor, but*).

Comma Splice	**Improved**
Disney World operates in Orlando, EuroDisney serves Paris.	Disney World operates in Orlando; EuroDisney serves Paris.
	Disney World operates in Orlando, and EuroDisney serves Paris.
Visitors wanted a resort vacation, however they were disappointed.	Visitors wanted a resort vacation; however, they were disappointed.

Tip. In joining independent clauses, beware of using a comma and words like *consequently, furthermore, however, therefore, then, thus,* and so on. These conjunctive adverbs require semicolons.

✓ Checkpoint

Revise the following to rectify sentence fragments, comma splices, and run-ons.

1. When McDonald's tested pizza, Pizza Hut fought back. With aggressive ads ridiculing McPizza.

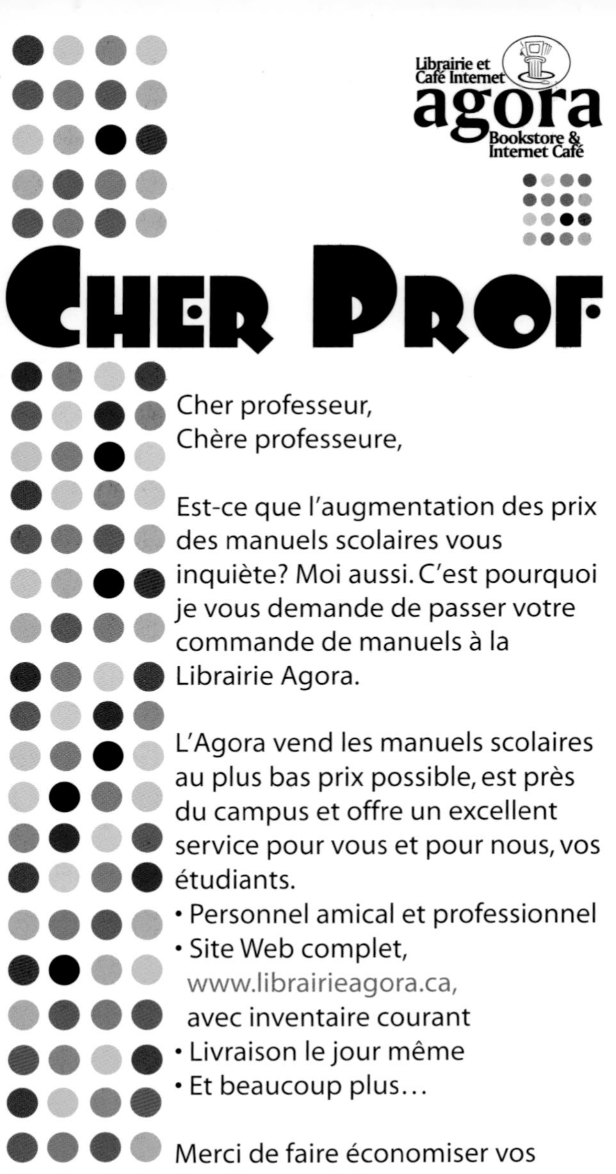

Cher Prof

Cher professeur,
Chère professeure,

Est-ce que l'augmentation des prix des manuels scolaires vous inquiète? Moi aussi. C'est pourquoi je vous demande de passer votre commande de manuels à la Librairie Agora.

L'Agora vend les manuels scolaires au plus bas prix possible, est près du campus et offre un excellent service pour vous et pour nous, vos étudiants.

- Personnel amical et professionnel
- Site Web complet, www.librairieagora.ca, avec inventaire courant
- Livraison le jour même
- Et beaucoup plus…

Merci de faire économiser vos étudiants en faisant une commande à la Librairie Agora.

(Signature)

Étudiants : Signez cette lettre et donnez-la à un enseignant qui n'a pas découvert l'Agora.

FÉUO SFUO
Fédération étudiante
Student Federation

DEAR PROF

Dear Prof,

Are you concerned about the rising cost of textbooks? I am too. That's why I'm asking you to order from the Agora Bookstore.

The Agora offers textbooks at the lowest possible prices, is close to campus and has excellent services for you and for us, your students.

- Professional and friendly staff
- An excellent website, www.agorabookstore.ca, with live inventory
- Same-day delivery
- And much more…

Thank you for helping students save money by ordering through the Agora Bookstore.

(Signature)

Students - Sign this letter and give it to a professor who has not yet discovered the Agora

FÉUO SFUO
Fédération étudiante
Student Federation

2. Aggressive ads can backfire, consequently, marketing directors consider them carefully.
3. Corporations study the legality of attack advertisements they also retaliate with counterattacks.
4. Although Pizza Hut is the country's number one pizza chain. Domino's Pizza leads in deliveries.
5. About half of the 6600 outlets make deliveries, the others concentrate on walk-in customers.

For all the Checkpoint sentences, compare your responses with the answers at the end of Appendix A (page A-22).

Grammar

Verb Tense

GUIDE 4: Use present tense, past tense, and past participle verb forms correctly.

Present Tense (Today I ______)	**Past Tense** (Yesterday I ______)	**Past Participle** (I have ______)
am	was	been
begin	began	begun
break	broke	broken
bring	brought	brought
choose	chose	chosen
come	came	come
do	did	done
give	gave	given
go	went	gone
know	knew	known
pay	paid	paid
see	saw	seen
steal	stole	stolen
take	took	taken
write	wrote	written

The package *came* yesterday, and Kevin *knew* what it contained.

If I *had seen* the shipper's bill, I *would have paid* it immediately.

I *know* the answer now; I wish I *had known* it yesterday.

Tip. Probably the most frequent mistake in tenses results from substituting the past participle form for the past tense. Notice that the past participle tense requires auxiliary verbs such as *has, had, have, would have,* and *could have.*

Faulty	**Correct**
When he *come* over last night, he *brung* pizza.	When he *came* over last night, he *brought* pizza.
If he *had came* earlier, we *could have saw* the video.	If he *had come* earlier, we *could have seen* the video.

Verb Mood

GUIDE 5: Use the subjunctive mood to express hypothetical (untrue) ideas. The most frequent misuse of the subjunctive mood involves using *was* instead of *were* in clauses introduced by *if* and *as though* or containing *wish.*

If I *were* (not *was*) you, I would take a business writing course.

Sometimes I wish I *were* (not *was*) the manager of this department.

He acts as though he *were* (not *was*) in charge of this department.

Tip. If the statement could possibly be true, use *was*.

If I *was* to blame, I accept the consequences.

Checkpoint

Correct faults in verb tenses and mood.

6. If I was in your position, I would have wrote the manager a letter.
7. You could have wrote a better résumé if you have read the chapter first.
8. When Trevor seen the want ad, he immediately contacted the company.
9. I wish I was able to operate a computer so that I could have went to work there.
10. Because she had took many computer courses, Maria was able to chose a good job.

Verb Voice

For a discussion of active- and passive-voice verbs, see page 121 in Chapter 6.

Verb Agreement

GUIDE 6: Make subjects agree with verbs despite intervening phrases and clauses. Become a detective in locating *true* subjects. Don't be deceived by prepositional phrases and parenthetic words that often disguise the true subject.

Our study of annual budgets, five-year plans, and sales proposals *is* (not *are*) progressing on schedule. (The true subject is *study*.)

The budgeted item, despite additions proposed yesterday, *remains* (not *remain*) as submitted. (The true subject is *item*.)

A salesperson's evaluation of the prospects for a sale, together with plans for follow-up action, *is* (not *are*) what we need. (The true subject is *evaluation*.)

Tip. Subjects are nouns or pronouns that control verbs. To find subjects, cross out prepositional phrases beginning with words like *about, at, by, for, from, of,* and *to*. Subjects of verbs are not found in prepositional phrases. Also, don't be tricked by expressions introduced by *together with, in addition to,* and *along with*.

GUIDE 7: Subjects joined by *and* require plural verbs. Watch for true subjects joined by the conjunction *and*. They require plural verbs.

The CEO and one of his assistants *have* (not *has*) ordered a limo.

Considerable time and money *were* (not *was*) spent on remodelling.

Exercising in the gym and jogging every day *are* (not *is*) how he keeps fit.

GUIDE 8: Subjects joined by *or* or *nor* may require singular or plural verbs. The verb should agree with the closest subject.

Either the software or the printer *is* (not *are*) causing the glitch. (The verb is controlled by closer subject, *printer*.)

Neither Montreal nor Calgary *has* (not *have*) a chance of winning. (The verb is controlled by *Calgary*.)

Tip. In joining singular and plural subjects with *or* or *nor*, place the plural subject closer to the verb. Then, the plural verb sounds natural. For example, *Either the manufacturer or the distributors are responsible.*

GUIDE 9: Use singular verbs for most indefinite pronouns. For example: *anyone, anybody, anything, each, either, every, everyone, everybody, everything, neither, nobody, nothing, someone, somebody,* and *something* all take singular verbs.

Everyone in both offices *was* (not *were*) given a bonus.

Each of the employees *is* (not *are*) being interviewed.

GUIDE 10: Use singular or plural verbs for collective nouns, depending on whether the members of the group are operating as a unit or individually. Words like *faculty, administration, class, crowd,* and *committee* are considered *collective* nouns. If the members of the collective are acting as a unit, treat them as singular subjects. If they are acting individually, it's usually better to add the word *members* and use a plural verb.

Correct
The Finance Committee *is* working harmoniously. (*Committee* is singular because its action is unified.)

The Planning Committee *are* having difficulty agreeing. (*Committee* is plural because its members are acting individually.)

Improved
The Planning Committee members *are* having difficulty agreeing. (Add the word *members* if a plural meaning is intended.)

Tip. In North America collective nouns are generally considered singular. In Britain these collective nouns are generally considered plural.

Checkpoint

Correct the errors in subject–verb agreement.

11. A manager's time and energy has to be focused on important issues.

12. Promotion of women, despite managerial training programs and networking efforts, are disappointingly small.

13. We're not sure whether Mr. Murphy or Ms. Wagner are in charge of the program.

14. Each of the Fortune 500 companies are being sent a survey regarding women in management.

15. Our CEO, like other good executives, know how to be totally informed without being totally involved.

Pronoun Case

GUIDE 11: Learn the three cases of pronouns and how each is used. Pronouns are substitutes for nouns. Every business writer must know the following pronoun cases.

Nominative or Subjective Case	Objective Case	Possessive Case
Used for subjects of verbs and subject complements	Used for objects of prepositions and objects of verbs	Used to show possession
I	me	my, mine
we	us	our, ours

Nominative or Subjective Case	Objective Case	Possessive Case
you	you	you, yours
he	him	his
she	her	her, hers
it	it	its
they	them	their, theirs
who, whoever	whom, whomever	whose

GUIDE 12: Use nominative case pronouns as subjects of verbs and as complements. Complements are words that follow linking verbs (such as *am, is, are, was, were, be, being,* and *been*) and rename the words to which they refer.

She and *I* (not *her* and *me*) prefer easy-riding mountain bikes. (Use nominative case pronouns as the subjects of the verb *prefer.*)

We think that *she* and *he* (not *her* and *him*) will win the race. (Use nominative case pronouns as the subjects of the verb *will win.*)

It must have been *she* (not *her*) who called last night. (Use a nominative case pronoun as a subject complement.)

Tip. If you feel awkward using nominative pronouns after linking verbs, rephrase the sentence to avoid the dilemma. Instead of *It is she who is the boss,* say *She is the boss.*

GUIDE 13: Use objective case pronouns as objects of prepositions and verbs.

Send the e-mail to *her* and *me* (not *she* and *I*). (The pronouns *her* and *me* are objects of the preposition *to.*)

The CEO appointed *him* (not *he*) to the position. (The pronoun *him* is the object of the verb *appointed.*)

Tip. When a pronoun appears in combination with a noun or another pronoun, ignore the extra noun or pronoun and its conjunction. Then, the case of the pronoun becomes more obvious.

Jason asked Jennifer and *me* (not *I*) to lunch. (Ignore *Jennifer and.*)

The waiter didn't know whether to give the bill to Jason or *her* (not *she*). (Ignore *Jason or.*)

Tip. Be especially alert to the following prepositions: *except, between, but,* and *like.* Be sure to use objective pronouns as their objects.

Just between you and *me* (not *I*), that mineral water comes from the tap.

Computer grammar checkers work well for writers like Lee and *him* (not *he*).

GUIDE 14: Use possessive case pronouns to show ownership. Possessive pronouns (such as *hers, yours, whose, ours, theirs,* and *its*) require no apostrophes.

All reports except *yours* (not *your's*) have to be rewritten.

The printer and *its* (not *it's*) fonts produce exceptional copy.

Tip. Don't confuse possessive pronouns and contractions. Contractions are shortened forms of subject–verb phrases (such as *it's* for *it is, there's* for *there is, who's* for *who is,* and *they're* for *they are*).

 **Checkpoint**

Correct errors in pronoun case.

16. Although my friend and myself are interested in this computer, it's price seems high.

17. Letters addressed to he and I were delivered to you and Ann in error.

18. Just between you and I, the mailroom and its procedures need improvement.

19. Several applications were lost; your's and her's were the only ones delivered.

20. It could have been her who sent the program update to you and I.

GUIDE 15: Use *self*-ending pronouns only when they refer to previously mentioned nouns or pronouns.

The president *himself* ate all the M & Ms.

Send the package to Marcus or *me* (not *myself*).

Tip. Trying to sound less egocentric, some radio and TV announcers incorrectly substitute *myself* when they should use *I*. For example, "Jerry and *myself* (should be *I*) are cohosting the telethon."

GUIDE 16: Use *who* or *whoever* for nominative case constructions and *whom* or *whomever* for objective case constructions. In determining the correct choice, it's helpful to substitute *he* for *who* or *whoever* and *him* for *whom* or *whomever.*

For *whom* was this software ordered? (The software was ordered for *him.*)

Who did you say called? (You did say *he* called?)

Give the supplies to *whoever* asked for them. (In this sentence the clause *whoever asked for them* functions as the object of the preposition *to.* Within the clause *whoever* is the subject of the verb *asked.* Again, try substituting *he: he asked for them.*)

 **Checkpoint**

Correct any errors in the use of *self*-ending pronouns and *who/whom.*

21. The boss herself is willing to call whoever we nominate for the position.

22. Who would you like to see nominated?

23. These supplies are for whomever ordered them.

24. The meeting is set for Tuesday; however, Jeff and myself cannot attend.

25. Incident reports are to be written by whomever experiences a sales problem.

Pronoun Reference

GUIDE 17: **Make pronouns agree in number and gender with the words to which they refer (their antecedents).** When the gender of the antecedent is obvious, pronoun references are simple.

One of the boys lost *his* (not *their*) new tennis shoes. (The singular pronoun *his* refers to the singular *One*.)

Each of the female nurses was escorted to *her car* (not *their cars*). (The singular pronoun *her* and singular noun *car* are necessary because they refer to the singular subject *Each*.)

Somebody on the girls' team left *her* (not *their*) headlights on.

When the gender of the antecedent could be male or female, sensitive writers today have a number of options.

Faulty

Every employee should receive *their* cheque Friday. (The plural pronoun *their* does not agree with its singular antecedent *employee*.)

Improved

All employees should receive *their* cheques Friday. (Make the subject plural so that the plural pronoun *their* is acceptable. This option is preferred by many writers today.)

All employees should receive cheques Friday. (Omit the possessive pronoun entirely.)

Every employee should receive *a* cheque Friday. (Substitute *a* for a pronoun.)

Every employee should receive *his* or *her* cheque Friday. (Use the combination *his* or *her*. However, this option is wordy and should be avoided.)

GUIDE 18: **Be sure that pronouns such as *it, which, this,* and *that* refer to clear antecedents.** Vague pronouns confuse the reader because they have no clear single antecedent. The most troublesome are *it, which, this,* and *that.* Replace vague pronouns with concrete nouns, or provide these pronouns with clear antecedents.

Faulty

Our office recycles as much paper as possible because *it* helps the environment. (Does *it* refer to *paper, recycling,* or *office*?)

The disadvantages of local area networks can offset their advantages. That merits further evaluation. (What merits evaluation: advantages, disadvantages, or offsetting of one by the other?)

Improved

Our office recycles as much paper as possible because *such efforts* help the environment. (Replace *it* with *such efforts*.)

The disadvantages of local area networks can offset their advantages. That fact merits further evaluation. (*Fact* supplies a concrete noun for the vague pronoun *that*.)

Faulty	Improved
Negotiators announced an expanded health care plan, reductions in dental coverage, and a proposal of on-site child-care facilities. *This* caused employee protests. (What exactly caused employee protests?)	Negotiators announced an expanded health care plan, reductions in dental coverage, and a proposal of on-site child-care facilities. *This* reduction in dental coverage caused employee protests. (The pronoun *This* now has a clear reference.)

Tip. Whenever you use the words *this, that, these,* and *those* by themselves, a red flag should pop up. These words are dangerous when they stand alone. Inexperienced writers often use them to refer to an entire previous idea, rather than to a specific antecedent, as shown in the preceding example. You can often solve the problem by adding another idea to the pronoun (such as *this announcement*).

✓ Checkpoint

Correct the faulty and vague pronoun references in the following sentences. Numerous remedies exist.

26. Every employee is entitled to have their tuition reimbursed.

27. Flexible working hours may mean slower career advancement, but it appeals to me anyway.

28. Any subscriber may cancel their subscription at any time.

29. Every voter must have their name and address verified at the polling place.

30. Obtaining agreement on job standards, listening to coworkers, and encouraging employee suggestions all helped to open lines of communication. This is particularly important in team projects.

Adjectives and Adverbs

GUIDE 19: Use adverbs, not adjectives, to describe or limit the action of verbs.

Andrew said he did *well* (not *good*) on the exam.

After its tune-up, the engine is running *smoothly* (not *smooth*).

Don't take the manager's criticism *personally* (not *personal*).

She finished her prescription *more quickly* (not *quicker*) than expected.

GUIDE 20: Hyphenate two or more adjectives that are joined to create a compound modifier before a noun.

Follow the *step-by-step* instructions to construct the *low-cost* bookshelves.

A *well-designed* keyboard is part of their *state-of-the-art* equipment.

Tip. Don't confuse adverbs ending in *-ly* with compound adjectives: *newly enacted* law and *highly regarded* CEO would not be hyphenated.

Checkpoint

Correct any problems in the use of pronouns, adjectives, and adverbs.

31. My manager and myself prepared a point by point analysis of the proposal.

32. Because we completed the work so quick, we were able to visit the recently-opened snack bar.
33. If I do good on the placement exam, I qualify for many part time jobs and a few full time positions.
34. The vice president told him and I not to take the announcement personal.
35. In the not too distant future, we may enjoy interactive television.

Punctuation

GUIDE 21: Use commas to separate three or more items (words, phrases, or short clauses) in a series.

Downward communication delivers job instructions, procedures, and appraisals.

In preparing your résumé, try to keep it brief, make it easy to read, and include only job-related information.

The new ice cream flavours include cookie dough, chocolate raspberry truffle, cappuccino, and almond amaretto.

Tip. Some professional writers omit the comma before *and.* However, most business writers prefer to retain that comma because it prevents misreading the last two items as one item. Notice in the third example how the final two ice cream flavours could have been misread if the comma had been omitted.

GUIDE 22: Use commas to separate introductory clauses and certain phrases from independent clauses. This guideline describes the comma most often omitted by business writers. Sentences that open with dependent clauses (often introduced by words such as *since, when, if, as, although,* and *because*) require commas to separate them from the main idea. The comma helps readers recognize where the introduction ends and the big idea begins. Introductory phrases of more than five words or phrases containing verbal elements also require commas.

If you recognize introductory clauses, you will have no trouble placing the comma. (Comma separates introductory dependent clause from main clause.)

When you have mastered this rule, half the battle with commas will be won.

As expected, additional explanations are necessary. (Use a comma even if the introductory clause omits the understood subject: *As we expected.*)

In the spring of last year, we opened our franchise. (Use a comma after a phrase containing five or more words.)

Having considered several alternatives, we decided to invest. (Use a comma after an introductory verbal phrase.)

To invest, we needed $100 000. (Use a comma after an introductory verbal phrase, regardless of its length.)

Tip. Short introductory prepositional phrases (four or fewer words) require no commas. Don't clutter your writing with unnecessary commas after introductory phrases such as *by 2007, in the fall,* or *at this time.*

GUIDE 23: Use a comma before the coordinating conjunction in a compound sentence. The most common coordinating conjunctions are *and, or, nor,* and *but.*

Occasionally, *for* and *so* may also function as coordinating conjunctions. When coordinating conjunctions join two independent clauses, commas are needed.

The investment sounded too good to be true, *and* many investors were dubious. (Use a comma before the coordinating conjunction *and* in a compound sentence.)

Niagara Falls is the honeymoon capital of the world, *but* some newlyweds prefer to go to more exotic desinations.

Tip. Before inserting a comma, test the two clauses. Can each of them stand alone as a complete sentence? If either is incomplete, skip the comma.

Promoters said the investment offer was for a limited time and couldn't be extended even one day. (Omit a comma before *and* because the second part of the sentence is not a complete independent clause.)

Home is a place you grow up wanting to leave but grow old wanting to return to. (Omit a comma before *but* because the second half of the sentence is not a complete clause.)

✓ Checkpoint

Add appropriate commas.

36. Before he entered this class Jeff used to sprinkle his writing with commas semi-colons and dashes.

37. After studying punctuation he learned to use commas more carefully and to reduce his reliance on dashes.

38. At this time Jeff is engaged in a strenuous body-building program but he also finds time to enlighten his mind.

39. Next spring Jeff may enroll in accounting and business law or he may work for a semester to earn money.

40. When he completes his degree he plans to apply for employment in Montreal, Ottawa or Toronto.

GUIDE 24: Use commas appropriately in dates, addresses, geographical names, degrees, and long numbers.

September 30, 1963, is her birthday. (For dates use commas before and after the year.)

Send the application to James Kirby, 3405 120th Ave. N. W. Edmonton, AB T5W 1M3, as soon as possible. (For addresses use commas to separate all units except the two-letter province abbreviation and the postal code.)

She expects to move from Salmon Arm, British Columbia, to Mississauga, Ontario, next fall. (For geographical areas use commas to enclose the second element.)

Karen Munson, CPA, and Richard B. Larsen, Ph.D., were the speakers. (For professional designations and academic degrees following names, use commas to enclose each item.)

The latest census figures show the city's population to be 342 000. (In figures use commas to separate every three digits, counting from the right. The metric system, as used in this book, uses a space instead of a comma.)

GUIDE 25: Use commas to set off internal sentence interrupters. Sentence interrupters may be verbal phrases, dependent clauses, contrasting elements, or parenthetical expressions (also called transitional phrases). These interrupters often provide information that is not grammatically essential.

> Medical researchers, working steadily for 18 months, developed a new cancer therapy. (Use commas to set off an interrupting verbal phrase.)
>
> The new therapy, which applies a genetically engineered virus, raises hope among cancer specialists. (Use commas to set off nonessential dependent *clauses*.)
>
> Dr. James C. Morrison, who is one of the researchers, made the announcement. (Use commas to set off nonessential dependent clauses.)
>
> It was Dr. Morrison, not Dr. Arturo, who led the team effort. (Use commas to set off a contrasting element.)
>
> This new therapy, by the way, was developed from a herpes virus. (Use commas to set off a parenthetical expression.)

Tip. Parenthetical (transitional) expressions are helpful words that guide the reader from one thought to the next. Here are representative parenthetical expressions that require commas:

as a matter of fact	in addition	of course
as a result	in the meantime	on the other hand
consequently	nevertheless	therefore
for example		

Tip. Always use *two* commas to set off an interrupter, unless it begins or ends a sentence.

 Checkpoint

Insert necessary commas.

41. Sue listed 222 George Henry Blvd. Toronto ON M2J 1E6 as her forwarding address.

42. The personnel director felt nevertheless that the applicant should be given an interview.

43. Employment of paralegals which is expected to increase 32 percent next year is growing rapidly because of the expanding legal services industry.

44. The contract was signed April 1 1999 and remained in effect until January 1 2003.

45. As a matter of fact the average North American drinks enough coffee to require 12 pounds of coffee beans annually.

GUIDE 26: Avoid unnecessary commas. Do not use commas between sentence elements that belong together. Don't automatically insert commas before every *and* or at points where your voice might drop if you were saying the sentence out loud.

> **Faulty**
> Growth will be spurred by the increasing complexity of business operations, and by large employment gains in trade and services. (A comma unnecessarily precedes *and*.)

All students with high grades, are eligible for the honour society. (A comma unnecessarily separates the subject and verb.)

One of the reasons for the success of the business honour society is, that it is very active. (A comma unnecessarily separates the verb and its complement.)

Our honour society has, at this time, over 50 members. (Commas unnecessarily separate a prepositional phrase from the sentence.)

 **Checkpoint**

Remove unnecessary commas. Add necessary ones.

46. Businesspeople from all over the world, gathered in Windsor for the meeting.

47. When shopping for computer equipment consider buying products that have been on the market for at least a year.

48. The trouble with talking fast is, that you sometimes say something before you've thought of it.

49. We think on the other hand, that we must develop management talent pools with the aim of promoting women minorities and people with disabilities.

50. A powerful reason for online purchasing is, that customers save time.

Semicolons, Colons

GUIDE 27: Use a semicolon to join closely related independent clauses. Mature writers use semicolons to show readers that two thoughts are closely associated. If the ideas are not related, they should be expressed as separate sentences. Often, but not always, the second independent clause contains a conjunctive adverb (such as *however, consequently, therefore,* or *furthermore*) to show the relationship between the two clauses.

Learning history is easy; learning its lessons is almost impossible.

He was determined to complete his degree; consequently, he studied diligently.

Most people want to be delivered from temptation; they would like, however, to keep in touch.

Tip. Don't use a semicolon unless each clause is truly independent. Try the sentence test. Omit the semicolon if each clause could not stand alone as a complete sentence.

Faulty	**Improved**
There's no point in speaking; unless you can improve on silence. (The second half of the sentence is a dependent clause. It could not stand alone as a sentence.)	There's no point in speaking unless you can improve on silence.
Although I cannot change the direction of the wind; I can adjust my sails to reach my destination. (The first clause could not stand alone.)	Although I cannot change the direction of the wind, I can adjust my sails to reach my destination.

GUIDE 28: Use a semicolon to separate items in a series when one or more of the items contains internal commas.

Representatives from as far away as Longueuil, Quebec; Vancouver, British Columbia; and Whitehorse, Yukon Territory, attended the conference.

Stories circulated about Henry Ford, founder, Ford Motor Company; Lee Iacocca, former CEO, Chrysler Motor Company; and Dr. Shoichiro Toyoda, honorary chairman, Toyota Motor Corporation.

GUIDE 29: Use a colon after a complete thought that introduces a list of items. Words such as *these, the following,* and *as follows* may introduce the list or they may be implied.

The following cities are on the tour: Toronto, Ottawa, and Winnipeg.

An alternative tour includes several western cities: Calgary, Saskatoon, and Edmonton.

Tip. Be sure that the statement before a colon is grammatically complete. An introductory statement that ends with a preposition (such as *by, for, at,* and *to*) or a verb (such as *is, are,* or *were*) is incomplete. The list following a preposition or a verb actually functions as an object or as a complement to finish the sentence.

Faulty	**Improved**
Three Big Macs were ordered by: Pam, Jim, and Lee. (Do not use a colon after an incomplete statement.)	Three Big Macs were ordered by Pam, Jim, and Lee.
Other items that they ordered were: fries, Cokes, and salads. (Do not use a colon after an incomplete statement.)	Other items that they ordered were fries, Cokes, and salads.

GUIDE 30: Use a colon after business letter salutations and to introduce long quotations.

Dear Mr. Duran: Dear Lisa:

The Asian consultant bluntly said: "North Americans tend to be too blabby, too impatient, and too informal for Asian tastes. To succeed in trade with Pacific Rim countries, North Americans must become more willing to adapt to native cultures."

Tip. Use a comma to introduce short quotations. Use a colon to introduce long one-sentence quotations and quotations of two or more sentences.

✓ Checkpoint

Add appropriate semicolons and colons.

51. My short-term goal is an entry-level job my long-term goal however is a management position.

52. Reebok interviewed the following candidates Joni Sims Simon Fraser University James Jones University of Saskatchewan and Madonna Farr Ryerson University.

53. The recruiter was looking for three qualities initiative versatility and enthusiasm.

54. Reebok seeks experienced individuals however it will hire recent graduates who have excellent records.

55. Mississauga is an expanding area therefore many business opportunities are available.

Apostrophe

GUIDE 31: Add an apostrophe plus *s* to an ownership word that does not end in an *s* sound.

We hope to show a profit in one year's time. (Add *'s* because the ownership word *year* does not end in an *s*.)

The company's assets rose in value. (Add *'s* because the ownership word *company* does not end in *s*.)

All the women's votes were counted. (Add *'s* because the ownership word *women* does not end in *s*.)

GUIDE 32: Add only an apostrophe to an ownership word that ends in an *s* sound—unless an extra syllable can be pronounced easily.

Some workers' benefits will cost more. (Add only an apostrophe because the ownership word *workers* ends in an *s*.)

Several months' rent are now due. (Add only an apostrophe because the ownership word *months* ends in an *s*.)

The boss's son got the job. (Add *'s* because an extra syllable can be pronounced easily.)

Tip. To determine whether an ownership word ends in an *s*, use it in an *of* phrase. For example, *one month's salary* becomes *the salary of one month*. By isolating the ownership word without its apostrophe, you can decide whether it ends in an *s*.

GUIDE 33: Use *'s* to make a noun possessive when it precedes a gerund, a verb form used as a noun.

We all protested *Laura's* (not *Laura*) smoking.

His (not *Him*) talking interfered with the movie.

I appreciate *your* (not *you*) answering the telephone while I was gone.

Checkpoint

Correct erroneous possessives.

56. Both companies presidents received huge salaries, even when profits were falling.

57. Within one months time we were able to verify all members names and addresses.

58. Bryans supporters worry that there's little chance of him being elected.

59. The position requires five years experience in waste management.

60. Ms. Jackson car is serviced every six months.

GUIDE 34: Use one period to end a statement, command, indirect question, or polite request. Never use two periods.

Matt worked at BioTech, Inc. (Statement. Use only one period.)

Deliver it before 5 p.m. (Command. Use only one period.)

Stacy asked whether she could use the car next weekend. (Indirect question)

Will you please send me an employment application. (Polite request)

Tip. Polite requests often sound like questions. To determine the punctuation, apply the action test. If the request prompts an action, use a period. If it prompts a verbal response, use a question mark.

Faulty	**Improved**
Could you please correct the balance on my next statement? (This polite request prompts an action rather than a verbal response.)	Could you please correct the balance on my next statement.

GUIDE 35: Use a question mark after a direct question and after statements with questions appended.

Are they hiring at BioTech, Inc.?

Most of their training is in-house, isn't it?

GUIDE 36: Use a dash to (a) set off parenthetical elements containing internal commas, (b) emphasize a sentence interruption, or (c) separate an introductory list from a summarizing statement. The dash has legitimate uses. However, some writers use it whenever they know that punctuation is necessary, but they're not sure exactly what. The dash can be very effective, if not misused.

Three top students—Gene Engle, Donna Hersh, and Mika Sato—won awards. (Use dashes to set off elements with internal commas.)

Executives at IBM—despite rampant rumours in the stock market—remained quiet regarding dividend earnings. (Use dashes to emphasize a sentence interruption.)

Dell, Hewlett-Packard, and Apple—these were the three leading computer manufacturers. (Use a dash to separate an introductory list from a summarizing statement.)

GUIDE 37: Use parentheses to set off nonessential sentence elements, such as explanations, directions, questions, or references.

Researchers find that the office grapevine (see Chapter 1 for more discussion) carries surprisingly accurate information.

Only two dates (February 15 and March 1) are suitable for the meeting.

Tip. Careful writers use parentheses to deemphasize and the dash to emphasize parenthetical information. One expert said, "Dashes shout the news; parentheses whisper it."

GUIDE 38: Use quotation marks to (a) enclose the exact words of a speaker or writer; (b) distinguish words used in a special sense, such as slang; or (c) enclose titles of articles, chapters, or other short works.

"If you make your job important," said the consultant, "it's quite likely to return the favour."

The recruiter said that she was looking for candidates with good communication skills. (Omit quotation marks because the exact words of the speaker are not quoted.)

This office discourages "rad" hair styles and clothing. (Use quotes for slang.)

In *Business Week* I saw an article entitled "Communication for Global Markets." (Use quotation marks around the title of an article; use all caps, underlines, or italics for the name of the publication.)

Tip. Never use quotation marks arbitrarily, as in *Our "spring" sale starts April 1.*

✓ Checkpoint

Add appropriate punctuation.

61. Will you please send me your latest catalogue as soon as possible

62. (Direct quote) The only thing you get in a hurry said the professor is trouble

63. (Deemphasize) Two kinds of batteries see page 16 of the instruction booklet may be used in this camera.

64. (Emphasize) The first three colours that we tested red, yellow, and orange were selected.

65. All letters with erroneous addresses were reprinted weren't they

Capitalization

GUIDE 39: Capitalize proper nouns and proper adjectives. Capitalize the *specific* names of persons, places, institutions, buildings, religions, holidays, months, organizations, laws, races, languages, and so forth. Don't capitalize common nouns that make *general* references.

Proper Nouns	**Common Nouns**
Michelle DeLuca	the manufacturer's rep
Algonquin Provincial Park	the wilderness park
College of the Rockies	the community college
CN Tower	the downtown building
Environmental Assessment Agency	the federal agency
Persian, Armenian, Hindi	modern foreign languages

Proper Adjectives	
French markets	Italian dressing
Xerox copy	Japanese executives
Swiss chocolates	Red River economics

GUIDE 40: Capitalize only specific academic courses and degrees.

Professor Jane Mangrum, Ph.D., will teach Accounting 121 next spring.

James Barker, who holds bachelor's and master's degrees, teaches marketing.

Jessica enrolled in classes in management, English, and business law.

GUIDE 41: Capitalize courtesy, professional, religious, government, family, and business titles when they precede names.

Mr. Jameson, Mrs. Alvarez, and Ms. Robinson (Courtesy titles)
Professor Andrews, Dr. Lee (Professional titles)
Rabbi Cohen, Pastor Williams, Pope John (Religious titles)
Prime Minister Martin, Mayor Tremblay (Government titles)
Uncle Edward, Aunt Louise, Cousin Vinney (Family titles)
Vice President Morris, Budget Director Lopez (Business titles)

Do not capitalize a title when it is followed by an appositive (that is, when the title is followed by a noun that renames or explains it).

Only one professor, Jonathan Marcus, favoured a tuition hike.

Local candidates counted on their premier, Ralph Klein, to raise funds.

Do not capitalize titles following names unless they are part of an address:

Mark Yoder, president of Yoder Enterprises, hired all employees.

Paula Beech, director of Human Resources, interviewed all candidates.

Send the package to Amanda Harr, Advertising Manager, Cambridge Publishers, 20 Park Plaza, Saint John, NB E2L 1G2.

Generally, do not capitalize a title that replaces a person's name.

Only the president, his chief of staff, and one senator made the trip.

The director of marketing and the sales manager will meet at 1 p.m.

Do not capitalize family titles used with possessive pronouns.

my mother, his father, your cousin

GUIDE 42: Capitalize the principal words in the titles of books, magazines, newspapers, articles, movies, plays, songs, poems, and reports. Do *not* capitalize articles (*a, an, the*) and prepositions of fewer than four letters (*in, to, by, for*) unless they begin or end the title. The *to* in infinitives (*to run, to say, to write*) is also not capitalized unless it appears as the first word of a title or subtitle.

I enjoyed the book *A Customer Is More Than a Name.*

Did you read the article entitled "Companies in Europe Seeking Executives With Multinational Skills"?

We liked the article entitled "Advice From a Pro: How to Say It With Pictures."

(Note that the titles of books are underlined or italicized while the titles of articles are enclosed in quotation marks.)

GUIDE 43: Capitalize *north, south, east, west,* and their derivatives only when they represent specific geographical regions.

from the Pacific Northwest	heading northwest on the highway
living in the East	east of the city
moving to the West Coast	western Quebec, southern Ontario

GUIDE 44: Capitalize the names of departments, divisions, or committees within your own organization. Outside your organization capitalize only *specific* department, division, or committee names.

Lawyers in our Legal Assistance Department met at 2 p.m.

Samsung offers TVs in its Consumer Electronics Division.

We volunteered for the Employee Social Responsibility Committee.

You might send an application to that company's personnel department.

GUIDE 45: Capitalize product names only when they refer to trademarked items. Don't capitalize the common names following manufacturers' names.

Sony portable television	Skippy peanut butter	NordicTrack treadmill
Eveready Energizer	Gillette razor	Kodak colour copier
Coca-Cola	Apple computer	Big Mac sandwich

GUIDE 46: Capitalize most nouns followed by numbers or letters (except in page, paragraph, line, and verse references).

Room 14	Exhibit A	Flight 12, Gate 43
Figure 2.1	Plan No. 1	Model Z2010

Checkpoint

Capitalize all appropriate words.

66. vice president ellis bought a toshiba computer for use on her trips to europe.

67. our director of research brought plan no. 1 with him to the meeting in our engineering research department.

68. proceed west on highway 10 until you reach the mt. vernon exit.

69. you are booked on american airlines flight 164 leaving from gate 5 at pearson international airport.

70. to improve their english, many new canadians purchased the book entitled *the power of language is yours.*

Number Usage

GUIDE 47: Use word form to express (a) numbers *ten* and under and (b) numbers beginning sentences. General references to numbers *ten* and under should be expressed in word form. Also use word form for numbers that begin sentences. If the resulting number involves more than two words, however, the sentence should be recast so that the number does not fall at the beginning.

We answered *six* telephone calls for the *four* sales reps.

Fifteen customers responded to the *three* advertisements today.

A total of 155 cameras were awarded as prizes. (Avoid beginning the sentence with a long number such as *one hundred fifty-five.*)

GUIDE 48: Use words to express general references to small fractions. Use words or figures to refer to periods of time or to ages.

When she reached *twenty-one* (or *21*), she received *one half* of the estate.

James owns a *one-third* interest in the electronics business. (Note that fractions are hyphenated only when they function as adjectives.)

That business was founded *thirty-five* (or *35*) years ago.

Tip. Exact ages and specific business terms should be expressed in figures.

Both Meredith Jones, 55, and Jack Jones, 57, appeared in the article.

The note is payable in 60 days.

GUIDE 49: Use figures to express most references to numbers *11* and over.

Over *150* people from *53* companies attended the two-day workshop.

A 114-mL serving of Haagen-Dazs toffee crunch ice cream contains *300* calories and *19* grams of fat.

GUIDE 50: Use figures to express money, dates, clock time, decimals, and percents. Use a combination of words and figures to express sums of 1 million and over.

One item cost only *$1.95*; most, however, were priced between *$10* and *$35*. (Omit the decimals and zeros in even sums of money.)

A total of *3700* employees approved the contract *May 12* at *3 p.m.*

When sales dropped *4.7* percent, net income fell *9.8* percent. (Use the word *percent* instead of the symbol %.)

Orion lost *$62.9 million* in the latest fiscal year on revenues of *$584 million*. (Use a combination of words and figures for sums of 1 million and over.)

Tip. To ease your memory load, concentrate on the numbers normally expressed in words: numbers *ten* and under, numbers at the beginning of a sentence, and small fractions. Nearly everything else in business is generally written with figures.

✓ Checkpoint

Correct any inappropriate expression of numbers.

71. McDonald's former McLean Deluxe, priced at one dollar and fifty-nine cents, had only three hundred ten calories and nine percent fat.

72. 175 employees will attend the meeting January tenth at one p.m.

73. The Nordstrom family, which owns forty percent of the company's stock, recently added four co-presidents.

74. Our three branch offices, with a total of ninety-six workers, needs to add six computers and nine printers.

75. On March eighth we paid thirty-two dollars per share to acquire one third of the shares.

Abbreviations

Abbreviations should be used only when they are clear and appropriate. Be aware that every field (such as technology and engineering) has its own specialized abbreviations. Therefore, be certain before you use such abbreviations that the receiver of your information is familiar with them.

GUIDE 51: Use abbreviations for titles before and after proper names.

Mr. Peter Mansbridge
Rev. Simon Brownsley
Hon. Judy Sgro
Joshua Paul, *Jr.*
Samford Amhas, *M.D.*
Ronny Muntroy, *Ph.D.*

GUIDE 52: Learn when to use periods with abbreviations.
Use a period with conventional abbreviations.

Mrs. Ms. Mr. Dr. Hon. Prof.

Acronyms (shortened forms), which are pronounced as a word, do not have periods.

AIDS scuba laser VIP UNICEF NAFTA

Latin abbreviations have periods.

e.g. i.e. etc. vs.

GUIDE 53: Use abbreviations for familiar institutions, organizations, associations, corporations, and people.

Institutions
UBC UWO WLU CNIB

Organizations and Associations
NDP CIA YMCA CAW CAPIC CMA
OPEC G8 OSSTF NHLPA CHRP CSIS

Corporations
IBM CTW CBC

People
PET FDR LBJ JFK

GUIDE 54: Remember your audience when using abbreviations. If the short form or abbreviation is not well known, spell it out it before using it throughout the discussion.

The CBE (Council of Biology Editors) documentation style is used primarily in the sciences. Consult a reference text for information about how to use CBE documentation.

✓ Checkpoint

Correct any inappropriate use of abbreviations.

76. My dr., Samnik Shanban, m.d., has wonderful credentials.

77. To save both money and time, the specialist recommended l.a.s.e.r. surgery.

78. The question was addressed to Prof Antle.

79. You should remember to use a large-sized font when preparing overheads, eg, 24-point or greater.

80. Mrs. Cathrick was n.a. for comment.

Key to C.L.U.E. Checkpoint Exercises in Appendix A

This key shows all corrections. If you marked anything else, double-check the appropriate guideline.

1. Pizza Hut fought back with

2. backfire; consequently,

3. advertisements; they

4. chain, Domino's

5. deliveries; the

6. If I *were* . . . I would have *written*

7. could have *written* . . . if you *had* read

8. When Trevor *saw*

9. I wish I *were* . . . could have *gone*

10. she had *taken* . . . able to *choose*

11. energy *have*

12. efforts, *is* disappointingly

13. Ms. Wagner *is* in charge

14. companies *is* being

15. *knows* how

16. my friend and *I* . . . *its* price

17. to *him* and *me*

18. between you and *me*

19. *yours* and *hers*

20. could have been *she* . . . to you and *me*

21. *whomever* we nominate

22. *Whom* would you

23. *whoever* ordered

24. Jeff and *I*

25. by *whoever* experiences

26. to have *his or her* tuition; to have *the* tuition; *all employees are entitled to have their tuition reimbursed*

27. but *this advancement plan* appeals (*Revise to avoid vague pronoun* it.)

28. may cancel *his or her* subscription; may cancel *the* subscription; *subscribers* may cancel *their* subscriptions

29. *his or her* name and address; *all voters must have their names and addresses*

30. *These activities are* particularly important (*Revise to avoid the vague pronoun* this.)

31. my manager and *I* . . . point-by-point

32. completed the work *so quickly* . . . recently opened (*Omit hyphen.*)

33. If I do *well* . . . part-time . . . full-time

34. told him and *me* . . . *personally*

35. *not-too-distant* future

36. class, Jeff . . . commas, semicolons, and

37. punctuation, (*No comma before* and!)

38. program, but

39. business law, or

40. degree, he . . . Montreal, Ottawa, or

41. 222 George Henry Blvd., Toronto, ON M2J 1E6, as her

42. felt, nevertheless,

43. paralegals, which . . . year,

44. April 1, 1999, . . . January 1, 2003.

45. As a matter of fact,

46. (*Remove comma.*)

47. equipment,

48. (*Remove comma.*)

49. think, on the other hand, . . . women, minorities, and

50. (*Remove comma.*)

51. entry-level job; my . . . goal, however,

52. candidates: Joni Sims, Simon Fraser University; James Jones, University of Saskatchewan; and Madonna Farr, Ryerson University.

53. qualities: initiative, versatility, and

54. individuals; however,

55. area; therefore,

56. companies'

57. one month's time . . . members'

58. Bryan's . . . *his* being elected

59. years' experience

60. Jackson's car

61. possible.

62. "The only thing you get in a hurry," said the professor, "is trouble."

63. batteries (see page 16 of the instruction booklet) may be

64. tested—red, yellow, and orange—were selected.

65. reprinted, weren't they?

66. Vice President Ellis . . . Toshiba computer . . . Europe

67. Our . . . Plan No. 1 . . . Engineering Research Department

68. Proceed . . . Highway 10 . . . Mt. Vernon exit.

69. You . . . American Airlines Flight 164 . . . Gate 5 at Pearson International Airport.

70. To improve their English, many new Canadians . . . *The Power of Language Is Yours.*

71. priced at $1.59, had only 310 calories and 9 percent fat.

72. A total of 175 employees . . . January 10 at 1 p.m.

73. 40 percent

74. 96 workers

75. March 8 . . . $32

76. doctor … M.D.,

77. laser

78. Professor

79. e.g.

80. not available

Appendix B

Documentation Formats

For many reasons business writers are careful to properly document report data. Citing sources strengthens a writer's argument, as you learned in Chapter 12. Acknowledging sources also shields writers from charges of plagiarism. Moreover, good references help readers pursue further research.

Source notes identify quotations, paraphrased passages, and author references. They lead readers to the sources of cited information, and they must follow a consistent format. Content notes, on the other hand, enable writers to add comments, explain information not directly related to the text, or refer readers to other sections of a report. Because content notes are generally infrequent, most writers identify them in the text with a raised asterisk (*). At the bottom of the page, the asterisk is repeated with the content note following. If two content notes appear on one page, a double asterisk identifies the second reference.

Your real concern will be with source notes. These identify quotations or paraphrased ideas in the text, and they direct readers to a complete list of references (a bibliography) at the end of your report. Researchers have struggled for years to develop the perfect documentation system, one that is efficient for the writer and crystal clear to the reader. As a result, many systems exist, each with its advantages. The important thing for you is to adopt one system and use it consistently.

Students frequently ask, "But what documentation system is most used in business?" Actually, no one method dominates. Many businesses have developed their own hybrid systems. These companies generally supply guidelines illustrating their in-house style to employees. Before starting any research project on the job, you'll want to inquire about your organization's preferred documentation style. You can also look in the files for examples of previous reports.

References are usually cited in two places: (1) a brief citation appears in the text, and (2) a complete citation appears in a bibliography at the end of the report. The two most common formats for citations and bibliographies are those of the Modern Language Association (MLA) and the American Psychological Association (APA). Each has its own style for textual references and bibliography lists.

Modern Language Association Format

Writers in the humanities frequently use the MLA format, as illustrated in Figure B.1. In parentheses close to the textual reference appears the author's name and page cited. If no author is known, a shortened version of the source title is used. At the end of the report, the writer lists alphabetically all references in a bibliography called "Works Cited." To see a long report illustrating MLA documentation, turn to Figure 14.3 in Chapter 14. For more information consult Joseph Gibaldi, *MLA Handbook for Writers*

FIGURE B.1 Portions of MLA Text Page and Bibliography

Peanut butter was first delivered to the world by a St. Louis physician in 1890. As discussed at the Peanut Advisory Board's Web site, peanut butter was originally promoted as a protein substitute for elderly patients ("History," screen 2). However, it was the 1905 Universal Exposition in St. Louis that truly launched peanut butter. Since then, annual peanut butter consumption has zoomed to 3.3 pounds a person in the United States (Barrons 46). America's farmers produce 1.6 million tons of peanuts annually, about half of which is used for oil, nuts, and candy. Lisa Gibbons, executive secretary of the Peanut Advisory Board, says that "peanuts in some form are in the top four candies: Snickers, Reese's Peanut Butter Cups, Peanut M & Ms, and Butterfinger" (Meadows 32).

Works Cited

Barrons, Elizabeth Ruth. "A Comparison of Domestic and International Consumption of Legumes." *Journal of Economic Agriculture* 23 (2005): 45–49.

"History of Peanut Butter." Peanut Advisory Board. Retrieved 19 Jan. 2006 <http://www.peanutbutterlovers.com/History/index.html>.

Meadows, Mark Allen. "Peanut Crop Is Anything but Peanuts at Home and Overseas." *Business Monthly* 30 Sept. 2005: 31–34.

of Research Papers, Sixth Edition (New York: The Modern Language Association of America, 2003).

MLA In-Text Format. In-text citations generally appear close to the point where the reference is mentioned or at the end of the sentence inside the closing period. Follow these guidelines:

- Include the last name of the author(s) and the page number. Omit a comma, as (Smith 310).
- If the author's name is mentioned in the text, cite only the page number in parentheses. Do not include either the word *page* or the abbreviations *p.* or *pp.*
- If no author is known, refer to the document title or a shortened version of it, as (Facts at Fingertips 102).

MLA Bibliographic Format. The "Works Cited" bibliography lists all references cited in a report. Some writers include all works consulted. A portion of an MLA bibliography is shown in Figure B.1. A more complete list of model references appears in Figure B.2. Following are selected guidelines summarizing important points regarding MLA bibliographic format:

- Use italics or underscores for the titles of books, magazines, newspapers, and journals. Check with your organization or instructor for guidance. Capitalize all important words.
- Enclose the titles of magazine, newspaper, and journal articles in quotation marks. Include volume and issue numbers for journals only.

FIGURE B.2 MLA Bibliography Sample References

Works Cited

Air Canada. *2005 Annual Report.* Dorval, QC.	**Annual report**
Berss, Marcia. "Protein Man." *Forbes* 24 Oct. 2005: 65–66.	**Magazine article**
Connors, H. Lee. "Saturn's Orbit Still High with Consumers." *Marketing News Online* 31 Aug. 2006. Retrieved 1 Sept. 2006 <http://www.marketingnews.com/08-31-06.htm>.	**Magazine article, online**
"Globalization Often Means That the Fast Track Leads Overseas." *National Post* 17 June 2005: A10.	**Newspaper article, no author**
Lancaster, Hal. "When Taking a Tip from a Job Network, Proceed with Caution." *The Globe and Mail* 7 Feb. 2004: B1.	**Newspaper article, one author**
Markoff, John. "Voluntary Rules Proposed to Help Insure Privacy for Internet Users." *The New York Times on the Web* 5 June 2005. Retrieved 9 June 2005 <http://www.nytimes.com/library/tech/02/05/biztech/articles/05privacy.html>.	**Newspaper article, online**
Pinkerton Investigation Services. *The Employer's Guide to Investigation Services,* 2nd ed. Atlanta: Pinkerton Information Center, 2005.	**Brochure**
Rivers, Frank. Personal interview. 16 May 2006.	**Interview**
Rose, Richard C., and Echo Montgomery Garrett. *How to Make a Buck and Still Be a Decent Human Being.* New York: HarperCollins, 2004.	**Book, two authors**
"Spam: How to Eliminate It from Your Workplace." *SmartPros.* 8 Aug. 2001. Retrieved 12 Sept. 2005 <http://accounting.smartpros.com/x10434.xml>.	**Internet document, no author**
Statistics Canada. *A Portrait of Persons with Disabilities: Target Groups Project.* Ottawa: Ministry of Industry, Science and Technology, 2000.	**Government publication**
Wetherbee, James C., Nicholas P. Vitalari, and Andrew Milner. "Key Trends in Systems Development in Europe and North America." *Journal of Global Information Management* 3.2 (2006): 5–20. ["3.2" signifies volume 3, issue 2]	**Journal article with volume and issue numbers**
Wilson, Craig M. "E-Mail Bill May Fail to Curtail Spamming." *eWeek.* 9 July 2006: 49. InfoTrac College Edition. Retrieved 26 Aug. 2006 <http://infotrac.thomsonlearning.com/>.	**Article from online database**
Yellen, Mike. myellen022@yahoo.com "Managing Managers and Cell Phones." Online posting. 26 June 2005. Technical Writers Listserv. 9 Sept. 2005 <http://www.techwr-1.com/techwhil/archives/>.	**Message from online forum or discussion group**

Note 1: If a printed document is viewed electronically and you have no reason to believe the electronic version is different from the print version, use the same format as for the print citation.

Note 2: To prevent confusion, you might add the words "Accessed" or "Retrieved" preceding the date you accessed an online source.

- For Internet citations, include a retrival date. Although MLA format does not include the words "Retrieved" or "Accessed," such wording helps distinguish the retrieval date from the document date.

American Psychological Association Format

Popular in the social and physical sciences, the American Psychological Association (APA) documentation style uses parenthetic citations. That is, each author reference is shown in parentheses when cited in the text, as shown in Figure B.3. At the end of the report, all references are listed alphabetically in a bibliography called "References." For more information about APA formats, see the *Publication Manual of the American Psychological Association*, Fifth Edition (Washington, DC: American Psychological Association, 2001).

APA In-Text Format. Within the text, document each specific textual source with a short description in parentheses. Following are selected guidelines summarizing important elements of APA style:

- Include the last name of the author(s), date of publication, and page number, as (Jones, 2005, p. 36). Use "n.d." if no date is available.
- If no author is known, refer to the first few words of the reference list entry and the year, as (Computer Privacy, 2005, p. 59).
- Omit page numbers for general references, but always include page numbers for direct quotations.

APA Bibliographic Format. List all citations alphabetically in a section called "References." A portion of an APA bibliography is shown in Figure B.3. A more complete list of model references appears in Figure B.4. APA style requires specific capitalization and sequencing guidelines, some of which are summarized here:

- Include an author's name with the last name first followed by initials, such as *Smith, M. A.* First and middle names are not used.

FIGURE B.3 Portions of APA Text Page and Bibliography

Peanut butter was first delivered to the world by a St. Louis physician in 1890. As discussed at the Peanut Advisory Board's Web site, peanut butter was originally promoted as a protein substitute for elderly patients ("History," n.d.). However, it was the 1905 Universal Exposition in St. Louis that truly launched peanut butter. Since then, annual peanut butter consumption has zoomed to 3.3 pounds a person in the United States (Barrons, 2003, p. 46). America's farmers produce 1.6 million tons of peanuts annually, about half of which is used for oil, nuts, and candy. Lisa Gibbons, executive secretary of the Peanut Advisory Board, says that "peanuts in some form are in the top four candies: Snickers, Reese's Peanut Butter Cups, Peanut M & Ms, and Butterfinger" (Meadows, 2005, p. 32).

References

Barrons, E. (2003). A comparison of domestic and international consumption of legumes. *Journal of Economic Agriculture, 23*, 45–49.

History of peanut butter. (n.d.). Peanut Advisory Board. Retrieved January 19, 2003, from http://www.peanutbutterlovers.com/History/index.html

Meadows, M. A. (2005, September 30). Peanut crop is anything but peanuts at home and overseas. *Business Monthly,* 31–34.

FIGURE B.4 Model APA Bibliography Sample References

References

Air Canada. (2005). *2005 Annual Report.* Dorval, QC. — Annual report

Atamian, R. M., & Ferranto, M. (2003). *Driving market forces.* New York: HarperCollins. — Book, two authors

Berss, M. (2004, October 24). Protein man. *Forbes, 154,* 64–66. — Magazine article

Cantrell, M. R., & Watson, H. (2003). Violence in today's workplace [Electronic version]. *Office Review, 26*(1), 24–29. — Magazine article, viewed electronically

Globalization often means that the fast track leads overseas. (2004, June 16). *National Post,* p. A10. — Newspaper article, no author

Lancaster, H. (2004, February 7). When taking a tip from a job network, proceed with caution. *The Globe and Mail,* p. B1. — Newspaper article, one author

Lang, R. T. (2003, March 2). Most people fail to identify nonverbal signs. *The New York Times.* Retrieved November 15, 2004, from http://www.nytimes.com — Newspaper article, online

Moon, J. (2001). Solid waste disposal. *Microsoft Encarta 2002* [CD-ROM]. Redmond, WA: Microsoft. — CD-ROM encyclopedia article

Pinkerton Investigation Services. (2003). *The employer's guide to investigation services* (3rd ed.) [Brochure]. Atlanta: Pinkerton Information Center. — Brochure

Wetherbee, J. C., Vitalari, N. P., & Milner, A. (2003). Key trends in systems development in Europe and North America. *Journal of Global Information Management, 3*(2), 5–20. ["3(2)" signifies volume 3, series or issue 2] — Journal article with volume and issue numbers

Wilson, G., & Simmons, P. (2003). *Plagiarism: What it is, and how to avoid it.* Retrieved July 4, 2005, from Biology Program Guide 2003/2004 at the University of British Columbia Web site: http://www.zoology.ubc/ca/bpg/plagiarism.htm — World Wide Web document with author and date

WWW user survey reveals consumer trends. (n.d.). Retrieved August 2, 2004, from http://www.cc.gatech.edu/gvu/user_surveys/survey-2001-10/ — World Wide Web document, no author, no date

Yudkin, M. (2003, July 4). The marketing minute: Truth is always in season [Msg. ID: ruf6kt0aiu5eui6523qsrofhu70h21evoj@4ax.com]. Message posted to news://biz.ecommerce — Message to online forum or discussion group

- Show the date of publication in parentheses immediately after the author's name, as *Smith, M. A. (2005).*
- Italicize the titles of books. Use "sentence-style" capitalization. This means that only the first word of a title, proper nouns, and the first word after an internal colon is capitalized.
- Do not italicize or underscore the titles of magazine and journal articles. Use sentence-style capitalization for article titles.
- Italicize the names of magazines and journals. Capitalize the initial letters of all important words.

Online Help

Various Web sites have been created to assist writers in creating the appropriate documentation. You may want to visit the following sites: <**www.easybib.com**>, <**www.noodletools.com**>, and <**www.workscited4u.com**>.

Citing Electronic Sources

Standards for researchers using electronic sources are still emerging. When citing electronic media, you should have the same goals as for print sources. That is, you try to give credit to the authors and to allow others to easily locate the same or updated information. However, traditional formats for identifying authors, publication dates, and page numbers become confusing when applied to sources on the Internet. Strive to give correct credit for electronic sources by including the author's name (when available), document title, Web page title, Web address, and retrieval date. Formats for some electronic sources have been shown here.

Key to C.L.U.E. Review Exercises

Chapter 1

1. In today's average business office, employees spend approximately 60 percent of their time processing documents.
2. My friend and I were surprised to learn that more information has been produced in the last thirty (or 30) years than in the previous 5000 years.
3. A typical manager, by the way, reads 1 million words every week, which is equal to reading one and a half full-length novels every day.
4. If you are defining *communication*, a principal element is the transmission of information and meaning.
5. When Ms. Diaz had three messages to send, she chose e-mail because it was definitely the fastest communication channel.
6. Five factors that make up your unique frame of reference are the following: experience, education, culture, expectations, and personality.
7. Just between you and me, who do you think will be recommended for the award?
8. To many workers, balancing family and work demands is more important than earning big salaries.
9. Matt felt that he did well (or had done well) on the exam, but he wants to do even better when it's given again next fall.
10. The grapevine may be an excellent source of employee information; however, it should not replace formal lines of communication.

Chapter 2

1. Companies are forming teams for at least three good reasons: better decisions, faster response times, and increased productivity.
2. Although they do not hold face-to-face meetings, virtual teams exchange information and make decisions electronically.
3. Successful self-directed teams are autonomous; that is, they can hire, fire, and discipline their own members.
4. We already have a number of teams; however, our CEO and several vice presidents are advising us to add more.
5. At last month's staff meeting, the manager and he encouraged a warm, supportive climate with praise and helpful comments.
6. When conflict erupted at our team's February meeting, we made a conscious effort to confront the underlying issues.
7. The best method for reaching group decisions involves consensus, but this method is very time-consuming.
8. The team leader and I think, however, that all speakers have a right to a fair hearing.
9. Seventy-five people are expected to attend the training session on May 15; consequently, she and I must find a larger room.
10. Lawyers in our Legal Services Department distributed an agenda for participants attending their January 3 meeting.

Chapter 3

1. Although listening is a principal activity of employees, experts say that many listen at only 25 percent efficiency.
2. When listening to instructions, be sure to take notes and review them immediately.
3. In a poll of over 9000 employees, only one third felt that their companies sought their opinions and suggestions.
4. Well-trained customer service representatives ask gentle, probing questions to ensure clear understanding.
5. The appearance and mannerisms of a speaker affect a listener's evaluation of a message.

6. Remembering important points involves three factors: (1) deciding to remember, (2) forming relationships, and (3) reviewing.

7. A list of suggestions for paraphrasing a speaker's ideas is found in an article titled "Best Listening Habits," which appeared in *Fortune.*

8. Skilled speakers raise their voices to convey important ideas; however, they whisper to imply secrecy.

9. One successful manager says that he can tell from people's eyes whether they are focused, receptive, or distant.

10. On March 5 the president of the company announced a casual dress policy; consequently, I must buy a whole new wardrobe.

Chapter 4

1. Gifts for the children of an Arab are welcome; however, gifts for an Arab's wife are not advisable.

2. In Latin America knives are not proper gifts; they signify cutting off a relationship.

3. Statistics Canada reports that one third of the foreign-born population of Canada is from Asia, the Caribbean, and the Middle East.

4. Although international business was already common among big companies, we now find many smaller companies seeking global markets.

5. On April 15 an article entitled "Practical Cross-Cultural Persuasion Strategies" appeared in *The Journal of International Business.*

6. Three executives agreed that their company's overseas project with France was taking twice as long as expected.

7. They recommend, therefore, that a committee study the cultural and language issues for a three-week period and submit a report of its findings.

8. The 300 representatives were told that the simple act of presenting a business card is something to which Canadians give little thought, but it is a serious formality in Japan.

9. Each of the 75 delegates was charged a fee of $40 to attend the cultural training session, although formerly the charge had been only $30.

10. Both the president and senior vice president agree that all staff members' suggestions should be sent to Human Relations. (Note: Capitalize the name of a specific department within your company.)

Chapter 5

1. If I were you, I would memorize the following three parts of the writing process: prewriting, writing, and revising.

2. A writer's time is usually spent as follows: 25 percent worrying, 25 percent writing, 45 percent revising, and 5 percent proofreading.

3. At least four or five members of our team will probably attend the meeting scheduled with our company vice president at 3 p.m. on Tuesday, March 4.

4. We're not asking the team to alter its proposal; we are asking team members to check the proposal's figures.

5. Writers may use computer software to fight writer's block as well as to help them collect information electronically. ("Writer's block" is an expression generally used in reference to a single writer.)

6. Will you please fax me a list of all independent publishers' names and addresses. (Note: A polite request ends in a period.)

7. Writers have many communication channels from which to choose; therefore, they should choose carefully.

8. Over 250 years ago one of Canada's founding fathers recognized a fundamental writing principle.

9. If you are trying to persuade someone, be sure that your proposal and request are beneficial to the receiver (OR *to that person*).

10. By substituting everyday, familiar words for unfamiliar ones, you can make your audience comprehend your ideas more quickly.

Chapter 6

1. Whether you are writing a short memo or a 30-page report, you should expect to conduct formal or informal research.

2. Our company vice president came to the president and me asking for help with two complex but separate desktop publishing problems.

3. Because neither of us is particularly creative, we decided to organize a brainstorming session.
4. To develop a better sense of design, we collected desirable samples from books, magazines, brochures, and newsletters.
5. We noticed that poorly designed projects often were filled with cluttered layouts, incompatible typefaces, and too many typefaces.
6. Our brainstorming session included the following individuals: Troy, Rhonda, Amanda, and Matt.
7. We encouraged participants to think visually, but most were reluctant to draw pictures.
8. One of our principal goals was to create 100 ideas in 30 minutes; however, we were prepared to meet up to one hour.
9. Because we know that ideas continue to incubate, we encouraged everyone to continue to submit ideas after the session ended.
10. Robyn Clarke's article titled "A Better Way to Brainstorm," which appeared in the magazine *Black Enterprise*, proved to be very helpful.

Chapter 7

1. Business documents must be written clearly to ensure that readers comprehend the message quickly.
2. The prominent chairman of Monsanto in Europe complained that his managers' reports were too long, too frequent, and too unread.
3. The report contained so many redundancies that its main principles requesting provincial and federal funding were lost.
4. The information was cited in a recent article entitled "What's New in Grammar-Checking Software"; however, I can't locate the article now.
5. All three of our company's recruiters—Jim Lucus, Doreen Delgado, and Brad Kirby—criticized their poorly written procedures.
6. To help receivers anticipate and comprehend ideas quickly, two special writing techniques are helpful: parallelism, which involves balanced writing, and highlighting, which makes important points more visible.
7. When you must proofread an important document, always work from a printed copy.
8. Have you already ordered the following: a dictionary, a reference manual, and a stylebook?
9. As we completed the final step in the writing process, we wondered how feasible it would be to evaluate our message.
10. It's almost impossible to improve your communication skills alone; therefore, you should take advantage of this opportunity.

Chapter 8

1. Today's organizations, however, are encouraging rank-and-file employees to share information and make decisions.
2. Because managers and employees are writing more messages than ever before, it's definitely important that they develop good communication skills.
3. Memos generally contain four necessary parts: subject line, opening, body, and action closing.
4. The Federal Trade Commission is holding hearings to elicit information about IBM's request to expand marketing in 21 cities.
5. Consumer buying and spending for the past five years are being studied by a federal team of analysts.
6. When you respond to an e-mail message, you should not automatically return the sender's message.
7. Wasn't it Dr. Ben Cohen, not Mr. Temple, who always wrote his e-mails in all capital letters?
8. A list of the names and addresses of e-mail recipients was sent using the "bcc" function.
9. Our Human Resources Department, which was formerly in Room 35, has moved its offices to Room 5.
10. The *Post Dispatch*, our local newspaper, featured as its principal article a story entitled "Smarter E-Mail Is Here."

Chapter 9

1. Although we've seen an extraordinary increase in the use of e-mail, some business letters must still be written.
2. She acts as if she were the only person who ever received a compliment about her business writing.

3. Good business letters are distinguished by three characteristics: clear content, a goodwill tone, and correct form.
4. Cynthia Jones, who I think is our newly appointed vice president, writes many business letters for our company.
5. After the office manager and he returned from their meeting, we were able to sort the customers' letters more quickly.
6. Even the best-run and best-loved businesses occasionally receive claims or complaints from consumers.
7. On Wednesday we received two claims; on Thursday we received four more.
8. We enclosed a refund cheque for $200; however, we worried that it was not enough to regain the confidence of the customer.
9. If you could have seen the customer's letter, you would have been as upset as Rona and I.
10. To express thanks and show appreciation, most people write a short note on special notepaper or heavy card stock.

Chapter 10

1. Successful persuasion results from two important elements: a reasonable request and a well-presented argument.
2. If we wanted to persuade a bank to lend you and me $10 000, we would probably use rational appeals.
3. Our senior marketing director and the sales manager want to send a sales letter to our current customers; therefore, they analyzed the product, purpose, and audience.
4. Four important parts of a persuasive message are (1) gaining the audience's attention, (2) convincing them that your purpose is worthy, (3) overcoming resistance, and (4) motivating action.
5. One of the biggest mistakes in persuasive requests is the failure to anticipate and offset audience resistance.
6. If the CEO and he had behaved more professionally, the chances of a practical settlement would be considerably greater.
7. An adjustment letter is a form of complaint; consequently, it's wise to use the indirect strategy.
8. Anger and emotion are not effective in persuasion, but many writers cannot control their tempers.
9. When we open our office in Montreal, we will need at least three people who are fluent in French and English.
10. A good news release looks and sounds credible; that is, it has no typos, no imaginative spelling, and no factual errors.

Chapter 11

1. When delivering bad news, you can reduce the disappointment by (1) telling the reasons for the rejection and (2) revealing the news with sensitivity.
2. It's important that you make sure the receiver understands the bad news and accepts it.
3. The indirect pattern consists of four parts: buffer, reasons, bad news, and close.
4. Undoubtedly, the indirect pattern cannot be used in every situation; however, it is often better than blunt announcements of bad news.
5. When the bad news is not devastating, references to resale or promotion may be appropriate.
6. If the vice president of our company must announce a big increase in each employee's contribution to health benefits, should he use the indirect strategy?
7. Most of us prefer to be let down gently when we're being refused something; that's why the reasons-before-refusal pattern is effective.
8. Publisher Malcolm Forbes said, "To be agreeable while disagreeing—that's an art."
9. When a well-known tire company recalled hundreds of thousands of tires, its president issued an apology to all injured customers.
10. If I were you, I would be more concerned with long-term, not short-term, returns on the invested capital.

Chapter 12

1. In a low-context culture such as North America, our values and attitudes prompt us to write many reports.
2. A reader's expectations and the content of a report determine its pattern of development.
3. The format of a report is governed by its length, topic, audience, and purpose.

4. If a report has ten or fewer pages, it's generally considered a short informal report.
5. Research reports from consultants to their clients tend to be formal; however, a conference report to your boss would be informal.
6. My colleague and I followed step-by-step instructions in preparing a work plan for our report.
7. If your report is authorized by someone, be sure to review its work plan with him or her (OR *with that person*) before proceeding.
8. Eric was offered $1000 to finish Robert's report, but Eric said the offer was "too little and too late."
9. To search the Internet, you need a browser such as Netscape Navigator or Microsoft Internet Explorer.
10. To illustrate report data, you may choose from among the following visual aids: tables, charts, graphs, and pictures.

Chapter 13

1. If you are conducting research for a report, you will probably face a jumble of data including printouts, note cards, copies of articles, interview notes, questionnaire results, and statistics.
2. Numerical information from surveys is usually summarized and simplified in tables.
3. Researchers use three statistical terms to describe data: mean, median, and mode.
4. When my boss and I use the word *average*, we are referring to the mean, which is the arithmetic average.
5. Readers of reports often turn right to the conclusions and recommendations; therefore, these sections must be written very carefully.
6. Report conclusions explain what the problem is; recommendations tell how to solve it.
7. In writing reports you will probably organize your data using one of the following five methods: time, component, importance, criteria, or convention.
8. The introduction to a report should tell its purpose and significance; it should also preview the main points.
9. You should, however, delay writing the introduction until after you complete the report.
10. To turn out professional-looking documents, be sure to design attractive pages and avoid using too many typefaces and graphics.

Chapter 14

1. Proposals are written offers to do the following: solve problems, provide services, or sell equipment.
2. Our company president and vice president worked together in developing two RFPs to solicit competitive bids.
3. To make an introduction to a proposal interesting, a writer should provide a "hook" to capture the reader's attention.
4. A central item in most proposals is the budget, which is a list of proposed project costs.
5. Any proposal delivered to the manager or me should definitely explain the specific credentials and expertise of key personnel for the project.
6. Lisa and he wanted to start their own business; therefore, they wrote a business plan that included a detailed market analysis.
7. Nicolas Scott, who is a member of our Research and Development Department, presented a formal report based on thorough investigation and analysis.
8. The principal section of the report is the body; it discusses the research findings.
9. If a report is 100 pages long, it may require a 10-page executive summary. (Note: Related numbers are written as the larger number is expressed.)
10. Only one of the executives was present at the June 10 meeting when the report was presented.

Chapter 15

1. The CEO's assistant asked my colleague and me to explain why our proposed method was better than the one previously used.
2. My friend and I were definitely inexperienced in making presentations; therefore, he and I decided to learn more about public speaking.
3. We learned that the introduction to a presentation should accomplish three goals: (a) capture attention, (b) establish credibility, and (c) preview main points.

4. In the body of a short presentation, which is usually 20 or fewer minutes, we should focus on two to four principal points.
5. One of the most important ways to end a presentation is focusing on what you want the audience to do, think, or remember.
6. Speakers must remember that listeners, unlike readers, cannot control the rate of presentation or flip back through pages to review main points.
7. In working with electronic presentation software, experts suggest choosing one transition effect and using it consistently.
8. The range of effects is staggering, but presenters using electronic slides must control their urge to pile on too many dazzling features.
9. Every good speaker adapts to his or her audience, and cross-cultural presentations call for special adjustments and sensitivity. (OR, *All good speakers adapt to their audiences* . . . .)
10. One study found that two thirds of telephone calls were less important than the work they interrupted.

Chapter 16

1. You can't hope to find the job of your dreams without first (1) knowing yourself, (2) knowing the job market, and (3) knowing the employment process.
2. Only about one third of the people currently employed work for companies with more than 500 employees.
3. If you're looking for a job, you should check classified ads as well as online job banks.
4. Preparing a résumé while you are still in school helps you recognize weak qualifications and gives you two or three years in which to bolster them.
5. Recruiters like to see career objectives on résumés; however, they may restrict a candidate's chances. (Note: To avoid confusion, you might prefer to replace the pronoun *they* with *such objectives.*)
6. Today's résumés omit personal data such as birth date, marital status, height, weight, and religious affiliation.
7. When listing job duties, skills, computer skills, and so forth, don't tabulate them into two- or three-column tables.
8. Did you see the article entitled "Which Is Better—A Functional or a Chronological Résumé?" in the latest issue of *Canadian Business*?
9. Although it's impossible to talk about yourself without using *I*, you should try to reduce *I* domination in your cover letter.
10. Before going to a job interview, learn something about the company's size, number of employees, competitors, reputation, strengths, and weaknesses.

Endnotes

CHAPTER 1

1. Hal Lancaster, "Learning to Manage in a Global Workplace," *The Wall Street Journal*, 2 June 1998, B1.
2. Thomas W. Malone, *The Future of Work* (Cambridge: Harvard Business School Press, 2004), 32.
3. "The Challenges Facing Workers in the Future," *HR Focus*, August 1999, 6; Paula Jacobs, "Strong Writing Skills Essential for Success, Even in IT," *Infoworld*, 6 July 1998, 86.
4. Dwight Cunningham, "The Downside of Technology," *Chicago Tribune Internet Edition*, 2 January 2000; "Wired to the Desk," *Fortune*, Summer 1999, 164.
5. "Behind the Numbers: E-mail Beats the Phone in Business Communication," *Information Week*, 19 May 2003, 66.
6. Canadian Telework Studies *InnoVisions Canada*, available <www.ivc.ca/part12.htm> (Accessed 28 May 2003).
7. Matthew Tartaro, "Best Practices for Supporting Home Users," *Network Computing*, 13 June 2003, 73.
8. Keith Naughton, "Designing Your Next Office," *Newsweek*, 28 April 2003, 46.
9. Andrew Denka, "New Office Etiquette Dilemmas," *CPA Journal*, August 1996, 13.
10. Susan Thea Posnock, "The Pros and Cons of a Virtual Office," *Folio: The Magazine for Magazine Management*, October 2000, 112.
11. Elaine Carey, "Gender Gap in Earnings Staying Stubbornly High," *Toronto Star*, 12 March 2003, A9.
12. Haroon Siddiqui, "Why Hugging an Immigrant Is a Good Idea," *The Toronto Star*, 27 March 2005, D1.
13. David Crane, "Census Figures Point to Three Economic Trends," *Toronto Star*, 12 February 2003, E2.
14. Vera N. Held, "Y Generation Takes a Different Approach to Work," *The Toronto Star*, 9 April 2005, D11.
15. G. A. Marken, "New Approach to Moving up the Corporate Ladder," *Public Relations Quarterly*, Winter 1996, 47.
16. Jerry Sullivan, Naoki Karmeda, and Tatsuo Nobu, "Bypassing in Managerial Communication," *Business Horizons*, January/February 1991, 72.
17. "Workers Suffering from Inbox Fatigue," *The Toronto Star*, 17 July 2004, D1, D6.
18. Dave Miller, "You've Got (Too Much) Mail," *London Free Press*, 21 September 2001, available <http://www.canoe.ca/LondonBusinessMonday/01b1.html>.
19. Leslie Walker, as quoted in "Coping With Communication Overload," *Association Management*, October 1997, 32–33.
20. Mitch Betts and Tim Ouellette, "Taming the E-Mail Shrew," *Computerworld*, 6 November 1995, 1, 32.
21. Marken, "New Approach to Moving Up the Corporate Ladder."
22. Thomas J. Hackett, "Giving Teams a Tune-Up: Reviving Work Teams," *HR Focus*, November 1997.
23. Stephanie Zimmermann, Beverly Davenport, and John W. Haas, "A Communication Metamyth in the Workplace: The Assumption That More Is Better," *Journal of Business Communication*, April 1996, 185–204.
24. Bob Nelson, "How to Energize Everyone in the Company," *Bottom Line/Business*, October 1997, 3.
25. Deirdre McMurdy, "Figures Show There's Plenty of Green in Being Green," *The Calgary Herald*, 23 January 2003, D4.
26. Tina Kelley, "Charting a Course to Ethical Profits," *The New York Times*, 8 February 1998, BU1.
27. Martha Groves, "Ethics at Work: Honor System," *Los Angeles Times*, 3 November 1997, Careers sec., 3, 15. See also Alison Boyd, "Employee Traps—Corruption in the Workplace," *Management Review*, September 1997, 9.
28. Based on Alison Bell, "What Price Ethics?" *Entrepreneurial Woman*, January/February, 1991, 68.
29. "Making Ethical Decisions—Common Rationalizations," <www.josephinstitute.org/MED/Medrationalizations.htm> (Retrieved 10 July 2000).

CHAPTER 2

1. Patricia Buhler, "Managing in the 90s: Creating Flexibility in Today's Workplace," *Supervision*, January 1996, 24–26.
2. Based on Cheryl Hamilton with Cordell Parker, *Communicating for Results*, 6th ed. (Belmont, CA: Wadsworth, 2000), 279; and Harvey Robbins and Michael Finley, *Why Teams Don't Work: What Went Wrong and How to Make It Right* (Princeton, NJ: Peterson's/Pacesetter Books, 1995), 11–12.
3. Frank Mueller, Stephen Procter, David Buchanan, "Teamworking in Its Context(s): Antecedents, Nature and Dimensions," *Human Relations*, November 2000, 1387.
4. James R. DiSanza and Nancy J. Legge, *Business and Professional*

Communication (Boston: Allyn and Bacon, 2000), 98.

5. Jon R. Katzenbach and Douglas K. Smith, *The Wisdom of Teams* (New York: HarperBusiness and Harvard Business School Press, 1994), 19.
6. The discussion of Tuckman's model is adapted from Robbins and Finley, *Why Teams Don't Work*, Chapter 22. See also Jane Henderson-Loney, "Tuckman and Tears: Developing Teams During Profound Organizational Change," *Supervision*, May 1996, 3–5.
7. Based on Kenneth D. Benne and Paul Sheats, "Functional Roles of Group Members," *Journal of Social Issues*, No. 4, 1949, 41–49; Hamilton and Parker, *Communicating for Results*, 308–312; and J. Keyton, *Group Communication: Process and Analysis* (Mountain View, CA: Mayfield, 1999).
8. Cheryl Hamilton with Cordell Parker, *Communicating for Success* (Belmont, CA: Wadsworth, 2001), 100–104.
9. Jean H. Miculka, *Speaking for Success* (Cincinnati: South-Western, 1999), 127.
10. I. L. Janis, *Groupthink: Psychological Studies on Policy Decisions and Fiascoes* (Boston: Houghton Mifflin, 1982). See also Shaila M. Miranda and Carol Saunders, "Group Support Systems: An Organization Development Intervention to Combat Groupthink," *Public Administration Quarterly*, Summer 1995, 193–216.
11. Allen C. Amason, Wayne A. Hochwarter, Kenneth R. Thompson, and Allison W. Harrison, "Conflict: An Important Dimension in Successful Management Teams," *Organizational Dynamics*, Autumn 1995, 20–35.
12. Parnell, "Teamwork: Not a New Idea," 36–40.
13. Katzennbach and Smith, *Wisdom of Teams*, 45.
14. Jon Hanke, "Presenting as a Team," *Presentations*, January 1998, 74–82.
15. Jay Robb, "More Gets Done in a No-Meeting Workplace," *The Hamilton Spectator*, 14 April 2003, D11.
16. John C. Bruening, "There's Good News About Meetings," *Managing Office Technology*, July 1996, 24–25.
17. J. Keith Cook, "Try These Eight Guidelines for More Effective Meetings," *Communication Briefings Bonus Item*, April 1995, 8a. See also Morey Stettner, "How to Manage a Corporate Motormouth," *Investor's Business Daily*, 8 October 1998, A1.
18. Eli Mina, "Meeting Minutes: Should You Record Meeting Minutes Verbatim?" *Office Pro*, June/July 2001, 4.
19. Hamilton and Parker, *Communicating*, 311–312.
20. Andrew Saunders, "Meetings: Would You Miss Them?" *Management Today*, October 2002, 54.

CHAPTER 3

1. Harvey Robbins and Michael Finley, *Why Teams Don't Work* (Princeton, NJ: Peterson's/Pacesetter Books, 1995), 123.
2. L. E. Penley, E. R. Alexander, I. E. Jerigan, and C. I. Henwood, "Communication Abilities of Managers: The Relationship to Performance," *Journal of Management*, No. 17, 1991, 57–76; R. P. Ramsey and R. S. Sohi, "Listening to Your Customers: The Impact of Perceived Salesperson Listening Behavior on Relationship Out-comes," *Journal of the Academy of Marketing Science*, No. 25 (2), 1997, 127–137; Lynn O. Cooper, "Listening Competency in the Workplace: A Model for Training," *Business Communication Quarterly*, December 1997, 75–84; and Valerie P. Goby and Justice H. Lewis, "The Key Role of Listening in Business: A Study of the Singapore Insurance Industry," *Business Communication Quarterly*, June 2000, 411.
3. Tom W. Harris, "Listen Carefully," *Nation's Business*, June 1989, 78.
4. L. K. Steil, L. I. Barker, and K. W. Watson, *Effective Listening: Key to Your Success* (Reading, MA: Addison-Wesley, 1983); and J. A. Harris, "Hear What's Really Being Said," *Management-Auckland*, August 1998, 18.
5. Eric H. Nelson and Jan Gypen, "The Subordinate's Predicament," *Harvard Business Review*, September/October 1979, 133.
6. "Listening Factoids," International Listening Association <http://www.listen.org/pages/factoids.html> (Retrieved 7 January 2001).
7. Patrice M. Johnson and Kittie W. Watson, "Managing Interpersonal and Team Conflict: Listening Strategies," in *Listening in Everyday Life*, eds. Michael Purdy and Deborah Borisoff (Lanham, MD: University Press of America, 1997), 126–129.
8. Michael Render, "Better Listening Makes for a Better Marketing Message," *Marketing News*, 11 September 2000, 22–23.
9. Georges Azzam, as quoted in Jonathon Kay, "Inside the Charisma Economy," *National Post Business*, 1 December 2001, 72–82.
10. International Listening Association, "Listening Factoids" <http://www.listen.org/pages/factoids.html> (Retrieved 12 January 2001).
11. Andrew Wolvin and Carolyn Gwynn Coakley, *Listening*, 5th ed. (New York: McGraw-Hill, 1996), 136–137.
12. "Effective Communication," *Training Tomorrow*, November 1994, 32–33.
13. Kristin J. Anderson and Campbell Leaper, "Meta-Analyses of Gender Effects on Conversational Interruption: Who, What, When, Where, and How," *Sex Roles: A Journal of Research*, August 1998, 2251; M. Booth-Butterfield, "She Hears: What They Hear and Why," *Personnel Journal*, No. 44, 1984, 39.
14. L. P. Stewart and A. D. Stewart, *Communication Between the Sexes: Sex Differences and Sex Role Stereotypes* (Scottsdale, AZ: Gorsuch Scarisbrick, 1990).
15. Jayne Tear, "They Just Don't Understand Gender Dynamics," *The Wall Street Journal*, 20 November 1995, A12; Alan Wolfe, "Talking From 9 to 5: How Women's and Men's Conversational Styles Affect Who Gets Heard, Who Gets Credit and What Gets Done at Work," *New Republic*, 12 December 1994.
16. Ray Birdwhistel, *Kinesics and Context* (Philadelphia: University of Pennsylvania Press, 1970).
17. "Casual Gone Too Far: U.S. Bosses," *The Toronto Star*, 20 September 2003, D24.
18. "Not Listening Is an American Thing," *HighGain Inc. Newsletter* <http://www.highgain.com/newsletter/back-issues/e-news/06-00/hg-enews-06-00.html> (Retrieved 17 January 2001).

19. Arthur H. Bell, "Using Nonverbal Cues," *Incentive*, September 1999, 162.

CHAPTER 4

1. Gabriella Stern, "Heinz Aims to Export Taste for Ketchup," *The Wall Street Journal*, 21 November 1992, B1.
2. Shona Crabtree, "Cultural Differences," *Eagle-Tribune* <http://www.eagletribune.com/news/stories/19990530/BU-001.htm> (Retrieved 13 February 2001).
3. Mary O'Hara-Devereaux and Robert Johansen, *GlobalWork: Bridging Distance, Culture and Time* (San Francisco: Jossey-Bass, 1994), 245.
4. Patrick J. Kiger, "The China Puzzle," *Workforce*, December 2003, 30.
5. Joseph Hall, "Weaving a New Canada," *The Toronto Star*, 23 March 2005, B1, B4.
6. Quoted in Pico Iyer, "Canada: Global Citizen," *Canadian Geographic*, Ottawa: November/December 2004, Vol. 124, Issue 6, 62, 64, 66, 68.
7. David Harvey, "Going Global," *Home Office Computing*, October 2000, 87.
8. Steve Alexander, "Learn the Politics of Going Global," *Computerworld*, 1 January 2001, S8–S10.
9. Adam Lincoln, "Lost in Translation," *ECFO*, Spring 2001, 38; Sari Kalin, "The Importance of Being Multiculturally Correct," *Computerworld*, 6 October 1997, G16–G17.
10. Lennie Copeland and Lewis Griggs, *Going International* (New York: Plume Books, 1985), 14.
11. Guo-Ming Chen and William J. Starosta, *Foundations of Intercultural Communication* (Boston: Allyn and Bacon, 1998), 40.
12. Iris Varner and Linda Beamer, *Intercultural Communication in the Global Workplace* (Boston: Irwin McGraw-Hill, 1995), 15.
13. Guy Rocher, "Culture," *1998 Canadian Encyclopaedia*, Electric Library Canada, 6 September 1997.
14. Joseph Brean, "Inukshuk Replacing the Maple Leaf," *National Post*, 25 April 2005, A1, A12.
15. Edward T. Hall and Mildred Reed Hall, *Understanding Cultural Differences* (Yarmouth, ME: Intercultural Press, 1987), 183–184.
16. Vivienne Luk, Mumtaz Patel, and Kathryn White, "Personal Attributes of American and Chinese Business Associates," *The Bulletin of the Association for Business Communication*, December 1990, 67.
17. Cynthia Gallois and Victor Callan, *Communication and Culture* (New York: John Wiley Sons, 1997), 24.
18. "Canada Business, Business Culture," *Canada Business*, Electric Library Canada, 30 June 1997.
19. "Canada Business, Business Culture."
20. T. Morrison, Wayne Conaway, and George Borden, *Kiss, Bow, or Shake Hands: How to Do Business in Sixty Countries* (Holbrook, MA: Bob Adams Inc., 1994), 44.
21. Susan S. Jarvis, "Preparing Employees to Work South of the Border," *Personnel*, June 1990, 763.
22. Gallois and Callan, *Communication and Culture*, 29.
23. Copeland and Griggs, *Going International*, 94.
24. Copeland and Griggs, *Going International*, 108.
25. Copeland and Griggs, *Going International*, 12.
26. Nicholas Keung, "Learning the Signs of Communication," *Toronto Star*, 22 May 1999, L1–L2.
27. Lillian H. Chaney and Jeanette S. Martin, *Intercultural Business Communication* (Englewood Cliffs, NJ: Prentice Hall Career and Technology, 1995), 67.
28. Gretchen Weber, "English Rules," *Workforce Management*, May 2004, 47–50.
29. *Do's and Taboos Around the World*, 2nd ed. (New York: Wiley, 1990), 71.
30. Robert McGarvey, "Foreign Exchange," *USAir Magazine*, June 1992, 64.
31. "The Way We'll Be," *The Toronto Star*, 23 March 2005, A1.
32. Graham Lowe, "Revamp HR Policies to Retain Older Workers," *Canadian HR Reporter*, Toronto: Vol. 17, Issue 19, 8 November 2004, 17.
33. "Business: A Monster Success," *The Economist*, London: Vol. 370, Issue 8368, March 2004, 66.
34. Uyen Vu, "FedEx Holds Managers Accountable for Diversity," *Canadian HR Reporter*, Toronto: Vol. 17, Issue 19, 3.
35. Carter Hammett, "Companies Win Through Team Building," *The Toronto Sun Career Connection* <www.canoe.ca/CareerConnectionNews/030213_teambuilding.html> (Retrieved 12 February 2003).
36. Sharda Prashad, "Corporate Diversity Pays Off, Conference Told," *The Toronto Star*, 11 April 2005, D1–D2.
37. Rae Andre, "Diversity Stress as Morality Stress," *Journal of Business Ethics*, June 1995, 489–496.
38. Lowe, "Revamp HR policies…," 17.
39. Genevieve Capowski, "Managing Diversity," *Management Review*, June 1996, 16.
40. Joel Makower, "Managing Diversity in the Workplace," *Business and Society Review*, Winter 1995, 48–54.
41. George Simons and Darlene Dunham, "Making Inclusion Happen," *Managing Diversity*, December 1995 <www.jalmc.org/mk-incl.htm> (Retrieved 9 August 1996).
42. Somporn Thapanachai, "Awareness Narrows Cross-Cultural Gap in Thai Management Training Courses," *Bangkok Post*, Knight-Ridder/Tribune Business News, 6 October 2003.
43. Karl Schoenberger, "Motorola Bets Big on China," *Fortune*, 27 May 1996, 116–124.
44. Based on Rose Knotts and Mary S. Thibodeaux, "Verbal Skills in Cross-Culture Managerial Communication," *European Business Review*, 92, no. 2, 1992, v–vii.
45. Makower, "Managing Diversity."

CHAPTER 5

1. Charles C. Manz, Christopher P. Neek, James Mancuso, and Karen P. Manz, *For Team Members Only* (New York: AMACOM American Management Association, 1997), 3–4. See also Edward M. Marshall, *Transforming the Way We Work* (New York: AMACOM American Management Association, 1995), 5.
2. Earl N. Harbert, "Knowing Your Audience," in *The Handbook of Executive Communication*, ed. John L. DiGaetani (Homewood, IL: Dow Jones/Irwin, 1986), 3.
3. Mark Bacon, quoted in "Business Writing: One-on-One Speaks Best

to the Masses," *Training*, April 1988, 95. See also Elizabeth Danziger, "Communicate Up," *Journal of Accountancy*, February 1998, 67.

4. For more information see Marilyn Schwartz, *Guidelines for Bias-Free Writing* (Bloomington, IN: University Press, 1994).
5. Leslie Matthies, as described in Carl Heyel, "Policy and Procedure Manuals," *The Handbook of Executive Communication* (Homewood, Illinois: Dow Jones-Irwin, 1986), 212.
6. Parts of this section are based on Kristin R. Woolever's "Corporate Language and the Law: Avoiding Liability in Corporate Communications," *IEE Transactions on Professional Communication*, 2 June 1990, 95–98.
7. "Effect of Product Liability Laws on Small Business: An Introduction to International Exposure through a Comparison of U.S. and Canadian Law," *Journal of Small Business Management*, 7 January 1998, 72.
8. Lewis N. Klar, "Torts," *The 1998 Canadian Encyclopedia*, Electric Library Canada, 9 June 1997.
9. Klar, "Torts."
10. Lisa Jenner, "Develop Communication and Training With Literacy in Mind," *HR Focus*, March 1994, 14.
11. 1996 Minister of Public Works and Government Services and the WWLIA "Misleading Advertisings Under the Federal Competition Act," <http://wwwlia.org/ca-compl.htm> (Retrieved 18 April 2000).
12. 1996 Minister of Public Works and Government Services and the WWLIA "Misleading Advertisings Under the Federal Competition Act," <http://wwwlia.org/ca-compl.htm> (Retrieved 18 April 2000).
13. Woolever, "Corporate Language," 96.
14. Lisa Jenner, "Employment-at-Will Liability: How Protected Are You?" *HR Focus*, March 1994, 11.
15. Judy E. Pickens, "Communication: Terms of Equality: A Guide to Bias-Free Language," *Personnel Journal*, August 1985, 5.

CHAPTER 6

1. Adrian Furnham, "The Brainstorming Myth," *Business Strategy Review*, Winter 2000, 21–28.
2. Dean Rieck, "AH HA! Running a Productive Brainstorming Session," *Direct Marketing*, November 1999, 78.
3. Kimberly Paterson, "The Writing Process," *Rough Notes*, April 1998, 59–60.
4. Based on information from <http://www.gapinc.com> (Retrieved 4 March 2004).
5. Andrew Fluegelman and Jeremy Joan Hewes, "The Word Processor and the Writing Process," in *Strategies for Business and Technical Writing*, 4th ed. Kevin J. Harty, ed. (San Diego: Harcourt Brace Jovanovich, 1989), 43. See also Lynn Quitman Troyka, *Simon & Schuster Handbook for Writers*, 4th ed. (Upper Saddle River, NJ: Prentice Hall, 1996), 49.
6. Maryann V. Piotrowski, *Effective Business Writing* (New York: HarperPerennial, 1996), 12.
7. Robert W. Goddard, "Communication: Use Language Effectively," *Personnel Journal*, April 1989, 32.
8. Frederick Crews, *The Random House Handbook*, 4th ed. (New York: Random House, 1991), 152.
9. "Creating the Right Environment," *National Post* Joint Venture Supplement with the Conference Board of Canada, 27 April 1999, CB1, CB3.

CHAPTER 7

1. Peter Elbow, *Writing With Power: Techniques for Mastering the Writing Process* (Oxford: Oxford University Press, 1998), 30.
2. Sonia Von Matt Stoddard, "Proofreading for Perfection," *Legal Assistant Today*, March/April 1997, 84–85.
3. Ralph Brown, "Add Some Informal Polish to Your Writing," *Management*, March 1998, 12.
4. *Business Week*, 6 July 1981, 107.
5. William Power and Michael Siconolfi, "Memo to: Mr. Ball, RE: Your Messages, Sir: They're Weird," *The Wall Street Journal*, 30 November 1990, 1; Ralph Brown, "Add Some Informal Polish to Your Writing," *Management*, March 1998, 12.

CHAPTER 8

1. "Canadians' Love Affair with Email Continues," Ipsos-Reid, 30 October 2001 <www.angusreid.com/media/dsp_displaypr.prnt.cfm?ID_to_view=1345> (Retrieved 18 June 2003).
2. Kevin Maney, "How the Big Names Tame E-mail," *USA Today*, 24 July 2003, 2A.
3. "Canadians' Love Affair with Email Continues."
4. John Fielden, "Clear Writing Is Not Enough," *Management Review*, April 1989, 51.
5. Joann S. Lublin, "You Should Negotiate a Severance Package—Even Before Job Starts," *The Wall Street Journal*, 13 March 2001, B1.

CHAPTER 9

1. Hugh Hay-Roe, "The Secret of Excess," *Executive Excellence*, January 1995, 20.
2. Dennis Chambers, *Writing to Get Action* (Bristol, VT: Velocity Business Publishing, 1998), 12.
3. Steven N. Spertz and Glenda S. Spertz, *The Rule of Law: Canadian Business Law*, 2nd ed. (Toronto: Copp Clark Ltd., 1995), 289.
4. Gary L. Clark, Peter F. Kaminski, and David R. Rink, "Consumer Complaints: Advice on How Companies Should Respond Based on an Empirical Study," *Journal of Services Marketing*, Winter 1992, 41–50.
5. Robert Klara, "Press 1 to Gripe," *Restaurant Business*, 15 May 1998, 96–102.

6. Marcia Mascolini, "Another Look at Teaching the External Negative Message," *The Bulletin of the Association of Business Communication*, June 1994, 46; Robert J. Aalberts and Lorraine A. Krajewski, "Claim and Adjustment Letters," *The Bulletin of the Association for Business Communication*, September 1987, 2.
7. Elizabeth Blackburn Brockman and Kelly Belanger, "You-Attitude and Positive Emphasis: Testing Received Wisdom in Business Communication," *The Bulletin of the Association for Business Communication*, June 1993, 1–5; C. Goodwin and I. Ross, "Consumer Evaluations of Responses to Complaints: What's Fair and Why," *Journal of Consumer Marketing*, 7, 1990, 39–47; Marcia Mascolini, "Another Look at Teaching the External Negative Message," *The Bulletin of the Association for Business Communication*, June 1994, 46.
8. Michael W. Michelson Jr., "Turning Complaints into Cash," *The American Salesman*, December 2003, 22.
9. Pamela Gilbert, "Two Words That Can Help a Business Thrive," *The Wall Street Journal*, 30 December 1996, A12.

CHAPTER 10

1. John R. Graham, "Improving Direct Mail," *Agency News*, January 2002, 47–50.
2. Dennis Chambers, *The Agile Manager's Guide to Writing to Get Action* (Bristol, VT: Velocity Press, 1998), 86.
3. Kevin McLaughlin, "Words of Wisdom," *Entrepreneur*, October 1990, 101.
4. Based on "PDA-Based Software Allows Realtors to Show Homes 'Practically Anywhere,'" <http://www.pdare.com/vertical/articles/article-460.xml> (Retrieved 2 July 2004); Michael Antoniak, "Buyer's Guide: PDA Software," *Realtor Magazine Online*, May 2003; and Frank Nelson, "Real Estate Agents' Best Friend," *Santa Barbara News-Press*, 6 June 2004, F1.
5. Anthony Marshall, "Technology Fees, Hidden Surcharges Cost Hotels Goodwill," *Hotel and Motel Management*, 5 July 2004, 8.
6. Virginia Galt, "Getting Fit on the Job," *The Globe and Mail*, 6 November 2002, C1 <www.globeandmail.com> (Retrieved 2 August 2003).

CHAPTER 11

1. Mohan R. Limaye, "Further Conceptualization of Explanations in Negative Messages," *Business Communication Quarterly*, June 1997, 46.
2. "Filene's Basement Bans 2 Shoppers Who Returned Too Much Stuff," *USA Today*, 14 July 2003, 7B.
3. "2004 Survey on Workplace E-mail and IM Reveals Unmanaged Risks," *The ePolicy Institute* <http://www.epolicyinstitute.com/survey/> (Retrieved 14 July 2004).
4. Sandra Swanson, "Employers Take a Closer Look," *Information Week*, 15 July 2002, 40.
5. Elizabeth M. Dorn, "Case Method Instruction in the Business Writing Classroom," *Business Communication Quarterly*, March 1999, 51–52.
6. Mimi Browning, "Work Dilemma: Delivering Bad News a Good Way," *Government Computer News*, 24 November 2003, 41; and Jeff Mowatt, "Breaking Bad News to Customers," *Agency Sales*, February 2002, 30.
7. Browning, "Work Dilemma"; and Bob Lewis, "To Be an Effective Leader You Need to Perfect the Art of Delivering Bad News," *Infoworld*, 13 September 1999, 124.
8. Jeanette W. Gilsdorf, "Metacommunication Effects on International Business Negotiating in China," *Business Communication Quarterly*, June 1997, 27.
9. Based on Gene Sloan, "Under 21? Carnival Says Cruise Is Off," *USA Today*, 29 November 1996.
10. Jordana Mishory, "Don't Shoot the Messenger: How to Deliver Bad News and Still Keep Customers Satisfied," *Sales and Marketing Management*, June 2004.
11. Andrew Ross Sorkin, "J. Crew Web Goof Results in Discount," *The New York Times*, 11 November 1999, D3.

CHAPTER 12

1. Joellen Perry and Janet Rae-Dupree, "Searching the Web Gets Easier With Engines That Try To Read Your Mind," *U.S. News & World Report*, 16 April 2001, 52.
2. Rona Maynard, "Making Your Life Simpler," *Chatelaine's Essential Web Guide*, Third Annual Web Guide, September 2002, 2.
3. Kimberly A. Killmer and Nicole B. Koppel, "So Much Information, So Little Time: Evaluating Web Resources With Search Engines," *T.H.E. Journal (Technological Horizons in Education)*, August 2002, 21.
4. Lisa Guernsey, "Mining the 'Deep Web' With Specialized Drills," *The New York Times*, 25 January 2001 <http://www.nytimes.com/2001/01/25/technology/25SEAR.html?ex=1090382400&en=9d85ad17e8811b27&ei=5070&ex=1090123200&en=bn83ce4c971d1b> (Retrieved 16 June 2004).
5. Google Inc., "Google Achieves Search Milestone With Immediate Access to More Than 6 Billion Items," press release, 17 February 2004 <http://www.google.com/press/pressrel/6billion.html> (Retrieved 10 July 2004).
6. Michael K. Bergman, "The Deep Web: Surfacing Hidden Value," *Journal of Electronic Publishing*, August 2001 <http://www.press.umich.edu/jep/07-01/bergman.html> (Retrieved 10 July 2004).
7. Alex Wright, "In Search of the Deep Web," *Salon*, 9 March 2004

<http://www.salon.com/tech/feature/2004/03/09/deep_web/index_np.html> (Retrieved 10 July 2004).

8. M. Theodore Farries, II, Jeanne D. Maes, and Ulla K. Bunz, "References and Bibliography: Citing the Internet," *Journal of Applied Business Research*, Summer 1998, 33–36.
9. Christopher Velotta, "How To Design and Implement a Questionnaire," *Technical Communication*, Fall 1991.
10. Daphne A. Jameson, "The Ethics of Plagiarism: How Genre Affects Writers' Use of Source Materials," *The Bulletin of the Association for Business Communication*, June 1993, 18.
11. Writing Tutorial Services, Indiana University, "Plagiarism: What It Is and How to Recognize and Avoid It" <http://www.indiana.edu/~wts/wts/plagiarism.html> (Retrieved 22 August 2001).
12. Gerald J. Alred, Walter E. Oliu, and Charles T. Brusaw, *The Professional Writer* (New York: St. Martin's Press, 1992), 78.
13. "On Target, American Retailing; America's Other Wal-Mart," *Economist (U.S.)*, 5 May 2001, 6.

CHAPTER 13

1. Charlene Marmer Solomon, "Marriott's Family Matters," *Personnel Journal*, October 1991, 40–42; Jennifer Laabs, "They Want More Support—Inside and Outside of Work," *Workforce*, November 1998, 54–56.

CHAPTER 14

1. Herman Holtz, *The Consultant's Guide to Proposal Writing* (New York: John Wiley, 1990), 188.

CHAPTER 15

1. Peter Urs Bender, *Secrets of Power Presentations* (Toronto: The Achievement Group, 1991).
2. Rod Plotnik, *Introduction to Psychology* (Pacific Grove, CA: Brooks/Cole, 1993), 484.
3. Wharton Applied Research Center, "A Study of the Effects of the Use of Overhead Transparencies on Business Meetings, Final Report" cited in "Short, Snappy Guide to Meaningful Presentations," *Working Woman*, June 1991, 73.
4. Stanford communications professor Clifford Nass quoted in Tad Simons, "When Was the Last Time PowerPoint Made You Sing?" *Presentations*, July 2001, 6. See also Geoffrey Nunberg, "The Trouble With PowerPoint," *Fortune*, 20 December 1999, 330–334.
5. "How to Avoid the 7 Deadly Sins of PowerPoint," *Yearbook of Experts News Release Wire*, 30 July 2004 (Retrieved 11 October 2004 from LexisNexis Academic database).
6. Jim Endicott, "For Better Presentations, Avoid PowerPoint Pitfalls," *Presentations*, June 1998, 36–37.
7. Victoria Hall Smith, "Gigs by the Gigabyte," *Working Woman*, May 1998, 114.
8. John Ellwood, "Less PowerPoint, More Powerful Points," *The Times (London)*, 4 August 2004, 6.
9. Dianna Booher, *Executive's Portfolio of Model Speeches for All Occasions* (Englewood Cliffs, NJ: Prentice Hall, 1991), 259.
10. Peter Schneider, "Scenes From a Marriage: Observations on the Daimler-Chrysler Merger From a German Living in America," *The New York Times Magazine*, 12 August 2001, 47.
11. Ronald E. Dulek, John S. Fielden, and John S. Hill, "International Communication: An Executive Primer," *Business Horizons*, January/February 1991, 23. See also Susan J. Marks, "Nurturing Global Workplace Connections," *Workforce*, September 2001, 76+.
12. Dulek, Fielden, and Hill, "International Communication," 22.

CHAPTER 16

1. "Small Business Sentinel," *National Post*, 4 March 2000, E8.
2. "Financial Outlook," *Maclean's*, 22 March 1999, 37.
3. Brian O'Connell, *The Career Survival Guide* (New York: McGraw-Hill, 2003), 11–12.
4. Anne Kates Smith, "Charting Your Own Course," *U.S. News & World Report*, 6 November 2000, 57.
5. Mitch Moxley, "Internet Job Sites a Hit," *National Post*, 1 July 2004, FP5.
6. Julia Drake, "Popular E-Recruiting Could Help You," *Canadian Grocer*, March 2001, Vol. 115, Issue 2, 9.
7. Mark Swartz, "Internet Job Boards Are Tricky," *The Spectator*, Hamilton, ON, 1 May 2004, E01.
8. Elizabeth Blackburn-Brockman and Kelly Belanger, "One Page or Two?: A National Study of CPA Recruiters' Preferences for Résumé Length," *The Journal of Business Communication*, January 2001, 29–57.
9. Tom Washington, "Improve Your Résumé 100 Percent" <http://www.nbew.com/archive/961001-001.html> (Retrieved 27 September 1998).
10. Robert Lorentz, James W. Carland, and Jo Ann Carland, "The Résumé: What Value Is There in References?" *Journal of Technical Writing and Communication*, Fall 1993, 371.
11. "As Graduation Approaches . . . ," *Personnel*, June 1991, 14.
12. Frequently Asked Questions, "Quintessential Résumés and Cover Letters," <http://www.resumesandcoverletters.com> (Retrieved 8 October 2004).
13. Marc Silver, "Selling the Perfect You," *U.S. News & World Report*, 5 February 1990, 70–72.
14. Jude M. Werra and Associates, publisher of the semiannual Liars Index, as cited in Drew Robb, "Résumé Writing," *Network World*, 8 October 2001, 65.
15. Diane Cole, "Ethics: Companies Crack Down on Dishonesty," *The Wall Street Journal, Managing Your Career* supplement, Spring 1991, 8.
16. "Managing Your Career," *National Business Employment Weekly*, Fall 1989, 29.
17. Joan E. Rigdon, "Deceptive Résumés Can Be Door-Openers but Can Become an Employee's Undoing," *The Wall Street Journal*, 17 June 1992, B1. See also Barbara Solomon, "Too Good to Be True?" *Management Review*, April 1998, 28.
18. Anne Fisher, "How to Ruin an Online Job Hunt," *Fortune*, 28 June 2004, 43.
19. Daisy Wright, "Tell Stories, Get Hired," *OfficePro*, August/September 2004, 32–33.

Acknowledgments

CHAPTER 2

p. 29 Tech Talk box based on David Armstrong, "Building Teams Across Borders," *Executive Excellence*, March 2000, 10; Deborah S. Kezsbom, "Creating Teamwork in Virtual Teams," *Cost Engineering*, October 2000, 33–36; Larry Greenemeier, "Teamwork Via the Web," *Informationweek*, 25 September 2000, 211; Steve Alexander, "Virtual Teams Going Global," *InfoWorld*, 13 November 2000, 55–56; and Cheryl Hamilton with Cordell Parker, *Communicating for Results* (Belmont, CA: Wadsworth, 2000), 320.

p. 30 Discussion of team development based on Jon R. Katzenbach and Douglas K. Smith, *The Wisdom of Teams* (New York: HarperCollins, 1994); Harvey Robbins and Michael Finley, *Why Teams Don't Work* (Peterson's/Pacesetter, 1995); Jon R. Katzenbach, *Teams at the Top* (Boston: Harvard Business School Press, 1997); and Jane Henderson-Loney, "Tuckman and Tears: Developing Teams During Profound Organizational Change," *Supervision*, May 1996, 3–5.

p. 30 Figure 2.1 based on Jon R. Katzenbach and Jason A. Santamaria, "Firing Up the Front Line," *Harvard Business Review*, May/June 1999, 107–117; and Suzanne K. Bishop, "Cross-Functional Project Teams in Functionally Aligned Organizations," *Project Management Journal*, September 1999, 6–12.

p. 31 Discussion of group and team roles based on K. E. Benne and Paul Sheats, "Functional Roles and Group Members," *Journal of Social Issues*, 1948, No. 4, 41–49; Cheryl Hamilton and Cordell Parker, *Communicating for Results* (Belmont, CA: Wadsworth, 2000), 309–311; Gerald M. Goldhaber, *Organizational Communication*, 6e (Madison, WI: WCB Brown & Benchmark, 1993), 247–249.

p. 32 Figure 2.2. Portions reprinted with permission of Peterson's, a division of International Thomson Publishing, FAX 800-730-2215. Adapted from *Why Teams Don't Work* © 1995 by Harvey A. Robbins and Michael Finley.

p. 33 Discussion of conflict and groupthink based on Stephanie Reynolds, "Managing Conflict Through a Team Intervention and Training Strategy," *Employee Relations Today*, Winter 1998, 57–64; Odette Pollar, "Sticking Together," *Successful Meetings*, January 1997, 87–90; Kathleen M. Eisenhardt, "How Management Teams Can Have a Good Fight," *Harvard Business Review*, July/August 1997, 77–85; and Erich Brockmann, "Removing the Paradox of Conflict from Group Decisions," *Academy of Management Executive*, May 1996, 61–62.

p. 34 Discussion about reaching group decisions based on Harvey Robbins and Michael Finley, *Why Teams Don't Work* (Princeton, NJ: Peterson's/Pacesetter Books, 1995), 42–45; and Steven A. Beebe and John T. Masterson, *Communicating in Small Groups* (New York: Longman, 1999), 198–200.

p. 37 Discussion of team-based presentations based in part on Jon Hanke, "Presenting as a Team," *Presentations*, January 1998, 74–82; Frank Jossi, "Putting It All Together: Creating Presentations as a Team," *Presentations*, July 1996, 18–26; and Jon Rosen, "10 Ways to Make Your Next Team Presentation a Winner," *Presentations*, August 1997, 31.

p. 40 Discussion on meetings based on Hal Lancaster, "Learning Some Ways to Make Meetings Slightly Less Awful," *The Wall Street Journal*, 26 May 1998, B1; Melinda Ligos, "Why Your Meetings Are a Total Bore," *Sales & Marketing Management*, May 1998, 84; Jana M. Kemp, "The Writing's on the Wall," *Successful Meetings*, August 1996, 74; Charles R. McConnell, "The Chairperson's Guide to Effective Meetings," *Health Care Supervisor*, March 1997, 1–9; and John C. Bruening, "There's Good News About Meetings," *Managing Office Technology*, July 1996, 24–25.

p. 45 Discussion on collaboration technology based on James R. Borck, "As E-Collaboration Tools Mature, They Can Help You Work Out a Competitive Advantage," *InfoWorld*, 27 November 2000, 73; Marion Agnew, "Collaboration on the Desktop," *Informationweek*, 10 July 2000, 87–94; Dennis Fisher, "Taming Web Projects: Project Management Software Embraces the Web, Opens Up More Choices," *eWeek*, 20 November 2000, 48; Steve Jefferson, "Groove Takes to New Level," *InfoWorld*, 30 October 2000, 29; Todd Coopee, "Outsourced Teamware Gains Ground," *InfoWorld*, 17 April 2000, 55–56; Howard Millman, "On Track and in Touch: You Want It When?" *Computerworld*, 26 June 2000, 88; Carla Catalano, "Web-Based Groupware," *Computerworld*, 7 June 2000, 105; Bradley C. Wheeler, Alan R. Dennis, and Laurence I, "Groupware Comes to the Internet: Charting a New

World," *Database for Advances in Information Systems*, Summer, 1999, 8–21; Steve Gillmor and Jeff Angus, "Teamware Comes of Age," *Informationweek*, 20 September, 1999, 69–78; and Craig R. Scott, Laura Quinn, C. Erik Timmerman, and Diana M. Garrett, "Ironic Uses of Group Communication Technology: Evidence from Meeting Transcripts and Interviews with Group Decision Support System Users," *Communication Quarterly*, Summer 1998, 353.

CHAPTER 3

p. 54 Tips for Workplace Listening based on Kenneth R. Johnson, "Effective Listening Skills," The itmWEB Site of Web Media Corporation <http://www.itmweb.com/essay514.htm> (Retrieved 15 January 2001); Shari Caudron, "Listen Up!" *Workforce*, August 1999, 25–27; and Hal Lancaster, "It's Time to Stop Promoting Yourself and Start Listening," *The Wall Street Journal*, 10 June 1997, B1.

p. 55 Listening to Superiors based on Lynn O. Cooper, "Listening Competency in the Workplace: A Model for Training," *Business Communication Quarterly*, December 1997, 75–84; Valerie Priscilla Goby and Justus Helen Lewis, "The Key Role of Listening in Business: A Study of the Singapore Insurance Industry," *Business Communication Quarterly*, June 2000, 411; and Michael C. Dennis, "Effective Communication Will Make Your Job Easier, *Business Credit*, June 1995, 45.

p. 55 Listening to Customers based on Nick Langley, "Looking After the Customers," *Computer Weekly*, 2 November 2000, 100; Jeff Caplan, "Golden Age Customer Service Returns," *Direct Marketing*, July 2000, 60; Rosemary P. Ramsey and Ravipreet S. Sohi, "Listening to Your Customers: The Impact of Perceived Salesperson Listening Behavior on Relationship Outcomes," *Journal of the Academy of Marketing Science*, Spring 1997, 127–137; Daniel Pedersen, "Dissing Customers: Why the Service Is Missing from America's Service Economy," *Newsweek*, 23 June 1997, 56; Michael Render, "Better Listening Makes for a Better Marketing Message," *Marketing News*, 11 September 2000, 22–23; Lynn Thomas, "Listening: So What's in It for Me?" *Rough Notes*, December 1998, 63–64; and Susan A. Timm, Timothy W. Aurant, and Rick E. Ridnout, "Listening Competence Within Marketing and Other Business Disciplines: Phase I —Measuring College Student Perceptions," *The Delta Pi Epsilon Journal*, Spring 2000, 78–89.

CHAPTER 4

p. 72 Tech Talk box based on Sari Kalin, "The Importance of Being Multiculturally Correct," *Computer World*, 6 October 1997, G16–17; B. G. Yovovich, "Making Sense of All the Web's Numbers," *Editor & Publisher*, Mediainfo.com Supplement, November 1998, 30–31; Laura Morelli, "Writing for a Global Audience on the Web," *Marketing News*, 17 August 1998, 16.

p. 75 Figure 4.1 based on J. Chung's analysis appearing in Guo-Ming Chen and William J. Starosta, *Foundations of Intercultural Communication* (Boston: Allyn and Bacon, 1998), 51; and Mary O'Hara-Devereaux and Robert Johansen, *Globalwork: Bridging Distance, Culture, and Time* (San Francisco: Jossey-Bass, 1994), 55.

CHAPTER 7

p. 137 Picture caption for Wall Street photo based on J. Peder Zane, "For Investors, an Initial Public Offering of English," *The New York Times*, 25 August 1996; U. S. Securities and Exchange Commission, *A Plain English Handbook*, Washington, DC, 13 January 1997.

CHAPTER 8

p. 156 The discussion on pages 156 to 159 ("Smart E-Mail Practices") is based on Dale Bowen and Bryan Gold, "Policies and Education Solve E-Mail Woes," *American City & County*, May 2001, 8; Reg Pirie, "Ask an Expert: E-Mail Etiquette," *CA Magazine*, December 2000, 11; Ruth Davidhizar, Ruth Shearer, and Becky Castro, "A Dilemma of Modern Technology: Managing E-Mail Overload," *Hospital Materiel Management Quarterly*, February 2000, 42–47; Margaret Boles and Brenda Paik Sunoo, "Don't Let E-Mail Botch Your Career," *Workforce*, February 1998, 21; Brenda Paik Sunoo, "What If Your E-Mail Ends Up in Court?" *Workforce*, July 1998, 36–41; G. A. Marken, "Think Before You Click," *Office Systems*, March 1998, 44–46; Howard Millman, "Easy EDI for Everyone," *InfoWorld*, 17 August 1998, 38–39; Joe Dysart, "Establishing an Internet Policy," *Credit Union Executive*, May/June 1998, 18–22; "Do's and Don'ts for E-Mail Use," *CA Magazine*, June/July 1998, 40; and Sana Reynolds, "Composing Effective E-Mail Messages," *Communication World*, July 1997, 8–9.

CHAPTER 9

p. 192 Discussion (adjustment letters) is based on Ed Foster, "Don't Blame the Vendor: Web Shoppers Are Not Always Innocent Victims," *InfoWorld*, 12 March 2001, 73; Kevin Lawrence, "How to Profit from Customer Complaints: Turning Problems into Opportunities," *Canadian Manager*, Fall 2000, 25; Jeffrey J. Roth, "When the Customer's Got a Beef," *ABA Banking Journal*, July 1998, 24–29; Geoffrey Brewer, "The Customer Stops Here," *Sales & Marketing Management*, March 1998, 30–36; Bill Knapp, "Communication Breakdown," *World Wastes*, February 1998, 16; Stephen S. Tax, Stephen W. Brown, and Murali Chandrashekaran, "Customer Evaluations of Service Complaint Experiences: Implications for Relationship Marketing," *Journal of Marketing*, April 1998, 60–76; Edmund S. Fine, "Are You Listening to Your Customers?" *Quality*

Progress, January 1998, 120; Robert Klara, "Press 1 to Gripe," *Restaurant Business*, 15 May 1998, 96–102; "Foiling the Rogues: 'Anti' Web Sites Are Great for Angry Customers, But Now Companies Are Trying to Fight Back," *Newsweek*, 27 October 1997, 80; Roberta Furger, "Don't Get Mad, Get Online," *PC World*, October 1997, 37; Gary Hren, "The Sales Behind the Scowl," *American Demographics, Marketing Tools Supplement*, March/April 1996, 14–17; Gwendolyn N. Smith, Rebecca F. Nolan, and Young Dai, "Job-Refusal Letters: Readers' Affective Responses to Direct and Indirect Organizational Plans," *Business Communication Quarterly*, March 1996, 67–73; Carol David and Margaret Ann Baker, "Rereading Bad News: Compliance-Gaining Features in Management Memos," *The Journal of Business Communications*, October 1994, 267–290.

p. 194 Internal picture (responding to claims) based on Kevin Lawrence, "How to Profit from Customer Complaints: Turning Problems into Opportunities," *Canadian Manager*, Fall 2000, 25.

CHAPTER 10

pp. 221–222 Discussion of e-marketing based on Stephan Spencer, "Email Marketing Tips," *Netconcepts* <http://www.netconcepts.com/bob04.htm> (Retrieved 27 June 2004); Jenny C. McCune, "8 Ways to Maximize E-Mail Marketing," *Bankrate.com* <http://www.bankrate.com/brm/news/biz/biz_ops/20020710a.asp?print=on> (Retrieved 27 June 2004); Pat Friesen, "How to Develop an Effective E-Mail Creative Strategy," *Target Marketing*, February 2002, 46–50; Steven C. Bursten, "E-Mail Marketing: Is It on Your Radar Screen?" *Franchising World*, July/August 2001, 60–61; and Karen Gedney and Joanna Belbey, "What Successful B2B E-Mail Messages Have in Common," *ClickZ Network* <http://www.clickz.com/experts/em_mkt/b2b_em_mkt/article.php/3293531> (Retrieved 7 June 2004).

CHAPTER 12

p. 278 Figure 12.6 based on Kim Zetter and Harry McCracken, "How to Stop Searching and Start Finding," *PC Magazine*, September 2000, 129.

p. 282 Figure 12.7 based on "Search Engines and Directories: The Quest for the Best," *PC Magazine*, September 2000, 131.

CHAPTER 14

p. 338 Career Coach box based on "The Business Plan—Road Map to Success," Small Business Administration <http://www.sba.gov/starting/indexbusplans.html> (Retrieved 21 September 2001) and "So You Wanna Write a Business Plan?," SoYouWanna.com <http://www.soyouwanna.com/site/sywsbizplan/bizplan2.html> (Retrieved 22 September 2001).

CHAPTER 15

p. 367 Career Coach box based on Bert Decker, "Successful Presentations: Simple and Practical," *HR Focus*, February 1992, 19; Lawrence Stevens, "The Proof Is in the Presentation," *Nation's Business*, July 1991, 33; Hal Lancaster, "Practice and Coaching Can Help You Improve Um, Y'Know, Speeches," *The Wall Street Journal*, 9 January 1996, B1.

p. 370 Discussion of vivid imagery based on Jeff Olson, *Giving Great Presentations* (Bristol, VT: Velocity Business Publishing, 1997), 32–37; Kevin Daley, "Using the Right Evidence for Effective Presentations," *Communication Briefings*, April 1997, 8a; Patricia Calderon, "Anatomy of a Great Presentation," *Windows Magazine*, June 1998, 203+; and Al Borowski, "To Connect with Audiences, Learn How to Build Rapport," Presentations.com <http://www.presentations.com/deliver/speak/2000/03/31> (Retrieved 31 May 2001).

p. 372 Figure 15.2 based on Dianna Booher, *Speak With Confidence* (New York: McGraw-Hill Professional, 2003), pp. 131–143; U.S. Department of Labor, "Presenting Effective Presentations With Visual Aids" <http://www.osha.gov/doc/outreachtraining/htmlfiles/traintec.html> (Retrieved 11 October 2004); and Shay McConnon, *Presenting With Power* (Oxford: How To Books, Ltd., 2002), pp. 38–43.

p. 386 Tech Talk box based on *The Office Professional*, June 2003, 8; Bill Quirke, "New Rules Needed as Technology Replaces Face-to-Face Meetings," *Personnel Today*, 11 December 2001, 1; and Susan Fox, "Conference Call Protocol," *Association Management*, January 1999, 93–94.

CHAPTER 16

p. 393 Searching for a job electronically based on Alan S. Kay, "Recruiters Embrace the Internet," *Informationweek*, 20 March 2000, 72–80; Gary M. Stern, "Applicants Use Web to Get Scoop on Firms," *Investor's Business Daily*, 13 June 2000, A2; and Michael E. Ryan and Ben Z. Gottesman, "Job Hunting and Hiring on the Web," *PC Magazine*, 25 May 1999, 159+.

p. 401 Figure 16.5 Action Verbs for Persuasive Résumés adapted from Yana Parker, *The Damn Good Résumé Guide* (Berkeley, CA: Ten Speed Press, 1996). Reprinted with permission from THE DAMN GOOD RESUME GUIDE by Yana Parker. Copyright © 1996 by Yana Parker, Ten Speed Press, Berkeley, CA. Available from Ten Speed Press by calling 1-800-841-2665, or online at <www.tenspeed.com>.

p. 404 Figure 16.7 Interpersonal Keywords Most Requested by Employers Using Résumé-Scanning Software. Source: Joyce Lain Kennedy and Thomas J. Morrow, *Electronic Résumé Revolution* (New York: John Wiley & Sons), 70. Reprinted by permission of John Wiley & Sons, Inc.

Photo Credits:

p. 12 © Bettmann/CORBIS; **p. 45** AP/Wide World Photos; **p. 58** © Ryan McVay/Photodisc; **p. 62, L to R** © Photodisc, © Andreas Pollok/Photodisc, © Javier

Pierini/Photodisc, © Jacobs Stock Photography/Photodisc; **p. 74** © Bryan & Cherry Alexander Photography/Alamy; **p. 76** Photo by Ken McLaren. Reprinted with permission of the Invitation Project. www.invitationproject.ca.; **p. 93** © Photodisc; **p. 121** © Lisette Le Bon/Superstock; **p. 137** © Reuters/CORBIS; **p. 153** Dick Hemingway; **p. 194** © Eyewire; **p. 240** © Giraud Philippe/CORBIS Sygma; **p. 280** © Andy Clark/Reuters/Corbis; **p. 311** © Royalty-Free/Corbis; **p. 343** © Ryan McVay/Photodisc; **p. 378** © Powerstock/SuperStock; **p. 418** © Javier Pierini/Photodisc.

Index

D

E

F

G

H

I

P

Q

R